The
LeannessLifestyle
by David Greenwalt

Proven Strategies to Sculpt Your Body, Heal Your Mind and Become Better Today

Library of Congress Cataloging-in-Publication Data:

Greenwalt, David 1965
      The Leanness Lifestyle / by David Greenwalt   4th ed.

     ISBN 0-9718198-0-7
     1. Exercise.   2. Physical fitness.   3. Health.   I. Title.

Printed in the United States of America

Acknowledgments

The Leanness Lifestyle started as a dream–a dream to help others transform in body and mind. The dream became a goal when I wrote it down, gave the dream clarity, and publicly committed it to dozens of people I know and respect. Goal or dream, there is no way this fourth, but first-bound edition, would have become a reality without the support and love of many individuals in my life.

Thank you first to my beloved mother. As my original mentor I am beyond grateful for your unconditional love. For making me feel special and talented but recognizing that we all must focus on what we do best, accepting that no one truly gets it all. For raising me to be a strong and independent person, filled with confidence and pride. For making me your favorite son when I was most in need. For teaching me how to laugh and keep life's challenges in perspective. For showing me the importance of recognizing the value of the simple things in life. For teaching me the true meaning of compassion for others. For always being there for me until the moment of your untimely passing.

Thank you to my father for teaching me the value of a day's pay for a day's work. For accepting the responsibility of raising me and providing for our family without reservation or appearance of burden. For showing me how to live knowing that all I have is always more than enough. For providing me the true experience of forgiveness that I now share with others. For simply being there day in and day out as I was growing up and giving me a sense of consistency and groundedness.

To my cousin, blood brother and childhood best friend Dallas. Even though you were only a few years older than me, it's hard to even imagine where I might be right now, had I not had you to look up to in my very early years. For helping me know it was good to do my own thing, not to conform to the peer pressures of youth, and being the first person to show me how to get a real bicep pump.

Thank you to my lovely wife Tracy. For sticking with me as a teenage bodybuilder. For putting up with all the foolishness that goes along with being the girlfriend of a guy who just "knows" he has to workout two hours a day, six days a week. For never leaving in times when you probably should have and for honoring our commitment to each other more than 20 years ago — through thick and thin. For letting me spread my wings and watching me start and fail many times in many endeavors. For delivering our three wonderful, healthy children. For taking care of our home, the children and me on a daily basis. For allowing me to watch you become more beautiful today than the day we met. For getting mad or upset *for* me when I'm not publicly allowed to do so. For laughing and crying with me during so many highs and lows over so many years. For being the love of my life and my one, true best friend.

Acknowledgments

I must thank my children for helping me keep a sense of perspective for what's truly important in life. For teaching me new meanings for patience, understanding and love. For providing a drive for me to become better than I would without you three in my life. For getting to experience all the joy of being your Dad.

To Snooky for asking me to train with his group in the Summer of 1982. For being the first to really show me what it took to grow muscle.

I must thank all the training partners and gym rats I've hung with, trained with, laughed with, laughed at and come to know in the past 20 years. The laughter and friendships created in the gym are cherished, and without question, helped keep my interest early on.

To especially the charter-coaching members—many of who are still with me today—but also the current members, of my coaching program. Thank you for sharing your lives with me. For allowing me to get to know many of you at a very personal level. For letting me share in your transformation journey. For setting me straight and allowing me to take original, yet scattered ideas, to create a complete system embodying all that is the transformation journey. For hanging tough with me when others were jumping ship with the slightest hiccup in the development of the program. For letting me share your stories with others so the honest message of transformation can benefit those who are about to begin their first or fifteenth weight loss program.

To those who worked directly with me on preparing the published work you hold today I thank you. Glenn, Colleen, Elisa and others helped turn my garbled initial drafts into a better looking, better flowing finished work.

Many hands were involved in the production of this, the fourth edition of The Leanness Lifestyle. There will be many more lives this edition will touch. The Leanness Lifestyle, as with the journey of your body and mind transformation, is ever evolving. As this edition touches the lives of what's sure to be thousands, I will have many more people to thank as the next edition develops, beginning with tomorrow.

Table of Contents

Table of Contents

Table of Contents

Table of Contents

Table of Contents

Introduction

If you're like most people who read The Leanness Lifestyle for the first time, you probably know very little about me—the author. Who is David Greenwalt and what gives me the right to claim to have enough valuable body transformation knowledge that I should feel compelled to write a book about it? If you would like to get a better feel of who I am, where I came from, and why I knew The Leanness Lifestyle had to be written, then get comfortable and allow me to properly introduce myself. I'll also discuss how The Leanness Lifestyle developed into what I believe is the most comprehensive body transformation guide ever developed for men and women.

Hello, my name is David Greenwalt, a midwestern-born and raised 37-year old (as of 2002), husband of wife Tracy and father to Steven, Christopher and Elizabeth. I don't define my role as husband and father in the first and second positions accidentally. My family truly comes first. But next in line comes my passion for fitness and helping others transform into all they are capable of becoming. Allow me to digress a bit and tell you where I've been before I tell you more about why I place helping others so high on my life's priorities.

My interest in fitness began in grammar school. My memory then was always being intrigued in those who were physically superior to others. In 5th grade I earned the President's Physical Fitness Award. Remember this award? Several events ranging from the standing broad jump to the baseball throw. I don't remember all the events but I do remember wanting that award badly.

I also have a vivid memory of one particular science class in 7th grade. My teacher asked the class who we thought were the most physically fit athletes. I was pretty shy and quiet in those days but as I listened to the other kids shouting their favorite team sports (football players!, baseball players! hockey players! etc.), I couldn't help but think that bodybuilders just had to be the most physically fit. How could they not be? I mean, look at them! I felt so strongly about it that I actually performed a rare act and raised my hand to answer. The teacher called on me and I answered "A bodybuilder?" It was pretty obvious in 1978 that I caught him off guard. He really didn't know what to say. It's not like bodybuilding was akin to apple pie or Chevrolet back then. Oh, the science teacher's answer? Swimmers. Now, some bodybuilders are really swimmers and just don't know it, and maybe that's who my teacher was talking about. I'm not sure.

Like many lifelong resistance trainers, I started piddling with weights at the early age of 14. I remember as a sophomore in high school, and recently-graduated student of the high school driver's ed program, doing curls at home until I thought I'd puke and then going out for a ride on my motorcycle so others could see my great bicep pump. Of course, no one paid any attention to my 13-inch guns but here's another vivid memory I have of those rides. "Man, if I could just hold this pump forever that would be awesome! It would be great to be *this* big all the time!" Jump to the present. I took a ride on my motorcycle (no, not the same motorcycle I owned then) today with no pump whatsoever and found myself still trying to see in the rear view mirrors if that bicep had the look I was after. It does. Twenty years later. But it does! I guess it's true that failure just cannot handle persistence.

I didn't really begin to train systematically or consistently until the summer of 1982, just prior to the start of my senior year in high school. I had dreamed of growing larger muscles but didn't know how to start, probably like many of you reading this today. I was a whopping 140 pounds. I was first introduced to hardcore resistance training and bodybuilding by local Adonis Richard Rutherford. Richard got me started by asking if I wanted to train with him and his circle of training partners. Together, we trained on ancient, smelly equipment at our local YMCA. As amazing as it may be for some, the few, simple pieces we trained on were all we needed to grow. After a few weeks of serious training I remember my first attempt at an all-out maximum single repetition on the bench press. It was 170 pounds and that's all I had in me. Within six months of starting, however, I could bench press 265 pounds and weighed 165 pounds. As many of you have observed or will observe, progress and success are contagious and addicting. As a senior I was so dedicated to my six days a week training regimen that my physical education teacher allowed me to skip regular P.E. so I could hit the weights. I mean, come on! Volleyball over weight lifting? No way! At least not for me. I still feel so incredibly lucky Richard asked me to train with him that summer day in 1982 but now for different reasons. Not only was he my original mentor for resistance training and bodybuilding but he is a great man and great friend to this day. For whatever reason, I tend to create or experience life-changing events in clusters. Not only did I begin serious bodybuilding training in 1982 but it was that same year I met Tracy and off we went on our very first date.

In 1986 I competed in my first bodybuilding competition at Western Illinois University. I dieted quite insanely and you will read more about that in Chapter 1. In 1987 I earned a Bachelor in Science degree from Western. I also married Tracy that same year. Hard to believe 15 years of marriage have gone by so quickly. In keeping true with my cluster of life-changing events, that same year I operated my first business by purchasing an existing, but failing, gym in my hometown of Dixon, Illinois. Co-Ed Fitness Center II was mine! At the same time I was a Dixon Police Officer. Even though I put in 40-50 hours of shift work per week as a police officer, the additional hours necessary to make Co-Ed II thrive were hours that really didn't feel like work to me. I believe I had a natural propensity toward entrepreneurship and also knew I loved being fit and being surrounded by others who sought the same.

Between 1987 and 1990 I continued to train hard and started coaching members of Co-Ed Fitness as well. I was sent to Northwestern University by the Dixon Police Department to participate in their "Physical Fitness Instructor Training for Police Officers" and really enjoyed it. Between coaching others and receiving specialized training in the field to evaluate and teach others, I felt I was coming into my own. Co-Ed continued to grow but I eventually sought and accepted a position with the Illinois State Police. As a young businessman, I hadn't established a business model that would afford me the opportunity to continue owning the gym while away at the State Police academy for six months. I sold Co-Ed Fitness center upon leaving for the academy.

After winning the award for Most Physically Fit cadet and graduating from the academy, I finally got to settle back in Dixon. I felt an emptiness, however, and knew I wanted to help people again within the fitness circles. It was time to start another business. It was in 1992 that I started a new company called The Power Store, which sold supplements to a few local people. Why "The Power Store?" I was involved heavily in powerlifting at the time and felt some of the basic supplements I took helped me create the "power" and strength I strived for. Over the years I've been a state champion powerlifter for the 220-pound class (more about how I got *that* fat in Chapter 1) and I promoted no less than ten powerlifting meets over a four-year stretch in the early to mid 90s. In 1995 my enthusiasm for powerlifting competitions waned in favor of bodybuilding competitions, and I continue to train as a natural bodybuilder today. I don't want to get ahead of myself so allow me to back up a bit once again. When I say I started The Power Store selling supplements to a few local people, I mean, very few local people! People were coming to my home to buy them or I hand-delivered all of them to their home and hoped they'd pay me in a reasonable time. To say my business plan was suffering is an understatement.

During The Power Store's formative years I took every call, ordered every product for inventory (3 shelves in a room 10 x 15), picked every product and packed every order. Tracy was working full-time during The Power Store's early years and we had two of our three beautiful children. So in between wiping snotty noses, giving hugs, changing diapers, reading stories and wrestling with my two boys, I worked full-time as a Trooper. I can still remember a common practice that makes me cringe a bit today and I wonder how I really did it back then. It wasn't uncommon to have two to four orders per day during this time and I always wanted to make sure the orders got out on time, regardless of the seasons or weather in Illinois. During the bitterly cold winter, the routine consisted of packing two orders that had to get out to be delivered on time. What did this mean for me then? It meant continuing to juggle the duties of a State Trooper with packing up one infant boy and a toddler in full winter gear into my beater car. After packing the whopping two orders, we were off to a UPS center 15 miles away so I could make sure the orders got out on time. The business did finally grow enough to ask UPS to come to my home. Thank goodness for that!

The Power Store continued to grow by word of mouth and small advertisements in magazines and in 1993 it had grown to a point where I had to move the business out of my home. Through the mid to late 90s, The Power Store became one of the largest sports supplement, catalog retailers in the country. In 1996 I resigned from the Illinois State Police to focus intently on my business.

While I enjoyed the success of The Power Store, I continued to feel a strong desire to help people and create real change in their lives. I had gotten a taste of this when I owned Co-Ed and I was hungry for that feeling again. During the time The Power Store was growing in the 90s, I began researching and writing a Power Store newsletter about dietary supplements, basic nutrition, and training. Although I earned a Bachelor in Science, it was through my own research that I learned about dietary supplements. I did so by reading everything I could get my hands on, and finding out what Medline was about, reading endless stacks of full research papers.

I researched and wrote because—although the magazines were good—there was plenty of room for honest to goodness truth in the supplement market. There's still plenty of room for that today. Since I began researching and writing in the early 90s, I've written hundreds of articles on supplements, nutrition and training. I've also been published in Muscle & Fitness, Peak Training, and been a ghost writer for others. I really believe that each article I published or had published was really the way I could help others see things more plainly, and helping clients sift through the muck that defines most of the marketing for supplements, stripping fat and adding muscle. I researched and wrote to positively affect the lives of others beyond making sure they had enough vitamins, protein and essential fatty acids in their meal planning.

As you will read more about in Chapter 1, the original seeds of The Leanness Lifestyle were sowed for many years but one major turning point occurred in 1998 that really gave The Leanness Lifestyle solid roots. It was in 1998 that I competed in my second bodybuilding show ever, but this time I applied the knowledge I had gained since my research into my precontest nutritional program. I wrote about that experience and printed it as an article in a magazine we were publishing then called *The Health & Performance Marketplace*. The article was titled *"Competition Becomes a Leanness Lifestyle."* Since then I've competed in 1999 and 2001. I plan to compete again when I am 40 (in 2005).

As you will read about in Chapter 12, *Lifestyle Booby Traps*, beginning in 1999 I began a year-long project of learning HTML programming as well as another programming language so I could build my own Power Store website. There were many functions I wanted the website to perform and I was not able to get the current programmers I knew to perform what I needed in a timely and cost-efficient manner. I really did not want to learn HTML or any other language at that time but I did learn it and from that I eventually created The Leanness Lifestyle Superfit Coaching program.

In 2000 I completed all requirements of the National Strength and Conditioning Association to become a Certified Strength and Conditioning Specialist (CSCS). I believe their programs for CSCS, Personal Trainer or others are among the very best alongside those certifications the American College of Sports Medicine offers.

The Leanness Lifestyle Success System (LLSS) was created to continually evolve as a comprehensive platform for the latest dissemination of my knowledge for many areas of life improvement. The LLSS is a member-based program consisting of this book, audio programs, regular e-mail and snail mail newsletters, and other wonderful tools thanks to the technology of the Internet. With The Leanness Lifestyle book and audio program in your hands, you can begin today to change. Beginning at www.leannesslifestyle.com you can further your progress and master two exceptionally important tasks you will read more about later: meal and exercise planning. You will also find free special reports, successful stories of others who have used The Leanness Lifestyle to transform from the "before" to the "after," grocery lists, recipe guides, workout program ideas to break boredom, a full encyclopedia, special calorie calculators to help you to more clearly set goals, and an entire network of support from fellow Lifestylers.

The experience of those who have traveled the Leanness road before you literally comes to life on the discussion forums for members. When you think you are the only one feeling a certain way or who has experienced a particular setback, you can rest assured you are not when you spend a little time lurking and eventually participating in the Lifestyle discussion forums. When no one physically close to you understands why you are so focused on your transformation, your Lifestyle support group will most certainly understand. By becoming and staying connected, you can be sure you never go through this process alone and without exceptional support. I honestly believe the LLSS is the most comprehensive body of transformation knowledge, tools and support ever amassed into one cohesive program.

The first edition of this book was written in 1999. This is now the fourth. It is no longer surprising to me—and I hope it won't come as any surprise to you—if, in this edition, I've amended some previous theories or guiding principles from former editions. Men and women can spend their entire lives seeking the solution to one unanswered question relating to some biological function occurring everyday within us all. As I continue to work closely with clients, my knowledge is ever increasing. This will continue to be a life-long process. As I put the finishing touches on this fourth edition, some who know I am doing so are already asking if there will be a fifth. As I ask all of you to seek true knowledge and not just information, to keep your minds open, to be willing to shift your position and move away from established, self-limiting paradigms, I must continue to do the same. While I cannot give an answer as to when, I cannot help but know that as my knowledge grows, and my love for helping others create their best body and life thrives by sharing my new knowledge, there must eventually be a fifth edition or some continuation through addendums.

Thank you so much for spending a few minutes getting to know me. I look forward to getting to know you through the various channels I've established within the LLSS. I especially look forward to the return of your Before and After packet and reading every word of your essay telling me of your journey to superfitness.

The best place to begin is the beginning. Turn to chapter one now and experience why The Leanness Lifestyle is beyond dieting—it's about the journey of transformation.

Your partner in living the Lifestyle,

David Greenwalt
The Leanness Lifestyle

Beyond Diet ...
The Journey of Transformation

"I continue to eat a variety of foods today and for some,
it might be considered that I am constantly now in a
pre-contest diet. It's not a diet though, it's life."
-- David Greenwalt 1998

The Surgeon General of the United States recently reported that more than 60 percent of America is overweight or obese. Any way you slice it this means more than 100 million Americans are currently losing the battle of the bulge. When you finish reading this book, it is my sincere desire that you are not only no longer one of the 60 percent, but that you finally recognize the terrific power within you to take control of your body and your weight.

The desire to "fit in" or "just be normal like everyone else" is strong. Going along to get along can indeed help you fit in and make you quite normal. I am confident you would not be reading this book, however, unless your intentions were quite different from the norm. Staying normal just is not in the cards for you. Anyone can fit in. Anyone can become or remain a member of the overweight 60 percent club. We all have our own definitions of normalcy and what it means to be normal. You may be asking "What's so wrong with being normal?" Please consider my definitions of normalcy in America before you truly decide you want to just be normal like everyone else.

Who Wants to Be Normal?

- Normal is being a man with 25-30 percent body fat. A healthy man will have less than 15 percent.
- Normal is being a woman with 35-40 percent body fat. A healthy woman will have less than 23 percent.
- Normal is walking around with a huge Goodyear® at your equator.
- Normal is getting by with your clothes on but knowing that your clothing is hiding a huge pile of dog dung underneath.
- Normal is huffing and puffing if you have to walk (only because the elevator is out) three flights of stairs. God knows you would never walk them just for the heck of it.
- Normal is earning the right to eat at all the best restaurants (which of course serve portions big enough for a family of four).
- Normal is spending five full minutes looking for the closest parking space at your favorite department store because you deserve it.

- Normal is giving one muscle a day exercise (your push button finger) because you have acquired some level of intelligence and have sought and found ways to optimally conserve energy. Well bully for you!
- Normal is being embarrassed poolside.
- Normal is having your kids embarrassed for you.
- Normal is having children mirror what mom and dad do–they too are fat.
- Normal is sitting back in your easy chair sucking down a "cool one" after cool one after cool one with your big ol' fat gut sticking out and rubbing that Buddha belly, proud that it truly has been bought and paid for–and it has.
- Normal is being the head of the household and having the others follow your lead. Like you, they practice disgusting behavioral practices and will also pack on 40-80 extra fat pounds so that, as a couple or family, you're a matched set of fat, glutinous, lazy, couch potatoes.
- Normal is waking up in a fog, dragging yourself to work, eating McDonald's for breakfast, doughnuts and coffee for a break, Burger King® for lunch (super size of course), going home to a big meal, then plopping yourself onto the couch with a half gallon of ice cream to watch some television.
- Normal is ordering a Big Mac® combo with a Diet Coke® because you're "watching your weight."
- Normal is the father who drinks after work with his buddies. Normal is the tension in the house when he comes home half-in-the-bag. Normal is the fear and confusion his children feel when they see their father drunk, feel the tension between the parents, and hear the arguing. Normal is having excessive drinking ruin times that should have been good.
- Normal is drifting through life without a plan and without any real goals, other than making it through the day.
- Normal is eating a whole box of Snackwells® or an entire bag of Baked Lays® because they are low-fat or fat-free.
- Normal is going to a buffet and eating as much as humanly possible because you paid for it.
- Normal is setting up social functions around food and drink.
- Normal is continuously rewarding your children with food for everything they do well.
- Normal is not becoming educated and falling for "one-fact diets."
- Normal is relying on your body to help you work your butt off in the office and with clients for 12 hours a day, but not making time for exercise and good nutrition for optimal daily performance.
- Normal is thinking that you must Either work hard at the office Or follow The Leanness Lifestyle.
- Normal is going home tired and crashing without taking a moment to tell the people closest to you that you love them and care.
- Normal is excuses, excuses, and excuses.
- Normal is claiming you are doing better than you were, so isn't that enough? Good enough almost never is.
- Normal is using junk "food" to make you "feel" better.
- Normal is getting a gym membership, working out for two weeks and giving up because you "just don't have time."

- Normal is going from one fad diet to another, losing weight, then gaining twice as much back rather than changing your lifestyle.
- Normal is looking at others who are heavier than you and giving yourself a pat on the back for not being as heavy as them, as you eat your Krispy Creme® doughnut.
- Normal is ordering the latest abs gadget and expecting it to "melt off the pounds" in just minutes a day!
- Normal is having a blood pressure of 145 over 100.
- Normal is having type II diabetes for no other reason other than excess body weight.
- Normal is having joint problems below the waist for one reason–excessive weight.
- Normal is a total cholesterol of 300+.

I have not painted a very pretty picture of normalcy in America but I also do not believe I have painted a false picture of overweight, out-of-shape Americans. Your level of performance is a choice. You can settle for mediocrity, or you can strive for excellence. But know this: you cannot make normalcy your goal and reach your potential. Not every depiction of normalcy in America has to fit you. What is important is you recognizing that, in America, being normal when it comes to your health and fitness is no goal worth achieving.

The Leannesss Lifestyle Is Not A Diet

From this point forward you will see me refer to The Leanness Lifestyle simply as the Lifestyle. The Leanness Lifestyle is not something you do for 12 weeks and then quit. It is not a diet. You will see I purposely distinguish the Lifestyle from dieting throughout this book. By using "diet" when I am referring to something improper or negative and "Lifestyle" when I am suggesting something proper or positive, you will be able to easily see what you should and should not be doing. I do not believe I am out of line when I say that diets are plans or scams for temporary weight loss. People start and stop diets everyday. The Lifestyle, on the other hand, is the fitness plan you work into your life for the <u>rest</u> of your life. The Lifestyle will not only help you shed the pounds but it will help you *keep the pounds off for life*. It is a plan you can teach your children and your grandchildren and con-fidently know you are teaching them the right way to fitness and better health. The Lifestyle really is the last weight loss book you will ever own if you implement the proven strategies in the chapters that follow.

Anything worth doing well is worth doing poorly at first. This may sound counterintuitive to common sense but you will need to accept this quickly so as not to become disheartened as you press onward implementing the Lifestyle into your life. Any first-time followers of the Lifestyle must accept there is a learning curve. Because the Lifestyle is truly an educational plan, you will not become a master of the Lifestyle in two weeks. You may quickly or slowly adopt the principles within the Lifestyle. You may go easily and accept you are reading the words of a fellow physique transformationist and qualified coach or you may resist and only go kicking and screaming. The important fact of the matter is that you keep going. Do not stop. Keep reading, keep learning the

Lifestyle, never give up and do not ever succumb to normalcy and complacency. This book is like Dorothy's ruby slippers. Now that you own it, you can come home to a better body and whatever level of fitness you desire anytime you want. You have always had the power within you to change and become the fit person you were destined to be.

I know you purchased this book looking for some support, guidance, encouragement and the knowledge to get yourself into the body you've always known you could have ... but for one reason or another just haven't achieved yet. You have the desire, maybe even the drive. If you're like most people I work with, you have at least some idea of what it is you want to do with your body ... but thus far you just haven't been that good at actually "doing" it. There are dozens of reasons, reasons unique to you I am certain, for wanting to start now. From the hundreds of clients I have helped change from the "before" to the "after," I have discovered some common themes initially driving them to the Lifestyle.

Why You Are Reading This Now?

- Perhaps you are simply tired of being tired. Maybe you are someone who was once in shape a long, long time ago. Remember how that felt? Remember the energy, the vitality, and how it seemed you could function almost effortlessly on six hours of sleep a night?

- Are you tired of your intelligence and competence being judged solely on the way you look? "If she can't take care of her body how can she take care of anything else?" You are smart; it is time your body matched your mind.

- Do you avoid people with good physiques? Do you feel awkward or even ashamed when you run into "old friends" because they hardly recognize you?

- Maybe you have turned 30 or 40-something and for the first time, you realized you are not invincible. Now the 20-year-old players are spanking you in every way and this irritates the daylights out of you. Are you really past your prime? No! I'll show you how to get in such great shape those 20-year-olds will be wishing you had never discovered this book!

- Are you successful in most every other area of your life but feel a bit embarrassed to admit that your own fitness is the one area in your life where you have had the least amount of control?

- Are you tired of wearing your shirts untucked and leaving the top button undone on your slacks and trousers?

- Maybe you are in that gargantuan class of individuals who are heavy just like their parents, grandparents, brothers or sisters and you are wondering if all hope is lost. Are you fighting a hopeless battle against heredity? I will tell you why later but for now suffice it to say, "No, you can improve tremendously!" Your heredity may load the gun but your environment pulls the trigger. You control your environment.

- Perhaps you want to be more attractive to the opposite sex and are in search of a mate. With the Lifestyle, you will see that you have total control over how much attention you attract from the opposite sex.

- Was a relationship with a husband, wife, boyfriend or girlfriend painfully severed? Don't you secretly, deep inside, want to show them what they missed by putting you on the receiving end of a "Dear John / Dear Jane" letter?

- If you've been married for five or more years there's a good chance you've come to the realization that food may be serving as far more than a source of nourishment and calories. Food satisfies emotional needs for overweight men and women. When you were courting, you were likely thinner than you are now. So what happened? Is marriage hazardous to your health? Is it mandatory that you gain 20-50 pounds over your married lifetime? The answer is "no," but until you understand why marriage appears to have such a detrimental impact on weight, you will not be able to take corrective action. As a married father of three children I will show you how your relationship affects your eating habits and what you can do to control food, instead of food controlling you.

- Maybe it is your dream to compete in a bodybuilding show or finish in the top three of a transformation contest. The Lifestyle is the perfect off-season companion but I've also included a chapter called "*Contest or After Photo Preparedness*" for the transformationist or bodybuilder as you approach the last four weeks and either need to have "After" photos taken or will be standing on stage. Imagine how great it might feel to be standing on stage in awesome shape with all of your family and friends cheering you on! Think for just a moment how wonderful showing off those after photos will be and how much better you will feel knowing you really did it ... you finally really did it!

- Have you recently suffered from a seemingly catastrophic health-related event? Perhaps the Herculean blow to the gut has been recently delivered about your high cholesterol, artery blockage, diabetes, or–dare we say it–cancer? Many times these life-altering messages and others delivered to you by your physician are finally the wake-up call you need to begin a healthier lifestyle. As you will discover in much detail shortly, sometimes these unnerving events will provide a strong emotion arousal–something I call "your click."

- Maybe you want to feel confident enough to go swimming with your kids instead of just watching them ... just because you are mortified to take your shirt off in public. Their "chubby dad" just does not care for water–or so they think. (Hey, I know the feeling!) Do you feel like you have been punched in the stomach when a friend calls and asks you to go swimming? Are you tired of making excuses not to go?

- Wouldn't it be great if the weight on your driver's license was *higher* than your actual weight?

- Maybe your dream is to give your significant other a present that really matters ... like a sexy, terrific physique! (I guarantee you they will not ever want to return that gift!)

- Are you tired of making darn sure the lights are off during any intimacy? "And whatever you do don't turn that way or touch that area because I'm really self conscious of those extra rolls."

- Finally, I promise I am not into witchcraft or voodoo but there are some who would say <u>you found</u> this book. However, I have a tendency to believe this book <u>found you</u> for a reason.

Regardless of your reason for reading this book, you want a fix. Something that will reverse or at least slow the aging clock and something that can make you as lean and muscular as you desire. Whether your body is borderline sexy or flat-out flabby, you hold in your hands the opportunity to finally make the permanent changes you deserve. Housewives, executives, doctors, dentists, lawyers, gardeners, athletes, salespeople, and others from every walk of life have used the Lifestyle to get the health, the body, and the look they want in as little as eight weeks. If it takes two, three or five times this long, you can confidently know the time it'll take to undo decades of overindulgence in only a fraction of the time it took to put it on.

After reading this book you will own a newfound understanding of the physical and emotional elements contributing to your unacceptable state of fitness. You will become free of the current myths holding you back and which you are mostly or completely unaware of at this point. All change is self-change and you'll soon learn, as hundreds of other clients I've worked with have, that properly matching specific processes to your true stage of change will propel you further and further until you reach your ultimate goal and have the body you've only dreamed of until now.

Will there be work? You bet! Will there be periods where you are taken out of your present comfort zone? Yes. But with the same certainty of those previous two statements comes my absolute confidence that with the tools I am providing you in the Lifestyle you can achieve far more than you ever imagined, and far more than you ever thought possible. I have the confidence where you may be lacking. Why? Because with the help of the Lifestyle you will discover your "Achilles heel," probably more than one, and you will finally understand that the power to change was within you all along. How can I be so confident?

Results–Not Theories

The Lifestyle is not theory-based teaching. Since 1999 when I wrote the first edition, I've been teaching, coaching and using everything you have in your hands to successfully help hundreds of clients through amazing physical and emotional transformations.

The Lifestyle will not only provide you with solid, factual information to guide you down the path of nutritional excellence, but will allow you to take control of your food once and for all, instead of your food controlling you. I have seen the most seemingly hopeless cases come alive and transform into lean, muscular success stories. Without the starvation and cravings that accompany the typical fad or "quick-fix" diets, you will understand how you can maintain permanent results instead of simply getting there and switching rails on a fast track back to obesity. A man will finally get to take his shirt off at the pool without fear of people running for their lives because of their wonder how a Sea cow made its way on land. As a woman, you will confidently enter any room and know that people are no longer looking through you, but at you. They are actually paying attention to what you have to say and all of a sudden, what you say matters and is important.

All I ask is that you give the Lifestyle your complete focus, attention, and most of all, your heart. Don't begin reading this book with thoughts of all the change and issues you'll have to face one to ten years from now. Just finish the book! Then move into accomplishing your first eight weeks with the Lifestyle as your fitness guide. Do not think in terms of what you will have to give up for an eternity beyond your first eight weeks. In other words, just try it on for eight weeks. If you do not like it, you do not have to live with it. Just finish the book and get through your first eight weeks. Truly amazing things can happen in only eight short weeks. The Lifestyle can show you the way to a lifetime of leanness, and as so many other success stories have revealed to me and other researchers in the field of weight loss, it is not an easy task to accomplish. Nevertheless, it is attainable and the victory is sweet and oh so worth it.

Not Long Ago I Was Also Flabby

Today my body fat percentage is rarely above eight percent, however, this was not always the case. Sure, until I really figured it out, I had visits with leanness but I certainly did not live there. In fact, I became infamous in my circle of friends and clients as saying, "We mortals can visit the land of super lean but we don't get to live there."

Until I was about 20 years old, I fought hard to gain weight–that's right–to gain weight. I had to eat anything that could not outrun me to gain weight during those years. In my twenties, I took up the sport of powerlifting. In the sport of powerlifting, you focus on three main lifts; the squat, bench press and deadlift. I realized early on that you could push or pull more weight if you weighed more. I also desperately wanted to be larger than the average guy on the block. "Why" is anyone's guess, but I have always had a fascination with a thickly muscled physique. As a child, The Incredible Hulk was truly a hero of mine.

In 1986, while a dirt-poor college student, I decided to compete in a collegiate bodybuilding show. The diet I used consisted of oatmeal, boiled chicken breasts, peas and popcorn for snacking. For cooking, I only had access to a hot pot that I could plug into my dorm room outlet. During my eight-week pre-contest training, I dropped from 215 pounds to 165! I thought I was going to die–I really did. I was ripped (body fat less than 6 percent) but ate such a one-dimensional, barbaric diet that I came in very flat, weak and

David Greenwalt Before

flat. Did I say I was flat, too? I placed second and vowed never again to compete in body-building. It was really a miserable experience. What I did not realize at the time was my vow was not to never compete again, but rather, to never repeat the barbaric diet I followed to compete in 1986.

After this short stint with unhealthy leanness, I became a bigger, stronger power lifter by eating and eating and eating. I accomplished my goal–or so I thought. After a few years of powerlifting, then in my late twenties and at a body weight of 230 pounds, I grew weary of my fat gut. It was hard work to be as fat as I was ... I had to eat a monstrous amount of food. In 1995, I leveled off at about 220 pounds by simply not eating as much as I had been. I knew something still had to change when I realized I still had a protruding belly lying flat on my back on the couch. I decided I would cut the fat off and become lean again. Wait just a minute–not so fast. Like many of you, I knew enough about weight loss to be dangerous and I certainly did not have fond memories of what it took to get lean for my bodybuilding show.

Secretly, deep inside, at 220 pounds I was unhappy about my state of leanness. Take my shirt off in public? What, are you nuts! I wasn't going to embarrass myself like that. How ridiculous considering I had been resistance training at that time for 14 years consistently and had acquired a fair amount of muscle! I could squat 600 pounds, bench press almost 400 and deadlift over 550 pounds. I was big and strong. The majority of long-term resistance trainers who are obese feel the same way though. You don't exactly see the average beach (Venice Beach notwithstanding) loaded with super lean resistance trainers, now do you? No, they are too embarrassed to reveal what they have created. With all the resistance training and self-pro-claiming that I was a bodybuilder, you could not see the muscles I had developed–at least not with any clarity. They were not chiseled. They were not sculpted like the guys in the magazines and when it came time to review my body in my birthday suit, I looked like a big tub of lard. As you can see from my before photo, at 220 pounds I didn't look like I had lifted a weight in my life, although I had been lifting for 14 years when that photo was taken.

Through basic moderation, I did lower my weight to 190 pounds by the summer of 1995 but I longed for the extra calories I used to be able to consume. I still longed for the high-fat, high-sugar foods that I thought made me a good, strong power lifter. I was quickly realizing what it was going to take to stay lean and I did-n't like it much, I'll tell you that right now. Never has it rung more true that if I knew then what I know now and am teaching you, I would have been much better off. I hovered around the 190 mark for a few months and then finally decided to take it down the rest

David Greenwalt After

of the way for a ripped look. I followed a low-carb/ketogenic diet to take my body weight down to 180 pounds and approximately seven percent body fat. It was through this process that I learned why low-carb diets are mostly fad diets and not something the vast majority will live with for long. It was also through this process that I realized it was probably counter-productive to health to eliminate entire food groups like most fruits, many vegetables and most grains.

After a short stint at 180 pounds and seven percent body fat, I climbed back up to about 200 pounds, where I comfortably maintained my weight at 12 to 15 percent body fat. I say it was comfortable because I could maintain it without much thought going into my nutritional program. Many researchers would call this my "set point." What I did not know at the time, of course, was that you can move your set point and what you currently have does not have to be what you are stuck with.

In 1992, I started a company called "The Power Store." I quickly realized that I had better become an avid student of the science of nutrition and training if I really wanted to service my clients. And so, I did–become an avid student of nutrition and exercise, that is. I began publishing my first newsletter in 1993 and realized the only way to really approach things was from a combination of science and pragmatism. Combining what science told us with what I knew worked for others and myself was the message I preached then and still do today.

In 1998, 12 years after my Neanderthal approach to weight loss while in college, I decided to compete in a bodybuilding show once again. I knew I wanted to pull everything I had learned up to that point together and really use a nutritional program that was healthy, multidimensional with plenty of food variety, and balanced. I had to be ripped by May of 1998 and I had at least 25 pounds to lose. It was through this contest preparation that the seeds of the Lifestyle were really being planted. In fact, in an issue of a magazine I published back then called "The Health & Performance Marketplace," I titled an article depicting my contest preparation as "Competition becomes a Leanness Lifestyle." Little did I know that I was creating the title for this book and success system. I concluded that article from the summer of 1998 with this passage ...

> *"I continue to eat a variety of foods today and for some, it might be considered that I am constantly now in a pre-contest diet. It's not a diet though, it's life."*

I did compete in May of 1998 and at my lowest body fat ever: five percent! Not only did I compete but I cut weight eating a wide variety of foods, never eliminating any food groups, always having at least one splurge meal each week, and never cutting back on water. To say this was vastly different from any dieting I had done in the past would be an understatement.

Joe Normal

I do not have an amazing metabolism. If you look up "average metabolism" in any medical textbook, you will see a photo of me. In fact, I consider my body unforgiving when it comes to food–probably a lot like you. If I am not careful, if I fall off the Lifestyle wagon for too long, I have the tendency to become fat easily. How do I know? I am human and have my full spectrum of bad, good and better cycles just like you, however, with practice and discipline, the swings in <u>my</u> cycles are not nearly as high or as low as they once were. I do pay for it when I do poorly however. I pay in the form of blurred abdominals and a thick feeling when I do an ab check. An ab check is a quick pinch of my skin around my midsection. When that skin is "thicker," I know I just caused myself additional work and focused thought toward my nutritional program.

Because I have average ability and genetics, I believe I have become a better teacher. It is important you are careful whom you trust when health and fitness advice is being dispensed.

"Never confuse natural ability and genetics with brains!"

I have never been gifted at any sport and have busted my backside to acquire every gram of muscle possible and to teach myself the methods I will teach you for lowering body fat and keeping it low. In other words, I am Joe Normal. I do not believe it does most clients any good to be taught by a super athlete who always excelled at what they tried and were always far above their competition for no apparent reason other than genetics. I am not the guy who eats two Sausage McMuffins® on the way to a bodybuilding show I am competing in <u>because I can</u>! Don't you just hate those guys in a green kind of way?

Since that first ugly contest diet I did back in 1986 (which some foolish bodybuilders still follow today), I have found the answers to my own leanness dreams. I guarantee that if you follow the guidelines I am laying out for you here you will never question again what it takes to get lean and stay lean forever! I have spent half my life practicing, making mistakes, devouring every thing I could read and finally understanding what it takes to create a lifetime of leanness.

As I said before, the Lifestyle is not theory-based teaching; it has proven techniques for leanness success. It works! Clients sometimes call the Lifestyle a workbook. It makes sense really. It is chock full of great information and you should feel comfortable writing in it, highlighting important points and truly making a mess of it. The more involved you immediately become, the greater your chances of success. The Lifestyle is also full of exercises that force you to think, dig deep inside and evaluate what you really want so you become involved in your own success at a level you never imagined possible. Too many books have you reading endlessly about protein, carbohydrates and fats and when you are done you are a more intelligent fat person and that's about it. The Lifestyle is about doing, not about postulating.

What The Lifestyle Is and Is Not

- The Lifestyle is foremost about *balance, moderation, substitution and consistency.* I know in our super-sized, extreme everything world those four terms may seem foreign but your acceptance of their simplicity and power is everything for being lean the rest of your life. It is true that for a period you might almost have to develop a maniacal attitude about your transformation. Let's face it. Things will be uncomfortable for a while and current priorities may take a backseat to your leanness goals. That's okay. It's natural and you will ease back out of the exceptionally focused mode you must attain for your transformation. The energy devoted to Lifestyle thought and preparation will decrease when you near your goal and realize you are the one in control.

- The Lifestyle is about displacing poor food choices with more vegetables, fruits, lean proteins, whole grains and essential fatty acids.

- The Lifestyle is about realizing you were in the driver's seat all along and your weight is a choice, not some predestined genetic anomaly.

- The Lifestyle is about teaching people their metabolisms are not broken and they are not some genetic mutants.

- The Lifestyle is truly a lifestyle you can live with.

- The Lifestyle is a plan you make your own. You will select foods that are tasty to you, which you can eat on a regular basis without an overwhelming feeling of loss and self-pity. As one client recently said "The great thing about the Lifestyle is no matter where you go, you can take it with you!"

- The Lifestyle is not about elimination, deprivation and living on rabbit food. Asian, Italian, Mexican? Doesn't matter. Favorite cultural dishes can still be eaten with moderation guiding you.

- The Lifestyle is not a quick fix diet plan. In fact, it is not a diet at all. A diet is something you start with little intention of continuing after a period. Isn't that how you have approached most diets in the past? Wasn't there a little voice inside your head telling you to just do it until you got there? The sooner you recognize that you manage your life and body with attitude and action, the sooner you will see that this Lifestyle is what your body was craving all those years anyway.

- The Lifestyle may not be a plan you have ever been taught but because of its simplicity and reasonableness, you can follow it forever without wondering if you are "doing the right thing." You can stop guessing what the right foods are, how to put it all together and you will finally know how to live with healthy choices that taste good.

• Finally, the Lifestyle is not about elimination. You will not hear me say anywhere that you cannot have _____. In fact, I will go on record right now as saying that you can have any non-trigger food (more about trigger foods later) you like, for the rest of your life, as long as you incorporate them into the Lifestyle when I say and not more than I say. I love this quote.

> *"There are no bad foods, only bad habits."*
> Jeanie Burke R.D.

Who Is The Lifestyle Really For?

The principles of the Lifestyle apply to anyone who wants to lose fat and gain muscle. I only make one assumption of those reading this book: you want to lose body fat and reshape your body, and the nutritional waters in your life have become muddied over the years with conflicting and confusing advice. You are seeking a solution for ultimate, lifelong leanness and muscularity you did not even know you had in you. I know you have it in you but allow me to answer more specifically, to whom in particular this book pertains.

If you want to lose 10 pounds or 100, it doesn't matter. The Lifestyle principles still apply. If you've tried to diet and failed on five or more occasions then welcome to the club because most ultimate success stories involve people just like you who've tried to lose the weight and keep it off and were unsuccessful on numerous occasions. In fact, if you have tried and failed to lose the weight and keep it off on numerous occasions, you are actually an expert just waiting to finally succeed. Whether you believe it or not, you are more knowledgeable now than you were with your first attempt. The brightest, richest and leanest people worldwide have also failed the most. Only those who do not try do not fail. Zig Ziglar is a favorite speaker and mentor of mine. I quote him often and cannot recommend his books and tapes enough. I completely agree with him when he talks about failures. He says

> *"A failure describes an event–not a person"*
> Zig Ziglar, *Over the Top*

If you have followed previous diets that required you to eat like a bird, then you are really going to love the fact that I highly suggest you eat four to six times a day! I'll explain why later but you need to know that yes, you will need to adjust your entire thinking about food, what it does for the body, and how you can control it, instead of it controlling you. Nevertheless, ultimately you will be able to eat what you want in moderation.

Competitive Bodybuilders Can And Should Use The Lifestyle

If you're a person who wants to compete as a bodybuilder, the Lifestyle is for you just as much as it is the person who has no intention of ever showing their body to anyone other than an intimate loved one. How can this be? The principles you are about to discover apply across all races, colors, ethnicities and athletic endeavors. Whether you have 100 pounds to lose or 10, it still takes the same adjustments of attitudes toward food, yourself and a permanent mental shift into believing you can do it and should do it. While there are some minor adjustments during the final few weeks or so of bodybuilding show preparation, they are only minor if you have already been following the Lifestyle.

As a natural bodybuilder myself, I strongly urge you to stay within ten percent of your contest weight and would preferably recommend you stay within five percent. You will come in tighter, fuller and will not feel like someone literally sucked the life out of you on contest day. The Lifestyle can easily keep you eight weeks away from entering any show you wish.

What If My Goal Is To Gain Weight?

In the 3rd edition of The Lifestyle, I provided a cursory overview of the mindset and strategies necessary for the hard gainer to pack on the pounds. I have decided to forego any focus on gaining weight in the Lifestyle other than the sections and chapters espousing the wonderful benefits of resistance training. The subject of gaining weight is as complex and diverse as losing weight and it really requires a completely separate book to properly discuss it. By not focusing on too many issues in the Lifestyle, you can be assured the focus of this book is about one issue: shedding the fat pounds, keeping them off permanently, and reshaping your body with lean, beautiful muscle.

I must address one issue that consistently rears its ugly head for many would-be leanness seekers: should I "bulk up" or "get ripped" first? Many would-be leanness seekers are fat but are also dissatisfied with their current muscularity. Narrow shoulders, stringy arms, wide hips and a thick waist are begging for a sound resistance-training program. Many confuse bulking up with adding lean, sexy, beautiful muscle. So while they are typically twice as fat as they should be to start, they believe they need to get *bigger* before they trim down. This may be true, but that does not mean they have to get *fatter* in the process.

Some actually believe that if they add a lot of quick weight they will look leaner because it will increase their thickness and make their waist look smaller. If this describes you, then I will strongly suggest you primarily choose leanness. A big part of the fat-stripping process will include a well-designed resistance-training program so you will continue or start the body reshaping process while you are bringing your body fat to a respectable, healthy level. By focusing on and achieving leanness first, you will succeed at one of two parts of a superb shape: getting rid of the fat.

The second part of achieving a head-spinning physique is adding lean, beautiful muscle. By using the right workout for you (see Chapter 14–*Resistance Training for Everyone*), you'll tone and tighten your thighs, narrow your hips, shrink your waist, round your shoulders, lift and thicken your chest, develop a v-taper from the back and your buttocks will no longer sag and resemble 25 pounds of chewed bubble gum! Adding muscle is approximately 50 times harder than stripping body fat. Don't ever fear adding too much muscle! Ever! As a natural trainer, it is not possible. And with that said I've just uncovered the first myth you may have held dear to your heart ...

"I'm afraid of resistance training because I believe I'll get too big"

Commit to leanness first and get off the fence once and for all. If you remain fence-bound, you will neither shed fat nor add muscle. The tug-of-war that occurs between the two can literally stagnate all progress if you are not focused on one or the other. This is not to say you cannot add muscle while losing fat–many neophyte resistance trainers can likely do just that. But if you don't commit fully, completely and with zealous disregard for the comments of spectators and current self-limiting beliefs about what you are really made of, you're likely to weigh the exact same a year from now as you do today, and neither of us wants that.

Mr. Skinny Fat

It is common, for men especially, to decide they will have to add significant muscle mass before they will be comfortable stripping body fat below a certain percentage. This typically occurs in men who have been thin most of their lives according to clothing size but who've gotten fatter with a high proportion of the added fat showing up around the midsection. It is typical for many men who wear a small to medium size shirt, and a 32-34 waist blue jean, to have a body fat above 20 percent. Family and friends still comment on how "Mr. Skinny Fat" is lucky to be so thin but Mr. Skinny Fat knows what hides behind his clothing. There is no question that the best "After" photos from a transformation–man or woman–are those which show the end result with at least a modicum of muscle tone and shape from resistance training. Undoing the "skinny fat" syndrome cannot be done with only aerobic exercise. You must place an equal or greater emphasis on resistance training.

If you're a man and you are absolutely certain you are not going to be happy if you end up skinny and without any visible muscularity, then here's my advice. Reduce body fat to approximately 12 percent using Lifestyle principles while incorporating the resistance training principles discussed later. Then, if you wish, maintain 12 percent body fat while progressively getting stronger in your resistance-training program for at least six months. After this period of time you can decide if you want to reduce fat any further or if you want to take another six months to add even more muscle. If you are living at 12 percent body fat and adding muscle, I can sleep at night knowing you are not obese and, in fact, are training at a body fat that is not only quite conducive for adding quality muscle, but also very healthy.

Ms. Skinny Fat

As a woman, it's imperative you realize that your hips, thighs and buttocks are not large because they are loaded with muscle. I swear to you ladies—your large thighs are *not* large because you were a cheerleader in high school. They are not large because you *used to* be a gymnast. And it unequivocally is not because you have too much muscle from your current resistance-training regimen! It is all about stored fat. Reducing your body fat to 20 percent while engaging in my resistance training—prescription for six to 12 months will ensure that you are going to bu...

...is capable of adding over a given period. It is a slower process than stripping fat, requires careful attention to details, a constant striving for progress and sometimes the patience of a saint. Even though I have made it sound next to impossible to add any quality muscle, I have only done so to make this point clear: you cannot possibly add too much muscle to your body. It is imperative that you resolve false perceptions about what it takes to look like a competitive bodybuilder and accept the fact right now that you will never have the body you truly desire without progressive resistance training. Never! That is a promise.

You Haven't Tried Everything

Not only do we all have baggage from our past to deal with but you and I are faced with fighting the daily barrage of infomercials, so-called health and muscle magazines and get-rich-quick schemes all playing off our inner need to be healthy, lean, and—not least of all—*our vanity*. You may believe because you have tried a dozen other programs that nothing works. You might find it hard to believe, after reading the Lifestyle thoroughly, that something so straightforward can work. "Where's the secret?" you might ask. "Where's the glitz?"

You may have tried many systems, products and programs but you have not tried "everything" as is so commonly claimed. Never forget that you can work very hard and diligently at doing the <u>wrong</u> things taught by misguided or purposefully deceitful trainers or advisors. Up to this point you may have been practicing to lose weight, however, there's a big difference between practicing, and practicing perfectly. Only perfect practice makes perfect and creates champions. You have not been. What you've done in the past isn't the equivalent of working very hard, in an intelligent, well thought out manner that applies scientific principles to weight loss. Maya Angelou perhaps said it best ...

> *"You did what you knew how to do,*
> *and when you knew better, you did better."*

It is time <u>you</u> knew better.

The Lifestyle is the next step regardless of where you are coming from. You have learned from your past but let us not dwell in the past. Yesterday really did end last night and today is a new day. The Lifestyle will take you to a new level when you commit to the program fully with Desire, Dedication, Determination and Discipline.

If you have never been lean in your life then the only disadvantage you may have is not believing in yourself enough to commit fully to the program. You have no idea how great it really feels to be lean and fit and therefore, you have nothing to compare your current lack of fitness to. I assure you that

Nothing tastes as great as being lean feels.

When I eat a cookie it takes me about five seconds to eat it. I enjoy it and derive pleasure from it for a maximum of another five seconds. While anyone can have a cookie, everyone agrees it would be foolish for me to advise *you* that eating a dozen per day is healthy or leanness promoting. Because I do not fixate on the short-term pleasure of excessively eating comfort foods like cookies, I am lean and have a nice six-pack most of the time. I wear my reward and derive pleasure from it 24 hours a day. That is 1440 minutes and 86,400 seconds of pleasure a day instead of ten seconds from eating the cookie. I focus intently and consistently on living within the reasonable bounds of the Lifestyle.

Successful transformationists are goal achievers. Failures in the
transformation process are tension relievers.

The Lifestyle will guide you every step of the way. This book will help you create an optimum eating plan for yourself. It is my sincere hope that this will become the last weight loss book you ever need. In that light, you should view the Lifestyle as an educational course with no real end. It is a lifelong program of continued learning and awareness of the effects of food on your health and well being. With practice and patience, you will not only <u>become</u> your best but also <u>continue</u> looking and feeling your best for a lifetime.

Finally, you are not a metabolically challenged person. Your metabolism is not "broken." You have not ruined your metabolism with yo-yo dieting. Scientific research clearly indicates that yo-yo dieting does not permanently lower your metabolic rate. And your past failures really were only learning experiences leading you up to this moment–nothing more, nothing less.

To summarize, the Lifestyle is a breakthrough nutrition and lifestyle program that will improve your energy, teach you to respond to natural, physiological hunger, and reduce food cravings by stabilizing blood sugars and stimulating the body to burn fat for fuel.

- Emotional stability
- Improved sleep
- Increased mental clarity
- Better concentration and memory

Medical Benefits
- Lower cholesterol, triglycerides, blood sugar, and blood pressure levels
- Reduced chest and leg pain
- Reduction or elimination of chronic medical symptoms such as PMS, headaches, asthma and intestinal disorders

Legal Duty

Before I get crankin' here I must first please my lawyers and suggest that anyone beginning a new eating regimen and exercise program should consult with their physician. Oh, the heck with it. Show this program to your doctor before you start it and she will be doing back flips for its simplicity and wholesomeness. Maybe she will even decide to do the Lifestyle and finally get rid of the 20 extra pounds of cottage cheese she has been carrying around since her first year of medical school! Anyway, I am not a doctor and I do not play one on TV, and more importantly, I don't have your medical history so talk to your doctor before starting this program.

I strongly recommend you do not skip sections of this book. Read it all from beginning to end. The flow is purposeful and logical. You must understand "A" before "B." You cannot reach the top of the building with a single leap. You will have to take each step along the way and every step counts. Miss one and you will stumble.

You will do me a disservice if you simply read this book and take no action. Jim Rohn said, "Don't let your learning lead to knowledge. Let your learning lead to action." Find out if you are ready for action in Chapter 2: *Are You Ready To Change?* It is a must read!

Summary

We Americans are as obese as we've ever been. It is common early on to feel sorry for ourselves when approaching a life-changing strategy like The Leanness Lifestyle. It is important you do not equate being a "normal American" with good or desirable.

There are a number of reasons many individuals have for reading The Leanness Lifestyle. Your reasons are all that matter to you and I certainly do not proclaim to have given you a comprehensive list within this chapter. It is quite possible you are already in very good shape, maybe practicing 90 percent of what this book is all about but just want to finish what you've started. You can.

Regardless of your present level of knowledge and experience with other programs I believe The Leanness Lifestyle is your springboard through the next steps to a new you. You certainly have not tried everything and it is absolutely time you became your full potential.

Take Action and Feel Great!

1. Read Chapter 2 and make certain you are in the right stage of change.

Are You Ready to Change?

.... every person, regardless of the change they go through, will pass through or recycle through at least five of six distinct stages of change: Pre-contemplation, Contemplation, Preparation, Action, Maintenance and Termination.

In this chapter, I will present these stages as they relate to your ultimate goal of a better, healthier body. My intention is that by providing a more scientific, yet easy-to-understand model, you will understand what stage of change you are in currently. This understanding will allow you to adapt to the stage and progress forward. If you attempt changes before you are truly ready, you will only set yourself up for failure. If you are ready to move ahead, but spend too much time simply raising "conscious awareness" or completing tasks you have already mastered, you may indefinitely delay moving forward. Neither scenario is desirable.

Will Power

Many people believe their lack of weight loss success is due to an inherent lack of will power. I do not believe this is true. I believe you have plenty of will power but may have lacked the power to harness and direct it for the right purpose.

Will Power n. The ability and strength of mind to carry out one's decisions, wishes, or plans.

You already possess tremendous will power and you are not lacking in this characteristic. For instance, when you awaken every day, do you rise when you feel like it? Or do you awaken with an "opportunity clock?" (Zig Ziglar refers to an alarm clock as an "opportunity clock," and I prefer that term as well.) Do you wake up late everyday? No. Is there anyone else in your home who relies on you to go to work, take care of the home, pay bills, get groceries, keep up with maintenance, or even take out the garbage? If not, do you not rely on yourself for all of these tasks? Do you fail at all of them? Are you late for work often? While at work, do you always let the boss down? Are you proficient at whatever earns you a living right now? When your children want your attention and you are tired, do you always tell them to go away and not to bother you? Do you call someone every time a decision has to be made, or do you rely on your own wisdom to make the best choice most of the time? You are self-sufficient and possess good judgment, I bet.

When you wanted to buy a car or a home did you have to save for it? How could you possibly have saved for a down payment if you did not possess will power? Do you invest in your retirement? It takes will power to sock money away every month into something you will not benefit from for 35 or more years! For all of these reasons and more, which all require will power, it is obvious that if there is one thing you are not lacking, it is will power.

Laziness

Without identifying which stage you are in and eventually progressing to the Action stage, the energy necessary to adjust your eating lifestyle and exercise regimen just will not surface. This can be perceived as lazy, however, with everything you are responsible for on a daily basis and how busy your life is, there is not a shred of doubt–you are not fat because you are lazy. Let's face it–being overweight is a real downer. Is there any question that your mindset as an overweight person can make you believe you are lazy, when in fact you are just depressed or afraid to move out of your comfort zone towards change? Once you identify which stage you are in, and you begin using effective processes to propel you into the Action stage, you will begin to feel more energized and positive about each step you take.

Lack of Time

The number one reason given for not exercising by those who do not is "not enough time." There is a limiting false perception that becoming fit will take an inordinate amount of time. Just think about "all that exercise" that you will have to do. The reality is once you have goals and a set program you will quit *wasting* time with immediate gratification and start being more productive. You will find time you never imagined you had! Couple that with the fact that becoming fit doesn't take more time–it gives you more time because you'll be goal oriented and able to accomplish more in less time. Voila! You have been stripped of the "not enough time" excuse. There is no doubt that all of us make time for the things that are most important to us. Any of the people who have been through a transformation before you had no more time than you have. They made the transformation successful because they planned ahead, and were willing to pay whatever price was required to make their transformation a reality. Once they invested the initial energy and time to learn and understand the principles within the Lifestyle, they found they had even more time. The Action stage is a tremendous learning phase and requires energy and more time than you are used to putting out for your fitness program. Maintenance, although still energy-intensive, requires far less mental energy and physical time because by the time you prove yourself worthy of achieving your goals and entering this stage, you will be far more efficient, knowledgeable and not losing weight. This is a very important point not to be missed! In Maintenance, as you will learn on the pages that follow,

Everyone on Earth is granted 24 hours in a day. You might believe there is no one busier on Earth than you. You are mistaken. You might also believe that while there might be someone, somewhere, busier than you, that particular busier person is not also trying to lose weight. You would be mistaken again. People far busier than you are losing 20 or more pounds in as little as 60 to 90 days.

Does it take any more time to eat better? Does it take any more time when you are working at your desk to eat a protein/energy bar instead of vending machine garbage? Does it take any more time to eat a chicken breast sandwich with mustard, lettuce and tomato versus a Double Grease Ball with Cheese? Being leaner and fitter will not take more of your time. It will literally give you more time. Once you start dropping weight by using the principles in the Lifestyle you will feel better and be able to do more with the resulting increased energy. You may not even realize it, but you are running at about half speed with a high body fat and additional, unnecessary body weight. When you drop the excess weight, you will wonder how you ever managed to function when you were where you are now.

Since you and I both know your current lack of weight loss success has nothing to do with an inherent lack of will power, laziness, or lack of time, where do you turn for answers to your weight problem? Your current lack of success has everything to do with matching the right activities with the right stage of change. As you'll read throughout this chapter, once you've truly reached the Action stage you will not only find the time and make the time, you will also become a better time manager. As is the case with every successful weight loss champion, you will do what it takes to make it happen!

Winding Road of Change

No one ever succeeds at getting the washboard stomach or developing a lifestyle of healthier eating habits until they are ready to change. I am fully aware that as you read this you may have no doubt you are ready for action! Over 90-percent of new coaching applicants I review are pumped and ready to roll! Or so they think. It is very common for the perception of readiness to not match the actual readiness needed to effect significant change. "Wanting it" is rarely enough and, at some much deeper level, you must have traveled through several earlier stages before reaching the Action stage.

The road leading up to the stage of change where the physical transformation occurs is winding and full of potholes. This road is also unique for every individual. There are similarities many times among individuals, however, every story is unique, and every past is different. It is important you have a better understanding of the stages of change so you know that there is never a reason to live without hope. As you will see in this chapter, it's exceptionally common for people to recycle through the stages at varying points in their life, however, these periods of recycling are always leading you further up the winding road to better health and fitness. Will there be hills and valleys along the way? You bet.

I strongly urge you not to skip this chapter. In fact, I suggest you read it, stop, take a day off and read it again before continuing. I believe it is easily one of the most important and if you choose to jump right to what you believe is the meat of the book, you'll truly be missing a very important concept I'm certain most of you have never considered, but need to.

Sam I Am

Sam came to me in the spring of 2001 with enthusiasm, excitement and a never-say-die attitude. His vocal commitment to his transformation was clear, strong and unwavering–or so it appeared. After only a few short weeks, Sam's communication with me began to wane so I checked in on him to determine if he was completing the assignments I had given him early on. After several days Sam responded. It was obvious he was struggling and had not completed the important assignments.

After a few weeks, Sam returned with a vengeance swearing he would never again allow himself to slip into the abyss of de-motivation eating. He dedicated himself by creating a website with his "Before" photos displayed, a daily log for all the world to see, and also vocally committed to the other members of my coaching program that he would finally achieve his dream of losing well over 100 pounds. The other members rallied around Sam as he posted messages and tidbits of inspiration for all, and a nearly daily recounting of how he was feeling and mentally progressing.

Slowly but surely, Sam began to drift away. At first, his messages decreased from ten or more per week to three or four per week. Then, within a very short time, his messages disappeared all together, and Sam was once again AWOL. Noticing his disappearance once again, I contacted Sam to see if he was completing the necessary food logging, analysis and exercise prescription I had given him. I had also asked him to secure his "cost" (also known as leverage and will be discussed later in this chapter) for continuing his journey. Sam's response was that his mindset was much better and he was feeling good about his progress. However, when asked specifically how much weight he had lost over the past few weeks, he never responded. *As an experienced coach, I know that in nearly every instance, no reply or failure to communicate is an indicator there has been no progress.* Most people at this point are ashamed of their lack of progress, and so they feel it is simply easier

Progressing Through the Stages

Why is it that some people can lose 20 pounds in ten weeks and others take six months or longer? What is the secret of those successful individuals, who seem to effortlessly lose all the weight they want without exceptional hunger and a deprived feeling all the time? The keys to an amazing transformation have always been matching the right activities with the right stage of change.

As I explain the six stages of change, I'd like you to reflect back on Sam's story and determine, when you're finished reading this chapter, what stage Sam was really in when he joined my coaching program as opposed to what stage he thought he was in. Then, more importantly, I would like you to take a hard look at the daily action steps you complete each day. Within just a few days to a week you will clearly see, for certain, which stage *you* are in. My goal with this chapter is to help you see your stage clearly, so you can continue to advance to the Action stage. That is where all the glamour and applause lies.

Research indicates that persons desiring change will typically do 80 percent better by including professional help when compared to those waiting for help. Hiring a coach or therapist to assist with changing is beneficial for many, however, even with their help, the person changing does 99 percent of the work during the hours and days where contact with the coach or therapist is not occurring. Therefore,

All change is self-change.

No matter how you decide to change (with or without professional help), you *must* apply the right strategy for the stage you are in.

It's the start that stops most people.

Pre-contemplation–Stage 1

It is important you realize that every person who changes anything always passes through at least five of the six stages of change. Pre-contemplation is the first. In the Pre-contemplation stage, there is a clear denial that any problem even exists. For the pre-contemplator, if any change is going to occur, it must come from everyone else around them because to them, there is no problem. During this stage you are likely to avoid any information that relates to your problem and will even turn the channel on the television if the talent brings up any solutions for, or discussions of, *your* problem. People have no intention of changing when they are in Pre-contemplation.

During Pre-contemplation you are likely to believe your weight problem is out of your control. Another common belief is that if God had wanted you to be fit, he would have made you fit. Genetics are quickly blamed, and there is little hope from within a pre-contemplator. Pre-contemplators are commonly demoralized and feel beaten. The phrases "ignorance is bliss" and "this is my fate" can define a pre-contemplator. They do not have a problem, so why learn about it? Never does it matter that everyone around them can easily see there is truly a problem that needs addressing.

Pre-contemplation is a safe place to be. For this reason, many people never leave this stage. It's a safe but miserable place to live. It is safe because if you never attempt anything new, you will not fail.

> *"To escape all criticism say nothing, do nothing, be nothing."*
> Elbert Hubbard, Designer and Writer

You cannot be criticized for trying and failing, because as a pre-contemplator you never try. Further, pre-contemplators are freed of any guilt related to their problem, because they will hear nothing of it. Society expects little of pre-contemplators, thus they are less likely to disappoint. To move out of the Pre-contemplation stage means being personally responsible for sinking or swimming and inviting social pressure to succeed and excel. In the end, however, I believe those who have significant weight or other problems, and who refuse to acknowledge them and move toward a better life, are really living a life of prison, not a safe life.

One of the most beneficial aspects of learning these stages is in knowing that every person starts at some Pre-contemplation level. Is there a spectrum for each stage? Sure. Not everyone is completely beaten down and demoralized when they start any change process. The spectrum is broad for each stage, but in general, the guidelines I am providing here will help you to see more clearly where you are. Do not wait until you "bottom out" to consider changing. Moving away from Pre-contemplation earlier rather than later, when the damage is more severe, is highly beneficial for success. By matching your needs with your stage of change, you will be able to progress to the next stage: Contemplation.

g..... quickly.

Contemplation–Stage 2

"I'm tired of being fat!" or "I'm tired of feeling sick and tired" are common statements some-one in the Contemplation stage would make. They recognize they have a problem they need to deal with, and are beginning to open their eyes and mind a bit more to help that may be available. Contemplators are seeking information. Consciousness-raising is the fuel that feeds their fire during this stage. Instead of turning the television channel, they will listen when the message relates to their problem. All of a sudden it'll appear to them as if all around them there are news articles, self-help books and people they know who can offer some bit of advice or knowledge relating to their prob-lem. Contemplators will feel as if all of this great information was never available before. We now know why they believe this is true. As a pre-contemplator they simply were not interested in hear-ing it. *Their antenna was down and their radio for help was off.*

Even though there is a marked difference between a contemplator and a pre-contemplator, the contemplator is not ready for action just yet. In fact, Prochaska says "Many people remain stuck in the Contemplation stage for a very long time. People who eternally substitute action for thinking can be called chronic contemplators." The latter part of this stage may even have the changer complete with all the knowledge they need to change, however, still nothing happens. They know what to do, but do not do it even though they know doing it is the right thing to do. "Some day" they will change … just not today.

Contemplators will wait for "just the right time" or "a little bit more conclusive data" before tak-ing the next step. A chronic contemplator wants to be fed (information) constantly. They aren't ready for the next step in the change process, but they will subscribe to three magazines on health, peruse every internet nugget they can find, and become so confused from all the mismatched stories on health and fitness that they remain catatonic. Anything that feeds them raw data without demanding they actually get up and <u>do</u> anything is good reading for many chronic contemplators. The bottom line for many chronic contemplators is that they are not interested in moving forward, just the next new fitness pearl to share with a friend. They can truly be quite educated, yet frightened, individuals.

FEAR is a major obstacle blocking many contemplators from moving to the next stage. Zig Ziglar says FEAR is really an acronym for

F - False   E - Evidence   A - Appearing   R - Real

Contemplators also feel anxiety over moving away from the known (their life as it currently exists) and toward the unknown (a more fit and energetic life with demands of being a better person). "What if I fail?" This explains why many contemplators remain stuck for months or years. This insight alone, which Contemplation brings to you, will not change your behavior.

> President John F. Kennedy said, *"There are risks and costs to a program of action, but they are far less than the long-range risks and costs of comfortable inaction."*

Waiting for Life to Level Out

The chronic contemplator's motto is "When in doubt, wait till tomorrow." If you wait for life to level out before you begin to take control of your life, you will waste a lifetime. Action creates motivation, not the other way around.

I believe many people who are stuck in a state of chronic Contemplation have a very backward way of thinking. Most contemplators have a genuine interest in improving their health and physique, however, they still do not act because they are waiting. For what, you might ask. They're waiting for life to level out, for the current crisis to pass, for work to let up until they have some more energy, after this semester at school, "you know how crazy this year has been?", when the summer is over and things aren't so hectic and disjointed, and in general, they're waiting for things to occur that never will. *The chronic contemplators would like to cure life instead of manage it.*

At the time of this writing, a commercial is playing on television projecting a place I believe many people try to live everyday. In this beer commercial, a couple uses a cell phone to prop up an unleveled and wobbling table as they gaze out upon a crystal blue ocean. An ever-so-gentle breeze cools them under the cover of a sun-beaten umbrella, and all the while, they peacefully sip their beers without a care in the world. No bills, no problems, nothing to stand in the way of pure ecstasy! Uh huh, not going to happen–so quit waiting for it!

The reality of the Corona vacation is that this same couple was stressed putting the vacation together. The stress was likely a two to three month affair. First the financial aspect: "How are we going to pay for it? It costs THAT much to go ... Wow!" Add the drive to the airport, finding a place to park, but first dropping the kids at grandma's, packing all their stuff, and getting traveler's checks. Kenneling the pets and that will cost ya! Who will pick up our mail while we are gone? "Honey, did you put a Stop Delivery Order in at the post office yet? What about the passports? Damn it! We

After a few days to weeks the energy will come. I never talk to anyone, *ever*, who says they have less energy after they begin a new training regimen and they get their food planning in order. I always hear people talking about waiting until they have more energy to start. Very simply, it does not work that way. It is like saying you are going to wait to start practicing the guitar until you play it well. Huh? No, you have to practice it for years *before* you play it well.

> ***Start practicing to feel better now.***
> ***Do not wait to feel better to begin practicing.***

If you want to change your body, start with a change in behavior. In other words, begin to act the part, as well as you can, of the person you would rather be, the person you most want to become. Gradually, the old, out-of-shape person will fade away. If you wait until you feel like it to try to change your body, you will never change. John Maxwell says it very well: "You have to act yourself into changing."

Might there be a crisis that is so overwhelming you feel emotionally crippled and unable to exercise and eat properly? Yes, but these exceptions are not the everyday living that most consider overwhelming. No matter what happens, you still have a choice to make. There is always a choice. You can either choose to make the very best of the situation and realize that how you feel is not about what happens to you, but what you <u>do</u> with what happens to you. On the other hand, you can make yourself miserable and play the victim. Everyday living is stressful, make no mistake about it, the hurdles of life are not going to change anytime soon.

> ***You must manage life and not try and cure it.***

If you are a chronic contemplator, it is time to put your knowledge to work and *do it* instead of thinking and talking about it. The life you are living is not a dress rehearsal. You never get another chance to live it again. *There is no do-over.* Beginning the Lifestyle is not nearly as hard as thinking about it. Procrastinating and continuing with the negative thoughts you have had in the past will always keep you at arms-length from success. Just do it! Get off the fence and become the great person you were destined to become.

Get it Just Right or "Nike" It?

It is important that you at least *start* the Lifestyle. Even if you are not totally ready in your mind. Even if you do not have every meal planned between now and Christmas. Even if you do not have a membership to the gym yet or your personal home gym loaded with all the fruit salad to make it a show piece. Even if you do not quite understand what foods are best, and what foods will be your trigger foods. Even if you are bewildered by dietary supplements and wonder what you should take, if anything. Regardless of all things you do not know and are presently unsure about–you need to start the Lifestyle today!

Here is a compilation of what several coaching members had to say about waiting to start until everything was just so versus getting started with what you already know.

Here's my point. At roughly the same time I saw a bunch of new coaching members join the club their posts kept mentioning how they were "getting ready" and how they were planning to get started. They were checking out supplements, devising meal plans for the months ahead, and planning workouts and asking lots of questions on the forum and talking a lot about their feelings. It seemed this went on for months, during which time I probably lost 20 - 25 lbs.

I'm not saying planning isn't important, but it seems to me you can get started with a good plan and do better as you go. Until you get a taste of it, planning every aspect of your transformation may be kind of unrealistic. You don't know what's going to really fit into your life. And too many people try to be perfect from the start. I think Dave warns not to do that. When I was well over 250, back before we had the Calorie Calculator (a tool available online), I figured 2900 kcals would be maintenance and cutting 10% would give me about 2600 kcals to consume each day. Then I lifted 3x a week for 45 minutes and did boxing class for one hour 2x a week. Cutting down to 2600 kcals (who knows what I was eating before) just meant getting rid of the ice cream, McDonald's and half-n-half from my coffee. It was easy.

Now, I'm eating much cleaner and healthier than I ever thought possible. And it's still pretty easy. But I'm a totally different person. I didn't change overnight; it took 7 months of weaning myself off of my high fat junk food diet.

When Dave offered a Diva challenge to 12 select women it immediately moved them off the fence. All of a sudden all these women who had been planning, got going, and the rest is history. If it wasn't for things like the leverage David helps us set and strong emotional

commitment to the goals I think some people
digital food scale is better.

Get a rough plan together and get going. Unles
don't worry about every little thing, like what kind of
sodium and fiber levels in certain foods. Don't try to figure
start. It's a moving target anyway, and you need to be flexible.

In my profession we learn about "sensitivity analysis." You set up an
cast, then play around with the components. You ask yourself, "What if my e
factor is off? How much does it effect my forecast?" And you figure which factors h
most influence on your outcome, and where you can be off, and where you have to be dead
on (i.e., you can be off on estimating how much broccoli you ate, but you better measure the
oil very carefully).

The biggest factor, in my humble opinion, in everyone succeeding in his or her transformation is doing the basic simple stuff:

- Logging your foods every day so you don't overlook calories,
- Finding some meals that you can use over and over that will work with your life
  (or at least until your initial 8 or 12 week goals are met)
- Making sure you lift at least 3x a week for 45 minutes while doing cardio 2-4x a
  week for about a half-hour.
- Adopting an attitude that "failing equals death" will help make sure that failing is not
  even a possibility. Those simple things will make the difference if you're new to this.

Once, a member asked Dave about a supplement that studies had shown resulted in a
loss of 3 pounds of fat on average over 3 months of use. Hey, it's interesting and I'm sure
statistically significant, but I can lose 3 pounds in a week just following the Calorie
Calculator in the coaching club tab. I'm just saying, don't lose sight of the forest for the trees.
Ask yourself when planning for your next several weeks, "What's really going to make the
difference in whether I succeed or not in losing 1.5 or 2 or whatever pounds a week?"

I'm not a religious person (I'm the doubting kind in general), but every journey takes a
little faith. You have to believe it will happen and believe enough in yourself to know you'll
handle the obstacles and figure out what needs to be done when the time comes. You can't
figure everything out in advance, or you'll never move from the planning stage.

Yes, get help and support from others. And plan, but keep it simple, because simple
works best. Yes, I'm still eating that less-than-pure instant oatmeal for breakfast instead of
the steel cut Irish oats cause right now it works for me, and I know myself. Some day I'll do
better. But for right now, I agree with Nike when they say, "Just Do It!"

Heat Seeking Missile

To succeed in your transformation you will, no doubt, need to be more meticulous than the average couch potato. I see myself as a heat seeking missile (no sexual innuendoes intended) or a torpedo. Yes, they have to be fired in the general direction of the target, but not with perfect aim, because they have guidance systems that are continuously tracking the target and making adjustments. In the beginning, those adjustments are large, but as the missile approaches the target, the adjustments become smaller (maybe more frequent) but just as important. Obviously, the further away the target, the more room you have to maneuver and the less accurate your "shot" has to be.

I guess I'm just saying you don't have to have the perfect plan to get going. With this transformation I started eating chicken breasts grilled on the George Foreman grill. Before this challenge, I ate the chicken breasts the way my wife prepares them dipped in eggbeaters and breadcrumbs and baked on a pan with some olive oil. Before that, my wife would sometimes use eggs to coat them, and I didn't really push her on how much oil she used, although I tried. Before that, I ate the chicken parmigiana style, same as above but with sauce and low-fat mozzarella cheese (sometimes with pepperoni slices). Before that I ate red meat more frequently than chicken. Before that was before I started the Leanness Lifestyle, and I usually ate bacon and eggs and/or sausage for breakfast (or an Egg-McMuffin with two hash browns and tons of catsup). Lunch was a Big Mac super-sized (sometimes with a Diet Coke if I was watching my weight LOL!). Dinner was meat and potatoes (no veggies) and a half-gallon or more of ice cream for dessert. And if you want to go back ten years (since I'm making my act of contrition), I used to drink to excess, take uppers so I could drink to excess without passing out, go to bars, sleep with women I met at bars, go to strip joints and brothels and I alternated between Chinese food and pizza for dinner every night.

So, if I started off doing the Leanness Lifestyle eating chicken breasts cooked on the George Foreman grill, I would have lasted about a week. I made changes in 10% increments, and I figured things out as I went along. There's no doubt I made a lot of mistakes, and I fell down a few times, but today I'm very close to my goal, after losing over fifty pounds. In the beginning I didn't have to be perfect to lose weight, and I doubt most people just starting out would have to be. Some of us, who have been in a transformation mode for awhile, need to be more exact in what we're doing as we get down the final pounds. Others might be new to this effort, and therefore, they need to just make the basic, though seemingly big, adjustments.

Animal flesh continuum
meat -> chicken in oil and cheese -> grilled with low fat cheese -> grilled

Turn That Tanker Around

Transformation analogies are helpful. One analogy may be the turning of a giant ship. Oil tankers don't turn on a dime. Rather they need to slow way down, then turn, then pick up speed going the other direction. In a similar vein, maybe someone starting the Lifestyle who has had years of horrible habits needs first to slowly rid themselves of the bad while acquiring the good. But that doesn't change the math -> 3500 kcal/deficit per pound. An Egg McMuffin with two hash browns = 550 kcal/28g fat/19g protein - not a great start to the day.

I guess my concern is for the vast majority of people who would start to make little changes and improvements but offset those with other caloric sources and then complain/give up because the "LL" doesn't work for them and they've "really tried" for several weeks. Growing up my parents' house was filled with fat-free this, low-fat that, you name it. My uncle used to call it a house filled with "food-free" food. My thinking was "Great! This ice cream is low-fat so I'll just throw a little extra in the bowl."

You don't starve on The Leanness Lifestyle. But it's easy to wipe out a week's gains in one sitting without much effort (especially eating out). And that is why my advice to newbies is to plan it out meticulously -> because who among us doesn't wish that is just what we'd done x pounds ago before it all got so out of control.

To this end, I offer my $.02. An airplane is OFF COURSE 90% of the time it is flying toward its destination. The pilot (you), co-pilot (David and other coaching club members), and auto-pilot (maintenance once course has been set), constantly need to adjust your course so that you DO land in the place(your goal) that you took off for. You must take off (Just Do It!) BEFORE you can be "off course" for the majority of your flight. Obviously, you need to file your flight plan (a well defined "plan") before you take off, but you WILL constantly need to adjust (not change or tweak...but "plan as you go") your flight plan along the way.

Whether you think of yourself as the "Nike" person, the "Heat-seeking missile", the "tanker" or some combination of all three, the important point is you must progress from the Contemplation stage to Preparation if you hope to eventually enter the Action stage and enjoy the physical changes that occur there. You must employ the processes of change (to be discussed shortly) to propel you forward. You truly must act your way through the stages of change. Move away from wishing for a new body with no consequences, to focusing more on the solution to your weight problem. Begin to focus more on the future than the past. When your focus moves from the problem to the solution, and towards the future and away from the past, this is a good sign you are moving into the Preparation stage.

Helping a Person in Contemplation

The contemplator is aware there is a problem that needs addressing. By doing your best to walk a mile in their shoes, being empathetic, offering support, and not pushing them too fast into the Action stage, you'll foster an even stronger relationship with the contemplator, thereby allowing them to continue to move through the stages at their own pace. Many contemplators are only just now coming to grips with the problem they face and are trying to gather knowledge about themselves and from others who have faced a similar problem.

Preparation–Stage 3

The Preparation stage is marked by taking those final steps, which will prepare the person to take Action within a very short time–usually a month or less. While their intentions are good, and there may even be a verbal commitment, ambivalence may still exist and has not quite been resolved yet. You might hear someone in this stage say "That's it! This weight is coming off once and for all!"

While the smell of anticipation is in the air for someone in the Preparation stage, rushing through this stage to Action will likely result in stumbling or recycling through it again at a later point. If you aren't fully prepared for action you can be "sick of this roller coaster" today and next week that same roller coaster–life–can set you right back on the chocolate, snacking, unaccountable sneaking food bandwagon. Taking the time to detail a plan with proper goals, true commitment, and leveraging will result in a more fruitful Action stage. If you are in the Preparation stage, now is the time to focus less on the problem and more on suitable action steps to correct the problem.

Learning the change processes and techniques for each stage will help solidify any missing resolve for the real work involved in the Action stage.

Action–Stage 4

Your actions are so loud I can't hear what you're saying.

I have referred several times to this stage and it is clearly the one that everyone desires to be in because it is the stage that gets you noticed. Those in the Action stage should recognize first that action without insight (Contemplation and Preparation) will likely lead to short-lived change. Without question, however, this is the stage where your behavior and surroundings are being modified most noticeably. You are using specific objectives to measure progress, and are no longer living with false perceptions about "how you feel" to guide your change. You are fully committed and full commitment to changing is evident in this stage.

The distinguishing difference between wanting to drop some weight, and really knowing why you will really transform this time, is the depth of the feeling and the drive that ensues from it. Thus, what happens not on the first day or week, but many weeks after, is that you have truly realized why you are going to transform. The person who truly knows why they must transform will be driving, full steam ahead, weeks after they have begun to take serious action. They will no longer be wishing and hoping for weight loss. The scale, tape measure and old clothes hanging in their closet will tell them undeniably that they have lost weight.

Transformationists in this stage weigh themselves frequently, measure body circumferences, and throw away junk in the house. They log their foods, exercise properly, write goals, and commit to them almost daily. These transformationists also surround themselves with positive peer pressure. They ignore the comments of ignorant bystanders, they realize they are doing this for themselves and no one else and, in short, they do all they have been preparing to do up to this point.

The unprepared "action" person will become charged up for a few days (this is what I refer to as having a hot flash) to a couple weeks, and then realize that it takes hard work and focus to really make it happen. Eventually some emotional episode or short-term illness will occur and since most hot flashers have not set any goals (realistic or otherwise), they fall off the proverbial wagon. Hot flashers want all of the good that comes with the transformation and none of the bad. Unrealistically, they believe they should not have to endure any cost dearer than money to make the change a reality. Hot flashers would love nothing better than to simply buy their way to a fit body with the next gizmo, gadget or miracle pill and powder.

The list of excuses and justifications when you are unprepared for action could fill a thousand pages. Since many of you have thought or spoken these excuses, I will not bore you with samples as they too are as diverse and varied as the individuals who think and speak them. When excuses and justifications for over-consumption, not analyzing your food intake, and not exercising dominate your thoughts and actions, then you are not truly in the Action stage. In short, your efforts were premature and without sufficient consciousness, preparation, and commitment.

During the Action stage, others will take notice of what you are doing. During this time you're likely to ruffle a few feathers, by creating uncomfortable or "different" eating arrangements, reducing the amount of time you spend doing now less-important tasks around the house, and no longer seeming as unselfish as you once were. This is *your* time. Because people will take notice of your action, they are likely to cheer or jeer you depending on how much your action steps affect *their* life. The less you affect another's daily grind, the more likely you are to receive cheers. The more you affect another's daily routine in what they perceive as a negative way ("Hey, I thought we always had ice cream on Friday nights?"), the more likely you are to receive jeers. Do your best to work with those closest to you, but ultimately you have to decide to firmly commit to your goals and let the chips fall where they may. There are critical times in life when you must throw your whole heart, mind, and body into what you are doing in order to succeed. You must forsake short-lived pleasures for the ultimate goal.

"Whenever you find something getting done,
you find a monomaniac with a mission."
Brian Tracy, *Success is a Journey*

I understand you need balance in life, but when you're going to break new ground in weight loss and body composition, you don't get to assign the transformation process the same priority as your other daily tasks merely to maintain some sort of perfect harmony with the earth. You have to take your transformation to the next level and prioritize it accordingly.

Instead of weight loss being number 60 on your "to do" list of priorities, it immediately moves to the top position or as low as position three or four. What might remain more important than your transformation when it is time for action? Husband, wife, significant other, career, and children, however, not much else and many times not even those. Partying with the boys, saying yes to the potluck lunch at work, swinging by McDonald's every morning on your way to work, sitting down to a nice, big bag of chips and dip at 11 PM at night and having your traditional, popcorn-sized bowl of ice cream every Friday night–all take a distant position somewhere below the success of your transformation. The "I just don't have enough time" and false beliefs that "I just do not eat that much" are looked at with a realism and conclusion that cannot be avoided. They are excuses and they do not hold water. There will truly be a disruption in your present routine and this may last for several weeks. Because your transformation is now taking a top priority, other areas of your life may suffer for awhile. If you clearly know why you must change, these disruptions will not seem as harsh. Being properly informed and prepared for the Action stage will help you keep your transformation goals a top priority.

The applause and cheers from your supporters will motivate you to push on and excel. The scary part, however, is it is typically only during this stage that you receive any recognition. The reason for this is that most people only recognize your change when you are overtly changing. People believe that action and change are synonymous. Although it is no less important when you move from Pre-contemplation to Contemplation, friends and family do not see these changes. You are not noticed and you do not "rain on their parade" until you enter the Action stage. In the minds of bystanders you are undeserving of encouragement until they see the physical changes the Action stage delivers. In actuality, however, in order to reach the Action stage, you've already changed significantly. Unfortunately, little recognition exists for the preparation and follow-ups surrounding the Action stage.

Many times the applause dies and encouragement stops as a transformationist approaches the end of the Action stage. While this is human nature, it is deleterious for the next stage–one that is just as important as the Action stage: Maintenance.

Maintenance–Stage 5

Change never ends with action. It's common knowledge among dieters that "losing the weight is easy, keeping it off is a nightmare!" Many dieters have single-handedly lost hundreds and hundreds of pounds over the years. They drop 20 pounds and put it back on. Drop it again, and put on 30. So the cycle continues. Even now I believe you can see how "recycling" through the stages of change is very common. Did you fail when you put the weight back on, or did you recycle through the stages once again?

Maintenance is mostly a continuation of the Action stage, but the emphasis is now on the positive reasons and benefits for keeping active and focused. During Maintenance, instead of focusing on all those wonderful foods you had to give up and all that dang exercise, you focus more so on how good you feel, and how by continuing to live the Lifestyle, your life can be better in so many ways beyond the physical transformation that occurred.

The Maintenance stage never ends for the person who has had a struggle with weight loss. There is no end to maintaining at least some degree of focus, commitment and action to stay on track. Without continued commitment to being the best you can be, you will surely relapse and recycle back to either the Pre-contemplation or Contemplation stage. Deliciously tempting foods and situations will always be around you. I firmly believe that no one who truly wants to be a stand-out, and has struggled with their weight, will ever get to the final stage in the stages of change: Termination.

Termination–Stage 6

Termination occurs when all desires and temptations to revert to old, negative habits are no longer an issue. You no longer consciously, or unconsciously, think about your problem, and you no longer see your daily routine as anything but what it is–a routine easily lived with. There essentially is no effort on your part during this stage to stave off the problem behavior. You have complete confidence in yourself and have no doubt you will never revert to your old ways. Termination is the ultimate goal for all changers. I do not believe we transformationists ever truly reach it. Prochaska and others agree.

First Attempt or Fifteenth Attempt, It Doesn't Matter. Keep Hope Alive!

Successful transformationists commonly recycle through the various stages of change numerous times before finally reaching the pinnacle of success. Relapse, unfortunately, *is* the rule and not the exception, but in knowing the stages of change and beneficial processes, you will increase your chances of ultimate success, thereby achieving the dream body you have always desired. The very idea that you are reading about the stages of change *while* you are seeking more information may also have a synergistic effect on your overall chances of success this time. With every recycle, you will have learned something. You will understand your body a little better. You will now know food a little better. You will know a little or a lot more about cardiovascular exercise than you did the very first time and you will know this will not be easy so more preparation will likely be taken this time. Never forget this:

> *When even a shred of hope is alive, you are still capable of changing your body and mind for the better. Life only passes you by when you give up on the idea <u>you can</u> change.*

Processes of Change

During the six stages of change, Prochaska has identified nine distinct processes. These processes can be used to keep progress moving forward and are more or less important depending on which stage you are in. For an in-depth review, I suggest you purchase a copy of the book *Changing for Good*, however, I will briefly cover the nine processes and the stage for which they are most appropriately used.

Process 1: Consciousness-raising. Any increased knowledge about yourself or the nature of your problem, regardless of the source, raises your consciousness. Increasing your consciousness increases your chances of success. Until you recognize a problem exists and you begin to see there really is a solution to your problem, no change can occur. Remember, Ms. Pre-contemplator is not actively increasing conscious awareness and has no interest in changing

   - Stages Best Used In: Pre-contemplation, Contemplation, Preparation

Process 2: Social liberation. When you begin to recognize how society has established helpful cubbyholes for people who really want to change, you are aware of social liberation. You will realize you really do have more alternatives and choices about where you can eat, spend your free time, exercise, and who you spend your time with at a community level. Recognizing the public support for the transformationist provides more information about problem behaviors and lets you know that you're not alone–others have experienced the same issues you are facing, and there really is help available when you truly desire change. No-smoking areas in restaurants and airports, self-help groups and coaching programs, bike paths and public walking trails are all examples of social liberation.

   - Stages Best Used In: Pre-contemplation

Process 3: Emotional arousal. This process is similar to consciousness-raising but on a deeper level. Emotional arousal can cause an audible "click" to be heard. "Getting to click" is a phrase I coined some time ago and it refers to a moment in time when you finally realize you will, or must, make your weight loss dream a reality. Instead of dreaming about weight loss, you commit–with complete, unshakeable focus–to achieving and living your dream. The level of focus achieved after a click is far superior to the traditional, weak "I want to be thin" wish.

Many transformationists will feel this arousal when they first view their "Before" photos or when they see another photo of themselves and are shocked by how they really look versus what the mirror tells them.

     Coaching member Sandi writes:
       "I look at myself in the mirror and think, 'Oh, you're doing so good,' and then look at my photo and say, 'Man, I thought I looked better than that!'"

Coaching member John writes:

"I recently took a set (photos) and noticed that somehow the EGO seems to get between the mirror and your eye more than it does between the camera and your eye!"

"Sure, you can console yourself and say, 'Well, the camera adds 5 pounds.' I weighed 292, so unless there were 18 cameras on me, I needed a better explanation."

"You can fool yourself looking in the mirror. When you look at yourself in the mirror, you focus on one thing, then another. You don't see the whole picture."

Below is an actual coaching client's note to me after he became emotionally aroused and heard his click.

"I have finally become enlightened.

I have finally realized that I cannot get away with free weekends any longer, even though I am strict during the week. Such a half-assed effort only leaves me with a larger ass (kind of ironic, isn't it?). That is why I am allowing myself one or two splurge meals a week. No exceptions - I will plan all of my meals.

I have finally realized I need to do AT LEAST 2 cardio sessions a week - 30 minutes each. I will aim for three.

I have realized I must keep with my training goals that the online workout generator has given me. I have been consistent with my lifting, and now I MUST stay consistent.

"I have finally realized I must be in control and even "selfish." That is, I need to dictate when, where, and what I eat, others cannot be a factor. I know this sounds strict, but I seem to give into others too easily.

I have finally realized that just because my company buys my lunch, it doesn't mean it is calorie-free also.

I have finally realized that being a smart (about fitness/diet), portly person is ridiculous. I need to apply the things I have learned and finally show everyone I know what I'm talking about.

I am not sure why it took me this long to realize these things, but I am glad I finally did. Now, I can finally take control, lose this extra weight and see my elusive abs.

In the past, I said these things because I wanted them to happen. This time, THEY WILL HAPPEN. GUARANTEED!"

Emotional arousal may also occur with the death of a family member, a diagnosis of, or recovery from an illness you know could likely have been prevented by practicing a healthier lifestyle.

- Stages Best Used In: Contemplation, Preparation

Process 4: Self-re-evaluation. This process requires you to give a thoughtful and emotional reappraisal of your problem, and an assessment of the kind of person you might be once you have conquered it. Self-re-evaluation enables you to see when and how your problem behavior conflicts with

your personal values. The result is that you come not only to believe, but also to feel that life would be significantly better without the problem. What will you lose by abandoning your problem behavior? No change comes without a price and any change worth anything will cost something dearer than money. Self-re-evaluation forces you to abandon all hope of finding an effortless route to change.
   - Stages Best Used In: Contemplation, Preparation

Process 5: Commitment. Once you choose to change, you accept responsibility for changing. This responsibility is the burden of commitment, sometimes called "self-liberation." Commitment includes not only a willingness to act, but also a belief in your ability to change, which in turn reinforces your will. The more entirely you throw yourself into a new way of behaving, the more likely you are to experience that way as being the best path to follow.
   - Stages Best Used In: Preparation, Action, Maintenance

I understand that you may feel a lot of anxiety about this process. No attempt at change is guaranteed. You may fail and recycle once again. For this reason, establishing strong leverage systems to help keep your focus and commitment is vital, while you transform from your present state of health and leanness to the person you know you must become.

> *"Depth of Commitment"*
>   *It is natural to become highly focused in a moment of extreme desire, frustration or anger. Yet, as the emotion of the moment begins to fade, that clear sense of focus can fade along with it. It is easy to become intensely focused shortly. Those who are able to maintain, and even intensify, a clear and driving focus over the long-term can truly achieve great things.*
>   *Focus is most effective when it grows stronger as time goes on. To stay focused and to grow even more focused, as the challenges grow more daunting, you must make that focus more than just something you do. You must make it who you are.*
>   *Dive into the depth of your character and seek to truly understand who you are. Ask yourself why you desire the things you desire, and keep asking until you have an answer that touches your fundamental, essential self. Forge that solid and irrefutable connection between who you are and what you desire, and the powerful, growing focus you need to achieve your goals will become a part of you."*
> Ralph Marston

Intentions Never Substitute for Commitment

It's been said that "The road to hell is paved with good intentions." Today you may have the fire, passion and commitment to push every destructive behavior to the side. On a day like today, no foods are tempting you, you are beyond temptation, and there is no way you will miss working out. You are focused and so ready and you have the best of intentions. There is no possible way you can fail. Not so fast. You may have forgotten about tomorrow, next week and how you might feel six weeks from now. You probably intend to keep the same fire then as you have today. But how? Let's be realistic here. If what you had attempted in the past worked, you would not be reading this book. You know that you have been fired up in the past. You have been zealous. You have been determined, and your intentions with each start were to finish and be the champion transformationist you have only read about or witnessed, but never experienced yourself up to this moment in your life. If you can accept that you do not know everything just yet, and you will admit that you have been fired up in the past without success, then you must be willing to move your position and trust me for the experience I bring to the table. What will it cost you? If I am wrong, you can always go back to less commitment, no leveraging, and doing it your way.

I am not a doctor but I am an avid student of human behavior. In my practical, hands-on, as well as academic experience, I believe the one thing that will stop you from truly committing and using leverage to reinforce that commitment is fear. I believe it's true that no matter how bad your current physical condition is, or how screwed up your current behavior patterns are, and how agonizing each day is when you realize you haven't lost a single pound and are in much worse condition than you ever imagined you'd be, *that pain is familiar and you can trust in it*. When you fully commit, you are accepting that you want more out of life. You demand more of yourself and with those demands come uncertainty.

Deciding you must become better is a decision to forego the status quo. You will enter unfamiliar waters and this is plain scary. What if you fail? What if you don't make it? Dr. Philip McGraw wrote in his book *Life Strategies*:

> *"The potential of trying new things, reaching for more and suffering a setback or a rejection, is something that, ultimately, you can deal with, whereas the fear of that event is formless, elusive, and difficult to fight. Fighting fear is like trying to sack fog; you just cannot get a handle on it. Giving your power away to fear is worse than suffering the consequence that you are afraid of. Choose to give yourself the chance. It's normal to be anxious and afraid, but you can't be dominated by the fear."*

Ultimately, you must decide that you deserve better and be willing to accept the temporary pain and uncertainty that is sure to surface. You must decide that you are worth the risk. The sense of security and safety you now cling to as a baby clings to a blankie must be disrupted in order to create meaningful change.

Before you read the next section on leveraging, I want to share with you a conversation I believe is necessary for you to have before proceeding. With some similar dialogue, I believe most have this conversation if they truly succeed at changing their body and mind for the better. This conversation is with yourself and, according to Dr. McGraw, goes something like this:

"There will be setbacks." I know it, and I will deal with them.

"You may not succeed." I may not win immediate success, but I will stay the course. To try and fail is not indicative of my worth.

"People will reject you." We do not always get what we want on the first try. Nevertheless, to continue asking, continue working until I get what I want, will be the ultimate acceptance.

"You'll be a failure." I will be a failure only if I stop trying in the face of my difficulties.

"Are you really worth it and capable of it?" Yes, I am. In any case, I guess I will find out, because I am going to do it.

Do not begin your transformation without full commitment. This involves a risk of failing. No one who has ever been massively successful and worth recognizing got it just right on the first try. Most bazillionaires and stars in any endeavor will unequivocally say their success is in direct proportion to their attempts and failures. Every failure is another opportunity to learn and nothing more. Do not repeat mistakes of the past by not fully committing to your transformation. Do not settle for status quo, and do not just provide lip service to your transformation. Commit with leverage and carve your transformation success in stone.

Leverage For Maximum Focus and Commitment

One definition of leverage, according to Webster, is the "power to act effectively." This definition is appropriate for the purposes of your Lifestyle program as well. As you read through the many leverage examples that follow, think of leverage as self-applied pressure to reinforce your focus and maintain your commitment through the journey. Ultimately, leverage can secure more benefits for you through rewards beyond the new body. But, more importantly, leverage establishes a cost for failing.

By establishing a strong leverage program you can provide yourself with better answers to the following questions:

- Besides you, who will care if you fail? Who knows about your desire to change, that you would rather die than let down?

- How will you really benefit if you succeed? If your answer is mostly about overall health or longevity, I can assure you, most of the time this just is not enough. Few of us really take our mortality seriously. Once in a great while, if your doctor has told you that you have only a short time to live if you do not act now, it will be enough to act. Even then, health and longevity goals are weak promoters for most successful transformations. There is always tomorrow to start and there is no pressing urgency to start, let alone carry on, unless you use leveraging.

- Will you benefit by not succeeding? Does your layer of fat protect you from the opposite sex? Does it keep you from having to stick your neck out and take risks? Does the fat you own make it acceptable for you to stay mediocre at work or your career choice? Is it just safer to stay fat? (See "*ambivalence*" in Chapter 12 – *Lifestyle Booby Traps*.)

- How much financial risk is at stake if you fail? Then again, is there a financial gain waiting for you if you achieve your goal?

- Is there a massive reward, other than money, for achieving your goal? If you believe the reward is the 20 pounds you are going to lose in 90 days, then you are seeking the wrong reward. There is no leverage in wanting to lose 20 pounds in 90 days. A sudden desire to change is also just not enough.

- Is there a massive risk for not achieving your goal?

- What are you willing to give up to get the body you desire? Partying? Fast-food? Television? Your routine? Candy? Wheat? Flour? Processed carbohydrates? Denial?

- Overall, what is your true cost (emotionally, physically, competitively, spiritually and financially) if you do or do not succeed? If your answer to this question or others is "Well, if I don't get it done this time, I'll just try something else I guess," then I must advise you now that you are not likely to achieve the level of leanness you are seeking at this time. Let's face it, "If I don't succeed I'll try again with something else" is just plain weak! There is no cost for you not making it if this is your response. When you are in the Action stage, there is no reason for you not to make it this time. You have to establish a better leveraging system than "I'll try again." You must stick with it. Instead of giving in, you have to dig in. Positive attitude qualities, overcoming discouragement and continuing with a solid plan in the face of disappointment are necessary to make a successful transformation happen.

No-Escape and No-Retreat

Leverage is a great tool to assist with creating what I call the "no-escape" or "no-retreat" clause of your transformation. You literally have to create such strong leverage and focus there is no possible way you can fail yet again. There must be no-retreat and no-escape. You fight and win or you die. (Only a metaphor here, okay? Don't kill yourself.) How strong should the leverage be? Here is an example of what I would consider a ten on a scale of one to ten. I would suggest you create leverage that brings you to at least an eight.

Do you think that you could achieve the body of your dreams if today someone told you that if you did not, all of the people you love on Earth would disappear forever? Is there any doubt whatsoever that you could achieve your goals and the body of your dreams if you would lose everyone you love if you didn't? There is no doubt whatsoever! You'd make it–no question. Losing everyone you love would be an example of a ten on the leverage scale and the reversed risk challenge is a nine. How can you create leverage equal to at least a eight to really help you stay focused? Weak leverage is worthless. The cost or benefit must be substantial for it to truly impact your progress.

Ultimately, all leveraging systems are put in place to accomplish one purpose—to keep your focus and commitment strong for long enough to see you through to a successful transformation. Leveraging doesn't teach you how to create your own success. Leveraging doesn't give you the necessary knowledge that other chapters of this book address. Leveraging begs you to answer one very important question with an answer that honestly can be rated as at least an eight on a one-to-ten scale (one being ineffective and ten being massively effective): What is my cost for failing? Unless you have strong leverages created that can provide you an answer to this question you'd rate as at least an eight on a ten scale, you should continue to think about your leveraging until you have made it strong enough to be effective.

Leverage Examples

Here are eight examples of leverage and how powerful they each can be to get you started and keep you focused throughout your transformation. As you read them, I suggest you start envisioning how you can use as many of these examples as possible to make your transformation dream a slam-dunk success. This is one of those rare cases where "if one's good, two is better." The more leveraging systems you put into place for yourself, the greater your chances of surviving past the first few hot flash days or weeks.

1. Risking public humiliation

Cindy sent me an address list of ten friends and relatives closest to her. We agreed that I would send all ten of those friends and relatives a copy of her Before photos if she did not achieve her ultimate goal. Cindy, like most women, would have rather died than show anyone those Before photos.

Don lives in a small town and thought long and hard about how he could up the ante and really create leverage against himself. Finally, in a moment of peace, it hit him. He contacted the local newspaper and asked them to publish a newspaper story about him and to follow up with him weekly to report his progress. Don admits the thought of this scared the daylights out of him. Can you imagine everyone in town knowing whether you are sticking to the Lifestyle or not? Whoa! To fail quietly and secretly is one thing. To fail and have the whole town know about it is certainly another. That is when I knew it was the right leverage for him. I encouraged Don to ask the local newspaper and told him he had nothing but ugly fat to lose and everything to gain. Much to his surprise, his local newspaper agreed to take his story and follow up with him weekly to check progress. Don was immediately submerged in a sea of leverage. Just like all the other successful clients I have ever coached, the leverage did not come to Don–he went out and got it. He made it happen, all the while developing a leverage system I had not even thought of before.

While Lana had been a devoted gym member for years, she was just not able to put it all together on her own to create the body of her dreams. She contacted her gym and asked them to profile her on bulletin boards while she progressed through her Lifestyle program. They agreed and her Before photos, starting weight and goals were made public to other members. Lana also agreed to have a staff member and any other members watch her weigh in every Tuesday at the gym. When I asked Lana what she believed her cost for failing with this leverage was, she quickly offered up that she was risking a tremendous blow to her character should she fail because of such a public form of leveraging. This potential threat to her character was perceived because of the public humiliation she would feel by letting all her fellow gym members down should she choose not to work the Lifestyle program properly, thus creating yet another failure in her weight-loss endeavors.

2. Make a bet with a friend or relative

Dave's brother made a $100 bet with him that he would not achieve the goals we set for him by the goal date. Dave suggested to his brother that they make it more interesting and raise the stakes to $1,000! Dave won the bet of course and this leverage actually had more value than an additional $2,500 Dave sent me to hold for reversed risk leveraging (to be discussed shortly).

3. Birthdays, reunions and other milestones

Are you about to turn 30? 40? 50? Is your class reunion a few months away? Are you getting married in eight weeks? Are you taking a cruise or flying to a warm, sandy beach for vacation? Will you be the focus of any public gathering in the next year? If you answered "yes" to any of these questions, then you are sitting on a gold mine of leverage.

Use any of these milestones to help establish an immovable date for your transformation ending. Read that again–an immovable date! You only get one shot to be your best for any of these events and this is a very positive source of leverage. It also helps to establish a no-escape clause, which I will discuss a bit later.

A good example of an immovable date is when I prepare for a bodybuilding show. My focus is so clear and vivid that I have no choice but to succeed. The show promoters are not about to move the show date because I decided to comfort myself with emotional eating three out of every seven days a week. The date is immovable, so I must stay true to the Lifestyle and my exercise regimen or I will enter the show fatter than I should have been. I have too much at stake in pride to allow this to happen. The immovable date is a very good source of leverage.

Immovable Date: A date that you cannot push further away. An event on a date, which can never again be duplicated.

Poor example: "I will be in shape by the first day of spring." This is a poor attempt at setting an immovable date because it is not an immovable date! What happens if the first day of spring comes and you do not reach your goal? Nothing! For that reason alone, above all else, this type of date setting is weak, and does not represent an immovable date.

Ask yourself now–do you have an immovable transformation date ending? Will it be easy to reset your goal on the date you set and could you say "Oh well, I tried but didn't make it, maybe I'll take up Yoga and Slimfast or maybe I'll try a ketogenic diet or maybe the Hollywood diet or maybe ...." You get my point.

4. Attach a major reward to your transformation success

The best example I've seen so far of using a truly major reward ONLY if the transformation was everything he wanted it to be comes from coaching client, Tim.

When I pressed Tim for something solid to base his transformation on, he thought about it for a few days and then told me what he would do. Tim had been seriously considering purchasing a new home for a few years and after saving and planning, he was about to make the plunge. Tim convinced me he was serious when he let me know he would not buy a new home, and would stay in his small apartment if he did not achieve the goals he set. Tim held true to his word and with this kind of leverage, he had no choice but to do well or look the fool for opening his mouth with such a bold statement to begin with. Again, an amazing transformation resulted. (See Center Section of photos.)

Another excellent example of attaching a major reward to a successful transformation comes from Bridget. She decided she could up the ante for her own transformation by holding her entire family back from taking their summer vacation if she did not make her goal. With her husband agreeing to go along with this and live with the consequences either way, she established strong leverage for success. With pressure from her husband and small children, and knowing the precious time with them on this vacation would be loaded with memories if they went, she had an ever-present voice in her ear to hold her steady and keep her true to the Lifestyle. Again, she applied strong leverage against herself to succeed. If she had not succeeded, she would have been the one responsible for the family not enjoying a vacation that summer! Ouch–that would have hurt.

The biggest catch with this form of leveraging is you must be truly honest with yourself and the others involved. If people are counting on you for any reason and you buckle and take the trip anyway, then this leveraging system is weak. If, however, you have a strong character and you truly will not go if you do not reach your transformation goal, then this major reward leveraging system is very, very powerful. No one wants to let family or close friends down.

Pay for the trip or a large part of the reward in advance? Very strong leveraging system.

Play it safe and wait to pay for anything until you are sure you are going to make it? Weak leveraging system.

5. Enter a transformation challenge

Today there are transformation challenges just about everywhere you look. Some offer large prizes, some small, but they are available if you keep your eyes open.

With a transformation challenge, you follow several steps and take action to commit to a specific date with the potential to win prizes such as national recognition, airfare, vacations, cars, and cash, clothing and dietary supplements. A typical transformation challenge doesn't offer a tremendously strong form of leverage but it can help you set goals, provide a defined time line to accomplish your goals, and set in motion many positive steps toward success.

The best source to find a transformation challenge is your local magazine stand. Magazines are the most common advertising venue for legitimate transformation challenges. Check out Muscle Media, Muscle & Fitness, Flex, Ironman, Muscular Development, Musclemag International and others. You can also do a search on the Internet as well.

6. Give someone you love and respect permission to question you

Public commitments are more powerful than private pledges. Create leverage against yourself by giving those you love permission to question you if you are eating poorly and not training consistently enough. Tell them what you are doing, why you are doing it and what you would like from them. Do not expect those helping relationships to read your mind. "Well, they should just know me well enough to know what I need to accomplish something like this." Give me a break! People who love you are willing to help, but do not always know how. Offer them a comprehensive list of "do's and don'ts." For example:

- Do not keep asking how I am doing.
- Do not nag me.
- Offer to help when I look overwhelmed.
- Tell me how proud you are that I am doing this.
- Do not be a silent supporter six days a week when I am doing really well and then on the one day I mess up, all of a sudden become vocal.

Do not ask for help without meaning it. When your helping relationship does what you have asked, they do not deserve a good scolding from you for doing so. This is a sure-fire way to end the helping relationship and sabotage your efforts. Tell them it is okay for them to lovingly question why you are eating cake when you said you were focused on change. "Why aren't you working out today? I thought you said you were going to work out five days a week," are positive types of leverage statements that might help you feel the positive pressure just enough to really make that day a success.

Barbara told me the story of how her husband of ten years used leverage against her to hold her true to the Lifestyle on a day she just did not think she could bare. Barbara admits it was her time of the month and, right on cue, the cravings for sugar were awaiting her. She conceded that she was also more emotional than usual due to the hormonal upheaval that occurs every month during her week.

Barbara really felt like giving in to a huge piece of strawberry pie. Just when she was about to, her husband reminded her, "Honey, I thought you were limiting yourself to two splurge meals a week?" Barbara admitted that at first this comment infuriated her, and her response to her husband was that she was just going to quit. By now, she was crying and upset at herself and the world in general. Now, here is the part that would put most men on very shaky ground with their wives. All the same, Barbara's husband knew her temperament well, knew what she could take, and also knew what he could say to really make her pay attention to what she was about to do. Barbara's husband told her, "If you want to quit, then fine, quit! But every time I see you eating the snacks and junk food you said you wouldn't eat during this transformation, I am going to moo at you (like a cow)." As you can imagine, these comments made Barbara extremely angry but it worked. She decided to forego the pie and instead did 40 minutes of cardio until her cravings passed. By the time she was done with her cardio she was no longer upset, no longer angry with her husband and was well aware that he had just done her a massive favor—one she had given him permission to do when she started the challenge.

I want you to be aware of one caveat with this accountability leveraging system for couples. Before giving this caveat to couples, I'd see women (mostly) who would decide to use their very successful, strong-willed husbands as sword-wielding accountability warriors. In other words, they would decide to give their husbands full authority to question them on everything, to be there during weigh-ins, and ultimately gave them permission to drop the hammer if they started to slip. I do not suggest doing this and here is why:

What is the point in having your husband watch you like a hawk except you get to be mad at him more for hounding you, which is never fun between spouses? What happens if you do not reach your goals? Nothing, except you get to be mad at your black-hat-wearing-whip-holder husband for trying to do as you asked, which is to really hold you accountable. I am not saying that your husband cannot help you. My hope is that he can be supportive. If he is a watchdog and has to hound you, not only will he grow tired of this, but you will also spend most of your days wondering what the ol' watchdog is thinking, instead of just loving each other as husband and wife.

Asking a husband or wife to be the watchdog, rather than simply giving them permission to lovingly hold you accountable, is really asking for trouble. The pressure of your transformation needs to rest squarely on your own shoulders, not your spouse's. If you want someone to crack the whip, then hire a qualified, neutral third party (a coach or personal trainer). When your coach hounds you or questions why you have not lost weight in three weeks, it will be okay if you are mad at him. After getting a butt chewing from your coach, you can go home and seek support from your spouse, as it should be. Hence, your relationship with your spouse is preserved.

7. Surround yourself with positive influences

When announcing to your friends, loved ones, and co-workers your plans to once and for all drop your excess weight, you will likely be hit from all sides with doubting remarks and negative comments about your chances, not to mention skepticism about how all diets are a scam. If you train at home and never speak to another living soul about fitness, your chances for success can still be hindered. Remember your options for social liberation, too. There are numerous supportive groups and activities available, if you will open your eyes to them.

I suggest that you either make it a point to join my coaching program, or simply find an avenue to socialize with other fitness goal-oriented individuals. Through this social contact, you may stay inspired, informed, and positive about your transformation. Coaching members under my wing are exceptional individuals who want nothing more than to cheer on those who are doing well, as well as encourage those who reveal they are having a rough go on a particular day. No matter how you do it, surround yourself with other positive, like-minded fitness enthusiasts who can understand what you are going through, give you a kick in the pants when you need it, check up on you, and finally, share with you in your ups and downs along the way. Going it alone is really a tough way to attempt a major transformation. When no one close to you understands what you are going through or why you are "putting yourself through all of this," you can rest assured that your Lifestyle friends within my online coaching program most certainly will.

8. Reversed risk leveraging

Reversed risk leveraging is created when you put up something of value (sentimental or monetary), thus placing you in an irreversible position—you either succeed or lose the item or cash. Like other forms of leveraging, there is a continuum of weaker to stronger forms I've seen utilized by successful Lifestylers. Generally, all forms of reversed risk leveraging are stronger than non-reversed risk forms. Unlike a body transformation challenge, where the only cost for failing is you "don't win the prize," with reversed risk leveraging you flat out lose something of value should you not properly work the Lifestyle program and fail as a result. What follows are several examples of reversed risk leveraging and how Lifestyle clients of mine have used this technique to create the body of their dreams with no-escape, no-retreat and maximum commitment by their side during their transformation.

A. Write a check and let the recipient cash it now

In 2001 I first used this technique on Brad, a client who just could not seem to move from Contemplation to Preparation and finally, to Action. Remember when I discussed chronic contemplators? Brad was a perfect example of this. After much thought, and much emotional exhaustion in working personally with Brad, I figured out the solution for him so he could move from Contemplation to Preparation. What did I do? I told this well-to-do, highly successful businessman and client to send me a check for $5,000 (no postdating allowed)! Here is how it worked.

If he succeeded at reaching his very reasonable goals (reasonable goals are a must) in 12 weeks, I would promptly send him back his $5,000. He had to prove his hard work through After photos and certified statements from a local personal trainer. In the event he did not reach his goal, I would send his $5,000 to the Make a Wish Foundation as a donation in his name. In other words, it was a reversed risk transformation challenge. Instead of being rewarded with cash, it would cost Brad $5,000 of his money if he did not make his goal. To say this proposition scared the living hell out of him at first would be an understatement! It also increased his commitment to the challenge, which was my intention.

After a day or two of pressure from myself and other coaching clients to accept the challenge, Brad agreed. It did not surprise me at all when Brad reached his goal of six percent body fat in 12 weeks. How could he not? He had so much to lose if he did not. This exceptionally powerful leverage proved to be very effective.

Do you have to send $5,000? No, not at all! The amount you agree upon does matter, but it does not have to be $5,000. It could be more or less. Only you can determine the amount that scares you and would be painful to lose but, at the same time, you could recover from if you did lose the money. My suggestion is that an amount of three to five percent of your annual salary is a good figure to use when determining what to put up in reversed risk dollars.

> *No excuses and no escape. It is the only way reversed*
> *risk leveraging can work.*

The following are the most common real-life excuses and examples of playing it safe I have heard from those I have challenged to use the reversed risk leveraging system. With few exceptions, not using reversed risk leveraging or trying to play it safe is a sure-fire way to show just how uncommitted you really are. There are virtually no valid excuses and unless you use this most powerful leveraging system properly, its effectiveness is weakened greatly, or worse, completely worthless.

Excuse #1: "I don't have the money right now but I'll sure save for it."

This excuse is about as lame as they come. Borrow the money! Right about now you might think I am nuts, but let me explain a second. Borrow the money to get into the best shape of your life? Yes! What will you lose? A few dollars in interest? Is your dream body worth a few dollars in interest for a 12-week loan of $1,000 to $5,000? Of course it is! So now, even if you do not have the money, if you can get the money, you have no excuse whatsoever NOT to use this tremendously powerful leveraging technique. Tell the bank you need a consolidation note. Hey, you will not be lying! Your body will consolidate as you have never seen once you use the reversed risk leveraging technique appropriately! Using this method halfway will result in no leverage, so don't skimp.

Write the check or borrow and then write the check, but make sure it's equal to at least three to five percent of your annual salary.

Excuse #2: "Sure, I could send $5,000 because I can afford it, but I like to remain liquid because, I'm sure you can relate, you just never know what deal's going to pop up around the corner and I might need the money. I also just don't feel comfortable with my money being in someone else's bank account."

If you are well enough off to be able to afford $5,000 or more for reversed risk leveraging, then you claiming to need that $5,000 for future deals is not a valid excuse. You know as well as I do that the $5,000 you'll temporarily allow someone you trust with your life to be held in escrow could be replaced in a second with a simple talk with your banker. What is really stopping you? You are afraid to trust in yourself and to really commit to the transformation. It has nothing to do with needing to be liquid. You must trust in your ability to lose the weight as long as the goals are reasonable. Everyone has the ability to do it–with no exceptions.

Play It Safe #1: "I'll send you the check, Dave, you just hang on to it, and if I don't make it then by all means please cash it."

Sorry, wrong answer. For reversed risk leveraging to be effective, the check has to be written to whomever is going to hold your money (father, mother, grandparent, brother, sister, etc.) and they must cash the check right away. Period! If you ask them to hold on to it until the end, you have just given yourself an out. At that point, you have just made this leveraging system worthless.

Play It Safe #2: "I'll write the check to the Make a Wish Foundation and I'll hang on to it. I'll even photocopy it for you if you want and if I don't make it, I'll send this bad boy off. You can count on me. My word is gold."

Sorry, wrong answer. Again, if you are holding the check, this is even worse than the first Play-it-safe. You have an absolute out instead of a no-escape and no-retreat leverage system. No one is questioning your credibility, however, everyone is questioning your commitment if you try to use this Play-it-safe method.

Play It Safe #3: "I'll make the check out to the Make a Wish Foundation and send it to you and if I don't make it you just send it directly to them."

Sorry, wrong answer. In this Play-it-safe example the potential problem is the person holding the check may go soft on you if you do not follow the program. Also, no real commitment has been made since nothing has really been given (the check is not cashed so no money is gone yet). Before you start justifying to me or anyone else all the reasons the person you are going to use will not go soft, just save all that nonsense and commit! Write the check to whomever is going to hold it, make it out in their name, tell them to cash it, and tell them that if you do not make it, they are to donate the money to the charity of your choice. Tell them not to return the money to you unless and until you reach your goal on or before your goal date.

Money Isn't That Important to Me

Finally, there are some who claim money just is not that important to them. Now don't get me wrong here folks, I am not saying that money is the most important thing in life, but as Zig Ziglar says, "It's reasonably close to oxygen."

The naysayers who claim the reversed risk leveraging system wouldn't work for them because money isn't that important are likely confused about how this leveraging system works. They will usually make statements about how they have spent hundreds of dollars on exercise equipment, only to have it sit without use for months at a time. They might even state they have wasted hundreds of dollars on toys without a care in the world. I believe the confusion lies in how much wasteful money they have spent on valuable items as opposed to how much money they have wasted on frivolous items. In nearly all cases, the majority of people will usually have some physical entity to show for the money they spent (for example, a Bowflex, new treadmill, fancy curtains, new car stereo).

Thus far, I have convinced any person I've spoken to about the power of the reversed risk leveraging system by simply pointing out the now more obvious points about what is involved:

- The risk must be or should be substantial (three to five percent of annual salary).
- There is no physical entity being purchased.
- You receive no money back if you don't follow the program and you don't reach your goal.

I firmly believe there is some monetary figure that will scare the living daylights out of you and will charge you up and commit you to your goal once and for all. Maybe it is not three to five percent of your annual salary. Maybe it is ten percent. Whatever the scary number is, that is the number you should pledge. At that point reversed risk leveraging will help create a no-escape, no-retreat contract between you and the lean body you desire–guaranteed.

B. Pay for Before/After photos in advance

"Then I took those dang pictures... now that was it!"

Coaching Member John writes:

"I'm so glad I have the early photos. When I take my pictures each month after losing about 10 pounds, I don't see much difference from one month to the next. Nevertheless, when I go back to my original photos, taken back in July when I weighed almost 290, I see the difference. A 10-pound loss shows just a little; a 40-pound loss shows, undeniably.

The photos help me from getting discouraged, and yet they keep me from getting complacent. When I look at my current photos, I'm always disappointed. I always look worse in the photos than I do in my clothes, or at the gym, or even undressed in front of the mirror. So, I look at myself clearly and see I have to keep pushing, and I want to keep pushing. The pictures motivate me, because I want to get to the point when I can see current photos of myself and feel satisfied and comfortable with the way they (and I) look.

But at the same time, the photos are another gauge of my success, along with the scale, my clothes and the body fat readings. From the old photos I can see that I'm succeeding, and if I didn't have them, if I skipped that step, then I would be disappointed when I took my current photos.

Even though I've lost a lot of weight (about 40 pounds) I'm only half way to where I need to be, and that's a dangerous point in any endeavor. That's when you start patting yourself on the back, and get complacent or sloppy. Or that's when you look in the mirror or at some photos and get down on yourself because you still have a ways to go. The photos stop that. They say, "Yes, you still have a ways to go, so don't get complacent, but, on the other hand, you have made a lot of progress, so don't get discouraged and give up".

Early in my transformation, I knew I was supposed to take them. I read that in The Lifestyle, but I didn't want to, I didn't think it was that important. I knew I was fat; I didn't need to embarrass myself with some photos. Dave says to do it, but it seems kind of gimmicky, and who the hell is David Greenwalt, anyway? I mean, I'm going to try this Lifestyle thing, but I'm not 100% committed, I'm not sure about it. I'll pick and choose and do the things I want, and screw the other stuff.

Man, I'm glad I did the photos. For those of you who are starting out, listen to me on this one (and believe me, because I am one of the most skeptical, insubordinate, questioning, won't take anyone's advice people out there): do the photos."

And this is a good lesson to take with you from this section, regardless of your current transformation status. Somewhere between the mirror and you is an ego and vanity, but, for some reason, as with us all, that separation disappears with a photo. The mirror can and does lie."

I can almost guarantee you that taking Before photos will be painful. I can also guarantee you it's very powerful and rewarding to look back on those photos, not only once you've achieved a successful transformation, but also along the way. I haven't met a person yet who took a look at their Before photos, moments after getting them developed or viewing them on their monitor, and felt jubilant about it. The mirror does lie and you might not be able to rely on what you see, or perhaps it's bettered stated what you "perceive to see." It is common, however, for someone to look at the Before photo and click because they are so disgusted by what they see.

In addition, you might swear you will never show the Before photos to anyone for as long as you live, but I promise you that's not true–and here's why. Once you have achieved a significant transformation and have taken your midpoint or final After photos, you will want to show the world what you have accomplished. You will literally want to climb a mountain and scream at the top of your lungs how happy and excited you are! Take your Before photos!

Before Photos–How?

I recommend you take your Before photos wearing a two-piece (ladies only obviously) or one-piece bathing suit and also some outfit that currently fits you but perhaps isn't all that flattering. While wearing your swimsuit, hold a newspaper (so it doesn't cover your body) while facing the camera, then in a relaxed side pose, and finally, while facing away from the camera (three total poses). In your fully clothed photo, take a straight-on front shot. It's important you take some full body photos and that you take up 90 percent of the photo. If you are too far away in the photo or the top of your head is cut off, you'll be disappointed later when trying to compare your Afters to your Befores. After you have at least taken these basic Befores, I would not hesitate to take a few more in different positions just in case you come up with something you like. Be creative. It doesn't cost you anything extra. (See Center Section of Photos.)

A great way to use leverage in the Before photo process is to pay a professional photographer to take your Before photos. While you're at it, pay him in advance, and set a date to take your After photos. Also, tell the photographer that, no matter what, she is not to give you a refund if you do not show up for the After photos. Most professional photographers will only charge you a sitting fee so the costs will be manageable. The act of paying in advance and setting a final date for the After photos is one way of applying leverage against yourself to increase commitment. This action step can really help make it happen. Do you really want to cancel the After shoot? Do you really want to lose the money you've already spent for the sitting fee of the After photos?

Excellent example: Mark, a coaching client of mine, set the Gold Standard for After photo leverage by flying from Ohio to California to have his After photos taken. Mark hired a professional photographer with a great deal of experience in photographing buff bodies. Was he expensive? You bet. Mark had to pay for the flight, hotel, rental car and the expensive photographer. Do you think for one second, after making all of these plans, weeks in advance, that he was about to let his hard-earned money go to waste by not showing up? No way! This 40-something-year-old's transformation was nothing short of amazing, just as you would expect from someone that I nudged a bit and used leverage to support the entire process. (See Center Section of Photos.)

C. Plan and pay for the event or trip in advance

If you respect someone so much you'd rather die than let them down and they live hundreds of miles away from you, then this is another perfect opportunity to use this respect as leverage. Here's how.

Jeremy, another coaching client, met a national celebrity of sorts in the transformation field and quickly grew to admire and respect him even more after the meeting. Jeremy told the celebrity he would return in 12 weeks with a completely transformed physique, even though Jeremy was horribly out of shape at the time. Jeremy returned home and immediately booked a flight, hotel and rental car for 12 weeks after that date so he could show his mentor what he accomplished. He had to keep his promise! Jeremy did create an amazing transformation, and part of the reason he was an amazing success is because he could not bear the thought of letting his new friend down, a friend whom he respected very much.

An important distinction, which increased Jeremy's chances for success, is that he paid for the trip back to see his mentor in advance. If you have a friend or mentor to whom you would like to show your new body, then do not hedge your bets. Commit by paying your trip to see them in advance. Pay for everything: flight, hotel, and rental car and you will see just how powerful this leveraging system can be. If you play it safe, and tell your friend you're going to see them next summer with a new body, but you believe you should wait until you really get the new body to pay for the trip, then this leveraging system is almost worthless.

Beth and Jason decided to book a trip to Las Vegas, something they had been dreaming of doing for years, however, they agreed they would not actually take the trip if they didn't reach their goal. The trip was paid for in advance.

Bob had always dreamed of biking across America, but since he was 50 pounds overweight, he knew he needed to improve his overall fitness level or he would never make it. Making the trip with a team of riders would cost him $4,000. This would include most of his expenses for the several week venture. Can you guess my suggestion to Bob when he came to me asking for help? You got it–I told him to write the check first! Bob was hesitant about committing at first, but when he wrote that check, he was locked in and had no choice but to be in the best shape possible. If he had not, his money would have been wasted and he would have been emotionally devastated. He just could not risk it. As you might have guessed, with my help and a lot of hard work on his own, he lost 50 pounds in 16 weeks just in time to make the trip.

Tonya and her husband were in possession of $4,000 tickets to the Winter Olympics in Utah. Yes, the trip was already paid for. Tonya is an avid skier and none of her ski clothes fit anymore. She also made a promise to her mother about finally getting rid of the weight and would be seeing her mother in Utah when they went to the Olympics. If Tonya did not reach her goal she and her husband (I verified the husband's agreement) would forego their entire trip and the $4,000 would have been a waste. Guess who went to the Olympics in 2002 with new ski clothes?

Pay in advance? Very powerful leveraging system.
Wait and see? Weak leveraging system.
Who do you respect enough to tell about your transformation without letting them down?

D. Buy a gift now and accept only when the goal is achieved

Sam and her husband decided he would buy the platinum, princess-cut 1.45 carat diamond ring Sam had salivated over for the past four years. Their 10th anniversary was approaching, and if she achieved her goals, she would get the ring on their 10th anniversary. If not, no ring.

Juanita wanted a new computer because she was tired of her old one taking ten minutes to boot up. She sent me $1,000 to hold while she proceeded through one particular leg of her transformation. If she succeeded at losing her next 20 pounds of weight loss I would return the money back to her. If not, I would send the money to the charity of her choice.

Set the money aside (outside of your possession) or purchasing the gift but not taking possession of it until your goal is achieved? Strong leverage

Say "I'll set the money aside." but still having control? Weak leverage

E. Put a prized or sentimental possession on the line

Glenn decided that since he didn't have much extra money and wasn't willing to take a loan out, he'd ask a friend to hold his most prized possession (a $1,500 set of Ping golf clubs). If Glenn dropped from 215 to 195 in 12 weeks, he'd get the clubs back just in time for the new golf season. If not, Glenn, who is a graphic designer, had to design the ad that would sell the clubs to the highest bidder on E-bay. Any proceeds would be donated to a charity.

Scott was awarded a ring for accomplishing significant sales in his career. He asked his best friend to hold the ring for him in a safe deposit box. If he did not reach his goal, the friend could mail the ring to his ex-business partner with a note that read, "Just thought you'd like to know that Scott failed and lost a bet." Scott and his ex-business partner no longer got along at all and the thought of Scott losing this prized possession to his nemesis really kept him focused.

Erin decided her transformation was important enough to put up her Celtic folk harp (a musical instrument worth $2,500) as leverage. She asked her sister to hold it and took it to her sister's house. If Erin had not reached her goal, her sister had strict instructions to put an ad in the paper and sell the harp. Any proceeds were to be donated to the American Cancer Society.

David was a guitar collector with over a dozen classic guitars in his possession. One particular guitar was worth over two thousand dollars. David took the guitar to his brother's house and told his brother how it would work. If David achieved his goals he got the guitar back. If he failed the guitar was to be sold and the proceeds donated to charity.

Doreen wasn't comfortable with taking a cash loan out to strengthen her leverage and she was short on disposable income at the time of her transformation. Although she was short on cash, she did own a beautiful butterfly pendant that was given to her by her grandmother. While she was unsure of the monetary value, the sentimental value was tremendously strong for her. She asked her best friend, someone she knew would not buckle under pressure, to hold the pendant for her. If she made her goal the pendant was returned. If she did not make her goal the pendant was to be pawned or sold for a donation to charity.

Tracy couldn't convince her husband that money would be a good thing to use as leverage. Her grandmother had given her a set of pearl necklaces, however, that not only were worth thousands but also had far more sentimental than monetary value for her. Tracy asked a trusted loved one to hold the necklaces with the proper directive of what to do with the necklaces should she not follow the Lifestyle program properly, thus not reaching her goal. If Tracy reached her goal she got the family heirloom back. If not, the necklaces were to be sold or pawned and the money donated to charity. Like so many others, there was no way Tracy was going to let her grandmother down by not first creating a strong plan and then following it.

Protect Your Relationships

Regardless of whether you choose a prized possession or cash for your reversed risk leveraging you must protect the relationship with your holder. I strongly suggest you first make it clear that if you do not make your goal they are to write a check to the charity you choose and in your name. This is in contrast to the holder getting to keep the item of value, heirloom or money if you do not reach your goal. The reason I suggest the holder write a check to a charity, versus them keeping the money to spend on whatever they want, is because there could be some serious resentment if you see your friend or loved one driving around on a new motorcycle or wearing some really sporting duds purchased with the money they received from you. For these reasons and more, it is important you choose someone you would trust with your life and who you know will properly handle your money. One more time–do not let them keep your money, they should donate it. This way, neither of you benefits financially should you not make your goal.

Some say reversed risk leveraging is like gambling, but what are you really gambling here? If you are serious about your transformation, what will you lose? Nothing, except a lot of ugly fat! If you have an escape or an "out," why should anyone waste their time believing you are really going to make it this time?

Vitally important is that you make sure you are clear to your holder about the consequences if you do not reach your goal. Be clear about how your success will be measured.

Are You Weak for Using This Leveraging System?

The use of this leveraging system does not violate any laws. There are no issues of morality, ethics or values being violated or infringed upon. If you do not reach your goal, then the money does not personally benefit either party (you or the holder); instead, it benefits those less fortunate through your donation to their charity organization. If we can agree for a moment that the only possible outcome is beneficial (either you reach your all time dream of being leaner and more fit or a charity gets a nice donation), then I'll move on to why using this leverage technique isn't a reflection of strength or weakness, but merely a show of strong commitment to the goal.

For as long as people have been losing weight and food has been plentiful, various tools and programs have been used to strengthen the resolve of the weight loss participant and increase the probability of their success.

- Are you weak if you lose weight following this or any national-chain diet program?
- Are you weak if you use a personal trainer at your local gym?
- Are you weak if you buy a high-tech home treadmill instead of walking outside?
- Are you weak if you purchase cassettes, CDs and use your automobile audio system to educate yourself about positive ways you can make your transformation a real success?
- Are you weak if you purchase some hand-held calorie counter device just to more closely evaluate your dietary habits?
- Are you weak if you buy a new food scale to properly weigh and measure your foods?
- Are you weak if you surround yourself with a positive support group (on- or off-line) and have to pay fees to do so?

The answer to all of these questions is a resounding NO!

Reversed risk leveraging finally answers the question of "when" you will commit to your transformation. The answer to that very important question is "right now"! Even though you know being lean and fit is better for your health, it is far too easy to start your program tomorrow without something pressing you to start right now. The consequences of inaction are substantial and painful if you use reversed risk leveraging. You will lose hard-earned cash for not taking action.

While it's an absolute fact that lean, sexy people are more productive, have more energy, are healthier, spend less time in health care centers, and have better sex more often, that doesn't prevent you from starting tomorrow what you really ought to start today. Reversed risk leveraging places your transformation goal high on your list of life's priorities and it causes this priority shift to occur right now–not tomorrow or the next day or the day after that. It helps to ensure you have a no escape and no retreat clause in your contract for a better body.

It takes a great deal of strength to put yourself in an irreversible position where you are risking a great deal to accomplish a goal. If you choose to use reversed risk leveraging as part of your Lifestyle system, it does not reflect upon your character in a negative way. Quite the opposite, it shows your character in a positive way. The fact that you are willing to do something that is legally, ethically and morally proper only shows you have strong character. Doing "what it takes" proves that you accept the fact that you will likely do better with help rather than on your own. The fact that you are willing to do what it takes to get the job done is not a reflection of weakness; instead, it is an indicator of someone with the intelligence, strength, and resolve to make his or her dream a reality.

Process 6: Countering. This process is the technical term for substituting healthy responses for unhealthy ones. If you determine you are a "night eater," is there something healthier you could do with your time rather than eat at night? Do you find you eat comfort foods more often when watching television or bored? Could you choose to eat something better or replace television with anything fun or productive? After a hard day at work, when stress is high, do you run to comfort foods to console your angst? Is there a better outlet for calming you down? Remember, most problem behaviors represent elaborate and indirect means of achieving relaxation and assertion. When you fight with your spouse or significant other, do you use food to show them who's in charge or to replace lost affection? Can you become more aware of this behavior, evaluate it a little more closely each time, and find healthy alternatives to reduce anguish and pain? There are many good countering techniques for trouble situations. The trick lies in finding the ones that will work for you.
  - Stages Best Used In: Action

Without conscious effort and evaluation, no one is strong enough to will themselves to substitute good behavior for destructive behavior. No matter how much of an intellectual you think you are, your emotions drive choices until you recognize repetitive behavior and associate negative consequences with the trigger situation. You must clearly discern that the cons of repeating the poor eating pattern when trigger situations occur far outweigh the short-term pros of feeling warm and fuzzy by finishing the entire bag, box, bowl or pan of whatever is within your reach.

If you believe it is best to simply tell yourself to "stop it!" and you do not establish a healthy substitute for the behavior you are stopping, you will fail. The risk of returning to old patterns remains high unless you replace negative behaviors with positive ones. Replace–do not eliminate.

Prochaska has identified five effective countering techniques that self-changers often employ. They are:

Active diversion. Active diversion is any activity that is enjoyable, healthy, and incompatible with your problem. Watching television does little to prevent you from eating so this is not a good example of active diversion. Playing an instrument, cleaning, exercising, working on a project, going for a walk, reading a book, listening to tapes or CDs, having sex and even calling a friend are all good examples of active diversion.

Exercise. There is no more beneficial substitute for problem behavior than exercise. Inactive people are in not only poor physical condition, but poor psychological condition as well. This reduces their coping ability to deal with stress that can accompany change.

Relaxation. Watching television is not a form of relaxation for our purposes here. The type of relaxation suggested is deep relaxation. Some examples include transcendental meditation, prayer, autogenic training, yoga, and progressive muscle relaxation. According to Prochaska, all of these relaxation techniques share these common elements:

- A quiet environment
- An internal focus
- A comfortable position
- A "letting go"

By practicing better forms of relaxation, ones that can be called upon in any situation, you will be relying on a healthy alternative to food as your only source of relaxation.

Counter-thinking. Many successful self-changers rely on counter-thinking more often than relaxation. It is quick, covert, and takes relatively little energy. It is common for all of us to play negative thoughts over and repeatedly in our heads. It is as if we are playing a tape but every time a negative thought is played, instead of letting the tape play forward to something that might be more positive, we hit the STOP button, then the REWIND button and then the PLAY button once again. This process is repeated over and over until we literally have ourselves worked up into a frenzy replaying the same negative message repeatedly and over again. In other words, we allow our thoughts to get the better of us.

Most negative thoughts that need to be replaced are irrational or gross over-exaggerations of what is really occurring or going to occur. It is also common for dysmorphic thoughts to find a home in our conscious psyche. Irrational thoughts are best countered with a dose of reality. An airplane crash is awful. The bombing of the twin towers in New York City was terrible. Burning the dinner is undesirable, but not horrible. Having a bad day at work or even getting a layoff notice is no fun, but it is also not a disaster. A spat with your spouse is unpleasant, but not the end of the world. There are several words and phrases we unconsciously choose when irrationality is about to get the best of us. Some of them include:

- Worst
- Awful
- Nightmare
- Can't resist the urge to...
- It's not fair
- Just no good
- Blew it
- Horrible
- What a disaster
- Why can't I...
- I don't deserve
- Can't stand it
- Terrible
- Can't control myself
- Can't stand the tension and craving when...
- I need to...in order to cope with...

There are many more you will find yourself saying, if you really try hard to catch them when they begin flooding your thoughts.

Most things other than sleep, nourishment, bodily needs and protection from the elements are desires. When desires are improperly classified as needs, we cry like a baby who did not get a toy when those "needs" are not met. Do not paint yourself into a corner by using "absolute" statements like

- I have to • I need to • I must

Practice counter-thinking and begin to increase your mental flexibility and your capacity for self-change.

Assertiveness. When people in your life apply any pressure for you to continue problem behaviors, it is time to whip out your assertiveness training and use it effectively. Instead of feeling helpless when you feel this external pressure, you should communicate your thoughts, feelings, wishes and intentions clearly. Not only will you counter feelings of helplessness, but you will also establish the fact that you are not a rug to be walked on.

You have many rights as a human being, but do not confuse being assertive with being aggressive. When you are passive, you are saying that "You count and I don't." When you are aggressive, you are saying, "I count and you don't." Assertive behavior is that which mutually respects both sides and clearly projects an understanding that both of you count and are important to the relationship. To make sure you were assertive and not aggressive, answer the following questions honestly:

- Did I express my right?
- Did I respect his or her rights?
- Was I specific about a behavior change?

If you do not verbally express to others what you want, there is no way you will ever get anything from them. People are not mind readers and they need to be informed of your needs and desires.

Process 7: Environment control. While countering adjusts the internal cues and response for behaviors, environment control regulates the external stimuli. Examples of environment control include:

- Throwing away junk food in the home
- Not eating out as much
- Carrying energy bars with you wherever you go
- Keeping your goals posted on the refrigerator door, bathroom mirror or screen saver
- Not shopping for groceries when you are hungry
- Asking a hotel for a fridge for the room

- Stocking the fridge with basic groceries purchased locally
- Not visiting family or friends as much if they trigger binge eating episodes
- Discontinuing drinking of alcoholic beverages

If the smell of Cinnabons® drives you crazy and you just cannot say no to them, then don't go to the mall. By being aware of the environment when you find yourself eating improperly, you can often choose to change the environment or avoid that environment for the duration of your transformation. Slowly, at some point in the future, you may be able to reintroduce some of the environmental stimuli, that you found to be problematic during your transformation.

- Stages Best Used In: Action

Process 8: Rewards. While punishing yourself after a slip is counterproductive, detrimental and demoralizing, rewarding yourself for every positive step along the way is very productive, motivating and uplifting. Many transformationists commonly make the mistake of holding back all rewards until the transformation is complete. This is a huge mistake! For some reason, no matter what part of the country a coaching client comes from, there is a belief that they are undeserving of a reward for breaking a bad habit or poor behavior they feel they should not have been engaging in anyway. Do not allow this thinking to prevail. Speaking positively to yourself, buying yourself a small gift, allowing family to give you compliments (by actually accepting the compliment), and even buying your children a small present with each small goal achieved will reinforce the behavior you are engaging in that brought you to that point in your transformation.

For many transformation wannabes, it is common to set the "final" goal and nothing else in between. This, in and of itself, is a mistake. If you weigh 200 pounds, can you possibly ever plan to get to 140 if you never reach 195 pounds? Then 195 pounds is an important milestone if you weigh 200 pounds now.

My suggestion to everyone is that you at least set five-pound weight loss goals along the way, and with each goal you hit on time, reward yourself with something desirable and positive (barring anything illegal or involving food). Women seem to be driven more toward pampering, clothing, shopping, and cosmetic fussing over and men seem to be driven more by music, gadgets and pampered relaxation. Whatever your "thing" is, it does not matter. Giving yourself, or even a loved one a little something every time you meet a set goal for a five-pound drop in body weight is worthy of being rewarded. Giving a little something to a helping relationship makes sense, does it not? Won't that motivate them even further to support your transformation and to keep an eye on you? Rewarding yourself and the most important helping relationships frequently is something you should do to help maintain commitment and motivation. If you fail to reward, then you have simply punished yourself.

- Stages Best Used In: Action, Maintenance

Process 9: Helping relationships. Although only you can change you, I would not suggest you attempt to go it alone. Using the support of significant people in your life is very powerful for continued progression through the change process. A helping relationship can come from a professional, a friend, a family member or the clergy. A "helper" is there to support, care, understand and accept you. They will also provide you with empathetic, yet honest, responses when they see you slipping up. And, you will slip. Everyone does.

Enlisting or eliciting helping relationships does not guarantee they will respond in the way you would prefer. As I have now said many times, the more vocal and assertive you are, the better the chances you will get the kind of responses you desire.

When possible, I urge anyone starting a transformation to extend the helping relationship process to partnering up. Some call it the "buddy system." If you are going through the transformation with someone you love and respect–even if you live thousands of miles apart–you can really help each other to stay focused and motivated. Who better to understand what you are feeling and going through than someone you love doing the same thing as you? By partnering up you can support each other with daily talks, share experiences and recipes, and sound the "crap detector" if you think the other is losing focus. Many partnering relationships will include innocent, but powerful, side bets and other forms of fun motivation to keep the transformation fire burning. Use your imagination because the possibilities are limitless once you enlist the support of a loved one.

- Stages Best Used In: Pre-contemplation, Contemplation, Preparation, Action, Maintenance

Summary

There are six distinct stages of change. Everyone must pass through at least five of them to enjoy lasting and significant change of any kind. By matching the correct process with the correct stage of change, you can move forward through the stages with continual progress. Leapfrogging a stage may only delay yet another failure and learning experience. Even though Action is the most overt stage you should never underestimate the influence and importance of the three stages passed through prior to it. As you work on becoming a better life manager, you'll no longer wait for life to level out. You will realize that a significant key to ultimate transformation success is not trying to cure life. By creating leverage and strengthening commitment you no longer rely on your good intentions. Through leveraging and the application of the processes presented in this chapter you can eliminate false starts and prove to yourself that you have had all the will power and time to effect a positive change all along.

Take Action and Feel Great!

1. Determine your present stage of change.

2. Write about any FEARs you presently have and that must be addressed and overcome for optimal transformation success.

3. Why must you begin your transformation now? Write out every painful thought or feeling for which you have control and which is associated with your present physical condition.

4. Make a commitment to purchase at least one book or audio tape series about becoming a better life manager from authors such as Zig Ziglar, Phil McGraw, Jim Rohn, Tony Robbins, Normal Vincent Peale and others. Do not rely on past practices to get you by.

5. Establish several leverages you will use (more is better) to reinforce your commitment and avoid false starts. Continue working on leverages until your commitment is at least a seven as described in this chapter.

6. Take your Before photos!

7. Visit www.leannesslifestyle.com and consider surrounding yourself with positive, like-minded individuals who share your passion for becoming the best you can be.

Body Composition and Obesity

*Although your genetics may load the gun, your environment and
daily activities pull the trigger.*

Obesity is now considered a disease—not a character failure. The Surgeon General warns that obesity may surpass smoking as the number one preventable cause of death. According to a 1995 report from the Institute of Medicine, "Obesity is a heterogeneous disease in which genetic, environmental, psychological, and other factors are involved. It occurs when energy intake exceeds the amount of energy expended over time. Only in a small minority of cases is obesity caused by such illnesses as hypothyroidism or the result of taking medications, such as steroids, that can cause weight gain." What does this mean in English? "although your genetics may load the gun, your environment and daily activities pull the trigger.

Public health concerns about this disease relate to its link to numerous other diseases that can lead to premature illness or death. Being overweight is a handicap at any age. Overweight individuals who lose even 5 to 15 percent of their body weight are likely to:

- Lower their blood pressure (and thereby the risk of heart attack and stroke).
- Reduce abnormally high levels of blood glucose (associated with diabetes). (Losing 15-20 pounds can actually reduce chances of getting diabetes by 58 percent!)
- Bring blood levels of cholesterol and triglycerides (associated with cardiovascular disease) down to more desirable levels.
- Reduce sleep apnea, or irregular breathing during sleep.
- Decrease the risk of osteoarthritis of the weight-bearing joints.
- Decrease depression.
- Increase self-esteem.
- Reduce anxiety.
- Improve psycho-social functioning, mood and quality of life.
- Benefit from a 40-50 percent drop in mortality from obesity-related cancers.
- Experience a prolonged and more fulfilling life.

Measuring Obesity

"Obesity" is the excess accumulation of body fat. For practical purposes, most overweight people are obese. "Overweight" is a less specific term used to define body weight that exceeds standard height and weight charts. Body weight includes muscle, bone, fat and water, therefore, a body-builder who has a lot of muscle, for example, may be overweight according to charts, but not necessarily obese because of his low body fat. Most people are not in this situation, so in this discussion I use the words obesity and overweight interchangeably.

Body Mass Index (BMI)

Until recently, body mass index (BMI), a mathematical formula based on an individual's height and weight, has been the most commonly used method for determining obesity. Physicians, researchers and insurance companies use BMI to project disease risk assessment. Over 90 million Americans are considered either overweight or obese by BMI standards. There is a lot of research that cannot be ignored correlating disease risk with BMI.

Disease Risk for Adult Women
- Low - BMI less than 18.5
- Medium - BMI 18.5-24.9
- Medium/High (Overweight) - BMI 25.0-29.9
- High Obese - BMI 30.0 +

Disease Risk for Adult Men
- Low - BMI less than 18.5
- Medium - BMI 18.5-24.9
- Medium/High (Overweight) - BMI 25.0-29.9
- High (Obese) - BMI 30.0 +

Some of the research shows that a person with a BMI greater than 35 has a 6.61 times greater risk of having type II diabetes than a person who is not overweight (BMI less than 25).

I have provided an easy-to-use BMI chart in the Appendix. Turn there now and find your height along the left side. Then run your finger across the row where it intersects with the weight column that matches your present body weight. To maintain consistency, you should weigh nude, first thing in the morning or whenever it is you crawl out of bed after your 6-8 hours of sleep. You should use the height that applies to you when you are not wearing shoes. If you are outside the range of the chart provided, you can use either of the official formulas shown below for the Metric and American systems.

Metric
- BMI = $w / h2$ (where w is weight in kilograms and h is height in meters. Since we Americans still haven't converted to the Metric system, I'll also provide you an easy way to determine BMI using the more familiar inches and pounds.)

American
- BMI = w x 703 / $h2$ where w is weight in pounds and h is height in inches.

I will provide my own BMI stats as an example:

Weight = 180 pounds   Height = 5'10" (70 inches)

180 x 703 = 126,540
(70 x 70) = 4900
126,540/4900 = 25.82 (26 if we're rounding)

BMI Does Not Measure Body Fat

One problem with BMI, however, is that it does not allow for a distinction between fat and muscle. New research now provides credibility for the use of body fat measurements over BMI as a more accurate measure of a healthy weight. A muscular person may have a very high BMI, but be far healthier than someone who has a lower BMI but a higher body fat percentage. Body fat measurements solve the problem of distinguishing fat from muscle and should be considered as significant an indicator of health as blood pressure and blood cholesterol levels.

Height and Weight Charts

Before I begin my discussion of body fat measurement, at least look at the Metropolitan Life Height and Weight Chart in the Appendix to see where you fall. What do the ranges on those charts mean, anyway? In a nutshell, they indicate that people who weigh within these ranges live the longest. That's it. It does not mean *you must weigh this amount to be healthy*! It is simply another guideline to provide you with an understanding of what is considered optimal for longevity.

Body Fat

Leading health care advocates generally agree that men with more than 25 percent body fat and women with more than 32 percent body fat are obese. Monitoring body fat percentage is no longer just a research technique. Today body fat can be conveniently measured at home or in a health club. Measuring body fat accurately can be difficult, but as you will see later, consistency is far more important than absolute precision. Knowing your body fat isn't just important for stating the difference for some transformation challenge contest, it is also a way to increase your awareness of any health risks associated with your body, as well as adding another objective tool in your arsenal of performance measures.

Recent research has identified the following risks associated with body fat percent in men and women:

Adult Women Disease Risk
Age 20-39
Low - Less than 21%
Medium - 21% to 32%
Medium/High - 33% to 38%
High - 39% +

Adult Men Disease Risk
Age 20-39
Low - Less than 8%
Medium - 8% to 19%
Medium/High - 20% to 24%
High - 25% +

Age 40-59
Low - Less than 23%
Medium - 23% to 33%
Medium/High - 34% to 39%
High - 40% +

Age 40-59
Low - Less than 11%
Medium - 11% to 21%
Medium/High - 22% to 27%
High - 28% +

Adult Women Disease Risk Age 60-79	Adult Men Disease Risk Age 60-79
Low - Less than 24%	Low - Less than 13%
Medium - 24% to 35%	Medium - 13% to 24%
Medium/High - 36% to 41%	Medium/High - 25% to 29%
High - 42% +	High - 30% +

Hydrodensitometry

The most scientifically accepted method of measuring body fat has been to weigh a person underwater (hydrodensitometry). Unfortunately, underwater weighing is a procedure limited to laboratories with special equipment. Hydrodensitometry is also not immune from human error, and is only as accurate as the instrument operator's skills and willingness to properly follow protocol for testing.

Bioelectrical Impedance Analysis (BIA)

Another method of body fat testing is bioelectrical impedance analysis (BIA). BIA sends a harmless amount of electrical current through the body, which estimates total body water. Generally, a higher percent of body water indicates a larger amount of fat-free mass, including skeletal muscle. Mathematical equations can translate the percent body water measure into an indirect estimate of body fat and lean body mass. BIA may not be accurate in severely obese individuals or bodybuilders with a substantial amount of muscle mass and it's not useful for tracking short-term changes in body fat brought about by diet or exercise. Does BIA sound like the type of analysis you want? No. BIA can be another tool, however, for measuring the *trends* in fat loss. As long as you do not rely on it solely to determine your fat loss progress, you can add BIA to your arsenal of progress measures.

BIA Home Devices

There are two popular home use BIA measurement devices. One is a handheld unit called the Omron Body Logic Pro, which retails for about $189.00. The other is a floor unit that measures body weight to the tenth of a pound and BIA at the same time. Tanita makes this scale (model TBF-521) and it retails for about $160.00.

*Skin is only 1/10th Of an Inch Thick.
What Else Is All That You're Grabbing?*

Skinfold

In the hands of a skilled trainer, skinfold is likely the most accurate, practical method of measuring body fat you have. Skinfold refers to the skin and subcutaneous (just below the skin) fat pulled away from the body by pinching and lifting firmly. Until recently, I always suggested those

I coached to purchase their own set of calipers and do their best to become skilled at taking their own body fat with skinfold. However, as experience dictates, I must now digress a bit and take you to the next level with more practical guidelines on whether you should even concern yourself with taking your body fat or not.

I have always been a big proponent of using as many objective measures of success as possible. Determining your progress "by feel" only sets you up for failure. I have harped heavily on everyone knowing his or her numbers–that is, scale/weight and skinfold/body fat (S&S). When I am personally working with a client over the Internet, I must have hard numbers to go on because I do not actually see the client other than in photos. I need good, accurate data to tell me what is going on when a client writes me with something like "I'm stuck. Help!" Regardless of whether you are a coaching client of mine, someone else's, or going solo, it is important you use as many objective measures as possible to determine your progress.

I have, however, repeatedly encouered a problem with accuracy with clients who become fixated on knowing their body fat and self-administering a skinfold test. Recall, skinfold is about as good as it gets for everyday, practical body fat testing, but only in the hands of a skilled tester. Can anyone become a skilled tester? Yes, although the reality of most people starting a transformation for the first or fifteenth time is that they are not skilled at skinfold measure. Lack of skill is the first problem that can really screw up your body fat results. The other is your level of obesity. The fatter you are, the greater your skinfold thickness.

Not Accurate for High Body Fat

The skinfold method of body fat measure is not as accurate when body fats are above about 15 percent for men and about 20 percent for women (give or take a few points). Even highly skilled trainers have a hard time accurately measuring men and women with the typical body fats I see most transformationists starting with. This is because the skin and fat lying just beneath the surface becomes too thick to accurately pinch and lift properly.

Hire a Trained Professional at Least Once

What, then, should you do, and how do you know if you are too fat to really get an accurate skinfold reading? Use the services of a trained professional in your area who has completed thousands of skinfold tests (check with your local health club, gym, or doctor's office). Once you find that person, stick with him or her. Two equally qualified trainers will likely give you two completely different body fat results. Ultimately, what you are seeking is the accurate measurement of "change." If you use three different trainers to check your body fat, you are negating the impact of the resulting data. When it comes to the scale and skin fold, it is important you use the same scale every time, and the same skinfold technique and person every time you measure. It certainly *is* worth the money they will charge you to find out what your starting body fat number is and, subsequently, what they become with approximately each 3-5 percent drop in body weight.

I suggest you use the services of a trained professional to obtain a starting body fat by multi-site (3, 4, 7 or 9) skinfold when any two of the following three criteria are met:

- You aren't a thickly muscled bodybuilder
- Your BMI is greater than 25
- Your weight is at least 25 percent more than what the height and weight charts (see the Appendix) suggest is appropriate for you

In the next chapter on weight, I'll show you how to calculate "What will I weigh when...?" If you are currently 35 percent body fat, you will see in the next chapter how to calculate what you will weigh when you are 15 percent body fat. Barring any rules of a contest you may have entered, you can skip taking any further body fat measures until you are approaching the weight calculated as about 15 percent for a man or about 20 percent for a woman. I would like you to focus more on weight loss, anthropometrics (measuring circumferences of body parts), and how you fit into your clothing. These three specific measures of progress are all you really need once you have a clear understanding of what your starting body fat is. While a high body fat is difficult to accurately measure with skinfold, a low body fat more predictably ensures an accurate skinfold measure. The thinner your skin plus subcutaneous fat, the more likely you are to get an accurate body fat measure by anyone.

Losing Fat or Muscle

I can already hear you saying "Well yeah, but I have to check my body fat more often because I need to know if I'm losing fat or muscle." If you are following all of the most basic guidelines I present to you in this book then you will not have to concern yourself with losing muscle instead of fat until your body fat reaches very low levels. These guidelines are:

- Incorporate progressive resistance training with a focus on "progressive."
- Consume adequate protein each day.
- Do not create too great a caloric deficit (more than 0.5 - 1.5 percent of your body weight each week or about two pounds per week, whichever is less).
- Get adequate rest.
- Keep stress under control.
- Choose nutrient dense foods and supplement when necessary.
- Balance meals each and every day.
- Be consistent in your plan.

When your body fat reaches 8-12 percent as a man and 15-19 percent as a woman, you should be more aware of whether your weight loss is more fat or muscle. As soon as your body fat reaches these very low levels you can concern yourself not just with what the scale says, but also with what your body fat says too. The reason for this is simple, and scientific research supports it. The fatter you are–assuming you are following the Lifestyle and not trying to follow my plan "cafeteria style" by picking and choosing some things you like, and skipping other important steps and guidelines–the more likely it is that the weight you lose will be fat and not muscle.

The leaner you are, the more likely it is that a greater percentage of the weight you lose could be muscle. There's no guarantee you'll lose muscle, however, your chances increase with every drop in body fat percentage once you reach the low levels I've discussed here. When your body fat is low, you run a greater risk of losing precious muscle.

Again, I must stress the caveats about how you do not have to worry yourself sick over body fat, but only if you are following the Lifestyle fully. Do not try to apply my guidelines about "not having to worry about muscle loss when you're really obese" if you are *not* doing all the other things that I teach in this book properly. You do not get to have it both ways.

- Diet without proper resistance exercise? Say bye bye to muscle.
- Diet without adequate protein? Say bye bye to muscle.
- Lose 3 percent of your body weight each week for a month? Bye bye!
- Overdo cardio? Bye bye!
- Diet without nutrient dense foods each day? Bye bye!
- Rely on four hours of sleep a day? Bye bye!
- Live on packaged and fast-food? Bye bye!

Do-It-Yourself Analysis

If you are starting my program when your body fat is already relatively low, or you are bound and determined to do it all yourself, I'll provide you with some illustrations and guidance for a proper skinfold measure for both men and women.

Skin thickness, compressibility of adipose tissue and hydration can all affect a skinfold reading and thus, the resulting body fat percent. Exercise also increases the extracellular (outside the cell) water accumulation in the subcutaneous tissue and thus will increase skinfold thickness. Therefore, skin folds should not be measured immediately after exercise, especially in warmer environments.

The following procedures will increase your reliability and precision when doing skinfold (SKF) measurements (Harrison et al., 1988):

1. Take all SKF measurements on the right side of the body.
2. Carefully identify, measure and mark the SKF site.
3. Grasp the SKF firmly between the thumb and index finger of your hand. The fold is lifted 1 cm (about 1/2 inch) above the site to be measured.
4. Lift the fold by placing the thumb and index finger 8 cm (about 3 inches) apart on a line that is perpendicular to the long axis of the skinfold. The long axis is parallel to the natural cleavage lines of the skin. For individuals with extremely large skin folds, the thumb and finger will need to be separated more than 8 cm in order to lift the fold.
5. Keep the fold elevated while the measurement is taken.

6. Place the jaws of the caliper perpendicular to the fold, approximately 1 cm below the thumb and index finger, and release the jaw pressure slowly.

7. Take the SKF measurement 4 seconds after the pressure is released. Write down the millimeter reading.

8. Open the jaws of the caliper to remove it from the site. Close the jaws slowly to prevent damage or loss of calibration.

9. Take a minimum of two measurements at each site. If values vary from each other by more than 10 percent, take additional measurements.

10. Take SKF measurements in a rotational order rather than consecutive readings at each site.

11. Take the SKF measurements when your skin is dry and lotion-free.

12. Do not measure SKFs immediately after physical activity because of fluid shifts to the skin.

13. After writing down the skinfold thickness in millimeters for each of the three sites measured, add them together to determine the "sum of skinfold." Determine body composition by referring to the Body Composition chart in the Appendix. Be sure and choose the correct row and column based on the correctly corresponding sum of skinfold, sex and age.

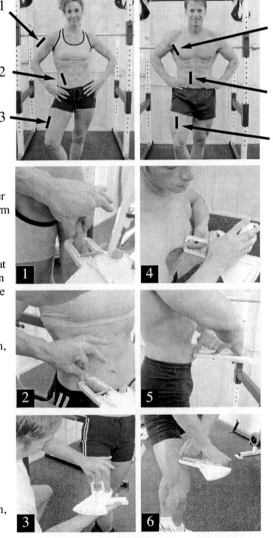

These photos show the most widely used Jackson/ Jackson-Pollock 3-site method.

Illustration 1: female [Tracy 3-site]
Triceps: a VERTICAL fold halfway between the shoulder and elbow joints, on the posterior midline of the upper arm (over the triceps muscle).

Illustration 2: female
Suprailiac: a DIAGONAL fold just above the iliac crest, at the spot where the anterior axillary line would come down (this is about 1/4 way between the midaxillary line and the umbilicus), at about 30 degrees.

Illustration 3: female
Thigh: a VERTICAL fold in the middle of the front thigh, halfway between hip and knee joints.

Illustration 4: male [David 3-site]
Axilla: a VERTICAL fold on the midaxillary line at the level of the nipple.

Illustration 5: male
Abdomen: a VERTICAL fold one inch to the right of the umbilicus.

Illustration 6: male
Thigh: a VERTICAL fold in the middle of the front thigh, halfway between hip and knee joints.

Other Important Points to Consider

I do not recommend using body fat equations that use one-site skinfold measures. Many companies will use a suprailiac (near hip bone) measure only to make life simpler for you. Unfortunately, dumbing down the analysis does not necessarily provide you with the best information. Your body fat is distributed differently across your body. My bias is toward the method I provide in this book. The sites are easy to find and men don't even need a partner to do theirs.

I don't recommend digital calipers that "beep" when you are compressing the fingers with the "proper" force. I have used these calipers and have found there is too great a variance between measures to even consider using them. Also, if your body fat is higher than 10 percent, just forget it. The accuracy is horrifically low.

Slimguide™ calipers by Creative Health Products are a quality set of plastic skinfold calipers. There are others and brands will come and go. You usually get what you pay for, so choose quality accordingly. The Slimguide™ calipers can be purchased for less than $25. You can easily spend several hundred dollars on a professional set.

Normal and Desirable Body Fat

As much as you will hate to admit it, you are likely fatter than you ever thought. Although it does not matter where you are starting, with the Lifestyle the focus is always about where you are going.

The following national standards were derived from data collected by The Cooper Institute for Aerobics Research. These guidelines should help you determine what is less than average (25th percentile) and average (50th percentile), and the three levels (75th, 90th, and 99th) leading you all the way to the highest percentile in your age bracket. If you are in the 90th percentile, this means your body fat is better than 90 percent of the rest of the American population in your age division.

National Percentiles for Men
Age 20-29
25th percentile 20.7%
50th percentile 15.9%
75th percentile 10.6%
90th percentile 7.1%
99th percentile 2.4%

Age 30-39
25th percentile 23.2%
50th percentile 19.0%
75th percentile 14.9%
90th percentile 11.3%
99th percentile 5.2%

National Percentiles for Women
Age 20-29
25th percentile 26.6%
50th percentile 22.1%
75th percentile 18.2%
90th percentile 14.5%
99th percentile 5.4%

Age 30-39
25th percentile 28.1%
50th percentile 23.1%
75th percentile 19.1%
90th percentile 15.5%
99th percentile 7.3%

National Percentiles for Men
Age 40-49
25th percentile 25.0%
50th percentile 21.1%
75th percentile 17.3%
90th percentile 13.6%
99th percentile 6.6%

Age 50-59
25th percentile 26.6%
50th percentile 22.7%
75th percentile 19.0%
90th percentile 15.3%
99th percentile 8.8%

Age 60+
25th percentile 27.6%
50th percentile 23.5%
75th percentile 19.3%
90th percentile 15.3%
99th percentile 7.7%

National Percentiles for Women
Age 40-49
25th percentile 31.1%
50th percentile 26.4%
75th percentile 22.4%
90th percentile 18.5%
99th percentile 11.6%

Age 50-59
25th percentile 34.3%
50th percentile 30.1%
75th percentile 25.8%
90th percentile 21.6%
99th percentile 11.6%

Age 60+
25th percentile 35.5%
50th percentile 30.9%
75th percentile 26.7%
90th percentile 21.1%
99th percentile 15.4%

I would be surprised if you really had a good idea before reading this section, what a good body fat was for your sex and age. Now you do. Most people I coach come to me somewhere between the 25th and 50th percentiles, and if they follow the Lifestyle prescription I am sharing with you, they will exit into Maintenance between the 75th and 99th percentile.

Like everyone else, you have a perception of what is lean, healthy and sexy. There really is no reality, only your perception of what is "right." I can tell you that if you want to live a healthy and vibrant life, you should aim for at least the 75th percentile. If you want to stand on stage or enter and win a transformation challenge, then I strongly suggest you plan on doing so when you are between the 90th and 99th percentiles, and I would lean more toward the 99th percentile if you want to be competitive.

Progressing Through Life Stages

Example–A Typical Female

This woman at age 45, through low-fat eating and periodic dieting, especially after pregnancy, has only gained 10 pounds in 22 years. Although pleased with only a 10-pound weight gain, she is not happy with the way she looks and feels. She has developed sagging, soft muscle in the arms and rear. She believes that the scale tells all and has never become aware of the importance of body fat measures. Because of her belief that the scale tells all, and that it is natural to become less toned as you age, she is not aware that she has become under-muscled and over-fat.

Let's see how this happened over time.

Age (yrs)	Weight (lbs)	Body Fat (%)	Muscle (lbs)	Fat (lbs)	Situation
22	125	20	100	25	Healthy no children
24	145	26	105	40	Post pregnant
25	128	23	98	30	Diet - low fat, no exercise
27	130	27	96	34	Busy child little exercise
28	150	32	100	50	Post pregnant
29	130	28	94	36	Low calorie diet
35	130	30	91	39	Inactive, watches food
45	135	33	90	45	

- Age 22: Single and fit. **20% body fat.**

- Age 22 to 25: Gained fat and muscle with the pregnancy and then followed a low-calorie, low-protein diet afterwards. She did lose almost all the gained weight but also lost muscle because of the low-protein and lack of resistance training. Her weight is now only 3 pounds more than pre-pregnancy but in reality, she is 5 fat pounds heavier and 2 muscle pounds lighter. **23% body fat.**

- Age 25 to 27: Gained 2 pounds weight but actually gained 4 fat pounds and lost 2 muscle pounds. **27% body fat.**

- Age 27 to 29: Another pregnancy and diet. She did not gain weight but gained 2 fat pounds and lost 2 muscle pounds. **28% body fat.**

- Age 29 to 35: Inactive with low fat diet. No weight gain but gained 3 fat pounds and lost 3 muscle pounds. **30% body fat.**

- Age 35 to 45: Followed a low-fat, high-carbohydrate diet with sporadic physical activity. She only gained another 5 pounds but actually gained 6 fat pounds and lost 1 muscle pound. **33% body fat.**

So, after 23 years, although she only gained 10 pounds of total weight, she really gained 20 fat pounds while simultaneously losing 10 muscle pounds. Her body fat went from a healthy, lean, 20 percent (5 pounds lean to 1 pound fat) to a very over fat 33 percent (3 pounds lean to 1 pound fat). **Because of the significant loss of muscle, her goal should be to gain muscle and lose body fat.**

By increasing her muscle, she will look and feel better and increase metabolism. She will be able to eat more food at a stabile, healthy body weight once she adds the muscle. If she only loses fat without gaining muscle, she would have to weigh 112 pounds in order to reach her ideal body fat of 22 percent. She would not only feel thin but would look gaunt because of the loss of muscle over the years. **If she weighed the same now as she did when she looked her best when she was younger, she would still be over fat.**

Example–A Typical Male

This is a man who at age 60 is only 5 pounds heavier than when he was age 20. Yet, he still has a small gut and his belt size is 5 inches greater. This once-muscular man now has narrow shoulders, a flat chest and thin legs. Most concerning to him and his family is how gaunt his face looks.

Age (yrs)	Weight (lbs)	Body Fat (%)	Muscle (lbs)	Fat (lbs)	Situation
20	175	11	155	20	College football player
30	180	13	157	23	Stays fit while single
38	180	16	150	30	Occasionally active
45	185	25	143	42	Off and on diets
55	200	32	135	65	Pot Belly
60	180	26	130	50	Low calorie diet

- Age 20: He was a very fit, muscular man. His diet was high in calories, protein, carbohydrates and fat. Because of his young age, regular activity program and large muscle mass he was able to stabilize blood sugar and burn fat for energy. **Body fat 11%.**

- Age 20 to 30: Although not as active as in college, he was able to maintain his body composition with periodic fitness training. **Body fat 13%.**

- Age 30 to 38: Married with kids and increased work responsibilities caused him to become less physically active. Yet, he was still able to maintain weight. He looked very fit to everyone else but he was beginning to notice a difference in his physique. He gained 8 fat pounds and lost 8 muscle pounds. **Body fat 16%.**

- Age 38 to 45: Further lessened his activity program. Although he only gained 5 pounds, his waist size was up 3 inches. Actually gained 12 fat pounds (mainly in his abdomen) and lost 7 muscle pounds. Because of his size, he still looked fit in clothing. **Body fat 25%.**

- Age 45 to 55: Occasionally went on low-fat, high-carbohydrate diets with little increased physical activity. Gained 15 pounds but actually 23 fat pounds while losing 8 muscle pounds. Waist increased 4 more inches. His cholesterol and blood pressure were elevated. **Body fat 32%.**

Therefore, from age 32 to 55, he had gained only 20 pounds of weight but in reality gained 42 pounds fat and lost 22 pounds of muscle. He increased waist size 8 inches and his fat percentage from a very fit 13 percent (7 pounds lean to 1 pound fat) to a very over-fat 33 percent (3 pounds lean to 1 pound fat).

- Age 55 to 60: Because of a family history of heart disease, elevated blood pressure and cholesterol, he finally stuck on diet and lost 20 pounds to get back to his weight at 30 years old, but of the 20 pounds lost, another 5 pounds were muscle.

- Age 60: Still 5 pounds more than his weight at age 20, and over fat at 26 percent body fat. People are telling him that he looks too thin. The problem is that he has lost 25 pounds of muscle since age 20. Over the years, facial shape was maintained with body fat. When he lost the fat on his diet, his muscle-depleted facial bones were apparent causing him to feel like a concentration camp victim.

Both the woman and the man portrayed above, could have prevented the distress of losing muscle by regularly participating in a progressive resistance training program and paying earlier attention to body composition, instead of only the scale. Now, no matter your age, you can turn back the hands of time more intelligently and understand why things are different now compared to when you were 20. Hope is not lost, regardless.

By incorporating a solid resistance training program as outlined in this book, you can add quality muscle and regain most or all of the youthful shape you once had, within a reasonable period.

Summary

Obesity is second behind smoking as the most preventable cause of illness and premature death. Obesity is defined as a body fat greater than 25 percent for a man and 32 percent for a woman.

BMI is a quick and relied-upon calculation for determining obesity, however, BMI doesn't take into account the thickly muscled bodybuilder or transformationist and, therefore, body fat is likely a superior measure when available.

There are many ways to measure body fat, however, two methods are most prevalently used by transformationists–skinfold and BIA. I recommend you consult with a personal trainer at least once who is skilled at taking multi-site skinfold measurements so you have a baseline body fat to go on. Depending on what the measure is, you may not need to focus on body fat for quite some time thereafter. Body fat becomes more important to watch when men and women approach very low body fat levels. The tug of war between the loss of muscle or fat is more of a concern once body fat as reached a certain low threshold. Regular body fat analysis is ultimately important once it is low because it helps tell you what your lean body mass is.

Throughout life it becomes all too common for men and women to focus only on the scale weight. As I clearly portrayed in this chapter, however, your scale weight at 40 to 60 years of age, even if the same or similar to when you were 20, may leave you with a body you still don't desire. If you haven't been focusing on resistance training to preserve and add lean body mass (muscle), there is little question you will see and feel the difference once you do. There is always an opportunity to start today and muscle can be accumulated at any age with a sound resistance training program as covered in later chapters.

Take Action and Feel Great!

1. Determine your current BMI.

2. Look at the height/weight charts in the Appendix. Are you over, under or at your proper weight?

3. Make an appointment with a certified personal trainer who has experience in taking multi-site skinfolds for body fat analysis.

4. Determine your present body fat.

5. Identify your disease risk according to your BMI and body fat.

6. Determine what percentile you fall into with respect to your body fat.

Your Weight–Everything You Wanted to Know But Were Afraid to Ask

Fat mass is the percentage of total body mass that is composed of fat. Fat-free mass simply refers to all body tissue that is not fat.

You step on the scale and your old, trusty enemy immediately feeds you data about your progress, or lack thereof. Many people allow the scale to completely dictate how their entire day will proceed. Your weight can have such a dramatic bearing on your day and mental attitude if you allow it. It's either a good day or a bad day from the moment after you visit the scale. It's not uncommon for individuals to stash their scale, throw it away, cuss it them, and even set the dial back 5 to 10 pounds knowing full well they've done so just so what is reflected back to them is anything but reality. Interpersonal relationships often suffer or benefit from three numbers delivered by an inanimate object: the scale.

Regardless of your current relationship with the scale, it's time you understand the two-component model and learn what is realistic in terms of adding one of the two components: fat-free mass. What exactly is the scale and should you even use it? If you do use it, should you weigh frequently or not? This chapter will address these questions head on. Finally, you need to know how you can determine what your approximate goal weight will be so you can transition smoothly from Action into Maintenance.

Two-Component Model

Transformationists will commonly refer to all nonfat gains or losses as muscle. If someone gains two pounds and their body fat does not go up, they will state that they have gained two pounds of muscle. First, they are really referring to skeletal muscle (and not cardiac or smooth muscle), and second, their reference is an inaccurate assessment of what has been gained.

Most researchers in the field of body composition have adapted the two-component model, which includes:

- Fat mass, and
- Fat-free mass.

Fat mass is the percentage of total body mass that is composed of fat. Fat-free mass simply refers to all body tissue that is not fat.

When a transformationist says, "I've gained 10 pounds of muscle," the more appropriate statement is really, "I've gained 10 pounds of fat-free mass." What transformationists typically call muscle is fat-free mass. Fat-free mass is a much broader class than you might think. Fat-free mass is composed of all of the body's nonfat tissue, including bone, muscle, organs, connective tissue, water and other bodily fluids. Basically, fat-free mass is everything other than fat.

Having a clear understanding of the two-component model is important because it helps explain the confusion many transformationists feel when either they, or advertisements report a 20-pound gain of "muscle" in just four weeks. By the way, some transformationists are truly confused, and others are simply steroid-using liars or charlatans.

We live in a fast food, fast-paced, "why should I ever expect to have to wait" world. I am sorry to report that none of that impatience matters to your body with regard to adding skeletal muscle, a major component of fat-free mass. Losing body fat is difficult, but adding skeletal muscle is at least ten times more difficult. Most people start a resistance-training program thinking that if they touch an iron bar they will literally rip out of their clothes like the Incredible Hulk. Ask any man or woman who has any appreciable muscle mass, how hard it is to add muscle. Most likely, you will get the same answer every time–"It's damn hard!" You must be persistently and diligently patient.

After over 20 years of competing in bodybuilding and power lifting, as well as training hundreds of transformationists, I provide for you, with great confidence, my ...

Maximum Muscle Accumulation Guide for the Drug-Free Resistance Trainer
Valid when weight is stable or weight loss is occuring. Not valid during weight gain.

Age & Gender	Experience - Never touched a weight before		Intermediate to Advanced (At least 2 years of progressive steady lifting)	
	Maximum Pounds Per Month	.1 .2 .3 .4 .5 .6 .7 .8 .9 1 1.2 1.5 Lbs	Maximum Pounds Per Month	.1 .2 .3 .4 .5 .6 .7 .8
Age 50 +				
Male	.6 - .9 Lbs per month		.3 - .45 Lbs per month	
Female	.3 - .45 Lbs per month		.15 - .225 Lbs per month	
Age 30 - 50				
Male	.8 - 1.2 Lbs per month		.4 - .6 Lbs per month	
Female	.4 - .6 Lbs per month		.2 - .3 Lbs per month	
Age < 30				
Male	1 - 1.5 Lbs per month		.5 - .75 Lbs per month	
Female	.5 - .75 Lbs per month		.25 - .375 Lbs per month	

Claims of higher muscle accumulation abound in popular muscle building comic books and Internet discussion forums. To say that I question their veracity would be an understatement. If you aren't sure yourself who to believe, then ask any person who claims you can add more muscle than what I suggest to provide a published, peer-reviewed study supporting their claim. Just make sure you don't hold your breath waiting.

Men claim to add 20-30 pounds of muscle in 4-8 weeks, and women claim to add 5-10 pounds of muscle a month. No research whatsoever will support these claims. How do we explain away the disparity between what is claimed and even believed true by some, and what is real? The following criteria are the roots of how the ignorantly held beliefs become the standard by which all must accumulate muscle, or be labeled a failure:

1. Body fat equation used: It is not uncommon for transformationists to perform their own body fat measures. This is highly unreliable for all but the elite few who have substantial experience at the skinfold technique. Others will seek the help of a professional, only to have a different, so-called professional measure skinfold at the end of their transformation. Unless the same person is doing the measuring, all bets are off. It is also not uncommon for transformationists to use one technique (e.g., skinfold) at the beginning of the transformation, and then–at the end–use a very different body fat method such as bioelectrical impedance. If two different body fat methods are used, the results may not be valid.

2. Changing scales during the transformation: For some reason it is very common for transformationists to change weight scales at some point during their transformation. Perhaps, with good intentions, they want a better scale they believe will be more accurate. Unfortunately, this negates the reliability of the data. Many transformationists will use their home scale one time, then the gym's scale another, and still their doctor's scale a different time. Which is accurate? As the saying goes, "*A man with one watch always knows what time it is.*" For a more accurate depiction of your true transformation success, start and end with the same scale.

3. Time of day weighed: It pretty much goes without saying that you will weigh less when you climb out of bed than at the end of the day, however, this denominator is not always held constant. You should always weigh at the same time of day.

4. With or without clothing: As hard as this might be to believe, it's not uncommon for people to weigh at times with clothing, yet at other times, without clothing and wonder why there is a disparity in the weights. Clothing can add or reduce scale weight by 2 to 10 pounds!

5. Water retention or dehydration at start or end: Both men and women will temporarily retain water for a period of 24 to 36 hours after an exceptionally high day of sodium consumption. It is also very common for additional water retention to occur for 24 to 36 hours after what Body-for-Lifers call their "free day" or what I call a "splurge meal." Women will commonly retain water equal to about 2 to 3 percent of their body weight during "their week of the month." Therefore, if a woman weighs 150 for three weeks of the month, it is not uncommon

for the same woman to weigh 153 for 4 to 7 days during "the week." Even mild dehydration can be responsible for a 1 to 2 percent body weight drop. With all of these confounding variables, it's not a wonder people start or end with unintentionally misrepresented data.

6. Supplements being used: We absolutely know that creatine monohydrate can add body weight quickly primarily in the form of intramuscular water. Other supplements, especially prohormones ("andros"), may also cause water retention. Were supplements used? When were they started? Were they taken as directed? Were they stopped mid-transformation? Were they started mid-transformation? For all of these reasons and more, supplements can cause transformationists to mistakenly believe they have added real muscle tissue when, in fact, they have added a minutely small amount of real muscle and a significant amount of fat-free mass in the form of water.

7. Not all of the weight ever lost is 100 percent fat, even if no muscle is lost. In the first week or two, weight loss might be comprised of 70 percent water, 25 percent fat and 5 percent from protein. After a few weeks, the quality of the weight lost for the obese person is usually more desirable with approximately 85 percent of the weight loss coming from stored fat and 15 percent coming from protein.

For a truer picture of just how much real muscle was added during any transformation, and before you talk yourself into a particular accomplishment or defeat, you should take another look at the confounding variables 1 to 7 above, and then take into consideration my *Maximum Muscle Accumulation Guide*. The interplay between all of the variables is massively influential on the alleged increase or decrease in fat-free mass (which some completely, and inaccurately, attribute to skeletal muscle tissue).

This interplay is also the reason why many gung-ho transformationists believe their heroes in the comic books and Internet discussion forums started with x percent body fat, lost 40 pounds (as an intermediate to advanced trainee), and gained 10 pounds of muscle in 12 weeks. Foolishness! Poppycock! Bunk! Or, as the English would say, rubbish!

Unfortunately, for honest and intelligent folk who report valid data and report actual muscle loss as one approaches superhumanly low body fats (e.g., 5 percent for men or 8 percent for women), you get punished by the transformation community for your attempts at accuracy and honesty.

Bob Takes a Beating

I want to briefly tell you the story of coaching member Bob, who started with a body fat he believed to be approximately 9.9 percent and who dropped it all the way down to 5 percent.

Bob says he started at 174 pounds and 9.9 percent body fat. This left him with 156.77 pounds of fat-free mass (not all of which is muscle, as you now know). At the conclusion of Bob's transformation he weighed 160 pounds and was measured at 5 percent body fat. That left him with 152 pounds of fat-free mass.

Bob all but apologized publicly for what he thought was a loss of muscle. But is that what happened ...?

There is little question that with skinfold body fat measurements, the leaner you are the more accurate the results. Research has proven this repeatedly. The thicker the skinfold, the less accurate the body fat measurement.

What if Bob's starting body fat was not 9.9 percent, but instead, it was really 12.5 percent (it is not uncommon at all for skinfold body fat measures to be off by 3 percent high or low, especially when the body fat isn't super low). That would have put his fat-free mass when he was 174 pounds at 152.25 pounds.

Look at his Before photo. [See Center Section]. Would it be crazy or unfathomable to believe he started his transformation at 12.5 percent? Of course not. Now, I have more of a tendency to believe Bob's 5 percent body fat because, as I said earlier, when body fats are low, skinfold is typically more accurate. Look at his After! Does he look like he is 2 percent (3 percent variance remember) or does he look like he is 8 percent? No. He looks like he is 5-something percent.

So, ol' Bob may or may not have lost muscle during his transformation. Nevertheless, he was punished (on several Internet discussion forums) as if he had. He was also blasted for–allegedly–losing the battle of muscle preservation and accretion while dieting. Utter foolishness! Bob may have lost a small amount of muscle. Is it certain he lost 5 pounds of muscle? Absolutely not! Most likely, he placed lower in a contest challenge he entered because of his honesty in providing data without manipulation. This is not always the case in transformation challenges.

As I see it, the problem is the unarmed, common man does not realize the extent with which some people and companies will go to be recognized. It has been said that, "Men will die for ribbons." I could not agree more, except that I would have to add women to the list, too. This lack of knowledge about what's truly possible in any transformation–man or woman–has created tremendous false hope with regard to how much real muscle can be accumulated in two or three months. The standard by which many are compared has been placed so high that unless you are willing to twist and distort the numbers, there is little hope of not feeling like a failure when you publicly report actual data. "Did you gain 20 pounds of solid muscle in eight weeks? No? What is wrong with *your* program? Not only didn't you add 20 pounds of muscle in eight weeks, you didn't reduce your body fat from 25 down to 5 percent? It took you five or six cycles (four weeks to a cycle) to achieve a 20 percent body fat reduction? What is wrong with your program?"

The reality is that there is nothing wrong with a program based on fact over fallacy. Unfortunately, most are not. There is likely little wrong with any weight-loss program that soundly promotes the retention of muscle and healthy eating behaviors, while reducing obesity and creating head-spinning physiques.

Seven Take-Home Maxims to Help Analyze Transformation Claims

1. Is the beginning body fat valid? For the reasons I have already discussed, most starting body fats of obese men and women are not accurate. Obviously, this means some initial body fats will be accurate. Are you willing to judge yourself or someone else harshly, however, when they don't "appear" to have "the numbers" of the man or woman in the magazine ad or on the Internet discussion forum?

2. There is a better chance the ending body fat will be more accurate, still there is no guarantee of this. Before you judge yourself, or anyone else, be sure to recalculate the fat lost and fat-free mass gained or lost by using a starting and ending bodyfat that is three to five percent higher and lower than what was reported. A margin of error between three and five percent is completely reasonable with few exceptions. The error itself, if there is one, could be much larger than three to five percent.

3. People are not robotic. When they are taking dietary supplements, they rarely do so with the precision of a Swiss watch. They start and stop supplements mid-challenge. They forget to take them. As I have mentioned, certain supplements like creatine monohydrate can totally change the fat-free mass to total mass ratio.

4. Unfortunately, not all people are honest. The chance to be a "recognized winner" is too alluring for some to swallow that "tell the truth" pill. It would have been very easy for Bob to say he was 12.5 percent body fat in the beginning (and he just might have been) and therefore he would have been able to claim ZERO fat-free mass loss while getting to 5 percent! Quite amazing, since he already had some experience with resistance training before starting his transformation.

5. Research doesn't support the idea that people who are at the top of their game (like me, for instance) with little room left in their genetic ceiling for growth can keep or add real contractile muscle tissue while dropping their body fat down to 5 percent. But, ol' David Greenwalt, with over 20 years of training experience, could take six months off (achieve a very detrained state) and then claim a massive muscle gain during a transformation, right? Absolutely! This occurs everyday in official and unofficial transformation challenges.

6. Authentic peer-reviewed research does not routinely support most beginners with having the ability to keep muscle while dieting from 20 percent down to 15 percent, let alone from 20 percent down to 6 percent!

7. Current research suggests the leaner people become, the more skeletal muscle they lose, when compared to when they were fatter. This means that when you are very obese you have a better chance of your weight loss being primarily fat, because the leaner a person is, the more fat-free mass they lose while dieting. In real world applications, this is precisely what we see.

The next time you see wild claims of 15 pounds of *muscle* accumulation in 12 weeks *while* dieting away 25 pounds of fat, you can count on this to be a hyperbole and not reality. If 15 pounds of real skeletal muscle are added in 12 weeks, then it did not happen drug-free. During a 12-week challenge there might have been fat loss and a fat-free mass addition, but remember, fat-free mass is not *just* skeletal muscle.

Before you talk yourself into believing *you* have added x pounds of muscle in 2-3 weeks, keep in mind the huge difference between real skeletal muscle and what appears to be left when you subtract out fat from your body weight (fat-free mass). I have said it repeatedly in this section but I must say it again:

Fat-free mass does not equal muscle!

Do not punish yourself if you do not end up with the "amazing" increases in skeletal muscle the magazine transformation winners' claim to. Think about all the possible inaccuracies that potentially exist from beginning to end. Make the best transformation possible, but keep it real. Keeping it real is what the Lifestyle is all about.

The Bathroom Scale: Friend or Foe?

Is it important to have your weight continuously staring you in the face? Some nutritionists say we focus too much on the scale and that it sets us up for disappointment and failure when we monitor our weight too closely. Some say to weigh once a month. I completely disagree for most individuals, and those who have lost weight and kept it off for more than three years agree with me.

Most people monitor their weight regularly while they are developing their personal plan for leanness. Once they are stuck, or see an increase in weight rather than a decrease, they abandon the scale because they are afraid of it. They do not want to confirm what their clothing and mirror are shouting to them on a daily basis. "You're not losing! You are gaining! You're getting fatter!" Abandoning the scale will not help you achieve your goal of losing fat and gaining muscle. It is merely another objective measure of progress.

Clothes and Mirror Only?

Fitting into an old, favorite, smaller pair of blue jeans is an awesome feeling. The mirror gives indications of change, but you do not see it all with the mirror. Together, the fit of clothing and the mirror are great guides to tell you how your body shape is changing, however, they may not provide enough objective evidence to accurately measure your planned progress.

Only the most self-disciplined, honest, self-critiquers are able to throw away the scale and rely solely on clothing size and the mirror to guide them. I once asked Dale Tomita, a professional fitness competitor and one of the nicest professional athletes I have ever had the pleasure of speaking with, what her body weight or body fat was. She admitted that she did not know. She said she only cared about what the mirror said, because on stage her weight did not matter, only her overall presentation and look. I think that once you have reached the level that Dale has, you are justified in using the disciplined technique of self-critique based solely on self-observation. Most people (like 99 percent of you reading this) have not reached this level of self-honesty, so you should use the scale.

> *You cannot change fat into muscle! You either lose fat or you gain muscle but you do not change fat into muscle. You also do not change muscle into fat.*

Some people avoid the common bathroom scale like the plague. I repeat: This is a mistake. If you believe the scale lies more than it tells the truth, then you have to accept that your current belief is false. If you refuse to let go of this myth, then you will not progress through your own transformation as successfully as you could have.

The Scale Makes Me Feel Bad

The truth is, most people aren't following an eating plan tight enough to make the desired changes a reality, and when they step on the scale, they are sorely disappointed by a lack of left-ward shift of the needle or downward direction of numbers displayed. Thus, they become depressed and avoid the scale like the plague. After all, it is the scale that is causing them to feel bad every time they step on it, right? Well, no. The scale provides no emotion. Scales do not make you *feel* bad. *You* make you feel bad. You control your thoughts, and your thoughts have a direct impact on your emotions and physiology. Once the scale numbers are revealed to you, it is completely up to you to turn that moment and the rest of the day into a "nightmare" or into a day of progress and disciplined action.

No Weight Loss Equals All Muscle Gain?

If there is no scale change in four weeks, and you have at least 10 pounds of weight to lose, you have not simply added muscle in place of fat. As I mentioned in the *Maximum Muscle Accumulation Guide for the Drug-free Resistance Trainer* section, the average man will put on, at best, about 1.5 pounds of muscle a month if he is a beginner resistance trainer, and even less as an advanced trainer. The average woman? At best, about half that of a man. If over a three- to four-week period the needle or numbers on the scale do not reflect a lower body weight than at the start, you are not doing what is necessary to achieve fat loss. Period! Do not kid yourself otherwise.

Just because you "know you are doing everything right" does not mean you are doing everything right. If the scale just will not budge, you are not paying close enough attention to the finer details of what is entering your mouth. When you've read about calories and the contribution of vigorous exercise to your plan, you'll learn that it takes 15 minutes or less to eat 2000 calories and five hours to burn those same 2000 calories off! *You truly cannot outrun what you can potentially eat.* If you are being active, then there is only one place left to blame: your fingers and your fork.

Weighing: How Often?

The question always arises as to whether you should weigh once a week, once a month, twice a week or what? I believe it is best to weigh once a day, every day, at the same time of day, nude, right after waking up. Why so often? Because, over time you will learn your weight cycle and this is very important. Your weight cycle is unique to you and but varies more for premenopausal women than any other group. Most premenopausal women don't know their cycle as well as they should or are irregular. If they happen to step on the scale when they are peaking with water retention, they may be sorely disappointed by the apparent lack of progress for all of their hard work. Regardless of whether you are a premenopausal women or not, you should learn your cycle and keep a close eye on the effects of certain food and drink on your weight.

Imagine being in the dating scene and having someone come in and snap a Polaroid of you the second your body is vertical in the morning. Imagine pillow lines in your face, hair looking like you combed it with a Mix Master blender, bags under the eyes, and even that weird eye droop that goes away shortly after your second cup of coffee. This photo will be the photo all the other singles are shown for "window shopping." This scenario would hardly be fair, would it? Is that snapshot really an accurate depiction of who you are? It is for those few minutes before you get your shower and bathroom routine done, but it is only a snapshot of you. It does not tell the real story. *Do not rely on infrequent snapshots of your weight to measure true progress.* Do not panic when the scale seemingly overnight reflects a change of two to five pounds. I assure you it is water weight.

Weigh daily, chart it, and assess your real progress over a period of three to four weeks.

Scales are Objective: No Personality

Do not fear the scale! It is what it is. Scales do not have a personality and they could care less who you are. Scales provide feedback and do not do it nicely or ask permission to slap you across the face if you have been unfocused about following the plan. Take the beating when the weight does not drop, and then give the scale a real smack when you win the war on fat and you truly are doing what is necessary to get the fat off.

If you are true to your hourly, daily, nighttime, weekend and other short-term goals, you will not and should not fear the scale. The scale is what it is: an objective measure of what is really happening. Run from it if you will, but it will not make you a thinner person by running. Even if you have had good results following someone else's plan up until now, I am completely confident, those results did not come because you consistently turned your back on reality.

Never use two different scales to weigh. That is nuts! Always use the same scale and always weigh at the same time in the same condition (nude) every time!

The trends in weight loss over time are what you are really looking for. Not the daily ups and downs, which will seem to occur sporadically at first. Once you have charted your weight, every day, for at least a month (use the graph I've provided in the Appendix), you will have a true picture of your progress. If you weigh only once a week, you leave yourself open to that *one weigh-in* being *the* day you are holding water (especially women during "their week" or anyone else a day or two after a splurge meal). If this occurs, you may choose to be depressed and not realize that it was only a snapshot of one day and not a true reflection of your real progress.

> Coaching client Erin wrote this about her experience with charting her weight on the graph included in the Appendix.

> *"Weighing in daily was hard at first. David, as you know, I spent several weeks crying about water retention and the scale going up. Then I used your chart - a graph actually, and I suggest that everyone do the same thing. I charted two months of daily weigh-ins in a chart and connected the dots. What I saw was that although my weight is up and down daily, the overall trend was right there in front of my face. Every time I dropped in weight, I also went up several days before it. Now I can almost predict my weight gain or loss on a daily basis. Up days do not upset me any longer because I know I am not eating enough calories to gain that weight therefore it is water retention. And for me water retention means a loss is coming.*
>
> *Try this... if you have a digital scale measure out 1/2 pound (8 ounces) of water. Now take a good look at it. About a coffee cup worth, right? Considering our bodies are about 70% water, isn't that a teeny-weeny amount of water? I'm not letting a couple of cups of water mess up my plans...or my mood that day when the scale reads higher than I think it should.*
>
> *I know this weight loss thing is a long process but my graph shows a steady movement of little peaks and valleys that are continually progressing downward.... even when I retain water or have a splurge meal. I will be successful in the end.*
>
> *And I want to publicly thank you, David, for being patient and helping me through that lesson."*

The Scale Will not Budge!

When you think you are doing everything right, what do you do when the scale refuses to budge? First, honestly assess your current eating plan and log your foods for at least three full days. Determine precisely how many calories you are consuming each day and what percentage of those calories comes from carbohydrates, proteins, fats and alcohol. If you are not already exercising excessively, add another 20 to 30 minutes of vigorous exercise one to two times a week (see the *Energy Balance* chapter). Ensure you are eating enough–but not too many–calories each day and that those calories are coming primarily from whole, unprocessed and unpackaged foods. Increase your servings of fresh or frozen fibrous vegetables as well as your lean sources of protein (see *Nutrients chapter*). Then look at the next two- to four-week block, and you'll be very pleasantly surprised at what happens.

Minor Adjustments -> Big Results -> Great Knowledge Gained

What Not to Do

Don't throw out the baby with the bath water! Do not throw away the plan or the Lifestyle. Just tweak the inputs and outputs and maybe, just maybe, the macronutrient ratios, to get the weight moving in the right direction. At least now you know for sure that you will not gain more than 1 to 1.5 pounds of muscle as a man or 0.5 to 0.75 pounds of muscle as a woman in any given four-week period. What you do with the data becomes the critical issue now.

Weight Loss Champions' Secret

The true champions of weight loss are those who not only take off the pounds, but also manage to keep them off for more than two years. The true champions frequently monitor their weight and quickly make adjustments to food intake before any more than five pounds creep up on them. It is true. Successful long-term dieters do not fear the scale. They use it as a tool for success. If you start to drift from the Lifestyle when you have gained four pounds, it is much easier to make some minor adjustments early on, than if you have not been paying attention (or purposely ignoring the dreaded demon scale) and you have gained eight pounds. At that point, it becomes quite easy to say "The heck with it. I have blown it. I can't do this!" Negative self-talk is destructive, and has never gotten you thinner, so stop it! As I was told growing up "'Can't' never could do anything."

Pay attention to the scale and establish a "trigger point" of five pounds. Once you reach your goal weight you can allow up to five pounds to accumulate above this, but that "point" should "trigger" you to take action before any more accumulates. Weigh yourself frequently and accept that any more than a five-pound increase is likely the result of adding some fat and it is time to tighten things up and get this book back out.

What Kind of Scale?

I suggest you purchase a quality digital scale that measures either in half-pound or in tenth-pound increments. A digital scale can provide encouragement when the weight is coming off slowly and it will not allow you to tilt your head to the right while standing on it looking down to get a "better" reading than what is true. It is like looking at the now old-fashioned needle-type speedometer when you are sitting in the passenger side of the car. It looks like you are going five miles per hour slower than you really are because of the angle.

What Will I Weigh When I am There?

In the two-component model, your body weight is made up of fat and then "everything else." We call everything else fat-free mass. Follow me through this example and let's see how many pounds of fat you have on your body. Then, if you have a good idea of what your body fat is, we'll see what you'll weigh when you achieve your goal body fat. If you do not have a clue what your body fat is, I will provide an easy-to-use formula to help you determine what might be a healthy weight for you.

I weigh 180 pounds and have approximately 6.5 percent body fat. This means I have 11.7 pounds of fat on me. It also means I have 168.3 pounds of fat-free mass (not all muscle). I could never get rid of all my fat nor would I want to because the body needs about 3 percent or so for proper organ function and support. What would I weigh to compete at 5 percent body fat? It's easy. Follow along and fill in the blanks.

Formula to Determine Fat Mass and Fat-Free Mass

(Numbers to the right of the blank spaces are my numbers and are only provided as an example.)

Enter your present weight	(A)_____	180
Enter your present body fat as a decimal	(B)_____	0.065
Multiply (A) times (B)	(C)_____	11.7
Subtract (C) from (A)	(D)_____	168.3

(C) is the amount of fat on your body in pounds
(D) is the fat-free mass you have on your body in pounds

What Will I Weigh When?

It is simple. Just plug in the numbers:

Re-enter your fat-free mass from (D)	(E)_____	168.3
Enter your body fat goal as decimal	(F)_____	0.05
Subtract (F) from 100	(G)_____	0.95 (100-0.05
Divide (E) by (G) to determine your final weight	(K)_____	177.16 (168.3/0.95)

(K) is the weight you will be at when you reach your goal body fat percentage (F) if you have lost no skeletal muscle and other fat-free mass. (Remember, numbers to the right of the blank spaces are only examples.)

If you have not grabbed a pencil by now, do it! Fill in the blanks above and get a clear picture of where you really are now and where you need to be. Do not be caught in a swoon of false hope and do not be down in the dumps unnecessarily about what you need to do because you are not armed with the facts. It is far too common for transformation hopefuls to begin with the idea that while they're a "big man" and they weigh 230 pounds, they'd like to "rip up" to 215 pounds or so. As if saying it makes it so. The reality is they are 230 pounds at 24 percent body fat, leaving 174.8 pounds of fat-free mass. If you plug in those numbers above you will see that if they have any hope of showing their 6-pack abs (which is about 7 percent body fat), they will have to weigh in around 188 pounds (174.8 / 0.93), not 215 pounds. Needless to say, a few bubbles might be burst in the beginning, but at least you will start with what is real. Might your "ideal" body weight vary by 5 percent higher or lower than what you project on this form today? Yes, but it is not worth quibbling over so write it down now.

I Don't Know My Body Fat, What is a Healthy Weight to Shoot For?

In the appendix, I have provided a standard height and weight chart. There is also another quick method to determine what is likely a healthy weight for you. Thickly muscled bodybuilders are not represented in the "healthy weight" guidelines below. While I cringe at what I'm about to say–because many heavy people mistakenly think they are "large framed" or "big boned"–I would be remiss if I didn't say that small- and large-framed men and women may be healthiest at a lower or higher weight than what these simple equations provide.

Men: 106 + 6 pounds for every inch over 5 feet tall.
(Example: a 5'9" man is 9 inches taller than 5 feet. 9 x 6 = 54 + 106 = 160 pounds).

If a man has been resistance training continuously for at least two years with no breaks longer than a week or two, he could likely use this formula: 106 + 7 to 8 pounds for every inch over 5 feet.

Women: 105 + 5 pounds for every inch over 5 feet tall.
(Example - a 5'6" woman is 6 inches taller than 5 feet. 6 x 5 = 30 + 105 = 135 pounds).

If a woman has been resistance training continuously for at least two years with no breaks longer than a week or two, she could likely use this formula: 105 + 6 to 7 pounds for every inch over 5 feet.

Water-Weight Fluctuations
1. Prescription Medicines

If a doctor prescribes you anything, you need to know the side effects. Water retention or weight gain is a common side effect of prescription medicines. Instead of running headfirst into a brick wall when you "all of a sudden" jump up five pounds after taking the new pill you were prescribed, you should read about the drug online or ask the doctor for a copy of the listing from the *Physician's Desk Reference*. All doctors have a current edition of this very large prescription drug book in their office. Talk to your doctor, and do not be shy about asking about all potential side effects. It is your right to know.

2. Premenstrual Syndrome (PMS)

If you're a premenopausal woman, it's important you know that it's more common than not to add 2 to 3 percent of your current body weight during the week before menstruation, the week of, or even a few days after menstruation ends. This will drive you nuts, if it hasn't already. I do not blame you for feeling like hitting something during this time, but your best weapon against going crazy is to chart your weight every day on the form I've provided in the Appendix. Once you understand *your* cycle, you will learn to take the weight gain in stride, you will not fear it any longer, and you will know that about three to five days after menstruation ends, the water weight will disappear. If you have been following the Lifestyle with the proper diligence and effort, you are likely to experience your lowest weight in a two-week period the week after menstruation ends. Things do not always work out this way, but these are the norms.

Anecdotally, women commonly report they see less weight fluctuation and feel less bloating and overall PMS symptoms if they consume 1.5 to 2 gallons of water every day beginning ten days prior to menstruation and continue until menstruation is complete. Water restriction is never a good practice but seems to exacerbate the symptoms of PMS. Women also report they feel less bloated if they eat less refined and processed sugars, zero chocolate (as in none) and keep their macronutrient (carbohydrate, protein, and fat) ratios as follows:

- Carbohydrates: 35 - 40% of total calories
- Protein: 40 - 50% of total calories
- Fat: 15 - 20% of total calories

* See the Energy Balance chapter for more details on how to better manage macronutrient ratios.

3. High Sodium Meal or Day

The recommended intake of sodium per day is 2400 mg for an adult. It is not uncommon for the average person to consume 8000 mg per day. Some transformationists will continuously blame a lack of weight loss on the notion they "must be retaining water" from the popcorn they had last week. If you find yourself saying this more than a few days a month, I must caution you and say that a lack of weight loss over a three-week period is not going to be because of the high sodium day you had more than a day or two ago.

After wolfing down movie popcorn, chips of any kind, fast food and other super-high sodium foods, it is very common to add two to three percent of your present body weight in the form of excessive water retention. The additional water retention will last for approximately 24 to 36 hours. It is important you increase your overall water intake by 25 to 50 percent for at least 36 hours after consuming any high-sodium food. Do not reduce water intake. Do not take a "water pill" or diuretic unless directed to do so by a physician. In the next chapter, *Nutrients*, you'll read about fluid balance and have a better understanding of how important proper water intake is to maintaining fluid balance and optimal performance.

One problem I have witnessed transformationists create for themselves is attempting to eliminate sodium from the diet. The well-meaning transformationist decides to restrict sodium in an effort to reduce "all that water bloating" they are always experiencing. I've observed individuals consuming less than 500 mg of sodium per day for several days who report feeling lethargic and dizzy when changing from a sitting or lying to standing position. Do not restrict sodium unless your doctor has specifically advised you to do so.

Sodium and potassium are the body's two major electrolytes. The concentrations of these two ions determine the water balance within the body's compartments. Sodium has many functions in the body and is essential for maintaining normal blood pressure, balance of body fluids, and for transmitting nerve signals and muscle contraction.

Electrolyte imbalance is the leading cause of death in eating disorder subjects.

Do not try to eliminate sodium from your Lifestyle! You need it to live!

4. Macronutrient Change–More Carbs Than Usual

As a studious follower of the Lifestyle, you will get very good at meal balancing. It may take a few weeks but with persistence you will develop meals that closely match my recommended 40:40:20 ratio for carbohydrates, proteins and fats. Like anything, after a period of time your body will adapt to these new ratios. I'll explain a bit more *how* in just a moment. If, on a given day, you consume 70 percent of your calories as carbohydrates, then you'll likely be in for a surprise the day or two after: a large spike upward on the scale may result. You may have had the best intentions not to consume such a high percentage of carbohydrates, however, it is quite common for even the best transformationists to find themselves doing so unintentionally on occasion.

Whether it's your splurge meal, a special occasion day, or you've engaged in unaccustomed aerobic exercise of any kind, you may find yourself desiring and consuming excessive "feel good" or "give me energy" carbohydrates (sugars). Many times I find that the types of carbohydrates consumed are well within the Lifestyle recommendations (i.e., fruit, whole grains, yogurt, etc.). So why is it then that transformationists see a spike on the scale after they've consumed the same calories as they have for the past four to five days, but the percentage of carbohydrates on the "culprit" day was much greater than those previous days? It's really pretty simple–it's all about glycogen.

As you will learn in the *Nutrients* chapter where glycogen is explained in detail, muscle and liver are the primary sinks for glycogen storage in the body. As you proceed through your transformation and create a proper relative caloric deficit, it is my sincere belief that your skeletal muscles are never completely saturated, or–perhaps it's better stated–glycogen-optimized. While losing weight you are probably only operating with 80 percent of the intramuscular glycogen stores compared to when you are in Maintenance and, therefore, not losing weight. Typically, this reduced intramuscular glycogen state doesn't negatively affect exercise performance at submaximal levels, but could if glycogen levels fall much lower. When glycogen stores are too low, typically caused by inadequate carbohydrate intake for too long, exercise performance and mental accuity will suffer greatly.

If you can imagine that skeletal muscle has grown adept at operating quite efficiently with less than 100 percent glycogen storage, then I hope you can conceive what may occur when you suddenly consume a higher percentage of your daily calories from carbohydrates; your body creates glycogen from those additional carbohydrates and they are stored in skeletal muscle and the liver. You might still be wondering what all this has to do with a weight gain, but it's quite simple from here. *For every gram of glycogen stored, three grams of water are stored with it*. And there you have it. One day of increased carbohydrate (as a percentage of total calories), compared to previous days or weeks, can significantly impact the scale weight for up to three or four days depending on the individual. This creates stress and angst in the transformationist but it's important to note that well over 95 percent of the increased scale weight resulted from additional stored water attached to glycogen.

After you finish reading the *Energy Balance* chapter, you'll know that it takes 3500 additional calories over and above maintenance to add a pound of fat. It's not uncommon, however, for transformationists to add three to five pounds overnight after living a day where 70 percent of their calories came from carbohydrate, versus prior days or weeks where 40 to 50 percent of their calories were derived from carbohydrates. Most unknowing transformationists panic over the weight gain believing they have blown it. They don't understand what you already know: *It's impossible to add three to five pounds of fat in 24 hours unless you overconsume calories by approximately 10,500 to 17,500 above maintenance!* So, if you know you didn't overconsume calories but you may have simply overconsumed carbohydrates, you can expect a "scale correction" in three to four days once you bring your major macronutrients back in line with Lifestyle suggestions. You also know that you didn't add three to five pounds of fat. More than likely, 95-99 percent of the weight spike is from water with only a very negligible amount of fat stored if total calories were kept in check.

It's my sincere hope that now that you know yet another reason the scale may go up for a few days, you will be less tempted to throw in the towel or beat yourself up believing you've blown it. Sure, you may experience a "fluffy" or "bloated" or "thick-skinned" feeling for a few days, but you haven't blown it. The best advice I can give if you find yourself suffering from the overconsumption of carbohydrates as a percentage of total calories is this: Use those stored carbohydrates (glycogen) to your advantage. Since glycogen is a major energy source during intense aerobic activity (as well as contributing during resistance training), it's important that you crank up the heat for your workouts and get ready to experience a day or two of workout bliss. That's right: Your workouts will absolutely rock! Your aerobic activity may feel effortless compared to days past and your muscles will feel full and more pumped during resistance training sessions. Work hard! Use this carb-bloat to increase your volume or intensity or both during aerobic and resistance training sessions during the day or two you really feel it. By doing so you will see that scale correction in no time. Finally, consume plenty of water during the days that follow a carb-bloat. The last thing you want to do is create a mild or moderate state of dehydration. Affective lipolysis (breaking down stored fat) relies on adequate water intake. Never forget to drink your water!

5. Diseased State

The amount of fluids retained can vary with disease conditions that affect the circulation. Some common ones include hypothyroidism, diabetes, high and low blood pressure, heart and kidney disorders, and diseases of the arteries and veins. Excess retention is much more common in women than men because of the effect of female hormones on the body's metabolism and circulation.

Summary

The scale is a powerful, objective tool that no longer has to be regarded as "the enemy." The most successful masters of weight control use the scale consistently to objectively monitor progress and maintenance. Your weight is best thought of with the two-component model. Many people believe that fat-free mass and muscle are synonymous, however, this is not reality. As you measure not only your progress, but compare your progress to others, it is important you know the many confounding variables that can affect what many report as a muscle gain. Once you know your approximate starting body fat, you can quickly and easily determine your approximate weight when you are at your goal body fat. Shifts in water retention are easily the greatest contributor to short-term weight fluctuations. Knowing the facts about what is calorically necessary to create a loss or gain of true body fat can help you evaluate more appropriately why the scale is reporting a seemingly odd loss or gain.

Take Action and Feel Great!

1. Based on your age and level of resistance-training experience, determine your approximate capability of muscle accumulation each month.

2. Find an advertisement in any magazine depicting massive gains of muscle or monumental losses of fat in 12 or less weeks. Evaluate the ad based on what you now know to determine where intentional or unintentional errors may have occurred.

3. Begin logging your weight each and every day using the graph provided in the Appendix.

4. After determining your approximate body fat as described in Chapter 3, calculate what you will weigh when you reach your goal body fat.

5. Think of positive steps you can take on a daily basis to minimize water-weight fluctuations. Become aware of the variables that affect it and use your weight graph to plot progress over time.

Nutrients –
The Fuel That Feeds the Body

You may never become what you could have been,
because of what you eat.

There is not a computer on the planet as smart or complex as the human body. There is not an automobile or home as precious as the joy your body gives you every day. You simply cannot put a price on being lean, fit, muscular, full of energy and healthy. Ask anyone who has lost their health to disease what they would give to have it back. There is not a material possession they would not give up.

Food is the fuel your body uses. You would not consider putting kerosene in a Ferrari, but you don't hesitate to do the same with your body day in and day out. Why in the world would you ever consider giving the most complex machine ever created the cheapest toxic waste that can still pass a government inspection and be called food? How is your body supposed to run on the garbage you feed it?

When the fuel source is cheap, the body breaks down. It starts sputtering at an early age, it runs daily at half speed, and gives up before the real race is over. You cannot possibly begin to feel the energy you have been missing and the growth that has been lacking until you accept the fact that you must improve the fuel your finely crafted, precision-tuned body needs. We have all heard the cliché, "You are what you eat." But I believe there is more to it than that. You may never become what you could have been, because of what you eat.

Nutrients are the chemical compounds and elements contained in foods that can be used to support growth, maintenance, vital body processes and to provide energy. The six classes of nutrients are:

1. Carbohydrates
2. Fats
3. Proteins
4. Vitamins
5. Minerals
6. Water

The body can make some nutrients for itself, at least in limited quantities, but it cannot make them all, and it makes insufficient quantities of others to meet its needs. Therefore, the body must obtain many nutrients from foods. The nutrients that must be obtained from foods are called *essential* nutrients.

The term "energy" brings to mind the energy you need to feel great throughout the day. But most nutritional textbooks refer to energy and calories synonymously. Only three of the six classes of nutrients directly provide energy (calories): carbohydrates, fats (lipids), and proteins. Water, vitamins and minerals are necessary for an "energetic" body, however, they contain no calories. Without properly feeding your body the right amounts of vitamins and minerals, you will become very sick or even die. Vitamins, minerals and water "facilitate" many bodily processes that keep your body in either an energetic or a life-sucking state. Vitamins facilitate the release of energy from carbohydrates, proteins and fats. Minerals help regulate the release of energy. Water is the medium in which all of the bodys' processes take place.

So, what nutrients are best for an energetic body? When carbohydrates are plentiful, your body will primarily use carbohydrate as an energy source. Lipids are second in line, and protein only becomes a major fuel when the other fuels are unavailable. Understanding where your body derives the majority of its energy from, and how you can eat and drink properly to supply the body with energy, is vitally important. During your 16 or more waking hours each day, you must know how to properly fuel your body for lasting energy.

Mom's Confusion Breeds Confusion

My children are actively involved in sports. During the soccer playoffs, children between the ages of 5 and 15 came to compete against one another one final time before the season end. I overheard a conversation between a 12-year old girl, Carrie, and her teammate. The conversation was about which was the best breakfast before the big game. Like many children, Carrie obtained her nutrition knowledge from her parents. Carrie told her teammate that her mother told her it was important to have a big bacon and egg breakfast before the game–you know, lots of protein–so she'd have plenty of *energy* for the hour-long game. I cringed when I heard this, but these conversations occur everyday in thousands of settings, not just among children,

Carrie's mother was obviously confused about the pecking order of energy supply and how the body converts carbohydrates, lipids and proteins into useable energy. Apparently, Carrie's mother was not aware that the easiest nutrient for the body to convert into useable energy is carbohydrate. With this knowledge, she might have been more apt to prepare a breakfast more like my daughter, Elizabeth's, which consisted of cereal, milk, toast with peanut butter and orange juice. Elizabeth's breakfast was high in carbohydrates, moderate in protein and low in fat. Because I understood nutrients and how they contribute to useable energy for the body, I was better able to help my daughter maintain high stamina not only during the soccer game but also throughout the entire day. Carrie, on the other hand, was being fed misinformation from a trusted source: her mother.

Are you teaching those you love the proper information about nutrition? Keep an open mind as I explain everything you need to know about nutrients, their relationship to calories, and how alcohol affects calories, yet provides zero nutrients. By the time you finish reading this chapter, I want you to be the antithesis of Carrie's mother by understanding the importance of what to feed your body, and how much. These are the factors, which determine the process of not only gaining and losing weight, but also for feeling great everyday.

Carbohydrates (Sugars)

Carbohydrates provide 4 calories per gram

Carbohydrates are the only *nonessential* nutrient class. Unlike lipids (fats) and proteins, there is not one carbohydrate that you must obtain from food sources. In fact, you can live on a zero carbohydrate diet. However, you must consume adequate carbohydrates if you want to have plenty of vigor for exercise and maximum energy throughout your day,

When carbohydrates are plentiful, they are the preferred energy source for most of the body's functions. The human brain depends exclusively on carbohydrates as an energy source. Your muscles rely on the simplest of carbohydrates–glucose–to fuel intense contractions. Athletes eat a high-carb diet to store as much muscle carbohydrate fuel (glycogen) as possible. Dietary recommendations urge people to eat carbohydrate-rich foods for better health.

No matter what it becomes or what it is called on your store shelf, nearly all foods providing significant carbohydrates are derived from plants. Milk is the only animal-derived food that contains significant amounts of carbohydrate. You are most likely to find foods with a high percentage of carbohydrates when the first, second or third ingredient is from sugars (i.e., sugar, sucrose, fructose, dextrose, corn syrup). Food labeling laws require manufacturers to list their ingredients by percentage. This means that the first ingredient on the package shows the ingredient that has the highest percentage, the second ingredient listed has the next highest percentage, and so on. Prepackaged foods high in sugar-laden carbohydrate sources are not forbidden in the Lifestyle, but are less desirable than whole foods naturally rich in carbohydrates. Limiting the packaged foods that contain some sugar as the first, second, or third ingredient is strongly urged. Until you have a good handle on what ingredients are in the foods you are eating, *you must become a tenacious label reader*. The sooner, the better.

Starches

All starchy foods are plant foods. Starchy foods (i.e., breads, cereals, rice, grains, legumes, pasta, potatoes, sweet potatoes) are considered complex carbohydrates because they are composed of long chains of sugars (mostly glucose). It is quite common in the transformation community for well-intentioned dieters to believe that "complex" equals "slow burning." However, foods that are composed of mainly glucose are not necessarily "long-lasting" or slow-burning carbohydrate sources if they have been refined heavily and are lacking in fiber. Starchy foods can be a part of a balanced Lifestyle, however, excessive consumption of starchy carbohydrates can quite easily lead to an undesirable insulin response and increased fat storage. Most starchy foods are very low in fat, but this does not ensure that overconsumption of them will not cause an increase in body fat (adipose). Finally, as you will learn in the *Triggers, Addiction and Self-Regulation* chapter, starches are a common trigger food.

Grains

When consuming grains, I strongly recommend you choose whole-grain breads, cereals and pasta. Forty studies have linked regular consumption of whole grains with a 10 to 60 percent lower risk of certain cancers, especially cancers of the stomach and colon. Several large studies have found greater use of whole grains associated with a lower risk of heart disease, too. Research indicates a 30 percent reduced risk of heart disease for consumers of even 2.5 servings of whole-grain foods daily. Keep in mind: a slice of whole-grain bread is one serving.

At breakfast, choose a whole-grain cereal, or whole-grain toast or bagel. Depending on your portion size, what represents a serving? If you have a sandwich at lunch made with whole-grain bread, you have already consumed two servings of whole grains. For other sources of whole-grain nutrition, choose brown rice, corn or whole-grain tortillas and whole-grain pasta. If you currently use mixes to prepare muffins and quick breads, make them from scratch and substitute whole-grain flour, which will take only a few extra minutes, yet result in lots of extra nutrition.

See Appendix for a listing of quality grains for Lifestylers.

> *A diet centered on white bread, fat-free cookies, pretzels and bagels is not the ticket to good health.*

The Food and Drug Administration (FDA) has made it a little easier to choose foods *"Rich in Whole Grain."* If you see the words "rich in whole grain" on the packaging of breads, cereal or pasta you can safely assume the following about that food:

- It has at least 51 percent whole grains
- It has at least 2.8 grams of fiber in a 50 gram serving
- It's low in total fat, saturated fat and cholesterol

Fruits and Vegetables (Fibrous Carbohydrates)

Not all that long ago I would have rather taken a direct kick to the groin than eat a vegetable. I am serious. A beating would have been welcomed over gnawing on a piece of broccoli. I used to watch in amazement as my lovely wife would purposely choose to add vegetables to a perfectly green lettuce salad. I mean, it wasn't even an accident. She meant to eat those vegetables. Of course, even back then, I sort of believed vegetables were good for you. Don't we all though? Didn't mom always tell us to eat our veggies? When I was a young boy, my mom even took it to a new level. She would say, "You know why rabbits never go blind, don't you? They eat carrots."

I know many of you share my former feelings about vegetables as you sit there reading this now. Before you completely ignore this section, or try to convince yourself that you "just can't stand vegetables," let me first share with you the many benefits of eating fruits and vegetables. Then I will explain how I overcame my old feelings, and today practice what I preach and consume vegetables every day.

I know anyone can acquire a taste for vegetables for two reasons: 1. I did it, and 2. Sometime around the year 1600, the Virginia colonists brewed their first batch of beer. My beer analogy works like this. I never liked the taste of beer–somehow I always knew there was nothing good in it for me–so I have pretty much avoided it all my life. I think I am close to achieving a new protected class of minority for doing so. Over my lifetime, I have come to know hundreds and hundreds of people who regularly consume beer. Some even like the taste of it. However, in listening to them regale their stories of how they got started drinking, a common precept began to emerge from their stories: they invariably disliked the taste of it when they first tried it. For whatever reason, they decided there was some value to be obtained from continuing to drink it. Perhaps there *had* to be something to it because they believed everyone else was doing it. Whatever the reasons, unique as they are, regular beer drinkers knew there was only one way they were ever going to get over gagging it down: they had to acquire a taste for it. So they did–acquire a taste for beer that is–by consuming it over and over again. Eventually, that nasty tasting beer didn't taste so bad. Finally, after the 143rd beer, it actually started to taste good. So I truly have no fear whatsoever that you too can acquire a taste, but this time for a nutritious food that actually adds value to your health and shrinks your waist. And unlike beer, with veggies there is actually a good reason to acquire that taste.

Another reason I am optimistic for you non-veggie eaters is that you may not have ever eaten *fresh* vegetables before. If this is the case, and you grew up on canned, boiled vegetables, then I must stress that you don't have a clue what real vegetables taste like. We could argue a month of Sundays over whether fresh, frozen or canned contain the most nutrients. We could also bury ourselves in the minutia over whether raw, steamed, or boiled vegetables are best for the body, however, when it comes to taste, the order is clear–fresh, then frozen, and then canned. There truly is no comparison between fresh vegetables and frozen vegetables. There is also no comparison between frozen vegetables and canned vegetables. The taste is immeasurably better the closer you get to fresh. If all you have ever eaten is canned vegetables then I can safely say you have never even tried vegetables yet. Today I can eat them cold and raw or steamed – with or without seasoning or dressing. As you now know, this was not always the case.

Baby Carrots–Baby Steps

When I first decided it was time I started practicing what I knew to be true, I introduced myself to vegetables smothered in cheese sauce. I knew the cheese sauce was horribly high in fat, but I decided it would be a good way to introduce vegetables into my meal planning. After a few weeks, I reduced the cheese sauce and after a few more weeks, I completely omitted it. I replaced the cheese sauce with low-fat or fat-free salad dressings or even Dijon mustard. For steamed vegetables, I now use a Lowry's seasoning that gives them a very nice flavor.

Fruits and vegetables are nature's *original fast food*. They are loaded with vitamins, minerals, antioxidants, phytochemicals and fiber. Research has shown that eating more fruits and vegetables can play a positive role in the reduced incidence of cataracts, diverticulosis, high blood pressure, chronic obstructive pulmonary disease, asthma, bronchitis, osteoporosis, cancer, heart disease, stroke and other illnesses.

> *The quarter of the population that eats the fewest fruits and vegetables has approximately double the cancer rate for most types of cancer when compared to the quarter with the highest.*

Eighty percent of American children and adolescents and 68 percent of adults do not eat enough fruits and vegetables.

A nutritional program including more fruits and vegetables can yield:

- Half the risk of developing cancer compare to those who do not consume adequate amounts of fruits and vegetables. In fact, eating a diet rich in fruits and vegetables could prevent more than one-third of the 500,000 cancer deaths each year. A review of over 200 scientific studies has shown that the types of vegetables that most often appear to be protective against cancer are raw vegetables, followed by allium vegetables (onions, garlic, scallions, leeks, chives), carrots, green vegetables, cruciferous vegetables (broccoli, cauliflower, Brussels sprouts, cabbage), and tomatoes. Substances present in vegetables and fruit that help protect against cancer include: dithiolthiones, isthiocyanates, indole-3-carbinol, allium compounds, isoflavones, protease inhibitors, saponins, phytosterols, inositol, vitamin C, D-limonene, lutein, folic acid, beta carotene, lycopene, selenium, vitamin E, flavonoids, and dietary fiber.

- A 20 to 40 percent risk reduction for coronary heart disease.

- A 30 to 40 percent reduced cancer incidence when combined with regular exercise.

- A 25 percent risk reduction of stroke.

- Better control of high blood pressure and reduced risk for blood clotting.

- A five-fold reduction in relative risk for cataracts among consumers of more than 1.5 daily servings of fruits, vegetables, or both fruits and vegetables.

- The best defense against the development of diverticulosis by providing the best sources of fiber.

- Enhanced ventilatory function (less asthma and bronchitis), thereby reducing the risk of chronic obstructive pulmonary disease.

- A contribution to the maintenance of bone mineral density via the fruit and vegetables' alkaline-producing dietary components, specifically potassium, and magnesium.

Produce and Phytochemicals

Many plant families also contain phytochemicals, natural plant substances that work with nutrients and dietary fiber to protect against disease. Some of the more common phytochemicals found in fruits and vegetables include flavonoids, quercetin, carotentoids, allium, and others. Phytochemicals can be found in the following fruits and vegetables:

Citrus Fruits

Phytochemicals in oranges, tangerines, and grapefruits may help the body resist cancer-causing chemicals (carcinogens), prevent harmful blood clotting, and avoid blindness.

Melons, Berries

Melons and berries of all varieties may assist the immune system and help lower blood cholesterol. This family includes kiwi fruit, cucumbers, squash, and pumpkins.

Grapes

Grapes (especially red grapes) may help resist carcinogens, protect DNA in cells, and prevent harmful blood clots that trigger heart attacks and strokes.

Cruciferous (Cabbage Family) Vegetables

Broccoli, cauliflower, Brussels sprouts, kale, bok choy, collards, turnips, mustard greens, kohlrabi, and watercress may lower the risk of hormone-related cancers, help protect DNA, and boost the body's ability to fight off cancer.

Deep Yellow and Orange Fruits and Vegetables

Phytochemicals in apricots, persimmons, cantaloupe, sweet potatoes, pumpkins, and carrots may help protect against cancer, fatty plaque in the arteries, blood clots, and loss of eyesight.

Leafy Greens

Spinach, kale, and dark, leafy greens may have similar benefits.

Tomatoes and Eggplant

Tomatoes and eggplant may prevent carcinogens from forming, shield cells from carcinogens, or neutralize cancer-causing free radicals. Tomato products may reduce prostate cancer and heart attack risk.

Onions, Garlic, Leeks, and Chives

This class of vegetables may help the body produce less cholesterol, block cancer-causing chemicals, control cancer cells, and eliminate other toxic chemicals.

Other Fruits and Vegetables

Vegetables such as artichokes and stone fruits, (e.g., peaches, plums, nectarines, and cherries), as well as pears, apples, mangoes, bananas, and avocados, provide fiber, folate, potassium, and other nutrients that reduce the risk of heart disease and cancer. The monounsaturated fat in avocados, like that in olive oil and tree nuts, does not appear to raise disease risk and may be protective.

Fresh, Frozen, Canned, Dried, Juiced

Frozen fruits and vegetables contain nutrients similar to freshly harvested produce. Other processed fruits and vegetables retain most of their nutrient, fiber, and phytochemical value. Steaming and microwaving helps to maintain the vitamin C content and folate content of vegetables.
(Source: California Department of Health Services, September 1998)

Five A Day? How About Even One!

Currently there is a national campaign called "5 A Day" with the purpose of making you not only more aware of the benefits of eating more fruits and vegetables, but also to get you to consume at least five servings per day. In my practical experience working with real clients, I have found that while it may be ideal to consume five servings of fruits and vegetables every day for health and weight control, most who begin the Lifestyle are consuming virtually no fruits and vegetables. I do not believe in asking for something that is destined to create a feeling of failure so I simply recommend this for a start:

- Consume at least one serving of whole fruit each day
- Consume at least one serving of whole vegetable each day

It is optimal, however, to consume several servings of fresh vegetables each day. Work into it slowly if you must, but do work into it. When you have a choice to make between having a starchy carbohydrate and a fibrous (i.e., vegetable) carbohydrate, the better choice nine times out of ten will be the fibrous carbohydrate. Fibrous carbohydrates, when fresh and unprocessed, are almost impossible to overeat, and are rich in nutrients and fiber. You simply cannot go wrong eating fresh vegetables.

What is a Serving?
A fruit and vegetable serving is smaller than you think. One serving can be:

- 1 medium-size piece of fruit
- 3/4 cup (6 oz.) of 100 percent fruit or vegetable juice
- 1/2 cup cooked or canned vegetables or fruit
- 1 cup of raw leafy vegetables
- 1/2 cup cooked dry peas or beans
- 1/4 cup dried fruit

Taking Proper Care with Fruits & Veggies
It will take no longer than 30 minutes to wash and cut a week's worth of vegetables and fruit.

- Scrub the skins of cantaloupes and other melons with water and a brush before cutting to prevent the transfer of pathogens from the rind to the flesh.
- Use fast-running water to wash berries, lettuce (pre-washed or not), and other non-scrubbable fruits. Friction created by the running water helps remove bacteria and is better than soaking.
- Wash fruit even if you plan to peel it. If there are microbes on the peel, they can contaminate the rest of the fruit when you peel it.
- Eat only cooked sprouts (including home-grown).
- Ask restaurants not to add raw sprouts to your sandwich or salad.
(Source: Nutrition Action Health Letter, October 1999)

Fiber–The No–Calorie Carbohydrate

Fiber is a carbohydrate. Most fibers are polysaccharides, just as starch is. Bonds hold the sugar units in fiber together that human digestive enzymes cannot break. Many of these have names like cellulose, hemicellulose, pectins, gums, and mucilages, as well as lignans. Fiber is a constituent of plant cell walls and is commonly classified as either soluble or insoluble.

Soluble Fibers	Insoluble Fibers
oatmeal, oatbran, nuts and seeds	whole grains • whole wheat breads • barley
legumes • dried peas • beans • lentils	• couscous • brown rice • bulgar
	whole-grain breakfast cereals, wheat bran, seeds,
apples, pears, strawberries, blueberries	carrots, cucumbers, zucchini, celery, tomatoes
Benefits: satiate appetite, decrease calorie and fat utilization, stabilize blood sugar.	**Benefits:** give the stool bulk by absorbing water and therefore encourage frequency of bowel movements. Detoxify, enhance excretion and decrease absorption of bowel toxins.

Stool Check—Adequate water is so important for regular bowel movements to hydrate the fiber in the colon and give bulk to the stools. Stools should float. If they do not, either you are usually not eating enough fiber or you are dehydrated.

Cellulose—an indigestible fiber found in the skins of fruit, vegetables and outer husks of cereal grains.

Adults should consume at least 20 to 35 grams of dietary fiber per day for the following reasons:

- It takes longer to eat foods that are higher in fiber thereby slowing digestion and absorption.

- High-fiber foods require chewing, which not only satisfies the need to chew, but tell the brain to balance the hormone system in a way that stabilizes blood sugar.

- High-fiber food leaves the stomach slower, leaving you full longer and again slowing absorption.

- Excess fat absorption is decreased.

Foods with fiber have the added advantage of decreased usable calories. Therefore, for the same amount of calories, you can eat much more of the same food with fiber than if the fiber has been processed away.

- A slice of white bread has 16 grams of carbohydrate, 0 fiber, and provides 64 calories.

- Whole grain rye bread has 16 grams of carbohydrate, 5 of which are unusable, calorie-free fiber. Therefore, it has only 11 usable carbohydrates, which provide 44 calories (11g x 4).

Fiber for Prevention of Heart Disease and Cancer

Supplementing with fiber will do you little good while eating white bread and sugar and low vegetable consumption. This "short cut" is not how you maximize the Lifestyle. Many complex carbohydrate foods are fiber-rich, but also contain lots of quickly absorbing carbohydrate. For example, bananas contain 3 grams of fiber but also 27 grams of rapidly absorbing carbohydrates. This is not a warning to avoid bananas, simply my first recommendation to you that you balance each meal with protein and some fats. I'll discuss the importance of doing so just a little later.

The medical community recognizes inadequate fiber intake as a link to:

- Gastrointestinal disturbances
- Colon cancer
- Constipation
- Increased risk of heart disease

Choosing foods high in fiber is a great guideline to ensure you are choosing foods that have not been processed beyond recognition. When you become a label reader, you will find that *the healthiest choices of carbohydrates always provide significant fiber* as well. The more heavily processed foods are, the lower the fiber content generally is.

> *If 10 percent of the carbohydrate grams listed on a package, high-carb food is not dietary fiber, you most likely have a highly processed, undesirable carbohydrate and should make a better choice.*

A food that provides 38 grams of carbohydrates is probably a good carbohydrate choice if it contains at least 3.8 grams of dietary fiber (10 percent of the total carbohydrate grams as fiber). Is a carbohydrate-rich food "taboo" or "bad" if it does not contain 10 percent of the total carbohydrates as fiber? I would not put a blanket statement out that would indicate that any one food is bad, however, I am telling you to strive to include more fiber-rich foods in your meal planning. By doing so you'll be insured of choosing more wholesome and nutritious, nutrient-dense foods that will keep you full longer, are great for the digestive tract, and may provide you with the many other health benefits as well.

How Many Carbohydrates?

I suggest a daily intake of not less than 30 percent and not greater than 60 percent of your total caloric intake from carbohydrates. *Ideally, I'd like to see you keep your daily intake of carbohydrates between 40 and 45 percent of the total calories you consume.* Remember, carbohydrates provide 4 calories per gram. To determine what percentage of your Lifestyle is derived from carbohydrates, you simply multiply the total grams of carbohydrates by 4 and then divide that number by the total calories you consumed for the day. Here are two examples:

Example 1: 1200 Calorie Per Day Lifestyle
150 grams of carbohydrates per day
150 x 4 = 600 calories from carbohydrates
600/1200 = 0.5
0.5 x 100 = 50 percent of that day's calories came from carbohydrates

Example 2: 1800 Calorie Per Day Lifestyle
175 grams of carbohydrates per day
175 x 4 = 700 calories from carbohydrates
700/1800 = 0.39
0.39 x 100 = 39 percent of that day's calories came from carbohydrates

I will further add the following minimum carbohydrate guidelines for men and women:

Men: Body weight in pounds x 0.75 = minimum grams of carbohydrates per day
Example for 180 lb man: 180 x 0.75 = 135 g per day minimum

Women: Body weight in pounds x 0.50 = minimum grams of carbohydrates per day
Example for 150 lb woman: 150 x 0.75 = 75 g per day minimum

Glycogen–Stored Energy for Muscle

Glycogen is a polysaccharide (many sugars linked together) composed of glucose. It is made and stored primarily in skeletal muscle and the liver. Glycogen is *not* a significant food source of carbohydrate and is not counted as one of the complex carbohydrates in foods.

Stored glycogen in the body only amounts to about 2000 calories. Exercisers who fail to consume adequate carbohydrates will suffer a fall of glycogen in the liver and skeletal muscle, leaving their workouts wanting, and their overall energy low. Insufficient consumption of carbohydrates will deplete glycogen and prevent you from pushing with the intensity necessary to see maximum body reshaping and progress in your workouts.

Carbohydrate Cravings Explained?

The importance of adequate, daily carbohydrate consumption is not limited to the fact that carbohydrates provide quick and sustained energy. Not only will incorporating intelligent meal planning into your Lifestyle ensure plenty of carbohydrate energy for daily activity and exercise, but your body has a built in "carbostat" that tells you to crave carbohydrates when glycogen is low. If you choose not to follow the Lifestyle or poorly plan your days and regularly eat a very low carbohydrate diet, you are likely to crave carbohydrates and binge at some point. This is not conjecture or simple hyperbole to bolster the Lifestyle. Rather, it is based on scientific evidence and an understanding of endocrinology and energy stores within the body.

Carbohydrate is the body's preferred fuel, however, recall that the body has a very limited store of carbohydrate (about 2000 calories) when compared to lipid (about 150,000 calories) or even protein (about 24,000 calories). Not surprisingly, we seek foods that contain plentiful carbohydrates. We constantly need to replenish depleted glycogen stores and provide adequate fuel for the brain and other organs. Here is where you really get your money's worth ...

Changes in carbohydrate balance from day to day reciprocally affect carbohydrate intake on the subsequent day.

In animals, including humans, if carbohydrate balance is positive (i.e., if on a given day more carbohydrate is eaten than burned for fuel), less carbohydrate will be desired and eaten the next day. Conversely, when carbohydrate balance is negative on a given day, the animal will eat more carbohydrate the next day. We have all experienced more or less desire for carbohydrates on various days. You now know that a good part of the reason may be directly linked to what you ate the day before. This relationship of carbohydrate balancing does not hold true for fats or proteins.

Glycemic Index

The glycemic index (GI) is a measure of the magnitude of how high blood glucose rises with a 50 gram serving of "available" carbohydrate from some food over a 2-hour period. So, the GI does not equate to a measure of blood glucose. White bread or glucose is typically used as the standard by which other food sources are compared. White bread and glucose have a GI of 100. A food with a GI of 70 will cause a rise of blood glucose equal to 70 percent of what 50 grams of carbohydrate from white bread or glucose will. Foods dominated by simple carbohydrates (i.e., sugar, dextrose, corn syrup) are usually presumed to create a more rapid rise in blood sugar than complex carbohydrates (i.e., whole grains, vegetables, legumes).

One might wrongly assume that complex carbohydrates, such as white potatoes and rice, are more favorable than simple carbohydrates that can be found in whole fruit (not fruit juice). In this example, the GI of white potatoes and rice is much higher than the GI of many whole fruits, even though the potatoes and rice are a complex carbohydrate source and whole fruits are primarily a simple sugar (fructose) source. This is because the simple sugar in fruits is primarily fructose and fructose does not convert readily to glucose, the sugar found in blood. Another example of the fallacy of solely relying on the GI to determine your food selection is revealed in the comparison of potato chips and carrots. Potato chips have a GI of between 50 and 60 and carrots have a GI over 90. Does this mean potato chips are a better choice over carrots?

The confusion over the GI has even given carrots a bad rap. Carrots have a high GI, however, don't forget how the GI is determined. The GI is determined after measuring the rise in blood glucose after consuming a portion of the food that yields 50 grams of carbohydrate. One large carrot has 7 grams of carbohydrates but also provides 2 grams of fiber. Remember, fiber is a carbohydrate, however, its effects on energy are negligible. The GI for carrots was determined by giving a portion equal to 10 large carrots (50 usable grams of carbohydrate)! This is simply an unrealistic serving. To become paranoid about eating carrots is ridiculous, unless of course you routinely eat 10 large carrots at one sitting.

> ### *You will usually be safe eating whole, unprocessed food.*

Here are some characteristics of foods that affect the glycemic index:

- Compactness: The more crumbly a food is, the faster it is absorbed. Pasta is absorbed slower than bread.
- Resistance to digestive enzymes: Grains with their outer husk still intact absorb slower than those without, e.g., whole-grain rye bread vs. pumpernickel, steel cut oats vs. instant oats.
- The form of carbohydrate: Fructose (fruit sugar) takes a longer time to convert to glucose.
- The amount of fiber present in the food.
- The amount of fat present in the food: Due to its high fat content, ice cream, although high in simple sugars, has a relatively low glycemic index.
- How much it is cooked: Some foods have to be cooked to make them more digestible. Try not to overcook your foods. It not only destroys many nutrients but also increases the glycemic index.

Finally, unless you are eating a carbohydrate-rich food without protein or fat, there is little value in worrying yourself sick over the GI of that food. The reason for this settling revelation is the fact that when you combine a carbohydrate-rich food with a protein-rich food and include a small amount of healthy fat (i.e., a mixed meal), you make the GI of any one of those foods almost meaningless. A high-GI food will not cause the rise in blood sugar you would expect from eating it alone if you combine that high-GI food with some protein and a small amount of healthy fat. For this reason, you should eat as many "mixed meals" as possible, vs. simply eating only a carbohydrate-rich food.

Insulin Management

The importance of insulin management warrants explanation so you will see the full value of choosing balanced, mixed meals and fiber-rich carbohydrates. By discussing the noninsulin-dependent diabetic, also called Adult Onset Diabetes, I hope you will take home the value and importance of managing your meal planning and resulting insulin response.

The classic case of insulin dysfunction is characterized by the person suffering from noninsulin-dependent diabetes mellitus (NIDDM). NIDDM affects about 5 percent of the population or approximately 13,500,000 people nationwide. NIDDM is usually preceded by obesity. An organ called the pancreas secretes insulin in response to elevating blood sugar. A person with NIDDM may experience normal insulin secretion and is not to be confused with the type I diabetic who is insulin dependent. In NIDDM, circulating levels of insulin may even be elevated, thus the problem for an NIDDM sufferer is not necessarily a shortage of insulin, but insulin *resistance* resulting from decreased sensitivity, poor responsiveness, or both. When insulin is not doing its job properly, chronic hyperglycemia (high blood sugar) is the result. Untreated NIDDM sufferers experience a vicious cycle of chronically elevated blood sugar levels and elevated, but improperly functioning, insulin. As you will soon see, this condition blocks fat loss and explains why untreated NIDDM sufferers may remain fat, even when their caloric intake is relatively low.

Insulin's primary role is to lower blood sugar to healthy physiological levels. Insulin has many physiological functions, including stimulating the production of glycogen, fatty acids, and proteins. Elevated insulin levels block the breakdown of glycogen (stored carbohydrates) and adipose (stored fat). For the purposes of this section, I only want you to recognize the following: *Chronically elevated insulin or repeated insulin spikes create an environment, that promotes fat storage and can completely block fat loss.* Now I should have your attention. The process works like this: Blood sugar goes up? Insulin is released to bring it back down. While insulin is elevated, fat loss is blocked. Chronic hyperglycemia can also lead to a number of complications including cataracts, sclerotic lesions in blood vessel walls, and general poor health associated with obesity. The aim of all regimens for the management of diabetes is control of blood glucose levels. A benefit of following the Lifestyle is control of blood glucose, and thus, insulin.

Stable Blood Sugar Keeps You Feeling Well

Food gives you the energy to live by providing you with the nutrients necessary to maintain stable blood sugar.

> *Dietary carbohydrates are digested to glucose,*
> *which in turn becomes blood sugar.*

In order for your body to use foods, you need to break them down, absorb the usable parts through the intestines, and disregard what is toxic and unusable through the stools. This is accomplished through the process of digestion. Chewing foods thoroughly and exposing them to mouth saliva, stomach acid, and intestinal enzymes break foods down into smaller particles so they may be absorbed and used by the body. (We do not have bread and meat floating through our arteries).

> *Glucose (or blood sugar) is an important fuel for muscle and*
> *the primary fuel that the brain relies on for energy.*

When glucose levels are stable and balanced in the bloodstream, the body is being nourished with fuel and your brain and organs are happy. You feel energetic, are not overly hungry, and can stay focused. If blood sugar levels become too low, your brain and muscles run out of glucose and therefore run out of energy. You start to feel tired, hungry, and lose concentration. Other frequent symptoms include:

• Carbohydrate cravings	• Headache	• Irritability
• Anxiety	• Depression	• Clumsiness and palpitations

When the brain, which relies solely on glucose for energy, senses low glucose levels, it sends you signals (hunger, cravings) to find food that will rapidly provide the body with glucose. The foods you will want are those that provide a lot of glucose to the body rapidly. It is no wonder you desire or crave starchy or sweet carbohydrate-loaded foods such as alcohol, sugar, chocolate, cake, ice cream, candy, juice, breads and pastas because these foods are absorbed and elevate blood sugar so quickly. Juice, a sweet sugary carbohydrate, is the first treatment for diabetics when they have a "low blood sugar" reaction.

Because it is necessary for the body to keep blood sugar stable, when blood sugar goes up quickly, the body responds by bringing it down quickly. When blood sugar falls rapidly, the body may overcompensate and once again leave you with low blood sugar. This causes you once again to crave sugary or starchy carbohydrates to elevate the blood sugar. So the pattern continues.

Initially, eating sugary or starchy carbohydrates may make you feel better, but they actually cause and worsen unstable blood sugars. The more you consume these foods, the more susceptible you become to these rapid and large fluctuations in blood sugar. Not only will you experience decreased energy, constant cravings and abnormal hunger, but you are also susceptible to more severe physical medical problems such as heart disease, cancer, diabetes and obesity.

Most of you are troubled only by minor fluctuations in blood sugar. These may still be severe enough to provide unstable fuel to the muscles and brain and cause you to suffer from fatigue, abnormal hunger, cravings and many other symptoms. None of them is severe enough to cause acute distress.

A less common problem, but one suffered by many, is the condition of reactive hypoglycemia. This is a worsening of unstable blood sugars. It is not a disease of dangerously low blood sugar, but a condition caused by excessive fluctuation in blood sugar causing fatigue, hunger and cravings but also severe or acute, physical and mental symptoms. These symptoms are not necessarily caused by the rapid drop in blood sugar, but by the body's attempt to elevate it. To elevate the blood sugar, body releases adrenaline, the "fight or flight" hormone. Adrenaline symptoms that occur with reactive hypoglycemia resemble the feelings you get when you are frightened. These feelings can be:

• Confusion	• Light headedness	• Rapid pulse	• Palpitations	• Anxiety
• Cold hands	• Queasy stomach	• Headaches		

If you frequently experience any of these symptoms when you miss a meal, or after eating too many starchy or sugary carbohydrates, the cause of your problem is likely reactive hypoglycemia and unstable blood sugar.

Do not confuse fluctuations of blood sugar with the medical illness of hypoglycemia (very low blood sugars). Hypoglycemia is a condition of rapidly reduced or chronically very low blood sugar, which can cause blackouts, seizures and severe incapacitation. This disease is caused by dysfunction in the hormones from the pancreas or adrenal glands, which play an important role in regulation of blood sugar. Tumors or medication are common causes of true hypoglycemia.

Because most programs do not focus on maintaining stable blood sugars even if the foods eaten are nutritionally rich, eventually you will lose control and fall victim to the blood sugar roller coaster. If you have not stabilized blood sugars, you will not eliminate excessive hunger and cravings, and are therefore destined to fail.

> *A primary reason you have failed on other diets and still today have decreased energy, abnormal hunger and cravings is because you eat the wrong foods, in the wrong combinations, at the wrong times.*

Even if your meals are full of nutrients and low in fat, if they do not stabilize blood sugar, they can be unhealthy. The meals below are nutritionally very healthy. They are full of vitamins, minerals, fiber and protective phytochemicals (plant chemicals) and very low in fat. Imbalanced, yet "healthy" meals, may lead to unstable blood sugars and trigger increased hunger, carbohydrate cravings, and decreased energy. For some, they may even lead to serious medical problems such as weight gain, high blood pressure and increased cholesterol.

Breakfast: Buckwheat pancakes with apple butter, a banana and a glass of orange juice.

Morning snack: Real fruit flavored yogurt.

Lunch: Carrot salad with raisins and non-fat mayonnaise, one slice of whole wheat bread and a pineapple fruit smoothie.

Afternoon snack: Rice cakes and fruit jam.

Dinner: A plate of pasta with homemade tomato sauce, small potato, a fresh squeezed glass of carrot juice, a non-fat oat bran muffin and a mango for dessert.

Stable blood sugar is achieved by eating carbohydrates that are digested and absorbed slowly, or combining quick-absorbing carbohydrates with moderate amounts of protein and fat thereby causing a slower rise in blood sugar. Meals that combine carbohydrate, protein and fat are also more likely to satiate the appetite. You are likely to feel more satisfied and fuller, for a longer period than by consuming a meal overly rich in carbohydrates.

The low-fat, nutritious meals above provide carbohydrate that causes a rapid rise in blood sugar. For many people, these meals will cause unstable blood sugar leading to hunger, cravings and fatigue.

> *Choosing foods that do not stabilize blood sugar is like playing "Russian roulette" with your health.*

In the past, you may have made general dietary choices. These choices may have been low in fat and rich in vegetables and fiber. Individual meals were most likely chosen based on availability, scheduling, preferences and mood. At times, foods were eaten because they tasted good when you were hungry; sometimes foods were eaten too frequently, and at other times not frequently enough.

Until now, you have only been taught to balance meals based on nutritional content providing "the four food groups." You were not taught to choose meals of protein, carbohydrate and fat in order to stabilize blood sugar. When your meals are primarily unbalanced and consist mostly of processed, sugary carbohydrate-rich foods, you may feel well after some meals and not so well after others.

> *Control the food you eat and you will control your blood sugar.*

When you learn at every meal to choose the proper amount of protein, carbohydrate and fat that meets your individual requirements, you will stabilize blood sugar and consistently feel well after eating. You will see food not only as a pleasure and something necessary to take away hunger, but also as a powerful tool necessary to achieve optimal well-being.

When you eat a meal, you will not just choose the food you want to eat, but you will also choose how much protein, carbohydrate or fat you need. Initially this may seem cumbersome, however, with a few simple rules and some practice you will develop your own personal food guidelines that will make this plan easy and desirable to follow. You will enjoy knowing how much food you need to eat to feel satiated and not hungry for two to three hours at a time.

Once you experience the power of eating this way, you will never look at food in the same way again. Even if you do not follow the plan at every meal, at least you will now have the knowledge to make properly informed decisions about what and how much you should eat. In addition, you will understand the consequences of how you felt afterwards.

Food that stabilizes blood sugar provides optimal fuel for the body.

To understand the concept of how food stabilizes blood sugars ... view food as fuel for the body. Compare the fuel that propels your body on its daily journey to aviation fuel propelling a single engine plane on a day trip.

When a pilot is planning his fuel requirements for a journey, he must know three things.

1. Is the fuel contaminated?
2. Is the grade of fuel necessary for the type of engine in the plane?
3. How long he can fly before he needs to refuel, and where he may do so?

The pilot will not take off on his journey if his fuel is contaminated, the proper fuel is not available or he will not be able to refuel before he runs out of gas.

So it goes with our body. You will not function well if you consistently:

1. Eat contaminated foods (those that are refined, processed, or nutritionally inferior).
2. Eat low octane foods (those that are high in quickly-absorbing carbohydrates and without protein and fat).
3. Do not refuel (missed meals or go too long without eating).

Therefore, in order to meet your goals for the program, you should strive to:

• Eat nutritionally superior food (foods as close to their natural state as possible).
   "The whiter the bread the sooner you're dead."

• Attempt to achieve the proper balance of protein, carbohydrate and fat at every meal in order to satiate your appetite for 2 to 4 hours, eliminate your carbohydrate cravings, and provide you with maximal energy.

• Learn how to read your fuel gauge by knowing your signs of low fuel. Not everybody gets the sensation of hunger. Other symptoms of "low fuel" include fatigue, loss of concentration, headaches, anxiety and irritability. Know these indicators and *avoid them* by eating before they occur!

Plan your day and week so that you either have the appropriate food or know where you can get it. If you are someone who takes off for the day with no concern about when or where you will eat, you are destined to crash. The pilot will never take off without knowledge of where along his route he can refuel, nor will he wait until he is out of gas to refuel. He will land one hour before.

Eating frequently is crucial for stabilizing blood sugars in people who experience hunger often, as well as in those who do not.

For those who are hungry often, frequent, small feedings will stabilize the up and down swings of blood sugar they get through the day. For those of you who can go all day without eating, it will stop the slow decline in blood sugar that causes you to crave foods and overeat later in the day.

Balanced Blood Sugar Simplified

Your first reaction might be to think of all the ways you can eliminate carbohydrates so you can reduce insulin to nothing and unlock the fat-loss process. You have learned, however, how important carbohydrates are as a fuel source, so this would be a mistake. Besides, insulin is always present in the blood of the non-diseased person and thus, is never completely absent. Instead of trying to improperly eliminate any insulin response by eating a very low carbohydrate diet, I recommend you manage insulin by choosing to follow the Lifestyle and by:

- Consuming balanced meals. By including protein and some fat with each carbohydrate-rich food, you will slow gastric (stomach) emptying. Not only will your blood sugar not go up as fast, but you also will not experience a rapid rise in insulin to battle it. You will avoid the crash that follows the rapid rise in blood glucose and insulin as well.

- Eating 4-6 times per day. By doing so you will maintain a more stable blood sugar, reduce cravings and wild swings in insulin.

- Choosing fiber-rich carbohydrates. Fiber can slow gastric emptying. Foods that are rich in fiber are typically the best carbohydrate sources you can choose. Fiber-rich carbohydrates are less likely to create a spike in blood sugar or insulin and will provide you with sustained energy instead of only quick energy.

Striving for balanced insulin management and reducing repetitive insulin spikes are important for weight control and overall good health. If you choose to create an unfavorable insulin environment by being a *carboholic*–not balancing your carbohydrate-rich foods with protein and fat–and choosing to eat once per day, you will suffer the physiological consequences and make your fat-loss process more difficult.

The most desirable carbohydrates to choose when following the Lifestyle are:

• Fresh vegetables • Fresh fruits • Legumes • Whole grains

See Appendix for a listing of carbohydrate foods for Lifestylers.

Lipids (Fats)

Fats provide 9 calories per gram

Fats are a primary energy source during low-intensity activity like sitting, sleeping and driving. Fats also become a more dominant energy source when carbohydrate foods are less available during prolonged, low- to moderate-intensity exercise (e.g., jogging or biking longer than an hour). Stored fats within the body are waiting to be used for energy, but unless you consume fewer calories in a day than you need to survive and thrive, your fat stores will not reduce and can easily increase almost limitlessly.

You probably know that too much fat in the diet imposes health risks, but you may be surprised to learn that too little does also. More than likely you will eat too much fat than too little. The average American diet yields approximately 40 percent of the total calories from fat.

Fat is a member of the class of compounds called lipids. In my discussion of carbohydrates, I stated the storage form of carbohydrates in the body is glycogen. I also said that glycogen stores are limited compared to lipids and proteins. In contrast, the body's capacity to store fat (triglycerides) for energy is virtually unlimited due to the fat-storing cells of adipose (your stored body fat).

How Much Fat Can We Store?

The ability of the body to store fat in adipocytes (fat cells) is tremendous. While carbohydrate and protein reserves are limited, it appears there is no limit to the amount of fat that can potentially be stored! The average 154-pound man has 135,000 calories available to be used as energy from stored fat. That is equivalent to 15,000 grams of fat!

As an adult, your adipocyte number is relatively fixed. You have all the adipocytes you are going to have as long as you do not become too obese. Adipocytes swell or shrink depending on your level of leanness. However, adipocytes can increase in number, even as an adult. If your total body fat exceeds 30 kg (66 pounds), adipocytes can increase in number. Once adipocytes are created, they are believed to be never lost. When a bodybuilder is standing on stage at 5 percent body fat, he's got the same number of adipocytes as he had when he was 12 percent body fat just ten weeks earlier–they're just smaller.

Did You Know That You Can Hear Fat Being Stored?

You can. It sounds like this. "Aaah boy, I shouldn't have had that last piece of ..." OR "Oh man, I don't think I could eat another bite." OR "I did it! I finished the 40-ounce T-bone, now I get my meal for FREE!" Now you know what storing enormous amounts of fat sounds like.

Although we Americans typically consume to much dietary fat, it is a vital energy source for the body. In addition to being a vital energy source, fat within the body plays other important roles.

Fat:
- Insulates the body against temperature extremes.
- Protects the body's vital organs from shock.
- Forms the major material of cell membranes.
- Is an essential nutrient.

Fat is classified according to the number of hydrogen atoms present in its specific carbon chain. The Lifestyle is not a medical textbook on nutrition, but it is important to understand the three classes of fats you are going to see in the Nutrition Facts of the food products you purchase.

Saturated fats are saturated with hydrogen. Because they contain the maximum amount of hydrogen possible, they are very heat-resistant, and have no flexibility at cold temperatures. Saturated fats such as coconut and lard are found in warm tropical climates and in warm-blooded animals.

Monounsaturated fats are missing *one* pair of hydrogen atoms. They are still heat-resistant, while retaining some flexibility at cooler temperatures. Monounsaturated fats such as olive or canola oil are found in warm climates such as the Mediterranean.

Polyunsaturated fats are missing *two or more* pairs of hydrogen atoms. They are very flexible in colder temperatures, but they are very heat-sensitive. Polyunsaturated fats such as fish oil are found in cold, northern and polar regions.

Monounsaturated Fat

Monounsaturated fats are recommended for most people as the primary fat source. They provide many of the benefits of fat with few of its potential problems.

Monounsaturated fats:

- Satiate your appetite by promoting the release of stomach hormones that tell the brain you are full.

- Increase your energy, decrease your hunger and reduce food cravings through control of blood sugar levels.

- Improve the taste of vegetables, thereby increasing their palatability.

- Have little effect on metabolism.

- Have little effect on hormone production.

- Are resistant to oxidative damage (less harmful free radicals) due to missing only one pair of hydrogen atoms.

- Improve the favorable, protective HDL cholesterol.

The most common sources of monounsaturated fat are:

- Olive oil
- Macadamia nuts
- Almonds
- High-oleic canola oil
- Peanuts
- Avocado

Saturated Fats

Saturated fats as found naturally and when eaten in moderation are not damaging to your health.

Saturated fats have taken a bum rap as the villain in the war against heart disease.

1. The current understanding is that oxidized fats and cholesterol are the major cause of heart disease. It does not make sense that saturated fats–a chemically stable, non-oxidized fat, which man has eaten for thousands of years and the body produces as a necessary component of life–are the cause of heart disease.

2. While it is true that eating excessive amounts of some saturated fats has been linked to increases in cholesterol, it is not clear that this increase necessarily results in heart disease.

3. Studies have shown that countries or communities that consume most of their fat as coconut or palm oil (two saturated fats) have no increase in heart disease. In fact, many older studies show adding these fats to the diet actually decrease cholesterol levels.

4. Many societies consume more saturated fat than the American populations yet have less heart disease.

5. Saturated fats are storage fats and, historically, the fat consumed by man was primarily saturated, animal fats and essential fatty acids. Man later adapted to monounsaturated fats, primarily olive oil. Biochemically, we are equipped to digest a variety of saturated, animal fats and olive oils.

Eskimos and the Masai tribe of Africa eat upwards of 50 percent of their diet as saturated fat, yet heart disease is a rarity. Until the early 1900s, modern man consumed large amounts of saturated fats in animal, butter and dairy, yet heart disease was practically nonexistant.

French Paradox

The French consume the same amount of calories as Americans, four times the amount of butter, and twice the amount of cheese. Their animal fat content is twice ours, and their vegetable fat content is two-thirds. Their cholesterol levels are 230 mg/dl as compared to our 193 mg/dl, yet we have two times the rate of heart disease.

> *Blaming saturated fats as the cause of heart disease is similar to blaming insufficient calcium on the cause of osteoporosis. You cannot take one factor out of the larger picture. Heart disease is a complex disease caused by many factors.*

Because the American population is blinded by the belief that saturated fat is evil, we call this the French paradox. Upon closer inspection, the reasons for the French reduction in heart disease become apparent. The French eat more fresh foods and less processed chemical, fat-laden, frozen foods. They also consume 95 percent less sugar, one-half the fruit, as well as more fresh vegetables and whole grains. They also consume red wine (rich in antioxidant phytochemicals), have increased community and social connections, and lead an active lifestyle.

The French are doing many things right. They are living a life and eating a diet more like our ancestors. They are avoiding the processed sugars and fat, which exist at the core of modern degenerative disease.

Are Saturated Fats All Good?

Saturated fats can be harmful when eaten in large amounts, especially when eaten with large amounts of processed carbohydrates. Excess amounts of saturated fatty acids can block the transformation of essential fatty acids (to be discussed shortly) into favorable cellular hormones.

Foods high in saturated fats include:

• Butter   • Beef   • Animal lard or tallow   • Coconut oil   • Palm kernel oil

Hydrogenation Produces Unnatural Fats (Trans Fatty Acids)

The greatest danger to our health comes not from naturally-produced saturated fats that provide fat-soluble vitamins and antioxidants, but from processed polyunsaturated fatty acids (PUFA).

To produce a longer shelf life for PUFAs in processed foods, the food industry in the twentieth century developed hydrogenation, a process of altering fats. Hydrogenation adds hydrogen to a double bond between carbons. By reducing the double bonds, the PUFA becomes more resistant to rancidity (oxidation) and is more solid at higher temperatures.

Unfortunately, like most man-altered natural processes, hydrogenation does not come without a price. While hydrogenated oils have certain advantages in cooking and baking, it creates free radicals and an unnatural form of fat for our bodies to metabolize.

Hydrogenation changes the shape of the fats from a "cis," a naturally curved comma shape, to a more straight "trans" form, similar to the shape of saturated fats. This changed shape causes a case of mistaken identity in the body. These trans fatty acids (TFA) can now displace saturated fatty acids or PUFAs in various locations and functions throughout the body. This changes the way the cell membrane works.

> *"The cell membrane is the outermost limit of a cell, but it is more than a simple boundary surrounding the cellular contents. It is an actively functioning part of the living material, and many important metabolic reactions take place on its surfaces."*

(Source: Holes Human Anatomy and Physiology)

The membrane is an extremely important structure. It defines each cell in the body and determines what shall enter and what must remain outside the cell. The membranes function best when they have fluidity and complexity. When TFA are part of the membrane, the complexity is diminished. Further, certain enzymes present in the cell membrane are affected. Over time, the cell's function is affected negatively.

If all cellular systems are not working optimally, your fat loss efforts will be hindered. The semi-permeable cell membrane is composed of fats. If you do not provide your body with essential fatty acids (good fats), then improper or unhealthy fats will displace the good fats in cell walls and cells will not function optimally. Your immune system can become compromised, recovery from exercise will be hindered, and overall health, energy and vitality will suffer.

> *By blocking cellular hormone formation, interfering with cellular function and increasing free radical activity, trans fatty acids play a role in many diseases, including heart disease, cancer, obesity, diabetes and immune disorders.*

Trans fatty acids in the form of partially hydrogenated soybean oil are found in nearly all commercial and prepared foods such as:

• Margarine and solid vegetable shortenings.
• Prepared cakes, cookies, pastries, candy bars.
• French fries and fried foods.
• Cake mixes and pie crusts.
• Extended foods (i.e., Hamburger Helper™).

As with the dairy industry pushing the need for calcium to meet its own needs, the soybean industry, in its interest to promote the use of hydrogenated oils, is partly responsible for initiating and perpetuating the misinformation regarding saturated fats.

> *Most dangerous to the body is not too much saturated fat, but the lack of essential fatty acids.*

Essential Fatty Acids

The human body can synthesize all the fatty acids it needs from carbohydrate, fat, or protein except for two: linoleic and linolenic acid. Both are polyunsaturated fatty acids and cannot be made from other substances in the body. They must be obtained from food and therefore are called essential. Linoleic and linolenic acids are found in small amounts in plant and fish oils. From both of these essential fats, the body makes important hormone-like substances that regulate a wide range of body functions including blood pressure, clot formation, blood lipid concentration, the immune response, the inflammation response to injury, and many others. These two essential fats also serve as structural components of cell membranes.

Linoleic and Linolenic Acid

Linoleic acid is an omega-6 fatty acid found in the seeds of plants and in the oils harvested from the seeds. Any diet that contains vegetable oils, seeds, nuts, and whole-grain foods provides enough linoleic acid to meet the body's needs. Even though vegetable oils are high in omega-6 fatty acids, I do not recommend using them for cooking. Research indicates the over-consumption of these polyunsaturated fats is the most likely to promote cancer.

Linolenic acid belongs to a family of polyunsaturated fatty acids known as omega-3 fatty acids. The typical American diet is heavy in omega-6 fatty acids and light on omega-3 fatty acids. The importance of omega-3 fatty acids has only recently been recognized. Researchers now know that omega-3 fatty acids are essential for normal growth and development, and they may play an important role in the prevention and treatment of heart disease, hypertension, arthritis, and cancer. The best sources of linolenic acid are fatty cold-water fish (e.g., herring, salmon, mackerel) and flax.

Dietary Supplements of Fish and Flax Oils

Flax and fish oils are concentrated sources of omega-3 fatty acids. Many people, who do not regularly eat fatty, cold-water fish, use dietary supplements containing flax oil, fish oil or popular blends to ensure adequate omega-3 essential fatty acids. If you are not a regular consumer of fish (at least two to three servings per week), then I believe that moderate supplementation with a combination of fish and flax is intelligent and healthy for most Lifestylers.

An alarming trend I have recently observed, however, is the overuse of flax oil with a belief that it is somehow void of calories or is even a negative calorie food. Some believe that the more flax they use, the more weight they lose. Unfortunately, this is a perfect example of how your perception can create a false reality and limit your progress. Keep your mind open and constantly be on the lookout for these fallacies of weight loss. This "flax myth" is also a great example of how misinformation can spread quickly across the Internet and by word-of-mouth. I cannot count the number of clients who have been consuming 8-15 tablespoons of flax oil per day because misinformed fellow dieters told them that it would "fix" their metabolism or help them lose weight. Not surprisingly, once the dosing of flax was reduced to 1 tablespoon per day, without changing anything else, they began seeing weight loss again–something they had not experienced for weeks before reducing the dose.

Like all lipids, flax oil provides 9 calories per gram. The over-consumption of flax, much like any calorie-containing nutrient or alcohol, can make you fat or keep you from losing stored body fat. Flax may be cardio-protective, good for the digestive system and even beneficial for arthritis, however, it is not a cure for what you may believe is a "broken metabolism." (I will address the myth of the "broken metabolism" in a later section.) Flax does not possess mystical, magical qualities that will somehow put your metabolism into overdrive. Flax is a concentrated source of omega-3 fatty acids and is therefore a healthy fat if supplemented in moderation. If consumed to excess, however, it is just as fattening as any other fat, including butter, lard or pork fat.

Essential fatty acids should be viewed as vitamins.
In fact, at one time they were called Vitamin F.

Refrigerate Essential Fats

Although essential fatty acids are important for health, because they are missing more than one pair of hydrogen atoms, they are very susceptible to oxidative damage and, therefore, the production of free radicals. These oils should never be used for cooking or frying. They should be used in small amounts and stored in the refrigerator.

Total Fat <30 Percent–Saturated Fat <10 Percent

Dietary guidelines recommend that *total fat intake should not exceed 30 percent* of the day's total energy intake. For those following the Lifestyle, I agree. Fifteen to twenty percent might be ideal. *Most successful Lifestylers choose low-fat foods if other than fish and then add small amounts of quality fats such as olive oil, flax and/or fish oil to meet their requirements.* Further, saturated fat should contribute 10 percent or less of the total fat intake. Polyunsaturated fats should contribute about 10 percent, and monounsaturated fats about 10 percent.

Dietary fat is only a known major health risk when eaten with
large amounts of carbohydrates as most Americans do.

To determine your dietary fat contribution to total daily calories, simply follow either example:

Example 1: 1200 Calorie Per Day Lifestyle
　　30 grams of lipids per day
　　30 x 9 = 270 calories from lipids
　　270/1200 = 0.23
　　0.23 x 100 = 23 percent of that day's calories came from lipids

Example 2: 1800 Calorie Per Day Lifestyle
　　60 grams of lipids per day
　　60 x 9 = 540 calories from lipids
　　540/1800 = 0.30
　　0.30 x 100 = 30 percent of that day's calories came from lipids

85 Percent Lean Ground Beef Is 60 Percent Fat?

It's important you understand how food labels are somewhat misleading with regard to a food's fat content. . Foods with a label stating they are 98 percent fat free will always contain more than two percent fat. It would make intuitive sense that 85 percent lean ground beef ought to contain 15 percent fat. It doesn't. It contains 60 percent fat! How can this be so?

The Food and Drug Administration (FDA) allows food producers to label the fat content of foods based on percentage of total weight and not on percentage of calories from fat. This is where labels become misleading to we consumers.

Labeling confusion: A pan-cooked patty made from 90 percent-lean raw ground beef derives about 47 percent of its calories from fat, compared to about 62 percent fat calories for a 70 percent-lean patty. So how can "lean" ground beef still have so much fat? The fat-by-weight labeling method underestimates actual fat content on a calorie basis for two reasons. First, ground beef is 55 percent water. If water weight were excluded, the percentage fat by weight would more than double. In addition, a gram of fat contains nine calories of energy compared to only four calories for protein and carbohydrate, so each extra fat gram has a much greater impact than you might expect on increasing the percentage of fat calories. For the same reasons, whole milk (3.3% fat and 88% water by weight) contains 48 percent fat calories, and seven percent fat/93 percent-lean ground turkey contains about 45 percent fat calories.

Become an avid label reader. Don't just look at the front of any package of food you buy and assume that, because it has a big, bold, colorful starburst telling you it's "93 percent fat-free!" it's only seven percent fat. I can assure you it likely is not. Turn the package around. Look at the Nutrition Facts. Do some quick math in your head or on a small, hand-held calculator and determine the percent of total calories provided from fat.

Determining fat as a percent of total calories:
Numbers to the right of the blank lines are only provided as an example.

Enter total calories per serving: (A)_____ 125

Enter fat grams per serving: (B)_____ 6

Multiply (B) x 9 and enter: (C)_____ (6 x 9 = 54)

Divide (C) by (A) and enter: (D)_____ (54/125 = 0.43)*

43 percent of the example food's calories are from fat.

Fats for Cooking, Taste and Salads

If your diet consists of more than one serving of fried food or gravy each week, then I will suggest you are not following the Lifestyle. There is so little oil used for cooking when following the Lifestyle, this section is almost a non-issue. In the event you wish to prepare a dish using some fat, let me make the following recommendations:

> *Avoid partially hydrogenated fats such as margarine. These contain trans fatty acids that are harmful to health, regardless of its source. Eating a form of fat that produces massive free radicals does not make sense.*

Cooking

Use butter over margarine if those are your choices. Butter is a saturated fat, however, for cooking, this saturation protects the fats from transforming into trans fatty acids. Trans fatty acids, found in high concentrations in baked goods, most fried fast-food and margarine, are perhaps the deadliest fats of all known.

Use canola oil. Canola oil is a monounsaturated fat and if used in moderation, likely affects your health neutrally; it does not hurt or help it.

Taste

Use "I Can't Believe It's Not Butter Spray".

Salads

Use olive oil and vinegar, fat-free dressings or a combination of fat-free dressings and a smidge of full-fat dressing. Olive oil is also likely neutral in its effects on health, and is a monounsaturated fat. There are a plethora of low-fat and fat-free dressings available in any supermarket. Some taste good; others leave much to be desired. I am confident you can acquire a taste for at least a few of them. It is worth your effort to do so.

Protein (Groups of Amino Acids)

Protein provides 4 calories per gram

People think of proteins as the body-building nutrients, the material of strong muscles, and rightly so. No new living tissue can be built without them for proteins are part of every cell, every bone, the blood, and every other tissue. Proteins constitute the cells' machinery–they do the cells' work. The energy to fuel that work comes primarily from carbohydrate and lipids.

Protein makes up 50 percent of your body weight, is present in every cell of the body, and is vital to all life functions.

Proteins are formed by complex configurations of amino (containing nitrogen) acids. There are 20 common amino acids making up all proteins in the human body. They are:

Alanine	Arginine (ch)	Asparagine	Aspartic acid
Cysteine	Glutamic acid	Glutamine (ce)	Glycine
Histidine	Isoleucine (e)	Leucine (e)	Lysine (e)
Methionine (e)	Phenylalanine (e)	Proline	Serine
Threonine (e)	Tryptophan (e)	Tyrosine	Valine (e)

(e) - Essential

(ch) - Essential in children

(ce) - Conditionally essential

The human body contains an estimated 10,000 to 50,000 different kinds of proteins. Proteins from food do not provide body proteins directly, but rather, supply amino acids from which the body makes its own proteins.

The body can make over half of the amino acids for itself; the protein in food does not need to supply these. There are other amino acids that the body cannot make, and some that it cannot produce quickly enough to meet its needs. The proteins in foods must supply these amino acids to the body; they are therefore called essential amino acids.

Also important to point out is that sometimes a nonessential amino acid can become essential. During illness or conditions of trauma, or in other special circumstances, the need for an amino acid that is normally nonessential may become greater than the body's ability to produce it. In such circumstances, that amino acid becomes essential (e.g., glutamine). Glutamine is now considered a "conditionally essential" (ce) amino acid.

Enzymes are Proteins

Enzymes are proteins essential to all life processes. They assemble smaller molecules into larger molecules and they disassemble larger molecules into smaller molecules.

When you consume a protein food, it is broken down into amino acids by enzymes. The amino acids enter the cells of the body, where enzymes put the amino acids back together in long chains determined by genes. The chains fold and twist back on themselves to form the proteins the body needs. Day by day, in billions of reactions, these processes repeat themselves, and life goes on.

Antibodies and Some Hormones Are Proteins

While it is common thinking to equate protein with skeletal muscle, the ten- to fifty-thousand proteins in the body are not present only to make you buff. In addition to enzyme proteins, antibodies are also proteins. Antibodies are major proteins in the blood acting against viruses, bacteria, and other disease agents. These proteins are so effective that if a million bacterial cells are injected into the skin of a healthy person, fewer than ten are likely to survive for five hours. Without sufficient protein, your body cannot maintain its resistance to disease. Hormones like thyroid and insulin are also proteins with important physiological functions.

Adequate Dietary Protein Necessary

In everyday life, tissue is broken down and replaced, some quicker than others. The body uses protein to build *all* of its new tissues and to repair damaged tissues. The cells that line the intestinal wall, for instance, only live for three days; they are constantly being shed and must be replaced. When tissues break down the amino acids in the protein, tissues are liberated and the body can reuse them. However, even though amino acids can be recycled from damaged and repaired tissue, you need to eat protein-rich foods every day to replace the protein you continuously lose.

National recommendations for adult protein consumption are approximately 0.8 g/kg of body weight per day. This means that, according to federal guidelines, the typical adult who weighs 150 pounds does not require more than 55 grams of protein per day [(150 / 2.2) x 0.8]. Allow me to explain why you are not typical.

I believe the federal guidelines for adequate protein consumption are inadequate for most people losing weight or actively using resistance training to pursue real skeletal muscle growth. Research is on my side. The totality of the research indicates that you should consume more than the federal guidelines for maximum success and muscle preservation when you are:

1. In a hypocaloric (less calories eaten than you need to maintain weight) state, or
2. Actively pursuing muscle growth with resistance training, or
3. Engaging in consistent vigorous exercise.

Most of the adult protein-needs research done by the World Health Organization and other National and International authorities has only involved sick or healthy, but *stable,* individuals. Once you reach the status of "adulthood" and have stopped growing, the belief by mainstream nutrition authorities is that your needs will not be greater than the federal guidelines discussed above. I can agree with this, however, if you are purposely losing weight, your condition is not considered stable. Further, if you are adding new skeletal muscle, you are also not considered stable.

Nitrogen State

Like carbohydrates and lipids, proteins are composed of carbon (C), hydrogen (H), and oxygen O) but proteins are different in that they also contain nitrogen (N). Researchers can trace nitrogen retention in–and excretion from–the body after test subjects consume protein-rich foods. Much of the research determining adequate protein needs for the dieter or athlete is centered around the concept of nitrogen balance–or more appropriately called "nitrogen state." You can be in a positive, neutral or negative nitrogen state. Most non-dieting, non-exercising healthy adults are in a neutral nitrogen state (i.e., nitrogen balance); they are using and excreting nitrogen at the same rate as it is being consumed. As you might expect, however, being in a positive nitrogen state is desirable for adding new muscle and being in a negative nitrogen state is undesirable. Here are some examples that I hope will make things more clear with regard to nitrogen status:

- Normal, healthy, non-dieting, non-exercising adults are in a neutral nitrogen state: neither positive nor negative.
- Growing children and pregnant women are in a positive nitrogen state.
- People who are starving or fasting are in a negative nitrogen state.
- People suffering from anorexia, sickness, and trauma are in a negative nitrogen state.
- When you are in a negative nitrogen state, your body will turn to its own proteins (muscle) for energy.

Lifestyle Guidelines for Protein Needs

My protein recommendations for anyone losing weight and/or actively pursuing increased skeletal muscle mass mirror those of respected protein experts in this country and abroad. The research is clear: Lifestylers need slightly more than twice the federal guidelines of 0.8 g/kg of body weight per day. It is easier to understand if I say that you should consume approximately 1 gram of protein for every pound of *fat-free* mass you have. On a percentage of calories consumed basis, it can best be said this way: *Consume 25 to 50 percent of your total caloric intake as proteins.* Here are two examples to help you calculate your protein needs as a Lifestyler:

By Fat-Free Mass

Example 1:
  Weight = 175 pounds
  Body fat = 35 percent
  Fat-free mass = 175 x 0.65 = 113.75 (0.65 comes from 100-0.35)
  Protein needs = 25 to 50 percent of total calories consumed each day OR 114 grams of protein per day

Example 2:

Weight = 215 pounds

Body fat = 30 percent

Fat-free mass = 215 x 0.70 = 150.5 (0.70 comes from 100-0.30)

Protein needs = 25 to 50 percent of total calories consumed each day OR 151 grams of protein per day

By Percent of Total Calories

Example 1: 1200 Calorie Per Day Lifestyle

114 grams of protein per day

114 x 4 = 456 calories from proteins

456/1200 = 0.38

0.38 x 100 = 38 percent of that day's calories came from proteins

Example 2: 1800 Calorie Per Day Lifestyle

151 grams of protein per day

151 x 4 = 604 calories from protein

604/1800 = 0.34

0.34 x 100 = 34 percent of that day's calories came from proteins

Protein Supplements and the Best Source

In the carbohydrate section, I stated that most carbohydrate-rich foods are derived from plants. In this section, now the animals get all the glory. The highest quality, complete, protein-rich foods are derived from animals. When you are following the Lifestyle, assuming you are not a vegetarian (I'll cover you later), you'll get much of your protein from low-fat animal flesh (e.g., chicken, turkey, tuna and lean beef), quality-fat animal flesh (e.g., mackerel, salmon, trout), egg whites, and dairy products (e.g., cottage cheese, fat-free cheese, 1% or fat-free milk). Leaving you with this simple explanation would leave many of you wanting because many of you will likely use some kind of protein supplement to meet your needs. Is there a "best" protein supplement out there?

A mixed diet is one in which the food consumption is broad. I believe food selection should remain varied to prevent a deficiency of any one required nutrient. While some athletes remain convinced that strict limitations, avoidance, and a narrow selection of principle foods is optimal for their performance ("meat and potato" people), research does provide credence to the notion that variety is truly the spice of life, health and optimal performance. Should there be a different mode of thinking when considering supplementation with protein-rich supplements?

Varieties of protein powders are currently available on health-food store shelves today. Historical practice and valid research indicating the increased need of dietary protein for athletes have now combined to create a tremendous demand for high-quality protein supplements. Athletes, who first supplemented with protein powders in the '80s, were subjected to inferior, awful tasting blends commonly referred to as "chalkboard dust."

Whey is currently the number one selling protein powder but is it truly the only protein worth considering?   Whey and casein proteins are two of the primary proteins derived from milk. Quality dietary supplements using these proteins are obtained from manufacturing facilities that produce cheddar cheese. During cheese production, the milk is curdled, separating the curd (casein) from the whey. Only after careful handling, temperature control and proper drying techniques will a quality protein powder evolve from curd or the watery, liquid, mother-whey that results during cheese production.

Since whey is enjoying a solid spot at the top of the supplement sales chart, I will review some of its strengths and weaknesses. Then you can decide if whey is really the only protein worth considering. Whey protein can be a rich source of immunoglobulins. Immunoglobulins are immuno-enhancing and considered a strong functional property of whey proteins. Of the known dietary proteins, whey proteins are the richest source of branched chain amino acids (BCAAs are L-leucine, L-valine, L-isoleucine), supplying 4 grams of BCAAs per 20 grams of whey protein. A BCAA load before intense exercise may offer athletes an anabolic advantage during intense training periods. BCAAs are depleted from muscle tissue during strenuous exercise and are believed to support energy-dependent processes during heavy training. Some quality whey proteins with minimal denaturation (denaturation occurs most commonly as a result of chemical interaction or excessive exposure to high temperatures during production) contain serum albumin. Serum albumin is also rich in glutamylcysteine groups. This compound may be an important promoter of glutathione production within the body. Glutathione is an extremely important and potent antioxidant. Finally, regardless of the protein quality measure used (i.e., P.E.R., BV, etc.), whey is a quality protein worthy of your consideration.

At this point, it would appear that whey protein is hands-down the best protein available and there should be no need to look further. As nature would have it, however, things are not perfect in whey land. Recall that essential amino acids are those amino acids that your body cannot produce and which you must obtain from food. Whey proteins are not a good source of the essential amino acid L-phenylalanine. Whey protein is also low in the conditionally essential amino acid L-arginine.

Whey protein concentrates (WPC) can vary in their protein concentrations by 60 percent with some of the low quality versions supplying 20 percent protein by weight and some high-end products supplying 82 percent protein by weight. Whey protein isolates (WPI) (defined as a whey protein providing not less than 90 percent protein by weight) are very expensive by comparison to a WPC, egg, soy or casein. Ion-exchanged whey protein isolate (IWPI) is the most expensive WPI today and while still considered a high quality whey protein, IWPI lacks the nativity of the milk proteins originally present and considered important for functional purposes.

If you will remember when I briefly discussed casein above, I said that casein was the curd portion resulting from cheese production. Cottage cheese is naturally loaded with casein protein but unless you purchase the low-fat or fat-free varieties, cottage cheese is also loaded with fat, sodium and some lactose. Currently, beliefs in protein circles are that casein can slow transit time in the gastrointestinal tract. This may be important because the protein travels slower through the small intestine allowing greater time for contact with the intestinal tract, and greater absorption of amino acids therein. This is in contrast to quicker passage by whey proteins. Casein is also a rich source of glutamine and glucogenic amino acids. Glucogenic aminos are those that can be converted into energy (ATP) to support all athletic and metabolic activities. Where whey is low in L-phenylalanine, casein is rich in this essential amino acid. Casein is not as rich as whey protein with respect to the BCAAs.

Another protein source still popular among bodybuilders and protein experts is egg. In fact, it is still considered a reference protein due to its amino acid profile and quantity of essential amino acids. Reference proteins are generally recognized as those that are of such high quality that other proteins can be compared to them when considering human needs. Before whey and whey combinations were studied, egg protein enjoyed a lengthy history of being recognized as the highest quality protein known. One problem with egg is that most of the research has involved whole egg, and not simply the egg white (egg albumen). One whole egg contains approximately five grams of fat. Protein powders containing egg do not contain the yolk portion (this is where the fat resides), but instead only contain egg albumen (white). Egg albumen, while still a quality protein, is generally recognized as having a lower value biologically than whole egg. The biological value is one measure of how well a protein is retained by an organism.

Just as we are advised to consume a widely, varied diet, the wisest recommendation can also be extended to concentrated protein supplements. The same ideology that proclaims that variety ensures the consumption of required nutrients with no deficiencies of any one nutrient, also applies to amino acids and functional properties unique to each protein you consume. The purpose of this section is not to leave you intimidated of your favorite egg, soy or whey protein powders. If you are following the Lifestyle, you are also eating a variety of foods containing protein, such as meat, milk, soy, fish or nuts on a daily and weekly basis. Achieving balance for required nutrients, health and performance is not difficult. Seek variety and don't search for the one "perfect" food or protein.

Vegetarians–Traditionally a Walking Protein Shortage?

Vegetarians may be at increased risk for protein deficiencies because animals provide the best, complete protein sources we know of today. There are three basic classifications of vegetarians:

- Vegan: consumes zero animal products. (Nothing that ever had a mother)
- Lactovegan: consumes some dairy products.
- Lactoovovegan: consumes dairy and egg products.

The greatest problem with nearly all plant proteins is their incompleteness. This means they are lacking one or more essential amino acids. Soy is an exception. Many vegetarians combine foods to ensure consumption of all essential amino acids. Some common combinations are milk and cereal, peanut butter and bread, beans and rice, beans and corn tortillas, and macaroni and cheese.

Strict vegans can meet their Lifestyle protein needs by consuming more foods such as soy protein powder, tofu, tempeh and soy nuts. Lactovegans and lacto-ovovegans can follow my advice for vegans plus make a concerted effort to consume more low-fat varieties of the limited animal products they are willing to eat.

Other nutrients commonly lacking in a poorly managed diet and that a vegetarian should be concerned with: Vitamin B12, Vitamin D, Riboflavin, Calcium, Zinc, and Iron. In addition to eating a variety of foods known to be rich sources of these vitamins and minerals, a quality multivitamin/mineral is recommended each day.

Protein and Kidney Strain

It is important to realize that you will not be eating excessive amounts of protein. You will be eating a very healthy amount to support increased muscle mass.

Eskimos, the hunter-gatherer, body builders and people who are very carbohydrate-sensitive have maintained higher protein diets for years without any kidney abnormalities. Many people are likely to realize improvements in kidney function by reducing the intake of refined carbohydrates and saturated fat while increasing protein to within the guidelines of the Lifestyle.

There are two classes of individuals who should concern themselves with the protein suggestions of the Lifestyle: 1) those with pre-existing kidney abnormalities, and 2) diabetics and others suffering from a disease known to negatively affect kidney function. Always speak to your doctor about the Lifestyle if there is any question about the health of your kidneys or you are being treated for any medical conditions that may be affected by a moderately high protein intake.

Protein and Osteoporosis

Although some studies show that increased animal protein causes loss of calcium in the urine, the amount that causes the increase is not specific. The amount is also variable and the results are still controversial. In fact, a recent study agrees with ancestral data, which linked increased amounts of protein in pre-menopausal women with increased bone density.

Let's look at this finding in context with osteoporosis as a whole, and our ancestry. This will show the problem of isolating study findings out of context.

For every complex problem, there is a simple solution, and that simple solution will be wrong.

It is well documented that calcium, the major component of bone, is essential to maintain strong bones. Americans, who drink more milk and eat more dairy than any other country, have one of the highest incidences of osteoporosis. Orientals who eat no dairy have virtually no osteoporosis.

The process of bone formation and maintenance is a complex physiological process. Drinking more milk or taking calcium supplements is not the entire solution for obliterating the problem of osteoporosis. This thinking is simplistic, naïve and wrong. Without going into an explanation of the physiology of bone formation, I will address a few of the major risks of bone loss and protective traits necessary for bone development and maintenance.

Bone is not only composed of calcium, but other micronutrient minerals just as important for proper formation. The more important ones include:

• Magnesium   • Potassium   • Zinc   • Boron   • Phosphorous

All of these minerals, especially magnesium, are important to orchestrate the formation of bone. No matter how much calcium you consume, there will not be adequate bone formation and maintenance if other dietary practices create a deficiency of these nutrients. Further, excess calcium that does not get absorbed into bone may find itself in the soft tissues such as the arteries, kidneys and joints. This can play a role in heart disease, kidney stones and osteoarthritis.

In order for the body to use calcium effectively, it needs approximately equal amounts of magnesium. Magnesium was found readily in the diet of our ancestors in nuts, seeds and vegetables, therefore, we did not need to develop the ability to store magnesium. Because calcium-rich foods such as dairy were not available thousands of years ago, the body developed the ability to store calcium.

> *The bottom line: Even if you do consume enough dietary calcium,*
> *if you do not have enough of the other minerals, it will not be used*
> *the most effectively.*

Our basic need for dietary calcium is not that high, however, because of many dietary habits highly prevalent in western societies, there is so much calcium loss that increased intake is necessary. Commonly eaten or used substances have also been clearly shown to affect calcium metabolism and bone formation as well. These substances and habits will interfere not only with calcium absorption, but can leech it from the bones and cause the loss of calcium from the body:

- Insufficient vitamin D obtained from adequate amounts of sun light
- Phosphorous–found in high amounts in soda, especially diet soda
- Excessive Sodium–found in large amounts in processed foods
- Excessive caffeine
- Excessive sugar

- Smoking
- Excessive alcohol consumption
- Antacids with aluminum
- Certain cholesterol medications
- Excess bran
- Physical inactivity—Studies show that if activity is increased, then bone uptake of calcium increases regardless if extra calcium supplementation is taken. Two weeks of bed rest is equivalent to 1 year of aging. It increases calcium loss 50-fold.
- Hormonal loss—menopause or loss of menstrual cycles, estrogen, progesterone and testosterone

The following are still controversial:

- Excess protein—especially that from animals may increase calcium excretion
- Fat inadequate diets—the essential fatty acids are crucial to bone formation

If you are a couch potato and drink diet soda and coffee to excess, enjoy your daily fat-free cookies, eat prepared and processed foods high in sodium and think that by keeping protein intake very low you'll be safe from osteoporosis, then you need to wake up.

A Case for Prevention of Osteoporosis

Populations with very low incidence of osteoporosis are very physically active in the outdoors and are exposed to plenty of natural sunlight. They eat the right type of fats and loads of fresh vegetables and fruit. They eat less refined sugar, less processed foods with excess sodium, do not smoke, don't binge on alcohol, and they don't live on caffeine and sodas high in phosphorous.

Even though laboratory studies show protein may increase calcium loss, anthropological studies of hunter-gatherer populations have found the bones of these people to be extremely strong, even stronger than their agriculturally-raised brothers. This occurred even though hunter-gatherers ate diets consisting of 50-60 percent animal protein. The difference in density between these two populations is so great that on excavation, researchers can distinguish immediately the bones of the hunter-gatherer populations from the farming agricultural populations.

Perhaps the hunter-gatherer populations were more physically active. Perhaps they consumed more of the essential fatty acids or avoided the phytic acid found in grains. The point here is you just cannot make recommendations for a complex illness based on the results of one study, or on one variable taken out of context of a complete lifestyle.

See Appendix for a complete listing of high protein foods for the Lifestyler.

Vitamins (Metabolic Spark Plugs)

Vitamins provide no calories (energy) but that does not mean you can do without the right amounts of any single vitamin and still expect to feel energetic. A deficiency in any of these metabolic catalysts (they assist millions of chemical reactions in the body) could cause a lack of energy and a compromised immune system.

Arbitrarily consuming fat-soluble vitamins, including vitamins A, D, E, and K, can cause toxicity. We store them in the body, whereas the water-soluble vitamins (e.g., vitamins C and B complexes) are relatively nontoxic even at high doses.

I recommend a variety of foods on a daily basis, but I also recommend you take a good quality multivitamin/mineral, formulated to close the gap between what you get from whole foods and what you need for optimal health and performance. I am not a supporter of mega-vitamin dosing (ten times the RDA or DRI) without the knowledge and participation of a qualified, licensed medical professional. Vitamins are powerful catalysts, and when consumed at mega-doses can become a pharmacological substance, exerting drug-like actions. Drugs, as you well know, all have side effects and vitamins are no exception.

Minerals (Frame Support but Much More)

Minerals also provide no calories and are used by the body for structural support (like calcium in bones) and regulation of body processes (like the iron in blood that transports oxygen to cells). Minerals with a known physiological function and which are well documented as required by the body include: calcium, magnesium, iron, phosphorous, sodium, potassium, chromium, zinc, iodine, and copper. My cautionary, anti-mega dosing guidelines above for vitamins also apply to minerals.

Water (the Hidden Miracle Nutrient)

Water makes up 60 to 75 percent of your body weight. To say that water is required is the understatement of the year! Among the millions of chemical reactions that depend on it, water is required to stabilize body temperature, carry nutrients to and waste away from cells, and is necessary for fat to be broken down.

The scientific term "lipolysis" means to break down fat and without an adequate supply of water in your nutritional program, this chemical reaction (hydrolysis) is severely compromised. As soft drinks, both diet and regular have taken over the fluid replacement programs of the majority, not coincidentally has energy levels plummeted. Obesity has also increased, and millions of people are in a chronic state of mild dehydration.

A water loss of even two percent of total body weight (three pounds for a 150-pound person) can severely compromise physical performance and perceived energy. Even a mild state of dehydration can slow the basal metabolic rate, something weight loss seekers cannot afford to have occur.

People working out will sweat more than the average slug. Active persons have an even greater need for increased water consumption over the sedentary individual.

I suggest consuming no less than one-half gallon of water (i.e., two quarts or eight cups) per day in addition to any drink that is not *just* water (i.e., coffee, soda, tea, Crystal Light etc.) and eight additional ounces (one cup) of water for every 20 minutes of vigorous exercise.

Water in Equals Water Out

For many new Lifestylers my recommendations will mean an increase in water consumption. This will send them to the bathroom with the frequency of a woman with two weeks left in her third trimester. Some beginners have conveyed to me they had read in other publications that after a period of time, the trips to the restroom to urinate would decrease because their body would "get used to" the increased water consumption. This is a myth. The body tightly regulates water volume and this means that water in will equal water out. This does not mean, however, you will urinate out exactly the same amount of water you consume.

Although drinking fluids is the number one source of water at about 60 percent, additional water can be obtained from moist food (30 percent). When your body metabolizes nutrients, water is created as a product of these chemical reactions occurring within the body (about 10 percent). Similarly, although most of you may think of urination as being the only way you excrete fluids, this is not true. Although urination is the primary method of ridding the body of excess water (about 60 percent), respiration (water lost in breath), evaporation from skin (about 28 percent) and finally water lost in feces and sweat totaling about 6 percent each respectively, also contribute to water balance. The formula looks something like this as an equation.

Simplified Fluid Balance Formula

Consumption + Metabolism = Urination + Respiration + Evaporation + Feces + Sweating Losses

What this formula tells us is the body will always attempt to be in fluid balance. If you consume three gallons of water each day you will ALWAYS be making many trips to the restroom since you will likely urinate 1.8 gallons (60 percent of three gallons).

Alcohol (Calories and No Nutritional Support)

Alcohol provides 7 calories per gram (milliliter) of 200 proof alcohol ingested. It adds calories (energy) to your diet but does not provide any nutrients. I realize that consuming alcoholic liquor is about as common as grass is green. I also realize that some alcoholic liquor is the "drink of choice" in many social settings. In coaching hundreds of transformationists I have come to fully realize how difficult it is to break the "social drinking" habit and to let go of those wasteful calories.

Trading Good Calories for Alcohol

If you have 200 calories from cocktails (other than during a planned splurge meal) then what 200 calories from nutritious foods are you going to give up? Are you willing to give up sitting on your duff in front of the tube to vigorously exercise for 30 minutes to burn off the additional cocktail calories? You might have to. Alcoholic beverages are a snack–a treat–junk food. Alcoholic calories count just like all others. If consumed in excess, alcohol will prevent you from reaching your goal. Nevertheless, if you truly enjoy it and anyone tells you not to have anymore, ever, then you will likely feel deprived, and thus set up for failure.

If you do not believe you can socialize without alcohol, then perhaps there is another issue needing to be addressed. Sometimes this simple assignment can help you visualize a more realistic approach to mixing and mingling without alcoholic beverages. Fill in this statement when you are about to "go out for drinks" and you just do not believe you can do it without partaking.

I am acting as if ...

... I will die if I don't.

... I can't live without alcohol.

... I can't feel good without alcohol.

You fill in the blank.

To be blunt–while you are hot and heavy in the middle of your transformation–you cannot afford to drink more than one to two drinks per week. If you displace good, quality, nutrient-dense foods with social liquor calories, you will rob your body of nutrients it needs and likely add more calories than you bargained for. There are a number of reasons I do not like to see the consumption of more than one to two drinks per week.

- Alcohol hinders the metabolism and the absorption of numerous vitamins and minerals.

- Alcohol can suppress glucose utilization for energy.

- Alcoholic beverages are calorically dense and nutritionally void.

- The calories in alcohol can become precursors for fatty acids and weight gain.

- Alcohol has a dehydrating effect on the body.

- Moderate amounts of alcohol can stimulate the appetite and *reduce your control and inhibition.* Let's face it, in most social settings where you are going to drink, there are likely to be many high-carb/high-fat foods waiting to be devoured. Even drinking until you are "tipsy" can reduce inhibitions, setting you up to run to the cupboards, fridge or even the store to find comfort, party-it-up, and "I deserve it" foods.

Because your body considers alcohol a toxin, it will metabolize the calories from it first. If you consume other foods (like chicken wings) with alcoholic beverages, the body will first burn the calories from alcohol and then decide if it still needs the calories from the food for body processes. If it does not need the energy from food, then it will store the energy contained in the food as fat. I recommend no more than one serving of alcoholic beverage per day and never as a post-workout drink, a fluid replenishment drink, or before exercising.

Feeling Good, Improving Energy, and Experiencing Normal Hunger

Everyone knows that certain foods are not "good" for you. Eating too much of these "wrong" foods will not be "healthy." You will gain weight, and you will not look good. Few people are aware that every time they eat the "wrong" foods, the effects go beyond how they look. The truth is, the foods you eat play an important role in determining how you feel–physically and mentally.

The right foods can make you feel good.

Picture this: After eating a balanced breakfast, you cruise through the morning feeling sharp. After a balanced lunch, the trend continues. You are full of energy and ideas during the afternoon office meeting. It is obvious to you that every one else is dragging. Sure, you are met with the daily struggles, but you manage them with less effort and distraction. You eat a mid-afternoon snack, find it easy to focus on your work, and leave the office feeling fine.

You arrive home and prepare a simple, balanced dinner. Because your hunger is well under control, you decide to take a walk before you eat. After the dishes are cleared, you dig into the project you have wanted to start for months. You have a small, balanced bedtime snack, go to bed a little bit late, but fall right into a sound and restful sleep. You awaken early the next morning feeling refreshed. You eat your breakfast, pack your snack and it is off to the office again.

The wrong foods can make you feel bad.

Picture this: You skip breakfast with just enough time to make a cup of coffee before you leave for work. When you arrive, you eat the granola bar stashed away in your drawer. You are hungry again by late morning, so you eat the doughnut you have been craving. After a quick bite of whatever is available for lunch, you find yourself feeling sluggish and struggling to keep your eyes open. The water cooler at work is out of water and the "dumb S.O.B." who is responsible for taking care of it is nowhere to be found. You are already frazzled, but knowing that you need to be alert for an afternoon appointment, you have another cup of coffee along with some frozen yogurt for "a little more energy."

At the end of the day, you drag yourself home from the office. You are too tired to make dinner and do not feel a bit like doing any exercise. You end up on the couch doing the only thing you have enough energy for–watching television and indulging your cravings for popcorn, pretzels and ice cream. You go to bed early, but have a hard time falling asleep. You wake in the middle of the night hungry, so you eat some cereal and go back to bed.

The next morning, you have to drag yourself out of bed–stiff as a board–after hitting the snooze alarm three times. You head right to the kitchen to start up the coffee. You overslept again and rush out the door without any breakfast.

> *By choosing the right foods to eat, you hold the power to determine not only how you feel and look, but also what you can accomplish.*

Although the same food can affect different people in different ways, everyone experiences three benefits when they eat the right foods. These benefits will act as signposts of progress toward your goal of achieving optimum health and living the Lifestyle. These benefits are:

- A significant increase in your energy level
- Reduced or normal recognition of hunger
- A dramatic reduction or elimination of your food cravings

You may find that as you progress through the Lifestyle, you will become aware of your own specific physical and emotional "hints" that tell you when you are not eating the right foods. Some of the more common symptoms include headaches, bloating, premenstrual syndrome (PMS) and emotional instability. You will notice that when you are eating properly, these symptoms will be relieved and when you are not, they will return. These symptoms will serve as incentives and motivational reminders to continue practicing the principles within the Lifestyle.

> *If you do not increase your energy, normalize your hunger and eliminate your food cravings, you cannot achieve optimum health and the body you desire.*

Improved Energy

Many people believe that because they are getting older, they should not have the energy they did when they were younger. This belief allows them to accept either consciously or unconsciously that this is normal. Young children have more energy than anyone does. Go to a playground and observe them playing. They run and jump constantly and effortlessly. I am not suggesting that you will regain all the energy of a young child, but it is reasonable to expect that you can have the energy you had when you were in your twenties. In primitive societies, the young and old performed the same amount of work throughout their entire life.

Although many other factors affect your levels of energy–including your overall state of health, stress, hormonal balance, sleep, mood, and genetic constitution–balanced eating and physical activity are the two most important factors. Remember, you control both!

The following are the benefits that result from having more energy:

- Less sleep needed and, upon awaking, feeling sharp, rested and refreshed
- An end to the mid-day "slump" or that longing for an afternoon nap
- Feeling naturally fatigued at night but not so tired that you can't keep your eyes open and fall asleep on the couch
- Natural interest in physical exercise
- Greater strength and stamina
- Increased ability to deal with stress
- More sexually active

As you continue practicing the Lifestyle, you will notice that over time your energy will improve in a systematic fashion as you fine-tune your Lifestyle to meet your individual needs.

> *Because you are unique, judge your improvements in energy compared to how you have felt at your best in the past. Strive to obtain the energy that will allow you to achieve all of your personal goals.*

Normal Hunger

The Lifestyle will help you to recognize when your body truly needs food and when your body has had enough.

You will be able to distinguish between three types of hunger:

- **True** physiological hunger that is associated with a real need for food–True hunger is a physical response. When your stomach growls, you feel lightheaded or lethargic, your body is telling you that it needs food. Real hunger does not disappear until your body is fed.

- **False** hunger associated with the need for water–This is caused by stomach acid causing the sensation of hunger and is relieved by drinking water. If you feel hungry before you think it is time to eat or are still hungry after eating a full meal, it is good practice to drink a glass of water.

- **Emotional,** psychological and habitual forms of hunger–This hunger is not related to your body's actual need for food. As you begin to eat in balance and you learn to recognize true hunger, the times when you have emotional hunger will not only lessen but become much more apparent.

If hunger is your body's physical signal that it needs food, satiation is the body's signal that you have had enough food.

Eating in balance will allow your body to feel satiated on the proper amounts of food. You will:

- Finish a meal feeling that your body has received the proper nourishment.
- Stop eating before you overeat.
- Eliminate your need to eat that undefined "something else."
- Remain full for two to four hours.

Everyone Experiences Hunger Differently

You may feel hungry all of the time and frequently think about your next meal, however, when you eat the proper combination of proteins, fats and carbohydrates, you will no longer:

- Feel terrible if you miss a meal or eat late,
- Feel the need to eat more after a full meal,
- Feel hungry and "out of fuel" shortly after eating,
- Feel full but want to eat more,
- Feel the need to eat continually or "pick at food" throughout the course of the day, or
- Think about when and what you are eating for your next meal, sometimes even while you are eating the previous one.

Or you may be someone who has to be reminded to eat during the day, rarely thinks of food and only gets truly hungry at night if you haven't eaten all day. You need to become aware of the hunger clues if you:

- Are rarely hungry for breakfast and sometimes forget to eat lunch,
- Can go all day without eating if you are preoccupied,
- Find if you do get hungry, the feeling will pass if you wait awhile,
- Find a cup of coffee is all you need to feel energetic,
- Tend to get more hungry in the evening, especially after dinner.

Although you may not get the typical "hunger growl" or lightheadedness that normally occurs with the lack of adequate food, you may experience other signs of hunger including fatigue, headaches, anxiety, irritability, loss of concentration or forgetfulness. These traits are individual. Pay attention to your body's hunger signals.

When you pay attention to your hunger signals, you will eat earlier and more frequently. You will have more energy throughout the day and have less hunger and cravings in the evening.

Nutrient Density

When you are following the Lifestyle, as a rule you will be seeking foods that are nutrient heavy (dense) and calorically sparse but adequate. For the type of lean, muscular body you are trying to build, you need a steady supply and a proper ratio of quality nutrients. If you do not choose foods that will supply your body with the nutrients it needs to go and grow, you will do neither. Because your ultimate goal is a sleek, sexy, muscular physique, you must pay close attention to your food choices. Settling for prepackaged, toxic waste will not supply the nutrients your body needs to transform into all you want it to become. It is of critical importance to being both lean and strong that the food choices you make are the most nutrient dense for the calories they provide.

Until now, many of your food choices have been calorically dense, not nutrient dense. You may have never heard of "nutrient density" before, so here is an example to make this concept a little clearer.

Strawberry Pie vs. Fresh Strawberries

In one hand you have a Dolly Madison® strawberry pie. And in the other, you have 2 cups of strawberries.

The strawberry pie provides:
Calories: 470
Total Fat: ....22 g
Saturated Fat: ....11 g
Total Carbohydrate: ....6 g
Dietary Fiber: ....1 g
Protein: ....3 g

Fresh cut strawberries (2 cups) provide:
Calories: 104
Total Fat: ....0.4 g
Total Carbohydrate: ....27 g
Dietary Fiber: ....6 g
Protein: ....1.2 g
Vitamin A: ....67 I.U.
Folic Acid: ....25 mcg
Vitamin C: ....62 mg
Calcium: ....24 mg
Potassium: ....220 mg

Can you lose weight eating a staple of strawberry pies? Yes, but if pies or similar products are a staple in your diet, you are *not* following the Lifestyle. An underlying principle of the Lifestyle is making good, nutritionally sound food choices that provide you with maximum nutrients in minimal calories (i.e., nutrient density). In the example above, the strawberry pie has four times the calories of two full cups of strawberries and it is nearly void of quality nutrients.

Evolutionary Eating

There are a plethora of books currently available that describe precisely what evolutionary eating is, however, I wanted to take just a moment to address it here as it directly relates to this chapter and others.

Our ancestors of tens of thousands of years ago did not rely on packaged and processed foods to live. Further, they consumed virtually no grains whatsoever. Many times a sharp stick or a rock was all that was available to hunt and forage with. A wide variety of fruits, vegetables, nuts and berries could easily be gathered or dug from the ground with simple tools and eaten without further processing. Almost any animal food, including small and large game, could be hunted successfully. It is believed that humans lived this way for over two million years. They were called hunter-gatherers. The period of time when all humans were hunter-gatherers is called the Paleolithic era. It lasted until about ten thousand years ago.

According to Ray Audette, author of *Neanderthin – A Caveman's Guide to Nutrition*, an evolutionary diet would consist of:

- Meats: beef, veal, lamb, pork, venison, chicken, turkey, duck, pheasant, quail, rabbit, all fish and any other form of meat.
- Fruits: nearly all varieties as long as they are fresh.
- Vegetables: nearly anything that is edible raw.
- Nuts: almonds, walnuts, pecans, Brazil acorns, hickory nuts, filberts, macadamia and any others that are edible raw (peanuts are a legume, not a nut and are excluded).
- Berries: grapes, blueberries, raspberries, blackberries, boysenberries, strawberries and any others edible raw.

If you were following an evolutionary diet, you would ***never*** eat:

- Grains: corn, wheat, barley, rye, rice, oats and all products made from them.
- Beans: all varieties of hard beans, lima beans, green beans, wax beans, peas, peanuts, chocolate, soy and all of the products made from them.
- Potatoes: all varieties of potatoes and yams, beets, taro, cassava (tapioca), turnips and the products made from them.
- Dairy: milk, cheese, yogurt, whey, butter and all of the products made from them – no matter what kind of animal milk was used to produce them.
- Sugar: fructose, sucrose, maltose, dextrose, lactose, corn sweeteners, honey, molasses and the products made from them.

For some time now there has been a trend that several authors have capitalized on which proposes that we return to our ancestral ways of eating. To do so would mean you would *never* eat another sandwich again. You would also never eat another pretzel or low-fat cookie or chip. You'd never eat any cottage cheese or any other cheese for that matter. And there certainly would never be any chocolate chip cookies! The reason for this abstention by the proponents of an evolutionary diet is because it has only been in the last ten thousand years that agriculture was developed to produce the foods on the "never eat" list. Their belief is that modern man is biologically no different than he was tens of thousands of years ago. Even though technology has allowed greater change in the food supply over the past few hundred years than the past tens of thousands, the body still thinks it is 80,000 B.C. and does not know how to process the massive choices available.

My position with regard to evolutionary eating and the Lifestyle is one of mixed emotions. As you will read in the *Triggers, Addiction and Self-Regulation* chapter, there are foods that can *trigger* episodes of bingeing and are even at the root of food addiction—much like alcohol, nicotine or stronger drugs. As you will learn, the foods creating a chemical addiction are always those foods that have only been available for the past few hundred years and are only available as a result of modern agriculture practices, milling and refinement. There are three main classes of addictive, trigger foods:

- Refined sugars (chocolate, candies, donuts)
- Grains (breads, pasta, donuts, pastries, cakes)
- Chips (all kinds but the saltier and crunchier, the better)

In working closely with hundreds of clients there is absolutely no doubt whatsoever that many perform better once they are able to abstain from the "never eat" list of foods. Many don't have to completely abstain from the "never eat" foods permanently, but must do so whenever they feel they are "stuck" and the weight isn't moving. This is undeniably true and I continue to experience this today in my coaching and counseling. Some will, however, for ultimate success, have to abstain from certain foods for a lifetime. I cannot and will not lie to you and say otherwise. I will refer you to the *Addictions* chapter mentioned previously for a more thorough discussion of the topic.

Many individuals, however, are not addicted to a food or food class and can reasonably follow a more traditional, modern, healthy-eating Lifestyle that incorporates plenty of whole grains, low-fat dairy products, beans, potatoes

What Counts As A Serving?
Food Groups

Bread, Cereal, Rice, and Pasta		
1 slice of bread	1 ounce of ready-to-eat cereal	1/2 cup of cooked cereal, rice, or pasta
Vegetable		
1 cup of raw leafy vegetables	1/2 cup of other vegetables, cooked or chopped raw	3/4 cup of vegetable juice
Fruit		
1 medium apple, banana, orange	1/2 cup of chopped, cooked, or canned fruit	3/4 cup of fruit juice
Milk, Yogurt, and Cheese		
1 cup of milk or yogurt	1-1/2 ounces of natural cheese	2 ounces of process cheese
Meat, Poultry, Fish, Dry Beans, Eggs, and Nuts		
2-3 ounces of cooked lean meat, poultry, or fish	1/2 cup of cooked dry beans or 1 egg counts as 1 ounce of lean meat. 2 tablespoons of peanut butter or 1/3 cup of nuts count as 1 ounce of meat.	

(Source: U.S. Department of Agriculture)

and the occasional sweet treat. I place myself in this class. But just because I am in this class does not mean you will be.

In the final analysis of this very brief review of evolutionary eating, I will simply say this: As you continue to read the Lifestyle and discover more about yourself than you ever have before, keep in mind that there truly are classes of foods that many individuals simply do not tolerate well for a number of reasons (i.e., sensitivity, intolerance, allergy, addiction). If you decide, in your final analysis, that you continue to "fall down" with foods of the modern age (many times called neo-foods), then do not continue to live in denial (which could stand for "Don't Even Know I Am Lying"). Adapt your Lifestyle, as necessary, to eliminate those foods causing problems, while still promoting an amazingly healthy and complete nutritional Lifestyle. Eating within the guidelines of the Lifestyle should never be construed as being restrictive regardless of whether you identify one or several foods you simply cannot eat. You have to commit to making lifestyle changes that will readjust how you feel about food and what it does for *your* body. For further reading about evolutionary eating, do a search at your favorite bookstore for words such as Paleolithic, Paleo, neanderthal and evolutionary, with the usual weight-loss words such as diet and weight loss. Dr. Loren Cordain has written a good book on the subject titled *The Paleo Diet*.

Macronutrient Chart & Lifestyle Food Pyramid

The Lifestyle probably wouldn't be a valid guide to the body of your dreams without at least few charts and illustrations in the Nutrients chapter. The pie chart (Figure 5.2) graphically represents what I typically suggest as "optimal" for most people following my program. Not everyone will need to vehemently adhere to the limited range of what I consider optimal, however, a majority of the clients who routinely perform and succeed the greatest do adhere to the percentages represented by Figure 5.2.

Figure 5.2

40 - 45% Carbohydrates

35 - 40% Protein

10 - 30% Fat

The final illustration is a representation of what the food guide pyramid for the Lifestyle would look like. I call it The Leanness Lifestyle Superfit Pyramid. If you've ever seen a standard USDA Food Guide Pyramid you will notice some marked differences between there's and mine.

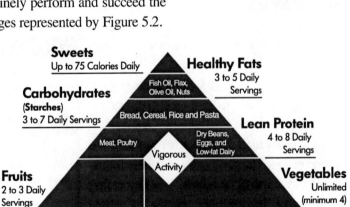

Sweets
Up to 75 Calories Daily

Healthy Fats
3 to 5 Daily Servings

Fish Oil, Flax, Olive Oil, Nuts

Carbohydrates
(Starches)
3 to 7 Daily Servings

Bread, Cereal, Rice and Pasta

Lean Protein
4 to 8 Daily Servings

Meat, Poultry

Dry Beans, Eggs, and Low-fat Dairy

Vigorous Activity

Fruits
2 to 3 Daily Servings

Vegetables
Unlimited
(minimum 4)

Leanness Lifestyle Superfit Pyramid
© The LeannessLifestyle and David Greenwalt C.S.C.S.

First, mine is modeled after the Mayo Clinic's Healthy Eating Pyramid with some subtle differences. While the standard Food Guide Pyramid might be okay for the general public, I believe it is suboptimal for our intentions–losing weight, adding quality muscle and becoming superfit. Instead of 6-11 servings of bread, cereal and starches being at the base, the Lifestyle Superfit Pyramid emphasizes vegetables and fruits. It is harder to overeat them, they provide tremendous nutrients per calorie, they are full of fiber and phytochemicals, and there is less susceptibility to intolerances, allergies and addiction than breads, cereals and starches. On the next tier I recommend lean sources of protein. The tier above that contains carbohydrates other than vegetables and fruits. These include breads, cereals and other starches. The next smaller tier includes added healthy fats such as olive oil, flax oil and fish oils. The upper most and smallest tier includes sweets and all other junk foods. Finally, as did the developer of the Mayo Healthy Eating Guide, Dr. Donald Hensrud M.D., I've included Vigorous Activity in the center to remind everyone that optimal health is only achieved with a sound exercise program.

It is important that as you review the Lifestyle Superfit Pyramid you realize it is only a guide and not an absolute. Many different varieties of healthy eating are accomplished by consuming more or less breads, cereals and grains. Other Lifestyle-oriented individuals do wonderfully well consuming a little less protein. However, overall, the Lifestyle Superfit Pyramid represents what I currently believe is optimal and what has become representative of what the most successful Lifestylers routinely are drawn to for long-term weight control.

Summary

The body is the most complex machine you will ever know. It is vitally important that you feed the machine the nutrients it needs to thrive with energy on a daily basis. Your health, productivity and happiness depend upon the fuels you choose to feed your machine.

There are six classes of nutrients and only three provide energy directly to the body. Carbohydrates are the preferred energy source so it is important to choose your carbohydrate foods wisely. Your increased knowledge of the proper fuels for the body will prevent you from spreading misinformation and confusing others. Incorporating more fibrous vegetables over processed, packaged starches is a decision you will never regret. A general rule of thumb when choosing moderate- to high-carbohydrate foods is to seek those foods that provide at least 10 percent of the total carbohydrates as fiber.

Some fats are essential for a healthy life. Contrary to popular belief, however, overconsumption of flax oil can expand the waistline just as easily as other forms of dietary fat. While saturated fats should be limited to 10 percent or less of your total fat intake, it is not the saturated fat found in a typical lean piece of beef that is creating your obesity or other health issues. Trans fatty acids created by cooking with polyunsaturated oils, as well as those created in the production of margarine, pastries, donuts and french fries are far more dangerous to your health and waistline.

Lean sources of protein provide essential amino acids allowing for retention and accretion of muscle. The Lifestyle does not promote a high-protein diet. The Lifestyle promotes an adequate-protein program based on research for individuals who are not couch potatoes.

Planning meals that yield a balanced mix of carbohydrates, proteins and fats will help control blood sugar and insulin levels.

While vitamins and minerals provide no direct energy to the body, they are essential nutrients that must be considered seriously for a healthy Lifestyle. A quality vitamin/mineral supplement is highly recommended.

Water is the miracle nutrient and drink of choice by Lifestylers. You should consume at least enough water to create four to five clear urinations per day.

The more nutrient dense and calorically sparse your food choices are, the more volume of food you will be consuming and the better your Lifestyle will progress.

Evolutionary eating can be a healthy modification of the Lifestyle when properly executed. Some individuals will need to strongly evaluate whether they must abstain from certain foods once in a while, most of the time, or for life.

Take Action and Feel Great!

1. Clean your cupboards and fridge of junk food. Throw it away or donate it to a local food pantry.

2. Use the grocery list at www.leannesslifestyle.com and make a grocery run.

3. Pick up a copy of a "Light and Tasty" cooking magazine for ideas on how to add zest to your low-fat, healthy dishes. You may also purchase a cookbook for preparing low-fat, protein-rich dishes at any major book store.

4. Prepare your vegetables and fruit after purchasing so they are readily accessible when you are hungry. They need to be as easy to eat as the finger snacks you currently eat but have thrown away by now.

5. If you are not currently taking a multi-vitamin, log on to www.leannesslifestyle.com for recommendations and guidelines on what to take or look for in a good quality multi-vitamin/mineral.

6. If you are not currently taking an essential fatty acid supplement, log on to www.leannesslifestyle.com for recommendations and guidelines on what to take or look for in a good quality essential fatty acid supplement.

Energy Balance

> ## *"I have been overweight all of my life and my body tends to hold onto everything."*

How many times have you spoken or thought those very same words? I predict this chapter will be in the top three of your favorites of the entire book. This chapter address the question everyone wants to know "How many calories can I have?" You are not alone if you, too, believe your body "tends to hold onto everything."

I find too many people sabotaging themselves by being hung up and confused by the equations calculating metabolic rate and the value of activity. Many people also associate some kind of "permission" to eat a certain number of calories each day based on some formula.

First Law of Metabolic Equations

> *All valid metabolic equations are scientific estimates of caloric need to cause the desired movement in body weight. Regardless of whose formula you choose to use, that formula is a "best guess" based on science or the experience of the presenter. Detailed analysis of your progression with appropriate adjustments will be necessary.*

As you progress through this section and work through the numbers to determine how many calories you should start your transformation with, I believe it's imperative to keep the first law in mind at all times. Think of it only as a starting block out of which you will run. Once you take off running, you must determine the precise number of calories you can consume through food logging and a detailed analysis of the numbers (i.e., calories, carbs, proteins, fats, scale weight, tape measure, body fat).

A difference of up to 40 percent is possible in the resting metabolic rate (RMR) between two individuals weighing the same with the same fat-free mass. Does this mean that one 180-pound woman with 35 percent body fat may get to eat 40 percent more than another 180-pound woman with 35 percent body fat? Yes. Precisely why has not been fully determined. Not knowing the precise reason does not change what is true.

Certain nutrients provide energy (calories) allowing your body to perform many biological functions. What is a calorie and how do you balance food and physical activity so that you consume the number of calories necessary to lose weight?

> One calorie is defined as the quantity of heat necessary to raise the temperature of 1 kilogram (1 liter) of water 1 degree Celsius (for example, from 14.5 to 15.5 degrees Celsius). Thus, a calorie is more accurately termed a kilogram calorie or

kilocalorie, abbreviated kcal. In layman's terms, I will simply use the common vernacular most are used to: calorie. If the caloric value of a medium banana is 100, this simply means that banana possesses the heat energy needed to increase the temperature of 100 Liters of water 1 degree Celsius.

When reading elsewhere about calories, you may also read about the joule or kilojoule (kJ), the international unit of expressing energy. To convert calories to joules, multiply the caloric value of the food by 4.2. The joule value of the banana, for example, would be 100 calories x 4.2, or 420 kJ. I will not address energy as joules further in this book and only reference this you'll know what they are saying if you come upon this term when reading elsewhere.

Remember that carbohydrate and protein provide four calories per gram and lipid provides nine calories per gram. By understanding calories, you can apply some basic understanding into why the Lifestyle places a strong emphasis on a low to moderate fat intake. Fats contain more than twice the energy value of carbohydrates and protein on a per-gram basis. While the energy (calories) from fat is not necessarily believed to be more fattening than the energy from carbohydrate and protein, it is simply much easier to over-consume total calories when poor quality, high-fat foods are a bigger proportion of your intake.

For example, to consume 100 calories from each of six common foods–carrots, celery, green peppers, grapefruit, medium-sized eggs, and mayonnaise–you would have to eat five carrots, 20 stalks of celery, six green peppers, one large grapefruit, and 1-1/4 eggs, but only one tablespoon of mayonnaise. If your daily caloric requirement demanded an intake of 2100 calories per day, you would need to consume about 420 celery stalks, 105 carrots, 136 green peppers, or 26 eggs, yet only 1 cup of mayonnaise or eight ounces of salad oil. These examples dramatically illustrate that foods high in lipid content contain considerably more calories by volume than foods low in lipid and correspondingly high in water content. (Source: Katch, "Exercise Physiology," 4th ed., 1996.)

Daily Energy Expenditure Needs

The amount of energy (calories) you need to consume each day depends upon four primary factors:

- Resting Metabolic Rate
- Thermic effect of physical activity
- Thermic effect of food
- Adaptive thermogenesis

(The terms thermic and thermogenesis refer to "heat producing." Basically, the human body is a skin-wrapped furnace and food is the fuel you use to stoke the furnace.)

Resting Metabolic Rate

Resting Metabolic Rate (RMR) is the rate of energy expenditure at rest in a supine position (lying on back with face upward), measured immediately after at least eight hours of sleep and 12 hours of fasting. The RMR reflects the minimum amount of energy required to carry out your body's essential physiological functions, including both awake and sleep conditions. Approximately 65 to 75 percent of all energy needs result from the RMR.

Your resting metabolic rate is determined primarily by fat-free mass (FFM) and body surface area (BSA). This means that the more FFM and BSA you have, the higher your RMR will be. Without any additional information, you may not have realized it but are now aware of the reason most women have a lower RMR than men. Typically, even if a man and woman weigh the same, the man will have a higher RMR because his body fat will be lower and he will possess more FFM.

Without a sound resistance training program, aging individuals lose fat-free mass and experience a drop in RMR of approximately five percent per decade. As a result, they suffer a lowering of their RMR, making it necessary to either eat less to maintain body weight, or continue eating the same as always with a concomitant gain of fat weight resulting. Individuals who over-diet, or don't include a resistance training plan in their weight loss efforts, will also lose precious skeletal muscle (part of FFM), thus undesirably slowing their RMR.

You may have glossed over the point I made above about "BSA," however, it's important to understand a bit about how BSA can affect your RMR too. The BSA also provides an explanation as to why a 225-pound person with 150 pounds of FFM will usually need more calories per day to maintain their weight than a person who weighs 185 pounds with 150 pounds of FFM. Although these two individuals have the same FFM, the heavier person will require more calories per day because:

- The 225-pound person has 33 percent body fat. The 185-pound person has 19 percent body fat. Adipose is metabolically active; although unlike skeletal muscle, it is active nonetheless. If you are larger (i.e., more BSA) because of excess stored fat, your RMR will increase even if FFM does not go up. Some energy is necessary to support the extra stored fat the 225-pound person possesses.

- The more surface area you have (the bigger, taller, or fatter you are), the greater the cooling area across the skin. In the example comparison, the 225-pound person will have a greater BSA over the 185-pound person partly due to extra adipose. This will increase the RMR a bit so that body temperature can be regulated properly.

- If weight is stable, the person with more BSA will consume more calories to maintain the weight. The "thermic effect of food" will be greater, and this increases total caloric needs.

- We are dynamic organisms and have varying activity levels. Most people would realize that it simply takes more energy to move a 225-pound person than it does a 185-pound person. If you weigh 185 and do not believe me, walk around for a day with two 20-pound dumbbells in your hands and never set them down.

For these four reasons, the person with greater BSA will usually have a greater RMR than someone who possesses equal FFM with less BSA. The importance of understanding not only the impact of FFM, but also BSA on RMR comes when you might ordinarily scratch your head and blame some mystical, magical slowing of the RMR after you drop weight without losing any muscle. Allow me to explain.

If you are the 225-pound person today and you have 150 pounds of FFM you will follow the lifestyle to lower your weight to 185 while striving to maintain all of your FFM. Because of a smaller BSA you will eat fewer calories when you are 185 compared to when you were 225. Unless you understood the effects of BSA, you may have blamed the reduction in caloric needs on a damaged and depressed metabolism, or some other incorrect thinking.

If you diet too hard, can you screw up your metabolism for a while? Yes. How? Cut calories drastically and drop about four to five percent of your body weight week after week after week after week. That ought to do the trick. I do not teach super-fast weight loss with the Lifestyle, and this is the reason why. This quick weight loss can really put the hormonal breaks on, because by crash dieting, you are starving. I like 0.5 to 1.5 percent (that's one-half of one percent to one and a half percent) of your body weight in loss per week unless the loss calculated is greater than 2 pounds per week. I rarely like greater than a two-pound loss per week. I prefer the slower weight loss best. No, the slower weight loss does not create the grand "After" photos as fast, nor does it shed decades of overindulgences overnight, but it definitely helps to maintain an effective, natural metabolic slowdown as opposed to a metabolic shutdown.

RMR by Total Body Weight

The RMR equation is different for men and women. The primary reason for the difference is that women typically have higher body fats and less fat-free mass than men do. Below are guidelines showing common ranges for both men and women:

RMR Range for Men:
Body weight x 9 (low)   Body weight x 17 (high)

This equation simply means that a man weighing 250 pounds could have a RMR as low as 2250 calories per day (250 x 9) and as high as 4250 calories per day (250 x 17). Based on my experience in working with hundreds of men who have successfully transformed, I prefer for all men desiring Lifestyle weight loss to use body weight x 13 as a starting point. Your RMR is *not* the total number of calories you will consume in a day for weight loss.

Example (185 Pound man): 185 x 13 = 2,405 (RMR)

Determine Your RMR (Men)
Body weight (nude, after sleeping for 6 to 8 hours) _____ x 13 = _____ RMR

RMR Range for Women:

Body weight x 8 (low)   Body weight x 16 (high)

This means that a woman weighing 200 pounds could have a RMR as low as 1600 calories per day (200 x 8) and as high as 3200 calories per day (200 x 16). For women desiring Lifestyle weight loss, I prefer to use body weight x 12 as a starting point. Your RMR is not the total number of calories you will consume in a day for weight loss.

Example (155 Pound Woman): 155 x 12 = 1,860 (RMR)

Determine Your RMR (Women)
Body weight (nude, after sleeping for 6 to 8 hours) _____ x 12 = _____ RMR

RMR by Body Surface Area (See Figure 6.1. RMR Nomogram)

I have included a nomogram and age factor chart based on the formula of Dubois and Dubois to help you computate your body surface area. To determine your RMR using the BSA method, you will first need to find your age in the chart provided, and then determine the factor to use first.

For example, a 35-year-old man has an age factor of 37.
The BSA method of RMR calculation works as follows:
Age factor x BSA (from nomogram) x 24

Example for Men: Age = 35   Height = 5'10"

Using the 185-pound man as an example again, we can first see that his age factor for this equation is 37. With a straight edge, find the 5'10" mark on the left column of the nomogram. On the far right column, find the weight of 185. Align the straight edge on the left (height value) with the weight value on the right. Look at the middle column; this number represents body mass in meters squared. You will see that your straight edge crosses the 1.99 mark.

This is all done only so you can plug in the numbers to the formula.

RMR = 37 x 1.99 x 24 = 1,767 calories per day
A 5'10" man aged 35 who weighs 185 will have a predicted RMR of 1,767 calories per day.

Age Factor (AF)

BSAF

Age (Men)	AF	Age (Women)	AF
1	53	1	53
2 - 3	52	2	52
4	51	3	51
5	50	4	49
6	49	5	48
7	48	6	45
8	47	7	44
9	46	8 - 10	43
10 - 12	44	11	42
13 - 15	43	12 - 14	41
16 - 17	42	15	39
18 - 19	41	16	38
20	40	17 - 20	37
21 - 25	39	21 - 45	36
26 - 30	38	46 - 52	35
31 - 52	37	53 - 59	34
53 - 60	36	60 - 73	33
61 - 69	35	74 - 80	32
70 - 76	34		
77 - 80	33		

Scale I Height — in / cm

Scale III Surface Area — m²

Scale II Weight — lb / kg

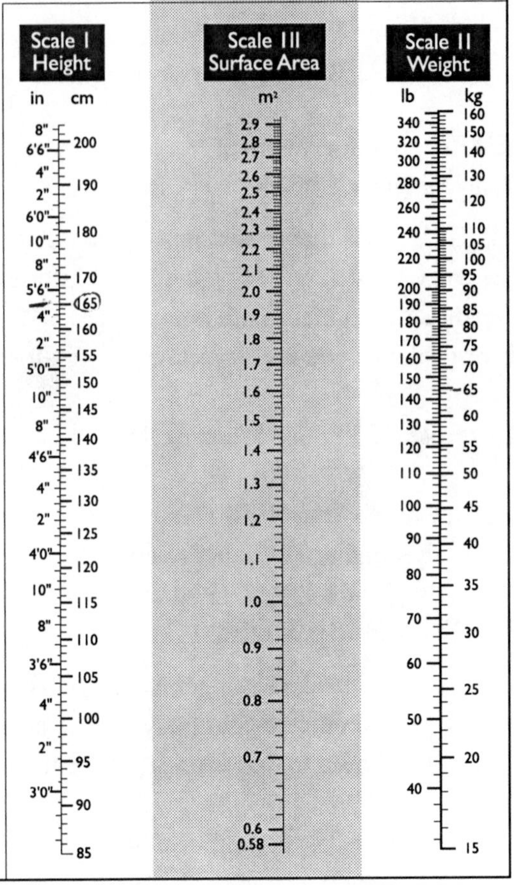

Figure 6.1. RMR Nomogram

Example for Women: Age = 40   Height = 5'5"

If we use our 155-pound woman, again we can first see that her age factor for this equation is 36. With a straight edge, find the 5'5" mark on the left column of the nomogram. On the far right column, find the weight of 155. Align the straight edge on the left (height value) with the weight value on the right. Look at the middle column; this number represents body mass in meters squared. You will see that your straight edge crosses the 1.74 mark.

This is all done only so you can plug in the numbers to the formula.

RMR = 36 x 1.74 x 24 = 1,503 calories per day

A 5'5" woman aged 40 who weighs 155 will have a predicted RMR of 1,503 calories per day.

RMR, When You Know Your Body Fat

There are a multitude of equations developed by researchers to determine RMR. A relatively easy and accurate estimate of RMR can be obtained by using fat-free mass. The generalized equation, applicable to males and females over a wide range of body weights, is as follows:

RMR = 370 + (21.6 x FFM)
FFM = Fat-free mass expressed in kilograms, NOT pounds.

Example: Our 185-pound man determines with relative accuracy that his body fat is 20 percent. This means he has 37 pounds of fat (185 x 0.20) on his body and 148 pounds of fat-free mass (185 - 37). To determine his fat-free mass in kilograms, he divides his fat-free mass (148) by 2.2.

148/2.2 = 67.27 kilograms of fat-free mass
The 185-pound example man would have an estimated RMR of:
> 370 + (21.6 x 67.27)
> 21.6 x 67.27 = 1,453
> 370 + 1,453 = 1,890
> RMR = 1,890

Example: Our 155-pound woman determines with relative accuracy that her body fat is 35 percent. This means she has 54 pounds of fat (155 x .35) on her body and 101 pounds of fat-free mass (155 - 54). To determine her fat-free mass in kilograms she divides her fat-free mass (101) by 2.2.

101/2.2 = 45.91 kilograms of fat-free mass
The 155-pound example woman would have an estimated RMR of:
> 370 + (21.6 x 45.91)
> 21.6 x 45.91 = 992
> 370 + 992 = 1,362
> RMR = 1,362

(Source: Mcardle, Katch, Katch, "*Exercise Physiology 4th Ed*")

Be careful when choosing to use this method of determining RMR. If you are not confident your body fat is reasonably accurate, then I suggest you use my total body weight formula or the BSA formula to determine RMR.

As you can see, the 180-pound man and 155-pound woman have three different predicted RMRs depending on the formula used.

185 Pound Man RMR Methods
- Total body weight: 2,405
- BSA: 1,767
- FFM: 1,890

155 Pound Woman RMR Methods
- Total body weight: 1,860
- BSA: 1,503
- FFM: 1,362

Remember, a formula is only a start–a baseline–not a rule that commands your "right" to any given caloric amount simply because it works out on paper. The RMR helps to determine a place to start, a place to revisit should you come unglued, and, best of all, it helps to determine whether your eating makes sense for the results you are or are not achieving. For future calculations throughout this chapter, I will refer to the total body weight method of determining RMR, only because it is the simplest.

Physical Activity

Physical activity profoundly affects your energy expenditure. It accounts for approximately 20 to 40 percent of the daily energy expenditure needs. World-class athletes nearly double their daily caloric outputs with three to four hours of hard training.

How about the rest of us who are not world-class? Can physical activity really allow you to consume 20 to 40 percent more calories per day to maintain or lose weight compared to a completely sedentary lifestyle? Yes, it can!

You are now keenly aware of the caloric value for carbohydrate, lipid and protein represented in every mainstream book, magazine and news article including this one. What you might not know is that those numbers are general estimates (technically called the Atwater general factors). The true caloric value of many foods is somewhat different from what we are accustomed to seeing. For example, fruits can provide 3.60 calories per gram of carbohydrate and cereals can provide 4.11 calories per gram of carbohydrate. Since everyone uses the Atwater general factors, the carbohydrates in both fruits and cereals are given a value of four calories per gram. The reason the Atwater general factors are used is because unless you are enrolled in a university study, the differences are insignificant and the Atwater factors are easier to use. Can you imagine the level of difficulty in analyzing your Lifestyle if you had to look up every food you consumed to determine whether the carbohydrates in that food yielded 3.60 or 4.11 or some other caloric value in between? What an arduous task that would be.

When calculating the true value of exercise, generalizations are also used. For your purposes, this generalization works exceptionally well and has been used by hundreds of Lifestylers with much ease and success. Before explaining my generalized exercise equations, it is vital to understand what "perceived exertion" means.

Perceived Exertion

In health clubs around the world, on the walls beside treadmills, stationary bikes and step machines, one often sees a scale going from 6-20. This is called a RPE Scale, which stands for "Rate of Perceived Exertion." It is a psycho-physiological scale, which means it calls on the mind and body to self-rate perception of effort.

The RPE scale measures feelings of effort, strain, discomfort, and/or fatigue experienced during both aerobic and resistance training. One's perception of physical exertion is a subjective assessment that incorporates information from the internal and external environment of the body. The more frequently these signals are felt, the more intense the perceptions of physical exertion.

Perceived exertion reflects the interaction between the mind and body. This psychological parameter has been linked to many physiological events that occur during physical exercise. These physiological events can be divided into respiratory/metabolic (such as ventilation and oxygen uptake) and peripheral (such as cellular metabolism and energy substrate utilization).

How is Perceived Exertion Measured?

The level of perceived exertion is often measured with a 15-category scale that was developed by the Swedish psychologist Gunnar Borg.

The Borg scale is shown below:

6	No exertion at all	13	Somewhat hard
7	Extemely light	14	
8		15	Hard (heavy)
9	Very light	16	
10		19	Extremely hard
11	Light	20	Maximal exertion
12			

© Gunnar Borg 1985

The Borg scale is simple to understand and very user-friendly, however, to use it effectively, it is necessary to adhere to these standard guidelines in measuring perceived exertion:

1. Perceived exertion should be understood as a method to determine the intensity of effort, strain, and/or discomfort that is felt during exercise.

2. The range of sensations must correspond to the scale. For example, number 6 should be made in reference to the feelings during rest, whereas number 20 should refer to the maximal level of exertion.

3. Either the RPE should be made specific to the overall body perception (e.g., when your whole body is tired after a grueling run or full body workout) or the perception derived from a certain anatomical region of the body such as chest, arms and/or legs (e.g., when your resistance training program calls for a hard effort on chest day).

How Can RPE Be Used?

Often the question is raised as to whether the intensity produced based on perceptual ratings is accurate. Several recent studies have attempted to answer this question, and these studies have determined that using a "target RPE" as a guide to regulate exercise intensity is valid.

Using the RPE can be especially important in two situations. If heart-rate measurement is difficult for some reason, or if the individual is on any medication that may alter normal heart rate response to physical stress, RPE can be an excellent tool to regulate and monitor intensity. The RPE scale continues to be a useful tool, offering subjective reflection of physiological responses during physical exercise, and enabling the individual to regulate effort to gain maximum benefit. (Source: American College of Sports Medicine)

Vigorous Exercise

Many of you are familiar with various charts and equations depicting the difference in caloric output among individuals for various sports or exercise activities. The problem with those charts and equations is that often they are complicated to use and many times, you will not find your favorite activity listed. I commonly find charts that do not list resistance training at all! After reviewing dozens of research papers and textbooks on the subject of energy expenditure and exercise, I have made some generalized conclusions that will forever simplify your view of the caloric benefits of exercise:

Any activity that is perceived as at least a 13 on the Borg RPE scale is vigorous exercise.

Men will burn about 10 calories a minute (300 calories every 30 minutes) with vigorous exercise. Women will burn about 8 calories a minute (240 calories every 30 minutes) with vigorous exercise.

The accuracy of this simple equation depends upon your understanding of the Borg scale, your character and integrity. Let's face it. If you perceive sitting on the couch as a 13, then nothing I am about to say is going to work. If you perceive a leisurely walk with the dog a 13, then again, all bets are off. You must be honest with yourself; otherwise, you are only cheating yourself.

Upon reading this section, some will get hung up in the minutia and argue over the fact that an elite athlete will have a higher pain threshold over a rank beginner and thus will "perceive" less pain while doing more work. Others will want to point a finger at my generalizations and talk about what they learned in their last exercise physiology course about how energy expenditure is also related to the weight of the individual performing the activity. I will simply say this: If you are inclined to argue the finer points of determining energy expenditure, I am not talking to you. I am *not* talking to the thickly muscled bodybuilder. I am not talking to the elite athlete. I am talking to the other 162 million overweight Americans who are more concerned with results than they are with crunching complex equations into fine dust.

Thermic Effect of Food

The thermic effect of food represents the energy used to process the body's food. This includes the work associated with the digestion, absorption, transport, metabolism, and storage of energy from ingested food. The contribution of the thermic effect of food to daily energy expenditure is approximately 10 percent.

Individuals who spend far too much time worrying themselves sick over the minutia of nutrition have chanted for years now that a calorie is not a calorie. They rant and rave about how a "mixed diet" will contribute about 10 percent to the daily energy expenditure costs, but protein contributes 25 percent, carbohydrates 15 percent and lipids almost nothing. Therefore–you guessed it–a high-protein diet is suggested. Why? Those who speculate far more than they act believe that if a high-protein, low-carb diet is consumed, your weight loss woes will end because of the increased thermic effect of food. Once again, I must stress that you should consider every source you hear, question their credentials and experience, and do your best to come back near the middle. Strive for balance and macronutrient ratios relatively close to the Lifestyle. High-protein, low-carb diets create more waste products, which stress the body, and protein is not an efficient fuel source for a continuous energetic state.

Adaptive Thermogenesis

The term "adaptive thermogenesis" refers to the alteration in metabolism that occurs due to environmental, psychological, or other influences. Some of the possible factors affecting adaptive thermogenesis are unconscious or spontaneous movements or activities (i.e., a nervous knee), hormone levels, responses to changes in nutrient and caloric intake, adaptations to changes in ambient temperature, climate and emotional stress. The contribution of adaptive thermogenesis to total daily energy expenditure is considerably smaller by comparison to the other three primary factors.

Can You Eat Too Few Calories?

The runaway majority of the Lifestyle will speak of the overindulgences that are far too common in the civilized world. Is it possible to eat too few calories when trying to lose body fat and maintain or add muscle? Yes.

When you restrict calories, your RMR slows. The body perceives a caloric deficit as a form of famine; this is believed to be an adaptive process to prevent starvation. If you restrict calories too severely–with or without exercise–you may achieve the opposite of your intended goal of fat loss and muscle gain. You may lose muscle and add fat. You may become weaker and not stronger. You may lose muscle rather than gain it.

Muscles require adequate energy (calories) to grow. Muscles are a nutrient-dense source of fuel the body can use if caloric restriction is too severe. When exercise and portion control (calorie restriction) is overly restrictive, muscle is used as a fuel and nutrient source. Muscle wasting becomes enhanced because your body needs even greater fuel than if you were *not* exercising. Not consuming the calories necessary to sustain your total daily energy expenditure will not only cause the body to *not* grow more muscle, but will also use the very muscle you're trying to add to as a fuel source. This truly undesirable scenario occurs daily in thousands of dieters nationwide.

Below is an example of what occurs when exercise accompanies severe calorie restriction:

1. Exercise occurs without sufficient energy intake.

2. Body adapts to inadequate energy by lowering RMR.

3. Weight gain or increase in body fat percent occurs because of increased metabolic efficiency (the RMR is slowing).

4. The exerciser reduces energy intake further to maintain desired weight and/or body composition.

5. Metabolic rate is further compromised, reducing the amount of energy that can still be consumed.

Over-Restriction and Women

For women, the problems of severe calorie restriction continue. Restrained eating is also associated with ovulatory disturbances that are related to bone health. Today it is well accepted that low-energy intake highly correlates to amenorrhea (absence or abnormal stoppage of the menses) and oligomenorrhea (infrequent menstrual flow) and that, in this reduced estrogen environment, women are at increased risk for the development of early osteoporosis. Amenorrhea and associated problems of poor bone development or maintenance may increase the risk of stress fractures (Source: ACSM's Health & Fitness Journal).

For these reasons and more, I place a bottom limit (a floor) on caloric restriction so you do not succumb to eating inadequate calories.

> *I strongly urge anyone following the Lifestyle not to consume less than 50 percent of their RMR in any given day.*

In just a moment, you will determine what your RMR is by completing the provided formulas. You will also find another calculation that will allow you to quickly see the absolute minimum number of calories you should ever consume in a day.

Relative Caloric Deficit

In order to lose weight, a relative caloric deficit (RCD) must be created. It is "relative" because not all of the RCD is necessarily created from food restriction. The RCD may be accomplished by one of three ways:

1) Reduce calories below your total daily energy expenditure, or
2) Maintain caloric intake and increase vigorous activity, or
3) Simultaneously reduce caloric intake and increase activity.

Ideally, the RCD will be created by a combination of reducing the consumption of calorie-containing food and drink, and increasing vigorous exercise.

To lose one pound of "fat" you must create a 3500 calorie deficit. This means that after you have considered all of the factors affecting total daily energy expenditure as well as analyzed all of the calorie-containing food and drink you consumed, there must be a negative balance. Let me say it in a way you have likely heard before and might be more familiar with.

You have to burn more than you eat and drink!

If you are into the "details" of this, you might be scratching your head wondering why is it that to lose fat only a 3500-calorie deficit must be created, and not a 4086-calorie deficit. Good computation skills will show that one gram of fat contains nine calories and there are 454 grams in a pound, that one pound of adipose would contain 4086 calories (454 x 9) and not 3500. Adipose, the stored fat you are most desiring to lose is not composed solely of lipid. It is only about 87 percent lipid. The rest of adipose is water and a small amount of protein. Refigured as (454 x 0.87 = 394.98 x 9 = 3554.82), you can see that a pound of adipose really contains about 3555 calories. Again, for the sake of simplicity, everyone teaches and uses 3500 calories per pound of body fat.

How Much RCD From Food and How Much From Exercise?

If you would like to lose two pounds a week, it is simple to see that you must create a RCD of 7000 calories a week (2 x 3500). However, how much of this 7000 RCD should come from calorie reduction and how much should come from increased vigorous exercise? The answer differs for men and women.

First, I'll start with men since they are the easiest to deal with. I suggest that 50 to 80 percent of the RCD should come from food, and 20 to 50 percent of the RCD should come from exercise.

Contribution of food and exercise for the RCD in males
Food: 50 to 80 percent
Exercise: 20 to 50 percent

For women I must lay a few facts down to help them understand why they aren't treated quite the same as men when creating a RCD. There really are some good reasons for treating men and women differently but you can believe me when I say that I know the reasons won't necessarily make you ladies feel better just because they are true.

Women were chosen to be the life-carrying vessels to further the human race. Since your body doesn't have a clue that it is the 21st century and still thinks it is 80,000 B.C. when food wasn't always plentiful, the genes controlling fat storage and fat release are essentially the same now as they were tens of thousands of years ago. Unlike men, a woman's body believes it needs enough fat stored at any given time to survive periods of famine for at least nine months - to carry a fetus full term.

By comparison to men, when women create a caloric deficit, their metabolisms put the brakes on probably twice as hard. This means that for every 100 calories she pulls out of her nutritional program, her body may react, compared to a man, as though she were pulling 200 calories out. Every single person who restricts calories at all will evoke a slowdown of their metabolism. Most times this slow down is tolerable and able to be managed while fat loss is occurring. However, when women create a deficit from food that is overzealous or similar to their male friends, they may set off a hormonal cascade–that can truly apply the brakes–stronger than almost any application of the gas pedal (i.e., more caloric restriction and exercise) except starvation. Women may only lose a half-a-pound a week or less while exercising 600 minutes a week and eating 800 calories per day when the body perceives too great a deficit from food and slams on the hormonal brakes.

The solution to this problem is creating a greater percentage of the RCD from exercise than from food. This means most women, across the board, will have to exercise more than their male counterparts. It is the only true way to create significant weight loss while not decreasing calories too much. In keeping with what you now know is true I recommend women strive for only 30 to 60 percent of the RCD from food and 40 to 70 percent of the RCD from exercise. Further, I strongly urge no woman, unless advised by her medical doctor, to strive for a loss greater than two pounds per week.

Contribution of food and exercise for the RCD in females
Food: 30 to 60 percent
Exercise: 40 to 70 percent

As you work through the formulas to determine approximate caloric needs, an explanation to determine if your calorie reduction and exercise are in line with the Lifestyle guidelines is provided for both men and women.

Putting It All Together

With your new knowledge of what an RCD is and how many calories there are in each pound of body fat you'd like to shed, it's really easy to determine how much of an RCD you'll have to create to shed the excess fat. Here is where you pull this chapter all together and determine the estimated calories you will get to eat to achieve your goal. Two important factors will determine how many calories you will get to eat each day:

1. Amount of weight you desire to lose each week.
2. Number of minutes of vigorous exercise you put in each week.

Earlier we learned that to lose a pound of body fat, an RCD of 3500 calories must be created. From here on, I will discuss the RCD in terms of weekly (7 days) values and I will then show you how to determine the daily exercise and caloric requirements to achieve your goals.

Minimum and Maximum Weight Loss Each Week

I recommend setting a weight loss goal of 0.5 to 1.5 percent (or 2 total pounds, whichever is less) of your present body weight per week.

Determining the Minimum Goal Per Week
Weight: _____ x 0.005 = Minimum Weight Loss Each Week _____

Determining the Maximum Goal Per Week
Weight: _____ x 0.015 = Maximum Weight Loss Each Week _____
(Maximum weight loss should not exceed two pounds per week)

With these calculations it is easy to see that the less you weigh, the less weight you should plan to lose each week. Once you determine how much weekly weight loss is reasonable, you can determine how much of an RCD you will need.

Exercise Six Out of Every Seven Days

While you are progressing intensely through your transformation, I recommend exercising six out of every seven days, taking one full day off from any vigorous activity for recovery. This doesn't mean you can't go for a walk or do something fun while remaining active.

A Healthy Weight for You (reminder)

A standard height and weight chart is included in the appendix of this book. There is also another quick method to determine what is likely a healthy weight for you. Thickly muscled bodybuilders are not represented in the "healthy weight" guidelines below. While I cringe at what I'm about to say (because many heavy people mistakenly think they are "large framed"), I would be remiss if I didn't say that small-framed and large-framed men and women may be healthiest at a lower or higher weight than what these simple equations provide.

Men: 106 + 6 pounds for every inch you are over 5 feet tall
(Example: a 5'9" man is 9 inches taller than 5 feet. 9 x 6 = 54 + 106 = 160 pounds). If a man has been resistance training continuously for at least two years with no breaks longer than a week or two, he could likely use this formula: 106 + 7 to 8 pounds for every inch over 5 feet.

Women:105 + 5 pounds for every inch you are over 5 feet tall.
(Example: a 5'6" woman is 6 inches taller than 5 feet. 6 x 5 = 30 + 105 = 135 pounds). If a woman has been resistance training continuously for at least two years with no breaks longer than a week or two, she could likely use this formula: 105 + 6 to 7 pounds for every inch over 5 feet.

Step 1 - Determine an RCD.

Pounds You Desire to Lose Each Week: (A) _____   (B) 3500
Multiply (A) x (B):   (C) _____
(C) is the weekly RCD (If greater than 7,000 then use 7,000. Do not exceed an RCD greater than 7,000 calories per week)

Step 2 - Determine Your Daily RMR.

Female body weight: _____ x 12 = (D) _____
Multiply D x 0.5   (E) _____
Male body weight: _____ x 13 = (D) _____
Multiply D x .50   (E) _____
(D) represents your daily RMR
(E) represents the minimum number of calories you should ingest on a daily basis. You should never eat less than (E).

Step 3 - Determine Your Weekly RMR.

Multiply (D) x 7 and enter: (F) _____
(F) represents your weekly RMR

Step 4 - Determine How Much You Will Exercise and the Value of Exercise Credits.

How many minutes per week will you realistically train with vigorous exertion?
Enter vigorous exercise minutes per 7 days (week)   (G) _____
Multiply (G) x 8 if you are a woman and by 10 if a man   (H) _____
Divide (H) by (C) = (I)   (I) _____
(H) represents the total weekly caloric contribution of your intended exercise plan.
(I) represents the percentage (expressed as a decimal) that your exercise plan will contribute to the total deficit. (I) for men should be between 0.2 (20%) and 0.5 (50%). (I) for women should be between 0.4 (40%) and 0.7 (70%).

Important for Men! If (I) is less than 0.2 (0.00-0.19), then you either need to reduce your intended weight loss in pounds for each week or increase your vigorous exercise minutes for the week. If (I) is greater than 0.50 (0.51-0.99), then, unless you are a well-condtioned individual, you may be running the risk of overtraining if your intention is to exercise as much as (I) represents.

Important for Women! If (I) is less than 0.4 (0.00-0.39), then you either need to; reduce your intended weight loss in pounds for each week, or increase your vigorous exercise minutes for the week. If (I) is greater than 0.70 (0.71-0.99) then, unless you are a well-conditioned individual, you may be running the risk of over training if your intention is to exercise as much as (I) represents.

Step 5 - Determine Weekly Total Allowed Calories for Lifestyle Success.

Re-enter (F):   (F) _____
Re-enter (H):   (H) _____
Add (F) + (H):   (J) _____
Re-enter (C):   (C) _____
Subtract (C) from (J):   (K) _____
(K) represents the total estimated weekly calories you are allotted when you desire to lose weight at the rate of (A) _____ pounds per week while exercising (G) _____ minutes per week.

Step 6 - Determine Daily Total Allowed Calories for Lifestyle Success.

Divide (K) by 7:   (L) _____

(L) represents the total estimated daily calories you are allowed when you want to lose weight at the rate of (A) _____ pounds per week while exercising (G) _____ minutes per week.

Quick Recalculation

Now that you understand where the numbers are coming from, I feel comfortable allowing you to quickly re-evaluate your goals by showing you the quick way to come up with the numbers for the equation. Simply repeat steps 5 and 6 by using the following quick calculations for the proper matching letter.

Men

(F) Body weight x 91

(H) Vigorous exercise minutes x 10

(C) Number of pounds you want to lose each week x 3500 (Should not exceed 7000 total)

Women

(F) Body weight x 84

(H) Vigorous exercise minutes x 8

(C) Number of pounds you want to lose each week x 3500 (Should not exceed 7000 total)

Zig Zagging

Zig Zagging refers to the daily increase or decrease of calories from the target average calories per day. In regards to zig zagging, I am taking a gross departure from what I said in version 3 of The Leanness Lifestyle. I found that too many people were placing too much emphasis on zig zagging, and not enough emphasis on their fork and exercise. If I had to put a figure on the importance of zig zagging compared to paying attention to total calories in vs. total calories out, I'd say zig zagging is about as important as taking a thermogenic dietary supplement (about a 0.1 to 1 percent benefit max for weight loss if you don't include benefits of muscle retention). If you compare your Lifestyle to a fine automobile, zig zagging can be thought of by using this analogy:

> *If the tires of your fine automobile are supposed to be inflated to 32 pounds per square inch for maximum fuel mileage and safety, and they only contain 30 or 31 pounds, you are probably only going to notice a minute difference in performance and fuel mileage. However, if you have a flat tire, you are not going anywhere at all.*

Zig zagging = tires at 30-31 pounds vs. the recommended 32 pounds per square inch.
Calories in and Calories out = flat tire

Obviously, the focus should be on calories in/calories out rather than zig zagging. Do not believe that there is something mystical or magical about the zig zag. Zig zagging will not fix your "broken metabolism," because your metabolism is not broken.

Zig zagging can still be used to build in a day that includes a splurge meal, however, I don't recommend that any one day be lower than your average daily caloric target multiplied by 0.80 nor greater than your average daily caloric target multiplied by 1.4. This means that if your daily average (represented by [L] from the equation in step 6) is 2000, you shouldn't eat less than 1600 calories on any day (2000 x 0.8) nor more than 2800 calories on any day (2000 x 1.4). Eating excessively low calories on multiple days per week just so you can consume a massive quantity of food in your splurge meal only sets up cravings and excessive water retention for days after the splurge. Further, excessive low-calorie days are not advantageous for retaining skeletal muscle or for maintaining optimal energy levels for those days.

Use the following guidelines to set up a seven-day schedule so you can enjoy a nice splurge meal. Pick two to three of the seven days and reduce the daily average by 10 to 20 percent. With this reduction, you will have plenty of calories for your splurge meal one day each week. Here is how it might work:

Average Daily Calories = 2000
Shouldn't go below 1600 (2000 x 0.8).
Shouldn't go above 2800 (2000 x 1.4).

Day 1	Day 2	Day 3	Day 4	Day 5	Day 6	Day 7
2000	1800	2000	1600	2600	2000	2000

Total for Week = 14,000 (average of 2000 per day).

Tom Follows the Lifestyle to Healthy Weight Loss

Thirty-eight year old Tom decides he is tired of being fat and tired all the time and wants to drop some body fat with the Lifestyle. After reading the chapter on Weight and using the simple formula in this chapter, he determines that an approximate "ideal" weight for his 5'10" frame would be about 175 pounds. He currently weighs 235 pounds. While glossing over this book he stumbles upon this chapter and decides he will take a stab at calculating the number of calories he will be able to eat to start the weight-loss process.

Tom first determines that his healthy weight loss range is between 1.1 (235 x 0.005) and 3.5 (235 x 0.015) pounds per week when he uses the 0.5-1.5 percent method. However, he quickly sees that 3.5 pounds per week is greater than the recommended upper limit of 2 pounds per week and adjusts his healthy weight loss range to between 1.1 and 2 pounds per week. Being impatient and wanting to shed 15 years of overindulgence as soon as possible, Tom decides to shoot for the full 2 pounds of weight loss per week for his first few weeks. Tom then simply follows the steps I have provided in this chapter and does the math.

In Step 1, Tom determines his RCD (represented by [C] in step 1) is 7000 (2 x 3500).

In Step 2, Tom sees that his RMR (represented by [D] in step 2) is 3055 (235 x 13). He also sees that the minimum number of calories he should consume on any given day (represented by [E] in step 2), is 1528 (3055/2).

In Step 3, Tom calculates his weekly RMR (represented by [F] in step 3) as 21,385 (3055 x 7).

In Step 4, Tom thinks long and hard about what is possible and what he is willing to commit to for vigorous exercise each week. At this point, he determines that he will do three resistance-training workouts for 30 minutes each for a total of 90 minutes per week of vigorous exercise.This just "feels" about right to Tom. Tom is aware that his workouts need to be vigorous. He is also aware of my definition of vigorous exercise. With this information, Tom then calculates the value of his exercise plan (represented by [H] in step 4) as 900 (90 x 10) calories for the week. He decides the percent of his weight loss that will come from exercise (represented by [I] in step 4) and he sees right away that it is 0.13 (900 / 7000). As he reads on, he notices that as a man anything less than 0.20 will require a decision whether to reduce his weight-loss goal or increase exercise for the week. In this case, Tom decides he will begrudgingly add in 30 minutes of aerobic activity and also back off the weight loss to 1.5 pounds a week.

Tom's goal now is to lose 1.5 pounds per week instead of 2. Additionally, because he has wisely chosen to add in 30 minutes of aerobic activity he has raised his exercise credits from 900 for the week to 1200 (120 x 10). Tom's new RCD (step 1) is 5250 calories (1.5 x 3500) a week and no longer the 7000 (2 x 3500) RCD needed when he wanted to lose two pounds a week. He then jumps back to step 4 and sees that when he divides 1200 by 5250 he gets a decimal of 0.23 (1200 / 5250), again (represented by [I] in step 4). He is overjoyed that at 1.5 pounds of weight loss per week, his exercise contribution (120 minutes a week) falls in line with Lifestyle suggestions.

In Step 5, Tom gets to use the values he has already calculated to determine his weekly caloric allotment (represented by [K] in step 5). Here is how he does it:

He re-enters (F):	(F) 21,385
He re-enters (H):	(H) 1200
He adds (F) + (H):	(J) 22,585
He re-enters (C):	(C) 5250
He subtracts (C) from (J):	(K) 17,335

He sees that (K) is 17,335, wonders what that has to do with anything at all, and why he ever bothered with this calculation.

In Step 6, Tom sees that the total calories he gets to eat each day (represented by [L] in step 6) is 2476 (17,335 / 7). He sighs, actually catches himself saying "Finally!" and knows that he must adhere to his plan to achieve his goal of two pounds of weight loss that week. Because he took the time to go through the process, he knows his weight loss for that week will be reasonable and safe. He also knows that his exercise contribution falls right in line with Lifestyle suggestions (20 to 50 percent of the RCD). The next step for Tom is to log his foods (see Chapter 7) and not reduce less than 2476 calories a day by more than 20 percent (1981) or over by more than 40 percent (3466). After seven days of food logging has been completed, Tom is aware that his total calories for seven days should not exceed 17,335 (represented by "K").

Julie Follows the Lifestyle to Healthy Weight Loss

Thirty-one year old Julie decides she is tired of never having anything to wear and always shopping in the Plus department. She wants to drop at least two dress sizes with the Lifestyle. After reading the chapter on Weight and using the simple formula in this chapter she determines that an approximate "ideal" weight for her 5'5" frame would be about 130 pounds. Currently, she weighs 165 pounds. While glossing over this book, Julie stumbles upon this chapter and decides she'll take a stab at calculating the number of calories she'll be able to consume in order to start the weight-loss process.

Julie first determines that her healthy weight loss range is between 0.8 (165 x 0.005) and 2.5 (165 x 0.015) pounds per week by using the 0.5-1.5 percent method. However, she realizes I suggest not losing more than two pounds per week and alters her healthy weight loss range to between 0.8 and 2. Being impatient and wanting to shed a decade of overindulgence as soon as possible, Julie decides to shoot for the full two pounds of weight loss per week for her first few weeks. Julie then simply follows the steps I have provided in this chapter and does the math.

In Step 1, Julie determines her RCD (represented by [C] in step 1) is 7000 (2 x 3500).

In Step 2, Julie sees that her RMR (represented by [D] in step 2) is 1980 (165 x 12). She also sees that the minimum number of calories she should consume on any given day (represented by [E] in step 2) is 990 (1980 / 2).

In Step 3, Julie calculates her weekly RMR (represented by [F] in step 3) as 13,860 (1980 x 7).

In Step 4, Julie thinks long and hard about what's possible and what she's willing to commit to for vigorous exercise each week. She has already been working out quite a bit, but has not seen the scale moving down in weeks. She settles on doing three resistance-training workouts for 40 minutes each and three cardio sessions at 30 minutes each (a total of 210 minutes a week). This is about what she has already been doing and she is comfortable with this plan. Julie is aware that her workouts need to be vigorous. Julie calculates the value of her exercise plan (represented by [H] in step 4) as 1680 (210 x 8) calories for the week. Next, she decides what percent of her weight loss is going to come from exercise (represented by [I] in step 4). Right away she notices that it is 0.24 (1680 / 7000). As she reads on, she notices that anything less than 0.40 as a woman will require a decision to reduce her weight-loss goal or increase exercise for the week. In this case, Julie sees she'll have to reduce her expected loss each week or increase her vigorous exercise minutes rather substantially. She decides to try a little of both to create the healthy weight loss the Lifestyle teaches. Julie decides to split her body parts up differently for resistance training, thus adding in another 30 minutes per week of resistance exercise. She also decides to add in another 25 minutes of aerobic exercise as well for a total of 55 additional minutes per week of exercise. She also decides to back off her expected weight loss to 1.5 pounds instead of 2 thus reducing her total RCD required from 7000 to 5250 (1.5 x 3500). She wonders if this half-pound difference per week will really matter and decides to plug in the numbers again and see.

Since Julie was willing to increase her vigorous exercise minutes for the week (from 210 to 265) she recalculated step 4 and now she sees that her total exercise contribution is 3120 (265 x 8), (represented by [H]), and represents 40 percent (2120 / 5250), (represented by [I]), of the total RCD. This new information allows her to feel better by knowing her numbers are correct and she is following the Lifestyle.

In Step 5, Julie gets to use the values she's already calculated to determine her weekly caloric allotment (represented by [K] in step 5). Here is how she does it:

She re-enters (F):	(F) 13,860
She re-enters (H):	(H) 2120
She adds (F) + (H):	(J) 15,980
She re-enters (C):	(C) 5250
She subtracts (C) from (J):	(K) 10,730

Upon finishing, she notices that (K) is 10,730 and wonders what this number has to do with anything at all, and why she ever bothered with this calculation.

In Step 6, Julie sees that the total calories she gets to eat each day (represented by [L] in step 6) is 1532 (10,730 / 7). Julie is happy with her 1532 average calories per day and decides to continue the process using the zig zag method so she can build in her splurge meal for the week.

Her first week looked like this:

Day 1	Day 2	Day 3	Day 4	Day 5	Day 6	Day 7
1532	1379	1532	1379	1379	1992	1532

Total for Week = 10,725 (average of 1532 per day).

Managing the 80-Percent-of-Average Days (Low-Cal Days)

Coaching client Tiffany wrote:

"Today was my low-cal day - 1152 calories divided by 6 meals. I do not like it, but it has gotten easier for me to deal with over the last few weeks (I am in week 4 of LL). Here are a couple of things that I do to help get through it.

1. It seems to have gotten easier if I do not focus on it being a low-cal day. I just eat a small meal and have about 16 ounces of water, and then I know I get to eat again in 2 to 3 hours or so. I focus on my next meal...not on the "few" calories I get to eat.

2. I drink a lot of water...especially if I start to get hungry. Today, I had nearly 11 glasses of water at 16 ounces each.

3. I think to myself that "the nice thing is, it is just one day out of my life each week - not so bad, and I can do that." I also consider it my tradeoff for my high-cal day; this helps to put it in perspective.

4. For meals, I may have an apple and a protein shake.... or some non-fat yogurt and a protein shake. These things are light in calories and hold me for that 2 to 3 hour period...downing lots of water as the hunger sets in around 1 hour 45 minutes to 2 hours.

5. A mental thing I started doing today was thinking that as I got hungry, I could almost visualize and feel my body calling on my fat reserves and using them up for energy.

6. I do not do my low-cal day on a lifting day.

7. When the day is over, think back and think to yourself "that wasn't as bad as I thought it would be" that way, you kind of set yourself up mentally for it not being such a big deal the next time. Mentally, if we do not make it a big deal, then it will not be one.

8. Stay very busy so that you do not focus on the "lack of food".

Any Calorie Can Make You Fat

In the 80s, there was a huge push for the development of low-fat and fat-free foods. Today in 2002, there is a huge push for high-protein, low-carb foods. What is the rationale behind each push, and is there any validity to either?

> *Whenever you eat more calories than your body can use, the extra calories you eat will be stored as fat. This goes for protein, carbohydrate and fat.*

In the 1980s, our government and other so-called experts projected to the American public that if you reduced fat intake you would lose weight. It was a nice thought. Since gram for gram, fat is more than twice as calorically dense as carbohydrate or protein, there was no way it should have failed. With hindsight, we know it did fail. The real message, which was one of energy balance, portion, and calorie control, got lost in the marketing of low-fat and fat-free foods. Consumers ate less fat overall, but gobbled up so much of the lower-fat and fat-free products, they ended up consuming more total calories each day than before they switched to the lower-fat products. The Lifestyle promotes a relatively low-fat food plan, but also stresses balanced meals whenever possible. Even though I stress a low-fat plan that is fully balanced, the same risks for overconsumption of calories exist if you do not pay attention to your numbers. Energy balance, meal balance, and meal frequency are the critical keys to consider. America has not focused on this, and 20 years after the low-fat product push, America is fatter than ever.

- You can eat nothing but lard (pure fat) and lose weight as long as your total caloric intake of lard is less than your total daily energy expenditure. Lard contains no protein or carbohydrate.

- You can eat nothing but table sugar and lose weight if your total caloric intake of sugar is less than your total daily energy expenditure. Sugar contains no protein or fat.

- You can eat only egg white protein and get as big as a barn, even though egg white protein contains essentially no carbohydrates and no fat.

These statements may run counterintuitive to what you have believed until this very moment. If this is the case, then I must point out that myths die hard. I know this. You are probably still a little skeptical about these statements. Once again, a choice has to be made: you can open your mind and shift your position or remain where you are today.

You might be saying to yourself "I thought it was the fat that made me fat." Nope. "It must have been the extra protein I've been eating." Nope. "I know those dang carbs are what's making me fat." Nope. You are fat because the combination of carbohydrate, protein, fat *and alcohol* you have been consuming have been providing more calories than you need for total daily energy expenditure. Your body has been conditioned to store the additional energy quite efficiently. You have been eating as if there was going to be a famine. Even if you do not consider yourself a big eater, you have been eating more than your fair share. Your body has been protecting you from a famine that will never occur. Your body is simply reacting to what you are feeding it. Over time, your body has slowly added fat weight and it will continue to do so unless you break the cycle and finally gain control over your energy balance.

Stuck Low-Carbers Today No Different Than Stuck Low-fatters of the 1980s

Like arachnophobia (the fear of spiders) and acrophobia (the fear of heights), carbophobia (the fear of carbohydrates) should receive its own psychological classification in the diagnostic and statistical manual of mental disorders. Low-carbing has reached epidemic proportions. Twenty years after we heard half the story about how we would get skinny if we would only switch to low-fat and fat-free foods, far too many people today are now living in fear of sugars and all carbohydrates. Given a nickel for every person I know who falsely believes that carbs are evil, would have long ago made me a rich man!

A current and predominant thinking among millions of dieters is that the best way to lose fat is to cut carbs. Men or women—it makes no difference. As I discussed in the *Nutrients* chapter, for the active person engaging in vigorous exercise, low-carb eating can reduce vigor and leave you feeling lethargic. I've coached many clients who cut carbs too much and guess what happens? Their energy goes down, fat loss slows or stops, and they can't figure out why. What do they do? They further cut carbs and calories. Oops, that didn't work either. Now what?

The protein-only dieters and super low-carb dieters nearly go into convulsions when they look at a food they'd like to try and they see it has 12 to 20 grams of sugars per serving. "Oh my goodness, whatever will I do? I am not buying that crap! I'll buy the low-carb food because I know that'll help me get ripped!" Give me a break! As much as we were duped by marketers and refused to listen to the entire message about energy balance in the 80s, people today are being duped into thinking that carbs are the problem. The truth is, unless you are not exercising at all, you need adequate carbs, and you should not necessarily run and hide from a food just because it has 20 grams of sugars.

Low-Carb Dieting–For Most a Diet, Not a Lifestyle

Low-carb diets can certainly provide a means to creating a caloric deficit. The way they are followed, however, and not even necessarily promoted, is usually counterproductive for health and an energetic state. Low-carb diets are also often high in artery-clogging saturated fat and short on nutrient-rich fruits and vegetables.

If you eat a meal full of fat (e.g., a bacon and egg breakfast) and it provides satiety (satisfies your hunger) for a longer period than what is normal for you, you will not be looking for the next snack as soon. If you are slimming down on a diet of bacon and butter, it is not because you have reset your metabolism as some diet gurus would claim. The truth is, people on low-carb diets average only 1414 calories a day, whereas the typical American who has not heard of the Lifestyle downs

2200 or more. With what you know right now, what do you think will happen if you eat a bacon and egg breakfast, a hamburger lunch (hold the bread, of course) and a polish sausage supper, if your calories ultimately are less than your body needs to live? You will lose weight.

Many of the low-carb diets are ketogenic. In the simplest terms, Lyle McDonald, author of *The Ketogenic Diet*, states that a ketogenic diet is essentially a diet where less than 75 grams of carbohydrate are consumed on a daily basis. While I do not promote ketogenic dieting I do not buy into the scare that eating a high-fat or high-protein ketogenic diet is harmful to your health. When a ketogenic diet is followed as precisely as some plans call for, there is little evidence supporting the idea that eating high-fat, high-protein foods in the near absence of carbohydrates is going to be the killer the high-carb promoters suggest. The evidence is just not strong enough to show that a ketogenic diet is harmful for most otherwise healthy, but obese, people. However, in the real world there are far too many people still mixing those high-fat, high-protein foods with sugary carbohydrates. This spells obesity, cardiovascular disease, stroke and diabetes.

A major reason people love low-carb diets is because initial weight loss is quick. The carbohydrate levels in them are so low that muscle starts breaking down muscle glycogen (a stored carb) so the body can fuel normal cellular functions. Every gram of stored glycogen in muscle has three grams of water attached to it. Therefore, when glycogen is broken down to fuel the body and muscular movement, water leaves with it. This will show up on a scale as weight loss, most of which is initially water. For some, this water-weight loss can amount to 7 to 10 pounds in one week. Anyone would love to lose 7 to 10 pounds in a week! That is, until they have no energy for workouts and they resume eating carbohydrate foods again. Their carbohydrate-starved bodies use the sugars as an energy source, but during the first 48 hours also stores as much of the sugar as possible as glycogen. As I have already said, water is attached to glycogen at a ratio of 3:1. What do you think happens to the dieter's body weight when they resume eating carbs again? It shoots right back up! Unless they have truly created a caloric deficit over the duration of the low-carb diet and lost fat weight, they may binge their way to a bigger, fatter body than before when carbohydrates are reintroduced.

Carbophobia

What follows are some real-life examples of statements from clients I have personally coached. I am sharing them with you so that if you see yourself in any of these statements, you can choose to stop the madness and come to grips with the reality of energy balance as opposed to seeking a low-carb miracle.

Example 1: Sugars in energy bars are scary?

"My final question is about the Opti-Pro Bars you recommended - the Peanut Butter in particular you mentioned. Although I have not tried that yet, the Blueberry Muffin is excellent as well. Noting the macronutrients, the 40 g of carbs are made up largely of sugars. Does this pose any threat to insulin spikes or such?"

This client's definition of "largely" was 38 percent because the Opti-Pro Meal Peanut Crunch bars by Optimum Nutrition contain 15 grams of sugars out of 40 total grams of carbohydrates. As I explained to this client, I consumed at least one of these bars a day as I prepared for my last bodybuilding competition. I competed at 4.8 percent body fat.

Example 2: This person's carbs are less than 100 grams per day, 4 out of 7 days a week! I also might add, this person is exercising like a madman.

"But the days are ROUGH - since I work out first thing in the morning, that's my "last gasp" and then it's swimming upstream all day - get that heavy weight around my eyelids, kind of feel like I'm sleep walking, that type of thing. I am getting through, the issue is not sticking to the nutrition plan or anything else, and it is the lack of progress. Carbs are low - I have most of my carbs on training days and then the bulk of them before/after training. So non-training days are really a drag. I'm not going low enough to kick into ketosis."

As I explained to this client, even if he had not told me how he was feeling, it would have been completely predictable. Can you guess why his eyelids were hanging all day? Through the vigorous exercise he was engaging in, he had drained his liver and muscles of glycogen and did not have enough available carbohydrate to fuel the brain optimally.

Example 3: The dangers of fruit consumption?

"Okay, about Fruits and Veggies. I am pretty picky. I do eat green beans sometimes, and peas, and broccoli and asparagus, and salads. I do love fruits, too. But a few different times I have heard that they are too high in sugar and I should not have them to lose fat. So what the heck? I cut-em out. I am used to that since I did Atkins for 6 months."

Even though the fruits were eliminated, this member was still "stuck" and had not lost weight in weeks. Hmmm - maybe it was not the fruit after all.

Example 4: Here is a nice goal for ya–eliminate sugars and then life will be good. Not REDUCE, but ELIMINATE sugars.

"Hi David, My goals for this 8 week cycle: I want to increase strength by 10%, therefore increasing muscle mass. Lose 2% body fat; eliminate sugar (you know this has been the hard thing for me.) I am taking Citrimax to help with the cravings and I have just about totally given up diet coke!"

Amazing as it may seem eliminating sugars was not high on my list of recommendations for this person. He wanted to increase strength by 10 percent, but eliminate sugars, too. This is like saying you want to earn six figures a year but do not want to work. It is putting oil and water together. It does not mix!

Example 5: Oh yeah, and let's make sure you NEVER eat carbs after 6pm too, because don't you know it's well documented that eating carbs after 6pm will KILL all chances of fat loss.

"One other thing, I'm pretty sure that right now I'm not getting enough carbs daily, any good advice on which foods are good to eat to add carbs, but not fat? Right now I get carbs from oatmeal at breakfast, some veggies at mid-morning, yogurt and wheat bread at lunch, and some from a meal replacement powder at mid-afternoon. I try to eat a dinner with little or no carbs since I have to eat so late, around 8 pm, (is that too late for a meal?) due to getting home so late because of my workout schedule."

Is it difficult to believe this person was stuck? I mean, after all, they do not eat carbs late at night and they do not eat ANYTHING after 8 pm. Gee, what could be preventing them from losing more body fat? Perhaps it is more a matter of energy balance.

Example 6: Taking things to extremes.

"Perhaps others are like me in their "fear" of carbs - having gone through Body for Life (BFL), Phillips mentions many times the dangers carbs pose for most Americans. They eat all of the fat-free foods and wonder why they are fat - because they overeat the fat-free foods, often rich in carbs. Perhaps Phillips stresses this too much, but I suspect others are careful of carbs, due in part to his book. In addition, since carbs are more easily converted to fats than protein, they do make me think before taking them in."

Well, it's good to think about any macronutrient before chowing it down but to be so hung up on carbs is unhealthy and propagates the myth that carbs are the root of fatness in America. This is simply untrue.

Overconsumption of *everything* is the cause of obesity in America. Let's be honest. We Americans can be gluttonous pigs!

It is hard to think in terms of moderation and balance, but if you truly want to shed the weight and live the Lifestyle forever, you have to begin thinking in these terms now. Do not "Well, yeah but" yourself into a corner you cannot escape. Be realistic with the decisions you make, and acknowledge the problem behaviors you need to focus on. Here are some common "Well, yeah but" examples I often hear:

> "Well, yeah but, I like pizza."
> "Well, yeah but, there's just so much good food all around us."
> "Well, yeah but, I am busy and have to rely on fast food daily."
> "Well, yeah but, the people I live with eat like total crap and I feel obligated to eat like they do so I don't offend them."
> "Well, yeah but, how can anyone resist all the cookouts and beer-swilling parties that are all around?"

"Well, yeah but, I eat 2 boxes of fat-free cookies (just like they say) and then have a 3/4 lb. burger, 44 ounces of regular Coke® with cheese and fries and pie. If I follow the guidelines half way won't it still work?"

"Well, yeah but, you just don't understand how busy I am."

"Well, yeah but, I have to keep snacks for the kids. I mean, why should I punish them for me being fat?"

"Well, yeah but, I'm just so hungry when I come home. I mean, starving yourself isn't good for building muscle, right?"

I don't want to be accused of exposing a problem with no solutions. Allow me to leave you with some maxims that will certainly help put anyone on the path to choosing better carbohydrate sources, achieving better health and a leaner body:

- Eat more fresh veggies.
- Eat more fresh fruits.
- Eat more whole-grains.
- Eat less processed and packaged foods.
- Follow and live the Lifestyle.

The Real Fear

- Do not fear carbs! Fear the processed bottom-feeder, toxic waste that barely passes a government inspection. Fear the overconsumption of any calorie-containing product (carbs, proteins, fats and alcohol).
- Fear imbalance.
- Fear the elimination of whole food groups.
- Fear fad diets.
- Fear teaching your children how to do everything to an extreme (Atkins).
- Fear having such a lack of control in your own life that your children follow suit.
- Fear looking like everyone else.
- Fear dying a very old person at a very young age.
- Fear forcing your relatives to watch and care for you as you suffer in agony during your last ten years of life due to the nutrition and exercise choices you make today.

If these maxims are the only benefit you get from this chapter, then you are still ahead of the game. I am in full agreement with a recent report from the U.S. Department of Agriculture. It stated, "Caloric balance (calories in vs. calories out), rather than macronutrient composition, is the major determinant of weight loss." There are all kinds of things to fear–carbohydrates should not really top the list. If you take things to extremes–stop it!

Fasting–Starvation on Purpose

For religious and other reasons, some believe fasting is healthy and beneficial for weight loss. Some use fasting to create what they believe is an inner strength or power that cannot be achieved through eating. I disagree, and believe fasting should be left to those who do not know better. After this section, you will know better too.

Absorption of nutrients from the intestines takes two to four hours. After this period, dietary glucose becomes unavailable and your body relies more on glucose from endogenous (within the body) sources. You need glucose at all times! Your body will provide it one way or another.

A few hours into fasting, insulin levels drop and glucagon levels rise. Glucagon assists with the breakdown of glycogen (stored carbs) and the creation of glucose. For those interested in maximum performance and the maintenance and development of skeletal muscle, wouldn't the loss of muscle glycogen be considered a negative? Yes, it is. Losing excessive muscle glycogen is something you want to avoid. Fasting causes excessive loss of muscle glycogen.

Since insulin becomes low, lipolysis (breaking down fat for fuel) is highly active and free fatty acids (FFA) are liberated from adipose for energy. The heart and other tissues begin to use FFA as a primary fuel source more so than before fasting. When FFAs are becoming a more predominant fuel source, glucose takes a back seat and–except in the brain, central nervous system and red blood cells–is no longer the predominant fuel source. The body reduces glucose utilization in most other tissues to ensure the brain has what it needs to function normally. To ensure that the brain has the glucose it needs, the body will produce what it needs, however, and glucose is used minimally in the body by other tissues and organs that do not critically need it.

Glucagon continues to break down glycogen stores in the liver and skeletal muscle. Liver glycogen stores can only last about 16 to 24 hours. After liver glycogen stores are depleted, circulating glucose is produced from something called gluconeogenesis. Gluconeogenesis is the production of glucose from non-carbohydrate sources. During early fasting, proteins in the liver increasingly break down. After a few hours, however, the breakdown of proteins outside the liver occurs to provide amino acids for gluconeogenesis. To produce about 100 grams of glucose, your body needs about 175 grams of amino acids. All proteins in the body have a function, and the loss of protein to provide energy is accompanied by a loss of functional capacity.

A 70 kg human (154 pounds) could live for over a month with only minimal fluids and vitamins, so how is this accomplished? During a short-term fasting, amino acids are used readily to produce glucose, but after a few days of fasting, the rate of gluconeogenesis from amino acids must slow if body protein is to be preserved. The body is concerned with preservation of proteins. They are precious! The body adapts and begins to manufacture ketone bodies. What you need to know about ketones for this discussion is that ketone bodies help spare protein loss after a few days into fasting. Keep in mind that ketone bodies really become effective *after a few* days of fasting.

With a one-day fast, you have little protection against skeletal protein losses. You will feel weaker, and you will actually become weaker. This weakness results from too little overall energy, and skeletal muscle being used as a fuel source to create glucose. Skeletal muscle will give up two amino acids primarily: glutamine and alanine. There is some release of most amino acids from muscle for gluconeogenesis during fasting. This is precisely the wrong scenario to create.

I will not kid anyone here. I am not a "fasting guru" in the sense of purposely practicing it myself. I do understand what happens in the body when you fast, especially with regard to where fuel is derived from. I do not give credence to the idea of giving up amino acids from skeletal muscle to fuel gluconeogenesis. You have worked too hard for the little muscle you have. You also should not care to give up over 50 percent of the amino acids as glutamine and alanine. A loss of glutamine from skeletal muscle has been associated with catabolic conditions. Yes, fasting is catabolic. What a shame with all those hours spent in the gym.

Maybe my colon would appreciate my fasting, and perhaps I'd feel at one with the universe, but I'll have to take a rain check until someone proves to me I won't lose any skeletal muscle during the process. I work too hard for what I have, and I will have to take care of my colon and inner peace with a healthier, higher fiber intake via better selection of carbohydrates. I will take up meditation or something. I am not going to fast. You should not either.

Yo-Yo Dieting

When you restrict your food intake, your resting metabolic rate (RMR) falls initially about ten percent in an attempt to conserve energy because it assumes that food is in short supply. However, this decrease is not permanent; the body adapts to the reduced food intake and the RMR increases within one to two weeks. In any case, it returns to its original level once normal eating is resumed. Hence, it is a myth that dieting slows down your metabolism in the long term.

Dieting, Exercise and Metabolic Rate

It has been suggested that exercise will help prevent this drop in RMR, however, studies have reported mixed findings. Some have found that exercise prevents or minimizes the reduction in RMR with dieting; others have found that exercise decreases RMR even more than dieting alone. To settle the debate, US researchers have recently analyzed the methods and results from 22 studies. The majority of studies involved women between ages 31 and 45 years who were fed a relatively low-fat, high-carbohydrate diet of less than 1200 kcal a day. The main prescribed exercise program was aerobic in nature: 31 to 60 minutes in duration, moderate intensity (51 to 70 percent of VO2 max) and performed 4 to 5 days a week.

A summary of the results of the analysis is as follows:

1. The RMR decreases significantly when an individual embarks on a diet or on a diet plus exercise program.
2. The drop in RMR with diet alone is significantly greater than with diet plus exercise.
3. Combining diet with a moderate intensity exercise program prevents some of the decrease in the RMR.
4. The size of the drop in RMR varies from one person to another. In general, the heaviest people experience the greatest drop in RMR. (This is most probably due to the fact that they experience the greatest deficit between calorie intake and output). When the results are expressed per kg of fat-free mass, the drop in RMR for diet plus exercise is relatively small, and less than that observed for diet only. What is interesting to discover is that the RMR expressed per kg body weight returns to pre-dieting values for both types of treatment. Essentially, the RMR does not stay permanently lower after dieting with or without exercise.

The previous studies on metabolic rate and dieting have produced variable results. According to the researchers who analyzed the data, this is due to differences in methods used and to poor reliability of RMR measurements. The researchers suggest a number of mechanisms to explain why exercise diminishes the drop in RMR with dieting:

1. Exercise prevents loss of lean tissue associated with dieting and therefore helps maintain RMR. Indeed, the results of the analysis show that the diet-only groups lost a greater percentage of lean weight (25 percent of weight loss) than the diet plus exercise group (17 percent of weight loss).
2. Exercise has a carryover effect on RMR, sometimes called an afterburn, causing it to remain elevated for awhile after exercise.

Is Yo-Yo Dieting Harmful?

The Lifestyle is not a diet. A diet is something you do to lose weight but which you know you will not stick with forever. While dieting usually produces short-term weight loss, most people regain that lost weight within a year. As a result, they begin another diet and so the cycle continues. According to research at Nottingham University, 40 percent of women embark on a diet two or more times a year. Is this "yo-yo" dieting harmful to health?

It has been suggested that yo-yo dieting leads to a drop in the metabolic rate, increase in percent body fat and an increased difficulty in achieving weight loss in the future. Exactly what are these suggestions based on?

The research to prove these negative effects of yo-yo dieting is a little inconsistent at this time, and the exact mechanism is unclear. In an attempt to clarify the issues relating to yo-yo dieting, the National Institute of Health (NIH) in the United States commissioned a panel of experts to review the evidence as part of the National Task Force on the prevention and treatment of obesity. They examined the methods and results of 43 studies. Their findings are summarized below.

Yo-Yo Research

Early studies with lab animals reported that repeated dieting caused a slowdown in the body's resting metabolic rate, making the body more efficient in storing food energy and reducing the amount of energy used in heat production. The theory was that once you stopped dieting, you would regain weight (fat) more readily, because your body needed fewer calories. Future attempts to lose weight would be harder because you would need to cut calories even further.

However, this theory is not supported by scientific evidence in humans. Most human studies show no relationship between number of dieting attempts and ability to lose weight. A study in 1990 found that yo-yo dieting produced no change in metabolic rate—just the opposite of popular belief!

The NIH concluded that there is no evidence that fluctuations in body weight produce a decrease in the metabolic rate.

Yo-Yo Dieting and Body Fat

It has been suggested that yo-yo dieting causes an increase in body fat stores, especially around the abdominal region, which in turn, increases the risk of heart disease. However, most studies have found no difference in body fat distribution between yo-yo dieters and non-yo-yo dieters. Other researchers have suggested that repeated dieting causes a loss of lean body mass (muscle and organ tissue), but again this has not been proven significant.

The NIH panel concluded that there is no evidence that yo-yo dieting causes an increased storage of body fat around the abdomen. They also said that there is no proof that yo-yo dieting has an adverse effect on body composition or on future attempts to lose weight successfully.

Yo-Yo Dieting and Heart Disease

Repeated weight fluctuations have been linked with an increased risk of heart disease, secondary diabetes, gall bladder disease and premature death. In 1991 studies carried out at Baltimore University in the United States concluded that the risks of repeated weight fluctuations are equivalent to the risks of being severely overweight.

A study of Harvard graduates found that those individuals whose weight had fluctuated by 10 kg (22 pounds) or more over 30 years had a significantly greater risk of death than those whose weight had remained relatively stable. This, researchers propose, may be due to increases in blood pressure, blood glucose levels, insulin levels, reduced glucose tolerance, increased risk of secondary (non-insulin dependent diabetes), increased blood fats or blood cholesterol.

The NIH panel has carefully examined the methods used in these studies and found that in the majority of studies there is no clear risk of heart disease or premature death associated with yo-yo dieting. They did concede however that some studies have shown that yo-yo dieting increases risk. They made no firm conclusions on this area.

Yo-Yo Dieting and Self-esteem

Yo-yo dieting can be bad for your morale and psychological health. Each time you regain weight, you experience a sense of failure that can lead to lowered confidence and self esteem. Indeed, many people have found that repeated dieting and weight gain causes a negative psychological state, depression and a sense of failure. Unfortunately, very few studies have been carried out on the psychological effects of yo-yo dieting and the NIH recommends that more research is devoted to this area.

Yo-Yo Dieting Conclusions

In conclusion, studies to date show that moderate intensity exercise performed 31 to 60 minutes a day, for 4 to 5 days a week, can reduce some of the decrease in RMR with dieting. However, more research is needed to ascertain the ideal type, intensity and duration of exercise or the ideal calorie intake. Including exercise can minimize the drop in RMR resulting from dieting. Both aerobic and strength training should be included. Aerobic exercise will increase calorie expenditure and cause a small carryover effect on RMR. Strength training will maintain or increase muscle mass and, therefore, increase total calorie expenditure.

Calorie intake should be reduced only modestly. See the guidelines I have provided in this chapter to determine how much of a caloric deficit you should choose. The combined result is a faster and more effective fat loss as well as preservation of lean tissue.

Yo-yo dieting does not cause a long-term drop in the metabolic rate and there is no evidence that yo-yo dieting increases body fat or reduces lean tissue.

(Source: *Complete Guide to Sports Nutrition (2000)* by Anita Bean BSc.)

Zero Calories–What If?

If you were only to consume a few grams of omega-3 and omega-6 essential fatty acids, a few grams of the eight essential amino acids, water, vitamins and minerals each day, what do you think would happen? I ask that you ponder this question not because I want you to remotely consider trying it. When I spoke of fasting earlier, I made it perfectly clear, I hope, that fasting is counterproductive to keeping the hard-earned muscle you have acquired or are trying to acquire. I am not pitching an idea that you consume near zero calories each day. In fact, I am telling you "Don't do it!"

The reason I am asking you to consider what would happen if you did so, is so you will realize the real power of energy balance for creating the leaner body you desire. If your initial thoughts are like many clients of mine to whom I have posed the same question, you are likely thinking along these lines:

- I would get weak.
- I would die.
- I could not do it.
- My body would give up all its muscle first and then, lastly, stored fat.
- I would lose weight until my metabolism slowed down and then I would stop losing weight.

Regardless of what you are thinking right now, I must share the one, best answer. Appropriately, it was an answer from a coaching client. I consider it the best answer, because I think it portrays a vivid picture in our minds of what would happen if you consumed a few grams of omega-3 and omega-6 essential fatty acids, a few grams of the eight essential amino acids, water, vitamins and minerals each day.

"Eventually you'd look like a concentration camp victim."

If you consumed only what I described a moment ago, you would likely be eating less than 100 calories a day. Yes, eventually you would look like a concentration camp victim. Eventually, like millions of Nazi concentration camp victims, you would even die. Long before death, however, you would feel lethargic, leaving you too little energy to even complete routine, mundane tasks. The bodies of anorexics and bulimics are also prime examples of what happens when energy intake is too low for too long. They are sickly and unhealthy. Many also die because of complications from starvation, dehydration and electrolyte imbalances.

As I mentioned in the fasting section, your body would do what it could to preserve precious body proteins, including skeletal muscle. Contrary to what many believe, after the first few days, your body would not look first to its skeletal proteins as a primary energy source as long as stored body fat (adipose) was sufficient to draw from. Eventually, as occurred with the starved concentration camp victims, stored body fat would fall too low and body proteins would be used as a last, but dominant, energy source. Your metabolism would slow, however, contrary to what you might think, it would not stop. Your metabolism would continue to function at the most basic level to keep you alive. Any movement from you would further draw energy from body resources.

The purpose of my initial question and the concentration camp victim imagery is to clearly show you the power of energy balance. *Somewhere between near-zero calories and what you have been eating lies the answer to leanness for you.* If we agree that eventually you'd look like a concentration camp victim if you actually practiced the "What if?" scenario I've presented here, then you must be willing to admit that somewhere between near-zero calories and what you've been eating will successfully take you to the realistic and healthy weight you've dreamed of for too long.

You may have doubts that you can actually become lean. You may have doubts that energy balance and creating the RCD will truly help you create the lean body you desire. You may have misconceived feelings of self-pity and remorse over "not getting to eat like everyone else." As I described in the first chapter, you really do not want to be normal anyway. You might feel sorry for yourself and believe you cannot eat less than you do now. Regardless of the feelings and self-pity you indulge in, you can never escape the one truth about energy balance and where you are versus where you want to go:

> *If you were to consume only a few grams of omega-3 and omega-6 essential fatty acids, a few grams of the eight essential amino acids, water, vitamins and minerals each day, you'd eventually look like a concentration camp victim. You would even get so thin you would die. Everyone has the power to be thin. You now have the power to be thinner and to do it the right way.*

Now that you know it is entirely possible to be thinner than you would ever want to be, you must choose to analyze what you are eating and how much activity you are engaging in. In doing so, you can determine how much you need to eat and how much you need to move to achieve the level of leanness you truly desire.

Now that you have a better understanding of energy balance, you can determine a healthy place to start your weight-loss process. As I said in the beginning of this chapter, any formula telling you how many calories you "get" is only a close guess at best. I believe my formulas will be very close to what most of you reading this will need in order to see the results you are looking for. Be careful, some other formulas in other publications are grossly exaggerated.

Now that you have the data, it is time to begin analyzing how many calories you are currently consuming from food and drink. The Lifestyle is not about filling your life with endless years of counting calories, but you will need to closely analyze the calories you are consuming for awhile. Analyzing with detail now will buy you the opportunity to not have to later. You will need to know how many calories you are consuming each day (hint: it's probably a *lot* more than you think). You will also need to know if you are consuming the right amount of carbohydrates, proteins and fats. In the next chapter, I will discuss why sometimes it is okay to *sweat some small stuff*.

Caloric Entitlement

Even though I've said you shouldn't rely on formulas once you have established your actual caloric intake, monitored weight loss for several weeks and have a real-life baseline to go by, most will still think of my formulas here and within the super-popular Calorie Calculator tool within the online coaching program as a form of entitlement.

After a period of several months I revised my online "calorie calculator" for coaching clients. The new formulas were implemented after further research and more hands-on experience.

Clients I had been working with for months, who had a proven track record to go on, began writing me asking, "Do I get to eat the calories the new formulas says I should eat?" At first, I was blown away by the questions, but I could not ignore the thinking when dozens of clients started asking me the same thing. Let me be clear. Clients with a proven, known track record of caloric intake, exercise and weight loss were now asking me if they got to eat more simply because my new formula was a shift upward in calories estimated from the previous formula.

The formulas within this chapter are *not* an entitlement. You do not necessarily get to consume a given number of calories in a day *because* a formula says so. The formulas do, however, provide a starting place and point of reference should you fall away and need to come back. They also help to make sense of it all. Are you really eating too few calories for your body weight and body fat? Or are you simply not paying attention to the finer details?

Jen Gets Real

Jennifer came to me at 35 years of age, a 5'3" frame, 260 pounds and an unknown body fat percentage. After reading many magazines and articles on the Internet, Jennifer was afraid of eating too few calories because she had been convinced in her readings that if she ate too few, she would sacrifice precious muscle and would almost stop her metabolism. Was she doing damage to existing muscle by eating "so few" calories? Would she "ruin" her metabolism by eating so few calories? These thoughts and many more concerned Jennifer, but she really wanted to get the weight off.

Based on the equations I have given you in this chapter, we determined her RMR ranged from 3120 down to 1963.

Total Body Weight Method
RMR = 260 x 12 = 3120

Body Surface Area Method
RMR = 36 x 2.272 x 24 = 1963

We further agreed that Jennifer would complete 300 minutes of vigorous exercise each week. This was calculated as having a value of 2400 calories for the week or 343 calories on average each day. Since Jennifer wanted to lose 2 pounds a week, we knew her RCD needed to be 7000 calories for the week or 1000 calories each day.

Therefore, we determined Jennifer would need to consume:

3120 + 343 - 1000 = 2463 calories each day. OR as low as 1963 + 343 - 1000 = 1306 calories each day.

Jennifer was consistent with logging her food and recording meals. After only a few weeks we determined that about 2400 calories was not only hard for her to eat but was not creating the weight loss desired. In fact, no weight loss was occurring. We continued to work closely together and determined she was realizing about a one pound per week weight loss at a caloric intake of about 1400 per day averaged over 7 days. If we had stuck to our guns and used *only* the total body weight x 12 method of determining RMR, we could have created a fear that eating so few calories was truly *undereating* when, in fact, she was not.

During the initial weeks Jennifer and I worked together, her weight had reduced from 260 down to 247 while eating 1400 to 1700 calories, on average, per day.

I convinced Jennifer that skinfold measurements at her present level of obesity would not be accurate. Like all victors who refuse to play the role of victim, Jennifer found another way to have her body fat tested other than hydrodensitometry (underwater). She decided, for fun, to have her body fat tested with an instrument called the Bod Pod®. This instrument measures whole body mass and volume. From there, using a technology called "air-displacement," it determines the fat-free and fat mass.

The results of her Bod Pod® test revealed she had a body fat percentage of 59.7 percent. This shocked, alarmed and depressed her *for a few hours* after hearing the results. Her reaction was very normal and acceptable. The difference between Jennifer and many others who get such "news" is she didn't let the news sink her–she chose to rise to the challenge and accept the fact she only had about 99.5 pounds of fat-free mass (247 x 0.403). She also admitted it was somewhat relieving to know that her goal body weight of 130 pounds could indeed be achieved.

Once she told me she had a body fat of 59.7 percent and fat-free mass of 99.5 pounds it further reinforced the reason that the number of calories she was routinely eating were effectively creating the weight loss she was enjoying, but not more. It also helped solidify the reasons that the "whole body weight formula" for RMR was just no good for her.

Since we now had the knowledge of a reputedly accurate body fat measure, my suggestion to Jennifer was to use the fat-free mass formula to check RMR another way.

99.5/2.2 = 45.22 kilograms of fat-free mass
21.6 x 45.22 = 976.91
370 + 977 = 1347 calories per day for RMR

Since Jennifer was working out 300 minutes a week, she was able to add on 343 calories each day for the value of exercise. She had been losing one pound a week eating about 1400 calories per day. Does this make sense? Was she starving? Was Jennifer "killing her metabolism?" Let's see.

Based on the new knowledge of her body fat and using the fat-free mass equation to determine RMR, I predicted a 1-pound fat loss per week as follows:

1347 + 343 - 500 = 1190 calories per day

With this estimate, it is clear that Jennifer was actually eating more calories than would be predicted for her 1-pound-a-week weight-loss rate. By using all three formulas to predict RMR, Jennifer was better able to accept the lower calories than are typically quoted in many health books, magazines and Internet web sites. She was not eating "below her RMR" as is commonly stated. She was not starving. In fact, she was eating more than I predicted for all equations other than whole body weight x 12 method.

No formula is likely perfect, but by using all three RMR formulas, a much better idea of the range can be achieved. By having this knowledge and putting it to use, you will have a better understanding of how normal you really are. Knowing these formulas can also protect you from eating far less than you should be. In the next chapter you will discover how you can determine precisely what you are consuming and why it is vitally important to the success of your program to sweat some of the small stuff.

Summary

Weight control by the numbers is not overly difficult. Simply create a proper, reasonable RCD, be true to the plan and the weight should drop about as planned. In later chapters, I will go into more detail about why "weight control by the numbers" is only part of the reason you are not totally svelte today.

There are many RMR formulas and it is important you understand that one may be more accurate for you than another.

By following the guidelines in this chapter for determining your RCD, you will be better prepared to begin your program with a realistic starting point. The two predominant factors other than RMR that will determine your daily allotted caloric intake are 1) number of vigorous minutes of exercise minutes you are willing to shell out each week, and 2) the total loss of weight chosen each week. I do not normally recommend anyone purposely attempt to lose more than 2 pounds per week except in some morbidly obese cases, and only then for one to two months. This does not mean that some won't do fine losing 1.5 percent of their body weight each week exceeding the 2-pound maximum recommendation while doing so, however, an excessive caloric deficit can create too little intake of calories and reduce metabolism more than is desired. This could make the process more difficult and, in the end, slow the total loss while you figure out how to increase calories without adding back some weight already lost.

Any calorie can make you fat. Anyone pushing super-low fat or super-low carb as the end-all, be-all of weight control should be ignored. Balance, moderation, increased activity and portion control are better suited for a Lifestyler.

Fasting equals starvation and should be avoided. Find something other than food to use as a fast if for religious purposes.

Many of you reading this have experienced yo-yo dieting for years. While it is truly healthier to get to and stay at a healthy weight, your metabolism isn't broken because you have yo-yo dieted a hundred times before. In fact, your metabolism isn't broken at all.

Remember that the formulas in this chapter or any nutritional textbook are only an estimate of your caloric needs. Use them as a reference, a base, a starting point only. Once you have mastered the next chapter, you will know what your body truly needs to create the weight loss you desire.

Take Action and Feel Great!

1. Determine your RMR by Total Body Weight method.

2. Determine your RMR by Body Surface Area method.

3. Determine your RMR by Fat-Free Mass method.

4. Determine your Relative Caloric Deficit using the formulas in this chapter.

5. Determine your total calories per day based on the formulas in this chapter and your goals for weight loss. Don't break the rules provided!

6. Know what level of Perceived Exertion is considered a minimal threshold for exercise to be considered vigorous.

The Small Stuff You Can Sweat

"You can't guess your way to fitness"

It's very common for the well intentioned dieter to feel as though the transformation process has a mystique about it. One of the most common and costliest mistakes is thinking that your ulti-mate physique is due to some genius, some magic, something or other that you do not possess. Some are hoping for divine intervention and will to melt the fat off their body. Often the dieter who isn't clear about why the body responds to what it's fed will use words and phrases such as:

- Hoping
- Keeping my fingers crossed
- Doing everything I can

- Wanting
- Giving it a try

- Wishing
- Praying

This isn't really surprising when you consider three things:

1. Most people get their information from mass media,
2. Most mass media wants to keep their reader's interest, sometimes at all costs, and
3. Most diets pitched in the mass media are afraid to tell you what I'm telling you in the Lifestyle.

In the movie, "A Few Good Men" with Tom Cruise and Jack Nicholson, there's a famous courtroom banter that occurs between the two men. The Colonel, played by Nicholson, is on the stand being cross-examined by the prosecuting attorney, played by Cruise. In this dialog, Nicholson asks Cruise in an overtly exasperated and loud tone "You want the truth?" Cruise yells back, "I want the truth!" Nicholson then delivers the million-dollar line in the movie when he yells, "You can't handle the truth!" Why would I go into telling you about a movie from 1992? Because at this point I must unveil more truths about why you are out of shape or why you are not in the shape you've longed for until now.

You Can Handle the Truth

The prevalent thinking often delivered from the diet industry is that there is no way you can really tell someone who needs to lose weight what it takes to actually succeed. No way can you ask them to honestly look at the finer details of what they are doing wrong because they simply won't. "Don't you dare tell them what it'll really take to lose the weight! They can't handle the truth!" I don't believe this is true. I believe you *can* handle the truth. *I believe that the only way you will ever know the real path to leanness is by first being told the truth, and then by accepting and living it.*

When I tell you that I believe you can handle the truth, it's because I have first-hand experience with clients who I've enlightened, then watched them grow stronger and more independent as a result. The saying "the truth shall set you free" has never been more appropriate.

The magical mystery that cloaks the superfit body of "the other guy" is only partly the fault of mass media and diet product hucksters. The other part is simply your acceptance of the fact that change is painful and that you've kept the blinders on for far too long. Allowing yourself to believe there are "secrets" that others know and you don't is too easy. Admitting that there aren't any secrets is an admission that you are poor at following through and that you are *choosing* to be as fat or out of shape as you are. Naturally, the mass media has attempted to oversimplify the process and has failed to address the specifics of the change process. However, you've known all along that eating poorly and not getting enough activity was the root of your weight problem. You'd be hard pressed to find someone not living in a cave who doesn't understand the simplest diet of all is only five words: "Eat less and exercise more." The five-word diet is simplistic and leaves gaping holes in helpful knowledge. You've known for a long time now that sitting on the couch eating boxes of caramel corn and ice cream by the half-gallon will not create a great body. Stop wishing, hoping, wondering, and "giving it a shot." Make it happen. Here's how ....

Finding the Truth

If I believe you can handle the truth, then what *is* the truth? The truth begins with the knowledge and understanding of how nutrients affect your health and overall energy. Learning that your metabolism isn't broken and how energy balance is truly created or changed is also important. If you're confused or "stuck" about how to progress, then the knowledge of equations for energy balance and creating a relative caloric deficit are absolute requirements to demystify how calories affect your weight. You can uncover these truths in the *Nutrients* and *Energy Balance* chapters. Understanding those two chapters helps give you control over your body.

I'll assume for a moment that you've read the *Nutrients* and *Energy Balance* chapters at this time. With an understanding of these two facets, it's now time to turn your attention to the details of self-analysis and self-evaluation. You see, even though you swear you "don't eat that much," you really are "eating that much." Telling yourself, "I'm definitely eating less than 3000 calories a day" might be grossly inaccurate. You may tell yourself that you "know your metabolism is broken," however, a careful review of the upcoming facts will provide plenty of evidence to the contrary. Even though it "seems" that you are eating a low calorie diet, I'm absolutely confident you're eating more than you think. I'm asking you to **pay attention to the details**. I know we've all been told to "not sweat the small stuff–and it's all small stuff," so let me clarify which details I'm referring to.

Sweat the Small Stuff?

The fittest people you will encounter are very detail- and goal-oriented individuals. The most unfit people you know are more like Gilligan on Thorazine. They are very disorganized and haven't a clue about what they are really doing. I believe that if you realistically emulate the positive actions of the most successful people on Earth, you stand a very good chance of becoming as good or even more successful than they are. It's no different for fitness. To become more fit, start acting like you are already that fit person who just happens to be zipped up inside a moon suit of fat. In less time than you think, you'll be well on your way to becoming that better fit person. But instead of instantaneously unzipping the moon suit of fat, you will peel away the fat layers more like the layers of an onion.

When the daily grind is threatening to beat them down, successful transformationists don't sweat the small stuff. The successful changers don't get all bent out of shape over having a hair out of place. They don't go nuts when someone cuts them off on the freeway. Their day isn't ruined when they lock their keys in the car. A spat with a coworker or a "look" from the boss isn't going to throw a successful Lifestyler into a tailspin. They don't berate their spouse for forgetting to pick up a gallon of milk. They don't scream at the kids for the "B" on the report card. They don't allow themselves to get depressed because someone in their life "let them down" again by not picking up their socks or taking out the garbage. *In essence, successful Lifestylers keep psychological distress to a minimum.* They do so not by trying to eliminate stress, but by managing the daily stress more effectively. Lifestylers look for better life management strategies. They don't look to cure life. Their perception more closely matches the reality and severity or insignificance of any given situation and they realize that very few things really matter and are truly horrific or terrible. It's also true that successful transformationists know their numbers. They know their formulas, and–most importantly–they know themselves. They aren't afraid to be honest with themselves first, and everyone else second. They possess great character.

> *"It's the little things that make the big things possible.*
> *Only close attention to the fine details of any operation*
> *makes the operation first-class."*
> J. Willard Marriott (1900-1985), Founder, Marriott Corporation

If you are stuck in a rut or just getting started, knowing your numbers is vital to your success. Zig says, "If it can't be measured, it can't be managed." You're not going to "sweat the small stuff," but you are going to analyze any calorie-containing food and drink entering your mouth with the utmost scrutiny and clarity. You're not going to do this forever, but until at least the first three to five percent of your body weight is gone, I'm recommending you properly log and analyze your food and drink. Through logging and analyzing, you will truly grasp the "why."

Logging your foods early on will buy you the opportunity to not need to do it later. You must become skilled at determining the values of foods and portions of the foods you commonly eat. By doing this process until at least the first three to five percent of your body weight has been lost, you'll be able to travel, attend the party, visit friends and have a night out without living in fear.

You will understand, once and for all, that your favorite dessert is simply a tasty food providing roughly 700 calories. Without a good understanding of how many calories that favorite dessert provides, you are likely to attach "absolute thinking" to your description of it. You might say, "If I even eat one bite of that, I'll see it on the scale in the morning." Or you might think, "This cream cheese product goes directly to my ass." These statements simply aren't true and the reason you perceive them to be true, if you do, is because you haven't been paying attention to the numbers and haven't been properly logging your foods. That one bite of your favorite dessert isn't going to cause your hips and belly to swell like Violet Beauregard in the movie "Willy Wonka and the Chocolate Factory." Through food logging, you'll eventually become a good judge of the caloric content of foods commonly eaten without looking up the values at all. Upon reaching that point, you can make an intelligent decision to share the dessert, eat half and throw the rest away, or simply not to order it and to substitute something else that's tasty but with less calories.

When You Don't Know What You Think You Know

Too many times I've counseled a dieter who "knew" the reason they were fat: it was because they weren't *quite* active enough. What they "knew" was wrong. So many times I've helped individuals who just "know" they have a problem with carbs, or fat, or protein and that's why they are fat. In order to be successful, they had to shift their position. I don't have enough hair follicles left in my head to count the number of people who were "sure" they weren't eating too many calories, but a thorough analysis revealed that this was certainly the case. Until you succumb to a thorough and detailed analysis of your food and drink intake, you don't really know as much as you think. Even if you've logged foods in the past and believe you have a good grip on it all, if you are "stuck," it's time to do it again.

Dietary Recall

I've learned not to ask clients what they eat. Instead, I demand they properly log their foods. Anytime I've asked anyone who "can't seem to lose weight" or "just doesn't understand why they are stuck" or "can't seem to *gain* weight" I always get the same kinds of answers.

"Well, I really don't eat that much. Today I had a cup of coffee for breakfast–you know I really don't like breakfast. I had some grilled chicken for lunch and a lettuce salad for supper. I usually eat pretty well but you know, like everyone I have my *occasional* snack or cheat meal." Wink, wink.

Memory is a huge liar. The description I get is undoubtedly *not* typical of their normal eating patterns, and more likely describes a best day. Even as a best day, it's still pretty pitiful. So I've learned not to ask what a person eats. Even if you know you are overeating, there is little doubt you still underestimate the extent of the overeating and drinking.

The phrase "dietary recall" is used in research, and is defined as the food and drink remembered by the participant. Somewhat amusing is the fact that while dietary recall is used for some research studying dietary intake, most research on dietary recall itself clearly indicates it's about as reliable as your crazy Uncle Fred who hasn't shown up on time for anything, including his own birth. People are not good at remembering what they eat and drink. When asked, many believe they eat the exact same five foods day in and day out. The reality is that they eat 15 meals a week with a few dozen foods making up those meals. "Gosh, I never really gave any thought to the coffee and creamer I have every day." Many people also just plain forget to add in those "little things" such as three table-spoons of flax oil a day (well over 300 calories). It isn't surprising that most comparisons of dietary recall vs. what was actually consumed has dietary recall almost always underestimating compared to the reality. The difference can be 50 percent or higher. Dietary recall (remembering without the assistance of actually writing down what was truly eaten and drank) is completely unreliable for your purposes. You must log your food and drink within minutes of consuming it, or at the latest, before you turn in for bed the same day.

Susanne Fights the Process

Another less than desirable method of "logging" food and drink is simply writing down what you ate and drank without assigning the proper values for total calories, carbohydrates, protein, fat and alcohol. In working closely with Susanne, a follower of a popular diet plan, I asked her to show me her food logs. She faxed them to me and I quickly realized she had never properly been shown how to log foods for maximum performance and enlightenment. She wrote down what she had eaten, and even the time and portion, however, there were no numerical values assigned to any food or meal. I had to ask why. Susanne told me that she had grown accustomed with her current plan of using fist and palm-sized portions to measure food intake. If you haven't assumed so already, the reason Susanne came to me is because her current plan wasn't working. I clearly explained to Susanne that I wanted her to log foods my way, and she shrunk away for weeks before coming back to me. Again, she was frustrated with no weight loss. I asked her immediately for her food logs, just as I had asked last time. She attempted, yet again, to send me the same type of food logs as before. I again had to be the bearer of logical news and tell her those types of food logs were meaningless. I needed her to take it a step further and determine the caloric values of all of those foods. She again shrank away for weeks.

The process of asking for change, and the dieter's utter refusal to accept the process, is very common. As I discussed in the *Are You Ready to Change* chapter, change is scary. Change requires effort. Susanne is also a perfect example of how a refusal on your part to shift your position and accept the Lifestyle will ultimately keep you precisely where you are right now. If where you are is where you want to be, then I simply thank you for purchasing my system and hope you still glean useful information. Nevertheless, if you want to change, then you must accept that some things you think you know–you really don't. Some things that you are comfortable with must become uncomfortable. Some strategies that you hold dear to your heart must be set free so you can grow and truly change to the After photo you desire to become.

After many attempts at getting Susanne to properly log her foods and stop kidding herself, she gave in and began logging foods the Lifestyle way. Susanne used my online Nutrition Analyzer and in just a few short days, she began to notice her pitfalls. She realized those habits that needed adjusting and began to feel a tremendous sense of control over her fitness vehicle. After several more weeks, and over 20 pounds of weight loss, she felt completely in control and knew she was no longer being towed. In fact, she was driving her convertible fitness sports car just where she wanted to. She no longer felt like the victim, and any time she felt she was stuck, she came back to detailed logging again. Sure enough, every time she repeated the process, she again saw the scale move. Today Susanne has lost well over 50 pounds and continues to lose.

It's Time To Start Logging

After I complete a hands-on challenge with a group of coaching clients, I ask them what they learned and what they believe was the single greatest factor contributing to their success. Inevitably, other than personal advice from me, they admit that the single greatest contributor is keeping a detailed record of their nutritional plan. They know their numbers! They know the calories they consumed, the carbohydrates, the protein and the fat. As I am telling you here, I also tell my personal coaching clients ...

> Keeping a detailed record of your food and drink intake for even a few days is like getting an Associates degree in Transformation–pretty darn good. Keeping a detailed record of your food and drink intake until three to five percent of your body weight is gone is like getting a Ph.D. in Transformation Excellence! Recording the details is a huge step, and one that simply cannot be ignored. It's that powerful!
>
> I am 100 percent confident that if you will take the time to properly log your foods and analyze what is going in your mouth every day, until at least three to five percent of your body weight is gone, you will be so enlightened and feel so powerful you'll wonder why you never accepted or thought of doing this before.

Coaching member Howard writes:
> "Something that I learned about myself these last days is that if I think I am trying hard, I can try harder; if I think I am giving it my all, I have more to give and knowing and understanding the numbers is the first key to getting a hold of the process."

Knowing why you are gaining and losing weight is a very liberating feeling. Eighty percent of the answers to "Why can't I seem to get things moving?" and "Why does this scale do this to me?" and "No matter what I do I can't lose weight!" are all in the details of your food analysis. The other 20 percent is revealed in an analysis of your daily physical activity. Logging your food and drink can provide the calming knowledge necessary to show just how in control you can be. Remember in The Wizard of Oz when Glenda, the good witch of the North, told Dorothy she always had the power to go home anytime she wanted? Proper food logging and self-analysis is like a pair of ruby slippers. When you're ready to change, you'll use this tool to evaluate where your pitfalls are and to hold you straight and true to the plan. This process is so powerful; it can literally bring you home to fitness. I believe the exercise of food logging, while tedious and intense, is so beneficial that if you choose to skip it, I can almost guarantee you will fail yet again. Come on, you've gotten this far, what are you going to do, stop now, or–worse yet–try and continue the Lifestyle by trying the Lifestyle "cafeteria style" without doing this exercise? It won't work!

The Right Tools for the Job

Having the right tools for the job is important. Logging your foods is no different. Would you go scuba diving without a mask, tank and fins? Would you play professional football without pads? Would you want your surgeon to use a pair of rusty tweezers to remove your appendix? Since the obvious answer to all of these questions is "no," then don't plan to fail by not having the right tools for the food logging exercise you must complete. If you don't own a kitchen food scale, I'd suggest you make a trip to your favorite department store and buy one. A kitchen food scale will help you log your foods, and will also be there later when you get "sloppy" and are using eyeball measures to determine portions. I prefer a digital scale that weighs foods in both grams and ounces, but any food scale is better than no food scale.

For recipes that are multi-ingredient, you will have to weigh and measure all of the ingredients that provide calories so you know the calories that the entire recipe actually provides. Then, you will determine how much of a serving you are taking from the entire recipe. Not only will you weigh the individual calorie-containing ingredients, you can also use the kitchen food scale to weigh your portion. A good, digital kitchen food scale will cost you less than 40 bucks. You are worth $40, so go get one.

Through my online coaching program I have developed tremendously powerful tools to help anyone through the process of nutritional analysis and logging. There are other software programs as well and books that list thousands of foods with the proper information about those foods. A "Nutrition Desk Reference" or "Complete Book of Food Counts" or "Food Values of Portions Commonly Used" can serve your purposes much like an automobile with no air conditioning is still reliable transportation. Small, pocket guides are inadequate for your purposes here. Many people do enjoy the ability to see a more graphic representation of their nutritional analysis (this is like an automobile with air conditioning) and my online Nutrition Analyzer can make the process less daunting and even fun. Finally, my Nutrition Analyzer can do the math for you, making it more about you actually doing the process, rather than ensuring you're a good mathematician.

How to Log

Here's what I need you to do. Beginning tomorrow, you need to log every single thing you eat in a day. You don't need to wait for Monday to begin a new you. When I tell you to log everything, I mean everything! You need to write down or enter every finger-lickin' morsel of food that enters your mouth. I don't care if you're dipping your little finger into the cookie dough to taste, or if you are literally pouring M&Ms in your mouth with a funnel. You need to log it without fail! Remember those bites of the kids' hot dogs as you prepared their lunch? That counts! Remember the bite of every kid's bowl of cereal? That counts. How about the flax oil in your protein shake? It counts! The 10 calories in a cup of coffee? It counts. When you were standing in front of the fridge and wolfed down three pieces of cheese? That counts too. It all counts. It all must be logged.

No food log is complete unless it contains at least the following data for each meal of each day:

- Calories (total)
- Carbohydrates (grams and total calories)
- Protein (grams and total calories)
- Fat (grams and total calories)

Wrong

Chunky chicken sandwich — 1 sandwich
Baby carrots — 6 carrots
Mandarin Oranges — 1/2 cup
Pears — 1 pear

Correct	Calories	Carbs (g)	Prot (g)	Fat (g)
Chunky chicken sandwich				
Whole-wheat bread, 2 slices	142	25	6	2
Miracle Whip Lite, 1 Tbsp	35	2	0	3
Honey-roasted chicken, 1.5 cups	184	4.5	33	3.75
Fat-free cheese slice, 1 slice	30	2.5	4.5	.2
Baby Carrots, 6 carrots	60	13.5	1.5	0
Mandarin Oranges, 1/2 cup	76	19	0	0
Pears, 1 pear	90	21	.5	.5

Totals	617	87.5	45.5	9.45
Percentages		57%	29%	14%

When You Fall Down

When you have "*the* weekend" or "*the* day" and you really feel you've blown it–first know that you haven't blown it. Jon, a coaching client of mine had this to say when he fell down.

> *"Well I have good news and bad news. The bad news is that I slipped for the first time since we started working together, Dave. The good news is I made a full recovery. Quite simply, I violated two rules today, the first being control and the second knowing exactly what you're eating.*
>
> *While at work today, there was a big bowl of Hershey's Kisses, which I casually estimated had about 12 kcal/piece. After consuming 17 of them (3 groups of 4,1 group of 5) I decided to actually look up the calories and discovered they had 25 kcal/piece. I realized right then that I had completely wasted 425 kcals for the day.*
>
> *Deciding not to panic, I played around with the online Nutrition Analyzer you built and adjusted the rest of the meals for the day and increased my workout time for the day. I have finished my day with the planned amount of calories in the appropriate ratios. My point is, although I fell off the horse, I dusted myself off, got up, and fixed the problem to the best of my ability."*

Jon provides a perfect example of how to "fail quickly" and "recover quickly." Jon also recognized that his falling down wasn't something that he should repeat often. He accepted what he had done and didn't ignore it. With character and integrity he logged his Hershey Kisses and moved on.

Write About Failures

It's important–at the time–to log those "fall down" moments and days. It's very tempting to not weigh yourself on the scale and to not log the day you strayed from the plan. I suggest you log this day too and include your feelings about overindulging at the time. Place what you write in a conspicuous place where you can easily find it the next time you feel like straying off the plan. As a true Lifestyler, it's important you maintain the highest degree of character and integrity. Being dishonest with yourself won't help your pain, and the guilt you'll feel from it will beat you down even further. Swallow the bitter pill when you fall down, get up, brush your knees off, admit to yourself that you fell down and log those foods to the best of your ability. Being completely honest with yourself is difficult, but your success depends on it. Those who are of high moral character and integrity succeed a far greater percentage of the time than those who refuse to accept reality.

Now that you know how to use the process of food logging to gain control over your weight, you can stop wishing, hoping, wondering and praying for it to happen. Instead, you will make it happen. You are responsible for your weight. You must now recognize you have a choice to make. Be detailed, and thoroughly log your food and drink, or remain as you currently are. Whatever you decide, you've now been stripped of your "broken metabolism" and "my whole family is fat" excuses. If you take this process and run with it, you'll know that what I said is true. If you don't, your excuses remain just that–excuses that you and I both know aren't true.

Summary

You truly cannot guess your way to fitness. While it is absolutely imperative that you become a great life manager, you can work on that while you are being detail-oriented and logging your foods.

Relying on dietary recall or incomplete, hand-written records to log your foods will set you up for failure. Dietary recall is unreliable and through the wonder and magnificence of the Internet, you have access to a Nutrition Analyzer I created precisely for this specific purpose and no longer have to put pen to paper every time you eat a sandwich.

You can either fight this process and shrink away for weeks wasting precious time or you can wrap your arms around this monumentally important exercise and hit the ground running even today!

When you fall down and take a small detour off the straight and true path of the Lifestyle, it is important you do not lie to yourself or avoid the truth. To the best of your ability log all the foods you ate during your detour and write about the experience and negative feelings associated with the detour. Do your best to refer back to those written statements the next time you consider taking the same detour.

Take Action and Feel Great!

1. Visit www.leannesslifestyle.com and review the benefits of using the online Nutrition Analyzer I created for this all-too-important exercise.

2. Begin logging your foods tomorrow at the latest. You do not need to wait for Monday to start. Starting on Monday hasn't helped you thus far. It won't help this time either.

3. Purchase a quality kitchen food scale. If it costs $40, that's okay. You are worth it and you need the right tools for the job.

4. Once you start logging, do not stop until you have lost at least three to five percent of your current body weight. Some find logging with the Nutrition Analyzer so liberating and comforting they use it until they have reached their ultimate lifetime achievement goal weight.

Meal Frequency and The Splurge Meal

One-meal-a-day diets are for losers–and not the kind of loser you want to be.

There are a number of ideas promoted in popular media suggesting reasons one should eat 1, 2, 3, 6 or more meals a day. Typically, each idea reflects the marketing position of the writer or the product owner. The average American consumes on average just over three meals per day. For you, a Lifestyler, I recommend four to six meals per day, every day. My goal in this chapter is to show you why I recommend the meal frequency I do, and not use clever spin to lead you to follow my recommendations. I will also define a splurge meal, the many pitfalls of poor planning, and how the mismanagement of your splurge meals can lead to stagnation.

As a Lifestyler, I recommend a relatively high meal frequency for several reasons. What may surprise you is the reasons are not directly related to changing your metabolic rate or directly influencing your body composition. Many popular sources want you to believe there will be some tremendous increase in your metabolic rate, or drop in body fat, simply from eating multiple meals per day (i.e., becoming a grazer). The scientific research on the subject does not provide much credence to these ideas. At the practical, hands-on, level, I do not see a major benefit of multiple meals in relation to the increase of metabolic rate or the reduction of body fat simply because of the increased meal frequency.

My reasons for suggesting four to six meals per day, however, are based on scientific research. A relatively high meal frequency has been associated with the following benefits:

1. Lower total cholesterol
2. Increased good (HDL) cholesterol
3. Reduced triglyceride levels
4. More stable blood glucose and insulin levels hroughout the day (this can promote a feeling of increased vitality, vigor and overall mood elevation)
5. Enhanced appetite control and reduced desire to gorge or binge
6. Increased likelihood of muscle being preserved
7. Possible reduction in cortisol (a major stress hormone that can cause excessive muscle breakdown if high concentrations are sustained)

In addition to the research-suggested benefits that are possible from eating four to six meals per day, I have personally observed one very positive behavior that can truly help reduce total daily caloric intake: frequent eaters feel less obligated to be a member of the "Clean Plate Club." Grazers have a higher tendency to push away from the table when satisfied instead of stuffed. Many grazers who had previously been conditioned as children and young adults "not to waste food" have now realized it's better to leave something on your plate every time, not some of the time. Recognizing the importance of portion control early on is a significant determinant of eventual success.

From people I have coached to my own children, those who become accustomed to eating many times throughout the day feel less obligated to stuff themselves until it hurts. If my children are enjoying an ice cream treat, they will routinely stop halfway through it because they are full. They know that every day, seven days a week, they will be eating within two to three hours after any meal or snack. For this reason, there is little desire to eat past the point of being satisfied. They do not have to eat as if it is their last meal because the next meal is right around the corner. As parents, we also do not push them to eat past the point at which they say they are full. It is actually foreign for our children to do so. By consuming several meals per day, you too can become conditioned to know that your next meal is only two to three hours away and that there is no reason to eat any meal as if it were your last.

As a Lifestyler, you will be eating 28 to 42 times per week. It does not mean you will eat 22 times on day one and then one time a day for days 2 to 7. You should strive to consume four to six meals a day, every day. You will not skip breakfast because you think you "do better" when you skip breakfast. You will not have "one good meal" per day because you seem to grow fatter slower by doing so. "One Meal Losers," as I call those who eat once a day, artificially create a 20-hour window of starvation.

What do you think the body does when it is faced with starvation (which is what you create when you skip breakfast)? Whenever you miss meals, you trigger the body's survival mechanism. In order to survive these periods, the body's survival mechanism reduces energy consumption (muscle metabolism) to conserve energy stores (fat). Because fat is the body's energy storage and critical for survival in times of famine, the body will try to conserve it at all costs. In essence, the body slows all metabolic functions that are not critical for survival to a screeching halt. Hey, it is just protecting you from the famine you have artificially created (see *Fasting* in the *Energy Balance* chapter).

The body has no idea of when it is going to get its next meal, so it just shuts down and waits for you to feed it. It also creates a horde of enzymes (protein catalysts) that increase the likelihood of additional, unnecessary calories being stored as fat when you finally decide to eat again. Why would the body create additional fat-storing enzymes? Because, again, it's been conditioned over thousands of years to be very adept at protecting us from famine. Unbelievably, there really were periods, much like uncivilized parts of the world now, when food was scarce. It took thousands of years to develop this fat-storing protective mechanism and it will not be changing anytime soon. Genetic changes occur so slowly that man is essentially the same as he was tens of thousands of years ago.

Eating 4 to 6 Times Per Day–How To?

If you can prepare lean proteins, vegetables and fruits ahead of time, you will have little trouble consuming four to six meals per day. Tupperware® and Ziploc® baggies are a Godsend for storing prepared Lifestyle meals to be eaten later.

Prepare enough food for multiple feedings each time you prepare it. Many Lifestylers will choose a few hours on a Saturday or Sunday to prepare all of their core dishes, vegetables and fruits for the week. This is smart living! It really is wise when you are grilling chicken breasts to grill a dozen rather than two. Preparing some brown rice for today? Make enough to last a week and refrigerate the rest. Bag and freeze all Lifestyle-friendly leftovers for easy preparation later. Anytime you create any Lifestyle-friendly meal, it's to your advantage to prepare extra and freeze the leftovers. It makes creating a quick meal later that much easier.

Benefits and Pitfalls of Basic Supplementation

In the event that your schedule, travel or willingness to consistently prepare extra isn't what we'd optimally like it to be, this is the time to consider nutrition bars and shakes for their portability, balance, taste, cost and ease of use. Let's face it; most do not prepare in advance five or six meals a day.

It is easier to focus on preparing three squares a day, rather than six, however, with dietary supplements you no longer have to "prepare" six solid meals per day. With the variety of protein energy bars available and easy-to-mix shake-and-go protein and meal replacement powders, it is easier than ever to keep on track. Supplements make your busy, hectic, hurry-up and wait world much saner to live in. Drop a 99-cent bar in your purse or briefcase. Throw a $1.99 shake-and-go drink in your gym bag, suitcase or lunch pail. When it is time to snack and fill in the gaps between breakfast and lunch, or lunch and supper, or supper and bedtime, supplements can add tremendous flexibility and taste, and can end cravings instantly many times. Dietary supplements can also make it easier to increase your dietary protein without all the fat.

I must point out the dangers, however, of living on dietary supplement bars and shakes instead of eating real food at least equally in frequency and volume. Dietary supplements are just that: supplements to your whole-food Lifestyle plan. Individuals who live on bars and shakes are not following the Lifestyle. They are dieting. There is no Lifestyle being created when bars and shakes are the primary staples of your day. If you consume two to three meals as bars and shakes, then you should be consuming two to three meals from real, whole-food, too. You are not learning to live a lifetime of leanness when the majority of your calories come from bars and shakes. It is short-term thinking if you choose to follow a diet such as this. Your body will crave food sooner or later, so do not even start trying to live on bars and shakes.

Another potential danger of trying to live on bars especially is that since they have now been formulated to taste like a candy bar, this may trigger your desire for sugary snacks and other trigger foods, even more bars. I personally know clients who planned to eat one bar between breakfast and lunch but ended up eating six because once they started, they could not stop. I also know clients who bought a box of bars from the health food store and *ate the whole box* before they got home! As is the case with your food selection, however, most do not have this problem. Personally, I have no problem at all stopping after one bar and most people seem to respond more like me. But if you notice that you seem to crave bar after bar after bar, or you crave other sugary snacks after having a bar, then you may have to abstain from that bar or all bars. If it is so, then do not fight it. Just accept it and rely on whole foods or try a protein or meal replacement shake. If you notice the same reaction, then again, do not fight it. Just know that you most likely will have to prepare plenty of food in advance so you will be able to consume four to six meals per day.

A common example of how I use bars and shakes for my own Lifestyle is as follows:

Breakfast: whole food
Snack: Bar or shake
Lunch: whole food
Snack: Bar or shake
Dinner: whole food
Snack: Bar or shake

It is best for basic nutrition to rely less on anything packaged, including dietary supplements, other than a multivitamin and essential fatty acids. I am fortunate in that I am not a food addict and do not have any known trigger foods. I do not assume the same for you and you should not either.

In closing this section let me say this: If given the choice between having a Lifestyler skip meals because they realistically will not or cannot prepare enough whole-food meals, and having them consume two to three meals per day as a bar or shake (barring any trigger or bingeing associations), I would much rather have a client consume the bars and shakes to ensure adequate calories and nutrient density.

Splurging–Not a Trigger, Not a FREE Meal

One or two of your 28 to 42 meals per week will be what I call the "Splurge Meal." A splurge food is a controlled indulgence. It is defined as any food you want as long as you consider the total caloric value of that food and can stop eating it when you need to. The splurge food is not the same as a trigger food. I will discuss trigger foods in more depth in the *Emotions, Addiction and Self-Regulation* chapter, but with a trigger food, once you start, you are likely to eat it until it is gone. The marketing slogan, "Bet you can't eat just one!" was developed for a trigger food: potato chips. This slogan fits the trigger food description perfectly. For many, trigger foods are sweet or salty foods (e.g., chips, cookies, baked goods, cereals). Trigger foods are not splurge foods but it may take you a few weeks to clearly determine what your trigger foods are. First things first. Finish this book and be armed with the knowledge you need.

A splurge food is also not a "free meal." This terminology connotes the idea that somehow the calories within the splurge treat are somehow less important than all the other calories you consume in a week. "Free" insinuates you feel there is no cost; somehow, the calories on the "free day" do not count. They seem magically invisible. You must change your mindset if you currently practice "free meal" dieting.

Bill Phillips writes in his book "Body for Life":

"Six days a week, you need to follow the eating guidelines I have been telling you about in this section. And on the seventh day? Forget about them. I mean forget them all. Eat whatever you want. If you want to have blueberry pancakes with syrup for breakfast or a cinnamon roll with coffee or milk, that is fine. If you want a Big Mac or two for lunch, go for it. If you want a thick pizza with everything on it for dinner, be my guest. If you want apple pie and ice cream for dessert, that's okay with me."

Bill is an extremely intelligent man and his program "Body for Life" (BFL) has driven millions of fence riders off the fence and into a fitness mode. How should we regard Bill's statements? Is he right? Is it okay to consume anything you want and as much as you want for 24 hours (one full day) a week? Am I therefore wrong? In my opinion, for the person who has a weight problem, BFL has extended the idea of splurging beyond what is reasonable. Here is why:

Jane is dedicated to weight loss. She exercises 300 minutes per week and eats clean six of seven days per week. She is 5'5" and weighs 150 pounds. She will need roughly 1600 calories per day to lose one pound of body weight per week.

Let's say Jane is perfect six of her seven days per week and then follows the BFL plan on the seventh day. Because she is a woman and is not used to totally pigging out, she has the following "Cheat Day" as BFL prescribes she can:

- Bacon and eggs with a frosting-dripping cinnamon roll
- Big Roast Beef with fries and medium Pepsi
- Pizza for supper with another Pepsi (three slices of deep dish)
- Moose Tracks ice cream with chocolate sauce (about two cups, let's be real)

On this cheat day, Jane has eaten over 4000 calories. Is there any problem with this? She did perfectly well on all her other days. It is her cheat day and BFL says anything goes. Not so fast.

Recall that Jane needs to average about 11,200 calories (1600 x 7) per week to stay on track and lose a pound. On 6 of the 7 days she was perfect–she ate 9600 calories (1600 x 6). But on the 7th day she said, "Hooray! This is my cheat day and I can have anything I want, and as much as I want!" On the 7th day, she ate 4000 calories in four meals instead of six (very conservative numbers by the way).

Including her cheat day, Jane's total calories for the week were 13,600 (9600 in 6 days + 4000 on the 7th). At this point Jane is going to become very frustrated. She is over the 11,200 needed by 2400 calories. Jane will not lose a pound of fat this week. She will likely only lose about a third of a pound of fat this week. If she does not own a scale that measures in tenths, she will see no change in weight on the scale. She'll start the new week depressed and disappointed by the lack of results, but by gosh determined that she'll be perfect again for six out of seven days per week with the full cheat day as BFL prescribes again on day seven. She may even be encouraged by other BFL followers to "be patient," some day that weight will come off if she's just patient long enough. This cycle may continue repeatedly until Jane becomes so frustrated that she gives up and recycles back to the Contemplation stage of change (see Chapter 2).

If the scenario above held true, then no one following the BFL plan would ever lose weight, but some do. So, how do they do it? I will suggest that those who have been ultra successful with BFL have modified their cheat day not to be "anything they want" but anything that will provide them with the results they want. Yes, the winners of Bill's contests and promotions have cheat meals but they do *not* have as much as they want and any food they want *all day long*.

No Free Meals–No Cheating

Free days are not recommended for the Lifestyler. Additionally, the splurges you'll have each week should not be referred to as "cheat meals." Cheating connotes something negative or sinful. Consuming a splurge meal is not sinful or negative. This means there is no reason to apologize to anyone for enjoying your splurge meal each week. I want you to use great care when choosing the words that describe what you do regularly, because they define within you who you are. If you have pizza or a warm, chocolate brownie drizzled in chocolate syrup once a week, you are not naughty, or a bad girl or a sinful little boy. You simply enjoyed a tasty treat according to plan. There is nothing negative about that.

The example I gave for Jane is common. In fact, it is more the rule than the exception. Coaching client Tiffany wrote about how she used to feel about "free days."

> *"I felt like I needed to get it all in one day or I was screwed for having to be so perfect the rest of the week. And, being the kinda gal that can throw herself into an eating frenzy in a heartbeat, the free day made me feel like I had a license to cram all my wishes and cravings into one day of sugar and fat overload."*

I know of men and women who take the "free day" so literally they set their alarm clock for 12:01 A.M. just because that starts their "free day." Then they gorge themselves with sweets and other snacks until they pass out for the night. Once they awaken, they spend all day stuffing their face until 11:59 P.M., finally ending their "free day."

In addition to the overindulgence on the "free day," a common trend I have observed among the transformation community following this plan is that they crave sweets and salty foods for days after their "free day." *Something about consuming trigger foods and gorging for the better part of an entire day sets up a psychological craving that is not quenched quickly thereafter.*

Don't Attach Human Thoughts to Your Chemistry

Another reason I do not care for the "free days" or for calling a splurge meal a "free meal," is that it makes people think their body is uncontrollable or reacting outside of their control. Does this sound familiar?

"Here I was losing weight just great, and *all of a sudden* my body decided not to lose any more. My metabolism just said, 'Nope! I'm not giving any more fat up no matter what!'" or "I guess losing 7 pounds the first week overwhelmed my body and it's taking a breather."

I've now heard enough of these statements to know that while making these statements is not necessarily a huge problem, and they help you to communicate with me and other coaches about your transformation challenges, I believe they're too far off base to be ignored. You are an individual, however, you are much more so a big, hairy, bag of chemicals that will react rather predictably if provided the stimulus necessary for change.

To help clarify, allow me to tell you about William, a client I helped see through a 40 pound weight loss after he claimed he had been stuck for two months. William was a "my body just decided all of a sudden" guy. William ate very clean for six out of seven days. He had great success for many weeks, losing 40 pounds before his "body decided" to stop losing weight. He could not, for the life of him, figure out what in the world he was doing wrong. After six almost postcard-perfect days a week, he then ate anything he wanted on the seventh day (24 hours in a day, remember).

Averaging an estimated 3500 calories per day, 6 out of 7 days per week, William deserved to feel as if he was doing well since he weighed 265 pounds, down from just over 300 when he started. He was exercising approximately 120 minutes a week, too. So, what about that doggoned seventh day? On that day, he consumed approximately 8000 calories!

A close estimate of his caloric needs revealed that William needed approximately 3600 calories per day to maintain (no weight loss or gain) his 265-pound body. Over the course of a 7-day period, this man consumed an average of 4142 calories per day because of his "free day" (3500 x 6 = 21,000 + 8000 / 7 = 4142). Recall that William had been eating this way for months, and had dropped 40 pounds doing so. Mysteriously, "all of a sudden his body decided" to quit losing weight. Here is what really happened;

1. It wasn't all of a sudden; and
2. He simply consumed more calories in a week than he needed for maintenance, let alone weight loss. It is simply science, thermodynamics and mathematics in action.

What would have happened to William if he had consumed 3000 calories six days per week and a whopping 5000 calories on the 7th splurge day? He would have been eating an average of 3286 (23,000 / 7) calories per day and been losing weight again.

William was stuck at 265 for a couple months before coming to me. He missed achieving his goal on time, was frustrated and disheartened because of one gluttonous day per week. I, of course, was excited because I got to tell him the good news: he hadn't failed, he was simply misled into believing that somehow those calories consumed on the "free day" were different than the calories on any other day.

Do not attach characteristics to your body chemistry as though it has a mind of its own. Your body chemistry does not have a personality. It does not "decide" or "all of a sudden" anything. You do. You are in control, not your overweight parents and grandparents. Not your overweight brothers and sisters, and–least of all–not the big hairy bag of chemicals kept from becoming a puddle of goo by layers of dermis: your body.

Splurge Meal Guidelines

Do not allow your splurge meal to turn into a splurge day. It's not uncommon for some well intentioned Lifestylers to simply let one splurge meal lead into another until an entire day is filled with splurge meals, much like BFL's "free day." If this occurs, it is important you fail quickly, learn from your mistake and take corrective action the next day. Write down how you felt for overindulging and choosing a behavior that is counterproductive to your goals. Commit to doing better the next time and refer to what you wrote when the urge to keep splurging rears its ugly head again. In the end, never forget: the splurge meal is not magical and your final calories cannot exceed your planned goal or you will stay the same or gain weight. Even though you may be saying goodbye to the days when you ate with reckless abandon, you will also say goodbye to the scale staying the same week after week after week.

One Splurge Meal Per Week to Start

While you are in the Action phase of your transformation, and until you reach your goal weight, you will be allowed one splurge meal per seven-day period. After you have achieved your weight goal, you will enter the Maintenance stage of change; at this point, you will be allowed two splurge meals per week, however, all the other rules of splurging apply during Maintenance.

Splurge is Not FREE

The splurge meal is *not* a free meal. In other words, a splurge meal *must* be accounted for just like any other food. It can be any *thing* you want but it might not be as *much* as you want. A "free meal" (i.e., BFL method) indicates the meal can be anything you want and as much as you want. This is *not* Lifestyle eating.

Restaurants and Splurging

Until at least three to five percent of your starting body weight is gone, you do *not* get any splurge food that you cannot fully account for with calories, carbohydrates, proteins and fats. If you have a favorite restaurant food and you do not know exactly what energy value that meal or food provides, then *you do not get it*. Once you get a firm grip on food logging and you have properly logged your foods until at least the first three to five percent of your starting body weight is gone, you'll be better prepared to judge what your favorite restaurant food actually contains. Your favorite restaurant will still be serving that favorite dish when you drop the weight and have a better grip on the caloric value of that favorite dish.

Women and Splurging

Many women and some men have little interest in splurging on the main course, but would much rather splurge on the dessert. This is *not* a problem at all. If you would rather eat a sensible dinner like chicken, veggies and a sweet potato and *then* have a warm brownie drizzled with chocolate syrup as the splurge, this is perfectly acceptable. Keep in mind that the dessert splurge counts just like any other calorie you eat. You must account for it.

Will I Do Better If I Never Splurge?

You might be inclined to think that any splurging is for sissies or the weak-willed. "I don't need no stinkin' splurge meal! I am strong! I'm a fighter!" If this describes your intention at this point, then there is another adjective to describe your possibility of success: *short-lived*. You will regain any weight lost and then some, <u>guaranteed</u>. Anyone who has ever dieted in the traditional fashion, where foods are forbidden, knows that cravings for favorite foods will cripple progress when you finally cave and gorge yourself with splurge and trigger foods. With overwhelming feelings of failure, you may decide you have "blown it" and may as well go back to your old eating habits. By eating one to two planned splurge meals per week, you will always know you are never far from having a favorite food. This is a lifesaver when it comes to your success as a Lifestyler.

"Yucky" After the Splurge

I understand the psychological warfare going on within your brain. I also understand that after you consume your splurge meal, you may still feel like you have blown it–and on purpose no less! Some clients have reported they feel bloated and "yucky" after their splurge meal, and they have moderate to strong feelings of saying "the heck with it" after experiencing these feelings. These feelings are normal and are to be expected for your first two to four weeks.

For a period of 24 to 72 hours after your splurge meal, you will retain water. With typical high-carb splurge foods, muscle and liver glycogen is at least partly refilled. Each gram of glycogen has three grams of water attached to it. Subcutaneous fat may also temporarily hold more water during this period. This will make you feel "thick." This is a natural and common effect after consuming a splurge meal. Do not panic when it occurs. Simply log the weight, chart the cycle of what happens to you when you splurge (use our weight graph provided), and grow accustomed to this bounce in water weight for one to three days after your splurge.

By knowing when this water weight will show up, you can also plan on what day of a given week you'll look your best and usually be your lightest. I can't say for sure what day you will feel the best and be your lightest, but I can definitely say you will *not* feel your best and be your lightest for a 24 to 72 hour period after your splurge meal. To put it another way, if you have a class reunion you are wanting to attend on Friday night, I would not suggest having a splurge meal on the Wednesday or Thursday prior. Is this yet one more reason to avoid the splurge meal? No. Accept this natural phenomenon, log your weight, chart your splurge meal weight cycle, and grow more in tune with how your body responds to the high-carb/high-fat splurge meals you choose. There is absolutely no reason whatsoever to be alarmed or to panic over this. Stay the course, keep your total weekly calories in check, keep exercising and within 36 to 72 hours after your splurge meal, your weight will drop as quickly as it rose.

Depending on the splurge meal and how depleted your body was of glycogen before your splurge meal, you could gain 1 to 4 percent of your body weight almost overnight–with 95 percent or more of this weight being water and 5 percent or less being fat. This means that if you gain five pounds in the day or two after your splurge meal, 4.75 pounds will be from water and maybe 0.25 pounds will be a true fat increase. Do not worry about it. It will come off and much more if you stay the course and do not cave in with an "I've blown it" mentality.

Planning the Splurge

The real trick with your splurge meals is to plan them. Remember, the splurge is a controlled indulgence. Part of this control is planning. By planning to indulge, you can retain control of your life and food. You did not "mess up." Your plans for Saturday night included spaghetti, garlic bread and ice cream at your favorite Italian restaurant. You are still in control with my recommendation for splurge meals and this is a key component of your success with the Lifestyle.

For clarity, let's use the John Example from the *"Energy Balance"* chapter. He determined that he needs to average 2200 calories a day to lose 1.5 pounds per week. John loves the taste of pizza, and it is his favorite splurge meal. After being diligently on track all week, John asks his wife to order-in pizza from a national chain pizza joint (that way he can look up what the calories in each slice are online).

Earlier in the week, John ate 15 percent less than 2200 on two days so he could build in some additional calories (660) for his splurge meal. The day of John's splurge meal, John ate relatively light but still consumed four meals before dinner totaling 1600 calories. Because John had backed calories off 15 percent for two other days during the week, he now had an additional 660 calories to eat on his splurge day (2200 + 660 = 2860). John had already preplanned all of this and was in great shape to really enjoy some pizza. He had 1260 calories (2860 - 1600 = 1260) remaining for the day. After determining that his Meat Lover's pizza had about 400 calories per slice, he knew he could eat three slices. He ate them slowly and enjoyed every bite knowing he was still totally on track for the week.

Here is what John's week might have looked like if he had pizza on Saturday night.

Mon: 2200
Tue: 1870 (building in a lower calorie day - 15% - for the splurge meal)
Wed: 2200
Thurs: 2200
Fri: 1870 (a 2nd lower calorie day - 15% - for the splurge meal)
Sat: 2860 (his pizza splurge night)
Sun: 2200

Average: 2200 - totally on track and doing great!

You have likely always believed that getting lean and in shape was an EITHER/OR contract. EITHER you are eating perfectly all the time OR you are not. EITHER you are starving all the time and eating nothing but rabbit food OR you are not. Not so. The reality of a lifetime of leanness is we all have to splurge. What we all splurge on, however, can be quite different depending on taste, intolerance, sensitivities, allergies, triggers and even addiction.

Summary

I recommend a meal frequency of four to six per day. This will yield total meals in a week of 28 to 42. While increased meal frequency may not boost metabolism, there are a number of other benefits to consuming small, but frequent, meals.

Dietary supplements of bars, protein shakes or meal replacement shakes can really add nutrient density and convenience to your Lifestyle, however, a word of caution about living on them is in order. Don't! Ensure you are consuming at least an equal number of meals and calories from whole, unpackaged foods when compared to your consumption of dietary supplements or any packaged foods.

Splurge meals are a necessary component of a successful transformation. Trying to cold-turkey your way through a successful transformation without enjoying some favorite foods is only a set-up for failure. The splurge meal should not be confused with "free days" and should not be called "cheat meals." You should anticipate a small spike in weight for up to a few days after a splurge that is overwhelmingly just water weight. Your splurge meals must be accounted for in your logging. One rule is quite simple. *If you don't know what you are eating with regard to calories, carbohydrates, proteins and fats, then you don't get that food–period*. Remember, a splurge meal is a planned indulgence. This means if you are striving for a particular per-day average number of calories, you may have to "build in" a few lower calorie days to compensate for your higher-calorie day that contains your splurge meal during the week. This is acceptable and even desirable when you follow the rules about doing so as stated in the *Energy Balance* chapter.

Take Action and Feel Great!

1. Plan all of your meals a day ahead. Now that you are logging, it is time you started planning ahead instead of only recording your meals after you have consumed the food and drink.

2. Plan no less than four and no more than six small, balanced meals for tomorrow. Continue eating four to six meals every day by planning ahead and doing your best to foresee situations and circumstances that might place you in a position where lengthy periods of food deprivation or poor food availability may otherwise occur.

3. Prepare as many of your meals today for tomorrow.

4. Consider purchasing some balanced nutrition bars or protein powder or a meal replacement powder to ensure that when you don't have a whole-food meal prepared, you still have food to complete your four to six meals per day. You should not rely on bars and shakes for more than two to three meals per day. You can visit www.leannesslifestyle.com for suggestions on balanced nutrition bars and shakes that fit the Lifestyle.

5. Plan your splurge meal for this week. What will you have? Do you know the macronutrient breakdown of that meal? If not, you should find another splurge meal.

6. Build in the additional calories for your splurge by following the guidelines outlined in the *Energy Balance* chapter for doing so.

A Collection of Successful Leanness Lifestylers to Motivate and Inspire

Tracy Greenwalt

154 Lbs 32% Bodyfat
01/01

127 Lbs 16% Bodyfat
07/01

123 Lbs 13% Bodyfat
07/02

123 Lbs 13% Bodyfat
08/02

Before Photos - How?

Front

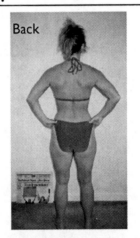

Back

Side

Fully Clothed

Stacie Piver

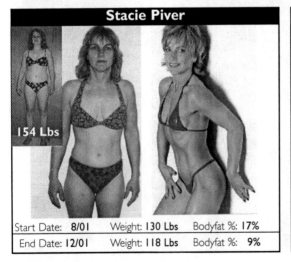

154 Lbs

Start Date: 8/01	Weight: 130 Lbs	Bodyfat %: 17%
End Date: 12/01	Weight: 118 Lbs	Bodyfat %: 9%

Bob Doyle

Start Date: 10/02/00	Weight: 175 Lbs	Bodyfat %: 10%
End Date: 12/18/00	Weight: 160 Lbs	Bodyfat %: 5%

Erin Ernst

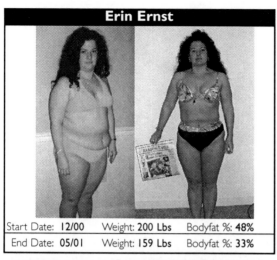

Start Date: 12/00	Weight: 200 Lbs	Bodyfat %: 48%
End Date: 05/01	Weight: 159 Lbs	Bodyfat %: 33%

Tim Barnby

Start Date: 1/06/01	Weight: 224 Lbs	Bodyfat %: 31%
End Date: 7/03/01	Weight: 172 Lbs	Bodyfat %: 7.5%

Tracy Anderson

148 Lbs

Start Date: 4/30/02	Weight: 117.4 Lbs	Bodyfat %: 18.3%
End Date: 7/09/02	Weight: 108 Lbs	Bodyfat %: 11.4%

Deb Baxter

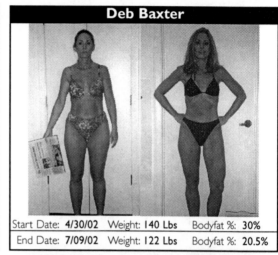

Start Date: 4/30/02	Weight: 140 Lbs	Bodyfat %: 30%
End Date: 7/09/02	Weight: 122 Lbs	Bodyfat %: 20.5%

Kailee Rainey

200 Lbs

Start Date: 8/14/01	Weight: 163 Lbs	Bodyfat %: 29%
End Date: 11/06/01	Weight: 137 Lbs	Bodyfat %: 18.5%

Tom Roehl

Start Date: 5/08/01	Weight: 192 Lbs	Bodyfat %: 22.6%
End Date: 7/24/01	Weight: 174 Lbs	Bodyfat %: 9.9%

Jason Duke

230 Lbs

Start Date: 12/00	Weight: 180 Lbs	Bodyfat %: 19%
End Date: 3/01	Weight: 153 Lbs	Bodyfat %: 7%

Sandi Porter

Start Date: 8/14/01	Weight: 159 Lbs	Bodyfat %: 26.9%
End Date: 11/6/01	Weight: 136 Lbs	Bodyfat %: 16.5%

Cindy Bonnell

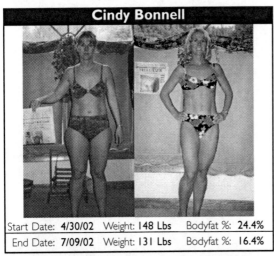

Start Date: 4/30/02	Weight: 148 Lbs	Bodyfat %: 24.4%
End Date: 7/09/02	Weight: 131 Lbs	Bodyfat %: 16.4%

Rick Cartwright

Start Date: 4/01	Weight: 241 Lbs	Bodyfat %: +30%
End Date: 5/02	Weight: 171 Lbs	Bodyfat %: 5.2%

Jeremy Likness

Start Date: 8/99	Weight: 245 Lbs	Bodyfat %: +30%
End Date: 6/01	Weight: 178 Lbs	Bodyfat %: 6.5%

Mindy Holloway

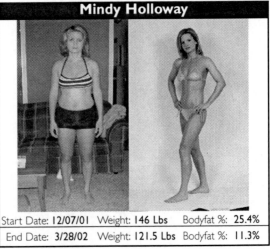

Start Date: 12/07/01	Weight: 146 Lbs	Bodyfat %: 25.4%
End Date: 3/28/02	Weight: 121.5 Lbs	Bodyfat %: 11.3%

Mark Domo

© Copyright Zach Taylor

| Start Date: 10/00 | Weight: 200 Lbs | Bodyfat %: 16% |
| End Date: 7/01 | Weight: 175 Lbs | Bodyfat %: 5% |

Kelly Jones

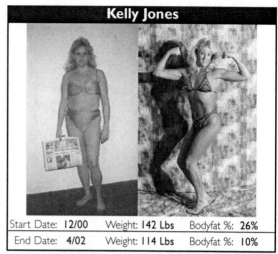

| Start Date: 12/00 | Weight: 142 Lbs | Bodyfat %: 26% |
| End Date: 4/02 | Weight: 114 Lbs | Bodyfat %: 10% |

Wendi Londos

| Start Date: 4/30/02 | Weight: 120 Lbs | Bodyfat %: 16.2% |
| End Date: 7/09/02 | Weight: 108 Lbs | Bodyfat %: 11.1% |

Julie Neumann

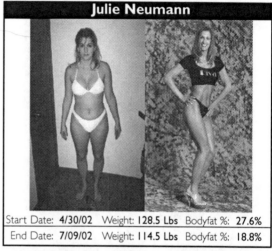

| Start Date: 4/30/02 | Weight: 128.5 Lbs | Bodyfat %: 27.6% |
| End Date: 7/09/02 | Weight: 114.5 Lbs | Bodyfat %: 18.8% |

Don Bender

| Start Date: 1/02 | Weight: 220 Lbs | Bodyfat %: 29% |
| End Date: 7/02 | Weight: 167.5 Lbs | Bodyfat %: 10.5% |

Pam Reeves

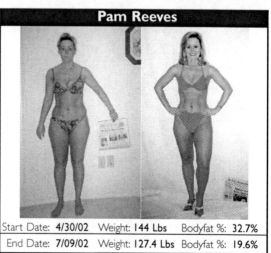

| Start Date: 4/30/02 | Weight: 144 Lbs | Bodyfat %: 32.7% |
| End Date: 7/09/02 | Weight: 127.4 Lbs | Bodyfat %: 19.6% |

Bridget Taft

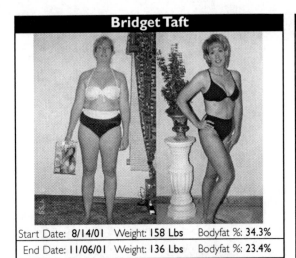

Start Date: 8/14/01	Weight: 158 Lbs	Bodyfat %: 34.3%
End Date: 11/06/01	Weight: 136 Lbs	Bodyfat %: 23.4%

Tony White

Start Date: 8/99	Weight: 216 Lbs	Bodyfat %: 24%
End Date: 11/99	Weight: 172 Lbs	Bodyfat %: 5%

Lisa Glover

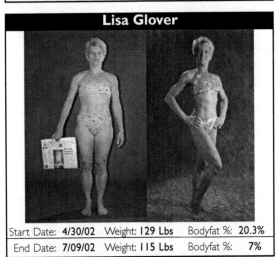

Start Date: 4/30/02	Weight: 129 Lbs	Bodyfat %: 20.3%
End Date: 7/09/02	Weight: 115 Lbs	Bodyfat %: 7%

John Delaney

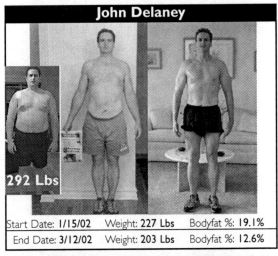

292 Lbs

Start Date: 1/15/02	Weight: 227 Lbs	Bodyfat %: 19.1%
End Date: 3/12/02	Weight: 203 Lbs	Bodyfat %: 12.6%

Estella Jones

Start Date: 4/30/02	Weight: 198 Lbs	Bodyfat %: 38%
End Date: 7/09/02	Weight: 173.2 Lbs	Bodyfat %: 31.1%

David Long

Start Date: 1/15/02	Weight: 197.5 Lbs	Bodyfat %: 21.2%
End Date: 3/12/02	Weight: 178.5 Lbs	Bodyfat %: 12.6%

Larry LaCoursiere

Start Date:	1/15/02	Weight: 196.5 Lbs	Bodyfat %: 17.5%
End Date:	3/15/02	Weight: 175 Lbs	Bodyfat %: 7.8%

Joan Roth

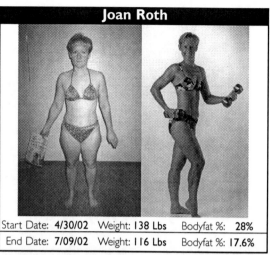

Start Date:	4/30/02	Weight: 138 Lbs	Bodyfat %: 28%
End Date:	7/09/02	Weight: 116 Lbs	Bodyfat %: 17.6%

Dana Tapia

184 Lbs

Start Date:	4/30/02	Weight: 153.5 Lbs	Bodyfat %: 33.4%
End Date:	7/09/02	Weight: 135.5 Lbs	Bodyfat %: 25.9%

Mark Drury

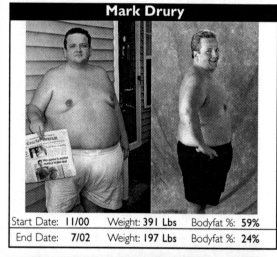

Start Date:	11/00	Weight: 391 Lbs	Bodyfat %: 59%
End Date:	7/02	Weight: 197 Lbs	Bodyfat %: 24%

John Jazwa

Start Date:	1/15/02	Weight: 183 Lbs	Bodyfat %: 20%
End Date:	3/12/02	Weight: 163.5 Lbs	Bodyfat %: 7%

Richard "Snook" Rutherford

Start Date:	1/26/00	Weight: 239 Lbs	Bodyfat %: 22%
End Date:	5/14/00	Weight: 197 Lbs	Bodyfat %: 5.5%

A Collection of Successful Leanness Lifestylers to Motivate and Inspire

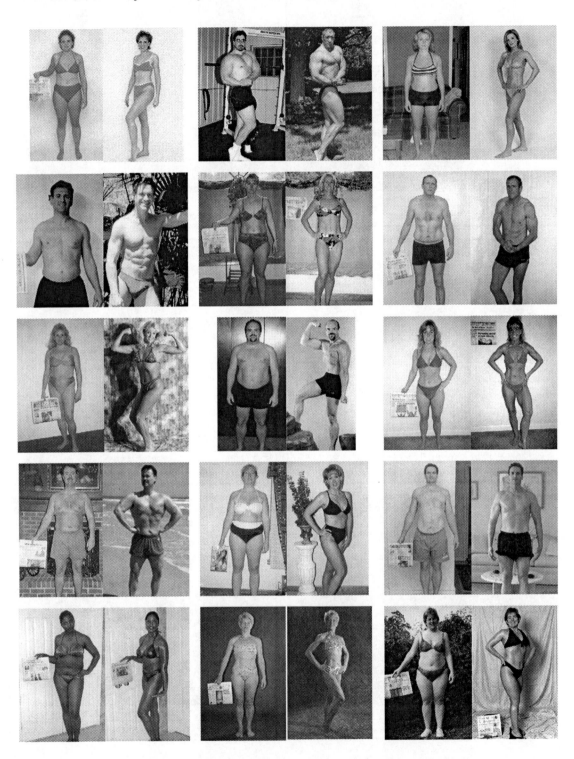

Goals Are A Must But You Better Know "Why"

An unwritten desire is only a dream.

The most successful people on the planet are faithful goal setters. Ask anyone who has achieved any measure of true success, and goal setting most likely is the one significant common denominator. Ever wonder why it is you'll plan a fishing trip or a vacation months in advance, but won't spend 15 minutes a day laying out a plan for your life or even a workout? Is it just "supposed to happen?" I can assure you *it does happen* and it will continue to happen until you set clear goals. This is precisely the reason you are looking to change now. Without goals and a *written* plan, you have only been following a plan to fail. Even if you decide not to choose, you still have made a choice. Until now, I suspect you have had no clear direction in what you want or even remotely how you might get there. While you would not dream of getting in the car and driving across the country without an atlas, you have been living every day without a personal fitness atlas. This can change today if you completely read this chapter and use goals to make your dreams a reality.

If you truly want to achieve the body of your dreams, then you must take your dream a step further and create goals. The difference between a goal and a dream is the clarity of the goal and the clear action steps identified to reach a goal. I could dream and say I want to travel the world. I could wish for a better sales year. I could pray that I get along better with my family. The dream, wish and prayer are a start, but without clarity and action, they are merely wandering generalizations and will never give me a strong foothold for true progress. Dreams and wishes do not have any teeth. When your goals are firm and clear, you are no longer just a spectator sitting back hoping that everything will turn out all right.

In order to travel the world I would need to set out, systematically, what I must do to achieve this dream. Some of these steps might include:

- Contacting the travel agent and performing research on the Internet to determine costs.
- Determining a specific projected date of departure.
- Opening my schedule for that period of time, and determining how other current obligations will be delegated or planned for before leaving.
- Beginning to save x dollars per week until the departure.
- Planning ahead to get passports in order.

It is clear that daydreaming about traveling the world is a far cry from establishing it as a true goal. You've got to vividly see yourself accomplishing your goal, take inventory of where you currently are, and take action steps to see it through to the end.

Choose Performance Over Outcome

Before you can achieve a goal, you must first clearly know what goal it is you are after. If you have read the chapters on *Weight and Body Composition*, you should have a good idea of what you will need to weigh, and how much muscle you will need to add to achieve your dream. Only once you have something that can be measured, can you manage your progress. Understanding the difference between an "outcome goal" and a "performance goal" is of utmost importance. An outcome goal would be stated in this way: "I want to blow away that snippy little secretary at the office with a really killer body." A performance goal would be stated in this way: "I will lower my body fat from 35 percent to 15 percent while adding 5 pounds of muscle by September 17th of this year–16 weeks from now."

If you have not read the chapters on *Weight and Body Composition*, I suggest you go back and do so now. Until you have a clear understanding of where you are now, what any human is capable of, and where you will need to be, you will constantly be fighting an uphill battle with no clear sense of direction. Should you drop ten pounds or thirty pounds? What will it really take for you to achieve your dream? Having clear goals based on performance, rather than outcome, is paramount for success.

All I Want

Eric Hoffer, known as the "Longshoreman Philosopher," once said "To become different from what we are, we must have some awareness of what we are." When people do not take inventory of their status and they have no clue about where it is they are going, they are likely to say things like "Well, Dave, all I want to do is look like you. You know, nothing big or anything, just cut and in shape." Meanwhile, as they say this, they don't realize that I am 180 pounds and seven percent body fat at a height of 5'10" (167.4 pounds of fat-free mass) and they are currently 200 pounds and 25 percent body fat (150 pounds of fat-free mass). They do not realize they are saying they want to drop 20 pounds of fat while adding 17 pounds of muscle. For a man with better-than-average genetics, the total time to accomplish both facets of the dream–dropping 20 pounds of body fat and gaining 17 pounds of muscle–is at least two solid years of diligent, consistent and concerted effort. The fat loss could occur in as little as 8 to 12 weeks, however, the muscle they need to acquire to achieve that "lean and cut" look will take much longer.

Another example of the "All I want" person is "All I want is to drop about 30 pounds of fat and add 15 to 20 pounds of muscle in my 12-week transformation." If you are a woman reading this and what I just said describes what you would have said before reading this chapter, then I have to break the news to you now. I cannot let you continue a minute longer thinking that this scenario is even remotely possible–it is not. It is not that the dream as a whole is bad or wrong. It is just that the time-line you have given yourself to achieve your dream is too short. As a refresher, I would like you to refer to the chapter on body weight, paying particular attention to the sections on the two-compo-nent model and what is realistic when desiring new muscle. When you complete those exercises, you'll quickly see that the average woman who vigorously and consistently uses resistance training in her transformation program might add 0.75 to 1 pound of muscle each month without the use of anabolic steroids. In three months (12 weeks), a woman *might* see three pounds of new muscle, not 15 to 20. Secondly, depending on your current body weight, you already know from the chapter on Energy Balance that you should not strive to lose more than 0.5 percent to 1.5 percent of your body weight each week. The question you must ask yourself now is, "Is all I want realistic?"

If either of the "All I want" individuals above would have taken stock of where they were start-ing, they'd know that "all they want" is truly a remarkable achievement, and not one accomplished in 12 weeks. They would know their proper weight to achieve their body fat goal and they would have realized that "all they want" is quite a reach from where they are. As I have said before, I am not an Adonis, nor am I gifted with the "muscle-building gene." It is quite possible that a man can achieve all I have and much more. A woman can be genetically gifted and rise above the norms as well. Unless you take stock of where you are starting and determine where you'll need to be (weight and body fat), you are trying to take a lengthy journey with no map and no compass. You do not have a goal if you are an "All I want" person.

Visual Help

On the pages of the top bodybuilding, health, and fitness magazines are photos of everything from fit runners to hulking, steroid-juicing freaks. Some magazines also focus on transformations and Before/After photos. Regardless of your personal tastes for what perfection is, I suggest you do your best to find a meaningful, specific goal by determining the height, weight, body fat and body shape of the person you admire. Find out the basic stats of your friend, family member, magazine stud or periodical goddess. Only then, compare notes and determine what it will really take to achieve a similar look. Even if you do not achieve it fully, you will be much better off than you are now, and that is nothing to sneeze at.

Height: Upon noticing that someone weighs 265 pounds and is in shape, it is important that you also know they are 6'5" tall. If you have a desire for quite a bit of muscle, you need to know that most men will not achieve a lean, muscular physique much past 106 pounds at 5 feet tall with 10 pounds added for every inch thereafter. A more detailed example is given in the body weight chap-ter. If you are 5'10" tall, there is little chance you will ever be lean (less than 10 percent body fat) while weighing more than 206 pounds (106 + 10 lbs for every inch above 5 feet). If you are a woman, then you must know that the minimum healthy weight would be about 105 pounds at 5 feet tall and 3 to 4 pounds for every inch above 5 feet. If you are a 5'5" woman, then I must suggest that shooting for a body weight less than 120 is probably unrealistic or undesirable, unless it is temporary for a photo shoot, fitness competition or bodybuilding show. Height matters! Do not ignore it when determining the statistics of your idols.

Weight: What does your idol weigh? You should not judge a book by its cover, and you should not guess at what your role model weighs. If you want to attain a meaningful specific physique, you have to have the specifics to shoot for. If you are a woman who stands 5'2" tall and your idol is 5'7" tall and 130 pounds, consider that she weighs 25 pounds more than 105 (the base 5 foot tall woman) and that means your idol has 3.57 pounds for every inch she is above 5 feet (25 / 7). I If you are 5'2" tall, then you might calculate what you would really like to weigh as 105 + (3.57 x 2) and this equals 112 pounds. Now you have created a meaningful and specific goal to shoot for!

Body Fat: Sure, the Coca-cola model looks buff and the beach babe is sexy, but besides the attractive face, what body fat do they have that creates "no jiggle" and "abs of steel?" Unless you know how low their body fat is, you might ignorantly assume you can achieve their look with a much higher body fat.

Body Shape: Most men are shaped like apples and woman like pears.
The hormone testosterone causes men to store excess fat mainly in the abdomen. Increased amounts of abdominal fat are a significant risk to health.

Apples have thicker waists, not much curve at the waists and thinner legs. If you are an apple man, you have always had a hard time achieving the infamous 6-pack and your legs may resemble those of a common barnyard chicken. In other words, your fat distribution is not even and you hold a great deal of fat around the midsection.

If you are an apple woman, you have likely always liked your legs more than your midsection. Even when apple women are out of shape, I often see them wearing shorts because they simply do not distribute a good percentage of their body fat on their legs (much like a man).

The hormone estrogen causes women to store fat in the hips and thighs. Although hip and thigh fat is more concerning to women than abdominal fat is to men, it is a much less risk to health.

Most men do not truly develop the pear shape of a woman, however, it is common for a man to distribute body fat to a greater degree on his thighs than on his abdomen. These men (I like to call them the lucky ones) will have rather large thighs–usually desirable by a man–and flatter abdomens. As with women, a skinfold analysis will clearly tell if your fat is distributed in this manner.

If you are a pear woman, you have likely always fretted over your hips and butt, while your waist has been relatively small by comparison. Some call this the hourglass figure.

Abdominal fat is easier to lose than hip and thigh fat.

Many women would call this a cruel twist of nature. Because of the predominance of estrogen over testosterone, women not only have greater fat stores and decreased muscle mass, but also find it harder to lose this fat. Because of the female body's genetic need to be prepared for pregnancy, it must maintain adequate stores of fat energy for nine months.

It is also interesting to note that the fat pattern in women changes after menopause. This results in the accumulation of fat around the middle and loss of the "figure." This is due to a loss of estrogen and therefore a greater influence of the male hormone, testosterone. Not only does the figure change, but there is also an increased risk of heart disease.

You can determine your pattern of fat distribution by taking body measurements at the belly button and the widest point around the hips and thighs and calculating a waist to hip ratio.

Example for men
Waist = 32 inches
Hips = 32 inches
32/32 = 1.0

Example for women
Waist = 32 inches
Hips = 36 inches
32/36 = 0.88

For men the ideal ratio is less than 1.0.
For women the ideal ratio is less than 0.80.

The important thing to note with shapes is it is important that you know the shape of the person you admire. If you are an apple trying to get the exact same shape as the pear, you might be fighting an uphill battle and vice versa. With the exception of the few, top models and bodybuilders, we all have an Achilles heel we would rather forget about. Do not compare yourself to someone with a different body shape. As the saying goes, "Compare apples to apples and pears to pears."

Where Have You Been?

Not only can you look to the periodicals for a guide to help you visualize what you'd like to look like, I would venture to guess that you might not have to look any farther than your own photo album. If you want to get a real idea of what it is you are absolutely capable of–not that you are not capable of more–find the one best photo of yourself since high school. Is there any denying you can look like that again or even better? The task of reviewing where it is you have already been is a powerful tool to show you at least what you are capable of achieving again. You have already been there!

Put the Goal in Sight

Though the marathon runner may be completely exhausted from the effort, when the finish line is in view her pace will quicken. When the goal is in sight, things change dramatically.

Those who can clearly visualize the goal from the farthest away are the ones who will surely reach that goal. When the goal is clearly in sight, there is a seemingly unstoppable force drawing you to it. You cannot help but make whatever effort is necessary to reach it.

When the goal is in sight, so is the path in which will get you there. The more precisely you can visualize your ultimate goal, the more clearly you will understand how to achieve it.

What are you working to accomplish? Precisely, exactly, specifically, what is it? What color is it? How does it feel when you touch it? What does it smell like? How does it sound? Make it real in your mind. See all the rich details. Visualize clearly, where you are going and you will find a way to get there.

Ralph Marston

And So It Is Written ... and So It Shall Be Done

Now that you have established a clear vision of your goal, it is important that you write your goals with purpose and specificity. No more sitting on the sidelines waiting for it to happen. It is time to get out of the bleachers and into the game. Either you will make it happen, or it will never happen. After writing your goals, you should post them in a conspicuous place where you will be reminded of them day in and day out. Start and finish your day by writing and reviewing your goals.

It is not enough to know the numbers, nor is it enough to "really want it." As I said in the beginning of this chapter, the difference between wishing, dreaming and goals is that goals have specific direction, steps and action statements to take you from point A to point B. Now it is time to change your wish and dream into a goal.

As a commitment device, writing your goals provides many great advantages. Truly magical is the act of writing your dreams down on paper and specifying the steps needed to achieve the goals. Once you put your commitment down on paper with action steps in place to achieve those commitments, you will live up to what you have written down.

Part of this magic comes from the fact that once you have written it down, you have clearly provided evidence that you are truly serious about changing. It is no longer a passing thought or whim. The opportunity to "forget" or "deny" that you actually want to change is stripped. The evidence becomes clear–it is on paper in black and white. Your own handwriting provides proof that you are serious and committed. The magic continues when you are compelled to act consistently with the words you put on paper. This is undeniable. Purely verbal statements do not provide such drive and clarity.

Coaching client Jeremy wrote me a reinforcing perspective on the importance of writing goals:

"Anyone who has played the game 'Operator' where one person delivers a message to the next and then you compare the final message to the original - you know how the message can change. When you do not write down your goals, you are playing operator with yourself. You might have a goal in your mind. Then you go to sleep and wake up in a different mood. This can slightly change your goal. After 12-weeks, it is like passing the goal through 84 people. Can you imagine how the original message might get lost?"

Coaching client Rebecca laminates her goals after writing them and keeps them in her pocket. Put them in your office at work on a big 8.5 x 11 piece of paper staring you in the face every moment possible. What about the dashboard of your car? The fridge? The bathroom mirror?

Writing down your goal shows that you care and are ready to take action. It provides you with a guide to refer to day by day and ensures that you keep the original message intact. If you have a bad day, instead of waking up the next day feeling down and deciding to change course, you can pick up your goals, read them, and get back on track.

"Until you commit your goals to paper, you have intentions that are seeds without soil." Anonymous

---

Lifetime Achievement Fitness Goal

Envisioning your Lifetime Achievement Fitness (LAF) goal is of utmost importance to a successful transformation. I am clearly making the distinction between the LAF goal and other lifetime pursuits of happiness goals, because I want your focus on this and this alone right now. Books and tapes by Zig Ziglar, Brian Tracy, Phil McGraw, Tony Robbins and others are perfect additions to your Lifestyle library, and I recommend you choose the books and tapes that you seem to be drawn to for better life management. For your purposes here, however, I want you focused on your LAF goal.

Ultimately, you need to decide where fitness happiness lies. Where is bliss? What are the specifics of your LAF goal? By demanding specifics, I hope to prevent you from writing something like "I just want to be thin" or "I don't want this gut any more" or "I want to stop jiggling and get rid of the cellulite." These statements can be a part of your LAF goal, however, they are far too general to have any meaning. What will you weigh? What will your body fat be? What dress size will you wear? What pants size will you wear? Where will you shop for clothes? What activities will you engage in, and how will these activities make you feel? Will you compete in a sport? The LAF goal is one you set realistically by taking into consideration at least the following factors:

1. What is the lowest body weight you have achieved for at least six months since high school? While it is true that you may be able to achieve a lower body weight than this, I have recognized that few actually achieve it. Anne Fletcher, author of "Thin for Life" states that most "Masters" recognize there is a point of comfortable, healthy living and the dream weight. Typically, the comfortable, healthy-living weight is slightly higher than the dream weight. Some may touch the dream weight shortly and then gain 5 to 10 pounds where they live quite comfortably. It doesn't mean the dream weight is unattainable, however, realistic expectations based on the performance of the Masters and clients I've coached tells me that setting a goal substantially below the weight you've maintained for at least six months since high school is potentially setting yourself up for disappointment. This is not a stop sign–it is simply a caution sign.

2. Throughout life, there are many windows of opportunities opening and closing all the time. If your LAF goal includes such things as becoming a ballerina or playing professional base-ball, then please take into consideration the reality of whether youth, skill and time are on your side. While it sounds simple enough, be real about what it is you will be doing when you reach your LAF goal.

3. It is okay to make your goal slightly higher than you believe you can achieve. Successful transformationists set goals just out of reach, but not out of sight. Some people will self-destruct almost invariably just before they reach their goal, no matter where that goal is. The inherent fears of success and the "I don't deserve to be happy and lean" thoughts are no laughing matters. Of the hundreds of clients I have coached, nearly all will do better when they shoot for the stars, even if they fall just a little short.

One-Year Goal

Take into consideration the guidelines I've given you for the LAF goal and again, being very specific, determine precisely what you'll weigh and what your body fat will be one year from now.

Six-Month Goal

Repeat the same steps for the six-month goal as you did for the one-year goal. What is realistic? Recall that I suggest a weekly weight loss no greater than 0.5 to 1.5 percent of your body weight. Never forget that any weight loss is great, and slower, consistent and progressive weight loss is usually better than quick weight loss.

Three-Month Goal (12 weeks)

Popular media has made this goal the most common to shoot for. Never forget that many magazines over-inflate the results of most programs. Advertisements are many times completely false and misleading. Use the guidelines I have provided in this book to help guide you to a realistic 12-week weight-loss/muscle-gain goal.

Two-Month Goal (8 weeks)

If you have a goal to lose 30 pounds in 12 weeks, you are not likely to reach that goal if you have not lost approximately two-thirds of that weight (20 pounds) by the 8-week mark. This makes the 8-week goal extremely important and not one you should overlook.

One Month Goal (4 weeks)

The same analogy applies to the 4-week goal. If you weigh 219 pounds and want to lose 30 pounds, you will be in trouble if you still weigh 219 pounds at the 4-week mark. The 4-week goal then, could be considered just as important, or more important, than the 8- or 12-week goals. Achieving your first goal magically lifts your spirit! Instead of dreaming, wishing and praying without results, when you set and achieve goals, you become an instant winner and you will feel the difference.

> Here is what coaching member Bethanie had to say about reaching her one-month goal:
>
> *"Yahoo! I made it! Right on the money. This morning I weighed in at 165! That was my goal and I got to it, it made me feel so good! So, I have now lost 11 lbs and cannot wait to lose the next 10. I am feeling so good about myself and I feel my attitude almost radiate everywhere I go. So once again - YAHOO!"*

Weekly Goals

The one-month goal is very important, however, you will never make your one-month goal if you don't consistently succeed at achieving your one-week goals. The second most important goal you set should be a complete layout of what you will weigh each week for at least 8 to 12 weeks. Many will lay out a weekly target goal weight every week until they reach their LAF.

I recommend weighing every day but I strongly urge you to plan your weekly target weight loss around a Monday or Tuesday weigh in. I purposely choose a Monday or Tuesday weigh in for my clients' weekly goals because it helps keep them honest on the weekends. If you binge and gorge yourself through a weekend those mostly water, and likely negligible fat pounds, will still be around come Monday or Tuesday. If you set Friday or Saturday as your official weekly target weigh in each week you have too great an opportunity to continue approaching a known danger zone—the weekend—with reckless abandon. After a successful Friday or Saturday weigh in you may feel liberated and free knowing you have all week to try and work off excessive consumption of food and drink from the weekend.

Don't allow yourself to fall more than a week behind. If you have set a course to lose 1.5 pounds per week and you currently weigh 180 pounds then at the end of your first week you should weigh 178.5 pounds. Assuming you achieve your first week's goal you're ready for week two. If you still weigh 178.5 pounds at the end of week two you are now 1.5 pounds behind in achieving your weekly goals. It's very important that you analyze your food and drink intake quite closely at this point. Determine if you truly followed the plan you set that week. Don't overlook factors that can temporarily create shifts in water retention as well (see Chapter 4 – *Your Weight*). Once you've completed these tasks it's time to be more diligent and consistent, while perhaps, increasing your vigorous activity slightly so as not to fall behind in your third week.

Today's Goal

When you are climbing the ladder to fitness, you cannot jump rungs on the ladder. Every little bit helps–and every little quit hurts. Every successful transformation is built by consistently assembling one successful, positively directed, focused moment after another. The obese and svelte body is both created and destroyed one bite at a time.

When you accomplish a small goal, you experience success. That is motivating! Daily repetition of this process becomes even more motivating! Today's goals are the most important goals you set. If you do not accomplish today's goal many days a week, you will not reach any of your other goals. You will never build momentum. John Maxwell writes in *The Success Journey*:

> *"Goals not only help you develop initial motivation by making your dreams obtainable, but they also help you continue to be motivated - and that creates momentum. Once you get going on the success journey, it will be very hard to stop you. The process is similar to what happens with a train. Getting it started is the toughest part of the trip. While standing still, a train can be prevented from moving forward by one-inch blocks of woods under each of the locomotive's drive wheels. However, once a train gets up to speed, not even a steel-reinforced concrete wall five feet thick can stop it."*

What one step can you take today that will bring you one step closer to realizing your 4-week goal? There are a number of today goals you can set for yourself, however, the scariest thing about a today goal is it needs to be done *today*. This may seem a bit overwhelming. Don't let it scare you into a catatonic state. Only so much can be done in any one day. The body you are dreaming of will not be created tomorrow but you have to make sure you do not put off until tomorrow what can be done today. Doing anything with purpose is better than many things haphazardly, so get moving. Your visual goal and your LAF goal are the result of setting and achieving smaller, equally important goals along the way.

Step 1: Write three goals you would like to accomplish today. Of these three goals, which goal is the most important? Second-most important? Third-most important? A popular saying is that you can do anything you want but you cannot do *everything* you want. Prioritize your three goals for today so you know precisely where your focus should lie. List up to ten action steps you can take today that will help to ensure you achieve your most important goal today. Write them out on a piece of paper.

Example:
Today's Most Important Goal: I will finish reading *The Leanness Lifestyle*.

Action Steps:
1. I will not watch television tonight.

2. I will spend quality time with the family until supper is over; then I will take the evening for me.

3. I will get three loads of laundry done, so I do not feel depressed and guilty when I am reading *The Leanness Lifestyle* tonight.

4. I will write a "to do" list early and check off each thing as I get it done. I will be focused on getting these things done so I can feel a sense of accomplishment and free my time for this evening.

As you can see, the action steps list does not have to include ten things to accomplish your goal for the day. However, the more steps you can list the better.

Step 2: Consider the action steps written. Which one is most important for you to achieve your goal today?

Step 3: Commit to or do the most important action step right now! If nothing else is done today, you will still have taken the most important action you needed to. By doing so, you will begin to realize that "by the yard it's hard, but by the inch it's a cinch." You have to start somewhere, so do the one thing that is most important today and start!

Be Specific

It is vital that your daily goals are clear and measurable. If you cannot measure it, then it is a dream. Dreams are nice. They are necessary to get things going. Nonetheless, dreams are not goals. Do not set a goal of:

- "I'll make better food choices." Instead of saying something like this try and finish this sentence: "I can begin to make better food choices immediately by ..." OR "One other thing I will do to improve my food choices is ..." OR "I will eat five times today and space my meals three hours apart, focusing on eating when hungry and stopping when satisfied."

- "I'll eat more fruits and vegetables." Instead of saying this, why not quantify your statement by saying "Today I will eat one whole fruit and one serving of vegetables."

- "I'll workout today." Instead of saying this, how about saying, "I will establish my maxes today for the bench press, lateral raise and standing barbell curl." OR "I will train according to the Lifestyle workout I've chosen and won't cut it short" OR "I will train at 75 percent of my predicted maximum heart rate on the treadmill for 30 minutes."

While the differences between generalizations and specific goals may seem small, the difference in results is huge. If you generalize or are not specific with your goal setting, you will never have a real goal to shoot for. You will still be wanting, wishing and praying without a plan.

Today's simple, three-step goal setting exercise should be repeated every single day of your transformation adventure. It is completely impossible to hit your 4-week goal if you do not start today. Can you begin eating one fruit and one vegetable a day if you never buy any? Is it time to make a grocery run? If your cupboards are still filled with your favorite treats, you are unlikely to reach your 4-week goal. Clean them out and throw that junk away today! If you have not made the doctor's appointment so you can get that "bum foot" examined so that you can exercise, you will not reach your 4-week goal. Call the doc today! Without a kitchen food scale and good, trusty bath scale, you will not have the tools to measure your foods and progress. If you are not using objective measures to end mysteries, you will not reach your 4-week goal. Go buy both tools today! Do you know what you weigh and what you should weigh? If your answer is no, review the chapters on *Weight and Body Composition*. You can do many activities today. You do not have to do them all but you must do at least one to start. To progress effectively, you must make daily visits to the three-step daily goal setting exercises.

If something happens in your personal life, a written goal can help you stay focused. Even in the face of tremendous adversity, goals can help you stay the course. Have you lost a dearly loved one? This does not mean you have to stop improving yourself. I can assure you your loved one would want you to continue and would never wish a life of disease and obesity on you. You should honor your loved one with your renewed vigor and commitment. You do not have to experience a painful loss to experience the benefits of properly writing and announcing your goals. When you feel down and out without reason, picking up your written goals can remind you of the original plan and, again, help you get back on track.

When you have attained your goals, frame them or throw them away, whichever ritual suits you, but make sure to write new goals. You should have a set of goals for every day, every week, every month, and every year. If you have not started, pick up that pen or pull up that laptop and begin writing!

Public Commitments–Not Private Pledges

When setting goals, it is simply not enough to keep it to yourself. You cannot keep it secret. You have to tell others. You have to go public. Public commitments tend to be lasting commitments. By telling other people what you are going to accomplish, how you are going to do it, and how important it is for you to accomplish your goal, you will set off an entire cascade of events that will immensely increase your chances of success. Going public greatly reinforces your commitment.

Dr. Cialdini writes in "Influence"...

"Once we have made a choice or taken a stand, we will encounter personal and interpersonal pressures to behave consistently with that commitment. Those pressures will cause us to respond in ways that justify our earlier decision. Whenever one takes a stand that is visible to others, there arises a drive to maintain that stand in order to look like a consistent person. Good personal consistency is desirable as a trait; someone without it could be considered fickle, uncertain, pliant, scatter-brained, or unstable; someone with it is viewed as rational, assured, trustworthy, and sound. For appearance sake, then, the more public a stand, the more reluctant we will be to change it."

Dr. Prochaska writes in "Changing for Good"...

"Don't make the mistake of keeping your commitment secret. Going public with your intended change increases anxiety, since you may feel embarrassed if you fail. Public commitments are more powerful than private pledges. When you go public, you enlist the sympathy of others, and allow them to understand your behaviors as they change.

Do not keep it in the family. Tell your colleagues and your neighbors, write friends and relatives. Some people even put a short advertisement in the newspaper, announcing that on a certain date they will quit smoking or start losing weight and that they will not be responsible for their moods.

It takes courage to go public but remember: Courage is not the absence of fear, but the ability to act in the face of fear."

Want to show just how serious you are this time? Make a list of all the people you respect and who you want to respect you and then get some business cards. Write on the back of each card "I just wanted you to know that I am committed to losing 30 pounds by April 1st. Feel free to check in on me and ask how I'm doing." Then hand-sign your name. Pass them out or mail them to everyone on your list. If you have any hope of truly convincing those around you that you are serious this time, then a remarkably great way to do that is to provide evidence in writing of your commitment. It is undeniable that people have a natural tendency to think that a written statement reflects the true attitude of the person who made it. Unless there is strong evidence to the contrary, people automatically assume that someone who makes a commitment on paper means it.

Not everyone you publicly tell will support you. Those who you firmly believe will support you fully may end up being your worst critic. Others who you currently believe will be your archrival will lift you and support you in ways you have never imagined. You probably have a good idea of who will support you and who will not, but you must know that what you currently perceive may not be the case once you let the cat out of the bag. No matter which people criticize you, or how they do it, do not let them take your focus off your goals.

David Competes and Builds a Website

In February of 1999, I decided to enter the "Show Me Naturals" body building show in May of 1999 in St. Louis. I really felt I needed a true reason to train harder. In August of 1998, I lost my mother in a tragic automobile accident. I loved her so dearly and in February of 1999 was still in a mental and emotional slump. Let me be honest. I was a pathetic mess in the gym. I told a friend at one point, shortly after my loss, that if I had the antidote for how I felt at that time I could bottle it and make millions because I was extremely catabolic and was losing muscle at an alarming rate.

Within 30 days after making the decision to enter the show, I had told no less than a dozen local friends and family members of my intentions. My workouts started getting better and I had a new fire once again for training hard. In March of 1999, after long deliberations with numerous Internet web design firms, I decided that the poor business models they were presenting to me and the unbelievably high prices they were charging for web design simply wasn't worth it. I knew what I wanted out of our web site and communicating with a designer on a regular basis carried a price I was not willing to pay. So, I decided to build the web site myself from scratch. Keep in mind that I did not know what Hyper Text Markup Language (HTML) stood for, let alone how to design a web page that I had repeatedly been told any 14-year-old could do. Nonetheless, I committed with my mouth and by pen that I would build my own web site and it would be far better than the one I was currently paying for. This commitment came with a steep price.

Beginning in March, I was literally reading four web design books at once, plus still searching for the right software and host for the new site. I was working 18-hour days, 7 days per week and getting 4 to 5 hours of sleep per night. By the end of March, the work and lack of sleep began taking a serious toll on my lean muscle. I felt flat. I was getting weaker and losing muscle much faster than I wanted to. Sure, I was getting leaner but the rate of muscle loss was killing me. Meanwhile, I'd get an e-mail or a phone call, or on rare occasions actually see a friend, and they'd all ask, "So, how's the diet and training going?" I would reply, "Not too bad, a little tired, but it's coming along." They would always nod with their approval and we would move on to the next subject. In my mind, let me tell you, I just wanted to quit.

On numerous days, I no more wanted to do the Missouri show than a man on the moon. I thought very seriously about *not* going but I could not back out. You know why? Because I had already told everyone who mattered that I was getting in the show. Now they were all asking me how I was doing. What could I say? "I am backing out because I'm killing myself working." No, that would not have been consistent with my words spoken only a month or so earlier. Another reason I couldn't back out was, as anyone who's ever been in a show knows, you have to set up your hotel arrangements weeks ahead and if you want your family and friends to have good seats you have to purchase them months ahead. I had done both. Again, another commitment in which I could not back out of. No refunds!

So what did I do? I backed off my workdays to 14 to 15 hours and around that same time things really started clicking for me on web design. I was getting the hang of it! I committed to getting more sleep, as I knew that was the culprit for my diminishing muscle, and I stabilized. I quit losing muscle. For a few weeks, I even got stronger. While I do not think I regained all the muscle I lost because of my work and stress overload, I entered the show in great shape and one pound heavier than my show the year before. I was pleased. The web site was up and running and ten times better than any site I had paid thousands for in the past.

I speak from first-hand experience. Written and verbal commitments are powerful weapons of influence and success.

A Price to Pay

For every decision you make there is a price to pay. H. Jackson Brown, author of *Life's Little Instruction Book*, said,

> *You pay a price for getting stronger.*
> *You pay a price for getting faster.*
> *You pay a price for jumping higher.*
> *[But also] you pay a price for staying just the same.*

Regardless of your choice, it is important to realize that there is indeed a price you pay, but there is also a reward for making the choice to change for the better.

So why is it that people do not turn their dreams into goals? People who have clear goals always outperform those who do not. They are richer, happier and lead more fulfilling lives. Companies, individuals, teams and others all need goals to be champions, so why don't they all do it? Heck, how hard is it to set a few goals? You take out a piece of paper or some index cards and you follow the guidelines I have provided in this chapter. It may take a couple hours the first time, but the daily three-step goal setting exercise takes less than 15 minutes a day and all but guarantees you will succeed if you do it. How tough is that?

Barriers to Setting Goals

In his February 1999 newsletter, Stuart Goldsmith, a rebel European author, provided some great insight into why people take no action with respect to goal setting. I quote:

"To set yourself a goal means to set yourself up for change. Any goal that you can think of, large or small reduces to the statement: 'I hereby promise to change in the following way...' People fear change - it is the unknown. Fear immobilizes. Fear stops you dead in your tracks. It is safer to stay well within your comfort zone.

Next comes our old enemy laziness, or inertia, and this, I believe, is the real reason people do not set goals.

Above everything else, a goal is a written contract with you to do something. To achieve even the smallest goal requires discipline, work and focus; all three in some measure. Despite all of that 'bounty from the infinite universe' crap, people know deep in their gut that you do not get something for nothing in this world. Since most people are home idle lazy, how do you think they react when faced with a contract containing the words discipline, work and focus. Why, they break out into a cold sweat. Their hands tremble and seem unable to grasp the pen. They go to sign, then draw back, then go to sign again. Suddenly, they feel faint. The pen slips from their numbed hand and clatters to the floor. They feel tired. Perhaps it is time for a lie down? They will sign that contract one-day very soon now - perhaps tomorrow.

I believe this is why people do not set goals. They still want all of the rewards and goodies which would have come their way had they set goals and applied the discipline, work and focus. Oh yes, they want all of these things, but they want them for free. They seek to short circuit reality, and now embark upon a path which leaves them prey to the happy-clappy, 'You can have it all' seminar snake-oil artist."

Zig Ziglar states in his book *"Over the Top"* there are four primary reasons people do not set goals:

1. Fear
2. Poor self-image
3. Never understood the benefits
4. Are unaware about how to set goals or complete the tasks to achieve them

Throughout this book, I have addressed all of the reasons Zig says you have for not setting goals. Overcoming fear of change is addressed in the *Are You Ready to Change* chapter. Poor self-image is addressed in the Emotions, Boobytraps and other chapters. The benefits received by setting goals and on which goals to focus are addressed in this chapter. The action steps necessary for achieving your fitness goals are also addressed throughout this entire book.

I want to challenge you to write down your goals. Do it right now! If you do not, there is a good chance you will not for far too long. Do not let another day, month or year go by without establishing a plan.

Know Your Why

Whether this is your first or fiftieth body transformation, it is very important that you know precisely WHY you are about to begin again. The Lifestyle is not inherently difficult. Once you understand HOW to create a negative energy balance, one where more calories are being expended than consumed, the path to superfitness is easy on paper. One may even ignorantly presume that you have all you need to succeed with some basic, simple formulas. An imbecile can do the math of energy balance. It's pretty simple really. Eat a little less than you are and exercise a lot more. So why is it so ineffective for me or anyone else to simply tell you to eat a little less and exercise a lot more? It works wonderfully well for rats in controlled studies. The answer lies in the fact that you are neither a rat nor an imbecile. The metamorphosis you are about to create doesn't occur from simply knowing "how" to transform based on energy balance formulas. It does not occur from me simply telling you to eat a little less and exercise a lot more. Emotional, physical, spiritual and social factors affect everyday living. Dynamic living as a free-thinking human in 21st century America is not the same as living the life of a rat in a controlled university experiment. When you consider these factors, even when you are completely aware of *how* weight loss and lifelong weight control is achieved, it becomes very important from the onset that you know WHY you must transform and ultimately serve the true purpose for your life.

Consistency and *persistence* are two strong values you must possess to succeed. Failure truly cannot handle persistence. Many times, when an individual starts a weight-loss program, they do so after some emotional arousal. I have referred to this process of change as "finding your click." Perhaps someone said something about your weight that again really hurt your feelings. Perhaps you saw a recent photograph of yourself and couldn't believe it was really you. You may have mastered many areas of your life and may even be in good shape now, but your current level of fitness is still the one area you haven't mastered and it feels like your life just isn't complete because of it.

Your "Why" Builds Self-Motivation

Unless you are self-motivated and driven by an exceptionally strong WHY, the daily grind and pain that accompanies all change makes it too easy to forget your intended purpose for starting. External motivators, such as encouraging words from friends, family and coworkers are never enough to see a Lifestyle plan through to completion. Attending meetings and participating as a member of a support group for weight control are never enough, by themselves, to see a Lifestyle plan through to completion. No matter how beneficial and supportive external motivators are, every external motivator is short-lived. The coolest thing about self-motivation over external motivation is self-motivation never leaves your side. You are never left "without" and it is you who controls it. You can draw upon your self-motivation daily, and even minute by minute but only if you build it first. Self-motivation is the motivation that comes from having a sense of purpose, a sense of self-esteem and self-determination. Creating a strong WHY adds to the strength of self-motivation.

Your "Why" Solidifies Commitment

Goals should be *written*–because they are a contract with yourself. Goals should be public commitments, not private pledges. There must not only be long-range goals, but mid-range, short-range and today goals as well. Goals must also be clear and date-sensitive. In effect, you must know precisely where you are going and when you will get there if you truly desire to get anywhere worth going to. After the goals are clear and firm though, what's the next step to take? The next step is to define why you must achieve those goals without exception, excuses or escape. Your WHY must affirm all of the reasons you absolutely cannot continue on the path you are currently living. Your WHY also clearly defines the positive expectations of charging ahead toward your goals.

Your WHY moves your flaccid, yet good, intentions from wishes to commitment. Only once your commitment reaches an irreversible, driving position, will you ultimately succeed at achieving the body of your dreams. While goals solidify your dreams, your WHY strengthens and solidifies your commitment. Your commitment must be solid because obstacles and the inevitable crises are lurking around the corner, waiting for the opportunity to slip in and thwart your forward momentum. When you've reached a level of commitment without compromise, you will move over, around and even through those obstacles. It's not important that you begin your transformation possessing some divine knowledge guaranteeing you will be all-knowing and all-seeing when obstacles cross your path. When your WHY is strong and personal, you will figure out the "how" in every instance. Instead of focusing on the obstacle or inevitable crisis, you will focus on why it's important to overcome it. Brian Tracy says, "*Your job is to be clear about your goal and flexible about the process of attaining it.*" With proper goals and an uncompromising commitment, instead of giving up when encountering the first, fifth or twenty-fifth obstacle, you will seek the wisdom and clarity to overcome each obstacle. You will maintain flexibility, so although the path to your goal will wind and weave, you too will bend, shift and change paradigms to keep focused on your goal while adapting the path to achieve it.

Writing Your "Why"

Your WHY must define the pain associated with living at less than your potential. It should include a history of the pains you've experienced for as long as you can remember. Your WHY should also include the positive emotions, activities and all the good that will come from you achieving your goals. As author Grace Speare says, "*Think and feel yourself there! To achieve any aim in life you need to project the end result. Think of the elation, the satisfaction, the joy! Carrying the ecstatic feeling with you will bring the desired goal into view.*"

I believe it is best if your WHY is written autobiographically in the form of a letter. You may be the only person who ever sees this letter but it is written to the most important person in your life—you. There are many questions that need to be answered in your WHY letter but only you can answer them. Some of the issues needing addressed and answered in your WHY include:

1. Why now? This first question addresses the very real problem for far too many chronic contemplators of waiting until just the right time to start. Since you are reading this now, however, there is likely a good, strong, positive reason for starting now versus later. If your answer is "there's no time like the present," this may be perfectly acceptable but continue reading anyway. Is there some other reason that is uniquely important to you addressing this first question of "Why now?" What most recently occurred that pressed you to think seriously about transforming your body and your life for the better? You can achieve *anything* you set your mind to, however, you cannot achieve *everything* you set your mind to. It's important that you define why beginning now is necessary and why it will be better than "okay" to put some other life's ambitions on the backburner for awhile. There is only so much you can focus on at any one time. It's okay to focus on you now. It's your turn. The noisy complications of daily life must be silenced a bit so you can give yourself some overdue attention.

2. What recurring mental, physical, emotional and social pains do you experience by living at less than you were destined to be? When did this start? What have you missed out on over the years? What haven't you participated in? What can you no longer put up with and tolerate that being better physically fit can solve?

3. Who else is impacted from you not being your best? How will you finally achieving superfitness positively affect others within your innermost circle of friends, family and loved ones? How does it negatively affect them now? While you must ultimately follow the Lifestyle primarily for you, there is nothing wrong with wanting to be more attractive to your soul mate. Do you feel your soul mate has been tricked or short-changed by your past dietary and activity practices?

4. How will you really benefit by becoming better fit? What innermost desires will be fulfilled once you achieve your ultimate body or state of fitness? There is likely a personal connection between your ultimate dream body and how you perceive you will feel once you achieve it. Don't be afraid to speak simply of the pride of being more fit than the average American. This is not the same as vanity and you are not conceited simply because you choose to be physically far better than average. It's okay for one of the many reasons for change to be very simply that you want to look awesome and be more attractive. The benefits, from your perspective and unique as they are to you, do not need to be filled with noble causes. They do need to be meaningful to you and reflective of what drives you. Ralph Marston says, *"There is enormous power in following a purpose which is truly yours. When there's something that makes the obstacles seem insignificant, you'll surely find your way around them. Know why, remember why, and find joy in fulfilling your most sincere purpose."*

If your answers are mostly about overall health or longevity, I can assure you that the overwhelming majority of the time these are not enough. Few of us really take our mortality seriously. Once in a great while, the urgent pressing of your family doctor to act now or suffer an untimely death will be enough. But even then, in my experience, it rarely is enough. Health and longevity goals are weak promoters for WHY most individuals truly persist through successful transformations. There is always tomorrow to start and there is no pressing urgency to start, let alone carry on, just because one will benefit with better health and longevity at some distant, undefined point in the future.

Revisiting Your "Why"

As life continues all around you and the Lifestyle seems too difficult, tedious and uncomfortable, your WHY can save you from faltering. Every decision you make is a choice. The reasons you start the Lifestyle will evolve with time but remain at the core of why you must continue to live it everyday. Keep those reasons in mind as you live out your daily and minute-by-minute choices that impact the outcome. You are not lacking in will power, energy or time to accomplish your most important goals. Keeping your WHY in front of you will afford you the willpower, energy and time to achieve the most important goals you have set your mind to accomplish. Remember, you can accomplish *anything* you set your mind to, but not *everything* you set your mind to.

On any given day, when you question why you are setting foot in the gym at 5:30a.m. yet again, or why you feel like you might grow feathers for consuming so much chicken, it's important you have your WHY conspicuously available. You will need to revisit your WHY frequently as a reminder that it's okay not to be "normal" like everyone else. I've discussed previously why being a normal American is not a very noteworthy goal in the first place but it becomes all-too-easy to go along to get along unless you draw upon your WHY as a powerful reminder. Never underestimate the importance of remembering why you started the Lifestyle. Use your written WHY to move ahead with a fresh, powerful, renewed sense of purpose anytime you are feeling weak or it seems the next healthy meal or exercise session is simply more than you can bear. If need be, rewrite your WHY again to reinforce your commitment to the Lifestyle.

What follows are three WHYS recently submitted to me by Lifestyle coaching members. These are not provided as some perfect examples of how to write your WHY, however, they are quite good. I'd be lying if I didn't say I am always deeply moved by the WHY submitted when they are written with care, thought and from the heart.

Female Lifestyler Defines Why

Well, first of all and most importantly, I wanted to do something for ME. I am a very generous and giving person to everyone but myself. I felt like being a part of this challenge and accomplishing my goals would be more beneficial for me than anyone. I was at a point in my life where I was determined to put the weight loss issue behind me once and for all.

From a physical standpoint, I was tired of my knees and feet aching every time I got up. Tired of being winded with a walk up a few flights of stairs. Tired of breaking into a sweat just from getting dressed in the morning; and tired of getting around like a woman twice my age. I do not have any of the diseases associated with obesity, but I knew it was only a matter of time.

From a psychological standpoint, I was tired of walking into a room and looking around to see if I was the fattest person there. Tired of missing parties and social events because of being embarrassed by the way I look. Tired of dressing like an old lady to camouflage my weight. Tired of shopping in the Plus-size department. Tired of looking like a kidney bean with legs. Tired of asking my husband, "How does this look? Do I look fat?" and tired of obsessing about food.

Then there is my husband. I wanted to do this for him. I have gained 70 pounds since the first day we meet. And for the most part, he has always been supportive of my weight loss. He always says stuff like "You're still pretty; you're not that fat; you just need to lose your stomach." Yeah right! I know he is just trying to be nice and he does not want to hurt my feelings. I don't even look like myself anymore. Next year is our 10-year anniversary and we are renewing our vows. And I want to look better than I did when we first met.

Male Lifestyler Defines Why Now

Why I will succeed this time and maintain my lower bodyweight throughout the rest of my life.

Last year I went through a divorce which left me as a single father of 4 children doing the roles of both mother and father while my ex-wife moved to a different state putting me in the position of providing for them 24x7 emotionally, physically, and in every other way. When we were first separated I went on the BFL program and lost 23 pounds. I felt better about myself which was important because my self-esteem was in the toilet. Why I started that program was that I have always wanted to lose this fat that I've become familiar with and it was the only thing in my life that I could control.

Throughout my life my weight is the only factor that I have not seemed to be able to get a handle on. My mom described it as the family curse, referring to the fact that everyone in her family was heavy. And indeed when I look around at everyone in both my father's and mother's families growing up, I was in the majority rather than the minority. While other children's grandmothers would give them a card with a five-dollar bill in it for their birthday, my grandmother gave me diet candy. I'll never forget the visit to the doctor's office when I was 8 years old and I was labeled with the dreaded "obese" label. How horrible that was for a young child who didn't know what to do to shred that label. In grade school and junior high I stuck to the non-athletic routes since I was too embarrassed to be involved in sports since I would be made fun of.

High School (1975 - 1979): Then there's high school, in high school, being overweight or right-fully obese screws up your whole social development. I never went to a dance, not a prom, not a homecoming, none, because I couldn't get a date. I asked girls but I'm sure I was asking "out of my league". I watch my two oldest kids going to the dances and every time one comes up, I'm glad for them but the dagger of the fat strikes me in the heart again. I never had my pictures taken before the dance, never went to the after dance parties. I think it was easier for my parents that I didn't engage in sports since that relieved them from having to provide rides and such for me so they never encouraged me to go out for any. I excelled in non athletic adventures and honed my ability to make people laugh as my way of fitting in. The summer before my senior year of high school I worked out and lost a great deal of weight and toned up my body. Unfortunately, my social skills weren't up to par so I didn't see myself in a new light, I saw myself as the pudgy fat kid still. As I write this tears are welling up in my eyes thinking of how much I've missed in my life.

College (1979 - 1983): I went away to college where I got a fresh start, I worked out at the gym but my nutrition was abominable so it didn't do much good. After a year and a half in college, my grades were pretty bad so I got kicked out. Being back home, I was lonely, depressed and wonder-ing what to do with my life. I went to the junior college and started working out and jumping rope, I remember I weighed 195 at that time and I felt incredible. That was in 1981, over 20 years ago. The thought of weighing that or less is exciting and scary all at the same time. I finished commu-nity college, went back to the school I got kicked out of and graduated with a higher gpa than most of my counterparts.

Work between college and marriage (1983-1989): I worked a lot of hours and became a gym rat, not keeping track of my weight, just piling the muscle on, going to the gym during my lunch hours. During this time I went out to Colorado to see what would happen if I moved, the economy experienced a downturn and it turned into a very unpleasant experience. My weight ballooned up to 260-265 range, after 250, I'd be darned if I was weighing myself. When I came back from Colorado, I brought my weight and my life back into order, I was dating a good deal and having a lot of fun. I fell in love with my ex-wife's kids as much as with her and I have a soft spot for chil-dren, seeing them live in a shack drove me to speed up the marriage process. In hindsight, mistake #1. My self-esteem has always lacked, mainly because of carrying so much extra weight constantly.

Married Life (1989-2001): Married life was so very difficult since I was trying my best to pro-vide for my family and my wife spent a lot of money which made me have to work more hours. I worked out almost the entire time but how foolish that seems in retrospect, without nutrition and supplementation, what was I expecting? Oh the wisdom that comes with age. Nutrition was impos-sible, I swear I think my ex wanted me to stay overweight. She would be upset if I wouldn't eat the fatty, high calorie meal that she prepared for the family and God help me if I criticized her cooking, I also have a weakness for M&M's, she would buy them by the pound bag load and put them in a bowl and darned if I didn't find my hand in that bowl time after time but of course those calories don't count right? Make no mistake, I put the food into my mouth but the house was filled with junk and I didn't have the resolve it took to get my nutrition under control.

Post Marriage (2001 - present): I have survived many of the scars that afflict someone that's gone through a divorce. I feel like I have a second chance, at dating, at life and it's not some mid-life crisis, it's my last chance to change the path I've headed on and change the things I can change which is the future.

If I want to attract a woman (eventually) into my life that embraces the fit lifestyle and a commitment to an active life, I have to be that myself since like attracts like. The discipline and commitment required to embrace the fit lifestyle does bleed over into other areas of life and makes for a healthier mind and body.

A BFL transformation success story turned me on to David and his methodology. I have to say that initially I thought it was bunk—20 pounds in 8 weeks? Maybe one of his other high-metabolism guys but not me. Well after logging my foods for 4 days in Dave's incredible Nutritional Analyzer, my eyes are wide open, I have increased my cardio, I bought myself a new pair of running shoes last night and I'm ready to do this. What the logging proved to me is that I can live on 1200-1500 calories/day and be quite satisfied. The kids are ecstatic with all of the fresh cutup fruit in the house. I'm happy to say that I've had to go out and buy fruit 3 times this week since they're eating all of it on me. They asked me if I was mad. I said heck no! That's a good problem for me to have. I stopped buying the junk food and I don't have Cheezits around—they are one of my major downfalls.

Dave was right when he said that everyone around you will try to sabotage you, not maliciously, they just feel like you're not joining in to the party. I've joined in to the party for too many years, now it's time to respect my body and my life. This was a good week to start a "trial week" if you will. I had to see if I thought that this could work and I made a cursory commitment to a week. Some co-workers were in town and we went to a White Sox baseball game, I turned down the beer, the fatty foods and I learned that peanuts will throw off my whole day's nutritional numbers. You would not believe all of the crap I caught for not drinking or eating a brat or nachos. There I am with my bottle of water and a hot pretzel and they're acting like Romans at the coliseum. Dave spent an hour on the phone with me last week to get me started, he said some really tough things for me to handle and made me realize I had really impotent goals when it came to weight loss. Dave gave me three tasks and I did them in the wrong order but after writing this, they'll all be done and I'll have my attack strategy laid out. I thought the goals for weight loss would be easy but I had to run through my history of weight loss and gain to realize that it's the only thing in my life that I have not controlled in the past but I will take control of starting yesterday. Oh and guess what, I came to grips with the fact that I'm a closet eater, or should I say I'm a recovering closet eater.

Why I will succeed? I have to succeed. Failure is not an option. I have also come to the realization through the Nutritional Analyzer that this is doable and a goal that is attainable in a healthy manner. Carrying extra weight and living obese is no longer acceptable. I choose to be a member of the lean crowd and I have started my journey towards that end today. I want to see those muscles that I have worked so hard so many years to develop. I think they're there and by shedding my obesity I will see the results that I have longed for so many years. I've been weightlifting for 23 years, you'd think the nutrition side would have struck me a lot sooner. There's an old saying that "when the student is ready, the teacher will appear." I'm ready, and Dave has appeared.

Female Lifestyler Revisits Her Why

To be honest, I am finding this exercise to be quite difficult. Why am I still here? The instinctive responses of "I am not a quitter" and "I finish what I start" pop into mind but it goes deeper than that. It brings a question to my mind, "where else would I be?" Living my life feels so very normal and right this way. I cannot think of another place to be than here, finishing this challenge and the next goal and the next, and doing what I do, eating right, exercising and looking after myself.

The Sunday afternoon when I cut my veggies and do a wee bit of fruit prep are automatic now. So much of "this" lifestyle is automatic now. So when I am asked why I am still here it is quite hard to answer because so much is instinctual now. I exercise. I eat right. I drink a lot of water. I take some basic vitamins and supplements. I get my sleep so that I can do my morning cardio. I read a menu in a restaurant and know what to eat, instinctively. This just IS. I am here because this is my life, where else would I be?

Yeah, I look to the future but this challenge was and is not going to bring me to my pinnacle, my end goal. I had an end goal before this challenge and focused on it quite intensely, at the cost of my then present. Now I do what I do today, trusting and knowing it to be right and while I might have goals for the future, I am truly living my life today, enjoying each success along the way, tending to each need and lifting each weight.

I will compete someday, for me that much is a given, I dream of creating dazzling routines like Russ and wowing the crowds with my physique. Bodybuilding, Figure - not sure. The Leanness Lifestyle is still helping me to uncover what naturally wonderful physique I have under this quickly dispersing fat and is building a foundation from which I will eventually begin to see a shape emerge.

Will it be physique or figure? Not sure as I have been fat all of my adult life. My 17-year-old swim team photo does not tell me what is under this layer of fat. I am still untrained to see through this fat and guess as to what basic structure I have to work with. It's the weight I lift today, the food I eat today, that shows me my true self, little by little and that is the joy—the discovery.

I once read a quote that mentioned something about the exquisite nature of having a perfect meal, balanced nicely and full of clean foods and water and then stringing that together with another and including a workout where you push with your all, where your mind is laser focused on and really feeling the muscle belly engorge with nutrients until the meals and workout become a day.. then stringing that day with another and another until it becomes a week ... combined with another week and another and another until you have a month of perfection, consistency, a true testament to the sheer joy and satisfaction that come from knowing you made those days turn to months.

Well that is truly why I am here, 7 weeks is not enough, I want more, I want a lifetime to look back on and to have learned from and through. The same way that I used to look back on the days and months where a crap meal preceded another and a sloth sedentary evening preceded another. While the memory of that time will never fade, I am enjoying building something to take its place from the forefront—from my recent identity and character—and soon I will look back upon this year as one full of splendor and perfection, a time where I will say my life began. No more plans for starting like I used to do over and over because this challenge has helped me to realize that I am never gonna stop and that is why I am still here, not the 10 weeks this is supposed to last, it has no end.

This DIVA II Challenge was originally a hope for me. A hope that I would learn, mentally, physically and instinctually the tools I will need in my never-ending journey of creating the leanest, tightest, best muscled body I can. I will be better at 31 than I was at 30 and at 35 even better and why? Because I have been able to practice the skills necessary to achieve my physique goals. Want to add mass? No worries. Want to lean out? No worries. I have the tools, the mystery is gone and at the end of this challenge I will be ready to continue conquering the flab.

To not be labeled "obese" by the bodyfat tests, that will be a nice perk of this challenge. To have lost the 25 lbs., that too will be a perk. But those things are not the end for me. It's the tools and knowledge and day in, day out practice that has drilled into me so many things, so much common sense and basic building blocks of knowledge about my body and what it needs to do what I want it to. The proven knowledge, which is much different than speculation or being told that my body does not have to be tortured, deprived or such to do what I want. I used to binge before "starting again." It is so nice to not have to think in terms of starting ever again, it is just a case of continuing, stringing one more day to this perfect journey to my best physique. Finally a sense of pride and accomplishment, as well as proving to myself that I can do this, that I can do what my mind's eye has yearned for and that it is not a magical pill or trick, these are side effects that while I did not start out aiming for, have come and are really jewels in this process. On a more practical level, why do I want to be superfit? Because to me that is what is "normal" these days and everything else looks wrong/feels wrong.

I was at the wading pool last Thursday on my day off, in the orange bikini I used for my Before photos (which looks better every day) with a pair of black shorts over the bottoms. I had Bain De Solei'd my body and tanned for about an hour prior and then took my child to the pool for dippins. I got there and looked around and was the slimmest adult there - can you believe it? Anyway, I said what the heck and took off my bottoms and tanned all the parts of me (sans rude bits). I remember really thinking to myself that soon I will hit goal and come to this same situation and have my body hard with shredded delts and visible muscles popping out at all of these "normal" people who, incidentally, were sitting around stuffing their faces talking about diets. I did not reproach myself for being overweight where normally I would have. Instead, I took pride in my current state with the comfort and confidence that I was indeed taking action and seeing results in my transformation. Taking pride in that I gave away my fat swimsuit never to return again. Taking pride that I had found the Leanness Lifestyle and am doing what it takes for what I want.

Why do I want to be superfit? Because it is feeling so good getting closer and closer and the idea of achieving what so few do really excites me, it is where my mind has been for ages and now the body is catching up. Before this challenge I would say that I cannot wait to be in that lean body but that is not true. I can wait. I can enjoy each day of my life, eating right and exercising and living, these are the jewels that I cannot wait for—another day to live the Leanness Lifestyle because it makes me feel so good inside and out.

Summary

The path to ultimate transformation success is through the use of clear, written, and public goals. Goals are several levels above dreams. With goals you are no longer wishing, hoping, praying or keeping your fingers crossed that life will "turn out."

It is vitally important that your goals are specific and measurable. By focusing on performance goals over outcome goals, you will be better prepared from the start. To choose a performance goal you must take inventory of your current status. You must also know specific physical attributes of an individual whom you idolize for their physical prowess.

A Lifetime Achievement Goal is necessary but contrary to some popularly held beliefs it is not necessarily the most important goal to set. It may be the most fun but that is typically because that goal is about "later" and not today. Setting short- and mid-range goals are just as important but there is likely no more important a goal to set, every day, than your "today" goal. Remember, you don't have to be good forever, just for today.

While it is true there is always a price to pay for setting and striving to reach goals, there is also a price to pay for inaction. A body worth bragging about will come at a price money can't touch. But that price is far less than living with a lifetime of shattered dreams and missed opportunities awaiting you at the end of your transformation.

Once your goals are clear it,s time to define WHY you must achieve your goals. It,s not enough to want to achieve your goals. You must need to achieve your goals. By opening up your heart and revisiting the pain of living with less than your true physical potential, you can strengthen and solidify your commitment to your goals. Expressing not only the pain, but the pleasure you see in your mind,s eye of living at your physical peak, will balance and strengthen your WHY.

Take Action and Feel Great!

1. Be sure you know your current weight and approximate body fat. Read or reread the Body Composition and Weight chapters if necessary.

2. Determine what type of body you have (apple or pear) and then find someone who also has your body shape who you admire for their level of leanness and muscularity.

3. Do your best to determine the height, weight, and body fat of your goal physique.

4. Go through old photos and find the photo of you that best represents your best physical conditioning as an adult.

5. Write your Lifetime Achievement Goal after taking time to self-evaluate where you are currently.

6. Write your 6-month goal.

7. Write your 3-month goal.

8. Write your 1-month goal.

9. Write your 1st week goal.

10. Using the three-steps provided in this chapter, determine the three most important goals for today. Write them down.

11. Determine the single most important goal that must be accomplished today and circle it.

12. Write up to ten action steps necessary to achieve your most important goal for today.

13. Take action and begin the first action step right away. Do not delay. Accomplish your most important today goal *today*!

14. After clearly writing your goals, it is time you shared your goals with those you love and respect. Send your goals and written commitment to friends, loved ones and coworkers who are most likely to support you. Tell them in the letter or e-mail what you are going to do and by when. If you have attached leverage to your goals and commitment, then tell them of your leverage as well. Enlist their help as helping relationships (See *"Are You Ready to Change?"* chapter) and take full advantage of the power of Public Commitments over Private Pledges.

15. Write your WHY.

Eating Well Wherever You Are

It's not about where you are, but what you've done to
prepare for where you are that counts.

Regardless of where you are, there are better ways to eat than you have been. The dinner party, Christmas dinner with the family, potluck at work, over-the-road, on-the-go and in-the-home times don't have to be disastrous to your plan and your waistline. Nutritionist Keith Klein says there are always "better bad" choices that can be made, and I agree.

Even when you haven't prepared at all, there are still plenty of better bad choices you can make that will do little harm to your plan and that you can easily make up for the next day.

Eating at Home

The concept of eating at home is becoming more and more foreign for Americans. In 1970, 26 percent of our meals were eaten outside the home. Today we eat away from home over 40 percent of the time. We're relying on restaurants (primarily fast food, no less) to supply us with low-fat, nutrient-rich dishes. Hence, we are the fattest nation in the world. If 40 percent of our meals are eaten away from home, it becomes easy to see then, that 60 percent of our eating is still done at home. However, there's no guarantee that the majority of your calories will be eaten at home. In this chapter, my goal is to help you see that putting a high priority on eating and preparing more foods at home will be advantageous to your Lifestyle.

It's easy to become overwhelmed as you think about "all the changes" that will be necessary to make your home fit the Lifestyle. To make this really work, will there need to be some changes made in your cupboards and fridge at home? You bet. If you just read that statement and the thought popped into your head, "Uh oh, now I have to be perfect," you are wrong and need to shift your position. No one is asking you to be perfect. No one is a perfect eater. No kitchen cabinets are perfectly filled with whole grains and all-natural foods. No fridge is stocked with only the freshest, purest fruits and vegetables. Before I advise you about how to stock your kitchen and prepare your foods, allow me to explain what living the Lifestyle at home means.

You might believe you have quite an appetite for variety. Then again, I've met many overweight people who admittedly eat with very little variety. They just "prefer" the lack of variety. Hey, live and let live, but that's not the Lifestyle. Some variety is necessary for maximum health, vitality and balance. In either case, you're probably not all that fired up about "all the ways you'll have to change" to make your home fit the Lifestyle. The reality is, you likely rotate in a given month through no more than 15 to 20 different meals.

You've gotten into a routine. We're all creatures of habit. You're no different. Unless you're a one-meal loser (you eat one meal a day), you currently eat one to seven different breakfasts, lunches and dinners a week. Sometimes you snack in between, sometimes you don't. The bottom line is that when you total up all the different meals you consume, you're really only looking at a total of 15 to 20 different meals a week. The exciting part about this is that you can start to think about finding 15 to 20 better meals that more closely match the Lifestyle. Don't waste time and emotional energy filling your head with misconceived thoughts about how you're going to have to spend a small fortune and all your free time buying cookbooks, with thousands of pages of worthless recipes, that you wouldn't feed your dog.

If you'll recall from the Nutrients chapter, the Lifestyle isn't rigidly fixed. I've asked you to eat meals that are fairly well balanced, but within a given range. You will be living the Lifestyle at home if you follow these simple guidelines for creating meals:

Carbohydrates: 30 to 60 percent of your meal and day (40 to 45 percent optimal)
Proteins: 25 to 50 percent of your meal and day (35 to 40 percent optimal)
Lipids: 10 to 30 percent of your meal and day (with less than a third of the fat being saturated)
        (10 to 20 percent optimal)

By the end of the day, you've been living the Lifestyle if you have 1) done your best to prepare meals that closely match the guidelines above, taking into consideration the total caloric guidelines I've provided in the *Energy Balance* chapter; 2) focused primarily on consuming whole foods and less packaged and process foods and 3) have consumed at least:

* 1 serving of fruit (1 cup cut up; not fruit juice or fruit packed in sugar) **2 to 3 is preferred.**

* 2 servings of vegetable (1/2 cup cooked or 1 cup cut up raw vegetable; fresh, frozen or canned without cream sauce) **4 is preferred.**

* 3 servings of whole grains (1/2 cup rice, pasta or cereal or 1 slice of bread is a serving)

* 4 servings of lean protein

The particular items you choose to prepare and how you choose to prepare them is up to you as long as you stay within the simple guidelines above. You'll notice that I never said you had to be perfect.

One of the most overwhelming aspects of adapting to a new food lifestyle is choosing your new favorite foods. Don't allow yourself to become overwhelmed from a limiting false perception of "all the work" that will be necessary to change. Don't continue eating the same old stuff when all you need is to find 15 to 20 meals you like and can live with within the Lifestyle. You're going to eat them day in and day out. Let's be real. You're a creature of habit. You're already doing it now!

Begin now by replacing the lousy meals with better meals that fit the Lifestyle. This is certainly a "today goal," so make it a goal today to find at least one better meal and you'll only have 14 to 19 left to create. If you just create one a day, you'll be done finding meals in 2 to 3 weeks. Talk about a bargain!

My Seven Breakfasts at Home

I rotate between the following seven breakfasts, day in and day out, week after week, month after month, and year after year:

Oatmeal: Slow cook or steel-cut with cinnamon, Stevia or Splenda™ and low-fat milk. I may mix 20 to 30 grams of protein with the oatmeal or mix a protein shake on the side to drink. Instead of a protein shake, I might also prepare 4 to 5 egg whites scrambled with one whole egg for a protein source to balance the meal. The objective is to balance the high-carbohydrate, low-protein aspect of the oatmeal with more protein.

Cocoa Wheats, Cream of Wheat, or other multi-grain hot cereal: I usually blend chocolate protein right into a hot cereal after I've poured it into a bowl.

Eggs: Scrambled with typically one whole egg for every 3 to 4 egg whites. I cook them in a non-stick pan with Pam®, salt and pepper to taste, and may add a slice of Kraft fat-free American cheese. You can also add any veggie, mushrooms, garlic and hot sauce. Because the eggs are very low in carbohydrates, I'll usually have a slice or two of whole-grain bread with low-cal jam, jelly or preserves (all-fruit is my preference) to balance the high protein with more carbohydrates.

Eggs: Over-medium in the same fashion as before, with one whole egg per every 3 to 4 egg whites. When I'm preparing my eggs in this fashion, I'm usually preparing them for an egg sandwich (on whole-grain toast with "I Can't Believe It's Not Butter™ spray).

Pancakes: High-protein mix that can be found at any reputable health food store. I cook my pancakes on a nonstick griddle, using Pam again, and use "I Can't Believe It's Not Butter™" spray or a thin coat of peanut butter. I top the pancakes with sugar-free or low-sugar syrup (usually providing 45 to 60 calories per 1/4 cup). There are even zero calorie syrups available.

Cereal: Any whole-grain, cold cereal you like will do. I pour fat-free milk into a bowl and add protein with 1 small ice cube. Then I whisk the protein with the milk and ice cube (the ice cube keeps the milk really cold during blending). I also add an appropriate amount of Shredded Wheat, Kashi or other whole-grain cereal.

MRP (Meal Replacement Shake): For my current recommendation visit the web site at www.leannesslifestyle.com. For breakfast I'll prepare it with a banana and Peanut Wonder™ or regular peanut butter and a flax blend of essential fats. Again, I'm striving for balance within the meal.

My Six Lunches at Home or Prepared at Home

Lunch is a time I frequently consume one or more servings of fruit or vegetable. The fruits and vegetables I consume from home have been cut up and prepared in advance, and are either sealed in Ziploc® baggies or Tupperware®-type containers. It's important that fruits and vegetables are as easy to eat when you are hungry as any other grab-and-go snack.

> *If I have to peel it, cut it or wash it when*
> *I'm hungry, you can bet I'm not eating it.*

Prepare everything before you are hungry. In the lunch examples I've given below, you can be sure I've added either a vegetable or fruit, or both to each main course. I typically eat my vegetables at lunch raw, and use Marzettis® Fat-free Dip, a fat-free salad dressing, or even a spicy mustard for dipping. I've also mixed traditional full-fat veggie dip with the fat-free dip to add flavor (a teaspoon of each).

I rotate between the following six home-prepared lunches day in and day out, week after week, month after month, and year after year:

Tuna: Packed in water and mixed with Miracle Whip Light®. I'll either prepare a tuna sandwich cold, or will grill the sandwich on a non-stick griddle with Pam®. I typically add one or two slices of Kraft American Fat-Free cheese for a tuna melt. Instead of butter, I always use I Can't Believe It's Not Butter® spray.

Salmon: Canned and then mixed with Miracle Whip Light®. I prepare it in the same fashion as the tuna, but I tend to add a couple of sliced dill pickles for improved texture and taste. Hey, it's your palate–get creative! Sam's Club also has pre-seasoned salmon patties that are quite delicious.

Lunch Meat: Packaged, deli, but always low fat. Sure the sodium is higher, but I don't unwittingly fear it. If you have hypertension, then paying attention to all sources of sodium is important; the rest of us will do well to get our meal planning to fit the Lifestyle, and not concern ourselves with a few hundred milligrams of sodium. Sodium isn't a killer–over-consumption of calories is. I prepare a sandwich on whole-grain bread, cold or grilled. I usually add one or two slices of Kraft fat-free American cheese.

Egg Salad: Hard-boiled eggs in a ratio of three or four white for every one whole egg. I mix Miracle Whip Light® and mustard, and eat on whole-grain bread.

Cottage Cheese: Sometimes I'll simply mix cut up fruit with 1 or 2 percent fat cottage cheese.

Soup: Chicken noodle or vegetable beef are my favorites. Check the label. There are a plethora of low-sodium and low-fat varieties. You're likely to find several soups that fit very well within the Lifestyle guidelines. As long as it's not creamed, you're probably going to be okay. Check the label for accurate details of the nutrition facts. Some creamed varieties still fit!

My Six Dinners at Home

Dinner is when I am most likely to consume my largest serving of fruits or vegetables. A nice dinner salad with spinach leaf, sliced carrots, egg whites, Kraft fat-free Cheddar cheese, broccoli and cauliflower is then topped with a low-fat or fat-free salad dressing. Steamed vegetables seasoned (Lowry's®) or raw veggies prepared the same as at lunchtime is also common. Fruits are rarely from a can, and are cut up and ready to eat. Your grocer's frozen foods section will offer quite a variety of ready-to-eat or ready-to-bake, seasoned vegetables.

In the dinner examples I've given below, you can be sure I've added a vegetable, fruit or both to each main course.

Turkey: Ground and formed into a patty. Seasoned to taste, and grilled on a non-stick griddle. We usually add A-1™ sauce for flavor, and will top with Kraft fat-free American cheese and sliced dill pickles on whole-grain bread. Also look for Jennie-O brand pre-seasoned and marinated turkey breasts.

Chicken: Breast, boneless and skinless. Once in a while we'll use a canned chunk chicken (98% fat-free).

1. Grilled over open flame after marinating in a fat-free dressing (Italian usually) or baked after being seasoned to taste. I never eat fried chicken with the skin on at home. In fact, we never fry anything at home.

2. Mix diced chicken breasts with Lipton seasoned rice mix (pick a packaged flavor that sounds good to <u>you</u>).

3. Spice Island's® Pasta Gourmet Alfredo goes well with diced chicken breasts and whole-grain pasta.

4. Barbecue sauces are what I'll typically dip relatively plain chicken breasts into.

5. Cream of mushroom soup, non-fat milk and Stove Top® stuffing make a great addition for baking chicken.

6. Parmesan cheese, oregano, spaghetti sauce from a jar, Kraft fat-free mozzarella cheese and Kraft Shake-n-Bake® makes a great chicken bake recipe as well.

7. Go to your local book store and choose a low-fat cookbook for preparing chicken dishes–there are plenty to choose from. Don't settle for plain, boiled chicken breasts. You don't have to!

Beef: Ground, roast or steak. About twice a week I eat red meat. Don't smother your beef in gravy or fat-laden sauces and be sure to account for the calories. You can't make me feel guilty over eating beef. It's a great source of protein and moderation is the key. Season and marinate to taste.

Spaghetti: Whole-wheat noodles, spaghetti sauces from a jar, and either turkey or the leanest ground beef. Once in a while we'll add Seapak™ marinated and grilled shrimp instead of turkey or beef.

Tacos: Chicken or lean ground beef. Prepared according to packaged taco seasoning instructions, with low-fat tortillas, or as a salad (bagged and shredded lettuce is super convenient). I then add Kraft fat-free shredded cheddar cheese, tomatoes, fat-free sour cream and whatever hot sauce I'm in the mood for.

Salmon: Tenderize filet with a fork and top with Golden Dip® Ginger Teriyaki Marinade; bake at 350 degrees for approximately 1/2 hour; cook brown rice according to package directions.

Green Peppers: Brown beef, drain, rinse, and return to skillet. Cook rice according to directions. Combine beef, rice, and tomato sauce. Salt as needed. Remove tops of peppers, and clean out seeds. Place peppers upright in baking dish, and fill with meat mixture. Bake covered at 350 degrees for 45 min. or until peppers are soft. Top with a little more tomato sauce and bake for 5 to 10 minutes longer.

That's it! Once in a while I'll be offered or treated to something different, but the foods above are all I eat at home well over 90 percent of the time.

Snacks at Home

Let's admit it, at home you are going to want some snacks, something salty or sweet. My favorites are usually energy bars or meal replacement drinks, but here are a few more suggestions when you get a craving for something sweet or salty:

- No-cook, low or no-sugar pudding with protein added during preparation.
- Popcorn: look for at least 95 percent fat-free varieties that are microwaveable or air-pop your popcorn with I Can't Believe It's Not Butter® spray and salt to taste.
- Go to your local bookstore and thumb through a few cookbooks or magazines on low-fat healthy snacking. Develop your own special treats that fit the Lifestyle!

Snacks for the Kids

Many of you who have children living at home will immediately dismiss this section because you "must keep snacks in the house for the kids." Fine, keep some snacks for the kids. But instead of keeping cookies in a cookie jar, buy the individually packaged cookies. Almost every conceivable popular kids' snack now comes individually packaged, so there is no reason why you can't keep kids' snacks in the home. Use a permanent marker to write your kids' name on it. At that point, the food becomes the property of your child. Don't steal from your children. It's their property now.

How far you're willing to bend to keep kids' snacks in the home is another issue. Do you have to keep ice cream in the house for kids? Labeling and individually packaging ice cream is kind of hard, right? What "kids" are you buying the snacks for? If you're a man, are you the kid? If you're a woman, are you the kid? Man or woman, if you are the one who does the shopping, are you buying snacks for the other adult "kid" in the home? Give some thought for which kid you are really buying "kids' snacks." Match your actions with the strong character you have or are developing, and leave your kids' snacks alone.

Finally, too many parents don't take the bull by the horns when raising their children. They allow their children to dictate what is purchased and prepared. While my children have plenty of common snacks, they don't choose what is purchased, nor what is prepared, the overwhelming majority of the time. Tracy and I share a philosophy I hope you can also make your own from this moment on:

> *Our children get to choose what we purchase and what is prepared when <u>they</u> are paying for it.*

Don't Keep Your Weak Foods In The House!

Most success stories from those who have lost and kept off a substantial number of pounds include the fact they don't keep their weak foods in the house with any regularity. This truly works, and it makes so much sense. If your freezer is full of Ben & Jerry's Chunky Monkey® and you have an ice cream weakness, you will eat it any chance you can. If your "thing" is cheese, and you routinely purchase a block of your favorite cheese every week, you are setting yourself up for failure. Don't do it!

The first time I threw away perfectly good food, I almost felt that I single-handedly caused world hunger. My upbringing taught me not to waste food, and anytime I didn't clean my plate I was reminded that there were children starving in third-world nations. These reminders made me feel almost dirty for throwing away a bag of chips, cookies or chocolates. I've long since gotten over these feelings, because I know that it's better to throw it away, than to wear it. The sooner the better that you realize that you aren't directly responsible for world hunger because you threw away a weak food that would have ended up on your gut or hips. After you do it the first time, it gets easier. Trust me. I recommend you do it now. It's most definitely a "today goal" activity. If you just can't bring yourself to throw away a perfectly good, unopened box, bag or bottle of whatever, then pack it up, and take it to your local food pantry. They will certainly appreciate it, and you can feel good about what you've done.

I used to treat myself to a mix of Gardettos®, popcorn and plain M&Ms®. I'd even go so far as to say I had a strong weakness for the salty-sweet combination. It would not be unheard of for me to eat a serving equaling a half-pound if it were a splurge night (about 1500 calories!). I have recognized this snack as a weakness, and I have asked my wife not to keep it in the house except on rare occasions. I am lucky enough to have a supportive spouse, and most of the time we don't have it lying around. Because it's not routinely available, I am more than happy to have something healthier.

Trolling for Food–If It's Available You Will Eat It

When you go trolling for food, you will eat what's available. Let's face it, that's what we do when we want a comfort food, right? We go on the prowl. It could be the minute you get home from work, or late at night after the kids and spouse are asleep.

For some reason, comfort foods just taste
better when no one's looking.

Again, let's be honest. You go to the fridge, yank open the door, and stand in amazement at the glory of choices you have available. "Nothing looks good." You move to the cupboards and with Cyborg-precise acuity (think Terminator movie) you scan the boxes, bags, cans and jars you chose to purchase at your last shopping venture. "Nothing looks good." Hey, it ain't over yet, folks. The trolling is only half over. Now it's time to check out the pantry or closet. "Any overstock lookin' good? Well, there's some Captain Crunch®, but that's not really what I'm in the mood for." Next it's time to go downstairs and check out the freezer or some other nook and cranny you know might have a comfort food stored in it. "Ah hah! It took several minutes of trolling, but I found it! A bag of M&Ms®! Just what the doctor ordered!" You then take the whole bag with you to the couch, so you won't have to get up again to "refill" and you eat your comfort food with mind-numbing indulgence as you watch whatever the boob tube is delivering that evening.

The only difference between the picture I just painted and the one that hits the canvas when you don't keep your weak foods in the house, is what happens when you find the M&Ms®. If there had been no M&Ms®, you would have likely done the right thing. You would have made yourself a shake, or eaten a bar, or chosen a higher protein, low-fat food. Perhaps you would have chosen to drink some more water, or waited 30 minutes until dinner, or–for a change–simply gone to bed for a good night's sleep. You may have felt sorry for yourself that day or evening, but you would have felt charged and in-charge the next day when you realized you did the right thing and didn't have any "making up" to do.

If you have a strong enough craving to leave your house, drive to the store, get out of the car, walk in, shop, pay for it, get back in the car, drive home, get out of the car and walk back into your house, then you probably should have the snack. Ninety-nine percent of the time, I do not have an urge strong enough to do this, and neither will you. Keep the foods in the house that you know you will eat, and which fit the Lifestyle. Keep candy in the freezer, if you "have to keep some around for the kids." You'll be less tempted to grab it, and you'll have to plan ahead unless you want to eat it rock hard.

Refrigerator A Mess–Cupboards Immaculate

Because you will be buying more fresh fruits and vegetables, you will be cutting them up ahead of time so you can snack on them when you need them (like when you want something right now!) Fresh fruits and vegetables require refrigeration. Most of the whole-grain breads that are the most natural and nutritious require refrigeration or they will spoil in only a few days. This takes refrigeration space. Ever wonder why that loaf of white bread can sit on your kitchen counter for weeks without getting hard? It's because of the added preservatives. White bread is about as nutritious as iceberg lettuce, which is only slightly more nutritious than the paper this book is written on. Low-fat yogurt, cottage cheese, salad dressings, low-fat or fat-free milk, and lean meats all require refrigeration. All are foods you will consume more of regularly if you are practicing Lifestyle eating habits.

Many of the food items currently in your cupboards are loaded with preservatives and are processed beyond recognition. They are not whole-grain foods. They are enriched, fortified, sodium-laden, sugar-filled snacks that you will learn to reduce if you really want to be successful in your fat-loss efforts. Read the labels and call me a liar. It won't happen. This paragraph and the one preceding it can take you a long way toward choosing foods that are better for you. That's all I'm really asking for here. No immediate, 180-degree turns–just improvement and consistent recognition of what has worked for other successful Lifestylers.

I strongly urge you to eat, or at least prepare, more of your meals at home (at least breakfast and supper) and as many in between-meal snacks as possible. You are more likely to take control over your portion sizes and you are far more likely to improve your food selection when eating foods prepared at home. For the times when it's simply not feasible to eat at home or bring a prepared meal from home, I am providing you with some surefire ways to succeed when dining out, eating fast food, and traveling.

Everyday Eating Away From Home

> *Always have a protein bar or Lifestyle-friendly food with you–something healthy to eat. When the time away from home is longer than you expect, these emergency foods keep you from getting so hungry that you settle for what's available.*

Now it's time to address the 40 percent of the time you're not eating at home. Every day many of you will be eating one or two meals away from home. How do you handle it? How can you make better choices?

Tracy and I have pretty much come to the conclusion–after looking around at 95 percent of the people at most greasy-spoon restaurants–that Lifestylers are a *huge* inconvenience to restaurants. Be prepared for this common attitude when you are dedicated to skipping the grease and eating healthy.

Waitress: "What would you like today?"
David: "I'll have six egg whites, one whole egg, scrambled, no butter, no oil, and a bowl of oatmeal with cinnamon and brown sugar."
Waitress: "Excuse me? You don't want any yolks?"
David: "Actually, I do want one yolk and 6 egg whites. No butter or oil too, please."
Waitress: "SIGH - And for you ma'am?"
Tracy: "I'll have three egg whites fried, not scrambled, no oil, no butter, whole wheat toast - dry - and hot tea."
Waitress: Rolls eyes and leaves.

When we're being good little Lifestylers, with the exception of some five-star restaurants, it's the same story wherever we go. Either the waitress is put out, or—if she's really friendly—it takes several repeats to make sure she has all the do's and don'ts down. It's still worth it.

Here are the basic Lifestyle guidelines for eating any meal not prepared or eaten at home:

Fast Food and Quick Stops

- Foods closely matching those you'd prepare at home are the foods you want to focus on eating away from home. Would you eat a sausage biscuit at home? Then don't make it a habit of eating one away from home.

- Forego the bacon and cheese. You must say, "No cheese, please."

- Skip the mayo or "special sauces." Stick with ketchup or mustard.

- Most Chinese food is not good Lifestyle food when prepared in restaurants. It's usually very high in fat and calorie-dense. If you don't know what your favorite daily Chinese meal provides for calories, carbohydrates, proteins and fats, then find out or acknowledge it's probably not a food you should dine on regularly. Better consider it a splurge food or simply off-limits.

- Sub shops are on every corner, in every city across America. Choose your favorite, and frequent it often when away from home. Again, skip the mayo, cheese and special sauces. Stick with mustards, lean meats and load up your sandwich with veggies. Choose a salad once in a while too at those sub shops.

- Choose baked chips or pretzels providing no more than 3 to 4 grams of fat per serving.

- Any fast-food restaurant will offer *something* you can order a better way and that will fit the Lifestyle. Remember, you have to ask! Don't settle and then play the "silly old me" game of "Gosh I didn't realize they'd put <u>that</u> much cheese on the butter-burger melt." Yes, you did, so special order every sandwich and stop kidding yourself.

- Chicken-anything without cheese or breading is usually a better choice than beef-anything.

- Paying for a large ice water and feeling bad about it because you didn't get the cola is essentially the same as refusing the keys to a brand new Cadillac because you paid for a Yugo. Water is best! It's okay to pay for the Yugo and get the Cadillac! Choose water even if you have to pay for it! If you must drink colas, then fill your cup to the top with ice before you add the pop. Choose diet soda over full-strength.

- Instead of ordering fries, double the chicken on the sandwich for a heartier sandwich, fold over, and so on. Or get two sandwiches if your appetite calls for it, but follow the Lifestyle guidelines for what is in the sandwich.

- Thin crust is better than deep dish. Cheese pizza is better than any other pizza with meat toppings. Pepperoni pizza is usually better than other pizzas with sausage and more meat. Pile on the veggies!

- Pancakes are a better choice over the "Big Country Breakfast."

- Never "Super Size!" The "value meal" is no value to your transformation. It'll cost you more of your precious time to take off the extra calories from the barrel-o-cola they'll serve you, and the thousand calories in french fries. It's not a bargain to take the gallon-sized cola because it's only 25 cents more.
- Veggie salads with fat-free dressings are smart choices.

- Anything you can do to reduce portion sizes is smart when quickly grabbing something on the go.

- Ask for fat-free milk vs. whole milk.

Work-Related Eating

- The FREE dinner provided by the company or with the boss isn't calorie free!

- When you dip your hand into the candy jar at work, you're being ultimately rude to yourself. Don't be afraid to say "no" to anyone offering work goodies. You don't have to indulge in anyone's poor behavior. By doing so you actually become an enabler for your coworker–you support the poor and destructive behavior they practice. Who do you respect more–the overweight secretary or yourself? The heck with her pathetic nutritional program and the candy. Say no! Did you ever stop and think they may be purposely sabotaging your efforts to keep you as fat as they are?

- Bring a healthy dish for potluck dinners. Use the Internet or your local library to search for recipes low in fat, great for the Lifestyle and that will leave your coworkers begging for more. No matter what your favorite dish is, there's a way to make it lower in fat and more nutritionally sound.

- Do you have a microwave at work? If so, there are dozens of decent microwaveable dinners found in your grocer's frozen foods section. Check them out. Find 2-3 that are low in fat and will provide you with the right number of total calories for your Lifestyle plan. If you need to eat two dinners or half of one, then so be it.

Sit-Down Restaurant Eating

- Don't be bashful; ask how an item is prepared.

- Peel the skin off chicken or turkey, and trim all visible fat from other meat.

- Leave all butter, gravy or sauces off the dish. Ask that your meals be prepared with no butter, gravy or sauces. Scrape it off if you have to! The second best is asking that it be served on the side.

- Look on the menu for the "Healthy..." meals. Many restaurants today are doing a better job of telling you which of their meals are lower in fat and healthier.

- Ask that your salad dressing be provided on the side.

- Bring a small container of your own salad dressing.

- Bring I Can't Believe It's Not Butter® spray.

- Ask for low-fat or fat-free salad dressing even if you don't see it anywhere.

- Lie to your waiter or waitress and tell them you're allergic to butter. Hey, if it makes a believer out of them, we've accomplished our mission.

- Request fresh fruit or vegetables. Demand your veggies *not* be cooked in any oil. Many times restaurants will offer fresh fruit or fresh veggies even if they're not on the menu. Ask!

- Select foods that are steamed, garden fresh, broiled, boiled, baked, roasted, poached or lightly sautéed or stir-fried.

- Broth based soups are better than "Cream of _____" soups.

- As a general rule, many restaurants attain a part of their "good" reputation by serving overly generous portions. Therefore, your general rule should be to eat one-half to two-thirds of what they serve. I've been to many restaurants where *my* meal was really enough to feed my entire family. In that case, I ate 1/3 of what they dished up.

- Get in the habit of not cleaning your plate when dining in a sit-down restaurant.

- Sherbert, low-fat frozen yogurt and fruit are your best choices for dessert.

- A non-calorie Perrier or club soda or spring water is your best choice for drinks.

- 6 ounces of dry white wine with seltzer (a spritzer) only has 50 calories, so this is an okay choice if you consume an alcoholic beverage.

- Give yourself a signal that you are done eating. Place your napkin over your plate. Ask the waiter to take your plate. Order coffee or tea.

- When you're stuck and there is truly nothing fitting the Lifestyle, then peel off the breading, scrape the gravy, and eat a smaller portion.

Holidays and Special Occasions

I believe it's important you continue to live and enjoy special occasions with family and loved ones. I also believe it's important that those closest to you know you are "transforming your physique," but that they also see you are still able to enjoy treat foods at rare and special occasions. It is not a step forward to project an image of extremism because you have a self-limiting belief that you can't enjoy birthday cake on your birthday.

You can accomplish the goals of living the Lifestyle, enjoying special occasions and projecting a positive image about the Lifestyle by preparing for these special events in advance. We can all agree that birthdays, weddings and holidays are the exception to your typical week, can't we? Sure, we all have a week or two a year when it seems there is a string of events all coming at us at the same time. At the most, however, that is one or two weeks out of 52. Therefore, if you'll just plan a bit more, you can certainly enjoy the foods being served without feeling awkward or offending the guests or the host.

Coaching client Kay wrote:
"Tonight I am going to a family wedding. You know the scenario - piles of great food, gallons of alcohol, and a complete lack of healthy choices, save for the limp veggies warming over the heater. I intend to bring my own food, and discretely refrain from wedding food. The hardest thing for me are the 'Saboteurs' who will literally be shoving food toward me, and then getting snippy, telling me I'm going overboard if I refuse it."

Coaching client Dave wrote:
"I almost fell off the wagon yesterday - it was my 41st birthday, and I had my wife make a cake and ice cream for the kids. My plan was to put one of the candles on a nutrition bar (to show the kids that while on a reduced plan, you could still make a game of it).

Well, all was good until I started cleaning up. That cake looked <u>really</u> good. I was able to hold off, though, and made it until this morning. I knew the cake was in the fridge, so I opened the door, and had some cake - or better yet, it had me. I forgot that I had put it precariously balancing on the top shelf. I opened the door, and the cake hit me square in the forehead - bam! It *overturned onto the floor, and it took me 10 minutes to stop laughing.*

After I cleaned it up, I put the surviving portions back in the fridge for the kids. I got over the craving, and am shooting for staying on plan all day today. Got to start off my 42nd year right!"

Neither Kay nor Dave needed to fear the celebrations they were attending. Dave ended up getting a good laugh out of his birthday stringency but he could have eaten a little of his own birthday cake. No matter whose birthday it is, you can always partake of a small piece of birthday cake and ice cream. I've known mothers who were trying to be so strict they didn't have any of their own children's birthday cake that *they* prepared! This is completely over-the-top in my view.

It was unnecessary for Kay and Dave to feel as though they simply couldn't partake of the foods for either of those once-in-a-lifetime celebrations. Enjoy weddings, birthdays and like occasions for the relationships and the fun. Food *can* be a part of that fun. Your weight problems aren't a result of eating a reasonable portion of wedding food–whatever is being served. Your weight problems aren't a result of eating birthday cake on anyone's birthday. Weight issues are much more a result of daily, emotional eating. Weight problems result from eating when you're *not* hungry and not stopping when you're satisfied. It's not the holidays and truly special occasions like a wedding or birthday that are "doing you in." It's the daily grind, repetitive poor behaviors, and comfort eating on a daily basis.

Tips for Enjoying Weddings, Birthdays and Other Once-in-a-Lifetime Occasions

- Eat a Lifestyle meal within an hour before attending the special event. Don't go there hungry.

- Eat light earlier and save calories for the event. If you are allowed 1200 calories for the day, then consume only half your calories up to the event so you have 600 calories left at the event.

- Many find that coffee or tea can blunt the appetite. Drink decaf coffee or tea, if you find you aren't hungry after doing so.

- Exercise an additional 30 to 60 minutes over and above what you normally would do on the day of the event and the day after the event.

- Enjoy the food but go light on portions.

- Drink more water and zero calorie drinks at the event to provide a fuller feeling.

- Toast with the others if you are an alcohol drinker. Keep other alcohol to a minimum.

- Don't carry a pocket calorie calculator with you. This is obsessive and unnecessary.

Remember, events like weddings and birthdays are one day out of 365 in a year. While it doesn't have to be a pig-out feast, it should be enjoyed without even drawing attention. If you teach those around you that you are a fanatic, they will see you as that, and will <u>never</u> want to join your Lifestyle party. Wouldn't it be better if you were able to show your family and friends that you lost 12 pounds in six weeks, and were still able to celebrate a bit on those special occasions? I think so.

As focused and intense as your passion for your transformation may be, I believe, on these rare and special occasions, it's just plain rude or weird *not* to enjoy the celebration and partake of a small portion of the food being offered. If you have a photo shoot or contest within a few days to a couple weeks away, then be extra careful, but do enjoy the celebration. It's okay to allow a little celebratory food on these few-and-far-between occasions. They are not the reason you are fighting the battle of the bulge.

From Thanksgiving Through January 15th

The period between Thanksgiving (near the end of November) and the second week of January is the toughest time for most Lifestylers. Instead of asking Lifestylers to be perfect little soldiers during this period, I suggest instead that you continue to practice good, daily Lifestyle habits. Unless your photo shoot or contest ends in December or the first couple weeks of January, you will be consuming more baked goods, sauces, gravies, alcoholic beverages, higher fat and more calorie-dense foods, therefore, more calories will be consumed overall. All hope is not lost. Here are some guidelines for you to follow for the period between Thanksgiving and January 15th:

- Bump weekly exercise up 30 to 60 minutes.

- You will be eating 28 to 42 meals a week. Keep at least 80 percent of your meals within the Lifestyle guidelines.

- Become more aware of true hunger and fullness signals. Resist the temptation to eat when you are not hungry. Stop eating when you are satisfied, not full. It'll be very easy to pack in twice the calories in half the time since the foods you'll be eating will be very calorie-dense and not nutrient-dense.

- Baked goods will provide about 120 calories per ounce. A 3-ounce cookie or brownie will yield about 360 calories. Go easy!

- Continue to weigh frequently and don't bury your head in the sand for two months. I've seen women gain 20 pounds in this period. I've seen men gain even more. Ignoring out-of-control holiday eating will only create more suffering and work come January 16th–about the time all the holiday treats and travels are finally gone and done with. By monitoring your weight, you can catch yourself before things get out-of-control.

- Maintain your pre-Thanksgiving body weight or within 1 to 2 percent. A 150-pound woman should stay 150 or not gain more than 1.5 to 3 pounds. A 200-pound man should stay 200 or not gain more than 2 to 4 pounds between Thanksgiving and January 15th.

- What you don't eat by the second day, you should throw away. Leftovers and massive platters of baked goods *will be eaten*, unless you throw them away or give them away once you've had your fill.

It's better to throw it away than to wear it!
My daughter Elizabeth once said "Waste it. Don't paste it."

Taking the Lifestyle on Vacation or a Trip

"Foods eaten outside of your home zip code have no caloric value."
Comment made in jest by a coaching client.

While it's important to discuss what you can do to improve your eating habits while you're away from home–but close to home–it's equally important to address how you survive a trip or vacation, beginning with travel to the airport or lengthy automobile trip.

After several months of living the Lifestyle, Susanne had this to say about how she planned for a recent trip:

"Here is what I have done so far. I told the hotel I have to have the option to take care of my food. I have ordered a fridge, ordered a shuttle to take me to the gym everyday, plus I am Fed-Exing frozen food over night so I have clean food available immediately when I arrive.

The hotel told me they would help with anything they can, including allowing me to use the kitchen to heat up anything I need. My 'care package' will include all my snacks and meal replacements that I will need.

I called a man that I barely knew that trained everyday at the conference last year. I asked if he would like to join me every morning at the gym before the training sessions. He was thrilled. I feel so much more in control this year. I really truly am in charge of my results."

Susanne is someone who understands the importance of planning before the trip.

Jeremy is another member who recently took the Lifestyle to Disney World® with him. Taking the Lifestyle on the road, even for a whole family, doesn't have to be disastrous to your plan. Here's what he had to say about his trip.

"My family just got back from vacation in Florida. We stayed the first week-end at my parents' home, then spent 5 days at the Polynesian Resort at Disney World.

At my parents' house, my dad has a homemade bench and some dumbbells. I brought my resistance bands, so we didn't have to miss a workout - for example, when we had to do 'narrow-grip cable rows' we wrapped a resistance band around the leg of the bench, then I sat on it while my wife performed the rows. Then she'd do the same for me. My wife and I also spent $10 a pop to workout at a local gym, and ran around the neighborhood for cardio.

At the Disney resort, we purchased a family membership to the health spa and fitness center at the Grand Floridian. It was $40 for the entire family to workout the duration of our stay. So my wife, son, and I took turns watching the baby in the morning. For example, I would wake up at 6 a.m., head to the gym and workout. When I returned, I'd watch the baby while my wife and son hit the health center. When they returned, we all took showers, ate breakfast, and hit the amusement park.

My wife requested a refrigerator in the room. We loaded the refrigerator with cottage cheese, peaches, apples, pears, and strawberries - all types of fantastic carbs. We also brought all-natural applesauce and a bucket of oatmeal - mix the applesauce and raw oatmeal and you've got a great breakfast. I also brought a shaker cup and container of protein powder, and we purchased 5-gallon jugs of distilled water. We'd fill our water bottles at night, stick them in the refrigerator, then pull them out the next day to bring to the park.

We also purchased a bunch of bars that we'd load into a backpack.

So a typical day: The family would workout. I'd purchase a pair of hard-boiled eggs from a local snack shop and eat those with a banana and a soy yogurt as a post-workout meal. We'd then head to the amusement park. For a mid-morning snack, we'd eat our protein bars. For lunch, we'd find a decent restaurant - for example, the steakhouse in Canada in the World Showcase at Epcot - order some nice steak, steamed veggies instead of the potatoes, a mixed-greens salad (dressing on the side) and take advantage of the awesome bread for a carb portion. Mid-afternoon snack might be a protein bar and an apple. Then, for dinner, find another restaurant and eat healthy again."

Traveling to the Airport

- Pack some high-protein energy bars.

- Purchase some bottled water at your local convenience mart.

- Hit the road.

Once You Get To The Airport

- Bars are a huge help to keep you from becoming ravenous.

- Shake-and-go or ready-to-drink protein or meal replacement drinks are also a great way to get some high quality protein quickly; they're low in fat and very convenient.

- Airports sell bottled water everywhere. This is your drink of choice.

- Bananas are available at many stands and restaurants.

- Fruit cups are becoming more popular, but you have to open your eyes to see them. Don't let the gargantuan Danish and muffins overshadow what you know to be true. They are big on calories and small on nutrients. Do not go by what a standard Nutrition Facts Desk Reference book says is typical for a Danish or muffin. The airport Danish or muffin is about three times larger than the typical serving.

- Many airport restaurant stands will offer grilled chicken breast or sliced turkey. These are your best bets, but you still have to let them know you don't want the cheese and, if possible, you do want them on whole-grain bread. Ask for it!

Once You Board The Plane

- Have a bar on the flight.

- Bring a banana with you onboard.

- Make the best bad choice you can while in flight.

- It's tough to resist that *delicious* airplane food but say "no" to a fat-laden airplane meal if you are not hungry, and you have alternatives packed with you (like bars or bananas).

- Drink water as much as possible.

- You don't have to be perfect, just make the best choices you can.

Breakfast

- Don't give in to the enormity of the buffet! Many hotel restaurants or any restaurants serving breakfast have huge buffets loaded with saturated fat, cholesterol and calories galore. Some do offer a nice fresh fruit spread though, and this is a good choice. Again, don't feel bad for paying $12.95 for the whole buffet and then only eating dry cereal, low-fat milk and fresh fruit. You are doing your body a lot of good, and unless you can get these kinds of foods off the menu, the buffet is a great choice! OR

- Order egg whites scrambled with one whole egg (tell them "no oil"), plus dry whole-wheat toast (you add the jam) plus 16 ounces of water AND

- If you do have the traditional scrambled eggs offered on most breakfast buffets, make your serving about the size of your palm.

- Skip the hash browns.

- Skip the Danish.

- If oatmeal is available, go for it! You can't lose with oatmeal.

- One or two poached eggs and a small bowl of oatmeal are safe foods, guaranteed to eliminate the cooking oil used by all griddle restaurants.

Lunch

- Find a favorite sub shop or other deli-style fast-food joint. You're likely to find better choices that fit the Lifestyle at these restaurants.

- Chicken breast not smothered in anything is a good choice.

- Skip the mayonnaise, bacon and cheese!

- Almost every restaurant is offering low-fat alternatives these days, and this is what your eyes should zero in on.

- Fresh vegetables and fruit, either off the salad bar or as a part of your meal, are always a good choice, but don't let them cook your veggies in oil!

- Sick of chicken? Do a lean steak, but skip the gravies and sauces, get a nice green salad with plenty of veggies, maybe two tablespoons of cottage cheese and drink water instead of pop. Since you're out of your environment, you'll want to drink even more water. Drinking water will save calories that may creep on to your travel menus.

Supper

- Look for the word "grilled" on the menu.

- No "batter-dipped" whatever.

- No "Cream of ____" or anything smothered in a cream sauce.

- Stay clear of breaded anything (remove it if necessary).

- Lean beef or chickens are good meat choices.

- Seafood, not deep-fried or batter dipped, is a good choice.

- Broth soups are better than cream soups.

- The salad bar is your friend, but don't ruin it by soaking your salad in 95 percent fat dressing. Find or ask for a low-fat or fat-free dressing. A little olive oil and vinegar is fine too.

- Plan to leave something on your plate. Most restaurants serve 50 percent more than you need for any single meal.

- When all else fails, make your portion smaller.

In-Between Meals

- Protein bars and meal replacement shakes are a great choice to keep you on track when traveling. If you choose to eat other snacks, you may be deficient in protein and overloaded with carbs and calories you can easily do without. You'll need two meal replacement shakes and one bar or one meal replacement shake and two bars each day. These would count as three snacks so plan ahead and make room in your suitcase.

In General

- Don't overdo it. Remember, eat until you're satisfied. As someone who spends a fair amount of time traveling, it's tremendously important not to lose sight of how easy it is to overeat on the road. Portion sizes are usually too large, so leave some on the plate and don't feel bad about it!

- Speaking from experience, I know the temptation is almost overpowering when you're out of town to kick up your heels and have a good ol' time. Your urge to eat more, drink more and splurge more is very real, but make as many better bad choices as you can, and as often as possible, stick as close to what you would eat if you were home. The urges are far more psychological than physical, so realize the power and don't crumble.

- If your environment doesn't suit the LL, then change the environment so that it does! Plan ahead and set up your environment for success.

Summary

You can take the Lifestyle wherever you go. Instead of focusing on all the changes you will have to make, instead focus on replacing one or more poor meals per day with a Lifestyle meal. Since you probably don't eat more than 20 different meals a week, you will have all of your meals replaced with Lifestyle meals in two to three weeks max!

Many parents use their children as scapegoats for why there are so many snacks in the house. It is important to be honest about who you are buying snacks for. It is equally important that you not keep your weak foods in the house. If they are available, you will eat them. Avoid this trap by doing a better job of controlling what is available.

No matter where you are, there are sensible choices you can make to improve your nutritional program.

Take Action and Feel Great!

1. Throw or give away the junk food in your home.

2. Take inventory of what snacks still remain and who they are really for.

3. Write your child's name on any snacks that belong to him/her.

Triggers, Addiction and Self-Regulation

"There are really only three reasons we eat:
hunger, emotions and addiction."

As I continue to coach transformationists at a very personal level, I continue to be amazed at the complexity of the emotional spirit within us all. Once you understand the basic principles of the Lifestyle, the concepts of how to lose weight are simple. As humans, however, we are very emotional beings. You may believe you are practical, logical and an intellectual first. The reality is you are an emotional animal first and a logical creature second. You might believe you make decisions based primarily on logic, but a close analysis of your decisions and habits will reveal your emotional side determines the majority of your day-to-day activities and decisions.

Coaching member Robert honestly wrote...
"I think sometimes I have eaten in the past to "deaden" my feelings and emotions, just as I used to go out and drink to excess and go to clubs with loud music to forget myself. Certainly, when I was eating a half- gallon of Edy's ice cream every night not too long ago, I was trying to push something down. You do not eat a half-gallon of ice cream because it tastes good (after a few scoops you can hardly taste it); you eat a half-gallon of ice cream to put yourself into a coma-like state. And there have probably been times in my life when I was miserable and thought going into a coma seemed like a good idea."

Let's look at a few examples and see if your decisions are logical or emotional. Then, let's look and see if your decisions begin primarily as one and then are justified by the other.

Do you drive the most basic, practical, fuel-efficient automobile there is? Did you purchase the automobile after carefully scouring every nugget of factual data about the 60-miles-per-hour braking distance, horsepower vs. gross weight rating, safety data from the National Highway Traffic Safety Administration and proven history of its resale value? Or did you buy the car because of some of this data and a much longer list of emotional factors relating to how owning and driving the car would make you feel? Is Ford better than Chevrolet? Is Chrysler better than Ford? Why do you believe whatever it is you currently believe? Why did you pick the color you chose? No matter your income and purchasing power, you had other choices for automobiles. The reasons, of course, are perception and the ensuing emotions resulting from your perceptions.

> ## *When making a purchase or an eating decision, we base our decision on emotions and justify that decision with logic.*

"Well, of course I got the AM/FM CD with 8-speaker surround-sound. It was the logical choice, considering it was only $250 more." Sure, you are logical all right.

"Who wouldn't have bought the slinky black dress? It was on sale! It is only logical to take advantage of a good sale and save money. Sure, I have a few other dresses, but when you find something that fits and there is an opportunity to save–you'd be a fool not to take it." Right, all logical, huh?

"Supersizing® is such a bargain; you'd be a fool not to take them up on it!" Right, the reality is you had visions of sugarplums dancing in your head and looked forward to how all that extra sugar and food would make you happy or feel better. Sure, you are logical all right.

At a more practical level:

- Do you buy the cheapest shoes you can find?
- Do you trust name brands over generic? Even if the exact same ingredients are in the generic?
- If you have any pets, are they animal shelter rejects?
- Have you ever spent more for a service when someone else in town was cheaper and might have been just as good?
- Have you ever cried watching a movie like Old Yeller or E.T.?
- Do you routinely run to food when you feel bad, sad, overjoyed, or depressed?
- Have you ever eaten foods out of spite?

The quicker you can begin to understand and accept how emotional an animal you are, the better you will be. There are many crevasses that can swallow a well-intentioned, but ignorant, transformationist. My discoveries came from working with real clients, as well as from reading and speaking with experts on a variety of emotional issues relating to the transformation process.

Earlier I devoted half a chapter to splurge foods, and how to incorporate them into your meal plans. Now I will teach you about the dangers of trigger foods and why they are different from a splurge meal. Next, I will discuss how identifying and feeding normal hunger with balanced Lifestyle meals is vitally important for your mood, emotions and daily energy. I will then discuss food addiction and close this chapter with a discussion about how self-regulation is a limited, energy-dependent resource.

Trigger Foods

Do you have certain special foods, groups of foods or food textures that:

- You look forward to on a daily or weekly basis?
- You have to have every day or you feel poorly?
- You frequently think about even when you are not eating them?
- You have a difficult time stopping once you start eating it?
- You would eat before anything else?

These trigger foods or groups of foods must be considered as an enemy. They are the foods that will cause you to lose control of your food choices and fall off the Lifestyle.

Everyone has different trigger foods. For one person it might be refined sweets, and for another it might be processed breads and grains. Some of you may have trigger foods that are crunchy, and for others it is the creamy foods that have you carving out the bottom of the bag, box or bowl.

Eating the right foods can be a more effective medication for eliminating the need for those special foods or the frequent thoughts of eating that food, especially if the cravings are for sweets or processed carbohydrates.

Betcha Can't Eat Just One

Every food has a certain probability that it will cause you to lose control. By this, I mean you will not be able to stop eating it, and you will then begin to eat other trigger foods. These foods, like marijuana leading you to harder drugs, will cause you to fall down in your Lifestyle eating plan. The plan becomes one where the foods seem to choose you.

Trigger foods are those that you might say, "betcha can't eat just one!" They lead to chain eating. These foods tend to be high in sugar, fat, or starch. They are widely accepted in today's society, and are readily available mostly in snack foods and fast foods. Some are even recommended as part of a healthy diet; including low-fat cookies (e.g., Snackwells®), bread, and pasta. There are few people whose trigger foods are broccoli and broiled, boneless, skinless chicken breast.

Trigger foods are the foods that you think you cannot live without.

You must learn to view your trigger foods as enemies that ruin your health, looks and life. No longer are these specific foods just treats, goodies, rewards, splurges or comfort foods. In the past these foods have caused you to fail on an otherwise healthy eating plan. You pay a high cost for the short, few minutes of pleasure that you obtain while eating these foods. In the end, they do you no favor, fail to bring you happiness and certainly do not better your life. Adapting a realistic mindset of the true harm of trigger foods is important.

For example, although a smoker may know smoking will cost him money and ruin his health, the pleasure of smoking or the addictive nature of the habit keeps the smoker coming back for more. But if you are a non-smoker, you do not see the pleasure in smoking. You only consider the negative consequences. You must learn to view your trigger foods in the same way that a non-smoker views cigarettes.

Consuming trigger foods drives you to eat even more trigger foods, and begin a cycle of bingeing. When eating trigger foods, one bite may be too many, and a thousand may never be enough.

Binging involves eating a greater-than-average amount of food, in a distinct period, and on a recurring basis.

The strong physiological and psychological nature of trigger foods will counter nearly any rational thought not to binge. In other words, for many, the trigger food sparks strong cravings (a physiological reaction by the body) for more. This reaction is then followed by obsession, compulsive eating (inability to stop eating the food with a reasonable portion) and bingeing. The physiological and psychological combination is much stronger than any will or commitment you possess.

Because they are linked to behavior, mood and situations, you will not succumb to all trigger foods all the time. You need to develop a better awareness of your limitations with these foods. Trigger foods cannot be dealt with by logic. Taste buds have their own memory and power.

The Control Test

Make a list of all your favorite foods. Include all types of foods, from soup to nuts and, of course, junk foods.

Review your list. Do you notice a pattern? Do any of the foods belong to a specific food category? Are they:

- Sweet foods (candy, cookies, cake)?
- Foods with a specific texture and mouth feel (e.g., crunchy foods like potato chips, creamy foods like ice cream).
- Finger foods?
- Salty foods (potato chips, pretzels, nacho chips, etc.)?
- All of the above? I doubt it.

Subject each food item that fits to the following nine questions. The answers will tell you if you have a consistent history of abusing that particular food.

1. Have you ever told yourself, "I'll just have one" or "just a little" and found it is impossible to stick to this commitment?
2. Have you ever tried to give it up entirely and been unable to stay away?
3. When you see this food, do you crave it?
4. Do you eat it even when you are not hungry?
5. Do you choose this food over other foods that might be available?
6. Have you ever eaten it instead of a meal?
7. Do you always eat it in certain situations (e.g., bread at restaurants, peanuts at a bar, cereal at night)?
8. When you tried to lose weight or change your diet in the past, did you give it up?
9. When you gained your weight back or fell off your new diet, were you eating it again?

If your answers to these questions–particularly the last two–are mostly yes, then you have most likely identified a trigger food.

Your Eating Print

What foods always prompt you to lose control of your eating?
In which situations?
In which moods?
Is it only a problem in your house?
Do you lose control only if you are angry and stressed?

Your eating print is your set of personal food habits. It is as individual as a fingerprint. Eating prints are developed through cultural upbringing, childhood food choices, your current lifestyle, beliefs, biological needs, and so on. It determines what, how, where and why you choose foods.

Your eating print is developed over a lifetime and is a complex blend of biological, behavioral, emotional and psychological components. Since these habits are strongly embedded in your personality, they may lessen, but will never leave you completely. Therefore, *prevention will be your cure.*

Understanding your eating print is vital. If you can recognize the foods, behaviors, situations and emotions that cause you to lose control of food, you can develop strategies to avoid pitfalls! This will allow you to incorporate the Lifestyle into your eating print.

> *Almost everyone who fails to maintain permanent changes in eating habits, fails with the same types of foods, in the same places, and even at the same time of day, week, and year.*

For one person, ice cream at a restaurant is no problem. However, in the kitchen late at night, on a gloomy day, all bets are off. For another person, ice cream is never a problem, but bread at a restaurant or homemade cookies will be the downfall. Your mouth does not exist in a vacuum. Unique, sometimes subtle or not so subtle situations will cause you to lose control.

Your individualized eating print consists of:

- Trigger foods
- Trigger situations
- Trigger emotions
- Trigger behaviors

I'll Just Have A Little

The goal of the Lifestyle is to not only teach you how to balance foods for maximum energy and hunger cravings, but also to teach skills that will lead to lifetime changes in health and weight. In order to have long term success, it is important to have positive goals and be regularly, physically active. Avoiding the great trap of "I'll just have a little." is also important.

To a trigger food, "I'll just have a little," is an invitation to disaster. The trap begins with one serving once or twice a week without difficulty, and then slowly and gradually over the course of 6 to 12 months, it slowly takes over your eating habits and takes up residence in your freezer.

Nobody intentionally says, "Okay, now I am going to begin to eat poorly again." Ninety-five percent of the people who lose weight and eventually gain it back have fallen victim to the trap of thinking, "One little bite won't hurt." Do not believe you won't as well. *When it comes to trigger foods, one bite is usually too much.*

Trigger Situations

At times, it is not just what you eat, but where and when you eat that causes difficulties. Trigger situations, along with trigger foods and behaviors, form the "Bermuda Triangle" of nutritional relapse. They cause you to get lost and relapse into bingeing. These trigger situations will prompt you to even eat when you are not hungry. Sometimes you eat without thinking.

Preparation of food and sharing present the most difficult situations. These include social events such as parties, buffets, and dining with family and friends. These situations will trigger unconscious, uncontrolled eating, particularly if you eat a trigger food. Most of these situations (e.g., weddings, vacation) will involve emotion and therefore provide a deep psychological link to food.

- Some people tend to have more problems when at home where they have few witnesses, more time, and the food is conveniently available.

- Others will have more difficulty outside their home at restaurants, parties and social functions.

- Many people eat to fill a void in their lives. Sometimes that void is as simple as boredom. Keeping the mind active (television does not keep your mind active) is an important step in the right direction for breaking the boredom trigger situation.

The problem is not the situations, but your reaction to them. You can develop a "Pavlovian" reaction to certain situations. Once you start on that pretzel or cookie without thinking, you have lost control.

Trigger Emotions

People often eat when lonely, frustrated, sad, or angry. Choose your emotion!

For some people, food is more comforting than for others. This is a big part of their problem. Instead of coping with the problem, food becomes their therapist and panacea. *When the going gets tough, stuff!*

Occasionally taking comfort in food is okay–for example, eating a bowl of chicken soup when you are sick on a cold winter's night. However, it is not okay if your one-word response to emotional stress is ... "Eat!"

Food therapy does not work. Food may make you feel better for ten minutes, but it will not solve your problems. Turning to food as solace confuses immediate pleasure with long-term happiness. Anyone who has battled obesity and monitored their weight in the process knows that ten minutes of "bliss" from trigger eating buys you a minimum of four days of "scale pain" from mostly water and a little fat. Even though a single bingeing episode might only equate to a one pound or less increase in true fat storage vs. water weight, the pain of stepping on the scale for the next four days or more is excruciating for most transformationists.

As with alcoholism, eating due to emotional stress is a destructive pleasure that makes you pay a high cost–your health and self-worth. Initially you eat for pleasure because you feel badly about something. Ten minutes later you feel even more upset (guilty) because you ate something you really did not need. Eventually, you feel even more upset (more guilty) and you eat some more. The cycle continues.

Do not let the emotional situation or person hurt you twice! Do not lose power over the situation and cheat your health. Take out your frustration against the destructive eating habit, not yourself. Replace the immediate pleasure obtained from foods with another pleasure such as a walk, whacking some golf balls, punching a heavy bag, taking a warm bath, listening to a favorite song, writing, calling a friend, etc. As discussed in the *Are You Ready to Change* chapter, use the concept of Countering. Developing strong Countering techniques is paramount to a successful Lifestyle.

Calories cannot make you happy, decrease your stress, and improve your coping skills or relationships. In fact, they do just the opposite. They make you dependent on an external means to cope. You become an emotional cheapskate. Instead of realizing that you can cope with these emotions and they will soon pass, you begin to believe that you are helpless without food.

As you can become more physically fit through exercise and healthy living, you can become more psychologically fit. You can learn to manage your health and weight by managing your life without turning to foods.

Again–The Importance of Your Why

Become your own therapist and spot your trouble situations and behaviors before they occur. Take steps before they occur to protect yourself. You can try to remember what your favorite foods and eating patterns have done to your life, but I believe it is better to create your "why." In your "why," you should write how being overweight makes you feel. How does it interfere with your interpersonal relationships? At the deepest, darkest levels, what have your favorite foods really done to you? Why is it important to keep bettering yourself? What pain does being less than your best really cause you? How long have you been suffering from living with less than your potential? Use your "why" to help you vividly remember what food did and did not do for you in the past. If you feel sorry for yourself at any point, and find yourself focusing on "all you've given up" in your quest for a better body and mind, you can remind yourself why you decided to begin the Lifestyle in the first place. Your "why" will remind you that your favorite foods and patterns of behavior made you unhealthy, and did not make you happy.

Learn Your ABCs

We subconsciously use food as a reward or to subdue the pains of life. We naturally turn to food as comfort when things go wrong. For this reason, we must always be aware of our daily emotions to prevent emotional eating. Examine your feelings every day. Are you feeling anxious, depressed or angry? Eating healthy becomes easier when you ask the right questions at the right time.

Being told to change your behaviors sounds nice, but I am a realist. When you are really ticked off or depressed, and chocolate cake or caramel corn is your trigger food and available, how do you stop yourself immediately–before the fact? How do you break the cycle of running to food every time any emotion occurs?

You cannot stop a problem behavior until you recognize it is a problem. Dr. Prochaska provides an excellent model for helping to determine why you eat when you are not hungry. If you are eating when you are not hungry, it is important to figure out why. In *Changing for Good*, Dr. Prochaska says you have to learn your ABCs.

A = Antecedent
B = Behavior
C = Consequences

Track the events that immediately precede and follow your problem behavior. Do you eat poor choice foods when you are lonely? Unhappy? Sad? Depressed? Frustrated? Frightened?

What happens right after an angry outburst? What makes you crave a piece of cake? How does eating it make you feel?

There are likely certain parts of your life that are out of control and need evaluating. Antecedents trigger a problem behavior, while Consequences reward or strengthen it, no matter how maladaptive it is.

> *Every human behavior is goal-directed. Most bad behavior is an elaborate device to secure relaxation or assertion.*

Poor food choices you make certainly do that. Give this some thought. Perhaps it seems a little deep, but it is so important, it is not even funny.

Take a moment when you "cave" and have a trigger food when you are not supposed to and list the Antecedents and Consequences. Pay attention not only to the external cues, but the internal feelings associated with each "caving."

- What did you tell yourself just before having that chocolate?
- When you were standing in front of the fridge, what did you think just before reaching for the ice cream?
- How did you justify or give permission to yourself to eat a trigger food?
- What "deal" did you make with yourself before you ate the food?
- What emotions were you trying to medicate?
- What activity were you engaging in just before you went on the prowl?

Try to stay primarily in the present with your analysis. Do not dive too deep into the past unless you feel you must.

Trigger Behaviors

Do you always eat all the peanuts or pretzels at a cocktail bar? Do you go all day without eating and then eat all night? Do you find a seemingly benign and pleasurable food like pizza is always followed a short time later by craving large quantities of sweets? Do you open the refrigerator door first thing when you enter your house?

Trigger eating often occurs in a semiconscious state. It occurs when your mind is inactive, like when you are daydreaming. Watching television is the number one time for trigger eating. Being aware of this will not change your behavior; nevertheless, it is a first step in recognizing a known danger zone. Vow not to eat while watching television. If you are going to eat, then make sure you are sitting down at a table with no television playing. Do not eat standing up.

Geneen Roth writes in her book; *When You Eat at the Refrigerator, Pull Up a Chair!*

"Imagine you... invite a friend over for dinner. Tell her that the two of you are going to eat the way you eat when you are alone. Explain that you are going to treat her the way you treat yourself. Lead her to the refrigerator. Open the door. Stare. Begin picking up Tupperware containers. Use your fingers. Graze through yesterday's Chinese food or last week's tapioca pudding. Make loud grunting noises of pleasure. Open the freezer. Try to chink off a piece of frozen cake with your fingers. When that doesn't work, hack it off with a carving knife. Notice the fine spray of sugar settling on your floor.

Now, imagine treating yourself the way you treat people you love. This means actually sitting in a chair when you eat. And although I do not recommend eating at the refrigerator, I urge you to sit down no matter where you eat. So, when you eat at the refrigerator, pull up a chair.

Sitting down allows you to concentrate and take pleasure from what you are doing. It also dispels the illusion that you are not really eating while you are standing — you just happened to be looking around, on your way to somewhere else, and yesterday's Chinese food landed in front of you.

Sitting down at the refrigerator not only allows you to be kind to yourself; it also allows you to be conscious. On a practical level, it keeps your teeth from being broken by fossilized cake."

These unconscious patterns lead to abuse of trigger foods and cause you to eat the wrong foods in the wrong amounts at the wrong times. They are hard to pin down because you may not be aware of them. These behaviors will be eliminated by a concerted effort on your part to recognize them, and following proper meal balancing, as I suggest in this book.

There are four main types of trigger behaviors. You may exhibit the traits of more than one behavior.

Picker: This is the most common problem. If you are a picker, you will eat more calories with your fingers than your forks. Your greatest enemy is finger foods. You may eat more calories between meals than at meals. Problem situations will be cooking meals, or baking for you or the family and times at parties.

Prowler: You are similar to the picker in many ways. If you are a prowler, you never eat your meals sitting at the table. You wander and snack all day on whatever is available.

Hoarder: This is a person on the layaway plan. If you are a hoarder, you do not eat all day. You are either "too busy" or on a "diet." Your downfall occurs when evening time comes; you are so hungry you will eat whatever is in your path and continue eating all through the evening. You will consume one to four days' worth of calories in the hours after the evening news because your body is starving for nourishment. Hoarders eat far more calories than Lifestylers do, even though they rarely will be seen eating when the sun is up.

Finisher: You are a member of the "Clean Plate Club." You make your grandmother happy. You're the one everyone points to when there's a half a pie left and they're looking for someone to finish it so it "doesn't go to waste." You believe it is wrong to waste food and it is important to eat because people are starving in uncivilized nations. You always need to get your "money's worth" at buffets.

The Solution

There is nothing simple about breaking a trigger food addiction or pattern of destructive behavior. Undoubtedly, however, it can be done! When faced with a desire or situation that puts you face to face with a trigger food, take a deep breath, close your eyes, envision your goal in rich detail, and think of the food and it's negative consequences on you. Say to yourself, "If I don't take the first taste, I don't begin and I don't have any trouble." The more you exercise this control, the stronger it will become.

> *In time, you may be able to eat certain trigger foods in certain situations, while others you may never tolerate well.*

Use your eating print to shed light on the overall pattern of your eating history. More than likely, you will see that you are not out of control with food in general, but with only a *few select foods in very specific situations*. Your eating print is a window of the past and a crystal ball to your future. If you abused food in the past, it is likely you will do the same in the future. Knowing your eating print can be very liberating. Changing your way of eating is not a mountain to climb, but a few specific patterns to master and, best of all, it is truly attainable.

If you succumb to a trigger food resulting in a binge episode perform these four steps immediately:

1. Review your ABCs immediately.
2. Do not berate yourself for more than a few moments. Let it go.
3. Begin speaking positively about what you learned from the experience.
4. Write out what you will do to strengthen your resolve when the next emotional trigger occurs.

Gratitude List

Regardless of your current position in life, there are many things to be thankful for. Most we all take for granted, but it doesn't change the fact that we all have many blessings to count. The gratitude list is a fun list to work on but one almost no one ever does. It is simply easier to expect and take for granted. The gratitude list is important, however, because when you find yourself feeling blue and as though all the world has been dumping on you, your gratitude list can really be just what the doctor ordered. Not only will you feel a sense of calm and warmth just from creating the list, but these feelings can be relived over and over again if you will take time to review your gratitude list when you feel like nothing's going your way and you aren't worth the time of day.

Simply write out who and what you appreciate and why. If you have enjoyed even a glimmer of happiness because of recent weight loss or improvements in former destructive patterns, write down how you feel about them. Your gratitude list can include everything from how you felt when you walked out to a perfect temperature day to family, friends, loved ones, coworkers or anyone else who says anything that makes you feel good for any reason.

The more positively you react to a lapse, the better you will be the next time. If you make a mistake, then make it quickly. In other words, make it, evaluate it (ABCs), learn from it and begin speaking positively about what you will do the next time the same trigger situation, emotion and behavior is likely to occur. Telling yourself you are a worthless pile of dog dung because you had an unauthorized trigger food will not move you forward. You have likely been beating yourself up for far too long. It hasn't worked yet, and never will. Write your gratitude list! Evaluate any lapse by following my four steps listed above. What do you have to lose? If it doesn't work, you can always go back to self-loathing.

17 Tips To Counter the Trigger Food Battle:

1. "Realize it's a major change. Ever since mom gave us a cookie for being good, we have associated food with rewarding ourselves. It is hard to change that mindset, but if you weigh that against a lifetime of being overweight, unhealthy and tired, the decision to change becomes easier. You may want to see a therapist who can help you learn to nourish your soul rather than fill your stomach."

2. "Calling a friend, taking a walk, eating a piece of fruit or something healthy has helped me some days."

3. "Try talking back to the little voice and suggest alternatives, such as a hot bubble bath with candlelight, music, and a small glass of wine ... reading ... shopping or doing something creative."

4. "I make myself drink a large glass of water before I eat anything. Many times, after I drink the full glass, I end up not wanting to eat anything because the water has filled my stomach."

5. "I would like to suggest exercise—like a kickboxing class or some type of a high-intensity aerobic class. This kind of class can clear your mind and help you forget about craving something."

6. "As long as you are eating the good stuff daily, it really isn't terrible if you eat the crappy stuff once in a while. If you are eating it regularly because you are regularly having crappy days, you need to change your life, not your diet."

7. "I tell myself to wait 5 or 10 minutes before I can go get the chocolate bar. By the time I can officially have the candy, I no longer crave it as madly."

8. "Create a journal and talk with your urge. It will say a host of crazy things. But let it speak. Let it go on and on. Ask it questions. Most of the time, it just runs out of steam. Nevertheless, the point is to hear it out. The food shuts it up, but allow your urges to be heard and understood."

9. "This may sound silly but I pretend I am someone I admire — either fictional or real. How would they handle it? Scarlett O'Hara wouldn't let herself pig out on ice cream."

10. "If it is nice weather and still daylight, go to a park and swing on the swings, or just watch the kids doing it. Just go have fun. And just because you had a bad day at work doesn't mean the rest of the day is shot. Tell yourself, 'I may have had a bad day up to this point, but I'm not going to let it ruin the rest of my day.'"

11. "I visualized the end result by going into the theatre of my mind and envisioning my body at 12 percent body fat."

12. "I substituted a good habit for the bad one (e.g., hot herbal tea and a great book instead of my evening pigout)"

13. "I asked myself if this choice protected my confidence, or pushed down my confidence (I'd look at the chocolate, or mashed potatoes with gravy, or whatever— and say, 'To eat that would push down my confidence' and I would choose something that protected it— like reading, walking, whatever)."

14. "Trickle eating helps tremendously with cravings to binge on high sugar, high fat foods. I found a significant difference in craving high carb, starches too."

15. I took an extra multivitamin and *no matter what* I worked out and found that the workouts nipped the urge to binge."

16. "I kept Dove Dark chocolates around to suck on instead of scarffing down 3 candy bars."

17. "I made myself aware as possible that it really was 'that time of the month' and that's why I felt like crap so I could mentally try and adjust (sometimes it worked, others it didn't but I'm better for trying because sometimes is better than no times)."

Identify Triggers and Control Cravings

As opposed to hunger, cravings have a strong psychological component. Although you may not be hungry, when you crave a food you salivate at the mention, smell or sight of it. And unlike hunger, cravings may pass after a short while, even if you do not eat.

In order to break these cravings, you must eat frequent, balanced meals. By abstaining from problematic trigger foods, you will find within a week or two that your desire and cravings for these foods will diminish or completely disappear. *It may be necessary to eliminate trigger foods for a period of several months at a minimum* because not only is it almost impossible to eat only a little of these foods, but you very likely have developed hidden food intolerances to them. It is also psychologically much easier to have none of a food you desire than to be limited to just a taste.

After following the Lifestyle for several months, you may be able to occasionally bring one or more trigger foods back into your eating plan. If you decide to do so, I suggest you start small and evaluate your ABCs each time. Still, for many, you will never again get to have a trigger food if your goal is control and fitness. You may find that eating that one trigger food, that one time, in that tiny little portion, leads to former, poor behaviors and binge eating. If you must abstain from a trigger food permanently, the key is not in focusing on what you are giving up, but on what you will have gained by finally having control over food, feeling great on a daily basis, and looking the part.

Food Addiction

For most of you reading this book, trigger foods are simply problematic indulgences you will have to learn to reduce, avoid completely or manage better. For the food addict, trigger foods can kill. Abstinence and elimination of trigger foods is the goal for the food addict. How do you know if you simply need to get better control over your Ben & Jerry's® and your Snackwells® or if you'll need to make your Lifestyle more closely fit the hunter-gatherer diets eaten all but the last few thousand years of man's existence?

Kay Sheppard, a self-admitted food addict, author of *Food Addiction - The Body Knows and From the First Bite*, and expert on food addiction, provides a list of 24 questions you should ask yourself:

1. Has anyone ever told you that you have a problem with food?
2. Do you think food is a problem for you?
    - Food addicts obsess about food.
    - Anticipating food predominates the thinking of many food addicts.
3. Do you eat large amounts of high-calorie food in short amounts of time?
4. Do you regularly eat over feelings?
5. Can you stop eating whenever you wish?
    - When you cannot stop eating and have lost control, this is a sure sign you have an addiction.
6. Has your eating or weight ever interfered with your jobs, relationships, or finances?
7. Do you weigh several times a day?

8. Do you judge yourself by the number on your scale?
9. Do you often eat more than you planned to eat?
10. Do you worry that you cannot control how much you eat?
11. Have you hidden food or eaten in secret?
12. Have you become angry when someone eats food you have put aside for yourself?
13. Are you routinely frantic about your size, shape, or weight?
14. Have you tried any of these methods to lose weight?
    - Self-induced vomiting
    - Laxatives
    - Diuretics
    - Fasting
    - Compulsive exercise
    - Amphetamines
    - Cocaine
    - Other-the-counter diet pills, gum and caramels
    - Orbital (for a laxative effect)
    - Chewing and spitting food
    - Acupuncture, acupressure
    - Hypnosis
    - Urine shots
    - Special food, drinks and supplements
15. Do you manipulate ways to be alone so that you can eat privately?
16. Do your friends and companions over-eat or binge eat?
17. Have you ever felt so ashamed of the amount of food you ate that you hide your eating?
18. Have you been so upset by the amount of food you eat that you wish you would die?
19. Do you overeat more than twice a week?
20. Do you invent plans in order to be alone to eat?
21. Do you seek out companions who eat the way you do?
22. Have you attempted to give up a "treat" only to find you felt worse when doing so and returned to eating it repeatedly?
23. Have you ever stolen food or money to buy food?
24. Do you work in a grocery store or restaurant?

Sheppard pulls no punches in saying there are only three ways a food addict becomes a nonaddict: they go insane, they die or they eliminate the trigger foods leading to obsession and bingeing. She writes:

> *"Food addiction is chronic, progressive and ultimately fatal.*
> *Food addiction involves the compulsive pursuit of a mood change*
> *engaging repeatedly in episodes of binge eating despite*
> *adverse consequences."*

Like any addiction, the condition never goes away. The only way to break the addictive behavior is to abstain from the substance the person is addicted to. Recovering alcoholics never introduce themselves as a "former alcoholic." Anyone addicted to any ingestible substance has one out: abstention from that substance. **Food is no different.**

Unlike drug addictions (e.g., alcohol, heroin, cocaine, nicotine), with food it is even more complex. Since no one can abstain from eating entirely, the food addict must first identify they are a food addict and submit themselves as powerless over the addiction. Second, they must identify which foods are triggering the addiction. With other forms of addiction the substance causing the addiction is rather easily identified.

Foods that are most problematic for food addicts are high-calorie, high-carbohydrate, high-fat foods with a texture that facilitates rapid eating. Not surprisingly, asparagus is not a problematic food for addicts. Refined carbohydrates affect neurotransmitters like dopamine, serotonin and norepinephrine. All of these chemical messengers affect the brain and, therefore, mood. The food addict literally craves foods that will bathe the brain in neurotransmitters that make them feel better temporarily.

The destructive comfort cycle for the food addict usually begins when any feelings occur other than bliss. Bliss is rare. They obsess about a particular food, and then compulsively seek it, binge-eat it, and feel completely disgusted afterwards for doing so. They beat themselves up hard for "falling off the wagon." Even though they know comfort eating is really no comfort and will lead to sorrow, even as they eat it many times, the need to medicate their emotions and feel better in the short term is overpowering. Most people would not dream of staying in a relationship with an abusive partner. But far too many people abuse their bodies by succumbing to trigger foods and comfort eating. There is no question: *the food addict eats to feel better those foods that make them feel worse every time.*

Instead of countering and finding healthy behaviors for stressful situations and emotions, the addict has one cure for everything: food! However, the food addict is not weak-willed, dumb, lazy, stupid or of low moral character for continuing the destructive pattern. *They are powerless as long as the addictive substance is present and ingested.* An important point here, however, is although the addict is powerless over the food they are addicted to, *they are not powerless over their life and behavior.* They still have a choice they can make. They can choose to recognize their addiction for what it is and seek help. Help is available.

The Lifestyle is pliable enough for the food addict to withstand the rigors of abstinence from many trigger foods. The food addict has no choice. She will die if she does not recover from her addiction. However, during recovery, she does not have to throw the baby out with the bath water and find a "new diet." Not this time. To get a better understanding of why refined, pasty, sticky, sweet carbohydrates and grains are problematic for the food addict, I need to discuss our ancestors again and a bit about nutritional evolution.

Neanderthals and the Food Addict

For over one million years, man was a hunter-gatherer, living on foods that he hunted such as large and small game, fish, eggs, reptiles, insects and foods he gathered in the wild such as roots, shoots, berries, seeds and nuts.

The change in diet from hunter-gatherer to agricultural resulted in significant decreases in health.

About ten thousand years ago, the human population began to outgrow the supply of wild animal. Out of a need to survive, man began to cultivate crops and domesticate animals. With this shift, man's diet changed from 40 to 60 percent animal protein and 20 to 30 percent vegetable and fruit carbohydrate to 15 to 30 percent animal protein and 60 to 75 percent vegetable, fruit and grain carbohydrate. His diet consisted of much less animal protein and much more dairy and whole grains.

Larger Meals Were Eaten

Larger meals became necessary since man worked in the fields all day and could not forage (snack). He needed to eat enough at mealtime to provide energy to sustain him through the day. The concept of breakfast, lunch and dinner did not appear until the industrial revolution. People had to work certain times so meals began to accommodate the schedule.

Studies of ancestral agricultural societies reveal these populations were free of degenerative disease and generally very healthy, but they were shorter, not as muscular, had weaker bones and more dental caries than the hunter-gatherer populations. Dr. Weston Price's research of modern day, primitive, agricultural societies also verified these findings by showing these populations to be, in general, very healthy. Those who ate less animal protein and more grains were shorter with more brittle bones, and suffered from more tooth decay, infections and some chronic disease. Studies of Egyptian mummies show that this society suffered from obesity and heart disease even though it existed on an abundance of whole-wheat bread, fruit, vegetables, nuts and little animal protein.

Grains and Dairy for the Food Addict

Man has only begun to eat grains and dairy over the past ten thousand years. While grains are an excellent source of fiber and B vitamins, and dairy is a good source of protein, calcium and vitamin D, these can all be obtained from other foods. For many people, eating grains and dairy can be the hidden cause of many acute and chronic medical problems.

If you were to eat only grains and beans, in the absence of any fruit and vegetables, severe and potentially life-threatening nutrient deficiencies would result. If you added fruits, vegetables and essential fats, even without animal protein, you could indeed be very healthy. You would surely be much healthier than the average American eating processed sugars, flours and fat washed down with alcohol and coffee.

Some people can thrive without animal protein if their diet includes fresh vegetables and fruit, but this means eating a large amount of beans and grains in order to meet protein needs. When you add lean animal protein to a vegetarian diet and reduce the amounts of grains eaten, health almost invariably improves. This is how you evolved to eat.

The Evolutionary Clock Ticks Very Slowly

Ten thousand years may seem like a long time, but in evolutionary time, it is a split second. Genetic changes occur so slowly that man is essentially the same as he was forty thousand years ago. For 99.8 percent of existence, man ate a diet of animal protein and wild plants and for only the last 0.2 percent of time has he reduced animal protein and eaten grains, dairy and legumes.

> *If you reduced man's two million years of existence to one year, man was a hunter-gatherer for 364 days and 12 hours and a farmer for only 12 hours.*

The last hundred years have seen the most radical change in diet and lifestyle and the deterioration of our health as a nation. Although changing from a hunter-gatherer to a farmer population resulted in less than optimal health, it has been the past one hundred years (0.02 percent of existence or the last ten minutes of our existence) that man has made dramatic and rapid changes in diet and lifestyle.

Even as late as the early 1900s, half the population lived and worked on farms. They raised and ate hormone- and antibiotic-free meats, whole grains, fresh whole dairy, fruits and vegetables. Physical labor was part of daily existence. Their diets were not low in fat, but rich in nutrient whole foods and void of processed fats, sugars and flours.

The American diet is now 25 percent refined sugar, 10 percent percent refined flour and 35 percent processed, refined and unnatural animal fats. Twenty-five percent of the population does not have a single serving of fruit or vegetable a day. The soil is depleted of minerals and the food is preserved with chemicals. Modern convenience and transportation make it possible to be completely sedentary and most people are not regularly physically active.

Our diet has seen the addition of processed cereal grains, refined sugars, refined and excessive amounts of saturated fats, and alcohol. A large percentage of the population eats only a doughnut or pastry for breakfast (highly refined flour, sugar and fat, artificial colors and flavors).

Dr. Price also documented dramatic changes in the health of populations that began to eat modern Western diets high in refined sugar and fat. Rapid increases in obesity and chronic disease were documented. Dramatic photographs of the first offspring of women eating Western diets revealed not only increased cavities but also significant deformation of the jaw and overcrowding of the teeth–problems commonly seen today in children requiring dental braces.

People do not live longer and healthier than in the year 1900.

Although the average age of death is 30 more years than in the year 1900 (75 as compared to 45), even with all the advances in medicine, the average life span for someone age 40 today is only 4 years longer than in 1900. In 1900, one-third of all babies died in infancy or childhood due to infection. Tuberculosis was the leading cause of death. Because of infection and disease, the average life span in 1900 is therefore artificially low. The majority of advances in life span in this century are not due to our advanced Western medicine, but to public health improvements and the discovery of antibiotics.

> *The chronic diseases such as heart disease, cancer, arthritis and immune disorders, now routinely suffered by the elderly and many people in their fifties or even forties, one hundred years ago were unusual and rare among the population as a whole, and literally unheard of at age 40 or 50.*

Paul Dudley White was the personal physician to former U.S. President Dwight Eisenhower when he suffered his two heart attacks. In 1943, Dudley wrote this in his textbook on heart disease: "When I graduated from medical school in 1911, I had never heard of coronary thrombosis ... which is now responsible for more than 50 percent of all deaths."

When you consider the drastic changes in food supply, environment, lifestyle, activity levels and social community, it is no wonder that obesity is an epidemic and we, as a nation, suffer from chronic, degenerative diseases unheard of 100 years ago.

Eating to Live

Our bodies have evolved to have stable blood sugars brought forth by eating meals with adequate protein, slow-digesting carbohydrates and essential fatty acids. Our bodies have evolved to need the chemicals, fiber and enzymes present in fruits and vegetables to protect itself and function at its natural capacity. Although our bodies have evolved to snack, they are not equipped to snack on pretzels, chips, ice cream, and flavored yogurt. So it is not surprising that the addition of unnatural foods to our diet, such as processed sugar, flour and fats with preservatives and chemicals, have not only destroyed the health of the American population, but created food addicts as well.

The message in this section is not that the Lifestyle needs to be a Neanderthal diet for everyone–far from it. The vast majority of you reading this will do well to choose a variety of wholesome foods as discussed in the *Nutrients* chapter and live the Lifestyle with balanced frequent, small meals. You will not have to abstain from dozens of foods to make the Lifestyle work for you, however, even the nonaddict may have to forego–forever–some trigger foods to stay true to a healthy Lifestyle.

No trigger foods you consume today, nor any foods the addict is commonly powerless over, existed several thousand years ago and most did not exist even a hundred years ago. The rapid change in food availability and quality has preceded our ability to manage the chemical consequences of consuming these trigger foods.

For the addict, however, trigger foods become a matter of life and death. Trigger foods are not just something keeping them 20 pounds overweight. The physical and psychological aspects of the addiction have a stranglehold on the addict. There truly is one choice: abstention from all trigger foods and recovery.

The largest departure from the standard Lifestyle for someone with a food addiction will be, according to Sheppard, the elimination of any food that lists at least the following ingredients on the label:

• Sugar (any)	• Caramel color	• Syrup (any)
• Fructose	• Dextrose	• Maltodextrin
• Honey	• Maltose	• Food starch
• Alcohol	• High fructose corn syrup	• Malt and malt syrup
• Malted ...	• Caffeine	• Wheat
• Flour (any)	• Glucose	• Sucrose
• Molasses	• Invert sugar	• Maple sugar or syrup
• Modified food starch	• Turbinado sugar	• Fruit sweeteners
• Rice syrup		

For a more in-depth reading of food addiction, I strongly recommend either of Kay Sheppard's books or a visit to your favorite bookstore. If there is any chance you are a food addict, the time spent investigating and reading will be the most valuable time you can spend–no question.

A food addict's problems will never go away until the addict is in recovery. You cannot "will your way" out of addiction. If you are a food addict, you cannot pound your fist on the table and vehemently state, "I will never eat doughnuts again!" It is never that simple–there is a process to recovery. The process is detailed, and therefore, beyond the scope of my intentions with the Lifestyle. If you are a food addict and your current focus is on losing weight, then your focus is on the wrong thing. You must educate yourself about food addiction, acknowledge you are powerless over your addiction, and focus on recovery. Instead of the Lifestyle being one of many "diet books" you own, I want the Lifestyle to be the last "diet book" you buy. For me to ignore food addiction would have been feeding into the problem instead of giving the food addict some guidelines on taking the first steps to identifying the activities and foods most likely to create the addiction.

Self-Control is a Limited Resource–Spend It Wisely

"I generally avoid temptation unless I can't resist it." Mae West

The capacity of the human organism to override, interrupt, and otherwise alter its own responses is one of the most dramatic and impressive functions of human selfhood, with broad implications for a wide range of behavior patterns. Self-control consists of taking a course of action that yields a more positive outcome in the *long* term than in the *short* term. For example, self-regulation affects crime and criminal behavior, smoking and dieting. Men with better self-control are less likely to become divorced. Children who are better at delaying gratification tend to be calmer, to resist frustration better, to be less irritable and aggressive, to concentrate better, and to get higher grades in school than children who are less able to delay gratification. Also, children who are better able to control themselves deal with stress better in adolescence and have higher SAT scores when applying to college. It is clear that self-control is related to success in many aspects of life.

Furthermore, the failure of self-control has immense personal and societal repercussions. Breakdowns in self-control are linked with depression, obsessive or ruminative (reflective) thoughts, and aggression. Many of the problems facing both individuals and society today, ranging from unprotected sexual behavior to addiction to school underachievement, involve regulatory failure. Therefore, it is important I take more than a moment to discuss some pertinent research and how you can develop better self-control.

What is Self-Regulation?

Self-regulation is the attempt to control or alter one's own responses. Because many responses have a motivational strength, the capacity for self-regulation requires strength to overcome them. Thus, in the standard example of dieting or resisting temptation in general, the person must exert strong self-control to prevent himself or herself from carrying out a strong but forbidden impulse. Most people describe this type of strong self-control as "having enough will power."

Self-regulation is not only about will power, but also involves exertion, consistent with a strength and energy model. Both strength and energy are limited resources. Self-regulation results in physiological arousal. For example, regulating one's emotions, due to either stable individual differences in emotional expression, or specific instructions to control one's emotion, is arousing. Inhibiting one's facial expression of emotion or pain also results in increased arousal. Additionally, research has shown that holding anger in or regulating its expression leads to physiological arousal, such as increased blood pressure.

Acting Drains Reserves

Regulating an emotion requires overcoming one's current emotional state and replacing it with a different one. Research clearly indicates that mood control and emotional regulation is effortful and requires exertion to succeed. Hochschild (1983) concluded that attempts to appear positive and friendly (for airline flight attendants) or to appear negative and threatening (for bill collectors) both require considerable amounts of acting and effort. Altering one's emotional state involves a similar exertion regardless of whether one is trying to alter it upward or downward.

It is now suggested that trying to alter one's emotional state, rather than the emotional state per se, is responsible for regulatory depletion. It makes no difference if a person is raising or lowering their emotional state. The effort to do so taps into self-regulatory energy and it is now evident this energy is a limited resource in a given period. While the resource is limited over any given period, it is frequently replenished. People will also feel more fatigued the more they exert regulatory control. This again, indicates the effortful nature of self-regulation.

Bite Your Tongue–Eat More Later

Attempting to suppress or avoid a thought requires much more effort than either deliberately expressing the thought or letting one's thoughts run naturally. Expressing a thought does not require as much effort as suppressing a thought. Therefore, it becomes reasonable to suggest that ineffective communication skills or repressed feelings and thoughts will drain the self-regulation reservoir much more quickly when compared to the individual who learns good communication skills, develops coping and effective listening skills, and communicates from a position of empathy.

Self-regulation and self-control are indeed limited resources that can become temporarily depleted. The capacity for self-regulation is depleted by multiple demands. *The more you act inconsistently with how you see yourself, the greater the load on self-regulation.*

Lowering Self-Regulation Reserves

The concept of self-regulation and self-control as limited resources helps us to understand a common phenomenon among transformationists: the strong ability to say "no" to almost any temptation in the morning and "I just don't have the strength or energy to say no" to the same "tempting" foods in the evening. Each event, task and interaction throughout the day carries with it the possibility of further draining the self-regulation resource.

Here are a few examples proven to <u>lower</u> self-regulation reserves:

- Self-control drops off after prior attempts at self-regulation. If you take a life position that "it's just too much" or "everyone's always dumping on me," then your reserves will be tapped the moment your eyes open each day. You can do little to keep life from throwing you zingers on a regular basis, however, your perception of what life delivers is everything for controlling your self-regulation resources.

• Research clearly indicates that unhealthy interaction (mismanaged communications) with others and "trying to make a good impression" is draining to self-regulation.

• Self-control falls when one becomes overly tired or fatigued. The ability to express one's self is diminished when tired and this is believed to affect self-control.

• Alcohol is a drug associated with many self-regulatory failures. Alcohol is a depressant and can reduce arousal. Since arousal is linked with exertion, alcohol interferes with one's ability to exert oneself. This results in poorer regulation of behavior and emotions.

• Succumbing to acute or chronic stress will lower self-regulation reserves. Stress is the experience of being subject to excessive, assorted demands. Coping with stress requires self-regulation. Ineffective stress management skills will deplete self-regulatory capacities more quickly than effective stress coping skills.

Maintaining Self-Regulation Reserves

Being calm, on the other hand, is associated with greater self-control as long as the self-regulation resource has not been previously depleted. Being calm indicates a high level of energy and potential for action. Feeling calm is also associated with a physical sensation of being rested and refreshed and not feeling fatigued, drowsy, or sleepy. Calmness is indicative of increased regulatory capacity, less fatigue, and, hence, better self-regulation.

Self-control is also improved if one has the arousal energy to exert effort. Since self-regulation is effortful, the ability to exert energy toward self-control is better facilitated when one is well rested.

Kay Sheppard writes in her book, *From the First Bite*, that we should remember the acronym HALT. She says we should never get too:

H = hungry   **A** = angry   **L** = lonely   **T** = tired

When you apply HALT to the concept of self-regulation as a limited resource, you can immediately see the benefit of doing so.

Feeling overly hungry is indicative of what occurs when you "fight off" hunger for too long. The act of inappropriately using self-regulation (not eating when hungry and not adjusting meal portions and balance to create appropriate hunger intervals) can drain the self-regulation reserves. If you are "always hungry" because you are eating too little, you eat no fiber-rich sources of carbohydrate, or your meals are not balanced, you are unwittingly draining a valuable resource.

Becoming overly angry or staying angry will also drain self-regulation resources. Feeling "out of control" is a sure way to quickly deplete resources.

Feelings of loneliness can reduce arousal, perceived energy and produce strong feelings of lethargy. Since self-control requires energy and an attentive state, managing periods of loneliness with productive, fun, and stimulating activities must be pursued.

Foregoing sleep on a regular basis is the quickest way to become fatigued. Much like being drunk, being overly tired lowers arousal and one's ability to exert one's self.

Drink or Go Light During the Day–Binge at Night

If you have ever been a person who thought that drinking shakes during the day with a "sound meal" at night was the way to go, I hope to shift your position once again. I am a proponent of making the Lifestyle simpler by incorporating meal replacement and protein shakes into your meal planning, however, we humans are drawn to chew, and drinking shakes does not satisfy this urge we all have. Not only do we all have a desire to chew, but also now, you know why your self-regulation reserves are highest during the day and typically lower at night. Take advantage of what you now know to be true.

On too many occasions, I have observed Lifestylers who claim to be following my plan when they consume nothing but shakes until supper. The Lifestyle is not a diet based primarily on shakes. Let me first make this point perfectly clear: the more whole foods, the better. Shakes are great for traveling, the quick-and-easy fix, and they can improve the nutrient density of your day. One important thing they do not do is satisfy the desire to chew.

Do not fall for the booby trap of drinking your meals all day when self-regulation reserves are high, and then, when self-regulation reserves are depleted at night, satisfy your desire to chew by bingeing all night. This is more common than you might think. The more real food you prepare or buy during the day that requires chewing, the better you will be at reducing the urge to chew mounds of food in the evening. Usually, when a Lifestyler has drunk their first four meals of the day, the urge to chew at night is usually accompanied by an urge to chew a lot–to binge.

Another booby trap for transformationists is being "strong" in the morning (now you know why you're strong in the morning) and consuming far less for the first few meals of the day only to more than make up for it with the latter meals in the day. If you weigh over 200 pounds and you decide to be "strong" at breakfast and only consume 200 calories, you are not being strong–you are being foolish.

Now that you know you are strongest in the morning when self-regulation reserves are highest, it is imperative you consume an equal number of calories in the first half of the day as the last. Sure, there might be an occasion when you will want to save a few extra calories for a special meal on some night, but this should not be the practiced norm. If your day calls for 2000 calories, it is important you pack in 1000 of those calories in the first 8 hours of your 16-hour waking day. Being "strong" in the morning only sets you up for being overly hungry and depleting self-regulation reserves more quickly. When the evening comes, your self-control is not likely to be on par with what it should be. Instead of consuming balanced meals with moderate caloric content, you are likely to succumb to overeating or bingeing.

To be forewarned is to be forearmed. Eat (chew) at least three of your meals each day and do not plan to do so just in the evening. Even spacing of whole foods and meal replacement or protein shakes will help you stay the course without over-satisfying your urges with nighttime binge eating.

Deconditioning

While it may be common to be conditioned to "celebrate" on the weekends, you can work to decondition yourself just the same. Even though you "always grab a doughnut" on your way to work, you can just as easily choose to take ten minutes at home and prepare a healthy Lifestyle meal. Even though you "always go out for a beer" after work, you can just as easily choose not to and do something productive or fun instead. Breaking the cycles and counterproductive behaviors will allow you to break free of the grip food has on you. This is paramount to not only losing weight, but also to living the Lifestyle with continued success.

Many can "fake their way through it" for 12 weeks. If you truly just cut calories and exercise you will surely lose weight. But unless you focus on your emotional self and how you see and react to the world around you, the chance of keeping the weight off and living a life full of energy and leanness is slim at best. If you truly begin to see food as nourishment instead of a panacea for every emotional outlet you need, you will be well on your way to a superfit life full of energy and vitality.

Self-Control Success

Self-regulation success depends primarily on two factors:

- Reducing prior demands on self-regulation
- Exerting greater effort at self-regulation

When I say that better self-control can be gained by reducing the prior demands on self-regulation, I am not saying you need to avoid life or try to find a cave to live in. In staying consistent with my position that life is only managed, not cured, you'll be far better off to become a better communicator, develop strong behavioral countering techniques, and better stress manager than to try and eliminate stress or the situations that we typically find causing it.

You are still going to argue with your husband. The boss is still going to be very demanding. That coworker is not going to keep her mouth shut. The kids are not going to pick up their rooms without being told at least three times. Life will just keep coming at you from all directions. Becoming a better life manager will reduce the perceived self-regulation load because your perceived stress will be reduced and all demands on self-regulation will be reduced. Reducing the demand on the limited self-regulation resource will allow you to exert better self-control later in the day.

Greater effort brings greater success at self-regulation. Unless you feel more energetic, self-control will break down because "I just don't have the energy to make the effort." You are not likely to exert enough effort at self-control at any time of the day if you are overly tired or intoxicated. Unless you become better at reducing the load on your self-regulation resource, you have to consider repeated dipping into that resource as another source of fatigue. Self-regulation requires exertion, which leads to fatigue and tiredness. Even if sleep and alcohol are under control, multiple self-regulatory episodes in a day will increase the likelihood of poor self-control later in the day.

Self-regulation resources are not depleted because of what others do or say to you. Self-regulation resources are depleted based on how you manage what others not only do and say to you, but what you are doing and saying to yourself on a daily basis. If you allow continuous thoughts of "awfulizing the Lifestyle" (see *Lifestyle Booby Traps*) to flood your thinking, you are not likely to practice the Lifestyle for very long. If you succumb to euphoric recall of the foods that "just don't quit calling your name," an amazing transformation simply will not occur.

It is important you have your "why" list and your gratitude list within arm's reach at all times. When you catch yourself feeling sorry for yourself and you have decided the Lifestyle is just too demanding, you can refer to your "why" for a dose of reality. Is not following the Lifestyle and living with regret better than experiencing all that living the Lifestyle promises to deliver?

Becoming aware of self-regulation as a limited resource can help you look for daily events, habits, rituals and interactions you need to work on to reduce the load. Although life will never stop throwing you curve balls, your willingness to educate yourself about how to become a better life manager–and then practicing what you learn–will not only make it easier to live the Lifestyle, but to become a better person as well.

Sources: (Muraven et.al. "Self-control as Limited Resource: Regulatory Depletion Patterns", J. Pers and Soc Psy, 1998) (Vohs et.al. "Self-regulatory Failure: A Resource-depletion Approach", Psy Sci, 2000)

Summary

We humans are very emotionally-driven animals. Becoming someone who is obese or who has fought weight in other ways did not occur because logic drove food decisions.

Trigger foods are those foods you typically cannot stop eating once you start. They may also mask themselves in a food you can stop eating, however, drive you to consume other foods you cannot stop eating. I used to say with near certainty that there were no foods a Lifestyler would ever have to permanently say "no" to. Let me be the first to say I was wrong. Thank goodness I have continued to study, learn and better myself as I ask all of you to do as well.

Your eating print is as individual to you as your fingerprint. When you eat, why, what types of foods, in what situations and your overall eating behavior are unique to you: you must become more reflective and use self-evaluation to uncover negative patterns of behavior you are currently oblivious to.

When you learn to apply your ABCs to episodes of lapse or bingeing, you will be better armed on the next go-round. Making sure you have a strong "why" as well as a gratitude list you continue to add to, will help keep you strong when you begin to "awfulize" the Lifestyle.

Food addiction kills. While you may have intuitively known for a long time that you or some-one you know is addicted to chocolate or chips, you may not have truly believed there could be such a thing as "food addiction." Once you submit yourself to some basic questions, it may be time to dig deeper, read books, or seek professional help should you decide you too are a food addict. There is no shame in getting well. If you determine you are a food addict and submit yourself as power-less over your addiction while seeking qualified help, you will be so much farther ahead than rely-ing on will power to beat this powerful chemical addiction. If you were addicted to heroin could you have "just a little?" The same idea applies to food addiction. Certain foods will have to be elimi-nated forever if you are truly an addict.

A key point worth repeating is there are no known trigger foods or foods that most addicts must abstain from on most evolutionary/Neanderthal diet programs. While most people will do well eat-ing a wide variety of foods from all food groups, some will not. If you are the "some," then do not fight it. Accept what is your reality and live the Lifestyle eating more like our ancestors did.

Self-regulation is an energy-dependent and limited resource. If you are like most, you can turn your nose up at about any food in the morning, however, by late evening your self-control has dropped to undetectable levels. The stress of the day, the fight with the coworker and the traffic jam can progressively reduce your daily self-regulation if you allow them. Becoming a better commu-nicator and life manager can greatly improve self-regulation at all times of the day. The self-control necessary to build momentum for a successful Lifestyle is effortful. By paying attention to self-reg-ulation drains and becoming better at managing those drains, you will reduce overall demand for self-control and have more energy available to exert self-control when temptation would otherwise get the best of you.

Take Action and Feel Great!

1. Take the "control" test and identify potential trigger foods in your life.

2. Follow my four-step plan the next time you succumb to a trigger food or a binge.

3. If you have not written your "why" and begun your gratitude list, then do so now!

4. Be sure you know what the acronym H-A-L-T stands for and do your best to eliminate it.

5. Identify current self-regulation drains in your life. Rethink how those drains can be better managed within your ability or how you could become more knowledgeable to increase your ability and reduce those drains on your self-regulation reserves as well as your life.

The 24 Most Common Lifestyle Booby Traps

"The events in your daily life have only the meaning that you assign to them. Put another way, there is no good news and there is no bad news; there is only news. You have the power to choose your perceptions. And you exercise this power of choice in every circumstance, every day of your life."
Phillip McGraw, Ph.D., *Life Strategies*

In this chapter, I want to talk about booby traps and how they can sabotage your good intentions if you are not aware of them. While working with hundreds of clients over the course of many years, I have become increasingly aware of the attitudes, relationship hurdles and repetitively poor behaviors that can stop all forward momentum. These booby traps can set you up for another notch in the failure belt instead of what could have been your ultimate transformation.

Lifestyle booby traps are those situations, verbalizations, thought processes, emotions and psychological games played on us, and which we play on ourselves. Lifestyle booby traps can stop momentum and cause you to falter before you reach your transformation goal. As you will see, there are many ways you can be blindsided or sabotaged. Sometimes you will self-sabotage, other times the words and actions of others can throw you off course. I believe to be forewarned is to be forearmed. This is not a chapter you want to gloss over. Get cozy and settle in for an interesting compilation of the many booby traps to the Lifestyle and how you can understand, cope with and combat each one.

Booby Trap #1: Living by a False Set of Nutritional Rules

The Anti-Stress Diet Rules
A break from the serious side of the Lifestyle

I've decided to keep the anti-stress diet rules in the Lifestyle because I believe we all see a little (or much!) of ourselves in these comedic portrayals of belief systems many have about foods and calories.

1. If you eat something and no one sees you eat it, it has no calories.

2. If you drink a diet soda with a candy bar, the diet soda cancels out the calories in the candy bar.

3. When you eat with someone else, calories do not count if you do not eat more than they do.

4. Foods used for medicinal purposes *never* count, such as hot chocolate, brandy, toast and Sara Lee® cheesecake.

5. If you fatten up everyone else around you, then you look thinner.

6. Movie-related foods do not have additional calories because they are part of the entertainment package and not part of one's personal fuel. Examples are Milk Duds®, buttered popcorn, Junior Mints®, Red Hots®, and Tootsie Rolls®.

7. Cookie pieces contain no calories. The process of breaking causes calorie leakage.

8. Things licked off knives and spoons have no calories if you are in the process of preparing something.

9. Foods that have the same color have the same number of calories. Examples are spinach and pistachio ice cream, mushrooms and mashed potatoes. Chocolate is a universal color and may be substituted for any other food color.

10. Anything consumed while standing has no calories. This is due to gravity and the density of the caloric mass.

11. Anything consumed from someone else's plate has no calories since the calories rightfully belong to the other person and will cling to his/her plate. (We ALL know how calories like to cling!)

Remember: Stressed Spelled Backwards Is Desserts

Booby Trap #2: Refusing to Accept That Your Reality is Within Your Control

Subjective Realism

The saying, "No matter where you go, there you are," could not be more fitting for this section. Many people have the idea that how they perceive an event or situation is *the* way to see it. It is as though there could never be another way to process the information or situation. Their way is *the* way. Right or wrong–it just is. And that's that.

I would like you to step outside yourself and ponder the following questions:

• Is it possible that you react to everyone and everything around you based not on some set of rules governing behavior, but on a set of filters and state of mind?

- Is the way you naturally respond to good, bad or indifferent news *the* way? Is your way just "common sense?"

- Should any idiot see that everyone ought to expect the reaction or response you give for any particular event?

- Is a "bad" day really bad?

- Is it "horrible" when the scale will not move?

- Is your girlfriend breaking up with you devastating, or is there any other way to look at such an event?

- Was your last embarrassing moment really a "disaster?" Was it really even embarrassing?

- Is this transformation stuff hard, or is it simply a series of steps that must be mastered gradually over time?

- Is news of a forthcoming financial downturn bad news? Does your blood pressure go up when you are the recipient of such news?

- Is it harder to live a life that delivers you a body fat of 15 percent vs. 35 percent?

- Is exercising 200 to 300 minutes a week hard?

- Is it a sacrifice to forego ice cream if it continually makes you feel bad every time you eat it?

Whether you answered "yes" or "no" to any of these questions is based completely on the fact that there are currently six billion realities on Earth, all of whom believe, like you, that they experience the one true reality. Most do not consider the one truism, which proposes that it is so only if you make it so. Your world is unique to you because of subjective realism–also stated as perception. How you perceive every event or sensory input experienced through your five senses (sight, smell, sound, taste, and touch) determines your reaction to those inputs. That becomes *your* reality, not *the* reality.

No one is holding a gun to your head to react a particular way. If you were in a good mood one moment and news of any kind was delivered to you, which you observed as changing your mood–you must recognize you had a choice to make at the moment the news was delivered. You could choose to accept that virtually every piece of news is neutral and it has only become positive or negative through our perceptual processing of the news. Or, you could succumb to the thinking that it's only *proper* to react in such a manner when that type of news is given.

Am I suggesting we all become drones, absent of feelings or emotions? No. Feeling is the part of living that makes the day-to-day existence all worth it. To be numb or unresponsive to all things is death. It's also irrational to assume that an injury or tragedy to your child or loved one is "good news." I am not asking you to improperly assign a smiley face to such an event. The message is one of *choice* and understanding that your subjective realism can be manipulated at the drop of a hat. When you understand that your perception makes it so, and your perception is a matter of choice rather than evolutionary inevitability, you can know in any moment that you don't have to feel fearful, angry, resentful, spiteful, depressed, hateful, embarrassed or oppressed to the point of your own undoing. You can choose to constructively change how you perceive the input, subsequently keeping balance at the forefront of how you process all news and sensory input.

- If you despise taking out the garbage, you now have a perfect opportunity to change how you perceive this so-called "menial" task. This task could also be perceived as showing you care about your home and your family. You are recognizing that your wife truly appreciates you doing so even though she never thanks you for it. Still it is important to her and the family, and sighs of exasperation are all of a sudden no longer necessary every time you see the overflowing can in the kitchen. It is not a menial or a "dirty job." It just is.

- Doesn't it just drive you nuts when the hubbie leaves his socks on the floor, and doesn't hang his coat up when he comes in the house? Without arguing the finer points of relationships, you have to admit that your blood pressure and mood change are not *really* related to his acts, but more of how you perceive his acts as disrespectful toward you. You do not have to feel this way. You can change how you feel. It is as simple as deciding to perceive his actions differently. He is not necessarily disrespectful for leaving his socks on the floor. Nor is he for hanging his coat on the back of a kitchen chair instead of on the hook, as you have told him a hundred times. Whatever he is, your attachment to your perception of his actions makes it so for you–nothing more, nothing less.

Rearrange your thinking and your reality changes.

She Found a Lump

Recently I put into practice what I am asking you to learn. My wife Tracy came to me one day and said "I found a lump." I could tell she was worried, and I could see she was doing her best not to appear overtly stressed or worried. I also knew her well enough to know she was indeed more than a little worried over finding the lump. We agreed to see her physician and see what he said.

A few days later, her physician found the lump right away. He commented, "Oh, yes, there is something there." The doctor scheduled an ultrasound and mammography at the local clinic. After her visit with the doctor, Tracy met me in my office.

Again, I could see that she was trying very hard not to appear overly concerned, but this time I could see it was more of a strain to keep things calm. After all, the doctor quickly found and even commented about the same lump she had found. She knew immediately she was not imagining anything. There truly was a lump of some kind.

My mind tried to leave the moment and race ahead. For fleeting tenths of a second, I imagined my life without her. "What if?" Then I came back. I forced myself to stay in the moment. Then again, while we were talking about the doctor's visit, my mind left the conversation yet again and raced ahead. "What about the kids? How could I ever tell the kids?" Again, I quickly came back to the moment–the here and now. I felt calmer when I returned to the moment vs. leaving the moment and projecting ahead. I noticed, however, that each time I left the moment, I began to choke up at the thoughts that momentarily flashed through my mind. I chose to stay in the moment. Not only was it better for Tracy, it was better for me.

I did my best to comfort her by saying what I knew was true. Staying in the moment, and forcing the choice to respond appropriately, is difficult to do. Many times when you are "in the moment," you feel like you are drowning. You feel like there is no other way you can feel, and there is nothing you can do to change the negative way you are feeling. This is not so. **You always have the power to choose to change how you feel.** Staying in the present and "in the moment" is necessary so you do not allow your mind to race with all the "what ifs" and "what about" that will try to fill your every thought.

My communication with Tracy was simply this: I told her the doctor's words and findings were completely neutral. We had no confirmation of what the lump was, and it would do neither of us any good to spend our time worrying about what it might be. The doctor's finding and comments were neither positive nor negative. There was no reason for us to respond to the doctor's visit in a negative way. We agreed not to live in worry and fret in the few days until the ultrasound and mammogram. Knowing there would be "what if" thoughts in the days that would pass, I told Tracy that if she had thoughts of "worst case scenario," she should do her best to stay in the present. I assured her that science and medicine have come a long way to obliterating breast cancer with early detection. Does this mean we each did not have fleeting thoughts of "what if?" No. We both did. However, we chose not to live in those thoughts for any period. We both recognized those thoughts as unnecessarily negative and unproductive in our busy lives.

Tracy returned to the medical clinic a few days later, and had her ultrasound and mammogram tests. The ultrasound found nothing. The mammogram indicated the tissue was normal breast tissue–perhaps some fatty tissue. A few days after the tests, the lump disappeared.

I realize this anecdote is not a portrayal of the death of a loved one, or any number of life's events that could be perceived as more severe. My intention was to show how choosing to perceive the information as neutral at all stages, and staying in the moment, will help you, as it helped Tracy and me, continue to live your daily lives virtually unscathed. We could have just as easily become emotional train wrecks, looking for some outlet (e.g., food, alcohol, or drugs) for the heightened sense of fear and impending doom our perceptions could have imposed upon us.

In order to properly process news and events in your life, you must evaluate where you might be out of balance or misinformed. If the biases and life-truths (things you no longer question and simply accept as fact) you follow are not based on sound information and judgment, then your perceptions of news and events can become distorted. When this occurs, you are likely to react inappropriately, seeking food or other sources of emotional comfort.

Recognize the self-imposed filters you have acquired through life's experiences, and by which you perceive the world around you. Only when you self-evaluate, can you begin to catch your biases and improper life-truths that are distorting your perception and making your reality unfriendlier than you deserve. You are accountable for everything that occurs from today forward. You are not responsible for dreadful acts of the past committed against you, but you cannot allow any distorted filters from dreadful or unspeakable atrocities against you to distort your perceptions of the news and events of today. If you allow your past to dictate your future, then you are committing the greatest atrocity of all: ruining your own life and giving the past and those in it the power.

As you progress through your transformation, consider how your filters, life-truths and beliefs might need to be re-evaluated to best serve your needs today. Since self-regulation is a limited resource, it's not hard to imagine how two people experiencing similar news and events on a similar day could drain or preserve self-regulation reserves by perceiving and reacting to the news and events in entirely different ways. Your health, relationships, energy, emotional control, self-regulation and self-control are all riding on what reality you choose to make your own.

Whenever you feel the Lifestyle is punishing you, whenever you feel the Lifestyle "just isn't fair," whenever you feel pity for yourself, whenever you feel you need to "start living again," whenever you think "I can have just one," whenever you feel that everyone else who is fit doesn't have to work as hard as you do; whenever these thoughts come to mind, you should get out your "why" and remind yourself why it's important you stick with the Lifestyle, and not feel sorry for yourself.

When you are feeling blue, your perception may be that "It's just too hard." Remember, your perception can change. You can change it. You possess this power to shift your perception and make a new reality. Recall that there is no reality, only your **perception** of reality. Shift your position, and accept the reality that a fit body, the one that takes you away from the pain, is only developed by following the activities described in the Lifestyle. You must act your way to change. You must act as if you are already fit. Follow the footsteps of those who have been successful, and be aware of what it takes. Shift your perception and begin living your dream, rather than only dreaming.

I sincerely hope and desire for you to more quickly come to terms with the specific tasks necessary to see a successful transformation through as just that–tasks you must complete to reach your destination. Giving up fried foods or refusing to eat at McDonalds five days a week is not difficult. It just is. Living at six to seven percent body fat is no more difficult for me today than it was for me to live at 15 percent body fat years ago. It just is. The actual calories I consume and activities I participate in aren't much different now from when I was traveling to six percent years ago. However, years ago, before I understood what subjective realism was, I felt like many of you will if you aren't careful–that you're "killing yourself" to get there. Recognize now that your perception is what makes it so. Exercise is not hard. It just is. It is not boring unless you make it so. It is not a dreadful daily duty. It's just exercise. You have the complete power to choose how you perceive every event and hoop you must jump through to complete a successful transformation and to live a fulfilling life of health and ultimate fitness. Whether you are miserable or pleasant during your transformation is completely up to you–it is your choice.

The tasks that all must complete to change from obese and unhealthy to lean and superfit are quite similar. Choose to rearrange your thinking, which, in turn, will help to rearrange your reality. By doing so, you will make your transformation experience and the experience of those closest to you a more rewarding and enjoyable process.

Coaching member John wrote:

"On one level, of course it gets harder, as we progress further through our trans-formation. On another level, no, I do not have to "admit" that. I feel like that would be going along with being recruited into a mindset that may not serve me. In some previous discussions with Coach, I came to understand that our own reality is a set of choices. As such, I am always working on choosing the thoughts and beliefs that will get me closer to my goals. In this case, my hallucination is that it does not get any harder, it is the same based on the formulas Coach gave us, and how those suit the individual. Part of that little equation is "blind faith." I feel like I made the deci-sion to make a great transformation, with Coach as my guide, so now, that deci-sion's already made, my job is to go do what I'm told.

Is it hard? Compared to what? Compared to a terminal illness, or a labor camp, etc.? Not really. Again, just my own choice of perspective. My hallucination is that I'll cruise all the way to 6-pack territory. If I get "stuck", I figure Coach has been there, done that and will get me past it. I hope all of us will cruise right to the fin-ish, and I know we've all got that in us."

John has already learned that his perception of everything becomes his reality. In knowing and accepting this, he realizes that all matters of feeling, emotion and reaction are a choice. Once his senses receive the information, the way he interprets and organizes that information becomes his perception–and thus, his reality.

Continue forward by staying in the present, allowing some things you have held dear as life-truths to be re-evaluated and be aware that there is truly no reality, only your perception of reality. Respect the fact that others are also governed by the same set of perceptions and filters, and learn to appreciate how each of us must see things quite differently. Indeed, there are over six billion real-ities on Earth today.

Booby Trap #3: Mutilating the Lifestyle Into a Diet

The Lifestyle is a commitment without compromise. You cannot expect success by adher-ing to a "diet" five days a week and then cancel it out by eating willy nilly the other two. You cannot workout two of the seven suggested times, and expect the seven times results. Fudging, cheating and tweaking your way through the Lifestyle until it no longer resembles the

Lifestyle does not work. Too many people claim to be following this or that diet plan, but the reality of it is they are following no plan.

- **Strike while the iron is hot!** This person will go overboard by restricting calories more than he should. "The strike while the iron's hot" woman will over-exercise because she's confident it's best to hurry up and get the 15 years of excess off "Exercise is good for you right?" Strike-while-the-iron's-hot individuals will go gangbusters for several weeks, then, as a result, will burn out and recycle for several weeks or longer.

- **Mr. Iron Will.** "I'm stronger than you think!" This person will forego splurges thinking they are doing justice to the Lifestyle. They are wrong. In a few weeks, they will crave favorite foods and may binge or begin "living again" with a full-blown relapse. "I mean, jeez, you have to eat real food once in a while right?"

- **Get it out of my system.** When a slip occurs, this person will allow herself to be deluged into thinking she may as well indulge/binge on the trigger food and "Get it out of her system." This person thinks she can gorge herself into a life void of cravings from the moment the final doughnut crumb is wiped from her chin. There is no such thing as "getting it out of your system." It's faulty thinking to binge and gorge yourself for days or weeks before starting the Lifestyle in hopes that it'll "tide you over" for the duration of the Lifestyle, or even your initial transformation process. The guilt and disgust felt after that "one last binge" will last a few days at most. It will not "hold you over." It never has in the past, and it never will in the future. Do not kid yourself. The Lifestyle is about self-evaluation and continuous progress of both body and mind.

I will take the Lifestyle "cafeteria style." You know how when you go into a cafeteria to eat you can select what foods you would like to try? My hands-on experience with clients tells me that you will likely read some, part, or all of this book. From what you read, you will find many ideas you like, and others you do not like. What you have to realize is the Lifestyle is not like a cafeteria.

- "Well, you know Dave, I like what you said about splurging, but I don't really care for the notion that I have to count those calories, too. So I'll take the first part, but not the second." You will fail.

- "Right on brother! I can work out as little as a couple hours a week! Now you're talkin'! But I still get to eat as though I was working out for four hours a week, right?" No, and if you do, you will fail again.

- "Okay Dave, I get the idea about maxing out to build a workout. But come on, can't I just wing it? I'm a good guesser, Dave. You don't know me." I do know you and you will fail if you try to guess your way to fitness.

• "Goals, huh? How about if I just will myself to a better body. I'm a strong person, Dave. You don't know me and all I've accomplished, except for getting fit. I'm headstrong. I am a success in so many other areas of my life. I will just tell myself to get going every day. I don't really care for that 'Writing it all out stuff.'" You will fail if you don't.

• "Log my foods? Every day? Until 3 yo 5 percent of my weight is gone? Man, I was hoping you would just tell me a few foods to eat and that would be that. Seems like a lot of work." At first, it is like trying to get a jet off the runway. A jet burns through hundreds of gallons of fuel just to get to lift off. Once a jet is only a few thousand feet up, however, the power is pulled back substantially. When a jet is cruising at 35,000 feet, it is only running at about 70 to 80 percent power. Starting takes a lot of energy, and it is the start that stops most people. If you do not get a good start and a good grip on food logging, you will fail (see the chapter on *Sweating the Small Stuff*).

Do not follow only parts of the Lifestyle and expect it to work. Do not skip any steps and do not choose what you like and do not like. Take it all and commit to following it fully for at least eight short weeks. Do not even commit beyond that time if you don't want to. As I said in the beginning, try it on, give it a fair chance by following it fully, and if you don't like it, then no one is holding a gun to your head to continue further. However, give your heart and will to the Lifestyle completely for the first eight weeks. Until you fully commit, you have not even started.

Booby Trap #4: Basing Your Commitment on Support From Loved Ones and Friends

> *"All the doubt in the world cannot stand up to one little positive action. Doubt has no power when you decide to act in spite of it, and doubt cannot stop you if you refuse it attention. It matters not who doubts you, or how much, or why. What matters is what you do."*
> Ralph Marston

Many people mistakenly believe that everyone they are close to will unconditionally support them during their transformation. They believe their loved ones will not only read their mind, but will also cheer them on with every step of their transformation. This is a false perception, and rarely occurs. The sooner you can accept a high level of indifference to your change, the better. Your transformation did not start because of someone else, and can never be dependent on them.

If indifference were the only saboteur, you would be in good shape. Unfortunately, purposeful and hurtful comments are coming from those close to you. Some may have given up, and are no longer interested in getting up again. Since they are no longer interested in getting up, their goal in life may be to pull someone else down, attempting to make themselves feel better. The way some people criticize the transformationists, you would think they were being paid for it. Many times, they haven't a clue what they are saying. Still other times they are precisely aware of their hurtful intentions. For these reasons, it is important you are aware of the indifference, hurtful words and sabotaging. The antidotes come in the form of conscious awareness, knowledge, full preparation, leveraging, commitment and a strong goals program.

It Hurts More in the Beginning

During the early stages of your transformation, your will and commitment are the most delicate. In fact, they are incredibly fragile. Much like soap bubbles floating close to jagged rocks on a windy day, your will and commitment, unless solidly anchored with leverage and written, public goals, can burst from the words and deeds of those close to you.

Your will and commitment are so fragile at this stage of the journey because they are so new. You have not had time yet to let them grow or develop. They are not fully established, and they do not have a record of accomplishment yet. John Maxwell writes in *The Success Journey,* "When a seedling oak is only a year old, a child can tear it out by the roots. But once it's had some time to become firmly established, even the force of a hurricane can't knock it down." So is the case with your will and commitment early on vs. how they are after you have been setting and achieving goals for months or years.

Your will and commitment are also more easily shot down at this point. Since close friends or family members are the only ones who know about your dreams, these people are usually the attackers. Although your will and commitment may weather the criticism of a stranger, they may have a more difficult time surviving when undermined by a loved one. In the beginning, you may feel hurt when your loved ones do not support you and try to tear you down as well. Many times, for those unprepared and without leverage and a strong goals program, the hurtful words of loved ones are enough to knock them off course. Don't let this be you!

Better With Time

Once you have progressed and acted in a manner consistent with your public, written goals, you will have an easier time convincing others that you are serious. Their words will still hurt, however, once your transformation gains some legs, they are not likely to deliver a lethal blow to your will and commitment.

Over time, with continued success in setting and achieving your little "stepping stone" goals along the path to your Lifetime Achievement Fitness goal, you will shut up the naysayers by your deeds. In fact, not only will you shut them up but also they are very likely to begin asking you what you are doing. They will become more inquisitive and this shows they are buying into what it is you have done–not what you said you were going to do.

> *You will never shut them up with your words alone. You must to commit, act and remain committed each day with daily goals.*

The longer you do this, and repeat this process, the greater your chances of succeeding. Also, the greater your ability to ignore the hurtful comments that may come from close friends and loved ones.

Ignoring Bystander's Comments

A client wrote:

"I went to work today and I was wearing shorts for the first time this year and this guy came up to me and asked if I had lost weight. I said yes. He said, 'It looks like you've lost 10-15 lbs.' But then he also said, 'You're looking skinny. It looks like you've lost all of your bulk.' I know that I haven't lost much muscle, if any lately, because my strength has not decreased. In some cases, it's increased. But to hear that I look 'skinny' and I've 'lost my bulk' is disheartening. It almost makes me want to start adding another 500 calories above maintenance to my diet and go bulk up.

It's made me more self-conscience of my appearance. I've struggled with my confidence/self image in the past (one of the reasons why I started working out with weights in the first place) and to hear this after I've made all of this progress puts a damper on my motivation, other than to get some 'juice' to add 20 pounds by May. I'll take any words of motivation you've got."

This is a perfect example of a confused spectator of the sport of transformation. It is quite possible the person making the comments is just shy of being a perfect specimen of the human form himself; however, he could never admit this to himself and simply be quiet. Instead, he feels he must make a guarded compliment, tainting it further with negativity. The person making the comment may be jealous of your achievements and inwardly be trying to "Level the playing field."

Here is a saying many of your naysayers live by:

> *"Never keep up with the Joneses. Drag them down to your level. It's cheaper."* Quentin Crisp (1908-1999)

On the other hand, from a more positive perspective, the onlooker may have no clue that what they said hurt you. We transformation buffs are sensitive about those comments and we take them to heart. Remember, in the beginning and until you have been a Lifestyler for a year or so, you are fragile. It takes time for others to adjust to your new, smaller, but leaner body. They might be used to seeing you as a "big man." What the onlooker does not know is the fact that you always covered up before because you were fat. They really have no clue just how fat you were.

I still get comments today from people close to me who "never remember me being fat." Look at my before pictures again, and tell me I was not fat! The trick though, is when I was fat I always stayed covered up. See how that works?

Covered up = "big man - me bulky - me strong"
Uncovered = "fat - obese - slovenly - never touched a weight in your life look"

While it is easy for fellow Lifestylers to see how the words of others can be hurtful or detracting, others simply do not get it, and that is okay. The reason it is okay is you have to quit making decisions about yourself based on the comments of others. Learn to let go of negative thoughts as easily as you let go of positive ones. In fact, hold on to the positive ones a little longer.

> *"It is not the critic who counts, not the one who points out how the strong man stumbled or how the doer of deeds might have done better. The credit belongs to the man who is actually in the arena, whose face is marred with sweat and dust and blood; who strives valiantly; who errs and comes short again and again; who knows the great enthusiasms, the great devotions, and spends himself in a worthy cause; who, if he wins, knows the triumph of high achievement; and who, if he fails, at least fails while daring greatly, so that his place shall never be with those cold and timid souls who know neither victory or defeat."*
> Teddy Roosevelt

Stick with the Lifestyle and do not let anyone get in your way. Be prepared for more comments like this as you continue to change from fat to lean. Don't ever kid yourself–you were fat before, and now you are leaning out and becoming healthier, more fit and will actually be able to take your shirt off some day in public without causing any great panic. Rather, you will be hearing plenty of "oohs" and "ahs."

Member Stacie wrote:
"Why do people insist on thinking they have a right to tell you how you should or shouldn't look?

*When I was fat no one came up (at least not very often) and said 'My, haven't we put on the pounds!' Why then, is it ok **now** to say...*
- 'My gawd, you're **wasting away** to nothing!'
- 'Jeez, just how **skinny** are you going to get?'
- 'Oh, come on, **eat already!**'
- "Are you ok? You're not getting **anorexic** are you?'
- 'You look older with your face **so little**'
- '**You'll be sorry** if you ever get sick.'

• 'Can you be healthy at such a low body fat?'
*I am sick of it! Okay, so I **love** the way I look, feel and that all my hard work has finally paid off, but damn it, what is with these people? I am finding myself getting a bit mean and defensive and I don't like that."*

Women have repeatedly told me, and I agree, that weight loss typically becomes the most evident first in the face, neck and chest. These are the three areas they rarely want it to disappear. Many times, when a very low body fat is achieved, a woman will look slightly gaunt. However, as long as the body fat is reasonable (see the chapter on *Body Composition*), it appears the body will rebalance over a period of a few months and the upper body look is improved. How the weight is dropped, whether resistance training is used, and how low you take your body fat, will determine your look.

The average woman's body fat is in the range of 30 percent. When a woman takes her body fat down to the 12 to 15 percent range, it can appear odd to the average person. If everyone wore swimsuits to work, the 12 to 15 percenters would be standouts for all the reasons they would like. However, since we humans use clothing to either draw attention or hide flaws, being lean can be perceived as sickly. To be forewarned is to be forearmed.

Booby Trap #5: Not Properly Addressing Ambivalence

Webster defines ambivalence as "the existence of mutually conflicting emotions or thoughts about a person, object, or idea," and "uncertainty as to what course to follow." The feelings creating ambivalence over changing your body can run deep, and are certainly less comfortable to approach than opening a refrigerator door. The reason ambivalence must be addressed in this book is because I have discovered how debilitating it can be for the otherwise well-intentioned transformationist. The internal conflict that arises literally paralyzes or stops progress right when things were really starting to look up. As the subconscious controls those feelings and emotions you consciously refuse to deal with, it can and does stop forward progress for many transformationists.

Almost as if some people have a thermometer of success on the wall, once they see the thermometer rise to a level just below *awesome*, they subconsciously self-destruct. Have you noticed this pattern in your life? Have you noticed that you feel undeserving of some of life's most simple pleasures? If you've ever wondered why it is you seem to self-destruct just before reaching your goals, or just when things were going so well, ambivalence toward reaching your ultimate potential is more than worth investigating–it could be the key to what's been holding you back all these years.

To gain a better understanding of just what ambivalence is, I believe it is important to read the words of those who have experienced ambivalence in many different ways. Truly, they say it best.

In the real-life examples that follow, pay close attention to the statements that contain the words "afraid," "uncomfortable," and deal with unanswered "What ifs." These are the statements most likely to convey some form of ambivalence. How many of these statements do you identify with?

Specifically I'm not totally sure what it is I'm afraid of. I know that my personality can tend towards arrogance if unchecked, and I can see myself 'going there' when my body matches my ideal. I am generally liked by people now, and sometimes a bit envied. I'm afraid that if my body matches my gifting as a person, I'll be despised. I'm uncomfortable with the amount of male attention that comes my way as I go down the scale. I know that remaining fat is also linked with a laziness. I see that in myself, as I don't push myself to the limits of my potential. I feel the stress of that a lot and though I sometimes dive in, most times I back off. I'm afraid of surpassing my fiancé. I've discovered since he's been here that he is a 'thin, fat person'. He and I have joked about that and he admits it, but it frightens me.

Right now, just typing the subject line, my hands are shaking and I can barely breath and I haven't even said anything!

The fear I would like to address today is the upcoming Women's Challenge. Is anyone forcing me to apply? No. But why does even thinking about it terrify me?

Fear of Failure:

What if I don't lose the 20 lbs? Putting myself "out there" just opens myself up for speculation and ridicule. Will I forever be labeled a failure if I don't make it? If I don't make it and I'm tossed out of the Coaching Club, what do I do then? What happens if I just don't have the balls, willpower and motivation? How will I recover from that? What if I REALLY find out I'm a failure, like I've secretly thought all along? How will I pick up the pieces when everyone realizes I'm a fraud? What if, in the end, I fail and NOBODY LIKES ME?

Fear of Success:

Okay, let's assume I do lose 20 lbs. I have a close friend, who's an MD, who is also 60-70 lbs overweight. She is constantly criticizing my methods of weight loss. I haven't even told her yet that I've joined the Coaching Club. Her opinions go beyond concern. "You are losing that weight too fast" or "You shouldn't lose that much weight" or "You're going to make yourself sick" and yada, yada, yada. Why must I defend my actions to her or to anyone? And will my other friends treat me differently?

Next is my husband. We've been married about 4 years and he's put on 40-50 lbs in that time. He's supportive of my fitness goals and yet he doesn't have any desire to share that area. He talks big, but when it comes down to it, he never manages to find any time to head to the gym and he only eats clean, because that's all I fix. Right now, he's none too happy that I've taken away our Free Day and replaced it with a splurge meal. How difficult will it be for me to reach my goals and maintain my goals, when I'm married to a man who doesn't care about the way he feels and looks? Will it change how I feel about him? Will I find him undesirable? I realize that may sound shallow, but it's an honest fear. And if I'm on a path to fitness and he's on a path to his first heart attack, how can I share that part of my life with him? And this sounds SO selfish, but I don't wanna spend my retirement years pushing his wheel chair. I want to stay as active as I can for as long as I can and even now, he runs out of energy.

And how can I justify devoting most (if not all) of my time and energy towards my goal? I'm a caretaker, I take care of others and it's what I do best. Most of the time, I put my own wants and needs below that of my family and friends. How can I selfishly think of putting myself first? How can I insist on making yet another chicken dish, when my family wants McDonald's? How can I force my healthy eating habits on my family when they would rather choose a Big Mac? Nobody is forcing this on me and I'd probably resent it if they did.

As joining this group and getting back into my workouts this time marks the 12th, 13th or 14th time I've done this in my life, I have to wonder what it is that causes me to balk and falter just when I'm starting to make progress, and can see the light at the end of the tunnel just up ahead. The closest I've ever been to reaching my fitness goals happened back in about '95, when I was the lowest I've ever weighed as an adult (286.) Could it actually be a deep-seated fear of success?

As twisted as it sounds, when you've become used to not getting all the things you want in life, to failure, disappointment and rejection, it becomes easier and easier to accept things "the way they are," and that nothing will change. But what about fear of succeeding, of making the goals you shoot for, or actually surpassing them?

With success comes a great measure of responsibility and the need to maintain a proactive outlook on your life. Once you succeed, you can't allow yourself to rest on your laurels and become satisfied with what you've accomplished. Once you've "tasted victory," doesn't it become addictive; leave you hungry for more, pushing yourself to the limits of your capabilities and beyond? This is an unknown quality to me as applied to my own life, and we all fear deeply that which we don't understand, or isn't familiar to us. Is this making any sense? Can anyone identify with the emotion I'm talking about? I believe that aside from getting the proper nutrition, supplementation, rest and getting in productive workouts, fear of success maybe the greatest obstacle I have to face. Anybody else ever feel like this?

And sometimes success is hard to accept, you know, that fear of success thing. In the back of my mind I'm thinking, "What if I get to 6%, and then what"? Also, I worry about how hard it will be, not just to get there, but to stay in control and not blow up and get fat after that. I am afraid that I won't be able to control myself after submitting to such an arduous undertaking, that I won't be able to sustain the effort.

I am afraid that even after getting to 6%, I won't like the way I'll look: maybe my muscles won't be big enough or my body balanced or something like that.

Shaming the Devil

"Tell the truth and shame the devil," the old saying goes, and Coach, now is the time to make Ol' Scratch blush to the tips of his horns.

I have the knowledge. I have the genetic predisposition to shed pounds and gain muscle quickly, even now at forty. (Forty-one next week.) I can redevelop the discipline and the drive I know is necessary to get my ass into the gym five days a week, devoting at least three of those days to resistance training.

But with all of that said; now it's time for me to come clean and fess up as to what the core of my fear truly is. Why with all of our correspondence, and all the support you've offered here, I still have all the hesitation of a wet car battery when it comes to making a solid commitment and getting started. And here it is, Coach, the whole truth and nothing but.

My partner is ten years my senior. He has been fitness-oriented before, but during times in his life that involved great stress, when he sought both running and the gym as a means of escape, meaning that it does not hold the best of memories for him. He went through a bad divorce, and even worse, got involved with a charming and charismatic guy he made friends with, who used that friendship as a means of emotional blackmail, and at one point got my partner involved in some very dark dealings, not the least of which was peddling illegal steroids to bodybuilders at the gym they both frequented many years ago.

Now to the point I need to make. This is the week I can start down the path and not look back. I know that I can do this.

But what of my partner and our relationship? He is the first person I have ever been involved with for an extended period of time, (five years going on six.) Our relationship was not based on appearances when we met, and it has had nothing to do with the love, affection and respect we have always had for one another.

But I have a clear-cut, mental image burned into my brain of what I can look like after just six months on a good, solid program of nutrition, supplementation and exercise, and it exhilarates and terrifies me at the same time, not because of what it could mean for my health and well-being overall, but because of what it could mean for us as a couple.

I don't know if my partner can (or even wants to) maintain the level of intensity and dedication I know I can "bring to the party." If he lags behind, or even worse, decides not to join me on my journey at all, I'm afraid of what that might mean for us. If I didn't care about him at all, it would make everything so much easier, but I have never been that kind of guy, and I am not making plans to change my personality now.

I've had a taste of what it's like to finally get noticed for all the RIGHT reasons. And I know what a life-changing experience realizing my fitness goals will be. But am I being foolish about my concerns as to how this will affect my personal life? Is this something I want, or even need to have happened to test the waters of where we are once and for all?

Most fitness books address everything EXCEPT this point. And it has been discussed here at some point in terms of what the achievement of different goals can do to affect the relationship of married or involved couples. The dynamics of my own involvement with my partner are definitely different, but the emotions, motivations and problems are not, at least not the way I see them.

I used to justify not quitting smoking because of concerns about gaining weight during quitting. I'd say, "If I could ever get my weight under control, then I'd quit smoking."

Isn't it true that when you get older you look much older when you're thin?

A few weeks ago, after some discussion with Dave, it became apparent that I would have to drop below 200 lbs to reach my bodyfat goal. I'm sure he knew it all along, but I had not really considered the possibility. This may sound funny, but I had a difficult time dealing with that. I had all kinds of 'internal' fears about getting too 'skinny'. Crazy to many, but I allowed this to consume my mental energies for a few days. After some mental housekeeping, I was able to move on with my goals.

I guess that's what I mean when I say I don't want to restrict my eating: I really don't want to control my emotions or find solutions to what gets me emotional or find substitutes for emotional eating.

Unlike you, I am not afraid of looking good, although I'm also not overly concerned with my looks. I do want to get in shape and look into changing my career, and I am afraid of making that move, so delaying getting in shape delays doing something I'm really fearful of.
I know I get comfortable with situations in my life, sometimes even if they are no good for me (like being overweight). Again why, because sometimes we find that it's easier to dance with the devil you know, than the devil you don't know (change, something new, etc.) Fear of the unknown (changing our body, or anything in our life, for that matter) is a little scary sometimes.

I have wondered if my excess weight is my security from getting pregnant again. You see, when my bodyfat gets high, I don't ovulate. Both times I have conceived, I have been at a good, healthy weight. If I don't conceive, then I can't lose another baby and be heartbroken, right?

Ambivalence is very common and very detrimental to a magnificent transformation. You can't want it/not want it and get there. With unresolved ambivalence you really do not know where *there* is.

Challenge yourself at an inwardly deep level, and answer a few questions honestly over a period of a few days. If, like so many others, you fear what may happen to the relationship with your husband, wife or life-partner, then I suggest you consider how long you want to remain in such a relationship. If your relationship is rocky, then a transformation might make it worse, or could even make it better. You can only change *yourself*. Either way, other things in life will eventually test that relationship. Being in good health will help you deal with those inevitable situations with a clear mind and a healthy attitude.

Like most complicated problems, there is not necessarily a super easy and "all-smiles" solution. There is, however, a right way to address it: face it head on. Dr. Susan Jeffers, Ph.D., says *Feel the Fear and Do it Anyway*, and has so titled a great book that you should own. What purpose does fat serve in your life? Compulsive eating expert Donna LeBlanc teaches an exercise where she asks her clients to fill in the blanks to these two simple questions with as many answers as possible:

Being fat is ...
Being thin is ...

Many have a perception of what thin people are:

- Conceited
- Overachieving
- Anal-retentive
- Braggarts

- Uppity
- Snooty
- Constipated (no fun)
- On the prowl

- High-brow
- Snobby
- Flaunting

In fact, it is more a matter of realizing who you really are and becoming that person, no matter what skin you are in. Every personality trait comes in every skin.

Well-written books, seminars, tapes or life strategy coaching can also help you develop the skills to cope with the fears of which you are overtly aware, including those you aren't aware of working behind the scenes to thwart your progress. Read, listen, study, think and self-evaluate. Rely on those who know more than you, who have paved the road before you, and who are paid to expose your hidden fears while providing you with the emotional skills to deal with them. You must learn about you!

Until ambivalence is resolved, you will never charge full-steam ahead. When you are not sure you will be happy with the results, or at least willing to give it an honest effort until you get there, you will most assuredly never get there. Once ambivalence is resolved or there is a sincere effort to open old wounds with the purpose of healing, you can become free of the shackles of ambivalence. When the subconscious has been freed and is acting in concert with your conscious self, you will be amazed at how you will succeed beyond your wildest dreams.

Big Man Gets the Smallies

"My mother thought I was sick, thought I had cancer and started crying when she saw me after my transformation. Then I showed her my beginning photo vs. my after photo and asked her if I looked sick? Not until then did she understand."

If you have been a big man most of your life, you are about to go through a real psychological road trip. Unless you are aware of them when you start, this trip will be filled with potholes and barricades. In fact, if you do not make yourself aware of them, I can all but guarantee you will sabotage your own efforts to fulfill the "big man" image you have had for years. Big men often succumb to a case of the "smallies." This form of ambivalence sets up a pattern of self-destruction, which begins the moment the transforming man begins to believe he is losing power directly proportional to his weight loss.

Today, I tell formerly big, fat men who are having a difficult time accepting their smaller, leaner size they are suffering from a case of the smallies. This term was given to me by coaching client and friend Tom Roehl, who also suffered from the smallies in his own transformation from fat to lean. What are the smallies, and what can you do to prevent them from blocking your success?

First, women rarely feel the smallies. Most, but not all women, who are overly large want nothing more than to be smaller. For many men this is rarely the case. The smallies occur when a large man loses a lot of size, causing him to feel less powerful and respected as a man. Many even feel quite meek and mild for a time until they adjust to their newer, smaller self.

For the large bodybuilder turned power lifter, or bodybuilder who has always been in the "bulking" stage and who's finally made a commitment to lose all the excess fat, there are powerful and influential psychological forces at work that, if he's not aware of them, can completely derail his chances of success. If you have been a size XXL for about as long as you can remember, you are used to a certain level of admiration among your gym buddies and your family. They have complimented you on your hugeness, and these compliments have always made you feel good. The comments about your large stature may have genuinely been a source of continued motivation to stay fat (I mean big, strong and powerful, right?).

When you receive positive reinforcement for an action, you are likely to continue it. This is not anything new in your psyche. In addition, you have always been bigger than those puny 180-pound guys who always hung in there around 10 percent body fat. Shoot, anyone can do that, right? Those 180-pound guys can't take their eyes off you because of your magnificence and hugeness. They are so totally in awe of you. "Wow! What a big guy!" Trust me, with few exceptions this is all in your head. Many 180-pound guys at 10 percent body fat would like to be as big as you look in clothes, but not one of them wants your gut. Not one of them wants to look like the beached whale you have become when you have no clothes on.

Inside every beached whale lifter is a bodybuilder. I do not care if you are the most hard-core power lifter that ever lived. Somewhere inside of you is a bodybuilder waiting to be released. No? Why are you staring at your reflection in the gym mirror as you strike a front lat spread or double biceps posing then? Why are you shaving your hairy back? Are posing and shaving necessary to increase your squat? Maybe you have read something I haven't, which told you to pose and shave on a regular basis to maintain your hulking physique. I doubt it. It is probably more a result of your desire to be both huge and ripped. For 99 percent of us, this wish will never come true without drugs. If you are ready to get lean, you have to let these demons go.

Whether you are a formerly large bodybuilder, or simply a man who always thought you were big-boned and have never touched a weight in your life, you have to commit to leanness. You don't get to ride the fence in an attempt to maintain your best-ever squat while losing 25 pounds of fat and five pounds of muscle along the way. You might get weaker during the transformation process. What most find, however, is once they reach a comfortably lean weight, they are many times–pound for pound–stronger than ever before, even if their max weight isn't quite as high as it was when they were 25 to 50 percent body fat.

It is common to lose an equal percent of strength for every percent of body fat you lose. If you are an experienced lifter with more than three years of consistent training under your belt, you are at 25 percent body fat right now, and you drop your body fat down to 10 percent, you might expect a 15 percent drop in strength. This would mean that a person benching 400 pounds for a 1-rep max, at a body weight of 200 pounds and 25 percent body fat, might expect to initially drop to a 340-pound bench when his body weight drops to 165 to 170 pounds at a body fat of 10 percent. However, I have witnessed the leveling and eventual increase in strength with only small increments in true lean muscle after a few months of adaptation. What I am saying is, "Expect a decrease in strength, however, any more of a loss than what I have portrayed above, and you are losing too much muscle. This would generally be indicative of a calorie restriction that is too severe, a protein consumption that is too low, stress in any form that is consistently pegging your stress alarm meter, or chronic sleep deprivation."

Letting go of the strength, your former unrealistic body image, and switching rails toward leanness is not an easy task. I understand it fully. When I was 230 pounds, I was large. I was thick. I was strong. I squatted 600 pounds, bench pressed 385 pounds and dead-lifted 570 pounds at a body weight of 210 pounds. All lifts were competition legal. However, I was well, I was fat. Even though at my heaviest I weighed 230 pounds because I wanted to, not because I was out of control, I had a hard time accepting I was as fat as I was. Once I accepted I was fat and did not want to be fat any longer, the next psychological task was realizing, after several weeks of applying Lifestyle principles, that I really was shrinking. I literally felt like the wicked witch of the West after Dorothy threw a bucket of water on her. "Oh my God! I'm melting! What will they think? What will they say? I will not be as huge as I was, and I will not be one of the biggest guys in the gym any more. Is this really what I want?" I answered "yes" to that one final question. I really did want to be lean, and I was sick of being fat. I handled the "verbal attacks" of the unknowing pretty well. What are unknowing verbal attacks according to a former power lifter or formerly big man?

- Hey, Dave, are you still lifting?
- Hey, Dave, I heard you were sick, have you gotten over it yet?
- Were you in a car wreck?
- Okay now, that is enough! I do not want you losing any more weight!
- You are so skinny. (From a relative - maybe a grandmother)
- Hey, Dave, eat a sandwich, man.
- Hey, you have lost a lot of weight, but when are you going to stop? Are you anorexic?
- You know, Tom looks good but he has lost a lot of weight, is he sick? Does he have cancer?

All of these comments will come for the once-huge guy who has been a regular at the gym for longer than a couple years, or, will be directed to he who has simply always been the big man on campus.

These comments are crushing at first, but you have to realize that it is only because they are seeing you in clothes. We all know that clothing hides a lot. In clothes, the huge guy is thick and powerful. At the beach, however, he is fat and slovenly. In clothes, the lean guy looks skinny and weak (even though he's likely more powerful pound for pound than when he was fat), but out of clothes he's chiseled, sexy, muscular and has the appearance that he's at least touched a weight in his life.

What is the bottom line with this message? Any man who was once "huge" will go through the psychologically treacherous path as he attains leanness. You should know the comments are coming, be ready to accept them and stay committed to the plan. Know that being lean offers you far more advantages in the long run over being a big fat guy who happens to look big in clothes. Get ready to buy some new clothes and accept that you may drop from an XXL to a large when it is all over. Perhaps you will be the guy who can stay an XXL and get ripped. Come on, big dog, don't do that to yourself. It cannot happen if you are doing it honestly, without drugs. You will drop at least one or two shirt sizes so get ready for it, and keep the vision of leanness burned into your brain. You will need this vision when the smallies come calling and times are tough.

Booby Trap #6: Improper Handling of Food Pushers (not saying no at least once)

No matter where you go, as you progress through the Lifestyle you will be met by the "food pushers," as I like to call them. Perhaps in the past you were the one the family could rely on to eat all the leftovers. Just because you have broken that cycle and have committed to a life of leanness does not mean everyone you know and love is onboard–far from it. If you have not informed many of your family and friends of your new resolve and commitment, this will empower the food pushers even more. Their ignorance of your stance will mean increased pressure from them to "dig in" and "oh, one is not gonna kill ya."

The more weight you lose, the more likely you are to encounter someone, somewhere, who is going to tell you that you really ought to eat a little more. They will try, without knowledge of what they are doing, to plant seeds of doubt in your mind. "Jeez, can a guy really be healthy at 10 percent body fat?" When a guy is 30 percent body fat, it is not a question of whether he will be healthy at 10 percent body fat. It's a matter of how reasonably fast can he move from the unhealthy and disease-prone 30 percent down to 10 percent. It is not *if*, it is *how* fast. If you are a woman with 40 percent body fat, it is not a matter of whether 15 to 18 percent body fat is really all that healthy. It is a question of how much longer you are going to play Russian Roulette with your life. How quickly can you exit the obesity danger zone? As I discussed in the section on Ignoring Bystander's Comments, it's important you are forewarned and have a plan when the food pushers line up to get you to keep "being one of the boys" or the "pleasant, but portly girl" they've all come to know and love.

Some people call it guts, others will say you've got to get some "cahoneys," but whatever you want to call it, the only way to deal with food pushers properly is to take a deep breath, look them straight in the eye and say "no thank you." You cannot allow others to run your life. By politely, but assertively, saying "no thank you," you will break the cycle. Eventually they *will* quit asking. But you have to do it the first time before you can break the cycle.

There is no doubt whatsoever that you are going to be castigated for how little you eat, "how skinny you're getting" and "how amazing it is that a person can live on so little." If you have doubts about why they will make these comments, then refer back to chapter 1 and reread what is considered "normal" in America. The last thing you want to be is just like everyone else.

> *"You laugh at me because I'm different.*
> *I laugh at you because you're all the same."*

You can explain that you are not dieting, but you are in training for a challenge. You are no longer losing weight, you are losing "fat." Sure, it's a play on words. I don't suggest you tell them you are on a diet, though. Everyone knows that a diet is something you do to hurry up and get the weight off with no intentions of keeping it off. Tell them "its just time I cleaned things up a bit and got healthy." What works for you will be unique to you. The bottom line is that you do not truly have to justify yourself to anyone but yourself. To make the food pusher situation more comfortable, however, I do suggest you think ahead of time about what you will say when it is time for the moment of truth and a food pusher says, "take that last pork chop, Johnny and have some extra gravy." This situation will occur.

Booby Trap #7: Relaxing the Lifestyle on the Weekends

If you were one who came from another program that pushes free-for-all days once or twice a week, you will find that you're in good company when you feel the pain of breaking the "weekends = party time" habits. Regardless of the programs you have tried in the past, it is common for the weekdays to be much more structured compared to weekends.

The problem with weekends is not necessarily that we are not busy, although many times we are not. It is more a fact that the structure is gone. During the week, you have a solid routine that takes you from sun-up to sundown and beyond five or more days a week. Keeping on schedule, staying on track and planning your meals become a matter of routine. Then the weekend hits–bam! Structure is gone and so is the Lifestyle unless you are aware of it and plan for it.

Not only is the structure gone on the weekends, but also there is no question that a pattern of behavior developed around the weekends from the time you were a small child. When did many family functions involving food occur? When did you go out to eat with mom and dad? What night did you spend at grandma's house? When did you go to friends' homes for birthday parties? You got it: the weekends. In yet another example of conditioning and the Pavlovian reaction, we salivate when the weekend draws nearer. We truly have been conditioned to do so.

Pavlov trained his famous dogs to associate food with the ringing of a bell, so they came to salivate when they heard one whether or not food was present.

Because you have been conditioned to "Kick up your heels, let loose, let your hair down" and "kick back," all based on food, you can recondition yourself just the same. It is only a habit because you have been conditioned for as long as you can remember to make it so. To decondition yourself away from gorging, bingeing or even fudging on the weekends, you have to start with one weekend. No one is asking you to be perfect, although you do need to break free from this vicious cycle and prove to yourself it can be done.

Focus intently on keeping busy with productive work, but take time to relax, too. The toughest part is in breaking the association of *relaxation equals food*. It only equals food because you have been conditioned to make the weekends and relaxation equal food. Plan, prepare for the weekend, and rely on your strong goals program to see you through your first weekend. Do not rely upon food as your sole source of entertainment and relaxation. Think about the countering techniques you should focus on, be aware of your ABCs, and stop yourself when you reach for the box, bag or bottle before you zone out, enter the semiconscious state of trigger eating, and set yourself back several days for a few moments of false pleasure. Write about your feelings over the weekend, no matter what happens, and refer to those written feelings when you enter the next weekend.

Remember, no one is asking for perfection. The Lifestyle is about progressively getting better and learning from mistakes. Do not berate yourself if you do slip. Slip quickly, do not succumb to "now I've blown it" thinking. Quickly evaluate what happened, review your ABCs, write about it, determine what you can learn from it, and move on immediately–the next minute. Do not wait for the next day, or even worse, Monday. The best time to start again is five minutes after you slipped.

Booby Trap #8: Perfectionism

It is common for the new transformationist to use a word such as "perfect" to describe how they feel they must conduct themselves to really transform.

- "I've been eating perfectly."
- "Well Dave, I slipped and wasn't perfect this week."
- "God, you really have to be perfect to make this work, don't you."

Before you use "perfect" to describe how you are managing your day-to-day Lifestyle, it is important you recognize this flaw in your thinking. No one is asking you to be perfect. No one's perfect.

> *By following the principles of the Lifestyle, it should be your goal to become progressively better–not perfect.*

If you are eating cleaner, logging your meals, not over-splurging, avoiding triggers foods, exercising and balancing, you are still far from perfect. You are living the Lifestyle of a person who truly desires to become fit. If you slip, you have not slipped from perfection. Since nobody following the Lifestyle is practicing a perfect life, a slip is simply a natural occurrence and one from which you can learn. A slip (or lapse) is a wake up call–an attention-getter–and should you choose to turn it into a positive experience, you will strengthen your foundation upon which you build from each day.

Booby Trap #9: Fighting What's Right

The knowledge you are gaining with each turn of the page can be your best friend or your worst enemy not only for losing fat and gaining muscle, but also for leading a more fulfilling, loving and rewarding life. Once you are given the knowledge to do what is best or what is right, it goes against your natural grain to do it any other way. It violates your internal barometer of self-respect to now do what you know is wrong. Oh, trust me, I know people do it every day, but it is not natural, and it doesn't feel right. There's a price to pay for not doing what you know is right.

When you act in a manner that is inconsistent with how you see yourself, it will not necessarily cause you to stop behaving poorly right away. The more you fight what you know is right, and while subsequent internal cues tell you to make better food and activity choices, the more you'll experience emotional swings, self-loathing and feelings of unworthiness of any good. These are further signs telling you to do what you know is right.

Continuing to behave in a manner that does not match the values you know to be true then transfers into your work and personal relationships. Instead of realizing that you are the one with the problem, that you are the one with low self-esteem, you blame everyone else for your inability to create loving and rewarding relationships.

Once you begin following a path bordering on righteousness, you will begin to feel much better about yourself. When your actions match what you know is right and true, you will first be able to love yourself. Once you can love yourself, your personal relationships will improve. Now you are able to love others more freely. Until you can love yourself first, no personal relationships can truly benefit from the love you are capable of giving.

Booby Trap #10: Playing the Victim Instead of the Victor?

Will you play the victim or the victor?

> Victims make excuses; victors make it happen. Victims whine about not having
>   enough time. Victors make the time for what is most important.
> Victims complain about money. Victors make do with what they have, and they find
>   a way.
> Victims feel self-pity relentlessly, and they succumb to emotional eating far too
>   often, because it is an "instant gratification." Victors are goal seekers, and strive
>   for betterment, not perfection. They will delay gratification for the larger prize.
> Victims will start "someday." Victors start today, even if it's not Monday.
> Victims are tension relievers. Victors are goal achievers.
> Victims look for pity. Victors look to get it done.
> Victims want to blame someone. Victors find solutions.
> Victims eat their way through every emotional struggle and punish themselves for
>   days after a slip. Victors develop healthy alternative activities to eating, and fail
>   quickly when they slip.
> Victims speak loudly with lip service and little action. Either victors do not have
>   much to say, or their actions are so loud you cannot hear what they are saying.
> Each day there are many opportunities to be the victim or the victor. The choice is
>   always yours, but it is not usually until you realize it *is* your choice that you can
>   transform from the victim to the victor.

Booby Trap #11: Living Your Life Looking in the Rearview Mirror

Creating personal relationships with coaching clients has allowed me the opportunity to look deeper inside the hearts and souls of those I have coached. I have discovered there is a tremendous amount of unresolved pain, many times still stuffed deep down inside. Improper and hurtful family relationships are usually the root of most of the pain I see. Today, decades after the tender childhood years are over, the emotional pain is bubbling near the surface. While many people older than 30 claim to have elephant skin (very thick), the reality is that their skin is a paper-thin crust with pain bubbling just below the surface. When people spend their lives looking in the rear view mirror, it is quite easy to break through the thin crust and expose the pain of the past with only a gentle tap on that outer crust.

It is hard for many of you to see yourselves in a positive light. The painful memories, ongoing abuse or repressed feelings can all be debilitating to the well-intentioned transformationist who does not fix what is broken. There is an entire history of verbal, physical and other abuse that many of you have experienced. The negative emotions and feelings you associate with these past and present experiences continue to limit you. You have allowed them to create a wedge between you and any positive thinking about yourself.

It makes sense that ongoing abuse must first stop before the healing process can begin. If you are in an abusive relationship, I strongly urge that you speak to a qualified expert on the subject, a help-crisis center or member of the clergy. The pain inflicted by any form of abuse cannot be covered in cheese sauce and chocolate-covered pretzels. It must first stop, before it can get better. No one deserves to be abused in any way.

I am not a psychologist nor am I a psychiatrist; I am merely an avid student of human behavior. There comes a time when you have to quit living your life by looking in the rear view mirror. Hate and pent up pain and frustration are more calorie-laden and weigh more on your hips and thighs than any trigger food you've ever dreamed of. By holding on to the pain of the past, you forsake a future that you were meant to enjoy.

Many of you have spent so much time listening to people who tell you what you cannot do in life, that you are shocked to see the results of your own transformation. You may continue to feel bewildered by all the other good that is in store for you as this weight is lifted, literally and figuratively. It is so very important to begin to appreciate the unique talents, qualities and abilities you have. Your image, the way you see yourself, has a direct bearing on your performance, whatever that performance may be. Dr. Joyce Brothers says that it is impossible to consistently perform in a manner that is inconsistent with how you see yourself. How you see yourself will affect how you treat other people. In this manner, the cycle continues.

It is time to quit living your life looking in the rear view mirror. Look ahead, your future is bright. Think of all the wonderful things you can appreciate in your life right now. Really, think about it. You have much to be thankful for, it is time to focus on the many blessings you have, and the positive things about yourself that are worth telling yourself everyday.

Self-talk is not anything new. It has been around for thousands of years. It is time that you paid close attention to the words you use to describe yourself each day. As the saying goes, it is garbage in and garbage out. Or if you will try just a little bit, it is love in and love out. Love yourself for the many good qualities you possess. And give yourself the most precious gift of all, the gift of forgiveness.

A book I suggest everyone read is called "*What to Say When You Talk To Yourself*" by Shad Helmstetter Ph.D. Don't procrastinate–put it on your today goal list and order it right away.

Booby Trap #12: Not Forgiving Yourself and Others

> *The pain of lingering anger is far worse most times than what the person did that let you down. Not forgiving or holding a grudge is like swallowing acid and hoping it burns the other person.*

You may believe it is impossible to forgive those who have been so cruel to you in the past. Forgive them anyway. You are not alone. Many others before you were also hurt in many ways much worse than you, and found a way to forgive and to quit living their life looking in the rear view mirror. Once you do forgive, you will find a weight is lifted, and for many, that weight can be lifted right off the waist, thighs and buttocks.

You forgive others, not for them, but for you. It is not necessary to tell them you forgive them. Their repentance is not needed in order to be forgiven–most will not repent. You, by choice, forgive those horrific deeds of the past, for you and you only. That does not mean what anyone did is okay, not at all. We all have a choice to make; carry that hate and anger with us forever, or let it go by forgiving–truly forgiving. In essence, you're saying, "Hey, you messed me up for years by doing this, that and the other thing, I'll be *damned* if you are going to keep messing me up now that you aren't a major influence in my life."

No matter how much you claim to have put negative feelings behind you, many are there, right at the surface, bubbling and waiting to boil over. Maybe this is what you call your major tempers. Somewhere along the way, someone has beaten you down, told you that you were not worth a darn and would never amount to jack squat. Know what? They were wrong!

Even if you suffered horribly as a child and young adult, it is time now to break the cycle. Do not allow the cycle to continue with your children and family. Become a well-balanced parent. Do not kid yourself that your children do not see and feel your pain–they do. Forgive the awful things said and done in the past and forgive yourself.

> *You do it for you–not for them. If not, they are still in control.*

Today I would like you to give yourself a big present–forgiveness. No one gets through this life without a tremendous amount of pain in one form or another, however, yesterday ended last night. Today is a new opportunity. There is so much hope in the future. Forgive yourself for the things you've said and done in the past, but make a sincere effort to do better and to be better in the future.

Forgive yourself for not having the body of a model or superhero, and forgive your parents for not endowing you with the genetics to have the pecs of Arnold, no hips, the butt of a boy and no cellulite on those thighs. You are here for a reason, and you were meant to be successful.

I truly believe that your life's experiences up to and including today are only preparing you to become the massive success you were meant to be. Nothing worth having comes easy.

> Brian Tracy says:
> *"Expect to meet many obstacles, difficulties, and temporary failures on your way to your goals. They are essential to your eventual success. You need them. They are each sent to teach you something vital that will help you."*

Why would your life's dream or your ultimate success dream be anything but on-the-edge white-knuckle tough to achieve? Would doctors be as highly regarded if they were able to achieve their degree by mail order in two weeks? Would someone who climbs Mt. Everest be as highly regarded as a doer, an accomplisher and an achiever if the mountain were 10 feet high instead of 29 thousand and 29 feet?

I really do want you to look in the mirror one day soon and see the beautiful person that you are. It is not only okay to say that you are beautiful repeatedly and over again, I highly suggest you do. Even if you are the only one who tells you that in a year, it is okay, it is true and you deserve it. Think about how you talk to yourself each day. Provide more than a little effort to speak positively about yourself. Change the garbage in and garbage out to love in and love out. Stop living your life looking in the rear view mirror; forgive your enemies, your family, your friends and most of all–yourself.

You were meant to be successful. Do not doubt your success as you successfully complete your transformation or any other area of your life. I believe that a happy person is not a person in a certain set of circumstances, but rather a person with a certain set of attitudes. Your self-talk can change your attitude about yourself. Accept the new you that is about to be unveiled. You deserve it. You are building it and you will own it.

Booby Trap #13: Becoming Just Like Your Negative Parent(s)

Compulsive eaters are people who continue to eat when they should stop, who go ahead and eat something they wish they had turned down. There is no question that the vast majority of us, especially compulsive eaters, were parented with punishment as the number one form of control. Get out of line? Expect a punishment. Let the parents down? Expect a punishment. Many individuals had overly critical parents with too little nurturing. Now, as an adult, you have an opportunity to re-parent yourself.

Without question, you are going to slip during your transformation. There are going to be times when you have the desired trigger/comfort food when it was nowhere to be found on your plan. Because you have been conditioned by many authoritative figures to beat yourself up relentlessly for having the "forbidden fruit," you will continue to do so unless you realize you will never, ever, become the person you want to be unless you stop this destructive cycle of negative self-talk and demoralizing behavior.

Donna LeBlanc M.Ed., *You Can't Quit 'til You Know What's Eating You*, believes we all have a parent, an adult and a child within us. The parent within us acts much the same as our parents acted. There is typically a critical parent and a nurturing parent. The vast majority of those who overeat and have a weight problem have an out-of-balance parent within them. The critical parent completely overshadows the nurturing parent. With every slip, the critical parent is there to blame, chastise, ridicule and demean. This sets up the all-too-common compulsive eating cycle (Figure 12.1.). Many of you will relate to this self-explanatory figure from LeBlanc's book. When behavior is good, however, the nurturing parent is nowhere to be found. There is no positive self-talk. There wasn't any when you were a child, so why would there be any now? Unless you have been an avid student of positive self-talk writers and lecturers, where would you have ever learned to talk positively to yourself?

Understanding where you developed the self-talk you use everyday is difficult unless you are willing to open up a potentially big can of worms. Reaching back into your childhood to remember the overly harsh and critical words and actions of a parent or guardian is not much fun. I'm not going to profess to know how deep you'll have to go, or how much time you'll have to spend thinking about how poorly you were treated as a child. I believe it is important you realize where things may have started, but then get back to the here and now. Use the past to be more aware of why you act and say the things you do about yourself. Use this introspective knowledge to change for today and tomorrow. Realizing you cannot change the past is very important so you can use it to help you understand "why" and then get and stay in the present to change who you are now.

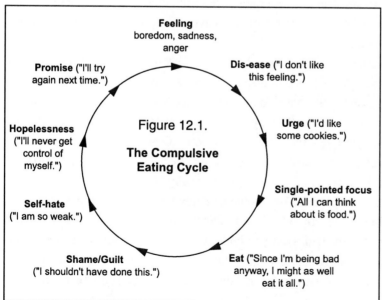

Figure 12.1.

The Compulsive Eating Cycle

Feeling boredom, sadness, anger

Dis-ease ("I don't like this feeling.")

Urge ("I'd like some cookies.")

Single-pointed focus ("All I can think about is food.")

Eat ("Since I'm being bad anyway, I might as well eat it all.")

Shame/Guilt ("I shouldn't have done this.")

Self-hate ("I am so weak.")

Hopelessness ("I'll never get control of myself.")

Promise ("I'll try again next time.")

When you slip–not "if" but when you slip, it is vital to your success that you become aware of any negative thinking and self-talk. When you slip, make a list of every negative feeling and thought you have. Really, write it out. Look at it. Then think about when this negative self-talk all started. Where is the compassion? Why is it easier to criticize than to empathize? Many times, you will have to look no further than who raised you. You are likely to see that you are now parenting yourself the same way your parents did. A big problem for the transformationist and overeater in general is continuing to parent in this fashion.

> *A few might lose some weight by continuously self-scolding and tough love, but no one ever keeps the weight off or sticks with a sound nutrition plan by doing so.*

When you eat the whole bag of chocolates or a dozen doughnuts, I am not telling you to pat yourself on the back and say "Atta boy, Dave! Way to go big guy!" However, I am telling you that negative self-talk past the minute you finish a binge-eating episode or other slip will only make matters worse. No one feels strong when he is beaten down. Negative self-talk beats you down and keeps you down. Self-regulation disappears quickly when you are depressed, tired and feeling blue. Negative self-talk and the critical parent within you must be muzzled, or you will suffer for it, not benefit from it.

While the critical parent is quick to judge and slow to praise, the nurturing parent within us is just the opposite. The nurturing parent is not a liar or someone living in a fantasy world. She recognizes a slip as just that–a slip. Sure, there was an opportunity to do better. However, the nurturing parent also realizes it's not the end of the world. We're all human, and the quicker you feel compassion for yourself, the quicker you'll get back up after being knocked down with the bloated, full, thick feeling you got from the off-the-plan indulgence. The nurturing parent knows that guilt and shame are inappropriate feelings for continued progress. You still need and deserve love when you slip. The nurturing parent knows you feel uncomfortable from eating too much and these feelings will be enough, over time, to prevent the same pattern of behavior from continuing. Will it happen overnight? For some, yes; for most, no.

In essence, the nurturing parent knows that the only way to break the cycle of compulsive eating, bingeing, triggers and more, is to befriend yourself and be more conscious of behaviors that repetitively keep you from achieving your goals. You not only must become your own best friend, you must become more aware of why you act the way you do and why you think as you do. Earlier, in the *Triggers, Addiction and Self-Regulation* chapter, I discussed how analyzing your ABCs (antecedents, behavior, and consequence) can help to make you more aware of why you ran to food for comfort and support, to break up boredom or to quench your thirst to be loved.

You must treat yourself like a best friend. You would certainly forgive a best friend for a mistake. You might even try to help your best friend to understand why they messed up. You would not treat a friend like a worst enemy. Nevertheless, if you criticize yourself for hours and days after a slip, that is exactly what you are doing–treating yourself like your worst enemy. And that is what you are if you continue this pattern of behavior–your own worst enemy. The real problematic patterns of behavior will not change until you learn to treat yourself like a best friend. You truly must learn to love yourself first.

Rewards are important for reinforcement. Many transformationists feel unworthy of any rewards until the final lifetime-achievement goal has been met. This is far too long to wait for your reward. This is also indicative of someone allowing the critical parent to do all the parenting. *Not rewarding is punishing*. It is time you gave the nurturing parent more than equal time.

You may not even be aware of things you can find pleasurable at this time because you have done without for far too long. Now is the time to begin experiencing life again. Self-indulgence with good, morally-straight gifts and activities must become a bigger and more consistent part of your everyday existence. It is time to pick out that necklace and put it on layaway. Pay a little on it each time you reach a weekly milestone. That motorcycle you have always dreamed about is only a few months away from being in your reach, if you start putting a little bit away each week for a down payment. Do you deserve it just for reaching your transformation goals along the way? Yes. Unequivocally–yes. Buy some special candles and bubble bath. Take it alone or with your honey. Get a massage, a facial, a manicure or a pedicure. Any pampering you would like to indulge in is probably a wonderful idea. Go for it! Pick out the CD you have been wanting. Get a new stereo system–put it on layaway if you must. Take a trip or start saving for one. Where would you like to go? What would you do when you get there? You deserve to go! Get that tattoo you have been wanting. Rewards, rewards, rewards. You have to get creative and do what you enjoy. You not only have to do it, you have to do those little things more consistently.

Booby Trap #14: Running on Empty Too Long

I believe it is necessary to keep learning. I do my darndest to surround myself with positive tapes, CDs and books by authors who don't blow smoke, but who speak the positive truth. We all need our tanks refilled regularly. No one fills up their car and expects it to run forever. That is exactly what we do with positive influences in our lives. The compliment you got last month will not tide you over more than a few hours, max. The compliment you gave yourself last year was only of value a few hours then.

Many times, you are so busy trying to take care of everyone around you that you forget about how important it is to consistently refill your tank with positive influences of many kinds. I am no different. That is why I read and listen to those who have more of life's experience than I do, and who have traveled the road before me, and who were successful at surviving all the potholes and roadblocks.

I recommend anything by Zig Ziglar and Brian Tracy without question. I also recommend a book called *The Speed Trap* by Joseph Bailey. Others enjoy Tony Robbins, Stephen Covey, and Napoleon Hill.

Booby Trap #15: Too Little Sleep

There is not a supplement on the planet that can overcome the catabolic effects of inadequate sleep. If everything else is right, but sleep is wrong, at a minimum your progress will come to a screeching halt. Inadequate sleep prevents proper recovery from exercise, reduces the strength of the immune system, and diminishes limited self-regulation stores.

Getting enough sleep just seems like good, common-sense advice, but I see too many transformationists doing all the other right things and foregoing sleep to be more "productive" or simply suffering from insomnia. Everyone has a night here and there when they just do not sleep well, however, if you chronically do not sleep well, you should seek the advice of your physician to rule out other, more serious, complications.

Science and my experience tell me the average transformationist needs at least six hours of sleep a night, and as much as nine hours a night to awaken refreshed and recovered from the day before. If your response to this statement was, "Heck, I don't remember the last time I got more than four hours," then I suggest you seek professional help. You are not doing your body and health much good on so little sleep.

A lack of proper sleep can cause the wrong kind of weight loss (muscle) and slow or stop fat loss. Sleep is very important to your daily energy, mental attitude, immune system and overall success. Get a grip on it.

Booby Trap #16: The EITHER/OR Syndrome

When you begin a new program like the Lifestyle, it begins a chain of psychological events that prompt you to say to yourself, "Okay, I'm on now. I am going to give it my all and nothing can stop me. I'm ready." These comments are inspirational, partly self-fulfilling and generally good. However, you probably have not ever thought about the EITHER/OR syndrome before, and you might continue with the same bad habits that the EITHER/OR syndrome perpetuates.

> Coaching client Phil wrote...
> *"When I started my business, I was still in the gym but soon found that with the demanding hours and the mental fatigue I was experiencing, something had to give. It did not take a rocket scientist to figure out that my creative talents were paying the bills, not my body."*

EITHER you work hard at work OR you work out? Most people who succumb to this self-limiting belief system have it in their head that living a life of health, fitness, vitality and beauty will require 20 hours a week of exercise. These self-limiting beliefs are precisely what are keeping this person from busting this EITHER/OR trap and becoming better physically and mentally fit. No matter how hard you are working, there is always time for exercise each week. Consistently doing something is far easier than starting gung-ho, stopping after a few weeks, and then restarting repeatedly. Anything is better than nothing. You have to start somewhere. Furthermore, if you choose to EITHER work hard at work OR work out you are limiting your performance at work. Undoubtedly, you will perform better at work if you are in great shape. The increased energy and positive mental attitude you will feel are certainly a major component of your productivity.

EITHER/OR and Nutrition

A female client recently came to me and said that she had begun the Lifestyle. She was enjoying it although it was quite a change from her *normal* way of eating. She never drank water before the Lifestyle. It was always pop, tea, or coffee. She said she knew I recommended at least a half gallon of water each day, plus another eight ounces for every 20 minutes of exercise and she said it was all she could do to force herself to drink the last few ounces of the half gallon each day. You see, for her it was EITHER she drank half gallon of water each day OR she failed the Lifestyle. In my mind, however, it was obvious this was not the case. I advised her that making such a dramatic change was very hard and that the Lifestyle was not about trying to create instant perfection, thus making you feel like a failure for not achieving it.

I have a general uneasiness about Aspartame. I am not saying it is Satan, but I am saying I am not convinced the FDA has really taken appropriate measures to protect us. If Aspartame is indeed the excitotoxin other scientists claim it to be, what does this have to do with my client? I felt very comfortable advising this woman to slowly build her water intake up to a half gallon per day by starting with a quart of fresh water and the next quart in Crystal Light® (this was a favorite of hers, but it does contain Aspartame). Slowly, I told her to begin eliminating the Crystal Light® and replacing it with the water. If she never gets to a half gallon or more of water per day, she is still doing far better than she was. She drank *no water* before the Lifestyle. Do not forget that. It became obvious to me that this woman was suffering from the EITHER/OR syndrome for water. Either she drinks the half-gallon per day, or she fails the program. This simply is NOT the case.

Another personal example is the method I used to begin enjoying vegetables. As I stated in the *Nutrients* chapter, only a few years ago I would not eat five servings of vegetables a year, let alone a day. Sound familiar? We have all heard that we should eat our vegetables fresh or lightly steamed for best nutritional preservation, right? Right. So what did I do? I bought pre-packed frozen vegetables in a cheese sauce. About four or five nights a week I would have my veggies smothered in cheese sauce, but over time here is what happened. I started cutting back on the "dipping" of the cheese sauce. Eventually, I cut the cheese sauce out and I traded it for fat-free salad dressings, spicy mustard, seasonings or veggie dip. On salads, I have a fat-free salad dressing or oil and vinegar.

I can guarantee you one thing: If I had chosen to try to eat perfectly from the beginning, I would have failed. I did not like vegetables. I figured in the beginning that if I at least started eating more vegetables, I'd get some benefit from them, and if I couldn't cut the cheese out of my veggie eating–well, then, at least I had tried. Now I eat several servings of veggies daily. I have acquired a taste for them. Anyone can acquire a taste for vegetables, but not until you take the effort to buy them fresh, cut them up ahead of time and really go for it.

I have told you about a woman who was able to break out of her EITHER/OR mentality by incorporating a more moderate approach to her water consumption, and I have told you how I broke out of a typical EITHER/OR mentality by starting with veggies in cheese sauce. What about some other common EITHER/OR mindsets that keep you from smoothly transitioning from where you are to a more healthy Lifestyle?

Other Common EITHER/OR Traps

- EITHER you have egg whites OR you have an omelet. The fix? What is wrong with having 2 whole eggs and 2 egg whites? Or, if you are a big guy, 6 egg whites and 2 whole eggs or 9 egg whites and 3 whole eggs?

- EITHER you are on a diet eating nothing but wheat grass, or you are eating pizza four nights a week. How about following the sensible guidelines of the Lifestyle?

- EITHER you eat your tuna with nothing OR it has to be a full-blown tuna salad. The fix? How about mixing your tuna with Miracle Whip Light® or half fat-free dressing and half miracle whip or full-fat mayo? Is there anything wrong with that? What about mixing your tuna with fresh pineapples?

- EITHER you mix your protein or meal replacement shake in water or milk. The fix? Why can't you mix your protein or meal replacement shake in 85 percent water and 15 percent milk for better flavor and consistency? What about using soy milk for lactose-intolerant people? Is there a problem there?

- You realize for the first time in your Lifestyle program that you are stuck. Things were going so well, but for the past three weeks, you have not lost a drop of weight. Well, I guess it is time to go from two chicken breasts at supper to one chicken breast right? EITHER you eat two OR one. The fix? Why can't you eat 1-3/4 or 1-1/2 chicken breasts instead of 2? Any problem with that, besides getting over the excessively common two or one mentality? Portions in general are cut in half when changes are made, and there is no reason for this. Instead of two scoops of protein, you will switch to one. What about one and a half? Think about it.

- For breakfast, you always have oatmeal, toast and orange juice, but again, you are stuck and have been for three weeks, so you know it is time for a change. What do you do? Normally you might cut the orange juice out completely, but now I think you know what to do. Instead of having 16 ounces of orange juice, a cup of oatmeal and two slices of whole-wheat toast with spray, non-fat butter, you have 3/4 cup of oatmeal, one slice of whole-wheat toast with sprayed non-fat butter and 12 ounces of orange juice. Think that this change will not be enough to matter? Think again. The difference between the two breakfasts I just described is roughly 100 to 150 calories. If you saved that many calories each day, your body would have almost no choice but to drop one pound more every 30 days. Small but significant, and you did not have to give up your favorite breakfast. No EITHER/OR to deal with.

There are a number of daily opportunities for you to fight the EITHER/OR syndrome. When you find yourself in the gym, on the treadmill or at the dinner table, you can make smoother, more progressive and less stressful changes to your life when you do not allow the EITHER/OR syndrome to back you into a corner. Life is not an EITHER/OR scenario. It is an adaptable journey that either we can make enjoyable, OR we can choose to continue living the same way, expecting different results. If I am not mistaken, this fits the definition of insanity.

Booby Trap #17: Making It About Him

Let me tell you about men in relationships with women who fight an ongoing weight battle. Since I am a husband of a former "weight fighter," I think I can speak from experience here. We are sick of it–very sick of it! The man in your life has seen you do this, that and the next thing. Still, here you are, fighting again, this time reading "another damn diet book" called the Lifestyle. You know it's not just another diet book now, but he does not.

Most times when you started a diet, you roared with enthusiasm. Your diets were begun by an announcement such as "I'm starting a new diet on Monday!" Now I digress to say that Monday-morning dieters are no better off than any-other-day dieters are, but there is something about starting a diet on Monday. An unfortunate reality is many gorge themselves on the Saturday and Sunday before to "get it out of their system." This never works. Two days of gorging will not "get it out of your system," however, it very well may set you up for tremendous cravings and hunger in your first week.

Your announcement came with food and supplement shopping, preparing and studying some new way of eating. Classes, trips to the doctor or meetings were begun to prepare for the new diet. The weight dropped or did not, but it was not long, and all we heard were the whimpers of defeat. The sounds of failure are much quieter than the uproarious fanfare attached to the start.

> *All the tries and failures before were leading you up to this moment with me, and I do not teach "tricks and secrets". I teach the scientific and emotional sides of health, balance and weight loss. Just remember, the man in your life does not know this yet.*

Do not expect the man in your life to rally too much around you until the results start showing up (like at least 5 to 10 percent of your starting weight being gone). When he consistently sees you getting up at 5:30 A.M. to get your workout in no matter what, he will see you are serious. When he sees you consistently weighing, measuring and experiencing results, he will start taking you seriously. When your actions are so loud he cannot hear what you are saying, he will know you are serious.

In the beginning, the man in your life will be resistant to change. He is sick of it. Why should he be any different from you or anyone else? We all resist change. The varying degrees of resistance are what separate successful people from failures. Those who are most successful will embrace change, accept that things rarely stay the same, and develop ways to manage it more effectively. In the beginning, however, he is rolling his eyes every time you mention the Lifestyle. Know this and approach him from a position of empathy.

Do enlist his support; he is a helping relationship in your life and you will need him to at least have a pulse. However, do not *demand* he support you. Do not demand he do this, that and the next thing. Do not demand he read your mind either. Refer to *Are You Ready to Change* chapter on how to handle Helping Relationships and seeking the support of others.

While you are being patient, do not be steamrolled into old behaviors you both may have enjoyed before you began the Lifestyle. If you have a Friday night ice cream ritual, it will have to become a solo event now. The man in your life can find his comfort foods outside the home–he does not have to find them in the home. Will this create some tension? Yes, in all likelihood it will, however, being an enabler for his poor behavior should not be a goal of yours. "Well yeah, but those foods make him happy." The reality is those foods medicate him as they have you. He uses them to temporarily feel better. In the end, however, they destroy his health because he overeats them, just like you.

I have given strong advice not to keep your trigger foods in the home. I have also discussed, in the *Goals* chapter, how to keep snacks for the kids. No one is asking you to eliminate all snacks from the home. Do not fall prey to the EITHER/OR syndrome. Some women can walk by a bag of Fritos® every day for a year without the slightest urge to dig in. Others eat a bag a day. *Your* triggers are the ones you need to abstain from. You cannot abstain if they are in the home; it is that simple.

There is a good chance you are the shopper and you prepare the dinner in the home. If this is true, then you have the power. Do not buy it for him if you know it will be too much temptation for you! Don't fall for the "Well, you'll just have to make two suppers from here on, cause I ain't eatin' that crap!" For one, yes, he will or he will make his own supper. Two, you can create healthy dinners that fit well within your Lifestyle day that you, the man in your life, and your children will enjoy. It will take some getting used to, no doubt. If you have been living on fried foods smothered in gravies or full-fat casseroles, then everyone will have some adjusting to do. Your children will fight you too, but this is also no reason to give in. You are doing them a massive favor by teaching them to live the Lifestyle. Wouldn't it be wonderful if your children grew up without the weight and self-esteem issues you have? Teach them how to eat those healthy foods that also taste good. They *will* adjust–you will just have to trust me on this. You can't roll over and play dead with the first, second, third or fourth grumbles you're sure to hear when you stop the sauce, gravy, butter and Wesson® oil meals you've been preparing for far too long.

If the entire process were easy, everyone would be thin and fit. Sometimes you just have to say "No, I'm not buying that food and keeping it in this house. You can get ice cream (or whatever the treat is) whenever you want it, but I'm not buying a food I know I can't say 'no' to." You will have to learn to say, "Honey, the Lifestyle is not overly restrictive. I can learn to prepare meals we will all enjoy. Give me a little time to make it work. It's important to me–please." And then, after you make your plea, make sure you follow through and prepare meals that you believe will best fit the Lifestyle while reducing grumbling to a low roar. Oh, the grumbling will continue for perhaps a few weeks, but eventually, both the man in your life and your children will adjust, and you will have the momentum you need and improve your chances of a great transformation.

When the results start showing, he will not have a choice but to stand up and take notice. Trust me, a gorgeously figured woman is a prize unlike any he has ever fantasized about. The thank yous and respect will come when the results are there, and those results are up to you.

When you commit to change, assuming you are prepared and armed with all the consciousness to do it, you will accept that no one is responsible for you but you. Helping relationships (I am a helping relationship for you, too) are great processes to help see you through the change, but it's all up to you, every day. If the man in your life thumbs his nose at your thousandth attempt, then so be it. He will come around soon enough.

Pay Him a Compliment

I have been dishing out advice that says to give men time, do not push them, and let them come around on their own. You stay true to your goals and mission, and just be patient. I need to emphasize a bit more how very important it is that you nudge, and not shove, the man in your life into support. He has to believe he is supporting you of his own free will. If he supports you only because you demand it, it will be short-lived. If he supports you because he truly believes in what he is doing, he'll support you in ways you can only dream of right now. Men and women alike have to believe they totally came around without being hounded, nagged and pestered into supportive submission. Some will come around sooner, while others will come around later, and some will never come around. Nevertheless, regardless of what he does, it is still up to you to make your transformation happen.

While you are engrossed in your transformation, be sure not to become so self-absorbed that you forget there is another person in your life. Sure, your focus will be on you. Sure, you must raise fitness to the number 1, 2, or 3 position in your life's priorities. Just do not forget to compliment the man in your life on the trivial, good things he says or does. Most men are pretty clueless when it comes to "what women want." If they do something good, or better yet, if they simply get up every day, go to work, earn a decent living, and try hard to support you or a family, thank them for the everyday things they do that you and they know are taken for granted most of the time. Do not wait for him to pay attention to your 2-pound weight loss to say something nice to him first.

It is easy when you are going through a transformation like this to keep the focus on you, but there is life outside of you, and it is going on all around you. Take notice and say "thank you." I do not do it enough either, so me saying it helps me to remember to take a dose of my own medicine.

Booby Trap #18: Making It About Her

While it's true that more women than men are dieting or concerned about their body, men who are transforming experience much of the same lack of support and understanding as women.

The same rules apply to men who are focused on a transformation as with women. You cannot "caveman" your woman into supporting you. Figuratively speaking, you cannot grab your woman by the hair and drag her into your Lifestyle. She will resent you for it. As I mentioned in the preceding section, it is important you realize she must support you of her own free will. You must also realize that she is likely the food buyer for the home. She has the power to make your life easy or difficult. She can create great tension or ease in the home. Face it, as the primary food buyer most of the time, it is easier if the woman in our life is watching out for us.

> Stephan tells the story of how he combats going on the prowl (trolling for trigger foods) with the help of his wife.
>
> *"I know I need my wife watching out for me. When I get on the prowl for food, I have to lock myself in the bedroom and call my wife (who is elsewhere in the house) on the cell phone to bring me items I need. I do this because I understand a pattern of behavior for me that sets me on a trigger-eating episode. When I am frustrated and looking for food to comfort my frustration, or when I simply walk into the kitchen, I am likely to grab something. I will stand in the kitchen and eat a half a bag of Fritos® staring out the kitchen window before I wake up and realize what I have done. Since I do not have to walk by the kitchen and grab something that will blow my plan I can stay the course. I would make the Lifestyle work for me no matter what but having a wife that watches out for me sure makes things easier."*

Instead of trying to rule the roost or be the king of your domain, I suggest you do something imaginative and ask the woman in your life for help. During a moment of peace, ask her to sit with you. Tell her how important your goals are to you. Tell her you need her help or you are likely to fail again. Ask her to consider ways she can have the goodies she wants without exposing you to them. Make a game out of it if you have to. The key is *asking her* to help you.

I have discovered five main reasons women do not support their transforming man. In contrast to popular belief, it is usually not because they are vindictive or hateful.

1. They have low self-esteem and are unsure about your commitment to them. It is your job to explicitly state your commitment to them and to recognize their fear. Reassure them about why you are doing this. They have to know they are important in your life and will remain important after your transformation.

2. They are unsure about your intentions and what you plan to do once you get the fat off. They may be asking "Are you going to leave me?" "Why now?"

3. They do not want their vices exposed. If she is a smoker and you are fat, or you are both fat and routinely eat Ben & Jerry's® by the gallon every week, who are you to talk about health or a better body? Some people hide what they really want and cover it up with jealousy or concern of you needing to put weight on or not needing to lose weight. Why? It makes them feel better. "Here, you eat and stay fat like me and then I will feel better about me." If you are fat and she is fat, who controls or initiates intimate relations? What will happen when you get lean? How will this change the dynamics of your intimacy? Express your feelings and remember to be assertive, not aggressive (see the *Are You Ready to Change* chapter).

4. They do not want to play second fiddle to your transformation. If you used to sit around watching television together every evening and now you don't because you are exercising, reading, or doing anything more constructive to keep your mind busy, she's likely to feel less important because you're taking away "us time". It does not matter that your together time was spent watching television and not talking to each other. You have disrupted the pattern and might be giving her less attention in other ways too. You can quell concerns over how much time your transformation is taking away from "cuddle time" with a little better time management on your part. The transformation will not take more time - it will give you more time, as you become a better time manager and set daily goals. You'll find that wasteful hours spent thumbing through magazines and newspapers, perusing the Internet, and rearranging your sock drawer will take a back seat to focused action on your daily goals.

5. The last reason is you have not clued her in on what you are doing, and she has not been asked to support you. Ask her for support but mean it. Give her explicit ground rules on what you would like from her and what you do not want from her. No helping relationship–and this includes me–is a mind reader. That is the stuff of fairy tales. Be explicitly clear about what you are doing, what you need, and what you do not need. Do not demand she support you. Ask for help–do not demand it. Let her naturally support you or not, but make sure you have told her what you are doing, how things might change a bit and what you need.

The women in our lives are under-appreciated much the same as we are. If you wait for them to "go first," you will wait too long. If they do anything that is positive for you, let them know how much you appreciate it–even if it is a little thing. Gifts are rarely a bad idea. Do not underestimate the power of giving and communicating how much you appreciate the little things she does and says.

No matter how rich you are, you cannot hire someone to do it all for you.

If you are the bread winner of the family, and you haven't shopped for groceries in five years, that's no excuse for there *not* being fresh fruits and vegetables in your refrigerator! Go get them! Wash them yourself. Take 30 minutes a week and prepare them, and I bet it won't take long, and your better half will start to believe how strongly you feel about what you're doing. Taking action can speak volumes when it comes to showing your personal commitment. Do not sit around belly-aching about how there is so much junk in your home and your wife does not want to eat healthy so you cannot. That does not cut it. When it comes to eating, you must grow independent of the unsupportive loved one. Eventually, you will more than likely see them begin to drift your way, but not until you take whatever initiative is necessary to get things started.

The buck stops with you, not everyone around you. Make it happen! Criticizing the woman in your life for not being exactly like you is harmful to your success, your happiness and your relationship. Let her be an individual, but you commit to what you now know is optimal for your own life.

In the end, when you have succeeded, she will see that in all regards it was well worth it: your feelings about yourself, your appreciative feelings about her support, her feelings about helping you win, and both of your feelings about the growth in your relationship.

As you read through booby traps 17 and 18, it should be quite clear to see that many of the ideas for one gender can quite easily cross over into the other. The five reasons I gave for women not supporting their transforming man could just as easily be applied to men who don't support their transforming woman.

Booby Trap #19: All Married People Get Fat

Gaining weight after marriage has reached epidemic proportions. Look around at your married friends and family members. You'll likely find that what authors Richard B. Stuart and Barbara Jacobson (*Weight, Sex & Marriage - A Delicate Balance*) found in a survey of over 25,000 married couples is true. After 13 years of marriage, the average woman gains 24.7 pounds and the average man gains 19.4.

Stuart and Jacobson reveal that men and women gain weight for different reasons. From the woman's perspective, overeating is principally a result of emotional triggers such as boredom, lone-liness, anger, anxiety or depression. There are a number of problems that can result for the married woman who decides she wants to be thin. Knowing what these problems are ahead of time can prevent a misfired attempt at the Lifestyle. I will briefly summarize the main concerns. For a more detailed explanation and a really fascinating read for married men and women, I highly recommend the Stuart and Jacobson book, and another book by Dr. Edward Abramson, Ph.D. titled *To Have and To Hold - How To Take Off The Weight When Marriage Puts On the Pounds.*

Housewives most commonly complain that the reason for overeating is boredom. It is not that there is not always plenty to do. Most housewives begin their day at dawn and end it completely exhausted after the ten o'clock news. It is that the work done is not appreciated, is tedious, is low on the social respect scale, and does not allow time for companionship and contact with other adults? Eating is a temporary solution, but it is not the answer to the problem. It only compounds feelings of depression and nibbles away at a woman's confidence.

Women who do not get hugs will substitute chocolate bars. Men need sex, and women need to be touched both in and out of bed. Affectionate words and gestures are many times more important to a woman than sexual intercourse. When a marriage lacks the sexual and affectionate expressiveness she craves, she may turn to food for love. Contrary to popular stereotypes, many women crave more sex than their male counterparts are willing or able to give. When a man is unwilling to seek help for physical impotence, or to communicate openly with his wife about her sexual needs, wives will many times cope with this frustration by overeating. A woman might feel hunger three or four times a day, but the emotional hunger might be her constant companion.

Earlier I stated that the average married woman gains 24.7 pounds over a 13-year marriage. Happily married women, however, have an average weight gain of only 18.4 pounds. Unhappy marriages produce a 42.6-pound weight gain for women on average. Happily married men gain 19 pounds; unhappily married men gain an average of 38 pounds over 13 years of marriage.

> *Unhappy marriages appear to be the ideal situation for excessive eating through emotional triggers.*

As a man, it is hard to imagine not being comfortable with catching the eye and praising word of a woman because of looks, but for many women, this is indeed a problem. A woman who has been overweight her entire life has likely not had much experience with flirtation and sexual innuendo. It is common for a woman to regain weight lost because of how uncomfortable she has become with her newfound attractiveness. It is also common for women to realize new desires for other men once they have attained a new level of power and self-worth. The strength of the marriage up to that point can be the strength she needs to maintain fidelity. Infidelity, on the other hand, may only be a symptom of the unhappiness she has internalized for far too long. Until the weight is gone and self-esteem has improved, she is unable to express her dissatisfaction to her husband.

Men, here is my advice. If you treat your wife poorly now, are not attentive to her needs and desires and she is overweight, there is a treacherous road ahead of you when she drops the weight. You had better start taking corrective action, even if it includes therapy or marriage counseling, *before* the weight comes off. If you wait until after the weight comes off, she may harbor resentment and bitterness toward your attempts to now be the nice guy she always wanted but was afraid to ask for.

Women do not want a guy with a gut! As much focus as we men like to put on keeping a woman attractive, women do have eyes, too. Women may regain weight lost if they suddenly decide they now find their husband unattractive. Why? Because they realize that by doing so, they will create an aversion to the man wanting sex. An easy way for a woman to avoid sex is to gain or regain weight.

Anger women feel for their husbands is many times swallowed in food. It prevents uncomfortable discussions and even physical abuse from weak cowards who still call themselves men. Many overweight women also find more tolerance to unreasonable behavior and demands placed upon them by their husbands, as compared to how they feel when they are thin. In an effort to maintain the marriage, weight gain is an option, and better in their minds, than dealing with the feelings of resentment and hostility.

Men and women who fear challenge and change will many times remain fat or regain weight lost because the social pressures of the thin are perceived to be more of a competitive nature. When you are fat, no one expects much from you. When you are thin, however, you are expected to lead the way, pave the path and make the right decisions–at least that is what we are taught by society. Stuart and Jacobson had this to say:

> *"Because she's fat, she doesn't compete; Because she doesn't compete she can't win; With no successes to her credit, she feels bad about herself; The worse she feels, the more she eats, and the heavier she grows; And with each pound she gains, her self-esteem falls even further."*

One of the most effective things we men can do to ensure our wives never lose weight is to *demand* they lose weight. Call it rebellious, or call it foolish expression of freedom. Call it whatever you want. If you demand it, you just sank the weight-loss ship. Nagging is not any better. Your smart little comments (that are really "just to help") will not cut it either. She has to decide it is time, and then you can help, but be careful. Helping your wife lose weight is a minefield, so watch your tongue.

As a woman loses weight, she normally feels better about herself. As self-esteem increases, she may grow more independent and confident. Many insecure men–those who like an oppressive approach to marriage–can't handle the woman getting all "uppity" because she's lost 30 pounds. When a man knows deep inside that he is insecure about his own appearance or ability to maintain a sexually attractive woman, he may purposely sabotage her attempts to lose weight. How? By doing something like:

- Complain about low-fat foods she makes.
- Complain about the purchase of exercise equipment or gym membership fees.
- Demand she make two meals.
- Demand she make only fattening suppers.
- Insist she keep weak foods in the house.
- Bring home gifts of chocolate for her weight-loss successes.
- Purposely create stress for her and more.

Some men and women are rather devious when you get right down to it. Most of the time, however, both men and women sabotage their partner's weight-loss efforts unintentionally because they just do not know what to do to help.

Men and women in marriages are usually matched pairs. It has been said that married couples really start to look alike after 15 years together. Why should their weight be any different? If one half of the relationship wants to lose weight, and the other partner does not want to participate in their own weight-loss, there exists another opportunity for the nonparticipating partner to sabotage the weight-loss efforts of the other. If the spouse who decides not to participate in the weight loss program was honest, you might here them saying: "Why should I have to change my routine; I have other bad habits like drinking and pornography and if you become thin I'll have to deal with those problems. Stay fat and quiet please. Although our marriage is a mess and I want nothing to do with you sexually, it is easy for me to use your weight as an excuse as to why I do not want to have sex with you. If you lose the weight, I'll lose my excuse; if you lose the weight and become more attractive you'll cheat on me."

"When women enjoy their bodies more, they think about them less. This frees them to redirect their attention to others, and husbands are the major beneficiaries."

Hey guys, here is something to think about as a rule. Women have sex more often and enjoy it more often after they lose weight.

Be aware that when you lose a substantial amount of weight, you will almost feel like you have been reborn with more confidence and assertiveness. Family members, coworkers and friends who have not gone through the physical and psychological transformation will not share your newfound attitude. You are going to experience life differently when you are lean and your perceptions will change. Be aware that it does not mean everyone around you will, too.

Never try to use weight loss to solve problems that are not weight related.

As a married father of three beautiful children, I am deeply entrenched in the midst of raising them with the knowledge that I am giving you in the Lifestyle. I also know there are mothers reading this who–up until this very moment–believed that being married, having kids and being a housewife or working-outside-the-home mom required a 25-pound weight increase because every one of your family and friends have done it. So untrue! Expect more out of life and deliver a shining physical example for your children and your husband. Do you really want your children to experience the same feelings you have about their weight? Is it fair to your "better half" that when you first met him you were trim and sexy, but now you are slovenly and physically unattractive? These are real issues and not ones most couples are one bit comfortable speaking to each other about.

Men and women also perceive the traditional marriage weight gain differently. Men look at their wives as weak, lazy and disrespectful toward their feelings and importance placed upon physical attractiveness. For most men, physical attraction was the first reason for pursuit. How can men be expected to completely dismiss this trait? Oh, wait, I know, because the vow was "for better or worse," right? Come on! "But I want him to love me for who I am, not what I look like." Does this even make sense? It is really all about perception. If you are approximately the same weight now as you were when you met (give or take ten pounds), then your spouse has no leg to stand on. You are the same person he married. However, if you have gained 25 to 100 pounds since marriage, there has been a little trick played on your spouse. Hey, don't get mad at me for telling you when they would not. That is how they feel! Address the physical, psychological and social issues relating to your weight gain head-on, and use the Lifestyle to deliver the old you or an even better physical you to your husband.

As I stated earlier, women are not the only ones packing on extra pounds after marriage. Men do, too. Nevertheless, women are more forgiving by nature, and visual stimulation is not as much a priority. Does this mean you have a green light to continue drinking, eating and sitting around? No! If you are reading this and someone is not reading it to you, I will assume you care about the physical side of your being and you cherish and respect your wife's unspoken desires for a more fit man. Many women have watched silently and tolerantly with disgust, as their husbands packed on the bought-and-paid-for Buddha belly. The Lifestyle can bring a new fire back into your marriage when you get into shape. It shows you care about her desires and her unspoken feelings of physical attractiveness.

Let me ask one question that I think will bring total clarity to the reasoning for getting into great shape and *staying* in great shape forever: What is the second major purchase after a divorce (besides a new car for a man and a new wardrobe for a woman)? A membership to the local health club, right? Absolutely! Why? Because it is time to get in shape for the next victim, I mean, spouse. Divorced people tan, they get a haircut, they buy new clothes, they diet, they work out, and they do everything within their power to become attractive to the opposite sex. This courtship process is not about telling the truth, the whole truth and nothing but the truth; it is about winning the dating game. It is an act. No act can be maintained for a lifetime. By applying the Lifestyle to your own life, you can create a real nutritional program that will not end after you say, "I do."

Why wait until you are divorced to become attractive? Do it now!

Married With Children

Many of you probably believe my kids eat lettuce and dirt for breakfast, tofu sandwiches and sparkling water for lunch, etc. Not true. Why? Because the Lifestyle is not overly restrictive and, is complete with substitution and moderation. I know the structure is there for them to use my principles for their entire lives. Do they eat candy like there is no tomorrow on Easter and Halloween? You betcha. Are there dinners when they eat fish sticks and I eat grilled salmon steak? Absolutely. While they are eating those breaded fish sticks they are also eating fresh-cut broccoli, carrots, cauliflower and other vegetables and dipping the veggies in some veggie dip. This is called eating realistically within the Lifestyle. I don't eat the fish sticks and they don't always have fish sticks when we have grilled salmon. But I strongly believe that by answering their questions and slowly and methodically incorporating fruits and vegetables into their diet, along with whole-grain breads and crackers, they will develop eating patterns that will carry them to their own Leanness Lifestyle as adults.

I'm not alone in my beliefs. A recent study published in the American Journal of Clinical Nutrition found that restricting children's access to foods they want might lead to over-indulgence when they are free to make their own choices. "This research does not imply that parents should let children have whatever they want whenever they want it. Structure is as important in child feeding as it is in any other aspect of parenting. Parents should provide their children with a variety of nutritious foods and with enough guidance to help their children make reasonable decisions about what and how much to eat." (Source: Fisher, Am Soc Nutr Sci, 1999)

We have to let our kids be kids, and if this means that McDonalds or other fast-food restaurants creep into their meal plan from time to time, then so be it. All you have to do is remember that there are no bad foods, only bad habits. If you make a habit of going to McDonalds for the kids every day, then that is a bad one. Go once a week? Fine!

Booby Trap #20: Assuming the Inevitable Crisis Will Become No Longer Inevitable

I discussed in the *Are You Ready to Change* chapter how the chronic Contemplator could be caught in the trap of waiting for life to level out before he begins his transformation. Another common booby trap that will surely cause you to stumble unless you are aware of it and accept it is the misconception that any day will not be filled with a chaotic series of events. If you have ever asked, "Does it ever end?" I can tell you the answer to that is, "No, it never ends." The barrage of chores, tasks, emails, faxes, errands and responsibilities are only managed, never ended. Life is not always a low but the inevitable crisis is right around the corner. Please make sure you do not have the mindset that "if life would only level out things would be so much better." Life will *not* level out. Stress is waiting for all of us everyday.

> *Life is a series of stressful events, broken up periodically by the*
> *occasional crisis.*

Sometime very soon, perhaps even today, you are going to experience what you would traditionally call "a real downer or nightmare." Whether you chip a nail, lock your keys in the car, have a purse stolen, get in a fight with a significant other, get a load of work dropped on you by the boss, experience conflict with a coworker, get a poor evaluation, get fired, get separated or divorced, or lose a loved one, something is going to happen–and soon!

The sooner you can accept that life is managed and not cured, the better you will be. The sooner you realize there are no excuses that can prevent you from achieving your transformation goals, the better. Do not let the tough times get you down. All of us are tested continually, every day, from the outside and the inside.

Remember that 99 percent of your own happiness and peace comes not from what stressors are thrown at you, but how you perceive and manage the stress. You can choose to accept or reject those stressors for what they really are, (usually minor blips) or you can choose a word like "catastrophe" to describe an event that truly is not. You can choose to counter and find something positive to do with the emotions, or you can decide that when you have had enough, "it's time to stuff." It is all a choice. Carefully consider your daily challenges, find the place deep in you that drives you, remember your "why" and tap into what it will take for you to succeed.

Booby Trap #21: Foolish Freedom

Don't you just hate it when someone tells you what to do? Have you ever reacted spontaneously foolish in a manner that is completely inconsistent with what you know to be right just to "show them?" If you are like most people, you can take direction and advice to a point, however, after a line is crossed, if you perceive the message to be coercive instead of helpful, you may inappropriately assert yourself just to maintain control. "I'll do most of what you say, Dave, but I just can't relinquish quite everything because you say so. Oh, sure, I agree with what you are saying, but there is only so much bossing around a guy can stand. You know?"

Transformationists may exhibit foolish freedom. That is, even when the direction or external message is purely helpful and sound, they feel a strong need to assert their "personal freedom." In an effort to maintain control or to not be influenced by others at all costs, and to not feel coerced, many will assert their foolish freedom, even if by doing so, their actions are to their own detriment.

The most common reasons people run to comfort foods are assertion and relaxation. When emotions are out of control and the sense of self is not clear, it is common for men or women to binge eat just to "show them who is boss." Been in an argument with the husband? You know he'd like you to weigh a little less and be in better shape. No problem; "I'll fix him, that son-of-a-gun won't ever get to see me fit. I will eat until it hurts. Jerk!" These emotional outbursts and reactions to relationships occur when self-esteem is low, and your character is being challenged, and when coping and countering techniques have not been explored and practiced. It is also another way of exerting foolish freedom.

Who are you hurting when you stuff your face after an argument? You, of course–and only you. The pain you feel from the argument is nothing compared to the lingering pain of self-defeat when the scale will not budge and your pants are too tight, again! Slamming down 2,000 calories in 30 minutes or an evening because he's a "no good S.O.B." not only won't make him a better man, but you'll pay with bloat and feelings of self-loathing for much longer than the ill feelings of the argument. Showing him or her who is boss with food is yet another way to swallow acid but hoping it will burn the other party. Establishing a stronger sense of self, as well as developing better coping and countering techniques, is paramount to matching your behavior with how you truly see yourself. If you **react** instead of **respond** to relationship woes, you are giving the other party the power and real control. As long as your self-esteem is beat down at all times, you cannot possibly ever, truly, have the upper hand, or, more appropriately, stand on even ground.

> A male coaching member wrote -
>
> *"As I once told Tom on the main forum, I'm doing this Leanness Lifestyle but I'm dragging my feet the whole way. He said something like you could not be resisting this lifestyle if you are losing all this weight. I know better. The few remaining trigger foods I am keeping around are my way of not being onboard 100%. They are the last vestiges of eating for emotional reasons as opposed to eating to fuel my body and improve my health."*

This is just one passage from many members who I see going through their transformation process kicking and screaming the whole way. Does it have to be this way? Is there a way for you to recognize that you are sabotaging yourself by resisting the best, well-intentioned guidance simply to exert foolish freedom?

> **In Changing for Good, Dr. Prochaska has this to say about foolish freedom...**
> *"It remains difficult to believe that many otherwise intelligent human beings actively resist becoming aware of the ways in which they are endangering, damaging, or even destroying their lives. You have no doubt heard the slogans of people who maintain their right to just such a foolish freedom. They go something like this: "No one can tell me how to live my life. I'll pull my own strings even if they hang me." "They're my children - I'll spoil them [or beat them] if I want to." "No one is going to tell me how to manage my money - even if I am going broke."*

Often those who have grown up with an over-controlling parent are especially vulnerable to this all-consuming need for control. These people seem to have vowed to themselves, "Never again will I let anyone control me. If anyone is going to be in control, it will be me."

It is quite possible that people have a hard time processing the many external messages delivered by media-blitzes on a daily basis. Who is really trying to look out for your best interests? Are you being "taken" again? Regardless of whether you had an over-controlling parent or not, everyone exerts a certain amount of foolish freedom in their lives. Being able to distinguish between what messages are harmful and what messages will truly benefit you, or are in your best interests to pursue, is a skill that can only be acquired once you recognize how you assert foolish freedom in your own life. Because many people have such a strong desire to be in control, they will resist even the most beneficial changes–and those that occur during a transformation are no exception.

It is important you recognize if you are living out of balance by exerting an "I will be in control at all costs" mentality. Freedom does not equal control. Some people believe that they are only truly free if their life is completely without influence. Prochaska states, "According to this notion, only acts of sheer caprice, performed in total independence of advantage or reason, can be free. Freedom becomes limited to actions that are truly spontaneous and unpredictable, totally unbounded, and yielding to no authority - not even reason." If you are bound and trapped to a life less than you deserve because you must control every situation at the highest level, then you can never be truly free. If you resist all efforts and messages to better your life because you just don't want to feel like someone else is telling you what to do, then you may be trapped to a life far more out of control than if you had listened to, and followed, the intelligent guidance to begin with. In other words, just because you exert your freedom and choose to resist intelligent guidance for your transformation, this does not mean you are properly controlling the situation or your life. If you are too afraid to read, listen to and follow the Lifestyle because you'll feel as though someone else is trying to control your life, then you will make the path from destructive behavior to true freedom much more difficult. If the guidelines of the Lifestyle are perceived as a coercive force rather than a freeing influence, you will likely invoke a defensive mechanism to resist at all costs.

You cannot consistently act in a manner that is inconsistent with how you see yourself. In order to sort out the external messages that are helpful from the messages that are truly harmful, you must know yourself. Self-re-evaluation is important so you can continue to sort through the many feelings you have as you progress through your transformation. The more consistently you act in a manner that is consistent with how you see yourself, the more true personal freedom and happiness you'll experience.

You must take a deep look at yourself and determine who you really are. Forget who is looking back at you in the mirror for a moment. What is it that you believe to be right and good? How do you really see yourself? Is the external message being delivered harmful to your sense of self? Do you consider yourself a rational person? If so, is the external message coercive if it too is quite rational? True freedom occurs when you are acting out of your identity, your self. You are not being coerced and you need not feel a loss of control if you identify with the positive qualities of the message or help being offered–in this case, the Leanness Lifestyle. Regardless of the source, it is important you trust your built-in protective mechanisms against harm. To maintain control at all costs, however, is damaging to your ultimate success.

"Responsible freedom is when you choose to change for the best of reasons, regardless of what you were conditioned to do, what you feel compelled to do, or what is most immediately gratifying to do. Our fullest freedom emerges when we have the opportunity to choose that which would enhance our life, our sense of self, and our society.

Foolish freedom is reactive–reacting just to keep from being controlled or reacting to immediate consequences. Responsible freedom is interactive–interacting with feedback and information about how changing our behavior can be beneficial to ourselves and to others. You do not have to resist if someone is trying to change you for good reasons. You can interact with the person and his or her reasons. If that person influences you to change for good, so much the better for both of you." (Source: Prochaska, "*Changing for Good*")

Booby Trap #22: Awfulizing the Lifestyle

Awfulizing the Lifestyle routinely occurs after a few weeks of diligent effort has been put forth. Whether results were as expected, more, or less than expected, the syndrome of awfulizing the Lifestyle is all too common. Awfulizing is negative self-talk that seems to make the Lifestyle seem unbearable while simultaneously creating the illusion that the old, unhealthy foods and habits really were much more enjoyable. Food addiction expert Kay Sheppard calls this "awfulizing with euphoric recall."

When you start the Lifestyle, you are full of hope, excitement, anticipation and confidence that this time is going to really be it! You are also very likely at a point in your life when you are sick to death of being fat. Every negative thought that could be had for having a less-than-desirable body filled your head in the early part of your transformation. Not only were you fired up with positive energy, you had fresh recall of the negative consequences and feelings of being too fat. And if you were really fired up, you followed my advice and wrote your "why" to remind you *why* you must change now.

Unless you create your "why" right away, however, sometime near the three to four week mark things change many times. Even with a nice variety of foods, adequate but not excessive exercise and the support of friends or loved ones, the syndrome of awfulizing the Lifestyle accompanied with euphoric recall of the old, favorite foods and habits begin to take a stronger position in your daily thoughts and actions.

Those who are best able to take an introspective look at their thoughts and actions are most likely to break the repetitively damaging cycle of awfulizing with euphoric recall. Transition is an uncomfortable process. We all want to "hurry up and get there." As I have said many times throughout this book, the pain of change is often more uncomfortable than the pain of being miserable right where you are. Even though life may be passing you by due to being unfit, the euphoric recall of how particular foods and drinks can instantaneously gratify you, can be very powerful.

The quicker you can catch yourself and stop awfulizing the Lifestyle while succumbing to euphoric recall of poor habits and food choices, the better. Writing and reflecting on your goals each day can also remind you of the reasons you desire to change. Maintaining your "why" while taking time for some serious introspection can help you break the cycle and realize that it truly is worth the pain of change to achieve the fitness goals you have. You have to believe that being leaner and more fit truly is more pleasurable than any food. Nothing tastes as good as being lean feels but you have to become leaner first to experience this for yourself. Falling prey to the trap of awfulizing the Lifestyle with euphoric recall of poor habits and food choices is an all-too-common booby trap but one you can overcome with knowledge and applied effort.

Booby Trap #23: Remaining a Professional Student

You have in your hands a gold mine of information that you can turn into useful knowledge. You may still choose to refuse it and seek another answer or the next new *solution* to weight control. When I am coaching an intense transformation challenge, I ask participants to limit their sources of outside nutritional and exercise information just for the 8, 10 or 12 weeks we are working closely together. I do so primarily to stop a vicious, but all-too-common, cycle of reading and regurgitating without action!

It is my sincere desire, that by including this booby trap in the Lifestyle, I will reduce the chronic desire some of you have to remain a professional student. Prior to this edition of the Lifestyle, I would routinely meet coaching clients who–although new to the Lifestyle with all the tools for success at their fingertips within the coaching program–would ask me a few days after starting if the latest workout in a muscle magazine would be good for them or not. It is quite obvious they had not even tried my proven workout programs but found great comfort in delaying their start by continuing to read and ask questions. Another example is the individual who reads that I suggest 40 to 45 percent of your total calories in a day should come from quality carbohydrates but wants to argue over whether 55 percent might be better. In fact, they'll many times offer that their nutrition professor or best friend who has a Ph.D. in God knows what says that 60 percent is probably even better. The question then becomes, "So Dave, what do you have to say for yourself?" *For these Chronic Contemplators, anything is better than action*. If you find that you would much rather read, argue, and spend your time talking instead of starting, then I implore you to run with the processes I described in Chapter 2 *"Are You Ready to Change?"* and move more quickly into the real Action stage. It really is time to get out of the bleachers and get on the field! It's time to play!

There will be some who will read this book for the sole purpose of bantering with others on Internet discussion forums. They may be morbidly obese, have a strong desire to change, but won't implement the strategies within this book because they spend far too much time sitting in front of their computer, reading magazines or the next new gimmicky diet book. It is not uncommon to avoid that one, single task that is clearly the most important and productive on any given day. The commonality of this truth does not preclude me from trying to get you out of your chair after reading the Lifestyle and truly applying the principles within it. When you do, you will clearly see how remaining a professional student (information without knowledge application) has been a downfall for far too long. Do not avoid the single most important and productive task necessary to begin your transformation. Once you finish reading this book, it is time to review certain chapters, take the action steps I've outlined to heart, and even add in others I've overlooked.

But in any event, you've got all you need. It is time to act!

Booby Trap #24: Depression and PMS

More and more people are intelligently seeking professional therapy and prescription medications to handle various forms of depression. Still far too many others suffer from seasonal, episodic, mild, moderate or severe depression and hope that some day they will be able to wish it away. These same people live far too many days wondering why they just can't be happy when they logically know they have plenty to be thankful for. In this section I will directly refer to premenstrual-syndrome (PMS)-related depression but I am also speaking to any individual suffering from any form of depression who refuses to seek treatment.

Millions of women suffer from PMS-related disorders each year. The major PMS symptoms I'm referring to are not so much the physical aches, pains and bloating, but more the depressive, lethargic, irrational feelings that can precede menstruation. Most of these feelings are a result of one or more neurotransmitters being out of balance (serotonin is probably the biggest). It is beyond the scope of this little section to explain everything serotonin is responsible for but suffice it to say that there is a good reason that most antidepressant medications directly affect serotonin so that it "hangs around" longer in the brain and doesn't get too low. I would strongly suggest you seek out more information on serotonin and all legitimate therapies for PMS before seeing your doctor. Don't delay seeing your doctor for more than a few weeks because you are dragging your feet on doing your own research. Don't be a Chronic Contemplator here!

Many women suffer from PMS 12 times a year but refuse to seek treatment because they don't want to seem weak-willed. Twelve times a year might not seem like much time, but when you break it down it gets ugly. If you are a "like clockwork" sufferer of PMS, then you really suffer about 23 percent of your current life directly from PMS and up to 50 percent from the repercussions of what is inappropriately said, not appropriately said, done inappropriately, and not done appropriately during the PMS period. The number of days a woman suffers with PMS will vary but it is quite common for it to last up to seven days a month. Since there are 12 months in a year, then we could reasonably state that 84 days a year a woman could suffer directly with PMS symptoms. That's 23 percent of the year! Depending on everything said and done, those otherwise supportive, helping relationships in your life may be quite upset for a period of time after the official 7-day PMS zone is passed. If you factor in all the additional negativity resulting from PMS-related events, it isn't hard to fathom that up to 50 percent of your life is unstable, unhappy and negatively impacting others.

If you suffer from depressive, lethargic and irrational symptoms relating to PMS, then you must realize that *it's not just you being affected!* Sure, you are the primary sufferer, however, if you are in a family of any kind, then every loved one around you is also negatively affected. I can speak from experience to my married colleagues when I say that irrational, hateful words and actions spoken during the five to seven days of PMS don't disappear in the minds of your spouse as quickly as the PMS does. Your kids will also suffer. Discipline is irrational and inconsistent with who you really are and, regardless of whether you believe in verbal or physical punishment, neither is proper if you can relate to this section and suffer from PMS. As for the husbands, when it is rare it is much easier to let it roll off. But when it is every month, like clockwork, it can really wear on both you and your spouse. Let's face it, if you are a PMS sufferer then when you are deep in the middle of a PMS period there is nothing your spouse can do but bite his tongue and hope for the best. There isn't a nice enough act the husband can do, nor a kind enough word from anyone that will make the PMS sufferer feel better. Well, that might not be entirely true. A super kind word or gift might make the sufferer feel better for 30 seconds, but what about the other 15 hours, 59 minutes and 30 seconds we're awake in a day?

What I've simply come to terms with in regard to neurotransmitters that affect how you feel is this: you can't will your way around them. Many people who are "in balance" chemically and hormonally can will their way through minor bouts of depression and minor PMS with positive daily affirmations and continued efforts to refill the mental tank with positive books, tapes and seminars. But, for those who are hormonally or chemically challenged, there is no will strong enough to overcome the negativity resulting from the imbalance.

Many women still believe they can will themselves around PMS. Normally this cannot be accomplished. Many women watched their own mothers suffer with untreated PMS for decades and have vowed to "stand strong and not be like mom!" It never works. When it is hormonally or chemically driven, you do not have a strong enough will to avoid it month after month after month after month.

> One coaching member wrote:
> *"I'm a little stubborn about blaming hormones (Just ask XXXX how many times I've railed at him for no reason, and then burst into tears because I thought he was hinting I was PMSing-I had a mom who blamed hormones for 3 weeks a month of bitchiness so I try to ignore it)...*
>
> *I've never been one who gave any credence to PMS, but after a few discussions with Dave, and hearing about the actual physical causes and consequences, I am pretty interested. I never thought I had any issues with PMS, I just thought my husband turned into a real antagonistic ogre a few days a month (but it certainly wasn't ME!!!).*

PMS is kind of a broad term for everything from true physical pain to unnecessary bitchiness, so I think it can be easy to mentally discredit a woman who is actually suffering from it. I know in the past, I would scoff at women who seemed to be "nothing but lazy" and blamed it on their body being out of whack. Now I know that what I thought was the true cause of their discomfort (being overweight, not exercising, fatigue) was very likely a symptom of an imbalance."

The bottom line here is that far too many people (men too) still try and grapple with hormonal, chemical and even many deep-seated emotional imbalances on their own. Many people believe there will be a stigma ("she's crazy") attached to them if they seek medical help for PMS or depression. I would like to stress that if you are a true sufferer of a chemical, hormonal or emotional imbalance, there is likely already a stigma attached to you for not seeking a solution. Personally, I think you are crazy if you do *not* seek help! I don't see the honor in living miserably because of a chemical, hormonal or emotional imbalance that is left untreated. I do see the pain, anguish, lack of motivation, disrupted lives, and good relationships gone bad for those who refuse to accept reality and don't seek the advice of a competent therapist or medical doctor who can properly evaluate the prescription opportunities best suited to the individual.

There is little doubt that increased activity, a good Lifestyle nutrition program, and specific vitamin, mineral and herbal therapy can all tremendously benefit the sufferer of PMS and mild depression. But if the best of the natural therapies does not work then I strongly suggest to any man or woman truly suffering depression or PMS that you seek the advice of a qualified clinical psychologist, psychiatrist and/or medical doctor for treatment.

For a great book on self-change with sound advice on how to locate a qualified therapist see *"Changing for Good"* by Dr. James Prochaska.

Summary

In this chapter I've described 24 of the most common booby traps that catch many well-intentioned transformationists off guard. For this summary, I believe it best to simply restate the booby traps by their title as a list:

1. Living by a False Set of Nutritional Rules

2. Refusing to Accept That Your Reality is Within Your Control

3. Mutilating the Lifestyle Into a Diet

4. Basing Your Commitment on Support From Loved Ones and Friends

5. Not Properly Addressing Ambivalence

6. Improper Handling of Food Pushers (not saying no at least once)

7. Relaxing the Lifestyle on the Weekends

8. Perfectionism

9. Fighting What's Right

10. Playing the Victim Instead of the Victor?

11. Living Your Life Looking in the Rear View Mirror

12. Not Forgiving Yourself and Others

13. Becoming Just Like Your Negative Parent(s)

14. Running on Empty Too Long

15. Too Little Sleep

16. The EITHER/OR Syndrome

17. Making It About Him

18. Making It About Her

19. All Married People Get Fat

20. Assuming the Inevitable Crisis Will Become No Longer Inevitable

21. Foolish Freedom

22. Awfulizing the Lifestyle

23. Remaining a Professional Student

24. Depression and PMS

Take Action and Feel Great!

1. As comprehensive as I've tried to make this chapter, there is little doubt that you have experienced other booby traps not addressed here. Visit www.leannesslifestyle.com and share your own booby trap experiences with me and others. By doing so you may get a booby trap published in a future edition of The Leanness Lifestyle and will certainly help thousands as I continue to spread the cautions of watching out for Lifestyle booby traps.

Benefits of Regular Physical Activity

If physical activity could be made into a pill, it would be the number one prescribed medication in the world.

You now hold in your hands the key to untapped leanness, health and muscularity through good nutrition and supplement habits, however, the plan is far from complete. In fact, the Lifestyle would be a joke if I didn't spend a fair amount of time discussing exercise, canceling myths and giving you some sound guidance on what exercises you can specifically use to reshape your body and add new muscle, regardless of your current level of fitness. I first want to tell you about the real benefits of regular, vigorous, physical activity.

Studies have confirmed that while dietary intake of quality nutrients is the single most important factor for getting the weight off, *exercise is the key to keeping it off?*

Recent studies have confirmed that a sedentary lifestyle is as strong a risk factor for disease as smoking, high blood pressure and diabetes. If you are unfit, you are no better off than if you were a smoker or had diabetes. If you have diabetes, you can improve your risk of disease to less than someone unfit *without* diabetes.

A Physically Active Lifestyle:

- Improves quality of life. The more physically fit you are, the more you will be able to do in life. The abilities to play a round of golf, play with your grandchildren, lift groceries, and garden are all improved greatly with regular, physical activity.

- Improves self-esteem. People who are fit and regularly active have a better view of themselves and the world.

- Prevents heart disease. Because it affects you in a similar way as a balanced Lifestyle, the results are very similar. Vigorous physical activity reduces the insulin response and increases muscle metabolism. Reductions in blood pressure and blood sugar, with increases in good (HDL) cholesterol, are commonly noted in those who participate in regular, vigorous exercise.

- Improves arthritis and osteoporosis.

- Improves sleep. If you are physically fit, you will fall asleep quicker and sleep more soundly.

- Improves immunity. As long as there is adequate recuperation and protein, immunity is improved. Otherwise, vigorous physical activity may decrease immunity.

- Improves stress coping ability. Regular physical activity can help you cope with stress. Vigorous physical activity is perceived as stress by the body. When the body perceives any unaccustomed stress, cortisol–a major stress hormone with a number of beneficial functions to the body–is increased. Too much cortisol can depress the immune system and rob you of precious muscle. So cortisol is a necessary hormone but too much of this hormone is *not* a good thing.

  An adaptive response to vigorous exercise involves the improved management of cortisol. A new, vigorous, physical activity program will be perceived as stress by the body. An interesting fact is that the body cannot distinguish between physical or mental stress. Because the body cannot differentiate the stress of exercise from the stress of life, the everyday problems will not evoke the same stress response. You will not get as upset about burning dinner, being late for an appointment or screaming kids. You're blood pressure won't rise as dramatically, you'll feel calmer and be better able to cope. These benefits are primarily derived from the body sensing less need to release cortisol with everyday stress. By participating in your new, demanding exercise program, you will cause the body to adapt to higher levels of stress. By improving the cortisol response to exercise stress, the body becomes better at managing cortisol during episodes of mental stress as well. In effect, by participating in a vigorous exercise program you are getting two stress-coping benefits for the price of one.

- Reduces reliance on antidepressants. Physical activity can not only be a powerful calming and anti-anxiety tool, but it is also one of the most powerful, natural antidepressants known. Through the release of certain mood-elevating brain chemicals such as norepinephrine, serotonin and dopamine, physical activity provides antidepressive relief only dreamed of by manufacturers of antidepressant drugs.

- Improves concentration. Physical activity also improves oxygen transfer to the brain. Increased delivery of oxygen to the brain improves concentration, thought and causes the release of hormones called endorphins, which are powerful mood elevators. If you are angry or upset, take a long walk or complete your workout right away. See how much better you feel afterwards.

- Physical activity also acts similarly to a balanced diet in that it directly improves blood sugar stability and decreases insulin levels.

- Physical activity enhances muscle metabolism and fat burning. It increases muscle mass. This is important because muscle is the engine that burns fat for fuel. Because muscle moves, it requires more energy as calories than any other organ. Muscle is 30 to 40 percent of the total mass of the body but it accounts for 90 percent of the energy used by the body. Muscle is the only organ that is able to increase its ability to burn fat for energy by increasing fat enzymes. Therefore, the more active you are, the more food you will be able to eat.

- Slows down the aging process. Recent research is showing that much of the decrease in function as you age is not as a result of aging itself, but due to a lack of physical activity. The changes that occur with aging are many times due to body misuse. As an arm in a cast for a few weeks atrophies and becomes stiff and sore, so does your body with many years of disuse. Studies have shown that 21 days of bed rest will decrease the body's ability to use oxygen with exercise similar to 20 years of aging. If you don't use it, you will lose it! Too many Americans practice getting old. They fulfill their own destiny by becoming inactive. Lack of physical activity has led to the increased disability of the elderly. Americans may be living longer but the quality of life and the ability to care for oneself at the end of life is severely impaired without implementing a vigorous exercise program.

The food you choose to eat, the stress you endure and how you cope, nutritional deficiencies, hormonal depletion and the loss of muscle mass due to inactivity are at the root of making individuals feel old before their time.

Although you cannot change your age:
- Muscle mass can be enhanced through physical activity.
- Hormones such as growth hormone, dehydroepiandrosterone (DHEA) and testosterone can be replaced.
- Nutrients such as chromium, magnesium, manganese, zinc, and vitamins A and E can be supplemented.

Many of the changes that occur as you age are related in large part to an inactive lifestyle.

- Increased body fat percentage
- Decreased balance
- Increased cholesterol
- Increased glucose levels
- Decreased ability to use oxygen
- Increased clotting of blood
- Loss of calcium from bone
- Decreased temperature regulation

Did you know? Most people do not end up in nursing homes because they are sick, but because they are physically weak. They lack the muscular strength and motor ability to live a functional, independent life.

As we get older, we generally get lazier. Does anyone disagree with this? Modern man has probably existed for at least 40,000 years to date. The transition from the lifestyle of roaming hunter and food gatherer to the less mobile farmer began some ten thousand years ago. Technological developments during the last one hundred years have introduced a rate of change far exceeding all that occurred during the preceding four million years of evolution. Technology has not only made our lives easier to live, it has reduced physical activity in millions of Americans by 50 percent since 1950.

If you have reached middle age, you are likely smarter than when you were in your teens and early twenties. For this increased intelligence, you have been paying a price. You have learned to work smarter, not harder, and this transfers into everything you do. Most of the time this is a good thing, but when it comes to being fit, it is not. You click the remote, do your laundry on the main floor at home, take the elevator, hire a gardener, take a cab when a walk is reasonable, have your groceries delivered, ask the kids to get you the newspaper and mail, and anything that can be auto-mated is automated. With a few simple clicks, you have what you need, when you need it, without ever leaving your chair. Hey, I'm a fan of technology and I am thankful that in the early part of the 20th century someone invented the refrigerator and all that, but your reliance upon the automated, motorized, push-button world we live in is making you fatter than ever.

With or Without Oxygen

Your body will use one of two types of fuel depending on the type and duration of activity you are doing.

Aerobic (with oxygen): a metabolic process that uses *oxygen for energy and fat burning*. This is achieved through any movement that involves the continuous and rhythmic use of large muscle groups that increase heart rate and oxygen demand without losing your breath. The energy produced during aerobic activity requires oxygen and is analogous to a fireplace burning logs for energy. It is a long, steady, hot, burn. Aerobic activity improves the body's ability to move more air through the lungs, move oxygen from the air into red blood cells, pump the blood to the muscles, deliver this blood to the muscles and use this oxygen to convert fat to energy.

Examples: walking, swimming, biking, jogging, rowing, dancing.

Anaerobic (without oxygen): a metabolic process that requires no oxygen for energy. This is seen in more explosive start and stop activities that leave you out of breath. This is analogous to a fireplace burning newspaper. It is very hot but only lasts for a short time. Resistance training is considered pri-marily an anaerobic activity. The greatest challenge of physical activity while also the most impor-tant is to increase your muscle mass. Only one type of activity can do that: resistance training.

Examples: resistance training, sprinting, skiing, tennis, racquetball.

> *Both aerobic and anaerobic activities are important to achieve*
> *"optimal metabolic health."*

Making Physical Activity a Part of Your Life

> *90 percent of the people who never have a weight problem or who lose weight and maintain their loss are regularly physically active.*

We are a nation of overweight, stressed people. We are too busy to eat and when we do, we eat processed carbohydrates for immediate energy. We live a sedentary life, and complain that we do not have time to be active, yet we have more health clubs and exercise equipment then anywhere else in the world. For every good reason there is for becoming regularly active, we all can come up with one more excuse not to. We need to start slowly, but in the end, we need to *just do it*!

Just as important as choosing the correct foods to eat, physical activity needs to become a way of life as important to you as brushing your teeth and washing your hair. When you are regularly active, you will develop a positive addiction. Regular physical activity is the best investment you will ever make. The time you take to be active will pay off with improved looks, increased productivity and more energy throughout the day and into the night.

Some Quick Facts and Tips to Get You Started Moving

- Choose activities that you enjoy and can see yourself doing consistently for at least a few months. Ask yourself this question: Can I see myself doing this activity for the next six months? If the answer is "no" but you can't think of any other activity, then do it, but know that you have got to find something you really enjoy doing (or at least believe you will enjoy doing for a long time!).

- Before attempting vigorous sport and recreational activities, you should use exercises that are better for overall conditioning first (e.g., walking, jogging, running, hiking, cycling, rowing, swimming and resistance training) to reach the desired level of fitness then, switch to the sport or recreational activity you think you'll enjoy. Alternatives to the standard conditioning activities include aerobic dance, boxing, Tae Bo, spinning, body pump, aqua classes and so on.

- Significant health benefits can be obtained by including a moderate amount of physical activity (e.g., 30 minutes of brisk walking or raking leaves, 15 minutes of running, or 45 minutes of playing volleyball) on most–if not all–days of the week.

- Any exercise is better than no exercise, but realistically we need to see a frequency of four to six days per week, although greater frequency in the early stages of your training might provide additional benefits.

- Exercise duration should last at least 20 to 30 minutes, but only if you are working at an effective threshold (which I'll discuss later).

- Strength decreases two percent per year after age 35. Endurance training does little to prevent the aging loss in muscle mass. Strength training, however, not only maintains or increases muscle mass and decrease body fat in young people, but also in older men and women.

- Aging appears neither to impair the ability to improve muscle strength nor to prevent muscle growth. Older people have considerable ability to increase their endurance capacity and strength with training.

- New research indicates that exercise may have to be conducted at enough frequency, duration and intensity to burn a total of 2800 calories per week (400 calories per day if training 7 days per week) for maximum weight loss and successful maintenance to continue. Until recently, researchers believed that exercise, that would burn a total of 1000 calories per week might have been sufficient.

Summary

Regular, vigorous, physical activity not only helps you lose weight, but also acts as a natural mood enhancer. It is a part of nearly every person's plan who has mastered weight control and lives a superfit life. You should not fight this overwhelming truth. Both aerobic and anaerobic activities are important for optimal metabolic health.

Take Action and Feel Great!

1. If you are not currently exercising, then it is important you seek activity you can see yourself doing for at least a few months.

2. Read the next chapter titled *"Resistance Training for Everyone"*.

Resistance Training for Everyone

Workouts are not like spouses. Be not faithful. Instead, be ever mindful of progression as the only true benchmark of success but be promiscuous along the way and reap the physical rewards of doing so.

When you are losing weight by following the Lifestyle, you want to make sure the majority of the weight you lose is fat and not muscle. If you lose weight without resistance training, you are likely to lose 50 percent fat and 50 percent muscle! This means that if you lose 10 pounds and you are not resistance training you may lose five pounds of fat and five pounds of muscle. This is truly an undesirable scenario because each pound of skeletal muscle you have or add burns between 30 and 50 calories per day regardless of your activity throughout the day. You can easily avoid losing 50 percent of your weight as muscle by incorporating an intelligent, yet vigorous, resistance-training program into your transformation plan.

Another major reason that resistance training must become an important element in your transformation is the natural loss of lean body mass as you age. After the age of 20, unless resistance training is a regular part of your physical activity, you will lose 7 percent of your lean body mass per decade. Not only does this slow your resting metabolic rate, it creates a different (softer, more saggy) body even if your body weight stays the same your entire life.

Finally, if you choose to rely solely on walking and aerobic training as your only exercise activity, you will never create the body of your dreams. It is that simple. Without incorporating resistance training into your program, you will never achieve the toned, shapely body you desire. The sooner the better that you can overcome fears of resistance training, learn and understand the proper fundamentals and form. To avoid learning the terminology and fundamentals of resistance training is just like saying, "I want to be thin and saggy!"

I implore you not to skim over this chapter. Even if your nutritional Lifestyle is dead-on true, you will never achieve what you're after unless you understand and eventually master the fundamentals of developing and practicing a sound resistance training program. Can I overstate this, or have I overstated this? Not even close. Resistance training is vital to achieving the body of your dreams. Give this chapter several reads and do not gloss over it - without question, your ultimate body is dependent upon it.

Resistance Training Benefits

- Improvements in cardiovascular fitness.

- Reductions in blood pressure in those who have high blood pressure or borderline high blood pressure.

- HDL (good cholesterol) goes up and bad cholesterol and total cholesterol go down.

- Your body becomes more efficient at delivering carbohydrates to muscle and other tissues and insulin functions better. The risk of diabetes and subsequent cardiovascular disease is reduced.

- Reductions in obesity! Resistance training increases muscle and reduces fat.

- Improves functional strength (the type of strength you need to do stuff around the house) and reduces bone loss (osteoporosis) in women. It may even reverse osteoporosis.

- Only known activity that can truly reshape your body with or without weight loss.

- Ladies: Resistance training can remove that huge flap of skin hanging off the back of your arm.

- Burns calories during the exercise session and increased calories burned for up to 48 hours post-exercise.

- Only activity that can facilitate the addition of muscle while losing weight. Running, jogging, step aerobics, the Stairmaster or treadmill cannot prevent you from losing muscle while losing weight. Only resistance training can!

Attention! Women Afraid of Growing Muscle!

Myth: You should fear looking like the professional woman body builder with all that muscle sticking out all over the place.

Truth: NO! It cannot happen. It will not happen. Your fear should not be adding new muscle because it is the muscle that will give you the sleek, sexy look you so desperately want. You do want to add muscle! You want it. You want it. You want it! Yes you do. I am telling you. You want it. You have to have it. It is the determining factor in you achieving your goal and getting the body you want. Muscle burns fat. You need it. Muscle reshapes your body. Muscle narrows the hips. Muscle shapes the thighs. Muscle is not bulky. Muscle is slimming. Muscle is not grotesque. Muscle is sleek and feminine. You cannot naturally add too much muscle. It is not possible. If you are not using steroids, you cannot add too much muscle. You will not get too big. Your muscle development is not what is keeping you from getting into pants sizes two sizes smaller than your current size. Fat is to blame. Your legs will not grow larger than they currently are with muscle. They will get smaller through fat reduction. Muscle is good. Muscle is sleek. Muscle is sexy. Muscle is what you want.

I went off on a rant because I have been told by more women than I have hair left on my head that they are deathly afraid to add muscle because it's "gross." When I drag them by the hand to a magazine and ask them to look at a fitness competitor, they say they really think these women have great bodies. When I then turn the page and show them the "he/shes" with muscle bulging out all over the place, they then say, "There, you see that's gross!" I should reserve judgment here in case someone reading this wants to look like the professional woman body builder, but you know what, I can't. They are gross! I agree! What I am saying is you have NO fear whatsoever of ever looking like them. You simply do not have the male hormones in your body that it takes to get to that level. In addition, like the men, these "women" are blessed with tremendous genetic potential to start with. You cannot look like them so do not fear it.

Resistance Training 101–Fundamentals of Hypertrophy

Very simply put, hypertrophy refers to the growth of skeletal muscle. A point I want to make clear before I continue with the fundamentals of resistance training is the goal of Lifestyle resistance training. Resistance training can serve a number of purposes and the goals of the trainee must be taken into consideration before adapting a particular routine for them.

I will be straight-up honest with you right now. If you purchased my system hoping to be handed a one-size-fits-all approach to better sports performance or if you were hoping to rehabilitate your knee post-surgery, then you likely purchased the wrong book. It is not my intention to create a world-class bench presser or Olympic gold-medalist weight lifter, to improve the 40-yard sprint time of an NFL running back, or some lateral change coordination indices of a national soccer player, or to prevent an injury of the groin to an NHL hockey player. In keeping the focus of the Lifestyle on my intended reader (the transformationist), the sole intent of resistance training is to deliver better health and increased muscle mass. This increase of muscle mass will be appropriately referred to as hypertrophy.

It is important for you to know now that when other books and magazines talk of toning, they are really speaking of, at least to some small degree, muscular hypertrophy. Depending on the intended audience, many authors will use the words "toning" and "shaping" instead of hypertrophy because they don't want to scare the reader into believing they are going to grow too much muscle. Instead of simply using appropriate terminology as I will do here, they may even inaccurately state that their program will tone and shape the body without adding any muscle size. Just know that all toning and shaping involves some hypertrophy. For my female readers, this does not mean I am going to try and make a man out of you–far from it. But it also does not mean that I will succumb to the wordsmithing that might make you feel better but will provide inaccurate information about what it really takes to reshape those thighs, lift the buttocks and flatten the tummy. In just a few moments you will read how we control hypertrophy and maximize it for our goals of achieving a leaner, sleeker and sexier physique.

Strength Improves First–Then We Grow (Neural Adaptation)

If you've never performed resistance training or it has been a number of months or years since your last go-round with it, then get ready to first train your neuromuscular system. During the first six to eight weeks of resistance training, you're going to get substantially stronger, however, you won't observe any significant hypertrophy during this period. How is this so? During the first several weeks of resistance training, your nervous system is coordinating with your muscular system to become more efficient at firing (recruiting) more muscle fibers–fibers that are unaccustomed to being called upon. If your nervous system does not send the impulse to the muscle fiber, then the muscle fiber does not contract.

Muscles are recruited only as needed. Your nervous system coordinates this recruitment. If you need to lift an iron or a crescent wrench, there are a minimal number of muscle fibers needed to do so. Even so, your nervous system coordinates with the muscle fibers needed to fire only those fibers necessary to get the job done. It is important that your nervous system not call upon more muscle fibers than necessary because skeletal muscle operates under the "all or nothing" principle. That is, when a muscle fiber is called upon, it contracts 100 percent or not at all. Therefore, it is imperative that your nervous system calls upon only the proper number of muscle fibers so as not to create movement that is excessive and dangerous. Can you imagine how difficult it would be to accomplish anything if you went to pick up the iron or crescent wrench, but your nervous system sent a signal to the muscles equal to what might be necessary for you to pick up a refrigerator? That wrench or iron would go flying across the room!

Already it should be quite easy to see why the average couch potato does not acquire any appreciable muscle. The "use it or lose it" principle is in full force. If you do not use a particular muscle, the body is not going to devote any energy to remodeling, developing or even maintaining it. Either you use it or you lose it. The perfect visual example of this is the leg in the cast. Anyone who has ever seen what happens to a broken leg when it has been cast for six weeks has witnessed what happens when a muscle is not used–it atrophies (gets smaller).

The body consistently acts in a manner to most efficiently use the energy available. To grow muscle without proper stimulation would be quite wasteful. From an evolutionary perspective, the body's main purpose is to survive long enough to procreate. Adding lots of skeletal muscle is a very energy-dependent process. No more muscle than is necessary will be created at any time. To do so would endanger the human species–at least that is what our bodies have been programmed to believe for tens of thousands of years. Think about it–it has only been the past few hundred years that food has been plentiful. Before that time there were many times when food was scarce.

Energy conservation, not waste, is the cornerstone of survival.

Through resistance training, you will boldly ask your nervous system to better coordinate with muscle fibers so you can stimulate untouched fibers waiting to grow. Once those fibers hypertrophy, they will shape your body for the better. Therefore, it is fair to say that initial gains in strength are largely the result of an increased ability to recruit more muscle fibers to participate in the overall force of a contraction. This adaptive response is termed *neural adaptation*.

After two to three months of consistent and progressive resistance training, you can expect to observe your first, real muscle growth. Your brain and nervous system will be coordinating nicely with your muscles and new muscle should be accumulating on your frame. With a proper resistance training program focused on progression, your muscles will respond by depositing more protein in the muscle bank than is being withdrawn (you're anabolic!). Scientists debate whether muscle fibers are growing in size (hypertrophy) or number (hyperplasia); to us it does not matter. One or both is occurring and this is the period when you will begin to observe improvements in muscle tone, size and shape.

Progressive Overload is Key to Strength, Toning and Shaping

Muscles specifically adapt to imposed demands (SAID) and only to those demands. Muscle does not grow haphazardly or because you will them to grow. Muscles do not grow because you put your time in the gym three days a week religiously. Anyone who has ever trained at a public gym can vouch for the fact that the herd does not change too much. That's why, in just a few months, you're going to stand out like a rose in a patch of thorny bushes–you will change for the better by striving for continual progress. The only path to increased muscularity, strength, toning and shaping is through consistency and progressive overload.

Myth: Muscle weighs more than fat.

Truth: Think about this statement a second. "Muscle weighs more than fat." Could this be any crazier? It is like the old joke "What weighs more, a pound of feathers or a pound of gold?" Some would answer "Gold of course!" Uh, well, they are equal. The more accurate statement is "a pound of muscle takes up one-third the space in the human body as a pound of fat." This is the reason that muscle is shapely and precisely the reason that many fitness competitors weigh more but also look more fantastic than the average guy or gal on the street.

Legend of Milo

According to Greek mythology, the first person to apply the theory of progressive overload was Milo of Croton. In his teen years, Milo decided to become the strongest man in the world, and embarked upon this mission by lifting and carrying a calf every day. As the calf grew and became heavier, Milo became stronger. Finally, when the calf had developed into a full-grown bull, Milo, thanks to a long-term progression, was able to lift the bull, and, consequently, became the strongest man on earth.

Whether you are a beginner or well on your way to a national or world bodybuilding title, the training workload must be progressively, yet gradually, increased if your goal is an increase in muscle size, strength, tone or shape. There is no other path to shapely greatness other than through progressive overload. Earlier I mentioned how inefficient it is for a body to add and maintain new muscle tissue. To the body, it is literally counterintuitive to build a single muscle fiber a micron larger or stronger than is necessary to accomplish the imposed demands placed upon it. Thus, you must coax and demand that your body build more muscle through progressively changing, and eventually demanding, more from your training sessions.

> *Progression is the most important measure for determining improvement and muscle growth.*

Workouts Should Be Goal Oriented– Not Seat Of Pants Generated!

There are a number of training variables that will be discussed in a moment. These variables will be adjusted to further progression, however, it's imperative you understand the importance of the one measure that matters more than any other: *safe progression is ultimately the only thing that matters*. Setting and achieving performance driven goals is paramount to you achieving the body of your dreams. Far too many people train "by the seat of their pants." These same people complain about the lack of results from their resistance-training program.

Likely, there are many of you who have put some substantial time into resistance training but are frustrated by the lack of results. If you've been resistance training for five years, I'd ask you to consider whether you have five years of resistance training experience or more like one year multiplied times five. Let me explain.

> *Quality time in training produces the best results–not the quantity of time in training alone.*

If you are the person who is still benching, curling, pressing, pulling, squatting, lunging, and leg-pressing what you were last month, last year and two years ago, then I would argue that you don't have five years of resistance training experience even though you may have spent the past five years consistently working out. If this describes you, then you have been training by the seat of your pants. You have had no formal goals and month after month after month after month, you have continued to use the same weights for the same exercises for the same repetitions completed. This has not been a complete waste of time, as all physical activity that is safe is good. However, if you are unsatisfied with your current shape or level of overall muscularity, then read this section carefully. It contains everything for how you can progress out of your current condition, regardless of your level of experience.

By setting performance goals, you will be able to rely more on what you have accomplished rather than whether you are able to drag your butt out of the gym with energy to spare or nothing left to give. Regardless of the unique vision you have of your body, creating the ultimate body, is only accomplished when you create workouts that are systematically progressive. The path to your dream body is not paved with stones of soreness, tiredness, the burn during a set, how much you sweat or how winded you were during the workout. The path to a great body is only paved with one kind of stone: progression.

Most people are aware of what the barbell bench press looks like, so let me provide an example of the importance of progression with that exercise. If you can bench press 100 pounds for 10 complete repetitions today but cannot complete the 11th repetition, we would say that your 10-repetition max (10 RM) is 100 pounds. The bottom line for creating the ultimate body is simple. If you cannot press more than 100 pounds for 10 repetitions or cannot press 100 pounds for at least 11 complete repetitions six months from now, and your goal is a physique transformation, then you simply have not progressed. Most likely, you have added no new muscle during that period. It does not matter if you were tired on numerous occasions. It does not matter if you sweated a lot. It does not matter if on numerous occasions your chest was sore to the touch. While it is not 100 percent accurate to say, it is close enough for our purposes - if you are not stronger in the 6 to 12 repetition range for any given exercise, you have not progressed.

When progression does occur, it will occur because of a host of variables over which you have control. Proper and ongoing measurements of results are necessary. Saying to yourself, "I think my shoulders are a little more rounded" is fine. Can you back up your statement with progressive accomplishments measured by the load and repetitions completed on an exercise affecting the shoulder (e.g., shoulder press, lateral raises)? If you can, then there's a great chance your perception is indeed reality. Otherwise, there is a possibility that your ego is getting between you and the mirror. Progression only occurs with dedication, commitment, perseverance and hard work. Rarely can you be complacent and you must always expect more from yourself. If you make a mistake, make it fast and keep moving forward.

What if:
- I supplement right
- I measure my lifts
- I have perseverance
- I make quick mistakes

- I eat right
- I have dedication
- I work hard

- I exercise
- I have commitment
- I am not complacent

and three months from now my barbell curl has not changed from 90 pounds for my 10 RM? It is safe to say I have not progressed and I have added no new muscle. While the time I spent in the gym or at home participating in resistance training was not a waste, it also did not further my goal to reshape or add new, quality muscle.

As I explain the variables affecting any workout system, keep the one truth, the resistance-training maxim of all maxims in mind at all times. No progress = no muscle growth = no addition of new muscle = no change in shape = no additional toning. Ask yourself these questions about any workout you create or that is created by a personal trainer for you:

Performance Goals Test
- Is this workout safely progressive from where I am now?
- Will I be stronger at the end of this cycle compared to where I am now?
- Is this program goals-driven?
- Will I judge each workout by what I accomplished and not by whether I am tired, sweaty or sore?

When you fail to plan you have certainly made a plan—a plan to fail.

Periodization Provides the Lifestyle Resistance Training Foundation

Contrary to the notion that there is one best way, there is no one right way to train. There are, however, many wrong ways to train. There are many cookie-cutter home gym pieces, machines, and free-weight combinations these days that will never apply to everyone reading this. Therefore, I want to provide a solid foundation for increasing muscle mass and strength by explaining principles that have proven time and time again to be effective for increasing muscularity, reducing injury and improving all around interest in resistance training

The answer to the question of "Which training program is best?" is really summed up in a term that only some of you are familiar with: periodization. Periodization describes a systematic approach to variety manipulation. While it has some boundaries, guidelines and structure, it is not overly restrictive but forces you, through goal setting, to make regular and spaced changes to your routine.

Many advanced male and female body builders and power lifters train intensely all the time. They seldom take a break, or, if they do take a break, it is too short to do much good. Each workout is full of 95 to 100 percent intensity and high volumes of work. While it's true that most of these lifters will be the strongest and biggest in any gym if they can stay healthy long enough, they are many times injured, over-trained and may suffer from burn-out. Also, many of these same lifters will experience lengthy plateaus in their muscular growth or strength before their genetic limit has been reached.

Plateaus are a marked time period when no progress appears to be occurring. Unless proper training methods like periodization are used, plateaus may last for years. When some resistance trainers hit a plateau, they often try to train even harder or longer. This further complicates their goal of increasing lean muscle or getting stronger by causing an injury or putting the body into an over trained state. Cycling periods of intense training with periods of less intense training can prevent plateaus or dramatically shorten their duration. Planning and cycling training periods is what Periodization is all about.

Periodization training, popularized in the United States by Steven Fleck and William Kraemer and backed by strong scientific support, provides a solid foundation for its use in resistance training. The foundation of periodization training is "a training plan that changes your workouts at regular intervals." That's it!

Do not train "by the seat of your pants" by stumbling around the gym wandering aimlessly from station to station without any purpose. Use Periodization training and you will have a solid base upon which you can build cycles of training. Some cycles are tough, some cycles are moderately tough, and some are borderline active rest. The important point I wish to make is that the cycles are planned. Without a plan, you will lose focus and you will likely follow a one-dimensional model where you choose the same exercises, same repetitions, same sets, and same rest intervals without changing for months. For the truly dedicated, hard-core lifter, this is not only sub-optimal for growth, but also may cause overuse injuries to occur. For the socially active weight lifter (someone who doesn't live and die by resistance training), the one-dimensional model will cause burn-out, boredom and eventual failure due to a lack of results.

Variation–Force the Body to Keep Adapting

During an interview I conducted with famous power lifting coach Louie Simmons, he said, "Everything works but nothing works forever." There is not a finite set of rules that will apply to all people across all muscle fiber types and all the varying degrees of intensity people are willing to shell out for a return of new muscle. Experts in this field call this "individual variability."

If we had divine knowledge of the precise needs of our body for optimal growth, I believe the variability of the program would appear haphazard to the unknowing mortals looking upon the workout. After even a few months of success, should this divine knowledge be lost, I doubt very seriously that we would be able to reverse-engineer the plan to determine just what we were doing that created each progressive step. If variability is this complicated, is all hope lost? Not at all.

There is no one best formula that works across the board for everyone. It just might take divine knowledge to create the perfect workout for all people, however, there are scientifically based foundations that can be relied upon to create a body that is not only worth showing off but that is much more functional for everyday living. It only makes sense to apply the most appropriate, scientifically-proven formulas in a systematic manner for growing the type of muscle that accomplishes both goals: creating a pleasing look and improving everyday functionality. An intelligent, scientifically based system should dictate that you know what you are going to do in the gym *before* you get to the gym. This system should force you to gauge your good and bad workouts not by how you feel when you are through with each workout, but by what you accomplished while you were there.

If you have an open mind that progressive overload is the key to your muscular or shapely success, then you may be tempted to simply believe that all you'll have to do to add muscle is to keep piling on the weight (increase the load) with each workout. That's progressive, right? Sure, that is progressive, however, the body will not allow that type of progression infinitely. If only things were that simple.

With the SAID principle in place, you know that the body will adapt to the demands placed upon it. Variability in your resistance training becomes quite important after only a few months of regular workouts. You could look at the entire process as a big chemistry experiment. In chemistry, you put things into a formula. In this case, those things are repetitions, sets, exercise selection, exercise order, rest intervals, volume, intensity, rest, recuperation, nutrition, tempo, supplementation, sleep, stress, workload, etc. The resulting product created from these ingredients are the various characteristics you're interested in achieving: capability to perform daily tasks effortlessly, muscle growth (hypertrophy), various measures of strength, improved fitness, better shape, firmer legs, more muscular arms, etc. Sounds pretty simple so far, doesn't it? However, providing a steady training stress (same exercises, weights, sets, repetitions, tempo, etc.) does not do anything to change the output of the experiment. We humans become well adapted and that is that.

As a studious follower of the Lifestyle, you know you need progressive overload to get results. If, however, you provide a steadily increasing training stress, with the rate of increase chosen so that you can continually adapt and get stronger, it turns out that this does not work forever. You simply cannot keep adapting to this kind of training stress, no matter how carefully it is chosen. Thus, although the story of Milo is a nice idea, it could not really happen. It turns out that the driving force, the training stress, has to be more complicated than that.

Why Variation Is So Important

Variation is important for many reasons:

- Your body is the master adapter. As soon as it adapts to a training stimulus it quits growing. Cycling everything forces your body to constantly continue adapting. It never knows what you are going to do next. This is good.

    "Dave, I've been using the same training routine for three years and I've always had good luck with it. That is, until recently. I seem to have plateaued and can't figure out why I've stopped getting bigger and stronger. Any ideas?" This statement is so common it is not even funny! Can you answer this person's question? You should be able to now.

- Cycling your sets, repetitions and exercises prevents boredom.

- Varying your intensity by way of time between sets, repetition and set quantity can prevent over-training and provide a continued stimulus for growth. Over training is a very real hazard to muscle growth. Beating your muscles to a pulp day after day without cycling your intensity through rep, exercise, set and a time adjustment is setting yourself up for no muscle growth. For some of you reading this, however, I want to caution you about interpreting the benefit of cycling as some kind of cop-out so you can give the same half-hearted, no-accountability efforts you may have given thus far. A constant lack of effort with inadequate stress placed upon the muscle also equals *no growth* or muscle tone. This goes for men and women.

Now comes variation and the idea of periodization, in which the intensity, volume, and various other characteristics of the training stress vary with time in planned waves that ratchet up over the long term. This idea works, generally speaking, although it often needs to be tweaked to suit a given individual, his/her current condition, and goals. It may be that periodization is the simplest type of driving force that will produce continual adaptation.

There are many questions that you will have as you create your first or fiftieth workout. You know you must progress and you know that there are a number of ingredients to the formula. Below is a guide to help you follow a periodization model should you choose to create your own workouts now or in the future. I will first define basic terminology, explain many variables you have control over, and finally I will close with eight steps anyone can take to create a massively successful periodization program.

I want to tell you early on that I have developed online tools that can rapidly and easily help you create a periodized Lifestyle workout. With my Workout Generator, you spend less time planning and more time doing. Thousands of clients have experienced the benefits of using this tool. Both my wife Tracy and I use this tool to create our current resistance training cycles. It is a valuable asset for the beginner to advanced trainer. You can visit www.leannesslifestyle.com for more information on my unique and powerful Workout Generator.

Repetitions

A repetition is one complete performance of an exercise, usually involving both a lifting and a lowering of the weight. One complete repetition of the bench press involves lowering the bar to your chest and then pressing the bar until your arms are fully extended.

The type of training I am teaching you in the Lifestyle will safely add new muscle in maximum quantities in the shortest amount of time. I am not teaching you to be a bench presser, power lifter or Olympic lifter. Because of this, I will focus on repetition guidelines that best support our goal of maximizing hypertrophy. While other authors will attempt to calm the ladies down by saying they must train substantially different from men so they don't get too bulky, I will simply restate the fact that it is impossible for a woman to get "too bulky" from Lifestyle resistance training without drugs. Women have a built-in thermostat that prevents them from adding too much muscle naturally. It is primarily due to low testosterone and high estrogen concentrations, the opposite of men.

Whether a novice, intermediate or advanced resistance trainer, it is accepted worldwide that for the greatest overall hypertrophy, the majority of your repetitions for each set should be in the 6 to 15 range. Beginners, especially, should focus nearly all of their training in this range.

Varying the number of repetitions per set over time will ensure that all available muscle fibers will be trained at some point. If one always sticks with the same repetition bracket (for example 10 to 12), much muscle tissue will be left untrained (i.e., unstimulated and still available for growth); this despite how hard someone works at performing those 10 to 12 repetitions. A sensible approach would be to include brief (two to four week) periods when sets are performed with three to five repetitions, six to eight repetitions, eight to ten repetitions, etc., accepting the fact that low-repetition training is not suitable only for power lifters. In fact, after a period of several months of vigorous training, other repetition ranges, such as one to five repetitions per set, become fair play for the novice too. Interestingly, those that appear to benefit most from incorporating some heavier loading with lower repetitions are those who have a foundation of resistance exercise experience but have never tried it!

Sets

A set refers to a group of repetitions performed in succession, after which a brief rest is taken.

Beginners should typically complete three to six sets for each body part until they complete 4 to 6 weeks of consistent training. Scientific and empirical evidence shows us that intermediate resistance trainers will benefit from three to six sets per exercise with a total of up to 12 sets per body part completed in a workout. Finally, advanced resistance trainers will benefit from cyclical periods of sets as high as 20 per body part in one workout. This is not to say that advanced trainers should incorporate several weeks or months of this high-volume training into their program, but there is no question that advanced trainers must cyclically ratchet up the volume to continue to progress.

Through periodization, set number will be varied in a cyclical pattern. Some cycles (you'll read about mesocycles in a moment) will incorporate one set per exercise to momentary muscular failure. Some cycles will incorporate multiple sets without quite going to failure and still other cycles will specify three to four working sets and finish with 1 more set to momentary muscular failure. With periodization, you will incorporate planned variability of your set number so you progressively overload the muscles being worked.

Momentary Muscular Failure

Momentary muscular failure is that point during a set when you cannot complete a repetition without assistance. If your target is ten repetitions and you are straining hard on number 9 but you get it, then you have *not* reached momentary muscular failure (no matter how hard the repetition was). If you attempt the next repetition (repetition number 10) and you cannot complete it no matter how hard you try, you have reached momentary muscular failure. Many authorities believe we need to incorporate effort that produces momentary muscular failure at regular intervals in our training. Periodization accomplishes this goal.

Volume

Volume relates to the amount of work performed during a workout. For the Lifestyle, we measure volume based on the total number of repetitions completed during the workout. Here are some examples of low, moderate and high volumes:

Volume	Repetitions per week
High	400 +
Moderate	150 - 400
Low	75 - 149

As you can see, there is quite a variation between a high-volume week (more than 400 repetitions) and a low-volume week (as few as 75 repetitions). Periodization manages volume variability quite effectively.

Intensity

According to standard periodization principles, intensity relates to the load being used relative to your 1 rep max (RM) for that exercise. If you can bench press 200 pounds for 10 repetitions but you cannot complete the 11th repetition, then your 10 RM is 200 pounds. 200 pounds is your 100 percent effort to complete 10 repetitions.

When you look at the "Find Your Max" chart included in the Appendix, you can see that a 200-pound load lifted 10 times is equal to a maximum single lift of 265 pounds. You can also see that

200 pounds for 10 repetitions is equivalent to 210 for 8, and 225 for 7, etc. This chart is illustrating relative strengths based on your 1 RM. Like volume, allow me to illustrate the differences between high, moderate and low intensities.

	Load equal to this
Intensity	percent of your 1 RM
High	95 - 100
Moderate	85 - 94
Low	60 - 84
Warm-up	40 - 59

Volume or Intensity, But Not Both

Generally speaking, you can either train with lots of volume or lots of intensity, but not both for any significant length of time. This means we should incorporate periods where we use high volume and low intensity, moderate volume and moderate intensity, low volume and moderate intensity, or low volume and high intensity. Only for brief two to three week cycles can we incorporate high volume and high intensity. Injury, over-training and burnout may result if we try to extend high volume/high intensity training periods beyond a few weeks.

Tempo

Perhaps the most overlooked aspect of effective program design is movement speed, or tempo. Training tempo is typically represented with a 4-digit system (e.g., 2-0-2-1) and has four phases:

- Eccentric: lowering portion (e.g., going down in the squat or bringing the bar to your chest in the bench press).
- Isometric: (pause).
- Concentric: lifting portion (e.g., pressing the bar from your chest in the bench press or flexing the elbow joint for the barbell curl).
- Contracted Pause: pause in the contracted position (e.g., when your elbow joint is fully extended during a triceps pushdown).

Each phase can be represented in terms of seconds taken to complete each portion of the repetition. For example, a 2-0-2-1 tempo indicates that a movement takes 2 seconds in the eccentric phase, 0 seconds in the isometric phase, 2 seconds in the concentric phase and 1 second in the contracted pause. For future reference, the "X" in a tempo scheme of 2-0-X-1 always means you should complete that part of the repetition as fast and powerfully as possible. Tempo should be varied periodically to shorten or extend the duration of a set, or simply to add variety.

Superslow Training

A type of training that has recently drawn the attention of the media is something called "Superslow Training." In a nutshell, SuperSlow is represented in tempo as 10-1-10-1. In an example of the bench press, this would mean you would take 10 full seconds in the eccentric (lowering) phase, 1 second in the isometric (pause) phase, 10 full seconds in the concentric (raising) phase and 1 second in the contracted pause phase. This is creepy slow to say the least. Proponents argue that Superslow Training is safer, reduces momentum and creates intense focus on the exercise.

While just about anyone could certainly use Superslow Training at some point in their resistance training life, research doesn't support Superslow for maximum effectiveness at creating hypertrophy or strength in skeletal muscle. If you are exceptionally immobile, have severely painful joints or are recovering from surgery, Superslow can certainly be used if your choice is Superslow or nothing–no question about it. However, for the rest of you reading this, I must caution you against buying into the hype of Superslow Training.

Skeletal muscle requires a proper neurological stimulus for growth and we need to train our nervous system to recruit as many muscle fibers as possible so that controlled damage is inflicted upon a larger cross section of muscle fibers. As you'll read in just a few moments, inflicting controlled damage upon muscle is necessary to cause that muscle to remodel and repair stronger and larger. It is an adaptive process. By moving the weight slowly during the eccentric and concentric phases of a repetition, you are ruining an opportunity to recruit large numbers of muscle fibers at one time.

According to the American College of Sports Medicine, "motor unit activity may be limited when intentionally contracting at slow velocity. In addition, the lighter loads required for slow velocities of training may not provide an optimal stimulus for strength enhancement in resistance-trained individuals, although some evidence does exist to support its use as a component part of the program in the beginning phases of training in highly untrained individuals."

When it comes to tempo, like most areas of your resistance training, variety is king. Maximum muscular performance is likely evoked from tempos with 1 to 2 seconds in the eccentric and 1 to 2 seconds in the concentric phases. Proper form is paramount for beginners and very important most of the time for intermediate and advanced lifters as well. Do not jeopardize good form by using incorrect tempo or an overly heavy load.

Time Under Tension

Time under tension refers to the length of time the muscle is strained (under tension) for each repetition or set. I commonly will rotate tempos of 2-0-1-1 for 12 weeks with a 4-0-X-1 for the next 12 weeks (the "X" means to move the weight as fast as you can). All things being equal, I feel stronger initially with the 2-0-1-1 tempos compared to the 4-0-X-1 tempos because I have decreased the "time under tension" for each set. Obviously, it takes less time to follow a tempo of 2-0-1-1 than it does a tempo of 4-0-X-1. Thus, the time under tension is less.

Time under tension is a variable we have control over and one we should change to keep stimulating growth and increased performance. Finally, the total time under tension per set should be limited to a maximum of 60 to 70 seconds. Sets lasting longer than this may be more suitable to the development of muscular endurance rather than muscular strength and hypertrophy.

Rest Intervals

Rest intervals refer to the time taken between consecutive sets during a workout. Rest intervals do not only refer to the rest taken between sets of the same exercise as many programs call for a series of different exercises to be performed one after another in succession with a proper rest interval between each exercise (i.e., circuit training).

It is not important that you have a full understanding of bioenergetics: the conversion of carbohydrate, protein and fat molecules into usable forms of energy by the body. However, there are a few terms that will give you a better understanding of why you rest a specific length of time depending on the load and repetitions you are completing for a set.

Adenosine triphosphate (ATP) is the energy currency that fuels all metabolic activity in the body, including muscle contractions. ATP is a very limited resource and must be continuously replenished. ATP in human skeletal muscle is replenished through three basic energy systems:

• Phosphagen
• Glycolytic
• Oxidative

The Phosphagen System

The phosphagen (anaerobic) system provides ATP primarily for short-term, high-intensity activities (e.g., resistance training and sprinting) and *is active at the start of all exercise, regardless of intensity*. ATP and creatine phosphate are the two primary phosphagens, but both are stored in muscle in small amounts. Therefore, the phosphagen system cannot supply energy for continuous, long-duration activities.

The phosphagen system is the primary energy source for activities lasting from 1 to 14 seconds. To fully restore lost phosphagens within muscle (e.g., ATP and creatine phosphate), the rest interval ranges from 1:12 to 1:20. Thus, if your set takes 10 seconds from start to finish, you may need to rest anywhere from 120 seconds (10 x 12) to 200 seconds (10 x 20) to fully restore lost phosphagens. Sets with heavy loads and few repetitions (high intensity) are most likely to use the phosphagen system as a primary energy source.

Sets that are truly high intensity and thus short in duration are not to be confused with a set where you "sandbag" your way through it. If you can complete 12 repetitions with 100 pounds for the squat but you do 3 repetitions and stop, this does not exhaust the phosphagen energy system as much as if you chose a load that allows you to complete 3 repetitions but not 4. The latter set would be short but very intense. The latter set would heavily tax the phosphagen energy system.

You may notice that within the phosphagen system I did not mention anything about carbohydrate, protein or fat utilization to create ATP. The glycolytic (anaerobic) system, however, relies on either stored carbohydrate (glycogen) or blood glucose to produce ATP. The glycolytic system supplements the phosphagen system for high-intensity muscular activity. Most sets of a resistance training workouts rely on a combination of the phosphagen and glycolytic energy systems to fuel muscular contractions.

The Glycolytic System

The glycolytic system becomes a more dominant energy source for activities lasting from 15 to 60 seconds. Replenishment of glycogen and available glucose for muscular contractions requires a rest interval ranging from 1:3 to 1:5. Thus, if your set takes 30 seconds from start to finish, you may need to rest anywhere from 90 seconds (30 x 3) to 150 seconds (30 x 5) to prepare the muscle for another set of similar duration. Sets with moderate loads and repetitions between 8 and 15 are most likely to use the glycolytic energy system as a dominant energy source.

Again, as with the phosphagen energy system, it is more accurate to say that the glycolytic energy system is called upon more strongly when you are choosing loads that create a momentary muscular failure with a repetition range lasting from 15 to 60 seconds. This is typically represented by 8 to 15 repetitions. However, if you choose a load that would allow you to complete 30 repetitions with a maximal effort and you "sandbag" once again and stop at 8 repetitions with that load, then you are not creating a work effort requiring you to match the set with the proper rest interval. You may be using more of the oxidative energy system when you consistently "hold back" and are not true to choosing the load most closely matches your program is design.

The Oxidative (Aerobic) System

The oxidative (aerobic) system is the primary source of ATP at rest and during low-intensity activities. It uses primarily carbohydrates and fats to create ATP. For the purposes of resistance training, the oxidative system is not typically a primary energy source. Of the three energy systems discussed, it is the only one that depends on oxygen to create ATP. The phosphagen and glycolytic systems are both anaerobic systems (do not require oxygen to create ATP).

The oxidative system is the primary source of ATP in activities lasting greater than 2 or 3 minutes. Standard cardio sessions depend most on the oxidative energy system, however, as you will learn in the Lifestyle *Aerobic Prescription* chapter, high-intensity interval training will use all three energy systems at different phases of the cardiovascular workout.

Rest Interval Variation

The length of time taken between consecutive sets of a particular exercise should be systematically varied like any other variable over which you have control. The greater the intensity (i.e., the closer the load compared to your 1 RM for that exercise), the greater the rest interval for optimal recovery between sets. If you can bench press 200 pounds for 1 repetition but cannot press 200 pounds for 2 repetitions, then 200 pounds is your 1 RM. If you are performing consecutive sets of bench press with 180 pounds for 3 repetitions (90 percent of your 1 RM), your muscles will likely require 3 to 6 minutes of rest between sets. When you think about this, it makes sense. A heavy load where only a few repetitions are possible will primarily use the phosphagen energy system. The phosphagen energy system has the highest active-to-rest ratio (i.e., 1:12 to 1:20). However, if the load is 140 pounds (70 percent of your 1 RM) for 12 repetitions, the rest between sets could be as short as 30 to 45 seconds. This should also make sense now. Because the load is lighter and the repetitions possible are greater, there is more reliance upon the glycolytic energy system than solely the phosphagen energy system. The active-to-rest ratio for the glycolytic energy system is 1:3 to 1:5, much shorter than the phosphagen energy system.

By now you should know that when I say "3 RM," I'm talking about a set where you have chosen the load (total weight lifted) that allows you to complete only 3 repetitions but that is too heavy for you to successfully complete a 4th repetition. If I say 12 RM, the load would be such that you can successfully complete 12 repetitions but not 13. If you complete 12 repetitions but could have completed 13 then this is not your 12 RM. Until you achieve a repetition that takes you to momentary muscular failure, you cannot accurately say what your repetition max is for that particular exercise and load.

It may seem odd that fewer repetitions performed with a heavier load would require a longer rest interval than a lighter load performed for more repetitions. In fact, your perceived exertion may be much higher after a set of squats where you complete 12 repetitions but could not complete the 13th (i.e., 12 RM) compared to a set of 3 repetitions where you could not complete the 4th (i.e., 3 RM). However, performing a 3 RM is much closer to your 1 RM than is a set where the load is adjusted down for a 12 RM. Because the energy systems used are different for a 3 RM set vs. a 12 RM set, you must pay attention to the energy replenishment guidelines (rest intervals) I've provided here to maximize your performance with each set in a workout.

Finally, and no less important, is the contribution of the nervous system with exercise of increasing intensity, and the extended time frame for recovery of this particular system. A 3 RM set in the squat will demand more of the nervous system than a 12 RM set in the squat. More muscle fibers are being called upon in a 3 RM set than a 12 RM set. The more your nervous system is taxed, the longer the rest needed to restore the impulses it sends to and feedback it receives from skeletal muscle. Also, a 10 RM set of barbell back squats will require more rest after the set than a 10 RM set of barbell curls. The squat is a complex movement, involving multiple joints, and is very demanding on your nervous system. The barbell curl is a single-joint exercise, relatively simple and creates much less whole-body stress.

Partners

During my early years of resistance training, I always trained with a partner. I was 17 years old when I started, in school, (even had a couple of friends) and I always worked out with at least one other person, and many times a group. My gains during the first few years of training with a partner were by far the greatest gains I have made, although I have progressed since then. Some of these initial gains would have occurred regardless because I had not yet reached my lifetime potential for new muscle growth. Accepted. However, there is little doubt that on many occasions, a training partner can give you things you cannot give yourself.

- Accountability: you are less likely to miss a workout.

- Friendly competition: you may develop a competitive edge, which can drive you to work for that extra repetition simply to beat your friend.

- Verbal support: positive comments during a set can make the difference between forward progress and staying the same. Cheering comments like "Come on big daddy! Get yo money! Show 'em who's boss today! Let's go big man!" "You go girl!" and many more can really motivate if you can keep from laughing.

- Safety: a partner can provide the spot necessary to keep you from wondering what to do when you are nearing failure. If you complete 7 repetitions with 100 pounds on the bench press and your workout calls for 8 repetitions but you are not sure if you can do it, a spotter can provide the encouragement and reassurance necessary to drive you to the 8th rep. If you do not have a partner and this same situation presents itself, you may simply rack the weight and not try it. I actually recommend this if you do not have a safety bar or pin as a back up. Obviously, you should not "go for it" and risk dying. In my youth I actually "went for it" on more than one occasion and I'd end up rolling the bar down my abdomen (usually with something like 275 pounds) and when it got to my waist, I'd stand up, pick the weight up off of me and throw it to the floor in disgust. So what do you do? With a partner, you always have someone who can help you if you are stuck on your final attempt and, as I will discuss very soon, if you want to do forced repetitions, negatives or strip sets, a partner is required.

Damage Muscle During a Workout Repair and Grow Muscle when You Rest

Contrary to popular belief, you do not build up muscle during a workout. You tear down muscle. If you believe this is not true, then you have to explain why it is that we get weaker as our workout progresses. If you were growing new muscle tissue as you worked out, you would get stronger as the workout progressed, not weaker. Since we know this is not the case, you must accept the proven physiological response of the body to progressive-resistance training.

Because we grow when we are *not* working out, we must typically allow adequate time for a particular trained muscle to recover and grow. This period is at least 48 hours and may last as long as 96 hours (4 days). This leads to the next discussion topic.

Muscle Group Priority and Exercise Order

Multi-Joint Exercise: Multiple-joint exercise is resistance training exercise where movement takes place at more than one joint and, therefore, involves more than one muscle group. Two examples are the squat (hip joint and knee joint) and the bench press (shoulder joint and elbow joint).

Single-joint Exercise: Single-joint exercise is resistance training exercise where movement takes place at only one joint and, therefore, predominantly involves one muscle group. Two examples are the barbell curl (elbow joint only) and the leg extension (knee joint only).

In most workouts, the major muscle groups are trained before minor muscle groups. The major muscle groups include the chest, back, shoulders, thighs and hamstrings. Smaller groups include the trapezius, triceps, biceps, forearms, calves and abdominal.

Major muscle groups are trained most effectively with multi-joint exercises, also known as "core" exercises. Typically, multi-joint exercises require more coordination, skill and concentration than single-joint (assistance) exercises. Resistance trainers who become fatigued are prone to using poor technique and, consequently, are at higher risk for injury. The multi-joint exercises also require significant energy expenditure. Therefore, it makes sense to place the multi-joint exercises near the front of your workout when you are most likely to be fresh, alert and without pre-fatigue.

Push-Pull Pairing

There are many ways to vary from this standard resistance training protocol and still create an effective workout. For instance, I personally like the "push and pull" pairing method. When using a push and pull exercise order, I will often pair up a multi-joint push exercise with a single-joint pull exercise, or vice versa. For example, I may complete a set of 10 repetitions on the bench press (a multi-joint push exercise) followed by a rest interval less than 30 seconds. Then, after the rest interval I will complete a 10-repetition set of standing barbell curl (a single-joint pull exercise) followed by a 60-90 second rest interval. I will then repeat this cycle the predetermined, preplanned number of times before moving on to the next pair. Pairing can speed your workout and reduce boredom.

Below is an example of pairing for a complete upper body workout.

Chest-Back
Triceps-Biceps
Shoulder-Trapezius

Notice that I still placed the larger muscle groups at the front of this workout before the smaller muscle groups.

Below is an example of pairing for a complete lower body workout plus abdominal muscles.

Thigh-Hamstring
Calf-Abdominal Muscles

Push-pull training is ideal for beginners or anyone wanting a change in their hypertrophy-focused routine.

Frequency

Frequency refers to the number of training sessions completed in one week. For the purposes of Lifestyle resistance training, frequency will always refer to the number of training sessions for a particular body part in one week. For example, if you train your chest on Monday and Thursday we would say your frequency for chest is two.

The ideal frequency based on scientific and empirical data lies somewhere between 1 and 3 sessions per week. However, if intensity is moderate and volume isn't too high, you may be able to train a particular body part (thighs for example) 5 to 6 days per week. Beginners may be able to handle a full body workout 3 times per week. In this case, we would say the full body has a frequency of 3. Other beginners and many intermediate and advanced resistance trainers can handle a maximum frequency of 2 for major muscle groups while still keeping a frequency of 3 for minor muscle groups. Still, many intermediate and advanced resistance trainers can handle no more than a frequency of 1 for all muscle groups. In this case, each body part would be worked once per 7 days. This is very common for successful, advanced resistance trainers and would likely be too little for beginners.

While it may sound counterintuitive when I say that advanced trainers can handle less frequency and not more frequency compared to beginners, the rationale is really quite simple. Whole body stress is increased the stronger and more advanced you become. Advanced trainers handle heavier loads than beginners. The heavier load places more stress on the muscles, joints, tendons, ligaments and nervous system compared to the loads of a beginner. More time in repair and recuperation is demanded from this increased stress. An advanced trainer's neuromuscular system is well coordinated and firing many muscle fibers at once. Not only does this create a larger cross-section of muscle fibers to be recruited and stressed, but the nervous system as a whole is also stressed and will need adequate recovery before the next workout. Finally, the mental capacity of the advanced trainer to push through positive pain and squeeze out one more rep is enhanced relative to the beginner. The first time a beginner experiences the "burn" of lactic acid and lack of oxygen to a working muscle (ischemia), they are likely to wonder what they are doing in the gym in the first place. An advanced trainer pushes through that positive pain to get the required reps as long as his form does not deteriorate.

Through periodization, we can adjust the frequency so that in some mesocycles (4-week periods), some body parts are being trained with a frequency of 3 times per week while other body parts are being trained once or twice. Many beginners will want to train the entire body 3 times per week. Still other beginners will want to train the upper body on one day, the lower body on the next day, and perform a total frequency of 2 for all body parts. When the upper and lower body are split into two different days this is known as a two-way split. A 7-day cycle might look like this.

Monday . . . . .Upper
Tuesday . . . . . . .Lower
Wednesday . . . . . .Off
Thursday . . . . .Upper
Friday . . . . .Lower
Saturday . . . . . . .Off
Sunday . . . . .Off

A host of variables will determine what frequency is best for you. Individual differences in ability to recover, nutrition, supplementation, sleep, genetics, mental drive and types of exercises can all play into what frequency is best. Here are some general guidelines, compliments of research and empirical data:

Beginners
Each body part 2-3 times per 7 days

Intermediate
Each body part 1-2 times per 7 days
Each body part every 5 days works well for many

Advanced
Major muscle groups 1 time per 5-10 days
Minor muscle groups 2 times per 5-7 days
Each body part every 5 days works well for many

Body Part Groupings

Listed below are some sample 2-way splits (total body trained over 2 different workouts). Notice that each workout structure allows for at least one complete day off every 7.

Monday . . . . .Chest, Back, Shoulder, Triceps and Aerobic training
Tuesday . . . . .Legs, Biceps
Wednesday . . . . . .Aerobic training
Thursday . . . . . . .Chest, Back, Shoulder, Triceps and Aerobic training
Friday . . . . .Legs, Biceps
Saturday . . . . . . .Aerobic training
Sunday . . . . .Off

Monday . . . . .Chest, Shoulder, Triceps and Aerobic training
Tuesday . . . . .Legs, Back, Biceps
Wednesday . . . . . .Aerobic training
Thursday . . . . . . .Chest, Shoulder, Triceps and Aerobic training
Friday . . . . .Legs, Back, Biceps
Saturday . . . . . . .Aerobic training
Sunday . . . . .Off

Listed below is a sample 3-way split (total body trained over 3 different workouts) for training the complete body once every 5 days. Notice that each workout structure allows for at least one complete day off every 7.

Monday . . . . .Chest, Shoulder, Triceps and Aerobic training
Tuesday . . . . .Back, Biceps and Aerobic training
Wednesday . . . . . .Legs
Thursday . . . . . . .Off
Friday . . . . .Chest, Shoulder, Triceps and Aerobic training
Saturday . . . . . . .Back, Biceps and Aerobic training
Sunday . . . . .Legs
Monday . . . . . . .Off
Tuesday . . . . . . .Chest, Shoulder, Triceps and Aerobic training
Wednesday . . . . .Back, Biceps and Aerobic training
Thursday . . . . . .Legs
Friday . . . . .Off
Saturday . . . . . . .Chest, Shoulder, Triceps and Aerobic training
Sunday . . . . .Back, Biceps and Aerobic training

Listed below are some sample 3-way splits (total body is trained over the course of 3 different workouts) for training the complete body once every 6-7 days.

Sample 1: This very common routine hits each body part every 6 days instead of every 7. It is very effective but you have to think about your training days more often and pay attention because you are not training the same body part on the same days each week.

Monday . . . . .Chest, Shoulder, Triceps
Tuesday . . . . . . .Aerobic training and abs
Wednesday . . . . . .Legs
Thursday . . . . . .Day Off
Friday . . . . .Back, Biceps
Saturday . . . . . . .Aerobic training and abs
Sunday . . . . .Chest, Shoulder, Triceps
Monday . . . . . . .Aerobic training and abs
Tuesday . . . . . . .Legs
Wednesday . . . . . .Day Off
Thursday . . . . . .Back, Biceps
Friday . . . . .Aerobic training and abs
Saturday . . . . . . .Chest, Shoulder, Triceps
Sunday . . . . .Aerobic training and abs

Sample 2: With this pattern, each body part is trained on the same day each week.

Monday . . . . .Back, Traps, Triceps
Tuesday . . . . .Aerobic training and abs
Wednesday . . . . . .Legs
Thursday . . . . .Off
Friday . . . . .Chest, Shoulder, Biceps
Saturday . . . . .Aerobic training and abs
Sunday . . . . .Off

Sample 3: I do not like this but it can work. The reason I personally do not like it is that I feel loose and flat by Saturday without some resistance training later in the week. In addition, I do not like the 3 days in a row of resistance training. Although this is an example of an effective way to train, your first workout of the week will always be your best and your third resistance-training workout of the week will likely be your worst.

Monday . . . . .Chest, Shoulder, Triceps
Tuesday . . . . .Legs
Wednesday . . . . . .Back, Biceps
Thursday . . . . .Off
Friday . . . . .Aerobic training and abs
Saturday . . . . .Aerobic training and abs
Sunday . . . . .Off

Sample 4: This is also a highly effective plan and allows you to train each body part on the same day each week.

Monday . . . . .Chest, Back
Tuesday . . . . .Aerobic training and abs
Wednesday . . . . . .Legs
Thursday . . . . .Off
Friday . . . . .Shoulders, Biceps, Triceps
Saturday . . . . .Aerobic training and abs
Sunday . . . . .Off

Well, Yeah But, Can I Try This?

As you continue to read this chapter and the next on the Lifestyle *Aerobic Prescription*, it is important that you understand just how varied things can be. I have said it before but I am purposely going to repeat myself: there is no one best workout. I have presented the basic, fundamental principles of resistance training. It is important you pay attention to the fundamentals, but if you come across a workout that interests you, and you can answer the following questions affirmatively, then you are absolutely entitled and even encouraged to use that workout to further your progression.

Performance Goals Test

- Is this workout safely progressive from where I am now?
- Will I be stronger at the end of this cycle compared to where I am now?
- Is this program goals-driven?
- Will I judge each workout by what I accomplished and not by whether I am tired, sweaty or sore?

If we were a group of professional hockey players like other trainers coach, maybe the answer would be "no" a lot more. But we are not. We are body sculptors. We are transformationists. You have to enjoy what you do and remain interested. There are as many varied workouts as your imagination and ingenuity will allow. Follow the Lifestyle resistance training fundamentals and apply the performance goals test to any workout you are considering. As long as it passes the test, you just found a workout worth implementing for 4 to 12 weeks.

Do Not Train the Same Body Part Two Days in a Row (Usually)

Not training the same body part two days in a row gets a little tricky and, while the headline above sounds simple, you need to know that we rarely work a muscle group in total isolation from other supporting muscles. This example illustrates my point. When you have gone through your chest work (typically consisting of a lot of pressing movements), your shoulders and triceps were being used extensively to support the chest movements. To apply the rule of not working the same body part two days in a row, we must also look at the primary supporting muscles worked for each major muscle group. Here they are:

Major Muscle Group	Primary Supporting Muscles
Chest	Shoulders and triceps
Back	Biceps and Shoulders
Thigh (if squatting)	Shoulders, chest, back

This list illustrates that if you're going to train the chest on a given day, it doesn't make much sense to expect optimal performance from your shoulders or triceps the next day. Shoulders and triceps are too much an integral/accessory part of your chest workout. They will be taxed seriously during your chest workout. If you train the back on a given day, you should be aware that training the back on the next day is counterproductive. Training your biceps the next day will likely result in less than optimal performance from them since they are an accessory muscle group for most back work. All of your back movements, with few exceptions are "pulling" movements, which requires extensive use (flexion) of your biceps.

The thigh example above may lead you to believe that I am nuts. If you are using a machine of some sort to do squats, then some of this will not apply. For the most part, however, squatting is squatting. Maintaining proper form and hand width, while supporting a bar on your upper back, requires a tremendous number of supporting muscle groups. Sometimes you barely recognize you are using them but you *are*.

- Your shoulders are strained to hold the bar in the proper position on your back.
- Your back is strained to support the weight as you lower your hips into the squat position.
- Your chest is strained when you drive out of the down position.

Let there be no mistake: your legs, hips, and buttocks are being worked like nobody's business but the accessory muscles are also working, too.

Too many times I have been subjected to the whining of some very hard-working and gifted lifters who train the squat on one day and then complain about how their chest workout sucked the next day. I have already said that your shoulders and triceps are needed to support most chest movements, and now I am saying the squat tremendously strains your chest and shoulders, too. It should now be painfully obvious that resistance training anything after a squat day is likely counter productive. The squat works everything, if not directly, then indirectly, and the next workout will suffer in some way if you try to force it. Do not force it!

An Exception

Notice I said "usually" in the main heading of this section. While the general rule is to never train the same body part two days in a row, and some rules were made to be broken, I must reinforce that this should occur only cyclically. Many women suffer from excessive lower body fat and are deathly afraid of creating larger thighs and plumper buttocks. I must vehemently state again that a woman's legs and buttocks are not large due to muscle, however. The goals of most women are to lose body fat while toning and shaping (hypertrophy) the thighs and buttocks. It would be acceptable for women to occasionally train lower body 5 to 6 days per week with low to moderate intensity loads and moderate to high volume. This may mean that a woman could train lunges, extensions and leg curls five days in a row if the load isn't too heavy and the volume isn't too high. What would this accomplish?

First, it would create a caloric expenditure when she might otherwise take the day off. This serves to further the number one goal: losing body fat. Second, it could replace or add to the aerobic activity. Instead of performing yet another boring 40-minute cardio session, she could perform 4 to 6 sets of lunges and 4 to 6 sets of leg extensions and leg curls. This would help satisfy goal number two, which is to tone and shape the thighs and buttocks with minimal hypertrophy. By keeping repetitions in the 10 to 20 range, one can be assured the intensity is not too high.

Duration

Duration refers to the length of time you spend exercising. Duration does not include warm-up, cool down, stretching or jaw-jacking. For the purposes of Lifestyle resistance training, there is no reason you should spend more than 60 minutes in any one resistance training session. In fact, research indicates that workouts lasting much longer than an hour will result in a drop in testosterone. After testosterone drops, it may take an hour or longer for levels to recover back to normal. If your session lasts longer than an hour, then your volume is too high or I have to agree with training guru Charles Poliquin who says, "You're just making friends."

Proper Form

Anyone who has been involved with resistance training has a horror story to tell about someone seen training like a complete fool. There are people who constantly sacrifice form so they can claim to be moving some "serious iron." In reality, however, they are just making a fool of themselves and sometimes even publicly.

Experienced lifters may be able to relate to the next anecdote. Picture in your mind the guy who sits on the 45 degree leg press and after he unlocks the safety pins, he grits his teeth, tenses up, spits occasionally, belts out some Ethiopian war cry and quickly lowers the platform 3 inches and returns it to its starting position. Everyone around the leg press can hardly keep from laughing, but the entertainment value alone is worth the price of admission, so you offer some inspirational comments when the fool is done like "Way to work!" or "Nice effort!"

Then there's the guy who needs no less than one spotter for every wheel (a wheel in resistance training language is a 45-pound Olympic plate) he has loaded on each side of the squat bar, leg press or bench press. If he has two wheels on each side of the bar, then he has two spotters, three wheels equals three spotters, until he reaches nine or ten wheels on each side and there is barely any room for the nine or ten spotters he requires to complete his set. Hey, at least he is getting the attention he did not get as a child or is not getting at home. I can do without this kind of attention and so can you. It is laughable and I have gotten many good laughs watching others use awful form.

Some intelligent people in this game would have you believe that form must *always* be perfect–that there is no room for sloppiness in resistance training! I disagree. Your warm-up sets should be nearly perfect. The weight should lower in a controlled fashion and your mind should focus totally on the muscle you are working–nice and strict. Complete the majority of your working sets using *excellent* form. Honestly, they really should not look much different from your warm-up sets. There should be no jerking, swinging, bouncing or other erotic movements while doing the set. Completed exercises should exhibit a full range of motion so the muscle worked moves from full extension to full contraction and back to full extension during each repetition.

Perfect-form training is highly recommended at all times for the beginner with less than six months of training experience, however, I do not advocate always using this type of form. When we cheat in a "controlled manner," we can increase the intensity and the variability at the same time.

There is absolutely no reason why, in a cyclical pattern, resistance trainers cannot occasionally jerk or sling the weight a little more forcefully so an extra repetition can be completed. You should always be aware of the potential for injury and you have to be smart enough to know when form has been sacrificed too much. If you do not, then you are bound for injury, which will likely cause a setback of months or even years. "Cheating" as we call it, should be reserved for occasional use and only after you have first acquired the ability to perform the lift correctly. This will take several weeks to months. Some expert power lifters never feel they master the techniques of their sport, so be patient and do not get sloppy too fast or too often.

Free Weights vs. Machines

This argument is as old as the first Nautilus machine. Which is better? Free weights (including barbells normally about 5 feet in length, cylindrical weights added to the bar, and dumbbells normally about 16 inches in length) or machines (anything working via a cam or pulley and tied to a load via a cable or strap or chain). The answer is simpler than most tend to believe. Look around you. Who looks muscular? What do they use?

There are no top bodybuilders (natural or drugged to the gills) who use machines only, however, some top bodybuilders use free weights only. Many athletes who drifted from free weights to the $4000 vertical bench press machine are going back to free weights. For building maximum muscle, free weights do offer advantages over machines. A lifter using free weights must control the weight being lifted, and in doing so will recruit more muscle fibers, not only in the muscle being trained but also in accessory muscles. Free-weight movements also mimic real-life activities more so than machines.

Machines, on the other hand, offer quick weight changes (by moving a pin usually) and offer the advantage of muscle isolation to the individual who is working through an injury or is being rehabilitated. Because machines typically only force the lifter to concentrate on moving the weight in a straight line (in contrast to free weights, which force you to control left-to-right and back-and-forward motion), you take less chance many times of re-injuring the tender area.

Basic exercises and equipment offer maximum muscle-building capacity and you do not need machines that cost $4000 to build a great body. If you have access to both free weights and machines, you have the ideal situation to move quickly through your workout while providing maximum stimulation for muscle growth. Most muscular men and women use a combination of both free weights and machines. I recommend both.

Finding the Right Starting Weight

Many beginners simply do not have a clue when it comes to determining starting weight amounts. In addition, those who find out how much their 1 RM will be, still self-select weights during training that are ineffective for producing muscular growth. A study published in Medicine Science in Sports and Exercise S214, 1998, concluded that many people training with weights do not choose lifting poundage for training that is high enough to produce muscular growth. In fact, the authors stated that men choose to lift between 50 to 58 percent of their 1 RM on average and women choose to lift 42 to 52 percent of their 1 RM. The authors concluded by saying that "self selection of lifting load is not an effective strength training methodology." What does this mean? It means that without some guidance, many of you are likely to choose loads that are not sufficient to cause hypertrophy to muscle fibers.

Generally, how much weight is considered necessary to minimally damage muscle for repair? About 60 percent of your 1 RM. Furthermore, the range for optimal muscular stimulation is between 60 and 90 percent of your 1 RM on any given exercise.

Tips to Help You Determine A Good Working Weight

1. Pay no attention to weights being used by experienced lifters. Do not compare yourself to anyone but yourself.

2. Warm up with 5 to 10 repetitions using 50 percent of an estimated 10 RM. In other words, choose a weight you believe is about one half what you could do for a maximum of 10 repetitions. If you believe you can bench press 100 pounds a maximum of 10 times, then choose 50 pounds as your first warm up and press it 10 times and re-evaluate.

3. After a minute or two of rest and some specific stretching, use about 70 percent of what you believe is your 10 RM and complete 10 repetitions.

4. Repeat step 3 and use what you now believe is 90 percent of your 10 RM.

5. After 2 minutes or so of rest, again repeat step 3, but this time, go to what you now believe is 100 to 105 percent of your 10 RM and complete it 10 times if possible.

6. If you complete step 5 and the weight still felt too light to be considered 100 percent effort, then start the procedure again after at least 1 or 2 days of rest. On your next day of determining your 10 RM max, start with a heavier weight but work through all five steps again.

Lifestyle "Find Your Max" Chart

Once you know, for any given exercise, a repetition maximum between 6 and 10, you can use the *Lifestyle "Find Your Max" Charts* (included in the Appendix) to determine your approximate 1 RM. It is simple to use. Look at it now. The first "max" listed on *the Intermediate to Advanced* chart is 155 pounds. Reading across the chart, you see that if you can lift 115 pounds for 10 controlled repetitions, your max is approximately 155 pounds. Simple, right? Another benefit beyond this chart's simplicity is that you do not have to kill yourself with a 1 RM lift to see how strong you are. Beginners are likely to injure themselves and advanced lifters also run a similar, albeit reduced, risk of injury. With the chart, you can quickly and easily determine your approximate 1 RM. You can also see how you are progressing as you get stronger without having to load the bar up for a maximal lift.

Included in the Appendix is another *"Find Your Max" Chart* for beginner to intermediate lifters. This chart goes down to a max of 25 pounds so you can determine your max at lighter weights. I can already hear you saying, "Well, yeah, but it says if my max is 25 pounds I should be able to do 4 repetitions at 25 pounds. How is that possible if my 1 RM is 25 pounds?" I hear ya. I hear ya. At the lower weights, it's not possible to provide you one-half pound increments, because you are probably *not* going to find dumbbells or barbell weights in increments less than 5 pounds (See *Microloading* in this chapter). If you can barbell curl 25 pounds for one repetition as a max, will you really be able to barbell curl 25 pounds for 4 repetitions? No. What, then, is the point here? The point is to provide a *guide* so you do not have to max out on every exercise with a single repetition to determine your 1 RM. Obviously, if you can barbell curl 25 pounds for 1 repetition, you would need to use less than 25 pounds to do 4 repetitions. Maybe it is 22.5 pounds.

Warm Up

In all honesty, I do not always warm up, but that doesn't mean I shouldn't. I am certain that some of the injuries I have experienced could have been prevented if I had only taken my own advice and warmed up a little. One of the nice things about getting older is that your body reminds you more often that you should warm up or your first few sets are going to be painful.

Warming up will increase your pulse, overall body temperature, blood and oxygen flow and it mentally prepares you for the damage you are about to inflict upon your muscles. Do not forget that you are going to properly damage your muscles in order for them to rebuild themselves stronger than they were before your workout.

The Top Five Types of General Pre-Resistance Training Warm-ups

With the following warm ups you should not be breathing so hard that you can't carry on a conversation at the same time. You should also be on the verge of breaking a good sweat after 5 to 10 minutes.

1. Riding the stationary bike. Warning! Do not do what I see so many people doing when they claim they are warming up while riding the bike. First, they are reading a magazine and second, if you count their revolutions per minute it would be less than 10. This is not warming up! There is a technical word for this and I am not sure if you will understand it, but I will try to explain it just the same: "Slug." I know that Webster has its definition, but I have mine.

   slug (slug) n. 1. A person who displays little passion for life and is dull in both activity and mental acuity. 2. Someone who wants to tell all their friends they "work out" but who really is just wasting oxygen and using equipment in a workout facility that Lifestyle followers are waiting for impatiently.

2. Rowing
3. Jogging in place
4. Skipping rope
5. Treadmill

Specific Warm-Ups

Perform one or two light, but progressively heavier, sets before resistance-training with heavy loads. If you're going to work chest and the bench press is your first movement, then you should warm up with a weight that is equal to no more than 40 percent of your max on your first set and you should do 10 to 15 repetitions in a very controlled manner. Then increase the weight to maybe 50 percent of your 1 RM for 10 repetitions. I know people who bench press well over 500 pounds who always–repeat always–warm up with 135 pounds for 10-15 repetitions, then they move the weight to 225 pounds and then onward and upward from there. This is the norm and is reasonable.

Stretch As You Go

There is not a fitness manual anywhere without a chapter or section extolling the benefits of stretching. For the person who is resistance training solely to improve their looks (for vanity's sake) and increase muscle mass, however, there is great controversy whether stretching is a benefit or a detriment or neither. Researchers do not agree on whether stretching before resistance training improves performance during resistance training. Some research has shown that stretching before a maximum lift can hinder the ability of the lifter to complete a maximum repetition. Some moderate stretching, however, as indicated in the following paragraphs are recommended for Lifestyle followers.

Stretching prepares the muscle for the damage your workout is about to inflict, and it can help you mentally focus on the muscle group you are about to work. Where I disagree with other fitness authors is *when* you should stretch. Most "experts" will tell you to stretch right after your general warm-up (like after riding the stationary bike for 5 minutes). You know what though? I have found that when I stretch right after warming up and I take the prescribed 5 minutes to stretch, I am cold again. This really stinks, too. After I've spent 5 to 10 precious minutes trying to get my heart rate up, my body temperature up and a nice warm feeling throughout my body, I have to stop and stretch only to get cold again? What a waste. I think there is a better way.

Instead of stretching right after your general warm-up, what has worked best for me is getting right to my specific warm-ups after my general warm-up. For instance, if I am training chest on a given day I will ride the stationary bike for 5 minutes and then I get right to the bench press for a nice, controlled specific warm-up. In between sets, I stretch. I will repeat this process for my first couple of sets of specific warm-ups. That way I do not cool down, my muscles are getting warmer and I am stretching a warm muscle with a warm body. If I do it the "experts' way," I start my first specific warm-up (bench press in this case) feeling just as cold as I did when I walked into the gym. Where is the benefit of this?

When you do stretch, you will want to use what is known as "passive static" stretching and not ballistic stretching. With the passive static form of stretching, you will not bounce or jerk your muscle into submission. You will slowly stretch the muscle to maximum tension without experiencing pain and you will hold it for 15 to 30 seconds. Perform 3 to 5 repetitions of each stretch.

First Working Set

After one or two specific warm ups, you are ready to complete your first working set. If you are using machines then you will be dealing with numbers or letters painted, hand-written or stamped onto plates, which are essentially meaningless except for giving you a reference. The principles for finding your starting weight still apply, however. If you find that your 10 RM is letter "J" on the machine chest press, then start your specific warm-up set at letter "G" the next time you're working chest (assuming G is four pin holes above J). Regardless of what the plate says, once you find your 10 RM you will start your first specific warm-up at four pinholes above your 10 RM (that's above as in vertically, not above as in amount of weight). There are so many variables on what the machine plates are going to say that you may have to use your head and the knowledge within this book to make the smartest decision. Many gyms and clubs have personal trainers on staff to help you as well. Do not be afraid to ask for help or to enlist their services.

Keep A Training Log!

Often I've witnessed the limp and lame efforts of many health club visitors who claim to be working out with weights. Instead, these people are only doing what they know is in vogue and they spend much of the time socializing. This is better than watching TV, but it is not Lifestyle resistance training. Why? Because mostly, they have not the faintest idea about their progression over a given period of time. They cannot show whether they are improving with each workout.

Instead of stumbling around the gym wondering what weight you used last time and how many times you completed it, write down your weight and repetitions in a good training log. If you start a resistance-training program and do not log your efforts, you will waste years simply going through the motions. I strongly recommend you keep a training log, but not just so you can say you are keeping a training log. Keep a training log so you can:

- Know what you've done in the past.
- Truly see progress from session to session.
- Know the difference between a successful and unsuccessful training program after you're finished.
- Map out small, but oh so significant, changes for future workouts.
- Understand why you are not progressing and when you have hit a plateau or begun to over-train.

Use your log wisely and do not simply jot some numbers down. I know dozens of people who have logged all their workouts since the dawn of time, and they have not progressed any better than someone not keeping a log but who is doing everything right otherwise.

Microloading–A Personal Best Every Week!

I was first introduced to microloading by Charles Poliquin, strength trainer extraordinaire. Following the Japanese Kaizen principles, Poliquin stresses the continuous advancement of training and even goes so far as to say that unless you plan on improving every workout by increasing your repetitions or increasing the weight for a particular lift, don't bother going to the gym. Poliquin believes that once progress has halted for a particular exercise, it is time to change the exercise.

"Platemates" are small, magnetic weights that attach to barbells, dumbbells, plates and weight stacks. Most experienced weight trainers have never given a second thought to how much of an increase in weight is required to advance at the typical gym. In most gyms, the smallest Olympic plate is 2-1/2 pounds, which means you must advance by 5 pounds (a 2-1/2 on each side of the bar). Most gym dumbbells also increase in 5-pound increments. Until someone like Charles or I hit you upside the head with the notion that it doesn't have to be this way, you accept the 5-pound jumps as law, and your progression is possibly hindered.

When you consider a few examples and think about what microloading can do for your training, the idea of smaller-than-normal increases becomes more appealing.

Inexperienced Lifters and Microloading

Neophytes cannot handle the same poundage as their experienced gym buddies. Microloading can be an important idea to consider for the new lifter. When you are curling 20-pound dumbbells for 10 RM, your calculated 1 RM is 26.66 pounds. Can you possibly lift more than 26.66 pounds if you can curl 20 pounds for 10? Sure, but it doesn't change the fact that if you are forced to jump to 25 pound dumbbells you have made a 25 percent jump in weight! Ouch! Your repetitions will drop significantly (likely to the 6 to 8 repetition range) and this is not always advantageous depending on the repetition structure you are striving for. Would it not make more sense to first increase your dumbbell weights from 20 to 21-1/4 pounds? Followed by an increase to 22-1/2 pounds? And then add weight to 23-3/4 pounds before jumping to 25 pounds? I believe it does. By making these small, yet significant, increases in weight, you can nudge the muscle into growth rather than attempting to jerk it into submission with a 25 percent increase in weight.

Experienced Lifters and Microloading

Experienced lifters have adapted so well to making 5-pound jumps that they don't know any other way. Shifting existing paradigms from 5-pound jumps to less than 2-pound jumps is difficult, but it makes tremendous sense. If you are an experienced lifter and can bench press 250 pounds for 10 RM, your calculated 1 RM is 333 pounds. Assuming you're as frustrated as those experienced lifters who haven't significantly increased their bench press in the past year or more, your next increase above 250 pounds is 255, right? No more. Again, for the inexperienced lifter your first increase should be to 251-1/4 pounds. I'd almost be willing to bet a case of protein bars that you will still get 10 repetitions at 251-1/4 pounds although it's an increase of 1-1/4 pounds above your previous personal best. If you do, you have not only called upon more muscle fibers through the increase in load, but you have also set a personal record (PR)!

Setting a PR has far-reaching value. Your current workout will benefit from the positive mental attitude you'll get from setting the PR. You'll also have more confidence for your next workout. Add to this the knowledge that you're able to increase your lift, even if only by 1-1/4 pounds. It is still a PR and it is still progress.

Do not underestimate the value of these small progressions. If you increase 1-1/4 pounds per week, you have increased 5 pounds in 4 weeks and almost 10 pounds in 12 weeks. Many experienced lifters do not progress on their 10 RM bench press by 10 pounds in two years!

Platemates are available in hex, donut and brick shapes. Visit the web site (www.leannesslifestyle.com) for examples of how these products are affixed to various barbells, dumbbells and weight stacks.

Advanced Resistance Training Methods

Forced Repetitions

Forced repetitions are repetitions that can only be accomplished with the assistance of a training partner. You have fatigued, reached momentary muscular failure and are still continuing to move the weight as originally planned, but with help. The proper way to do forced repetitions is to allow yourself to reach failure on your own and then your spotter will apply just enough force on the bar to keep the weight moving fluidly without stalling. There's nothing worse than watching a foolish spotter yank the bar from the unsuspecting lifter as soon as he stalls, or not apply enough pressure to the bar and the lifter is subjected to a 30-second repetition! Ouch! Forced repetitions should be used sparingly. I recommend forced repetitions for no more than one or two repetitions, and no more than one exercise per body part per training session. Excessive forced repetitions not only burn out your training partner, but also can easily place you in an over-trained state. Do not use forced repetitions on anything other than your last set of an exercise movement, when muscles and tendons are completely warm.

Drop Sets

Drop sets are sets that allow you to complete as many repetitions as you can in a particular movement. Then when you reach momentary muscular failure, you "drop the weight," reduce the load being used, and continue with more repetitions. Again, like forced repetitions, drop sets are an effective means to an end if used judiciously; however, they too should not be used more than one set of one exercise per body part. Repetitions will vary. As with forced repetitions, only use drop sets on your last set of an exercise.

Negatives

Negatives relate to the eccentric (lowering) portion of a repetition. During the bench press, the negative portion is when you are lowering the weight to your chest. Negatives are commonly accomplished by adding 10 to 15 percent more weight than you could handle for an all-out single repetition max (if my max is 300 pounds then I would likely try a negative with 325 to 350 pounds). Negatives also require a spotter or two and can be very hard on them because you will be controlling the negative portion of the lift by lowering the weight very slowly (during the bench press negative you would take 5 to 7 seconds to lower the weight to your chest), but when the weight gets to your chest, you are almost completely spent and there's nothing left to complete the concentric portion of the movement. Therefore you will need a spotter or two to complete the raising of the weight, even though you may be pushing the weight as hard as you can to help return the weight to the starting position.

Because negatives cause more damage to muscle than concentric movements and are likely the easiest way to overtrain, I do not recommend negatives more than one set per exercise per mesocycle (4-week period).

Pre- and Post-Workout Nutrition for Resistance Training

By following the Lifestyle nutrition strategies, you will not concern yourself about consuming a pre-workout meal. Since you will be eating 4 to 6 times per day, your pre-workout meal will likely be the last meal you had before your workout. The term "pre-workout meal" is usually thought of as the single meal consumed just before your workout. This is really a misnomer. Your resistance training or aerobic training performance will be dictated not only by the last meal you consumed, but also by the dozens of meals you consumed before your workout on the day of your workout and previous days. If you've been eating poorly, skipping meals, restricting calories too severely and you have hopes of making up for it all with a pre-workout meal, then you can flush those hopes right down the drain. The pre-workout meal will not make up for a dozen poorly balanced, nutritionally void meals consumed over the two days before this day's workout.

One question I frequently get about the pre-workout meal deserves mentioning. If you wake at 4:00 A.M. and train at 4:40 A.M., should you eat before training? In other words, if you're an early bird and train at or before the crack of dawn, should you train on an empty stomach, or should you consume a full five-course breakfast, an energy bar, or a protein or meal replacement shake?

Many people train first thing in the morning on an empty stomach and do very well. Others will consume a small protein or meal replacement shake, and still others will consume a light breakfast from whole-food sources. I have heard from every camp and all claim they do fine. The answer is simple, but a word of caution is warranted. If you feel energetic and most comfortable training on an empty stomach, then do so. If you can consume a shake or light breakfast before training without gastrointestinal discomfort and this makes you feel better and more alive while training, then do it!

There is potential concern for those who consume carbohydrates, protein or protein/carbohydrate combinations 30 to 60 minutes before a vigorous resistance training session. A resistance-training workout can lower blood glucose (blood sugar). Both proteins and carbohydrates can raise blood sugar. We know the body's response to increased blood sugar is the release of insulin in non-diabetics to lower blood sugar. The concern about having a carbohydrate, protein, or protein/carbohydrate meal within an hour of working out is that insulin will be released to lower blood sugar and the working muscle will ALSO lower blood sugar for a possible hypoglycemic event (blood sugar that's too low).

For resistance training workouts lasting less than one hour first thing in the morning, I'd still recommend you do what makes you the most comfortable, however, watch for symptoms such as fatigue, anxiety, headaches, difficulty concentrating, sweaty palms, shakiness, excessive hunger, drowsiness, abdominal pain, and depression. Those experiencing any of these symptoms may be experiencing reactive hypoglycemia and should seek a quick source of carbohydrates and/or medical attention.

What is absolutely *not* a concern is whether eating will disrupt the "fat-burning benefit" of training on an empty stomach. It is far more important to consider the caloric burn value of the workout itself rather than the fat-burning value during the workout. There is a wonderful balancing act occurring within your body at all times. Essentially, the trend is this. If you train on an empty stomach, there is a good chance you will burn more fat *during* the workout. Typically, this means you will rely more on carbohydrates as a fuel source in the hours afterwards. If you train with a mix of carbohydrate and protein eaten before the workout, then you may burn less fat during the workout, however, you may also burn more fat after the workout. Yes, it is true. More glycogen and glucose burned during the workout usually creates a shift to fat burning after the workout. It is not universally true, but the trends are there and worth noting.

More important than deciding whether your workout should be completed with or without a pre-workout meal for the purposes of burning fat during the workout, is how your pre-workout meal affects your overall performance and energy *during* the workout. If you are a fireball on an empty stomach at 5 A.M. and eating anything upsets your stomach during the workout, then by all means, train on an empty stomach! If, however, you'd rather take a nap, your energy is low, and you can hear the rumbling of your empty stomach over what's playing in your headphones, then the caloric burn of your workout will be less than if you had a settled stomach and energy for your workout. Plan to eat or drink something containing a blend of carbohydrates and protein and your early morning workouts may come alive. If they do, then you have truly accomplished something worth noting.

Post-Workout Meal Paramount for Success!

You already know that you grow when you are not lifting. Therefore, when you're working out with weights and you're actually working toward increases in strength (either repetitions or load lifted) with each workout, you are getting stronger. Muscle is being damaged and remodeled stronger with each workout. An effective nutritional strategy to promote recovery from exercise is vital for all athletes. Remodeling muscle tissue to enhance its power-generating capacity and growth is a vital part of the adaptation to training. How do we best accomplish this goal? What post-workout dietary strategies are necessary and why is it important to facilitate maximum tissue remodeling with fluid, electrolyte (sodium, potassium), amino acid and glycogen replenishment?

First, Replace Fluid Lost in Sweat

Exercise increases body temperature. The body's response to this increase in temperature is sweating. As water accumulates on the outside of the skin, we become more efficient at cooling as the outside air runs across the wet surface of the skin. Our first focus both during and after a workout then is to replace lost sweat.

What is sweat and what are we replacing? Sweat is primarily composed of water, sodium, chloride and potassium. How much fluid do we lose when we sweat? The range is broad but a well-published and acceptable guideline is to replace 8 ounces of water for every 20 minutes of exercise. Exercising in extreme heat and humidity, however, can multiply this requirement by a factor of 6. It is now accepted that we must not only replace what we lose in sweat, but we should consume 50 percent more fluids than we lose in sweat to effectively re-hydrate the body. If we lose 8 ounces of fluid during a 20-minute workout, we should consume 12 ounces of fluid as a replacement. As I discussed earlier with respect to water and hydration, even a small decrease in hydration status can cause a significant decrease in performance.

As I have indicated above, sweat is not only water but it is composed of electrolytes. Research does provide credible validity to the notion that it is not enough to simply replace water for sweat loss. That is not an even trade. You must replace lost electrolytes as well. Therefore, it is important to recognize the need for sodium and potassium (a good guideline is 10 percent of daily values for each electrolyte: 240 mg for sodium and 350 mg for potassium for each hour of work) in a well-formulated post-workout meal.

Next, Replace Lost Glycogen with Mixed Carbohydrates

Carbohydrate is the primary energy source used during prolonged high intensity exercise, but the body's carbohydrate stores (glycogen) are rather small. While the average 154-pound man has 135,000 calories stored as fat, the same man only stores 1500 to 2400 calories in the form of glycogen. Glycogen stores can be depleted with high intensity training and it is our goal to replenish lost glycogen between workouts. If we do not, we are sure to experience a decrease in exercise performance at subsequent workouts.

Many factors should be considered when deciding how many grams of carbohydrates are necessary to replenish lost glycogen and the variability among athletes. Essentially, the amount and timing of carbohydrate replenishment are the two critical factors for ensuring proper glycogen replacement. Current research indicates there is a "window of opportunity" to ensure glycogen is replaced fully and rapidly.

The "window" is approximately 30 minutes to 2 hours post workout. Therefore, it is very important that we consume a meal or beverage that contains mostly simple carbohydrates quickly after a workout if we are to reestablish optimal glycogen levels for our next workout. Failure to take advantage of this window of opportunity may result in glycogen being replaced at a much slower and inefficient rate for continuous, high intensity training.

At least 35 to 100 grams of simple or a combination of simple (glucose, dextrose, sucrose) and complex carbohydrates (maltodextrin, starches) should be consumed during the window of opportunity. I do not recommend fructose-only based drinks because of their lower glycemic index (a measure of the sugar's speed at raising blood glucose). I must also stress that not all glycogen is replaced in the 2-hour window. Therefore, you should not skimp on carbohydrates during your remaining meals on a workout day. With the exception of your post-workout meal, however, I do not recommend you vary from the Lifestyle food selection guides I have previously addressed. Consuming simple carbohydrates is great as a post workout meal but consistently consuming simple carbohydrates outside of your window of opportunity may be detrimental for fat loss. The "window" is the one time you can consume simple sugars and not feel one bit guilty about it.

Glycogen is replaced primarily in the first few hours after intense exercise if we provide our body with carbohydrate, however, full glycogen replenishment may not occur for 24 hours or slightly longer. Failure to incorporate carbohydrates in enough quantity and at the right time post workout may significantly hinder your next workout.

Finally, Make Sure Your Post-Workout Meal Contains Protein

Yes, carbohydrates are primarily responsible for replacing lost glycogen after an intense workout, but protein (which provides amino acids) can assist with glycogen replenishment and is also crucial for delivering amino acids to muscles during the remodeling process. The addition of protein to carbohydrate post-workout meals can increase the rate of glycogen synthesis above that which is observed after consuming carbohydrate alone. Researchers believe this is a result of increased insulin secretion.

I have said repeatedly throughout my Lifestyle that we tear down muscle when we work out and we rebuild it stronger when we rest. This is an adaptive process and while researchers continue to remain baffled about how the body does this exactly, we do know that synthesis of new proteins is a response to resistance training. Why is it important to include protein (amino acids) with your post-workout meal? Not only does the addition of protein assist with muscle glycogen replenishment, but also protein in your post-workout meal provides amino acids at a time when muscles are literally starving for these building blocks to remodel your muscle. Yes, glycogen replenishment is a primary goal after a workout, but synthesis of new proteins should be seen as being of equal or even greater importance.

Insulin Is Anabolic

The consumption of carbohydrates causes a non-diabetic person to release insulin from the pancreas. Stay with me now, I will not go too deep here. Insulin is an anabolic hormone, meaning that it activates cellular processes that facilitate new protein synthesis and the transport of amino acids into cells. Cool! Insulin's ability to facilitate increased protein synthesis depends upon the presence of high levels of amino acids in blood at the same time insulin is present in high concentrations. After a workout, we are trying to elicit an insulin response (by consuming simple carbohydrates) and thereby increase our overall anabolic state. When our blood has high concentrations of amino acids necessary to make new proteins and insulin is also present, our chances of increasing our anabolic activity is significantly increased!

In conclusion, I want to stress that I have simplified this highly complex area to a level that is pragmatic and effective. After each workout, drink at least eight ounces of fluid within the first hour and eight more ounces for every 20 minutes of exercise. Consume 35 to 100 grams of carbohydrate, 17 to 50 grams of protein, and sodium and potassium at approximately no greater than 10 percent of our daily requirement (240 mg of sodium and 350mg for potassium for each hour worked). This regimen will replace lost fluids, maximize glycogen replenishment and facilitate optimal protein synthesis. Damaged muscle tissue will be repaired, rebuilding it stronger and larger than before.

Delayed Onset Muscle Soreness (DOMS)

Delayed onset muscle soreness (DOMS) is induced primarily by unaccustomed exercise volume, intensity or both, and from overstretching a particular muscle group. What actually causes DOMS is not known definitively. DOMS normally occurs 24 to 72 hours after the exercise session.

We do know that DOMS is exercise-induced muscle damage followed by an inflammation-induced increase in fluid in the muscle. If your legs feel "thicker" after a hard squat workout, it is not your imagination–they probably are thicker from the temporary fluid retention in the damaged muscle. Many avid resistance trainers almost live for the swelling that occurs during the hours DOMS is active in a particular muscle group. I would be lying if I did not include myself in this mix. For us, moderate DOMS is almost like feeling the workout pump all over again.

Eccentric muscle actions induce the most DOMS. DOMS is associated with a reduction in muscle strength. DOMS is not an indicator of forward progress, however, I've never met a person with substantial muscle mass who still doesn't get sore after most workouts and who hasn't experienced DOMS after most workouts in their resistance training career. This may seem contradictory, however it is not. Never forget the rule: The only measure of true forward movement is progression through improved performance and strength over time. Nowhere in that definition did I say that DOMS must be present a certain percentage of the time. DOMS is not a goal of a workout, however, I know many resistance trainers who grow addicted to that pain and swelling.

I am Still Sore. Should I Train?

If a muscle group is still sore, that does not mean you *cannot* work it; rather it is a signal that the inflammation and damage caused by the last workout is not fully repaired. If you are sore (uncomfortable), then do not work that body part again until that level of soreness is manageable. This perception will vary between individuals. You don't have to wait until a muscle is totally pain-free before you train it again, however, it's pretty common for a sore muscle *not* to function as well as it does when it's fully recovered.

If there's any doubt whether you have DOMS or an undesirable injury, always side with caution and do not train. If the pain persists longer than about 72 hours after the workout or is not measurably better by 72 hours, seek medical attention and determine the root of the pain.

To Squat or Not to Squat–There is No Question

Because you are a transformationist and not an Olympic lifter, the squat is likely the hardest resistance training exercise you will ever encounter. It requires balance, coordination and creates a level of whole-body stress most are unaccustomed to. Now that I have terrified some of you, I must now tell you why–unless injured and completely unable–*you must learn to squat*!

The squat is so monumentally beneficial to you as a resistance trainer that not squatting is like refusing to invest in America Online (AOL) in 1995. The dividends that squatting provides are unmatched by any other leg or upper body exercise. I'm sure it's been said more than a million times by avid resistance trainers that if they had to choose only one exercise, they'd choose the squat for its whole-body training benefits. Can millions of squatters be wrong? No, this is one time the masses are right.

If you are a man, you need to squat to avoid looking like a cartoon character. Most muscular cartoon characters have an enormous upper body and the legs of Popeye's true love Olive Oil. Since most men have small legs because they distribute their fat around the waistline, it's imperative you grow those legs so you can look good not only in a short-sleeve polo shirt, but also in a pair of shorts.

Ladies, can you imagine a backside that is flat or just kind of sags there? Can you relate to the hips that are just too wide for comfort? Are your thighs currently bigger than those of that special guy in your life? If any of these statements are true, then you can put away your toys (foo-foo exercises) and use squats to correct all of these disconcerting areas. It is true. This is one case where one size fits all and it truly helps correct every problem I mentioned and more.

My coaching clients now quote me constantly as saying that the definition of a good leg workout is any leg workout that incorporates properly performed squats. Today I still believe this to be true. As an aside, it may be interesting for you to know that while massive variety is necessary for upper body training, the same doesn't hold true for lower body. Why this is so we do not really know, but the lower body will continue to respond to similar workouts more so than the upper body. You know what this means? You can squat nearly every leg workout! Aren't you excited? I know I am, because once you learn to squat you won't have to wonder if your leg workouts are accomplishing all of those lower body goals you have. You can trust that if you are performing the squat properly you are absolutely creating the lower body of your dreams.

By now I hope I have earned your trust, but if not, once you use all the Lifestyle strategies for nutrition and exercise, I am sure you will see progress. I say this because if you are not squatting, then you must trust me to teach you how to get started. There is no excuse, other than injury or immobility, for not squatting. Your legs, hips and buttocks are not large because they are thickly muscled. You may believe they are, but they are not. If your legs, hips and buttocks are large, it is because the little muscle you have is covered with a thick layer of adipose (fat). As discussed in this chapter, squatting with loads while incorporating periodization principles for variation will not make your legs bigger if you are losing weight. In fact, the result will be the opposite if you squat consistently.

You may also believe that your leg training must involve lots of additional isolation butt, inner thigh and outer thigh work to really hit all the problem areas. This thinking is erroneous and will cause you hours of wasted time in the gym if you do not jettison it immediately. I am not saying that if you choose to do additional abduction, adduction and hip extension work that you are wrong for doing so. All I am saying is if you choose to do three to four exercises in place of the squat, you are wasting your time by comparison. If, however, you absolutely cannot squat, then other exercises will be necessary to help you shape your legs, hips and buttocks.

With squatting, your legs will become more shapely, sexy, firm and toned. Your hips will narrow, your buttocks will lift and become firmer, and you will enjoy the caloric burn benefits. Squatting is a core exercise that burns more calories per minute than any other resistance training exercise you will perform.

See "*Strength Training Anatomy*" by Delavier for an accurate depiction of what a proper squat looks like and how it is performed as a start. I highly recommend, however, that you employ the services of a certified personal trainer who regularly squats as a part of his or her own training program to teach you how. You do not have to marry this trainer and get into a $1,000 package, but it is well worth it to pay for a few sessions to at least learn the form of the squat.

Can We Change Muscle Shape?

The shape of your muscle is predetermined. The length and shape of the muscle belly (what you commonly think of as your skeletal muscles) vs. the length and attachment of the tendons will determine the shape. So why do all the different exercises for muscle groups? Many muscles have more than one attachment. Muscles usually play more than one functional role as well. A few examples are:

- Hamstrings: extend hip, extend trunk/pelvis, flex knee, rotate tibia, rotate the hip.
- Gluteals: posterior rotation of the pelvis, extend the hip, externally rotate the thigh, assist in knee extension in its connection to the iliotibial band.

In the biceps, you have a long and short head. Changing the arm position changes the emphasis on muscle bellies. If you take into account that the bicep group flexes the elbow, flexes the shoulder, supinates the forearm (turns the palm upward), and much more, it is clear that the position of the arm makes a big difference in what part of the bicep gets worked. Position will affect what part of the muscle gets used as well as the total number of motor units firing.

When you think of the arm (continuing this example), you have more than just the biceps in front. You have the coracobrachialis, brachioradialis, and brachialis (see "*Strength Training Anatomy*" for details). Take any one of these and work them correctly, and the appearance of the arm will change though the shape of the muscle is the same. The brachialis will add some width as well as height to the front of the arm. You can apply the same concepts to the back, calves, chest, thighs, and so on. There are so many different attachments of muscles that the exercise position can affect emphasis.

By adding overall muscle mass to your frame, your shape will take on a new form that will always be more appealing than what you had before. Do not get caught up in isolation, single-joint shaping movements (concentration curls, cable crossovers, etc.). You can do them but do not rely solely on them thinking you are really going to create a new shape by doing so. The multi-joint basic movements will ultimately be your best time served in the gym.

Maxims to Help Guarantee Your Resistance Training Success

- Train between 60 and 100 percent of your target RM via a periodized plan.

- Keep your repetition ranges within the guidelines I have set forth in this chapter.

- Only three to six working sets are needed for each exercise.

- No more than two to four exercises per muscle group are necessary in any training session.

- Add some variety to your routine every one to four weeks (it really can vary this much) to confuse and stimulate new muscle growth.

- Strive to progress the load (weight x repetitions) with each workout cycle.

- Training longer than one hour is not advantageous and may be counterproductive.

- Consistently trying to move the weight slowly during the concentric (lifting) phase of the movement is counterproductive for growth. Superslow training should be reserved for the injured and elderly.

- Train larger muscle groups before smaller muscle groups when training them on the same day (chest or back before shoulders, triceps or biceps).

- Basic multi-joint exercises (bench press, squat, dead lift) are best for overall mass (which is what you want - including women) when compared to single-joint isolation movements (pec deck, leg extension and and Good Mornings).

- If you are going to resistance train and perform aerobics consecutively, then resistance train FIRST! If you do aerobic activity first and immediately go into your resistance-training workout, the resistance training workout will suffer.

- Beginning trainers may be able to train five to six hours per week (1 hour per day x 5 or 6 days per week) due to lighter loads moved and less overall damage inflicted upon muscle. Beginners may be able to train each body part 2 to 3 times per week.

- Advanced resistance trainers make fantastic progress training a total of no more than 4 or 5 hours per week. Advanced trainers should train each body part no more than twice per week and many recover best training each body part once every 5 to 7 days. All lifters only advance when they train with progression as the foremost measure of success.

- On a given day, if you must make a choice whether to work out with weights or do aerobic activity, choose weights! By stimulating new muscle growth, you create an annuity of reserve energy expenditure even when you are not working out.

Remember, every pound of muscle you add burns 30 to 50 calories per day when you are doing nothing! When you do aerobics, you only burn calories while you're training and for a very brief time after you are through training aerobic activity (see the *Aerobic Lifestyle Prescription* chapter, which follows).

Exercise List and Selection

Before I offer you a list of dozens of exercises most commonly executed to build the best physiques in the world, I must revisit our old enemy: Mr. EITHER/OR.

What would you do if you injured a deltoid (shoulder) or pectoralis (chest) muscle? You have heard and told yourself for 3, 5, 8, 10 or 15 years that you must bench press to have a big, strong chest. Now, you have an inflamed shoulder joint that will not allow you to train the barbell bench press without excruciating pain. What do you do? Many will simply take time off completely. Many beginners with less than a year's experience may become so disheartened that they quit lifting all together, never to return. Hey, if I cannot bench press, then I cannot have a big chest. If I cannot have a big, strong chest, then why lift? After all, the bench press is what everyone is measured by when they first start lifting. EITHER I can bench press, OR I cannot lift.

For the lifter who injured her shoulder and cannot bench press, the EITHER/OR mindset can prevent her from moving forward or even continuing. Why can't our bench press person choose other lifts to support the pectoral muscles? What about the incline barbell bench? God knows that if there is an area lacking on most bodybuilders, it is the upper chest (an area taking up about one third of the total chest area). What about dumbbell flyes, incline dumbbell flyes, pec deck, cable cross over, seated chest press, incline seated chest press, decline bench press, decline dumbbell press and others? Aren't these all alternative chest exercises? Sure they are. But no one asks you how much you can pec deck, do they?

I lived through a shoulder injury that lasted for two years. I could not flat barbell bench at all without pain. Luckily for me, my EITHER/OR mind was saying EITHER you figure out a way to keep training chest, OR you suffer severe psychological trauma for losing the only area of your body that grows easily–and for me it was my chest. I used to say that it was the only body part I was *given* and even then, the term "given" must be taken loosely. I still worked darn hard to build the chest I have. The point is, you must break out of the EITHER/OR syndrome if it is keeping you from moving forward.

What follows is a list of exercises most commonly selected by beginners to advanced resistance trainers.

The (M) or (S)

The (M) or (S) after each exercise indicates whether the exercise is multi-joint or single-joint. If you have a choice or are in doubt, choose a multi-joint (M) exercise over a single-joint (S) exercise for a given body part.

The "•••••" Mark

I have added a "•••••" after some exercises to help you find the most effective exercises for a given body part. In the resistance training workout examples on the pages that follow, you may find that you don't have access to the equipment to properly complete a given exercise, or you may find, on a given day, that others are hogging all the equipment you need to perform the exercise intended. If my workout suggestion calls for "barbell bench press" but you don't have the equipment to perform that exercise, you can find another chest exercise that is multi-joint (M) and that has the "•••••" associated with it. In doing so, you can feel confident that you have chosen an exercise that is likely as effective. If you have a choice or are in doubt, incorporate more exercises that have the "•••••" associated with them rather than not. If I have not added the "•••••" to an exercise name, then I have no reason to believe it is any better or worse than any other exercise that doesn't have the "•••••" mark. In other words, those exercises that have the "•••••" will provide the best bang for your buck, If there is no "•••••" mark, feel free to use those exercises to break boredom, add variety and overall balance to your program.

For a detailed description of the exercises listed and specific muscles worked for each, please refer to the "*Strength Training Anatomy*" book by Delavier.

Abdominal Exercises

Abs Crunch Machine - (S)

Any Abs Wheel with Handles - (S)

Crunches Alternating Bicycle - (S)

Crunches Alternating to Each Knee - (S)

Crunches Feet on Floor/Hands Reaching Front - (S)

Crunches w/Feet Flat On Floor - (S)

Crunches w/Feet Up and Crossed - (S)

Crunches w/Feet Up on Bench - (S)

Crunches w/Legs Extended in Leg Lift - (S)

Dumbbell Side Bends - (S)

Hanging Leg Lifts - (S)

Lying Leg Lifts - (S)

Back Exercises

Barbell Bent Over Rows - (M) •••••
Barbell Deadlifts - (M) •••••
Barbell Stiff Leg Deadlifts - (M)
Dumbbell Bent Over Rows 2 Hands - (M) •••••
Dumbbell Deadlifts - (M)
Dumbbell One Arm Rows - (M) •••••
Dumbbell Stiff Leg Deadlifts - (M)
Kelso Bar Deadlift - (M) •••••
Kelso Bar Stiff Leg Deadlifts - (M)
Lying Barbell Pullovers - (M)
Lying Dumbbell Pullovers - (M)
Palms Facing Each Other Pull Downs
    Front - (M) •••••
Partial Deadlifts - (M)

Pronated Close Grip Chin Ups Front - (M) •••••
Pronated Close Grip Chin Ups Rear - (M) •••••
Pronated Wide Grip Chin Ups Front - (M) •••••
Pronated Wide Grip Chin Ups Rear - (M) •••••
Pronated Wide Grip Pull Downs Front - (M) •••••
Pronated Wide Grip Pull Downs Rear - (M) •••••
Seated Cable Rows - (M) •••••
Seated Machine Pullovers - (M)
Supinated Close Grip Chin Ups Front - (M) •••••
Supinated Close Grip Pull Downs Front - (M) •••••
T-Bar Rows - (M) •••••
Good Mornings - (S)
Hyperextensions - (S)
Stiff Arm Pull Downs - (S)

Bicep Exercises

Barbell Preacher Curl - (S) •••••
Barbell Standing Curl - (S) •••••
Barbell Wrist Curls - (S)
Cable High Pulley Curls - (S)
Cable One Arm Curl - (S)
Cable Preacher Curls - (S)
Cable Two Arm Curl - (S)
Dumbbell Concentration Curls - (S)
Dumbbell Hammer Curls - (S) •••••

Dumbbell Preacher Curl - (S)
Dumbbell Reverse Curls - (S)
Dumbbell Seated Curl - (S) •••••
Dumbbell Standing Curl - (S) •••••
E-Z Curl Preacher Curl - (S) •••••
E-Z Curl Standing Curl - (S) •••••
Lying Supinated Cable Curls to Forehead - (S)
Spider Curls - (S)

Calf Exercises

Donkey Calf Raises - (S)
Leg Press Calf Pushes - (S)
One Arm Dumbbell Calf Raises - (S)

Seated Calf Raises - (S)
Standing Calf Raises - (S)

Chest Exercises

Barbell Bench Press - (M) •••••
Barbell Close-grip Bench Press - (M)
Barbell Decline Bench Press - (M) •••••
Barbell Incline Bench Press - (M) •••••
Dips - (M)
Dumbbell Bench Press - (M) •••••
Dumbbell Decline Bench Press - (M) •••••
Dumbbell Decline Flyes - (M) •••••
Dumbbell Flyes - (M) •••••

Dumbbell Incline Bench Press - (M) •••••
Dumbbell Incline Flyes - (M) •••••
Dumbbell Lying Pull Overs - (M)
Vertical Chest Press - (M)
Vertical Incline Chest Press - (M)
Barbell Pull Overs - (S)
Cable Crossovers - (S)
Dumbbell Pull Overs - (S)
Pec Deck - (S)

Forearm Exercises

Barbell Reverse Curls - (S)
Barbell Wrist Curls - (S)

Dumbbell Wrist Curls - (S)
Reverse EZ Curl Preachers - (S)

Hamstring Exercises

Stiff Leg Dead Lifts - (M)
Lying Leg Curls - (S)

Seated Leg Curls - (S)
Standing Leg Curls - (S)

Shoulder Exercises

Barbell Seated Back Press - (M) •••••
Barbell Seated Front Press - (M) •••••
Barbell Standing Back Press - (M) •••••
Barbell Standing Front Press - (M) •••••
Barbell Upright Rows - (M)
Dumbbell Seated Back Press - (M) •••••
Dumbbell Seated Front Press - (M) •••••
Dumbbell Standing Back Press - (M) •••••

Dumbbell Standing Front Press - (M) •••••
Log Clean & Press - (M)
Standing Log Press - (M)
Standing Push Press - (M)
Dumbbell Front Raises - (S)
Dumbbell Rear Lateral Raises - (S)
Dumbbell Side Lateral Raises - (S)

Thigh Exercises

Barbell Free Standing Back Squat - (M) •••••
Barbell Free Standing Front Squat - (M) •••••
Barbell on Shoulder Lunges - (M)
Dumbbell Squats - (M)
Dumbbells in Hands Lunges - (M)
Hack Squat - (M)
Leg Press - (M) •••••
Partial Squats - (M)
Sissy Squats - (M)
Smith Machine Back Squat - (M) •••••

Smith Machine Front Squat - (M) •••••
Squat Press - (M)
Zercher Squats - (M)
Cable Abductions - Outer Thigh - (S)
Cable Adductions - Inner Thigh - (S)
Cable Back Kicks - (S)
Hip Abduction - (S)
Hip Adduction - (S)
Leg Extensions - (S)
Machine Hip Extensions - (S)

Trapezius Exercises

Barbell Shrugs - (S)
Dumbbell Shrugs - (S)
Kelso Bar Shrugs - (S)

Machine Shrugs - (S)
V-Bar Shrugs - (S)

Tricep Exercises

Close Grip Bench Press - (M) •••••
Barbell Lying Triceps Extension - (S)
Barbell Seated Triceps Extension - (S)
Dumbbell Bent over Kick Backs - (S)
Dumbbell Lying Triceps Extension 1 Hand - (S)
Dumbbell Seated Triceps Extension 1 Hand - (S)
Dumbbell Seated Triceps Extension 2 Hands - (S)

E-Z Curl Lying Triceps Extension - (S)
E-Z Curl Seated Triceps Extension - (S)
Over Head Rope Kickouts by Pulley - (S)
Pronated Triceps Push Down Rope - (S)
Pronated Triceps Push Down Straight Bar - (S)
Pronated Triceps Push Down V-Bar - (S)
Supinated Triceps Push Down Straight Bar - (S)

Eight Steps to Creating a Massively Effective Periodization Program

1. An effective periodized workout will focus primarily on multi-joint exercises for the large muscle groups, giving them priority over single-joint exercises.

   You must ask: "When available, have I chosen at least one multi-joint exercise for each major muscle group?"

   Yes? Continue developing your program.
   No? Choose at least one multi-joint exercise for all large muscle groups.

2. An effective periodized workout will balance exercise number across muscle groups when overall fitness and muscularity is the goal. If you choose to perform two exercises per muscle group, you should generally choose two exercises for every muscle group, not just the large muscle groups.

   There are exceptions to this rule. An important note before listing the exceptions is one of priority and time management. During a workout, it is important you place the most emphasis on multi-joint exercises for the large muscle groups. Smaller muscle groups and accessory muscles will be recruited when you do. As busy Lifestylers, I realize you will want to maximize your 30- to 60-minute workout. If your particular workout calls for two exercises for each body part, you'll quickly find that your workout could easily run over on time. Therefore, for practical, real-world purposes, I will let you in on the common exceptions to the rule of exercise number balance.

   Exceptions may include the abdominal muscles, trapezius, shoulders, forearms, hamstrings and calves. Abdominal muscles are trained often with higher repetitions in many varied schemes and may not fit the traditional "set" structure as other muscles do. Shoulders are frequently overtrained and are used as an accessory for many large muscle group movements. Lateral and rear shoulder work is imperative, however, as well as rotator cuff balance (see www.leannesslifestyle.com for a document title "*The Shoulder, Basic Structure and Why it Hurts*" by Rick Kring, PT). Shoulder work can often many times be lessened compared to other large muscle groups overall if specific attention is given to the middle and rear deltoid. For time's sake, forearm work is many times omitted if bicep work is sufficient. Hamstrings fatigue rapidly and can respond with fewer sets than other large muscle groups. Calf work is important for stability and whole-body balance, however, unless your goal is to create diamond-shaped competition calves, many find they do quite well with fewer overall exercises. Keep in mind: These are only guidelines, not absolutes. Your mileage may vary.

   You must ask, "Am I completing the same number of exercises for chest, back, thigh, bicep and triceps?"

   Yes? Continue developing your program
   No? Balance the exercise number for the chest, back, thigh, bicep and triceps.

3. With periodization for the transformationist, it is easiest to think of a mesocycle as a 4-week period of training. It is also easy to think of a macrocycle as a 12-week period. When creating your Lifestyle resistance training program by implementing periodization principles, your first 4-week mesocycle of each 12-week macrocycle should include repetitions for each exercise ranging between 9 and 15. Further, your total volume should be moderate-high to high (see definition of "Volume" in this chapter). Remember, a fundamental principle of periodization and appropriate resistance training is that one can train either intensely or with high volume, but not both for any extended period of time. A rep range of 9 to 15 ensures the intensity is relatively low; therefore, it is important the volume is relatively high.

You must ask: "In the first mesocycle of my program, are most of my repetitions performed in the 9- to 15-repetition range? Next, is my total volume, as defined in this chapter, moderate-high to high?"

Yes? Continue developing your program.
No? Select loads that will cause near-momentary muscular failure for any exercise on the last set in the repetition range of 9 to 15. If volume is too high, reduce exercise number per muscle group or total sets per exercise. If volume is too low, increase total exercise number per muscle group or total sets per exercise.

4. During the second mesocycle, a shift toward increased intensity (repetition ranges between 6 to 8) coupled with less volume is warranted to further progression and add variability to your plan.

You must ask: "During my second Mesocycle (weeks 5 to 8) am I choosing loads that cause me to work very hard, many times at or near momentary muscular failure, in the 6- to 8-repetition range? Is my total volume moderate during this phase?"

Yes? Continue developing your program.
No? Choose loads that will cause you to struggle greatly to complete 6 to 8 repetitions for each exercise. If volume is too low, either add more exercises for each body part or add more sets for each exercise. If volume is too high, either reduce the number of exercises for each body part or reduce the number of sets for each exercise.

5. During the third and final mesocycle (weeks 9 to 12), a further shift toward increased intensity (repetition ranges between 5 to 7) coupled with less volume is warranted to further progression and add variability to your plan. During the final mesocycle, one of the weeks may include a period of higher intensity (5 to 7 reps for each exercise) coupled with high volume.

You must ask: "During my third and final Mesocycle (weeks 9 to 12), am I choosing loads that cause me to work very hard, many times at or near momentary muscular failure in the 5- to 7-repetition range? Is my volume slightly less overall than in weeks 5 to 8? Have I included one week where my volume is high?"

Yes? Continue developing your program.

No? Choose loads that will cause you to struggle greatly to complete 5 to 7 repetitions for each exercise. If volume is too low, either add more exercises for each body part or add more sets for each exercise. If volume is too high, either reduce the number of exercises for each body part or reduce the number of sets for each exercise.

6. Periodization and fundamental resistance training principles dictate that between 3 and 6 sets be completed for each exercise.

   You must ask: "For the exercises selected, am I completing a minimum of 3 sets and no more than 6 sets?"

   Yes? Continue developing your program.
   No? Adjust the set number accordingly for each exercise.

7. Through periodization, we allow the repetition prescribed (within 1) to dictate the load used. If a particular exercise calls for 11 repetitions, one should choose a load that, on the final set, will be a struggle but will allow a full repetition to be completed for at least 10 of the 11 prescribed. If a load is chosen that is too heavy, thus not allowing the 10th or 11th repetition to be completed, the load should be reduced on the next workout to allow for the successful completion of all the repetitions prescribed. Continuing with the 11-repetition example, if the last repetition of the last set for that exercise is completed with little perceived effort, the load should be adjusted higher on the next workout to ensure proper stimulation of the targeted muscle fibers. Many adjustments may be necessary to the load during the first several weeks for inexperienced trainers. This is quite common until one gets a feel of what they are capable.

   You must ask: "Am I allowing the prescribed repetitions to dictate the load I am choosing? Am I successfully completing the repetitions prescribed within one and am I approaching or reaching *momentary muscular failure on the last repetition of the last set for each exercise?*"

   Yes? Continue developing your program.
   No? Adjust the load to successfully complete the prescribed number of repetitions without choosing too light a load.

8. Through periodization, it is well established that changing the tempo periodically can facilitate less or more demand upon the working muscles. Many individuals never change their tempo, but instead commonly follow a 1-0-X-0 sequence. Never changing tempo is sub-optimal. Therefore, it is intelligent in designing your program to include a tempo change with each macrocycle at a minimum (every 12 weeks).

You must ask: "Is my tempo for this 12-week macrocycle different from the last macrocycle?"

Yes? Enjoy your workout!
No? It is time to change your tempo!

When you apply the principles presented in this chapter to your resistance training program, you are well on your way to creating the lean, muscular body of your dreams. It is important you recognize the tremendous variables you can control to keep forward progress in motion. This chapter was written primarily for the beginner to intermediate resistance trainer and I respectfully acknowledge the plethora of advanced training options that have also proven successful to thousands of resistance trainers worldwide.

Summary

Your investment of time in learning to develop and execute a proper Lifestyle resistance training workout is monumentally worth it. Resistance training can deliver what no other exercise can: a better shape, improved strength and an annuity of calories burned each day.

Hypertrophy is the goal we all must have to reshape our bodies. Some authors will use terms such as toning and shaping and avoid words such as hypertrophy and muscle growth. But neither toning nor shaping will occur without some hypertrophy of skeletal muscle.

Periodization provides the fundamental principles upon which a Lifestyle resistance workout is based. The concept of periodization is simply centered around the idea of planned variation within a cycle of training. With periodization, you no longer exercise by the seat of your parents. Through periodization you can accomplish the most important goal of resistance training: progression. Progression is truly the single greatest indicator of your eventual success at building muscle and reshaping your body.

When you invest a little of your time to understanding the terminology of resistance training, you will be able to create your own workouts or understand whether any workout is likely to deliver you the results you are looking for.

Take Action and Feel Great!

1. Visit www.leannesslifestyle.com for free examples of Lifestyle resistance training workouts for beginners to advanced athletes.

2. If you are new to resistance training, I strongly recommend you make an appointment with a certified personal trainer who regularly engages in vigorous resistance training. Take a package of at least six sessions to learn the fundamentals of form with hands-on help. This, too, is money very well spent for the beginner!

3. After visiting the website, print out a workout you would like to use and take it with you. Ask the personal trainer to show you how to perform the exercises. Once you know proper form, you can use the Workout Generator to build an unlimited number of workouts on your own. Always remember the rules in this chapter and follow the eight-steps for creating a quality periodization workout.

4. Do not fall into the trap of avoiding the most difficult and most effective, multi-joint exercises (squats, lunges, bench press, incline bench press, deadlifts, bent over rows etc.). The load you use can be quite light until form is good, however, the sooner you "Eat That Frog" the better. "*Eat That Frog*" is a book by Brian Tracy that deals with attacking the single, most important task of the day head on and I highly recommend it to everyone. Do not avoid learning the complex multi-joint exercises. To do so will only prolong your lack of progress and reshaping necessary to achieve your goals.

Aerobic Lifestyle Prescription

"Endurance training produces similar gains in aerobic capacity in healthy people throughout the age range of 20 to 70 years, and this adaptation is independent of age, sex, and initial fitness level."

Aerobic training is any training that primarily uses oxygen as a fuel source. Most of you reading this have your own thoughts of what aerobic activity normally involves. Aerobic activities typically associated with improving aerobic performance and fat loss include:

- Walking briskly
- Jogging
- Swimming
- Rowing
- Stepping
- Cycling
- High- and low-impact step aerobics
- Spinning
- Body pump

For some of you, aerobic training is the step class you signed up for last fall. For others it is a ride on a stationary bike, a run through your neighborhood, the treadmill, Stair Master or rowing machine that serves your needs. Nearly all of you have a perception of what benefits you are receiving by doing aerobics, but many of you are likely wrong about how aerobic activity can benefit your goal of fat loss or improve health.

The Real Benefits of Aerobic Training

There are benefits for everyone who engages in regular aerobic-powered exercise. To receive the benefits listed below, the minimal sessions needed are two to three per week at a minimum of 20 minutes each. Training more will not necessarily improve any of the benefits over training the recommended two to three days per week, however, increased duration or frequency may benefit those who seek superfitness and ultimate leanness. I'll cover those specifics in more detail later. Here are some true physical benefits of aerobic activity, which are well anchored in science:

- Cellular structures called mitochondria (the primary source of adenosine triphosphate- ATP) grow in number and size in muscles used for aerobic activity.

- Within muscles used to generate the aerobic movement, there is an increased ability to mobilize and use fat for energy. This is likely a result of an improved and increased blood flow within the muscles. This additional efficiency and use of fats for fuel is thought to spare carbohydrates, a real benefit for resistance trainers or endurance athletes needing the explosive power at the end or any part of the workout or race.

- Type I muscle fibers (generally thought of as the endurance muscle fibers, which don't hypertrophy enough to get someone recognized as a resistance trainer) will grow in size. This can allow the endurance athlete to perform better.

- The heart grows in size and weight.

- Heart rate during rest and submaximal exercise decreases with regular aerobic activity. It is common for a resting heart rate to drop 10 to 20 beats per minute with regular aerobic activity.

- The ability of the heart to pump more blood with each stroke is improved. Because the heart can pump more blood with each stroke, it can also deliver more oxygen per stroke (carried in the blood) to muscles and other tissues.

- The ability of active muscles to "extract" oxygen from the blood is improved, thus allowing for an increased ability of the muscle to fuel movement and exertion.

- A reduction in both systolic (top number) and diastolic (bottom number) blood pressures is noticed among regular users of proper aerobic strategies.

- Having an efficient aerobic system might allow for faster recovery between resistance training workouts because of increased blood flow within muscles and the ability for waste to be cleared faster and more efficiently. This improved recovery ability may allow more work to be performed during training, which may lead to greater strength improvements during resistance training.

- Improving your aerobic capacity may improve the ability for hormones and nutrients to get to the muscles during both exercise and recovery.

The Fat Burning Zone and Morning Aerobics

There are two erroneous beliefs held by many who engage in a quest for a great physique transformation. They are interconnected and are:

1. You must exercise in some "fat burning zone" to see significant fat loss.
2. You must perform aerobic activity first thing in the morning on an empty stomach.

The "fat burning zone" is some mysterious place where you allegedly have all your fat loss worries taken away. Many of you have seen a chart on the treadmill or your aerobics teacher talked about this fat burning zone as though it were the end-all be-all to your physique transformation. Actually, the fat burning zone is more like an urban legend that just will not die, rather than a truly functional parameter to which you should give more than a moment's thought to. At the worst it is a lie, at best it is only misleading. Performing your aerobic training first thing in the morning on an empty stomach is also suggested for the same reason: because you burn more fat during the exercise session when you train on an empty stomach.

Today, as you sit in your chair reading this book, you are in the fat burning zone. It is true! At rest and during low-intensity, long-duration events, the greatest contribution to overall metabolism comes from fat. Why aren't you thin and superfit? Why isn't cellulite disappearing from your body like nobody's business? It is because the total calories burned at rest and during the low-intensity activities you typically engage in are not enough to offset your consumption of calories. Even though fat wins as the major contributor of "sitting still" and low-intensity activities, there aren't enough calories being burned during these times to offset the calories being consumed.

It is true that aerobic training on an empty stomach, first thing in the morning, can burn 300 to 600 percent more fat *during* the activity over training with ample carbohydrates before training. This sounds good on advertising hyperbole but what substrate is used for fuel during exercise nets little contribution to overall *weight loss*. Your goal is not to ensure that fat is burned as a primary fuel source during exercise. Your goal is weight loss while preserving or adding lean body mass. This is achieved by creating a reasonable relative caloric deficit. The more consistently you engage in vigorous exercise activity, the more calories you will burn during and after that activity. This has a far greater reach than whether you burned more fat than carbohydrates during the workout.

Exercising at a higher level of intensity offers many benefits over low-intensity training. The harder the exercise, the greater the total number of calories expended per minute. Although the contribution of fat to fuel activity goes down as the intensity of the activity goes up, your total caloric expenditure increases. Vigorous aerobic activity increases your aerobic capacity and conditions your heart. Aerobic exercise conducted with purpose and effort pushes you, making you fitter and more conditioned–and a more conditioned person is a more efficient fat burner during her non-exercising hours.

Ignore the fat burning zone and concern yourself with caloric expenditure–it is what really matters.

After all I have said thus far on the subject, I must state that I agree it is best to train first thing in the morning if these conditions exist:

1. You have plenty of vigor and energy to perform the activity.
2. You are a morning person or have a tendency to skip workouts if put off until later in the day.
3. Performing morning workouts invigorates you for the rest of the day.

I further believe it is wise to train on an empty stomach if you feel ill by consuming food or drink before morning exercise.

Since the total caloric contribution during and after the workout is what matters, you must take into consideration your schedule, the type of person you are (i.e., morning, afternoon or evening), how not training in the morning affects your exercise compliance and consistency, and whether you have the energy to create a significant caloric burn during the workout. If you would rather have bamboo chutes be jammed under your fingernails than train at 5 A.M. and at that time your energy level is the equivalent of a sedated Jabba the Hut, then you are probably not doing yourself much good by training at that hour. You might do better once you have had your cup of coffee and some food at a minimum.

At the end of the day, at the end of the week and when all the chips have been cashed in, the bottom line is calories. We can't rule out all the personal differences and qualities attributed to training at various times of the day when our energy is highest and we are running at peak. For weight-loss/fat-loss purposes, there is no metabolic advantage to striving for a fat burning zone or first-thing aerobics on an empty stomach.

Myths and Realities of Aerobic Training

Myth: Aerobics are the key to fat loss.
Reality: Aerobics help burn additional calories.

Myth: Doing low intensity aerobics is better for fat loss than high intensity aerobics.
Reality: Low intensity aerobics burns fewer calories.

Myth: Aerobics burn hundreds of calories after you are through with the exercise.
Reality: Traditional aerobic work will burn an insignificant number of calories after you stop.

Myth: The pros do 45 to 60 minutes of aerobics twice per day 5 to 7 days per week. That must be their secret to fat loss and staying lean.
Reality: The pros use a good nutrition regimen, resistance training and many times illegal drugs to get or stay lean and many pros don't know any more about exercise physiology than you. Oh yes, it's true. Some do 45 to 60 minutes of aerobic activity, twice per day, 5 to 7 days per week only in the final 4 to 8 weeks of show preparation.

Myth: I will likely burn 600 calories per hour doing aerobic activity. I know because the monitor on the treadmill I use tells me so.
Reality: Women will burn 240 to 480 calories per hour and men will burn 420 to 600 calories per hour. The average person reading the latest Danielle Steele novel while walking on the treadmill is likely to burn 150 to 200 calories per hour of aerobic activity.

Myth: Research says that if I do aerobics first thing in the morning, I will burn 300 to 600 per-cent more fat than if I do my aerobics after eating or later in the day. That means I will lose 300 percent more fat by doing aerobics in the morning before eating.

Reality: Research does indicate there is a fat mobilization benefit to completing aerobics in the morning on an empty stomach, however, it is not the extra fat being burned that matters. What matters are the total calories burned vs. the calories consumed per day. In the end, it is all about calorie balance and creating a reasonable relative caloric deficit without invoking a primordial, hormonal roadblock to fat loss.

What Is Effective Aerobic Activity?

For the purposes of a body transformation, aerobic exercise involves continuous, uninterrupted movement causing a heart rate between 60 and 90 percent of your predicted maximum for at least 20 minutes.

Determining Your Target Heart Rate

Two formulas are frequently used to determine the predicted maximum heart rate and target heart rate for training:

- Karvonen method
- Percentage of Maximal Heart Rate method

Karvonen Method
Formula:
Age-predicted maximum heart rate (APMHR) = 220 - age
Heart rate reserve (HRR) = APMHR - resting heart rate (RHR)
Target heart rate (THR) = (HRR x exercise intensity) + RHR

Example:
A 35-year-old woman with a RHR of 65 beats per minute (BPM) wants to perform aerobic activity at 70 percent of her APMHR.

APMHR = 220 - 35 = 185 BPM
RHR = 65 BPM
HRR = 185 - 65 = 120 BPM

Target Heart Rate = (120 x 0.70 = 84) + 65 = 149 BPM

In this example, the 35-year-old woman would target a heart rate of 149 beats per minute. This can easily be figured by doing a 10-second pulse check. To determine a 10-second pulse check, simply divide the THR by 6 (149/6 = 25). In a 10-second pulse check, this woman should strive for 25 beats.

Percentage of Maximal Heart Rate Method

Formula:

Age-predicted maximum heart rate (APMHR) = 220 - age

Target heart rate (THR) = (APMHR x exercise intensity)

Example:

The same 35-year-old woman wants to perform aerobic activity at 70 percent of her APMHR.

APMHR = 220 - 35 = 185 BPM

THR = 185 x 0.70 = 129 BPM

In this example, the 35-year-old woman would target a heart rate of 129 beats per minute. Again, to determine whether she is on target during training, she can do a 10-second pulse check. Using this formula, she would strive for a target 10-second heart rate of 22 beats.

Since most of you don't have access to laboratory equipment that can measure your functional capacity and true aerobic power, you'll have to use the above formulas as a guide only. Those who have considerable experience may lean toward the Karvonen method. Beginners may want to veer toward the Predicted Maximal Heart Rate method. Others may want to choose a number somewhere in the middle. As long as your physician clears you for take off, either formula can be used with similar results for traditional aerobic training.

A typical aerobic workout used by tens of thousands of fitness enthusiasts across the country is 30 to 45 minutes in duration at 70 percent of predicted maximum. This 70 percent of predicted maximum level is also commonly called "conversational exercise." Conversational exercise can be effective for improving aerobic capacity and it is "conversational" because it is not so strenuous that it limits your ability to talk during it.

The Prescription

Research indicates that men and women differ little in their aerobic training needs. However, in my practical experience in dealing with hundreds of clients hands-on, there indeed is a greater need of aerobic training for women over men. It probably has something to do with the fact that evolution has given women the role of carrying a fetus until full term and she needs about nine months' worth of stored fat to ensure she doesn't die during pregnancy. This is not to say that men are cleared from performing aerobic activity, however, most men do not have issues with stubborn fat on the lower extremities and most women do. Women need to do sufficient aerobic activity to mobilize fat stores, especially lower-extremity fat stores. What is sufficient will vary among women, but in most cases, it will be more aerobic activity than necessary for most men. The typical man's fat stores are distributed primarily around the waistline. While this type of fat distribution is more dangerous and increases his risk of cardiovascular disease and stroke, it is also more easily mobilized and reduced. Let's not forget, too, that a man does not have the same genetic coding to keep a nine-month supply of stored fat on hand at all times.

This is a good time to look once again at the *Energy Balance* chapter. In that chapter I list specific formulas for determining the total exercise time you'll need to perform to accomplish a specific weight loss each week. I want to emphasize a few points, however, to ensure you have a clear understanding of the aerobic requirements before you.

- Any activity where oxygen is sufficient to fuel the movement is aerobic. So yes, walking, leisurely biking, canoeing and hiking all burn calories and are all aerobic activities. Your focus should be on performing more aerobic activity at the intensity outlined in this chapter (heart-rate focused) and the *Energy Balance* chapter with respect to the Ratings of Perceived Exertion Scale.

- Your total duration each week is determined first by following the formula in the *Energy Balance* chapter. How many total minutes you should engage in vigorous exercise is individual, however, guidelines for a start are provided in that chapter. The duration of each session should be somewhat balanced and spread out throughout the week.

- The frequency of sessions will be determined on an individual basis but must follow the rules as set forth in the *Energy Balance* chapter and the *Resistance Training for Everyone* chapters. Resistance training is performed before aerobic training if they are performed successively. This is not to be confused with performing aerobic activity in the early morning, then later in the day (at least 2 to 4 hours later), performing resistance training. This is common among successful Lifestylers and acceptable.

  It is quite common for women engaged in Lifestyle weight loss to perform 30 to 45 minutes of aerobic training at a frequency of 4 to 6 sessions per week. It is true as well that many fitness competitors who achieve single-digit body fats will perform 90 to 120 minutes of aerobic activity 6 or 7 days a week in the last 4 to 8 weeks before a show. They do not otherwise perform aerobic training at this frequency and duration, however. The good news is that once maintenance is achieved, it is quite common to reduce aerobic training to one-half your weight-loss frequency and duration, or even less.

  Men also benefit in the fat loss department from engaging in aerobic training. It is quite common for men to aerobically train at a frequency of 3 to 5 sessions per week, with each session lasting 20 to 30 minutes. Again, once in maintenance, many men can reduce aerobic training to almost nothing or 1 to 2 sessions per week.

- With regard to total vigorous exercise minutes, your aerobic training must not completely eclipse your resistance training minutes. Many women and some men perform 90 to 100 percent of their vigorous exercise as aerobic activity and are sorely disappointed at what they look like when the weight is gone. I recommend you spend a maximum of 70 percent of your vigorous exercise in aerobic training. This means a minimum of 30 percent of your total, vigorous exercise time should be engaged in resistance training. If your total, vigorous exercise time for a week is 300 minutes then at least 90 (300 x 0.30) of those minutes should be engaged in resistance training with the remaining 210 (300 x 0.70) in vigorous aerobic activity. The closer you can split your training equally between resistance training and aerobic training, the better.

Aerobic Training and Muscle Loss

There is a very good reason that you feel like giving the typical, competitive marathon athlete a sandwich: Many are waif-like and have little muscle mass. There's also a very good reason the fastest man in a world-class 100-meter sprint will have substantial muscle mass, especially in his legs. As I discussed in the *Resistance Training for Everyone* chapter, the body specifically adapts to imposed demands (SAID). I also mentioned that muscle is very energy dependent and the body will not deposit one gram of protein to new muscle if it is not coaxed heavily into doing so. The marathon runner does not need substantial muscle mass. Her body has specifically adapted to the imposed demands by becoming an aerobic machine. It's more efficient for the body to be light and for type I muscle fibers (endurance fibers) to be engaged and enhanced through specific, adaptive processes that are unimportant for this discussion. The sprinter, not unlike you as a transformationist, requires strong, explosive muscles to power the start and propel the runner a short distance as fast as possible. Stay with me. I will show you where all of this is leading next.

If you want to look like a marathon runner, you ought to eat, train and perform like a marathon runner. This would involve hours and hours each week engaged in aerobic training with little emphasis on resistance training. Conversely, if you want to look like a fitness competitor or Calvin Klein underwear model or simply want to drop some body fat while becoming buff, then you cannot train like a marathon athlete. You must follow my recommendations for total vigorous exercise time as outlined in the *Energy Balance* Chapter and also pay strict attention to the percentage of your exercise as aerobic training. In essence, the closer you can split your resistance training time and aerobic training time the better.

I will no longer apply an arbitrary cap to how much total time is allowed with respect to aerobic training to minimize or prevent muscle loss. In years past I used to say that if you were performing aerobic training longer than 90 or so minutes per week, you were likely to lose substantial muscle mass. In working with hundreds of clients hands-on, taking into consideration the plethora of aerobic training methods those clients engaged in, the multitude of starting body fats, wide variety of experiences in resistance training, and individual differences in ability to add and preserve muscle through genetics, nutrition, supplementation, lifestyle and stress management, I now simply say this:

> *The body will become what you most engage in. If you spend your vigorous exercise minutes almost solely engaged in aerobic training, then you will become more like those who train that way (marathon runner). If you spend your vigorous exercise minutes almost solely engaged in resistance training, then you will become more like those who train that way (bodybuilder). If you achieve near balance between aerobic training and resistance training as they contribute to total, vigorous exercise time, then you are most likely to become more like those who train that way (fitness competitor, Calvin Klein underwear model, and natural, entry level bodybuilder).*

Regardless of whom you choose to become, as dictated by the contribution of your aerobic and resistance training, you can shorten the total aerobic training time by incorporating a method of training known as "interval training."

Interval Training for the Advanced Transformationist

So far, I have discussed the standard aerobic workout. Another form of training involves aerobic training that is not constant or continuous. Instead, the training intensity is varied throughout the session and the session is normally shorter than traditional aerobic workouts. This type of training is commonly referred to as interval training.

The low intensity aerobic workout (that supposedly burns more fat than high intensity aerobics) is not important for fat loss; rather, it is the total caloric expenditure. However, while the caloric expenditure *during* the workout is what matters most, there is a potential caloric-burn benefit beyond the training session for those willing to engage in interval training.

The contribution of excess caloric burn above your resting metabolic rate after a workout is referred to in scientific jargon as excess post-exercise oxygen consumption (EPOC). The EPOC of traditional aerobic activity (conversational aerobics) is quite low. There is little residual caloric burn post-workout after a typical cardio session. However, while resistance training typically yields between 5 and 9 calories per minute (including rest periods between sets) *during* the workout, you may burn well over 100 additional calories in the 24-hour period *following* an intense resistance training session. Thus, you not only benefit from the calories burned during a resistance training workout, but from the additional calories expended through repair and remodeling of damaged muscle tissue in the 24-hour period following as well.

Interval training also provides a residual benefit after the workout is complete (similar to resistance training) and may therefore significantly affect weight loss over traditional aerobic activity. Research has shown that when two groups of individuals were trained with either traditional aerobic activity or interval training, the group who trained using interval training lost 9 times the fat but only spent 27 percent of the time doing the exercise (60 minutes per week vs. 3.75 hours per week). Talk about time management!

Three Interval Training Cautions

First, those who were inactive before reading this book should not use interval training. Because it will take your heart rate to near maximum repeatedly, it is not advised that anyone with any pre-existing cardiovascular disorders attempt this program without first consulting with their physician. Again, everyone should seek a complete checkup by his or her physician before beginning the Lifestyle.

Second, interval training is far more intense than the type of aerobics you may be used to. Because of this additional stress on the body, there is a chance cortisol (a stress hormone responsible for tearing down muscle if secreted in excess) may elevate if rest between sessions is insufficient.

Third, interval training is likely to cause a strength or net muscle loss if done more often than two to three times per week, likely due to a change in stress on muscle fiber types and the body's overall stress response.

The Interval Solution to Boring Aerobics

Interval training commonly lasts from 5 to 20 minutes and involves periods of high intensity alternated with periods of low intensity. The Lifestyle Interval Solution will involve a total of 20 minutes of work. Here is where the traditional aerobic workout and interval training differ:

- Traditional: Continuous low to moderate intensity for 20 to 60 minutes.
- Interval: Alternating low to very high intensity for no more than 20 minutes.

- Traditional: What you burn is what you get.
- Interval: What you burn is usually higher than traditional plus you get increased metabolism in the hour or so following the interval training.

- Traditional: You can carry on a conversation during the full session and even read a magazine sometimes without focusing on your exercise.
- Interval: You will have no desire to speak when you are training near maximum effort.

The 8-week program that follows describes how you can incorporate the Lifestyle Interval Solution into your training regimen with safety and effectiveness. Because the effort you are going to put forth during the high intensity portion will be quick, there is no accurate way (commercially) to measure your heart rate. Therefore, the high intensity portion of the interval training should be some increased effort that is subjectively measured (Ratings of Perceived Exertion from the *Energy Balance* chapter at a 19 or 20), which takes you to a level that matches the percentage of effort I have listed in the program.

The low intensity periods of the Leanness Lifestyle Interval Solution are slightly lower than what you are typically used to for traditional aerobics (60 percent of maximum heart rate vs. 70 percent).

Always Begin the Interval Training Workout with 3 Minutes of Steady Work At 60 Percent of Maximum Heart Rate

---

HI - High Intensity   LI - Low Intensity

Week 1: Three high intensity levels at 70% maximum heart rate (MHR) for 0:30 with 5:30 of low intensity levels between

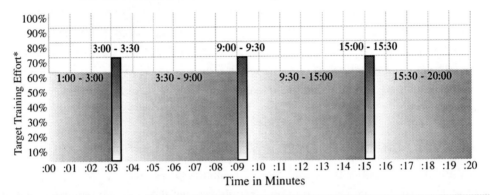

* REMEMBER!
Your Maximum Heart Rate Is 220 minus your age!
Percentages shown on charts (Target Training Effort %)
are a percentage of your maximum effort.

An 8-Week Interval Training Program Defined

I will describe the chart for week one in detail. All charts that follow are simply a variation in length of interval and intensity level.

Week One

During Week One, you start in minutes 1 through 3 with an intensity level at a measurable 60 percent of your maximum heart rate (MHR). This is low intensity. At precisely the 3-minute mark, you increase your effort by 10 percent for 30 seconds until you reach the 3 minute and 30 second mark. At that time, you will drop back to an effort that equaled 60 percent of your maximum heart rate at the start of the session. Will your heart rate drop all the way back down to 60 percent of your MHR? Probably not. Nevertheless, your effort during the low periods should correspond to the guidelines provided. You must become subjectively good at determining what level of exertion is necessary to reach the target efforts and heart rate percentages or you use equipment that helps you measure these guidelines through RPMs or other new, digital means. Investing in a heart rate monitor at some point might also be a wise idea.

Week 2: Four high intensity levels at 70% MHR for 0:30 with 4:30 of low intensity levels between

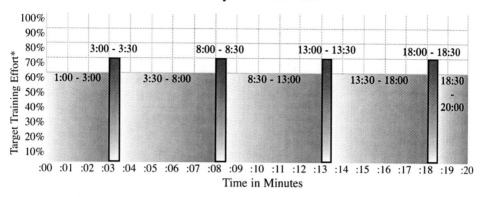

Week 3: Five high intensity levels at 75% MHR for 0:30 with 3:30 of low intensity levels between

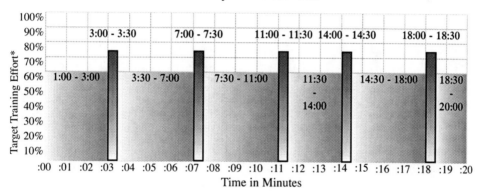

Week 4: Three high intensity levels at 80% MHR for 0:30 with 5:30 of low intensity levels between

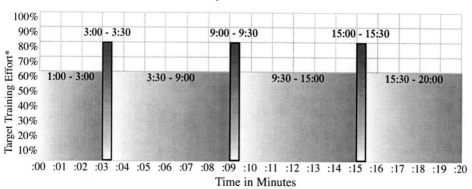

Week 5: Five high intensity levels at 80% MHR for 0:30
with 3:30 of low intensity levels between

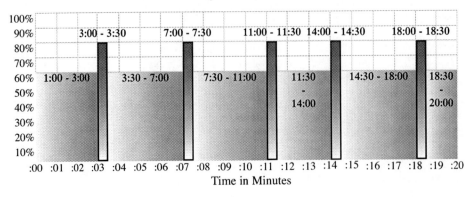

Week 6: Five high intensity levels at 90% MHR for 0:30
with 3:30 of low intensity levels between

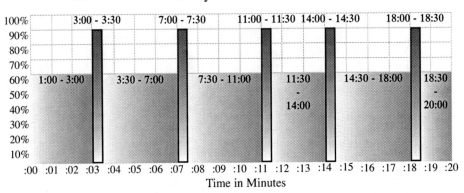

Week 7: Four high intensity levels at 80% MHR for 0:60
with 3:00 of low intensity levels between

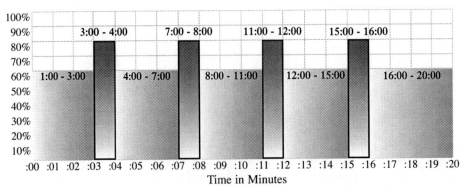

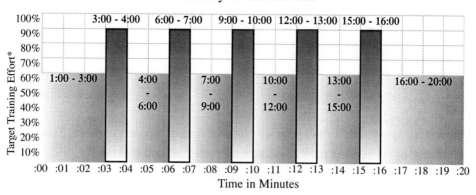

Week 8: Five high intensity levels at 90% MHR for 0:60 with 2:00 of low intensity levels between

Week Eight

By week 8 (with consistent two or three times per week aerobic activity plus resistance training), you will have developed a substantial increase in performance adaptation. Notice that not only are your high intensity periods longer, but they are more frequent than week one. Also, notice that the high intensity periods (which are 1 minute long now) require a 90 percent effort. What is 90 percent? Since trying to measure your heart rate during this 1 minute of borderline agony will be next to impossible, you have to gauge your effort based on your max. At a 90 percent effort, you are only training 10 percent less than an-all out effort. Therefore, 90 percent is not an all-out effort but it is not much less than all out. In other words, these one-minute high intensity sessions will be a real bear, but you must trust that each interval session is far more effective than traditional aerobics. By comparison, this type of aerobic activity *will allow you to cut your training time in half or even by two-thirds.*

To conclude this chapter, I want to state that considerable arguments exist over whether it is best to train aerobics on the same day as resistance training or on alternate days. Some argue that it is best to resistance train first (I totally agree) and then–on the same day–do aerobics immediately after. The idea with this exercise model is you will be able to take an entire day off with no exercise stress on the body during off days. Others state that training aerobically on resistance training off days is better because it allows you to focus on each training day more intensely. For some, the additional 20 minutes of aerobic exercise added onto a 45- to 60-minute resistance-training workout is beyond the time allotment they have available. Still, for others who are training intensely with weights for 30 minutes, the additional 20 minutes of aerobic activity on the same day might fit nicely into the schedule.

My recommendation at this point, until further research clearly tells me which way is best, is to always do aerobics training after resistance training if they are completed successively on the same day. With regard to aerobic training on the same day as resistance training or not, no clear strategy has been proven better than another. In many cases, especially for women, some aerobic activity will have to be completed on the same day as resistance training or there won't be enough days in the week to get it all in.

Summary

Aerobic activity is any activity that primarily uses oxygen as an energy source. There are a number of real benefits of performing aerobic activity for both men and women.

Contrary to popular belief, whether you train in the "fat burning zone" or on an empty stomach first thing in the morning bears little impact on your success or failure with the Lifestyle. Whether you burn more fat than carbohydrates during a workout is truly unimportant. What is important, however, is how many calories you burn during the workout and any residual burn in the hours afterwards.

While I recommend you train within a proper target heart zone, it is not so you are burning more fat during the workout. It is used as a gauge to determine if you are working hard enough during your aerobic workout, nothing more.

During weight loss, most women will require more aerobic and total activity than men. Through hormonal balance and a host of other complex yet integrated factors, women are genetically programmed to store about nine months' worth of fat to carry a fetus to full term. Her body isn't about to give up what it sees as "essential" too easily. Please do not confuse this essential fat to carry a fetus with your current total adipose if you are obese. One does not have to be obese to carry a fetus. Therefore, your strides to become very fit are well within your control and are not up to some genetic, evolutionary trait over which you have no control. The greatest output for total exercise time, however, will likely come when the body senses you are encroaching upon the "safe zone" for survival. Survival, for a woman, includes carrying a fetus to full term. The "protect the fetus" rules do not apply to men. Therefore, they will likely do far better with less total activity at all stages. This may not be fair but it doesn't negate the reality of what is true.

It is important that you do not focus so much of your time on aerobic activity that it totally eclipses your resistance training minutes. Cardio kings and queens never get the total body look they seek once the fat is gone, if they neglected resistance training along the way. Try and work toward an equal split between aerobic and resistance activity.

While the total number of aerobic minutes will vary for each individual one sure-fire way to reduce total aerobic time is through a training technique called interval training. With interval training, you ratchet up the intensity of your aerobic session in periodic bursts, eventually nearing an all-out effort. Each session is no longer than about 20 minutes, however, the total caloric value of the workout and post-exercise burn can really blow traditional aerobic activity away.

Take Action and Feel Great!

1. Take a look at the *Energy Balance* chapter and make sure you know how many total minutes of vigorous exercise you need to complete each week.

2. Be sure and review the Ratings of Perceived Exertion as defined in the *Energy Balance* chapter. If using this scale to determine the proper intensity of your aerobic activity, you should train between a 13 and 17 quite consistently unless you are training with interval aerobic activity. In that case, follow the guidelines for perceived effort as outlined in this chapter.

3. Begin an aerobic program today or within a few days at the latest.

4. Make sure your aerobic program is within your target zone or as prescribed by your physician.

Contest or After Photo Preparedness

"I think I feel so good from knowing I found what would work long-term, that the work of the Lifestyle is nothing compared to the work of doubting what I am doing."

As you approach the last few weeks of your transformation many questions will come to mind about whether you are a competitive bodybuilding contestant or transformationist (CT). "Should I cut back on sodium? If so, when?" "Should I eat less carbs for a while and then carb up?" "Do I need to take a water pill or cut back on water intake for my show or photos?" "What supplements should I take to really lean out before my shoot or contest?" These questions and many more are on the minds of those about to shoot their after, intermediate or "work-in-progress" photos as well as those who plan to compete in bodybuilding, fitness or swimsuit competitions.

Four Weeks Left Until the Show or After Photos

I hope that things have been progressing well up to this point. Your transformation will have significant impact on the judges or camera if you have dropped significant weight and body fat. There is no question whatsoever that your best asset on stage or in front of the lens will be a superbly low body fat. Even if you are thickly muscled, not having a body fat low enough to be noticed will kill any chances of placing well or having After photos you will be proud to show everyone. To compete you have to be ripped! This means that if you are a man competing in bodybuilding, you must attain a body fat less than six percent. If a woman, your body fat must be less than 10 percent. If you are competing in fitness or swimsuit, your body fat must be less than 12 percent.

Those who have attended any amateur bodybuilding show have likely heard or uttered these words after viewing an out-of-shape competitor, "Man, he's really holding a lot of water." Or, "She seems to have a lot of loose skin." The reality of it, usually, is although someone may be holding subcutaneous water (water under the skin) or have loose skin from being morbidly obese in years past, they are far more likely to simply be overfat on contest day.

A body fat that is too high is the number one enemy of the competitive bodybuilder, fitness competitor, or transformationist on After photo day.

First it is important I state that you need to make sure you are comparing apples to apples in your Before and After photos. For example, if you took your before photos fully clothed or the only Before photos of you are fully clothed, then no matter how lean you are, you need to take some After photos also fully clothed. This is not to say that you shouldn't take after photos in a swimsuit or flattering outfit exposing more flesh, but you must take those fully clothed shots if your Before photos were fully clothed. *No matter how far you have come, you are in much better shape than when you started.* All progress is wonderful progress! Unless you are very lean, however, shooting After photos with a lot of flesh showing when your Before photos were not taken the same way will not do your transformation the justice it deserves.

Very simply, here are the minimum photos you should take depending on what you started with:

Before	After
Swimsuit	Swimsuit
Fully clothed	Fully clothed (nice fitting or custom fit clothes)

When you are shooting After photos with a lot of flesh exposed, a low body fat will project the most significant impact to you and others as well. The very best Before and After photos are those that show the greatest relative change in body fat. I consider a significant change–one the camera will see–as at least 25 percent of your current body fat percentage. For example, if you started your transformation at 40 percent body fat, the camera will pick up a very noticeable change when your body fat has dropped to 30 percent (25 percent less than the forty you started with).

If your starting body fat was 20 percent, the camera will likely pick up a significant change with a nice impact when you have dropped your body fat to about 15 percent (25 percent less than the 20 you started with).

Far too often, I see the disappointed looks on the faces of transformers who drop from 25 percent body fat to 21 because they expected a world of difference. It is also common for those going through a transformation to take photos each week. This is usually a waste of time.

> *If you want to take photos to document your in-progress changes,*
> *I recommend taking them with each ten percent drop in total body*
> *weight or 25 percent drop in total body fat.*

For example, if you started your transformation at 245 pounds, I would recommend your first "in-progress" photos when you have dropped about 24 or 25 pounds. If you started your transformation at 150 pounds and 25 percent body fat, I would recommend your first in-progress photos when you've dropped to either 135 pounds or reached about 18 percent body fat (i.e., 10 percent drop in weight or a 25 percent drop in body fat). With each successive 10 percent drop in body weight or 25 percent drop in body fat I believe you will be pleased with what the camera lens reveals to you.

Even when your body fat reaches much lower levels, the same rules apply. Even then, the change is no less amazing. For example, if your starting body fat was 10 percent and you are currently 7.5 percent, the change will be quite noticeable and substantial to the camera lens. The change from 7.5 percent to 5.6 percent (i.e., another 25 percent drop in body fat) is also significant and will show well for the camera.

It is next to impossible to say precisely what your body fat must be to do well in a physique transformation challenge. So much of the impact depends on where you started, the categories being judged and what the judges are looking for on a given day. No matter how far you've come or how far you have to go, any positive changes for the better have brought you a step closer or fully to your dream. That is perhaps the most important take-home message in this entire chapter. Since most of you want to not only look and feel great, but compete well or have a great set of Before and After photos, I will now teach you what will be required to make it happen beginning with four weeks left before your event.

With four weeks left, it is imperative that you have done your homework. At this point you should have no more than three to five percent body fat left to drop or three to five percent of your present body weight left to lose. If you are currently 18 percent body fat and you are hoping to drop to less than 12 in the last four weeks, I'd say you either needed more time or you wasted too much precious time before now. You do not have enough time to properly drop six percent body fat with only 4 weeks remaining. Miracle powders, pills, potions, lotions and other concoctions are not the answer to your prayers at this point. If your goal was to be 150 pounds and you are 175, I'd suggest you either didn't have enough time and overestimated what could be accomplished or you wasted time early on in your transformation and now don't have enough time to reach your goal on time.

Remember, at four weeks out you should be no further than one or two percent body fat or three to five percent body weight from your goal.

Professional Photographers and Poses

Some entering a transformation challenge will want to engage the services of a professional photographer. I cannot recommend strongly enough that you choose a photographer with experience at shooting individuals as you want to be represented. If you have the best wild-game photographer in the country living in your town, he might not be worth a darn at shooting human physiques. Ask for examples of their work. If all they show you are high school graduation shots and weddings, you need to find another photographer. You can visit www.leannesslifestyle.com for suggestions on professional photographers who have a good reputation for shooting transformation physiques. There is no guarantee one will live close to you, but you can be guaranteed of finding a photographer who knows what he or she is doing.

One of the most stressful tasks for the transformationist is finding poses that will be appealing to the lens. Regardless of whether you choose a professional photographer or opt to go self-serve, it is imperative that you review hundreds of other Before and After photos on the Internet and in magazines. Print and clip as many pleasing photos as possible. Bring those poses with you to the photographer and tell her what you like about this or that photo. Snap a few dozen shots off with a digital camera a week or two before your photo shoot and see how you look. Sure, you will feel utterly ridiculous, but it sure beats waiting until the real day to make a first pass at posing. The more research you do, the better prepared and comfortable you will feel on shoot day. Knowing more closely what you want will help the professional or the friend you begged to take the best After photos possible.

Dietary Supplements

Psychologically, in your last four weeks, you will likely feel increased angst and stress as you realize how close you are to "the date." Let's face it, you may feel stressed to the max! You're worried about how you're going to look on stage or in your After photos. If there is ever a time when you are going to foolishly try something new, this is it–no question. The urge to try or do anything to help the fat loss/muscle preservation system is extremely high! Knowing this, I want to make sure you use supplements with at least a modicum of chance of getting a positive result.

I'll briefly cover the basics of supplementation as well as supplemental strategies to help maximize the final fat-loss phase once you have achieved a relatively low body fat by diligently following the Lifestyle. Just as I don't believe you should rely on the last four weeks to strip off excessive body fat you could or should have stripped before this point, hoping dietary supplements will make up for overeating and under-exercising is foolishness.

Supplementation basics indicate just about all of us will need some form of supplemental protein (e.g., bars, shakes), a multivitamin/mineral, essential fatty acids (e.g., flax and fish oils) and 500-1000 mg of extra daily calcium for women. Other than these three basic supplements, there is little need to fill your counter with esoteric fringe products until your body fat is lowered to the following levels:

Men	Women
10 - 12 percent	15 - 18 percent

Once your body fat has reached these low levels, you will have to focus even more on whether the weight you are losing is muscle or fat. Dietary supplements can assist with stripping off the last little bit of body fat while preserving muscle. If you have been diligently following the Lifestyle, there is little concern for excessive muscle loss until your body fat reaches the levels described above for men and women. The leaner you get, the greater the chance the weight you lose will be muscle.

What a shame it is when bodybuilders and transformationists work hard for years to develop a certain amount of fat-free mass, only to lose an excessive amount of it as they drop their body fats to ultra-low levels, as seen in magazines and bodybuilding shows.

Best Supplements in the Sprint to the Finish

When sprinting to the finish, there are a few supplements that should be considered in addition to supplemental protein, a quality multivitamin/mineral and essential fatty acid supplements.

Ephedrine/Caffeine (EC)

Ephedrine and caffeine (EC) are central nervous system stimulants. Taken together they are powerful thermogenic (heat-producing) agents. An increase in body temperature, heart rate and blood pressure has been noted in studies, however, in otherwise healthy individuals, not enough to cause alarm. EC are anorectic compounds (a substance that diminishes the appetite). When taken together, they have also exhibited the ability to preserve lean mass while following a hypocaloric diet (less calories than maintenance). Taking the proper EC can reduce your appetite and assist in preserving muscle while losing weight. It is believed that 80 percent or more of the positive weight-loss benefits attributed to EC combinations are related to its anorectic qualities.

EC products can not only be effective during the final four weeks of weight loss in preparation for a show or After photos, but also during the first few weeks of following the Lifestyle too. During this period, hunger signals will be increased and intense. Lifestylers commonly report reduced hunger after the first two to three weeks, however, and the choice is personal whether an EC product is used at all or continued past the first few weeks. If you do decide to use an EC product, it is imperative that you properly log your calories each day so you do not under-eat. In the *Energy Balance* chapter, I provided very specific formulas for giving you a caloric guideline to start with. Until you learn your body, metabolism and have mastered the principles within the Lifestyle, a word of caution is warranted for those of you who decide to use an EC product. *Do not miss meals!* If your plan calls for four, five or six meals per day, make sure you get in those meals and do not under eat. Unnecessary undereating can indeed slow metabolism undesirably.

It is now well established in research and bodybuilding circles that 20 mg of ephedrine plus 200 mg of caffeine taken three times per day can benefit the person wanting to shed extra fat. Empirically, however, lower doses of ephedrine and caffeine have resulted in positive weight-loss outcomes as well.

Will adding aspirin help the mix? Few studies have indicated it would and, even then, aspirin was only beneficial for obese women taking ephedrine and caffeine but not for non-obese women. Aspirin can prolong the effects of ephedrine and, thus, possibly reduce the amount of ephedrine necessary to cause the effect desired. Some people are allergic to aspirin, however, and for others aspirin upsets the stomach. If you decide to add aspirin, I recommend no more than a baby aspirin per dose.

Because a proper EC combination is likely to help reduce hunger cravings and aid in the preservation of lean mass when body fat levels are dipping to ultra low levels, I do recommend this combination for bodybuilders and transformationists during the final four weeks of preparation as long as there are no pre-existing medical conditions or prescription medications being taken. While taking any EC product is optional at any stage, many Lifestylers do favorably report more controllable hunger pains and increased energy when taking a properly formulated EC product during the first few weeks of their transformation as well.

Read all labels carefully and consult with your physician if you are being treated for anything or are taking any other over-the-counter or prescription medicines. I also do not recommend EC if you are capable of becoming pregnant.

Dose: Do not exceed 60 mg of ephedrine and 600 mg of caffeine (includes all forms of caffeine) per day. Divide into two or three doses (i.e., 20 mg ephedrine and 200 mg caffeine or less per dose).

Phosphatidyl Serine

Many researchers now use the testosterone:cortisol (T:C) ratio as a marker of anabolic vs. catabolic activity. Increased stress can acutely increase cortisol, a stress hormone, and thus reduce the T:C ratio. This is undesirable. During the final four weeks there is no doubt that stress will be elevated. You are very likely going to be nervous about either standing on stage or taking those After photos.

As you probably know, testosterone is the king of anabolic hormones. When present in excess, cortisol is at least a knight with respect to catabolic (tearing down) hormones. A high T:C ratio (greater testosterone than cortisol in serum) is associated with an anabolic status and a low ratio is associated with a catabolic status. Let me put it another way: you want to be more anabolic than catabolic and the last four weeks of preparation can create just the opposite effect on the T:C ratio.

Phosphatidyl serine may help provide the higher T:C ratio by limiting cortisol production during high-stress and intense training.

Dose: 300 - 800 mg per day in divided doses.

CLA

Conjugated linoleic acid (CLA) is the common name of a group of fatty acids found in the past in dairy products and meat. Even though the name is similar to the omega-6 fat linoleic acid, CLA is not an essential fatty acid. Over the last 50 years, changes in livestock development practices have largely removed naturally-occurring CLA from our diets. In several recent studies, however, CLA has received considerable attention due to its apparent metabolic properties in animals and humans. The effects include reduced body fat content, reduced abdominal obesity, improved serum lipid profiles, decreased aortic lipid deposition, and enhanced glucose metabolism. CLA may also assist with adding fat-free mass in the form of skeletal muscle when used in conjunction with a solid resistance-training program.

CLA is not a miracle supplement, but it is climbing the weight-loss ladder as something with potential and as a supplement worth adding to your regimen during the final four weeks. Will it make up for living on chocolate and pizza? No. Will it make up for missing workouts? No. Might it help just that little bit more? Maybe.

Dose: 2 - 4 g per day. The Tonalin® raw material is commonly used in studies.

Glutamine

Glutamine is considered a conditionally essential amino acid. It is conditionally essential because most of the time our bodies will manufacture adequate quantities and we consume it from food. Under periods of heavy physical stress, post-surgery or with a compromised immune system, glutamine stores may be reduced to sub-optimal levels. Low serum (a part of blood) glutamine levels are correlated with the overtraining syndrome and muscle glutamine levels are correlated with an anabolic or catabolic state. Consuming glutamine in a postworkout formula has been shown to increase glycogen formation and storage. Recall from the *Nutrients* chapter that glycogen is the body's storage form of carbohydrate. Restoring glycogen after a workout is paramount to continuously training at an intense level.

Skeletal muscle is the primary sink for glutamine in the body. The immune system is a heavy user of glutamine on a regular basis. If various organs and tissue need more glutamine than is being provided through synthesis and consumption, skeletal muscle will donate glutamine. This may be considered a catabolic condition and is not beneficial for preserving or adding muscle tissue. Your body cannot distinguish psychological stress from physical stress. During your final four weeks you will be training intensely with more perceived mental stress as well. This may tap your immune system harder than usual and glutamine needs may be increased. Therefore, during your final four weeks, I recommend supplemental glutamine daily.

Dose: 2 - 6 g three times per day.

Creatine Monohydrate

With well over 250 studies to date, creatine monohydrate is still the king of muscle performance supplements. Supplementers of creatine monohydrate routinely report increased muscular performance and increases in strength. Adenosine triphosphate (ATP) is the energy currency for muscular contractions. ATP is in limited supply at any given time. With only a few ounces of ATP in the body, it must constantly be recycled and synthesized. Creatine assists with these important processes for maintaining maximal muscular energy production. Through increased muscular performance, it is believed creatine monohydrate may increase muscle hypertrophy.

Most who have supplemented with creatine will report some weight gain. Until recently it was believed all of the weight gain was a result of increased intramuscular (inside the muscle cell) water, however, some recent research suggests water may not account for all of the weight gain observed. An increase in skeletal muscle after several weeks of use may also result when combined with an intelligent resistance training program. Some do not gain weight with creatine supplementation.

With only four weeks left, I do not recommend you begin supplementation with creatine monohydrate because the overwhelming majority of users do report an increase in scale weight, presumably from increased intramuscular water retention. This increased scale weight can really play with your perspective of weight loss progress since you might be losing body fat but not losing scale weight in the first few weeks of creatine supplementation.

If you are going to supplement with creatine monohydrate, I recommend you start taking creatine when you have at least 12 weeks until your show or After photos. You must realize that you may see no scale weight loss for up to three weeks after you begin taking creatine. After a few weeks if you are not losing weight, it is not because of your creatine supplementation. I do not recommend you *start* taking creatine with only four weeks remaining.

Dose: 0.1 - 0.2 g per pound of fat-free mass per day. If you have 150 pounds of fat-free mass, you would take 15 to 30 grams per day (150 x 0.1 OR 150 x 0.2).

Putting the Supplements All Together Four Weeks Out

In addition to any protein, multivitamin/mineral and essential fatty acid supplements, consider including these supplements:

Ephedrine-Caffeine
1 - 3 doses daily (5-6 days per week) (take with food)

Phosphatidyl Serine
300 - 800 mg daily in divided doses (take with food)

CLA (Tonalin brand)
2 - 4 g per day in divided doses

L-glutamine
6 - 18 g daily (take when hungry and prior to the meal)

Tan

There is a reason you do not see ghostly white women and men in the bodybuilding and fitness magazines. It is not appealing to readers! I am fully aware that tanning is not looked upon as one of the most healthy endeavors you can do, but if you don't tan for your After photos, you will simply not look as good. You will not look as tight and your definition will not be enhanced to the fullest. If you don't tan another time in your life, then fine, but tan now.

I recommend a tanning salon with tanning beds or a sunless tanning dye or cream over using natural sun. It is too hard to get a uniform tan lying out and there is too much chance you will fall asleep and get roasted.

See your tanning salon employee for specific guidelines about how to start, evaluating your skin and potential for burn, etc. If I have not tanned for a few months, I always start at 8 to 10 minutes but I do not tan longer than 20 minutes in any session. Beds are different, however, and some may allow you to tan a maximum of 30 minutes. A good rule of thumb is to start very low and slowly work your way up to the maximum time.

Many tanning packages are sold in groups of 10 sessions. It is common for 10 sessions to cost between $30 and $50 depending on the type of bed and area of country you live in. Plan on buying 20 sessions or try to convince the tanning personnel that you will be starting with half sessions so you will not burn and see if they will allow you to count it as a half session instead of a full session at half the time. Good salons will be fair with you. Find one that is. When you decide what date you want to take your photos, mark on the calendar four weeks prior and begin tanning then. Tanning seems to work best when you tan enough not to get burned so you can go daily, increasing your minutes as you determine you can do so without burning. In the end, the darker, the better.

It's important you don't take your After photos or step on stage with a sun burn. Not only will your color be off but you are likely to hold subcutaneous water as the body sends fluids to a damaged organ –the skin! Regardless, your last tanning session should be two or three days before your show or After photos.

There are currently a number of sunless tanners on the market for those who refuse to take any risks associated with ultraviolet radiation. Some tanning salons are even offering sunless tanning options that have been reported recently to work very well. See your local salon for ideas on achieving a dark but natural-looking tan to suit your needs.

Other Considerations Four Weeks Out

1. Do not cut back on sodium. If anything, salt foods to taste. Sodium is the primary extracellular (outside the cell) electrolyte and is necessary for a myriad of functions. If you hold a little water during this period, then so be it. You can use the extra fluid around your joints as your body fat drops anyway.

2. Do not avoid wheat bread because you think it will raise estrogens. It will not. As long as you tolerate wheat ordinarily, then there is no reason to cut it out now.
3. You should still have one splurge meal per week. That does not mean you eat an entire large pizza by yourself. It means you can consume any food you like in moderation as long as you account for your splurge.

4. Do not eliminate carbs. Carbohydrate moderation and an eventual reduction in simple carbohydrates may be necessary during the final two weeks or so, but carbohydrates are vitally important to your muscle fullness and energy levels at this stage. Do not let carbs drop to less than 30 percent of total calories on any day.

5. You can still eat at restaurants by following the basic guidelines of the Lifestyle. Continue to live, train and eat.

Putting It All Together Two Weeks Out

At two weeks out, many transformationists begin to reduce simple sugars like fruit and pop and exchange them for fibrous vegetables like broccoli, cauliflower, spinach, bell peppers. A slight reduction in carbohydrate as a percentage of total calories (but still not less than 30 percent) may also be warranted with a concomitant increase in protein as a percentage of total daily calories consumed. The typical Lifestyle suggestion is 25 to 50 percent protein, 30 to 60 percent carbohydrate and 15 to 30 percent fat. My suggestion for you at two weeks out is to take protein to 50 percent, carbohydrate to between 30 and 40 percent (mostly from fibrous carbohydrates) and fat down to no more than 15 percent of total caloric intake.

For those who want to use tanning makeup, I would recommend you order it no later than now and have it on hand during your last week.

The Last Week

If you're a competing male bodybuilder, then your body fat should be no higher than six percent at the beginning of this week. If you are a female, your body fat should be no higher than ten percent. Whatever I say after those two sentences does not count, unless you are ready in the body fat department.

Assuming your contest or After photo session is on Saturday and today is the Sunday before, I will suggest the following day by day:

Sunday to Thursday: Keep supplements the same. No change in food intake unless slight modifications are necessary to reduce body fat further (i.e., a slight reduction in calories consumed). Drink at least a gallon of water today.

Thursday: Shave. For many men shaving all body hair except around the pubic region may seem effeminate. Get over it. Please, don't get stuck in that mental rut when it comes to taking your After photos. Hair covers the skin obviously and in doing so, covers ripped muscle. Because your goal is to reduce body fat and to increase muscle mass to best show off the muscle you've acquired, you must get rid of body hair to do it properly. Both men and women should shave all body hair on flesh that will be exposed in the photos or on stage. Women will want to shave appropriately for any bikini photos.

There are a number of products on the market that purportedly remove body hair: creams, sprays, electrical devices, buzzers, zappers, etc. For our purposes, none work as well as shaving the hair off. Here are some guidelines to hair removal that work well for me and thousands of others who have competed or been featured in the magazines:

- Use electric or battery-powered clippers to remove all long hair off the arms, legs, back and underarms before shaving with a razor. It will take forever plus one day to shave long hair with shaving cream and a razor. Follow all safety precautions recommended by the clipper company. I recommend Wahl® as a great brand of clippers. They can be purchased at most major department stores.

- After all long hair has been removed and the stub is all that's left, use a shaving gel (like you'd use for your legs or face) and lather up one body part. I recommend a lady's razor to shave the entire body. I have found the men's razors cut the heck out of my legs. Not sure which lady's razor to get? Buy two different ones and see what you think. I am not going to make a recommendation because there are a number of good ones and you will just have to find one you like.

- Slowly shave the lathered body part, preferably while standing in the tub or shower. Rinse the razor very frequently with hot water.

- Assuming you are a hairy guy with back hair, I would allow at least 1 hour for shaving the entire body. You will need a partner to do the back so get cozy with someone and have them clipper cut and then razor shave your back as needed. Get rid of that hair!

Friday: Reduce sodium intake to no more than 500-750 mg total. This means you will be eating very clean with virtually no packaged foods. Many people want to cut sodium out completely for days before the show. This is a mistake. In the *Nutrients* chapter, I discuss the importance of sodium. Cutting it out is a mistake at any time.

Don't Cut Sodium Out

While we think of the kidney as an organ of excretion, it is more than that. It does remove wastes, but it also removes normal components of the blood that are present in greater-than-normal concentrations. When excess water and sodium are present, the excess quickly passes out in the urine. On the other hand, the kidneys step up their reclamation of these same substances when they are present in the blood in less-than-normal amounts. Thus, the kidney continuously regulates the chemical composition of the blood within narrow limits.

Reducing sodium intake is unnecessary and foolish if done so for more than 24 to 48 hours. The body will tightly regulate sodium balance. When sodium is too low for days or weeks before your show or After photos, you are accomplishing nothing. Once sodium intake is reduced, the body will quickly begin releasing hormones such as aldosterone to preserve your life and to conserve sodium. Without sufficient sodium in the blood, many physiological functions are hindered. When dietary intake of sodium is nearly nonexistent, aldosterone signals the kidneys to conserve more sodium instead of excreting it. You cannot fool the body for very long so do not try. Do not completely cut sodium out and do not cut it down too early.

The following low-sodium foods are recommended for the period 24 to 48 hours before a shoot or show:

- Oatmeal
- Brown rice
- Sweet potatoes
- Eggs and egg whites
- Protein powders
- Turkey breast

- Vegetables (all that are fresh and whole)
- Fruit (moderate and should be fresh and whole)
- Chicken breast
- Lean beef
- Low-sodium tuna

Be sure and consider all sources of sodium. Read all labels. Consume nothing where you are not certain of how much sodium it contains.

Begin drinking only distilled water. Drink two gallons today. Distilled water contains no electrolytes or minerals. It is unnecessary to drink distilled water for more than 24 to 48 hours.

Begin taking a potassium supplement (most capsules are 99 mg of elemental potassium). Do not exceed 2500 mg per day and spread your dosing to every three waking hours.

Increase ratios of protein to 55 percent, decrease carbohydrates to 30 to 35 percent and eliminate all fats possible to reduce fat intake to no more than 10 percent of total intake.

Saturday: Show Time! Assuming your prejudging or photo shoot is at noon do the following:

6:00 A.M.: Wake up and have a portion of oatmeal cooked in distilled water with a portion of low-sodium protein powder added to it. Continue to avoid all other forms of sodium. Consume 200 mg of potassium. Drink a quart of distilled water.

If you would like to sauna before applying tanning makeup, now is the time to do so. I cannot make a recommendation to sauna, however, some report they believe they look slightly more defined for a few hours after taking a 20- to 30-minute sauna. I suspect this is related to a temporary reduction of subcutaneous water. Any benefit, if any, will only be realized for a few hours at best so do not expect sauna use during the day(s) before to provide any benefit on the day of the show or shoot.

Tanning Makeup?

Now that you have a good base tan and the hair is gone, I would recommend taking some photos as a test if you are taking After photos. Bodybuilders have no choice but to use tanning makeup. It doesn't matter how dark you think you are, the stage lights will wash you out and you'll look ghostly if you don't use tanning makeup.

Transformationists should snap off 12 shots or so, have them developed at the one-hour lab, or view and print them off your computer if you used a digital camera. Are you dark enough? Were your facial expressions pleasing and natural or do you look like you are about to lay an egg? After you get back your photos and make an evaluation, you can decide if you need to use tanning makeup.

If you decide after reviewing your photos that your skin is still a tint of alabaster, then you may need to apply a commercial cosmetic tanning makeup.

If you are going to take your After photos on Saturday, apply your tanning makeup Saturday morning. Do not shower after applying the tanning dye until after your shoot or contest. Pro-tan Competition Tan by a company called Muscleup works well but there are others too.

Use Skin Scrub or some other exfoliate to remove tanning make up after your show or photos.

7:00 A.M.: Take 200 mg of potassium. Drink another quart of distilled water. This is your last water except for small sips until after prejudging or at least part way through the photo shoot.

8:00 A.M.: Take 200 mg of potassium.

9:00 A.M.: Take 200 mg of potassium. Consume about 0.50 g per pound of body weight of carbs from sweet potatoes or brown rice. Consume 0.25 g per pound of body weight of protein.

For example, if you weigh 150 pounds, you would consume about 75 grams of carbohydrate from sweet potatoes or brown rice and 35 grams of protein. This is your last meal unless you are famished by the time your shoot or prejudging session begins. Do not eat anything within 30 or 60 minutes of your first After photos or stepping on stage. It is a good idea to bring additional sweet potatoes, rice, chicken or turkey with you in case you get hungry during the shoot.

No more water (except for sipping) until after prejudging or the photo shoot is done.

10:00 A.M.: Take 200 mg of potassium

11:00 A.M.: Take 200 mg of potassium. At this time, you will want to add a very light sheen to your body to help the lights reflect better. Most After photos are taken with a slight glistening of the skin. The most practical and yet effective way to do this is to use plain old Pam®, non-stick cooking spray. Yep, spray vegetable oil! A very light coat is all that is necessary and it works really well. It is also available everywhere. Whether you are a bodybuilder or shooting After photos, you'll have to make sure the sheen is even everywhere skin will ever be exposed during your poses. **Do not go too heavy!** Do spray on and lightly spread it around. If you go too heavy, you will reduce definition. Not only that, it looks silly to look like a grease slick!

Pump Up

If you have muscle that will show, you will want to pump up a bit. This will engorge the muscle with blood and make it appear fuller and harder. It will also improve vascularity as well.

I suggest you plan on taking 20 minutes or so to pump up. Do not go too light to pump up or too heavy (something that would cause failure at about 15 to 20 reps is good). Plan to complete three or four sets of a few exercises before hitting the stage or your first poses. It is common to pump up by doing a circuit of push and then pull exercises (e.g., bench press, lat pull downs, incline presses, seated rows). Concentrate primarily on basic multi-joint exercises such as:

* Flat/incline bench or dumbbell presses
* Close-grip palm-up lat pull downs or seated rows

and single-joint exercises such as:

* Barbell curl
* Triceps push-down
* Lateral raises (shoulder)

Do not pump your legs at all. If you have calves you want to stand out more, then *do* pump them a bit. If you are a bodybuilder, it is smart to flex your calves quite hard in different positions a dozen or so times over a few minutes to prevent cramping on stage. You are only pumping your upper body and calves if you are going to pump up at all.

If you do not have access to real weights backstage or at the photo shoot, make sure you bring some dumbbells with you. A friend, a towel, bands and pushups can work in a pinch. Use the friend to sit across from you while seated on the floor with the balls of your feet pressing against each other. Do seated row towel pulls. As he/she provides resistance to you, it is like the weight stack that would normally provide the resistance.

12:00 P.M.: Take the stage or shoot the After photos. Nutritionally, you are ready!

After Prejudging and Before the Evening Show

For the transformationist who finishes the After photos, there are no more worries for the day. This is normally a time of bliss and celebration. For the bodybuilding competitor, however, there is still a question of what to eat after prejudging. The show has essentially been decided at this point but you will still want to look good for your family and friends in the audience later that evening. Here is what I suggest:

Eat whatever makes you comfortable. I know bodybuilders who consume huge splurge-type meals after prejudging and there are those who feel better eating more conservatively (grilled chicken, fresh fruit, etc.). In the short time between prejudging and the evening show, the visible difference to your physique will likely be so small that I feel comfortable telling you to eat whatever makes *you* feel comfortable. Personally, I have done it both ways and had equal success.

You must accept that the competition is basically over (unless you are in a match for the overall) and on stage, changes in this three- to four-hour window aren't going to amount to a hill of beans. If you are nervous and want to eat light, then eat light. If you believe you have no chance of winning, then have a great afternoon! Enjoy! If you believe you have a shot at winning your class or the overall, then go light, keep sodium relatively low (although not as restrictive as you were), consume another half gallon of distilled water, and have a great time at the evening show. In any event, you should consume one to two quarts of distilled water in the afternoon to keep your muscles full.

One hour before the evening show, consume 300 mg of potassium. Get ready to have fun with your routine and support group in the audience.

Four Common Questions About This Method of Pre-Contest/After-Photo Preparedness

Q: *I thought I was supposed to restrict my water intake beginning a few days before the show and then I was supposed to eliminate water the day of the show. You advocate drinking lots of water, even on show day. What gives?*

A: Muscles are made up of approximately 70 percent water. They need water to remain expanded, thus providing fullness. As national bodybuilder Skip Lacour once told me, think of your muscle as the inner tube and your skin as the tire. If you do not consume enough water as a natural bodybuilder, your inner tube will be deflated and will not be pressing hard against the tire. This can make you look flat and less defined. To prevent this from occurring we need to drink water.

Q: *I thought I was supposed to carb-down and then carb-up in the last few days before the show to make my muscles full and hard. You do not say anything about that. Why?*

A: Carbing up and down takes tremendous skill, experience and trial and error. If you carb-down too much, you will sacrifice muscle and feel lethargic and flat. If you over-carb during the carb-up phase, some of the carbs will spill over, creating adipose with excessive subcutaneous water retention. Many national level bodybuilders no longer carb-down and carb-up. They find they do just as well without it.

Q: *I should stay away from soy and wheat bread right? They might cause my estrogens to increase, right?*

A: No. Soy and wheat are fine and any naturally occurring phytoestrogens are likely to act as an anti-estrogen, if anything. Their naturally occurring estrogens will displace your body's naturally produced estrogens and, because they are weaker at the receptor, you might expect less estrogenic activity, not more. I know this is complex but it is becoming clearer as research continues to mount.

Q: *Why do I restrict sodium while increasing potassium in the last 24 hours?*

A: Potassium is the major intracellular (inside the cell) electrolyte. Sodium is the major extracellular (outside the cell) electrolyte. Wherever potassium and sodium go, water will follow. For a brief time (probably less than 36 hours), we are attempting to shift the fluid balance inside the muscle cell (causing it to swell) while reducing fluid outside the cell (to prevent the look of water retention). If you restrict sodium too soon, your performance will suffer. If you restrict sodium too soon and then add potassium trying to get this effect, your body will have too much time to compensate and the fluid balance will normalize. The body wants to maintain homeostasis (constant balance) at all times and it will secrete hormones, increase or decrease metabolism, and preserve or increase excretion of compounds to maintain home-ostasis. The sodium-restriction/potassium-load method is experimental still, but at least it makes physiological sense. The trick is not doing the sodium restriction and potassium load too soon. If you do, you just wasted the technique.

Summary

The greatest preparation necessary for After photos or a bodybuilding or fitness competition comes in the months and years prior to the shoot or competition. You must build a base of muscle and reduce body fat to competitive levels to do well.

The basics that will bring you within four weeks of a shoot or competition are not to be thrown away in those final four weeks. There are some minor adjustments necessary in the final few weeks, but if what you've been doing has been working, keep doing it!

Prepare for your After photos by researching for a quality photographer, reviewing hundreds of other Before and After photos on the Internet and in magazines, finding poses you like, and taking practice shots with either a digital camera or one-hour developing.

A few additional dietary supplements over the basics can potentially benefit the transforma-tionist or competitor in the last few stressful weeks because they can help control cortisol, liberate additional stored body fat, and help with muscle preservation. Visit www.leannesslifestyle.com for more information on dietary supplement recommendations for ultimate transformation success.

Take Action and Feel Great!

1. Continue to make each day count as you count down to four weeks away from your contest or photo shoot. What you do today is the most important determinant of whether you have great After photos and a good time at a competition.

2. Research qualified photographers in your area or visit www.leannesslifstyle.com for sugges-tions if you are going to use a professional.

3. No matter how many weeks, months or years you are away from taking After photos, now is the time to begin clipping photos for poses you think you might like. Keep a file of them; that file can never be too large.

4. Consider how you will tan and investigate tanning beds or professional sunless tanners in your area.

5. If you are going to add in the supplements I suggest in this chapter, order them well in advance so you have one less thing to stress over. The last thing you need is increased stress in your final four weeks before a show or photos.

Maintenance and Beyond

Your heredity is not your destiny!

Hundreds of pages ago you began a journey–a journey toward a better you. As we conclude this edition of the Lifestyle, it is important you understand where you will be when you "get there", what it means to be in maintenance and, finally what's next.

As I discussed in the goals chapter, it is vitally important to your transformation for you to have clearly defined goals. No matter how clear or blurred your ideal of the perfect body is, you are certainly destined to go there. Clear hourly, daily, weekly, monthly and long-term goals allow you to determine where you're likely to be at all stages of the transformation and finally to tell you that you've made it.

If you were taking a trip from Illinois to Florida you would probably also pick a precise city and even an address to stay in Florida. This is like having your lifetime achievement goal clearly envisioned in your conscious and subconscious self. Without at least a specific city in mind, you are liable to settle for a win as anything south of Louisville, Kentucky. It is true that you must have a well-defined lifetime achievement goal in place so you will know whether you are finally "there." Where is "there?" What happens when you get "there?" The answers are relatively unique to the individual, however, I believe strongly in a few basic philosophies for those who have successfully achieved the goals of at least an 8- or 12-week transformation.

After Photos and the Honeymoon

Many times the act of competing or taking those After photos are followed by a feeling of depression and sadness. You should first know these feelings are normal. It is like all the preparation that goes into a wedding. After hundreds and hundreds of preparatory hours, in only a few short hours it is over. At the completion of your show or After photos, you have just completed the honeymoon. After the honeymoon, the real work begins.

Can you imagine putting hundreds of hours into a typical formal wedding, including thousands of dollars for the wedding and honeymoon, only to believe that once the honeymoon was over you were done? Whoa, big fella! You have only begun! Now it is time to make the marriage work! You have to work on it daily to improve it. In a marriage or your transformation, no matter how much you know about yourself right now, you still have much to learn. You have to stay committed to your marriage. You have to focus on each other. You must learn more about the real differences between men and women. You must read about relationships and listen to those who have been successful at them. If you are not working on your marriage and making sure good communication is in place, your marriage will become ill and it will fail. Your transformation is so similar it is almost scary.

It is natural to feel a let down after such an intense focus on the publicly overt Action phase. The important distinction of those who are successful at weight maintenance or taking it to an even higher level is not allowing that feeling of let down to last for more than a few days max. It is time to think about the next step. Unbelievably, with few exceptions, there is a clear next step waiting for you. It is time to think of "What next?" It is also time to focus on doing what is necessary to truly reset your set-point.

Set-Point Theory of Weight Control

During the late 1940s and through the 1960s, behavioral theories of body weight were abundant. Why did you overeat? Well, it could be because eating was a psychological compensation for a conflict in your life or unresolved issues from early infancy. On the other hand, perhaps it was caused by the fact that you ate too fast, or skipped meals. Whatever the reason, the underlying reason was behavioral or psychological.

Beginning in the early 1960s, studies from animals began to show what a powerful influence the brain played in determining the amount of food one eats. Not only did these studies show rather dramatic effects on food intake and body weight, but also the pharmaceutical industry began to take notice. With the increase in the incidence in obesity, an increase existed in the consumer demand for drugs that would help people lose weight.

The current theory of body weight that is held by most experts is the Set-Point Theory of the regulation of body weight. It grew out of the experiments in the 1950s and 1960s in which very small lesions in the hypothalamus of the brains of rats would cause enormous changes in food intake and body weight. Various areas in the brain were first described as "feeding centers" because, if they were removed from the brain, the animal would not eat. If they were electrically stimulated, a non-hungry animal would begin to feed. Another area was the "satiety center"–an area which, if removed, would cause an animal to overeat and gain enormous amounts of weight. If it were stimulated, a hungry animal would stop eating. Everything was fine until a quiet, little scientist from Cambridge University, demonstrated that these areas in the brains were not "feeding" or "satiety" but were rather areas that seemed to determine the amount of body fat the animal maintains on its body.

The way the system worked was that fat cells were supposed to produce a signal that would be sent through the general circulation to the brain. In the brain, the hypothalamus would read this signal and communicate with other brain centers. These brain centers would contain information about how fat you should be, information placed there by your genes. These centers would then compare the amount of fat you do have and the amount that you should have and translate the difference into eating behavior. So if you decided to diet, your hypothalamus would know that you do not have the amount of fat that your genes say you should have and would make you hungry in order to get you to increase your food intake.

The major problem with the Set-Point Theory of body weight was that no one knew how fat cells could communicate their size to the brain–not until leptin was discovered. Leptin was discovered by a geneticist who examined the differences between obese and thin mice. He, and several other scientists, observed that fat mice produced far less leptin than thin mice. This observation fit perfectly with the Set-Point Theory. The hypothalamus of the fat mice never received the signal that their fat cells were full. Therefore they responded as if they did not have enough leptin and eating behavior was stimulated. That is why they were fat, or so the theory goes. Moreover, if leptin is injected in to these fat, leptin-less mice, their food intake is reduced and they lose weight.

All sounds quite perfect at this point as leptin appeared to be the wonder drug millions of obese Americans had been hoping for! You could almost hear the cash registers ringing with the discovery of leptin. Just feed overweight people leptin and all should be well. Their brains will think they have more leptin than they do, they will reduce their energy intake and lose weight. Best of all, the people (consumers) would have to take leptin for the rest of their life, if they wanted to remain thin.

However, several problems quickly arose. First, obese humans produce more leptin rather than less leptin. Leptin deficiency is very rare and when leptin is delivered to large people who do not produce leptin, the body-weight loss is relatively small (less than 10 percent). Although leptin is still being researched and believed to be part of the obesity problem, it is not the panacea for weight loss researchers had initially hoped for.

Set-Point Within Your Control

The Set-Point Theory of body weight is depressing if it is so far out of our control. I believe it is not. The roll-over-and-play-dead advocates of the Set-Point Theory of weight control make us slaves to our bodies. I like to think that I am the controller.

The Set-Point Theory cannot account for why we are getting fatter as a nation. And not just we, but also the whole world. Surely our brains cannot have changed so dramatically in only 50 short years. How about migration studies that show when Asians move to the U.S., they get fatter than if they had remained in their native countries? Then there are the socio-economic effects. Almost everywhere in the world, the richer and more educated people are, the thinner the females. This cannot be biologic. Most importantly, the critical aspect of the set-point, the biological communicator from fat cells to the brain, has not been identified. Maybe it does not exist.

However, arguments and facts do not destroy theories, only alternative theories replace theories. What I propose to you is that your set-point is set, however, quite labile. It is as movable as the counterweight on a balance scale. Just as you can move the little weight to the left or right to determine your accurate body weight, you can adjust your set-point.

Why, then, do so many people lose weight only to regain most, all, or even more weight after a weight-loss program? What I find is that in the minds of most dieters, they believe there is a finish line they can cross to stop doing all the "nonsense" like regular exercise and caloric/portion control. In the *Are You Ready to Change* chapter, I clearly spelled out what the Maintenance stage is. I also told you there is no such thing as a Termination stage for those of us who have battled weight and desire a truly exceptional physique. That is a true difference between a real Lifestyler and dieter. A Lifestyler knows there is no finish line where he gets to say, "Thank God it's over!" It is never over if your goal is an energetic, healthy, lean and sexy body. It gets easier with time but it is never over.

> Coaching client Don had this to say about his past experiences with weight loss and relapse...
> *"I'm starting to realize that many of my past goal achievements I've allowed to slip back into 'lazy subsistence'- career-related things, personal things, spiritual things. Well, just about everything! The common thread in that regression is the lack of forward vision to 'what's next.' I've always been, 'Look at what I accomplished!' and then assumed that things would automatically continually improve BECAUSE of that achievement. Maybe that's why I've done three BFL challenges and have always ended up at the same weight and fitness level each time."*

Proponents of habit creation will tell you it takes 21 days to create a habit. Sure, that might work if your goal is to rise at 6 a.m. every morning instead of 7 a.m., however, for creating the type of lasting behavioral patterns necessary to re-set your set-point, I believe the patterns of behavior must be sustained for more like 21 months, not 21 days.

Your body weight may be actively regulated, however, you can change how your body actively regulates your weight. So, while it's true that your internal gyroscope will try and pull you back to center (i.e., back to your most frequently visited weight over the past months or years), this can change with persistence, introspection, continued learning, striving for the next goal and behavior modification.

Obesity is not a trait like eye color, which is determined from the moment of conception and does not change. A "tendency" for obesity is inherited. This tendency needs to have an environment that will nurture its development before it becomes a reality. Just as your weight is actively regulated by hormonal signals, ultimately you are in control of your weight because you control your environment. Genetics may load the obesity gun, but your environment and reaction to your environment pulls the trigger. Your heredity is *not* your destiny!
(Source: David Levitsky, Ph.D., Cornell University)

What's Next?

There are no guarantees that re-setting your set-point will keep you thin for life. There is, however, substantial credence to the theory I have proposed here about re-setting it. The longer you work at living leaner, the greater your chances of living lean for life. You must know or consider what is next after each 8- or 12-week transformation period.

You must focus on "What's next?" right away or you are likely to rebound either:

- A bit,
- More than a bit, or
- All the way.

You will notice that in none of my options did I list "stay the same as the end of your challenge." Why? Because unless there is a "What's next?" answer it will be one of the three responses above –*period!*

Many people will resist thinking about what is next. "God, isn't it enough that I bet my brother, sent David $5,000 for reversed-risk leveraging and accomplished my goal? Jeez, do I have to plan my meals days or weeks ahead of time from now on or what? What? Do I have to leverage myself until the day I die? Must I enter contest after contest after contest after contest? When do I get a break? Will I ever really be 'there'? When do I get to stop thinking about my stupid weight? When do I get to just be happy where I am and quit working so hard?" Every question here is real and considered by many who finish their first or second transformation.

In the analogy of the marriage, I stated you have only begun after the honeymoon. Like a marriage, a fit body only stays fit if you put a little something into it every day. Ask every question I have posed in the paragraph above as if you were speaking of your own marriage, regardless of your present marital status.

> "God, isn't it enough that I spent $5,000 on the wedding and attended the reception?"
>
> "Jeez, do we have to plan to spend quality time together no matter how many kids we have or how many events seem to interfere with us? Why can't it just be spontaneous?"
>
> "What? Do I have to continuously show my love with tokens of appreciation and affection until the day I die?"
>
> "Do I have to take out the garbage, earn a living, wash dishes, do the laundry and cook dinner after dinner after dinner?"
>
> "When do I get a break from this marriage?"
>
> "Will I ever get to just be happy in this marriage without working at it?"
>
> "When do I get to stop thinking about this stupid marriage?"

Resting on your laurels is a guaranteed way to fail–in your marriage or body transformation. It completely sets you up for divorce/relapse after the honeymoon/show or After photos.

Preferably, before your show or After photos, you should already know what is next. There are many activities you can do to keep you actively maintaining or moving forward.

- Enter another transformation challenge. This may not be a strong motivator if you just finished a challenge, but if you did your transformation solo and still have a substantial amount of weight or body fat to lose, maybe it's time you used your newfound knowledge and entered a physique transformation contest.

- Re-establish very strong leverage. This one drives people nuts but you have to simply get over it and realize the power of leveraging when done properly. Regardless of the stunt, money, bet or public exposure you created as your initial leverage, its time to get creative and do it again. Leverage is a very powerful weapon in your arsenal of commitment. It is worth it every time.

- Maintain ties with the group, club or support network that helped you get where you are. If you belonged to a group or club, now is *not* the time to thank them and say goodbye. Stay "in the loop." Continue to surround yourself with positive influences that understand what you have gone through and felt. Become a teacher or mentor to others in the group and begin honing your own coaching abilities. Helping others is a big step in maintenance.

- Enter a bodybuilding, fitness, physique or swimsuit competition. Many will never step on a stage; however, some will. If it has only been because of your new level of leanness that you are able to even consider entering a show, then I suggest you visit several shows (ask the local gyms where they are) and see what they are all about. If you have developed a fair amount of muscularity, there is likely no better motivator than public exposure in a posing suit or swimsuit in front of hundreds of complete strangers. A show really has so much of what I talked about in the leveraging section of the *Are You Ready to Change* chapter. The promoters will not move the date for you. You will suffer public embarrassment if you do not come in with a reasonably low body fat and you will publicly tell your entire support network you are going to enter. It is a very powerful weapon of commitment.

- Create or enter an event where you are likely to be judged physically by others within a few months to one year maximum. Go to meet other physically fit friends who live far away. Hire the services of a professional photographer who you know has taken shots of others with desirable outcomes. What is even better is when this event forces you to get on a plane to make it happen.

- Create or enter a charity event involving a fitness-related activity. Tell your local clubs and groups you are willing to speak to them about your transformation just to share the message. The more action steps you take that reinforce who you are at the core level, the more likely you will live consistently with those actions.

- Enroll in a certification program for fitness training. It is very common for people to transform themselves because they want to look and feel the part for another dream they have–to coach others. To any transformationist who wants to teach, coach, train or mentor, you have to do it first yourself! I really believe this. You will be able to relate to those you are teaching so much better after you do it. Doing it is like getting a Master's degree in body transformation. I do not care what degrees you already have or what you have read or think you know. Doing it counts for so much more. By assuming accomplishments in other areas of your life will transfer nicely into your physique transformation, you are asking for trouble. Don't assume—act your way to super fitness without some preconceived ideals about how great you've been at business, baseball or raising children. Once you have done it, you can search for organizations on the Internet or in fitness magazines that offer certification programs based on your level of education or experience.

I'm absolutely convinced that you must do more than give strong consideration to thinking about what's next—you've got to take action and create the environment that will keep you moving forward or at least hold you in true maintenance. Remember, **maintenance is not the absence of action**. Maintenance is simply a furtherance of action with a focus on the future and all the good that being lean and fit will bestow upon you rather than belaboring how much you've had to give up to get there.

I Need a Break

It is common to finish a transformation phase and feel the need to settle in a bit. You might need a chance to get comfortable with what you have accomplished. Change can be overwhelming, even good and positive change. If you have made a major transformation but have not reached your lifetime achievement goal yet, you need to really think about how that makes you feel. Many feel somewhat discourage by it. The progress you have made, no matter how large or small, has brought you a step closer to leaving obesity or entering super leanness. Sometimes you simply need to go into maintenance (plateau) for a while and let it all sink in. You can't sit back on your laurels and hope your past accomplishments will somehow magically stay with you without thinking about it, but there's a big difference between charging full-steam ahead and holding steady. Perhaps the desire to lose more weight—now—just is not there. Not only do I believe this is completely acceptable, sometimes it is necessary to keep from completely burning out and relapsing. I often see clients feeling a need to maintain their present weight after a weight loss of 20 to 30 percent of their starting weight, but it is different for everyone.

It is common for transformationists to finish an 8-, 10- or 12-week cycle and lose their sense of urgency. At every stage, it is common to weigh the costs and benefits of pushing further and taking the next step—whatever that may be for you. It is at this point where knowing why you want to change really matters. Is being comfortable with a tight size 12, after always shopping in the plus-size departments, your long-term goal? Is dropping from size 46 waist pants to 38s enough? When you've reached a certain level of success and feel as though you need a break, you need to refocus using introspection to help you determine what is truly desired, and make a decision.

Many "ideal" physiques are not created in 8 or 12 short weeks. The reality of many transformations is that people are in far worse shape than they ever imagined when they began the journey. This means there may be several cycles necessary before the "ideal" physique is realized. These cycles can be consecutive, but many times, they are spaced out over weeks or months.

If you have 50 pounds to lose, is there anything wrong with losing 25 pounds and then maintaining for six months before you take off the next 25? Not at all! In fact, it may be more desirable than doing it in one long cycle. It is really a personal preference. When I originally lost weight at nearly 230 pounds, I dropped to about 200 pounds and held this weight for nearly a year before I dropped another 20 pounds. Could I have lost all the weight in one long cycle? Sure. I needed a mental break from caloric restriction and took it. Do not feel pressured to do it all–all at once.

Moving Toward Hunger and Fullness

In the *Sweating the Small Stuff* chapter I clearly defined the importance of logging your foods and monitoring caloric intake until at least three to five percent of your body weight is gone. I promised you then, however, that you would not necessarily have to rely on calorie counting forever.

The Lifestyle is not, as some diets preach, one where you will never feel hunger again. If you do not experience normal hunger, I would have to ask what is wrong with the program. There is something wrong if you are not feeling hunger with regularity. Ideally, I would like to see you experiencing hunger four to six times per day and responding to each episode of hunger by eating a Lifestyle-balanced meal. It should go something like this:

1. I am hungry. I am not eating for emotional reasons. I have consumed plenty of water.
2. I eat enough to satisfy hunger for 2-1/2 to 3 hours, but then I know I should feel hungry again.
3. I make sure I am hungry for the right reasons. I eat something again.
4. The cycle continues.

Eating does not mean you must sit down to a six-course meal. Eating doesn't mean you sit down to a meal that you've prepared right then, but it could be a meal that you prepared a week ago or three days ago and stored in Tupperware®. A "meal" could be something that is frozen. It could be something that is prepackaged. Whatever it is, eating every 2-1/2 to 3 hours is *the* way you control hunger, stabilize blood sugar and keep from becoming famished or ravenous. Eating every 2-1/2 to 3 hours keeps your metabolism running optimally and keeps you feeling maximum daily vitality and energy. When you eat every 2-1/2 to 3 hours based on hunger, you do not worry over what your pre-workout meal is going to be. You don't have to because your last few meals before a workout were all important in determining the energy you were going to have available for the workout.

Most lifelong transformationists who successfully remain in Maintenance do not count calories on a daily basis. They continue to be label readers, they remain concerned about nutritional density, but they do not regularly count calories. Lifestylers in Maintenance know the importance of eating small but frequent meals. They have also become more aware of the real cues for nutritional hunger vs. emotional or thirst hunger. With conscious awareness and concerted effort to pay attention to feelings of hunger and satiety, you too can free yourself from the tasks of calorie counting when you know how true hunger feels as well as satiety.

Indeed, some do need more than a "feeling" or "rumbling" telling them it is time to eat. Like any learned skill, becoming more in tune with hunger and satiety takes practice. Many newcomers say they eat when they are hungry and stop when they are full. They eat every 2-1/2 to 3 hours. What is the problem when they are not experiencing any weight loss? The problem is that every person needs to redefine what hunger and fullness mean to him or her. Do you eat when you feel the slightest twinge of hunger or when you are ravenous? The proper time is actually somewhere in the middle. Do you stop when you are bloated, stuffed and could not eat another bite, or when you are still hungry? The proper time to stop is actually somewhere in the middle. The difference between true maintenance and a slow but steady relapse could be how you define your hunger and satiety signals.

Some people claim they do not "feel hunger" at all and must eat according to a plan to stay on track. Some never do appropriately perceive the true signal of what satisfied is. In somewhat of an obsessive-compulsive manner, once they start eating a particular food, they carve out the bottom of the box, bag or bowl. Planning may still be necessary to ensure you get in all of your meals each day and to ensure you do not overeat. It may just be easier to eat according to a plan, taking 10 to 15 minutes a day to prepare, than to rely on your senses of what hunger and satiety are. If this is what works for you, do not rebel against it or fight what works! There are worse things than having a plan and sticking to it–things like obesity, lethargy, high cholesterol, cardiovascular disease, diabetes and poor self-esteem.

Ideally, you want to eat enough food so that you start to feel the first signs of hunger about 2 to 2-1/2 hours after your last meal. By 3 hours after your last meal, you should be eating again. You should only eat enough to provide satiety for 2 to 2-1/2 hours. Most people who become better at eating according to hunger and satiety signals know precisely how big a portion of any food is likely to satisfy them at the moment and for a sustained period not lasting longer than about 3 hours.

Ensuring your meals are balanced will help prolong satiety. Remember from the *Nutrients* chapter that just because a meal is high-carb and low-fat, does not mean it is balanced or most appropriate for reducing hunger or prolonging satiety. When you've eaten what you know is a reasonable number of calories at a given meal and you are "starving" 30 minutes later, it's really important you give proper consideration to the percentages of the major macronutrients that made up that meal. Did you have enough protein (25 to 50 percent of the meal is preferable)? Were there any monounsaturated or essential fatty acids present (15 to 30 percent of the meal is preferable)? Were the carbohydrate sources complex or simple sugars? Were the carbohydrate sources fiber-rich or packaged and processed beyond recognition? It is not enough to simply eat "X" calories and assume your hunger will be in control and lasting. Balancing the majority of your meals is just as important a consideration as determining how many calories the meal should provide in the first place.

Even though you're likely to become so in tune with your body you will not have to count calories for a lifetime, I can say with confidence you will likely have to revisit food logging and calorie counting at various points in your life. Whenever you believe you are doing everything perfectly and nothing is making sense on the scale, it is time to count calories again. If you know you aren't doing everything perfectly and want to quickly get back on track, there's no better way to do so than to be honest with yourself and count every morsel that enters your mouth for a few days at the least.

If Things Don't Turn Out as You Planned

It is okay if you fall down as long as you learn something as you get up. The length of time you remain down is important. I am never down, I am either up or getting up.

Regardless of how your first or fifteenth transformation venture turns out, you are better for trying. If you find yourself falling down yet again and not achieving the goals you set, it's wise to bring this book back out and reread it in its entirety or at least the following chapters:

- *Are You Ready to Change?*
- *Energy Balance*
- *Goal Setting and your "why"*

In *The Success Journey* by John Maxwell, Bobb Biehl provides a good list of questions to ask when you fail. Instead of blaming someone else or being too hard on yourself, ask yourself these questions:

- What lessons have I learned?
- Am I grateful for this experience?
- How can I turn the failure into success?
- Practically speaking, where do I go from here?
- Who else has failed in this way before, and how can that person help me?
- How can my experience help others someday to keep from failing?
- Did I fail because of another person, because of my situation, or because of myself?
- Did I actually fail, or did I fall short of an unrealistically high standard?
- Where did I succeed as well as fail?

Setbacks are Normal–Keep Trying!

I am confident that with this book you have a massively powerful tool in your arsenal of weight control. There are few things as pathetic as seeing someone finish a transformation period with less than expected results saying "I am never gonna try again." The only time your efforts must absolutely work perfectly is the last time you try. This may or may not be your last attempt–but if it ends up falling short of your dream transformation, it will only be because you allowed day-to-day life to get in the way of some very clear goals you set or should have set early on. Even if this occurs, there is always another time, always another chance to get back up and do it again, but smarter than before. I am not saying you will have a setback of months or years, but if you fall off the horse for a few days or a few weeks, do not take the attitude that once again you have failed–you have not. You only fail if you give up, throw in the towel and truly never try again. You can *always* start again. Learn from your mistakes, resolve personal issues and become a better life manager. Start your next transformation the next day or with the next meal. Either is a great place to start! Do not ever forget this.

Do Something Everyday You Don't Want to Do

By now, you know the Lifestyle processes. You understand the formulas. You know the psychological crevasses to look out for and you know no one is responsible for your transformation but you. Now you want results! Hey, I don't blame you. However, before you will get those results you have to be willing to do things on a daily basis you would rather not do.

Everyone wants results but where many are tripped up is in their willingness to do things everyday they would much rather not do to get those results. Transformationists who have been the most successful have done what I said in this book, almost to the letter. They did it even though, deep down inside, they would have rather not done the 400 minutes of exercise that week, and even though they would have rather had pizza instead of a salad with chicken. They did it anyway. They keep doing it anyway. They remain successful.

When I was a young boy, I did not really want to go to school. I didn't really care much one way or another about it, but did well enough to get by with a B-C average without studying and that was that. Many days I did not want to go. I went anyway and I am better for it.

After I finished high school, I did not want to go to college and I was tired of school. I wanted to be a policeman though, and knew that a degree of some kind would be good to have to enter the ranks. However, I really did not want to go. I went anyway and I am better for it. I first earned an Associates degree and then went on to earn a Bachelor in Science. Neither degree did I want, but I did the work and I am glad I did.

I think you see where this is going, but let me drone on a bit more before I finish. From 2000 to 2002, I was the den leader of one of my boy's Cub Scout dens. For anyone familiar with scouting, they were Webelos. For quite some time I watched other parents be leaders and was damn glad someone else was doing it. Then the time came when no parents were available to be a leader. It was time for me to decide if I would step up and become a den leader. It meant hours of time spent preparing for meetings, taking part in things that seemed oh-so-trivial and meaningless outside of spending time with the boys. It required time I personally would rather not have given to the cause. However, I joined. I joined and committed, I gave a very good effort and reaped many rewards I never would have gotten had I not raised my hand and said "yes." I did it even though I really did not want to in the beginning and I am glad for it.

In 1999 The Power Store's website stunk. It was time for a facelift and there were many things I wished the website could do better. I shopped around and determined it would cost me about twenty thousand dollars to get the site I wanted, and then there would likely have been two thousand dollars a month in maintenance with everything I wanted it to do. As a coach, entrepreneur and a businessman, not a programmer or web site designer, I did not want to spend thousands of hours learning hypertext markup language (HTML) and another more complex programming language. To be honest, I would have much rather sat on my duff hanging out than build some website. I really did not want to learn it. I felt the costs were too high for me to pay someone else to do it, so I learned HTML and a programming language. I am glad that I did. It was hard work, I lost countless hours of sleep, but it is undoubtedly one of the best investments of time I have ever given. I built everything my coaching clients use, and without learning it myself, I never would have been able to offer the many benefits of the coaching club.

I have lifted weights on Christmas Day and every other holiday you can think of. I've lifted when I have been sad, happy, depressed (that's the toughest time for me to lift by the way), angry, alone, partnered, with nice equipment, with crap equipment, in dungeons and in the nicest places on earth. There were so many days that I did not want to workout, but I did it anyway. Because I did it anyway, I get to proudly wear my badge of honor every day knowing that no matter where I go, not withstanding a bodybuilding show or expo, I am probably going to be a standout. I am 37 years old as I close the last chapter of the 4th edition today. I am 5'10", 182 pounds and 6.5 percent body fat. There just aren't many of me around, and I say this *not* to toot my own horn but to make the point that this is the case only because I put in quality time. I put in time when others wouldn't, and I did it even though I didn't want to.

One Day in David's Life

Now I know most of you think I climb out of bed each day, immediately drop to the floor, assume the one-armed push-up position and salute a life-sized poster of Arnold Schwarzenegger, as I crank out push up after push-up after push-up. Well, not quite.

I went for a run before supper tonight. As I went outside in full running apparel (t-shirt, shorts and old running shoes), I really did not want to run. I almost dreaded it. For some reason, I just did not care about it today, and felt as if I could have laid down and taken a nap. I yawned my way to the end of the driveway, where I actually begin running, and I took off with a slow pace.

I kept this pace for about a mile. Then, out of nowhere I got some energy, I felt more alert, more alive and I sped up to what is a very fast pace for me. I finished the last 1-1/2 miles very fast, and man am I glad I did it. I did not want to do it at first, but now that it is done, I am glad I did. I know I have helped my continuous leanness life and overall health.

Tonight Tracy made a fantastic chicken dinner in the crockpot and it was delicious, however, to be honest, I would have rather had pizza. Why? I have no idea. I just would have and it doesn't matter why. I really didn't want the veggies she took the time to prepare. I ate the chicken, it was good, I ate the veggies, and now as I sit here I am glad I did. I do not feel guilty because I ate another pile of "keep me fat" pasta or "watch my belly jiggle casserole." I don't feel bloated and disgusting because I stuffed myself until it hurt. I feel good about tonight's meal and I am thankful it was prepared. I did not really want it but I ate it and I'm glad I did. I have eaten many meals I would have rather not have in lieu of something else, but did anyway and was usually glad afterwards.

Lead Legs

During the early stages of your transformation, when you're unaccustomed to exercising with vigor and frequency, your internal gyroscope is going to do its best to pull you back to the couch and rest. Don't let it.

You need to anticipate that after a vigorous day of exercise you may not "feel" like training the next day, even if you are intelligently training a different body part or using a different form of exercise. Many feel like they have "lead legs" after walking, jogging, or doing other cardio or resistance training. The body will tell you "don't do it. You are already tired. Aren't you going to harm yourself further if you work out when you're already tired?" There are many games your mind will play with you in the early stages of your transformation. If you're just tired, you're thinking, "You know what? I just don't feel like 35 to 40 minutes of cardio or whatever. I just don't feel like it!" If you just don't feel like it, you're not sick, and other than being tired or a little sore, everything else is going okay, *do it anyway!*

There is a difference between being sick and being tired. If you have the flu, get medical attention and plenty of rest. However, if you're simply tired from a previous day's workout or from another "long, stressful day," then you need to get your exercise in. Do not miss! When you feel you "just don't have the energy to do it," but you are not medically sick you *have* to get your exercise in.

You are going to train the body and it's going to adapt to the new physical stress that you are placing upon it. It's not used to this. It doesn't like it now but will love it later. It's trying to tell you, "Hey this is out of my norm. Stop trying to be something you're not! You have never treated me like this before. I'm gonna let you know it. I'm gonna be sore. I'm gonna make you feel tired." You have to get up, get to the gym or get outside and get that exercise in. You have to press through it. The body will adapt to the additional stress by becoming stronger and more resilient to the physical demands you place upon it. If you slough it off, it will adapt to this as well. So please, do not slough it off, *just do it.*

If you press through it, the body will adapt and you will become stronger, you will have more energy and you will wonder, "How in the world did I ever get by on so little activity? How did I sit around like a couch potato all the time? How did I just sit like a bump on a log? All those months and years as life passed me by." Remember, you need to act your way into change and you have to begin acting like and doing the things fit people do on a regular basis. Fit people do not miss workouts because they don't want to do it. They know that many times, even though they don't want to do it, they will feel better once they get going and will feel better about themselves because they accomplished their plan for the day. Never underestimate the power of accomplishing the daily goals you have.

Just Be Good Today

Unless your good judgment tells you that you will do more harm than good by exercising when you don't want to, you must take advantage of today. You can never get this day back. Take the mindset that *you don't have to "be good" forever–just for today.* When you have one or two weeks left to reach your 10-week transformation benchmarks, and you have 15 pounds to go, you're going to look back at today and what you missed in the weeks up to this point and wish you had not missed. You're going to be saying, "Man, I wish I would have done my cardio. I wish I would have done my resistance training when I didn't feel like it. I wish I would have done it! I wish I ate fewer calories then, so I don't have to starve myself now." You can lie to yourself until you are blue in the face, but you cannot turn back the hands of time and not eat that chocolate cake that you scarfed down, or make up that session of cardio that your mind talked you out of. Every minute of every day matters. You cannot get today back, and if at one week out, you still have 10 pounds to go, you will wish you could go back and clean up your eating a little bit better, or do 40 minutes of cardio instead of 30.

Champions Do It Anyway

During the course of your transformation, you will be faced with sorrow, heartache and tiredness, and probably even mild depression for one reason or another. Many times, you won't want to work out when you could or eat what you should.

During the course of your transformation, you will suffer a spat with a loved one. You will have moments when you want to pull yours or someone else's hair out. Will you let this affect whether you do what you were supposed to with food and exercise?

Still, no matter what, some of you just won't put in the time necessary to ensure a great transformation. "It's hard. It's boring. It hurts." The packaged food lovers who refuse to incorporate more whole vegetables and fruits into their meal planning will be saying, "Do I really only get to eat that much? It's hard to cook the good foods. It's hard to find time. My husband does not like it. My house is in disorder. I have a headache, I have a backache, and I don't have the time I need to get in my exercise." I make no apologies when I tell you that you must overcome these mental and physical obstacles to get the job done. Perhaps it is better said this way–*those who are the best at transformations do what it takes to make it a lifestyle and get the job done no matter what.*

Many more of you will make an amazing transformation in spite of it all! You will simply do what I have asked and the weight will fall off, almost like clockwork. You will do what I have asked, many times in spite of your own beliefs about food and exercise, and most definitely during times you would have rather gone out for cocktails, had a pizza, and really whooped and hollered your way to a five-pound water weight gain the next day.

You will just do it and you will be so glad when you see the changes. You'll understand and appreciate every minute of cardio and weights you did, every last drop of chicken, tuna and veggies you ate. You will become the success you were meant to be. You and I, and hundreds of other successful Lifestylers, will wear our greatest reward every day with countless people asking us how we did it.

The bottom line is that transforming into the person you envision in your mind today will happen because you did many things you would rather not have done–all in knowing that it would be the best for you in the end. Instead of settling for the short-term pleasure, you will hold out for the bigger reward–the one you get to wear every day.

Every single person reading this has tremendous heartache, sadness, mild depression, anger and frustration. We're all pressed for time, have "had it up to here" with the world on a given day, but the champions know that none of this matters in the end. They have their priorities in order. They refuse to be derailed for any reason and for all the right reasons they will be success stories in their homes and neighborhoods making others envious of their accomplishments. "What was your secret?" others will ask. Maybe those who are the most successful with the Lifestyle will say, "I did a whole bunch of things I didn't want to do and you have no idea how glad I am that I did."

Closing Maxims From Lifestyler Tom Roehl for a Final Reality Check

1. I was worse off when I had started my first challenge than I ever thought.

2. You can make dramatic changes to your body in a short period but it takes persistence and long-term commitment to really be outstanding.

3. You can sabotage your own progress because of your own false beliefs and fears.

4. When you are a size 38, size 34s seem a long way off and when you do get there you feel lean.

5. You are not as lean in 34s as you think.

6. Yes, lean muscle looks bigger in the buff than muscle that has fat on it.

7. You can get over the "smallies" if you are honest with your self, believe no. 6 and have support from a good coach!

8. I do not have as much muscle as I thought I did.

9. I will not be competing in any bodybuilding shows in the near future but may in several years.

10. The mirror can lie because you can see yourself as you want to be rather than how you really are. Pictures give a more accurate impression.

11. A good body fat measurement helps you realize where you are along with pictures. You may find it hard to believe you are 30 percent or more body fat, but that is of no consequence here. I find it hard to believe we sent a man to the moon. So what. We did—end of story. Accept the objective specifics that will provide a truer picture of where you are starting so you know where a reasonable ending is.

12. Others can tell you things about training and nutrition, but until you personally experience them, you will never really understand.

13. You must have a solid goal and target date. One that will motivate you enough to do what you must do to reach your true potential; a goal that is strong enough to give you the strength to carry on even when it seems you cannot. The goal must be worth the extra effort and discipline required.

14. You need support from good friends and others who are honest and really have been there in order to make it through those "tough times."

15. There is a big difference between 16 percent body fat and 10 percent body fat and an even bigger difference between 10 percent and 6 percent.

"This Is Just Me Now"

Not too long ago a client who had transformed using the Lifestyle and my coaching program said the very words in this subtitle of The Leanness Lifestyle. After living the Lifestyle in maintenance for several months, she wrote, "This is just me now." Those words rang true to me in many ways and I believe it is befitting to close the Lifestyle with how powerful these words are and what they can mean to you.

There are many lessons learned along this journey toward a superfit physique and each person must learn them in his or her own time. Many times it doesn't matter how many times warnings and flares have been sent up by myself and others—you just have to experience the process, pain, exhilaration, discomfort, and joy yourself.

As you succeed in achieving a transformation worthy of who you really are, I believe you will begin to see yourself as a different, better person. However, at your core it is quite likely you'll just be a "fat-guy or gal fakin' it." This is in no way a personal attack on you or some preconceived notion about how big a failure anyone was before finding the Lifestyle. It is just my personal experience of the mindset of myself and hundreds of transformationists over the years when they get lean the first time.

If, as you begin to feel the success that living the Lifestyle is certainly capable of delivering, you realize that at your core you're just a "fat-guy or gal fakin' it" know that you're not alone. It takes quite a long time to undo the many years of negative self-talk and hurtful words and actions of others. If you have never been fit or even remotely thin as an adult it would be foolish to expect that after an 8-, 10- or 12-week challenge, all would be perfect and you would feel like someone who has been fit their whole life. It is not likely to occur. *It may only take a few months to become the body you desire, but it may take much longer for your "self" to adjust to the new, slimmer, and more buff you. In the meantime, you will feel and look much better until your "self" catches up.* It's important for you to recognize these feelings as normal and to know that when you live the Lifestyle only for today, then one day it truly will become who you are and you'll no longer be the "fat-guy or gal fakin' it." In the meantime, I have this to say; *Fake it 'til you make it!*

By faking it until you make it, you will stay lean and live the Lifestyle until you truly see yourself as the superfit person you are. If you have been fat most of your adult life, should you become a thin-thinking svelte person deep down because of a few months of outstanding weight loss? No way–it doesn't work that way. You will most naturally act in a manner most consistent with how you really see yourself and this is probably not what you project to most of the world. Most people show the world the outer layer only. In those outer layers, lies are told, however, at the core, the truth is guiding you subconsciously all along the way.

Through consistent, positive self-talk and taking each Lifestyle day one at a time, you can adapt to the new you and know that you are no longer living what seems like a lie. You're no longer a "fat-guy or gal fakin' it." One day, perhaps, you will just realize, like the client who provided the subtitle of this section, that this is truly who you are.

When the Lifestyle is truly who you are, you cross a bridge from theatrics to living your dream life. You will no longer be the soap bubble floating next to jagged rocks. Your family will be more accepting of the new you. Never forget you are not the only one adjusting to your new body and mindset. The hurtful comments will diminish because those closest to you will have had time to adjust to the new you. You will likely keep many of your old friends, but also will broaden your circle with new friends who share your philosophies on fitness. As you do, you will find it more enjoyable to spend time with those who think and act as if you do.

David's Epiphany

By January of 2001 I had mastered my own Lifestyle to the point where I found it quite comfortable living at eight to ten percent body fat. That body fat afforded me many opportunities to mow down a half a bag of Gardettos from time to time as a splurge, or a half a box of chocolate cake when I really felt "naughty." I was also able to do absolutely no aerobic training and I was quite content in most ways–except that at my core I still was not quite acting consistently in a manner that was consistent with who I was–an even better fit man and role model for others. There was no good reason to consume 1500 calories in Gardettos or cake. There were plenty of reasons to do a moderate amount of aerobic exercise on a regular basis.

In May of 2001, I competed in a bodybuilding show in Rockford, Illinois. I had lowered my body fat once again to five percent and did precisely the things you read about in this book to get there. What were those things?

1. Consumed frequent, balanced meals each day.
2. Maintained adequate protein.
3. Consumed plenty of quality, whole, low-processed foods, vegetables, fruits and grains.
4. Maintained a wide variety of foods and meals.
5. Drank no less than a half gallon of water each day.
6. Performed 60 to 90 minutes of aerobic exercise per week.
7. Continued to use resistance training as a primary tool for keeping lean body mass (three or four workouts per week).
8. Got quality rest within reason and improved my life management skills to better my stress-coping abilities.

In getting prepared for the competition, I started hearing a little voice asking me a question about the preparation. It asked:

> *"What is it about your current regimen that is so extreme or unbalanced that you shouldn't do it more often or all the time after the show?"*

When I ran down the eight-item list in my head, I could not find anything extreme or unbalanced. Then, a second question followed when I could not find anything extreme or unbalanced with my contest preparation. It asked:

> *"If there isn't anything unbalanced or extreme in what you are doing, and you are simply living a super-clean Lifestyle getting ready for this show, emulating everything you talk about and teach others to do, what excuse would you like to conjure up after the show to return to your old, good but improvable, habits that kept you living at 8 to 10 percent body fat?"*

I did not like the sound of the thoughts that followed and I realized that any excuse I would give would be just that–an excuse–and not anything valid worth repeating to me or anyone else. Simply put, not being the best I could be more often was only an excuse to eat more junk and be lazier than who I had fully become all the way down to my core. I had fully transformed! At my very core, I was a superfit, healthy man. I was no longer "Dave the power lifter" or "Dave the bulk monster" or "Dave, the fat guy faking it."

Since the bodybuilding show, I've maintained a body fat less than seven percent, and will only add more body fat should I desire more lean body mass or if I deem it absolutely necessary. There is much debate over whether it is possible to add appreciable lean body mass when the body fat is less than ten percent for a man. At the time of this writing, I am quite content with who I am, what I have accomplished and my overall state of fitness and muscularity. Yes, it is a wonderful place to be!

If someone quotes me as saying, "We mortals can visit the land of 6 percent but we don't get to live there," they are absolutely telling the truth. However, it is probable they did not hang around long enough to hear the rest of the story or find out how it ends. It ends by David saying he was wrong then. It ends by David saying we all control our fitness destiny. I used to justify eating a half-pound bag of Gardettos because being nine to ten percent was good enough, however, I no longer crave Gardettos and I fully understand what they mean when they say, "good enough rarely is." I eat to live and do not live to eat. I am superfit and loving every minute of it! I wish the same for you and know you have the power within you to achieve a body you will truly be proud of.

Summary

If I didn't get the point across in the body of this chapter, I must clearly state the real purpose of this chapter here: You cannot have an attitude of "I'm done" or "When will I be done?" and achieve the great body you desire. Just as a successful marriage requires continuous attention, so does your body transformation and maintenance of your new body created through the transformation process.

The Set-Point Theory of weight control proposes that we are all somewhat destined to be a particular weight, however, many researchers do not agree that we are destined to be obese regardless of our genes and I agree. We control what we weigh. It requires effort, consistency and putting into practice the principles with this book for much longer than 21 days. Adopting the mindset early on that you control your body and fitness destiny will make the process more fulfilling and successful. It may be overwhelming to think about how long you will have to live a fit Lifestyle, especially in the beginning. Therefore, I recommend you only live the Lifestyle for today. If you approach every day with this attitude, you will be leagues ahead of your dieting acquaintances.

When you begin your transformation it's okay to set up the initial phase for two or three cycles (eight or twelve weeks) and not look too much further down the road than that. But once the initial phase is complete it's very important that you know "what's next?" Do not sit back and rest on your laurels once your initial eight or twelve weeks are complete. Paddling upriver takes a lot of energy. If you stop paddling, you will float downstream without question. The same goes for the new body you will create. The good news is that although paddling upstream is hard, it takes far less effort to stay in place on that same river. This is Maintenance. But as you visualize this, it is important you keep in mind that at all points of your superfit life, it will require some paddling to keep from being swept away by the current. There will be times when the river is raging due to torrential downpours. There will be other times when the current is barely detectable and the river is low. The same holds true for you during your transformation and once you reach the transitional Maintenance period. Never stop paddling. It will always take some effort to hold your position.

Once you achieve maintenance and perhaps long before, you will likely no longer be counting calories. From your efforts early on at properly logging your food and drink, you will have earned the right not to count every morsel that enters your mouth. You will become more aware of how your body signals hunger and fullness and you will respond accordingly to satisfy each.

Along the path of fitness there will be many tasks and responsibilities you'd much rather not do. Champions do them anyway and they do them more consistently than those who lead mediocre lives. Always strive to become a goal achiever rather than a tension reliever.

With time I am confident the Lifestyle can become who you really are and you will no longer be the fat guy or gal faking it. It's not reasonable to assume that everyone will reach this grandiose place with their first 8- or 12-week transformation. You can transform your body and shed decades of overindulgence in only two or three cycles, however, it may take more than a year for your mind to catch up with the new body you create. Give it time to do so. Continue to work on being a better life manager and never leave self-worth to chance. Work on becoming more positive and living the rest of your life proud of who you are and what you've become.

Take Action and Feel Great!

1. Begin thinking about "what's next?" now, regardless of where you are in the transformation process.

2. Review commitment and leveraging in the *Are You Ready to Change?* chapter.

3. Life the Lifestyle to its fullest!

4. Give someone you love the gift of hope and send them their own copy of The Leanness Lifestyle Success System.

Appendix

Beginning to Intermediate
Find Your Max Chart

Your Max	Reps 10	9	8	7	6	5	4	3	2	Your Max	Reps 10	9	8	7	6	5	4	3	2
25	20	20	20	20	20	20	25	25	25	165	125	130	130	135	140	145	150	155	155
30	25	25	25	25	25	25	25	30	30	170	130	130	135	140	145	150	155	155	160
35	25	25	30	30	30	30	30	30	35	175	130	135	140	145	150	155	160	160	165
40	30	30	30	35	35	35	35	35	40	180	135	140	145	150	155	160	160	165	170
45	35	35	35	35	40	40	40	40	45	185	140	145	150	155	155	160	165	170	175
50	40	40	40	40	45	45	45	45	50	190	145	145	150	155	160	165	170	175	180
55	40	45	45	45	45	50	50	50	50	195	145	150	155	160	165	170	175	180	185
60	45	45	50	50	50	55	55	55	55	200	150	155	160	165	170	175	180	185	190
65	50	50	50	55	55	55	60	60	60	205	155	160	165	170	175	180	185	190	195
70	55	55	55	60	60	60	65	65	65	210	160	165	170	175	180	185	190	195	200
75	55	60	60	60	65	65	70	70	70	215	160	165	170	175	185	190	195	200	205
80	60	60	65	65	70	70	70	75	75	220	165	170	175	180	185	195	200	205	210
85	65	65	70	70	70	75	75	80	80	225	170	175	180	185	190	195	205	210	215
90	70	70	70	75	75	80	80	85	85	230	175	180	185	190	195	200	205	215	220
95	70	75	75	80	80	85	85	90	90	235	175	180	190	195	200	205	210	215	225
100	75	80	80	85	85	90	90	95	95	240	180	185	190	200	205	210	215	220	230
105	80	80	85	85	90	90	95	95	100	245	185	190	195	200	210	215	220	225	235
110	85	85	90	90	95	95	100	100	105	250	190	195	200	205	215	220	225	230	240
115	85	90	90	95	100	100	105	105	110	255	190	200	205	210	215	225	230	235	240
120	90	95	95	100	100	105	110	110	115	260	195	200	210	215	220	230	235	240	245
125	95	95	100	105	105	110	115	115	120	265	200	205	210	220	225	230	240	245	250
130	100	100	105	105	110	115	115	120	125	270	205	210	215	225	230	235	245	250	255
135	100	105	110	110	115	120	120	125	130	275	205	215	220	225	235	240	250	255	260
140	105	110	110	115	120	125	125	130	135	280	210	215	225	230	240	245	250	260	265
145	110	110	115	120	125	125	130	135	140	285	215	220	230	235	240	250	255	265	270
150	115	115	120	125	130	130	135	140	145	290	220	225	230	240	245	255	260	270	275
155	115	120	125	130	130	135	140	145	145	295	220	230	235	245	250	260	265	275	280
160	120	125	130	130	135	140	145	150	150	300	225	235	240	250	255	265	270	280	285

Intermediate to Advanced
Find Your Max Chart

Your Max	Reps 10	9	8	7	6	5	4	3	2	Your Max	Reps 10	9	8	7	6	5	4	3	2
155	115	120	125	130	130	135	140	145	145	380	285	295	305	315	325	335	340	350	360
160	120	125	130	130	135	140	145	150	150	385	290	300	310	320	325	335	345	355	365
165	125	130	130	135	140	145	150	155	155	390	295	300	310	320	330	340	350	360	370
170	130	130	135	140	145	150	155	155	160	395	295	305	315	325	335	345	355	365	375
175	130	135	140	145	150	155	160	160	165	400	300	310	320	330	340	350	360	370	380
180	135	140	145	150	155	160	160	165	170	405	305	315	325	335	345	355	365	375	385
185	140	145	150	155	155	160	165	170	175	410	310	320	330	340	350	360	370	380	390
190	145	145	150	155	160	165	170	175	180	415	310	320	330	340	355	365	375	385	395
195	145	150	155	160	165	170	175	180	185	420	315	325	335	345	355	370	380	390	400
200	150	155	160	165	170	175	180	185	190	425	320	330	340	350	360	370	385	395	405
205	155	160	165	170	175	180	185	190	195	430	325	335	345	355	365	375	385	400	410
210	160	165	170	175	180	185	190	195	200	435	325	335	350	360	370	380	390	400	415
215	160	165	170	175	185	190	195	200	205	440	330	340	350	365	375	385	395	405	420
220	165	170	175	180	185	195	200	205	210	445	335	345	355	365	380	390	400	410	425
225	170	175	180	185	190	195	205	210	215	450	340	350	360	370	385	395	405	415	430
230	175	180	185	190	195	200	205	215	220	455	340	355	365	375	385	400	410	420	430
235	175	180	190	195	200	205	210	215	225	460	345	355	370	380	390	405	415	425	435
240	180	185	190	200	205	210	215	220	230	465	350	360	370	385	395	405	420	430	440
245	195	190	195	200	210	215	220	225	235	470	355	365	375	390	400	410	425	435	445
250	190	195	200	205	215	220	225	230	240	475	355	370	380	390	405	415	430	440	450
255	190	200	205	210	215	225	230	235	240	480	360	370	385	395	410	420	430	445	455
260	195	200	210	215	220	230	235	240	245	485	365	375	390	400	410	425	435	450	460
265	200	205	210	220	225	230	240	245	250	490	370	380	390	405	415	430	440	455	465
270	205	210	215	225	230	235	245	250	255	495	370	385	395	410	420	435	445	460	470
275	205	215	220	225	235	240	250	255	260	500	375	390	400	415	425	440	450	465	475
280	210	215	225	230	240	245	250	260	265	510	385	395	410	420	435	445	460	470	485
285	215	220	230	235	240	250	255	265	270	520	390	405	415	430	440	455	470	480	495
290	220	225	230	240	245	255	260	270	275	530	400	410	425	435	450	465	475	490	505
295	220	230	235	245	250	260	265	275	280	540	405	420	430	445	460	475	485	500	515
300	225	235	240	250	255	265	270	280	285	550	415	425	440	455	470	480	495	510	525
305	230	235	245	250	260	265	275	280	290	560	420	435	450	460	475	490	505	520	530
310	235	240	250	255	265	270	280	285	295	570	430	440	455	470	485	500	515	525	540
315	235	245	250	260	270	275	285	290	300	580	435	450	465	480	495	510	520	535	550
320	240	250	255	265	270	280	290	295	305	590	445	455	470	485	500	515	530	545	560
325	245	250	260	270	275	285	295	300	310	600	450	465	480	495	510	525	540	555	570
330	250	255	265	270	280	290	295	305	315	610	460	475	490	505	520	535	550	565	580
335	250	260	270	275	285	295	300	310	320	620	465	480	495	510	525	545	560	575	590
340	255	265	270	280	290	300	305	315	325	630	475	490	505	520	535	550	565	585	600
345	260	265	275	285	295	300	310	320	330	640	480	495	510	530	545	560	575	590	610
350	265	270	280	290	300	305	315	325	335	650	490	505	520	535	555	570	585	600	620
355	265	275	285	295	300	310	320	330	335	660	495	510	530	545	560	580	595	610	625
360	270	280	290	295	305	315	325	335	340	670	505	520	535	555	570	585	605	620	635
365	275	285	290	300	310	320	330	340	345	680	510	525	545	560	580	595	610	630	645
370	280	285	295	305	315	325	335	340	350	690	520	535	550	570	585	605	620	640	655
375	280	290	300	310	320	330	340	345	355	700	525	545	560	580	595	615	630	650	665

The Metropolitan Life Insurance Company Height / Weight Chart

Women

	Weights at ages 25-59 based on lowest mortality. Weight in pounds according to frame (in indoor clothing weighing 3lbs.; shoes with 1" heels).		
Height Feet Inches	Small Frame	Medium Frame	Large Frame
4' 10"	102-111	109-121	118-131
4' 11"	103-113	111-123	120-134
5' 0"	104-115	113-126	122-137
5' 1"	106-118	115-129	125-140
5' 2"	108-121	118-132	128-143
5' 3"	111-124	121-135	131-147
5' 4"	114-127	124-138	134-151
5' 5"	117-130	127-141	137-155
5' 6"	120-133	130-144	140-159
5' 7"	123-136	133-147	143-163
5' 8"	126-139	136-150	146-167
5' 9"	129-142	139-153	149-170
5' 10"	132-145	142-156	152-173
5' 11"	135-148	145-159	155-176
6' 0"	138-151	148-162	158-179

Men

	Weights at ages 25-59 based on lowest mortality. Weight in pounds according to frame (in indoor clothing weighing 5lbs.; shoes with 1" heels).		
Height Feet Inches	Small Frame	Medium Frame	Large Frame
5' 2"	128-134	131-141	138-150
5' 3"	130-136	133-143	140-153
5' 4"	132-138	135-145	142-156
5' 5"	134-140	137-148	144-160
5' 6"	136-142	139-151	146-164
5' 7"	138-145	142-154	149-168
5' 8"	140-148	145-157	152-172
5' 9"	142-151	148-160	155-176
5' 10"	144-154	151-163	158-180
5' 11"	146-157	154-166	161-184
6' 0"	149-160	157-170	164-188
6' 1"	152-164	160-174	168-192
6' 2"	155-168	164-178	172-197
6' 3"	158-172	167-182	176-202
6' 4"	162-176	171-187	181-207

Body Composition by Three-Site Skinfold
(from Chapter 3—*Body Composition and Obesity*)

Sum of Skinfold (mm)	Body Fat Percentage for Men Age 18 TO 22	23 TO 27	28 TO 32	33 TO 37	38 TO 42	43 TO 47	48 TO 52	53 TO 57	58 & UP	Body Fat Percentage for Women Age 18 TO 22	23 TO 27	28 TO 32	33 TO 37	38 TO 42	43 TO 47	48 TO 52	53 TO 57	58 & UP
8 to 10	1.3	1.8	2.3	2.9	3.4	3.9	4.5	5.0	5.5									
11 to 13	2.2	2.8	3.3	3.8	4.4	4.9	5.5	6.0	6.5									
14 to 16	3.2	3.8	4.3	4.8	5.4	5.9	6.4	7.0	7.5									
17 to 19	4.2	4.7	5.3	5.8	6.3	6.9	7.4	8.0	8.5									
20 to 22	5.1	5.7	6.2	6.8	7.3	7.8	8.4	8.9	9.5									
23 to 25	6.1	6.6	7.2	7.7	8.3	8.8	9.4	9.9	10.5	10.8	11.1	11.4	11.7	12.0	12.3	12.6	12.9	13.2
26 to 28	7.0	7.6	8.1	8.7	9.2	9.8	10.3	10.9	11.4	11.9	12.2	12.5	12.8	13.1	13.4	13.7	14.0	14.3
29 to 31	8.0	8.5	9.1	9.6	10.2	10.7	11.3	11.8	12.4	13.1	13.4	13.7	14.0	14.3	14.6	14.9	15.2	15.5
32 to 34	8.9	9.4	10.0	10.5	11.1	11.6	12.2	12.8	13.3	14.2	14.5	14.8	15.1	15.4	15.7	16.0	16.3	16.6
34 to 37	9.8	10.4	10.9	11.5	12.0	12.6	13.1	13.7	14.2	15.2	15.6	15.9	16.2	16.5	16.8	17.1	17.4	17.7
38 to 40	10.7	11.3	11.8	12.4	12.9	13.5	14.0	14.6	15.2	16.3	16.6	16.9	17.2	17.6	17.9	18.2	18.5	18.8
41 to 43	11.6	12.2	12.7	13.3	13.8	14.4	15.0	15.5	16.1	17.4	17.7	18.0	18.3	18.6	18.9	19.2	19.6	19.9
44 to 46	12.5	13.1	13.6	14.2	14.7	15.3	15.9	16.4	17.0	18.4	18.8	19.1	19.4	19.7	20.0	20.3	20.6	20.9
47 to 49	13.4	13.9	14.5	15.1	15.6	16.2	16.8	17.3	17.9	19.5	19.8	20.1	20.4	20.7	21.0	21.4	21.7	22.0
50 to 52	14.3	14.8	15.4	15.9	16.5	17.1	17.6	18.2	18.8	20.5	20.8	21.1	21.4	21.8	22.1	22.4	22.7	23.0
53 to 55	15.1	15.7	16.2	16.8	17.4	17.9	18.5	19.1	19.7	21.5	21.8	22.1	22.5	22.8	23.1	23.4	23.7	24.0
56 to 58	16.0	16.5	17.1	17.7	18.2	18.8	19.4	20.0	20.5	22.5	22.8	23.1	23.5	23.8	24.1	24.4	24.7	25.0
59 to 61	16.8	17.4	17.9	18.5	19.1	19.7	20.2	20.8	21.4	23.5	23.8	24.1	24.4	24.8	25.1	25.4	25.7	26.0
62 to 64	17.6	18.2	18.8	19.4	19.9	20.5	21.1	21.7	22.2	24.5	24.8	25.1	25.4	25.7	26.1	26.4	26.7	27.0
65 to 67	18.5	19.0	19.6	20.2	20.8	21.3	21.9	22.5	23.1	25.4	25.7	26.1	26.4	26.7	27.0	27.3	27.7	28.0
68 to 70	19.3	19.9	20.4	21.0	21.6	22.2	22.7	23.3	23.9	26.4	26.7	27.0	27.3	27.6	28.0	28.3	28.6	28.9
71 to 73	20.1	20.7	21.2	21.8	22.4	23.0	23.6	24.1	24.7	27.3	27.6	27.9	28.2	28.6	28.9	29.2	29.5	29.8
74 to 76	20.9	21.5	22.0	22.6	23.2	23.8	24.4	24.9	25.5	28.2	28.5	28.8	29.1	29.5	29.8	30.1	30.4	30.8
77 to 79	21.7	22.2	22.8	23.4	24.0	24.6	25.2	25.7	26.3	29.1	29.4	29.7	30.0	30.4	30.7	31.0	31.3	31.7
80 to 82	22.4	23.0	23.6	24.2	24.8	25.4	25.9	26.5	27.1	29.9	30.3	30.6	30.9	31.2	31.6	31.9	32.2	32.5
83 to 85	23.2	23.8	24.4	24.9	25.5	26.1	26.7	27.3	27.9	30.8	31.1	31.5	31.8	32.1	32.4	32.8	33.1	33.4
86 to 88	23.9	24.5	25.1	25.7	26.3	26.9	27.5	28.1	28.7	31.6	32.0	32.3	32.6	33.0	33.3	33.6	33.9	34.3
89 to 91	24.7	25.3	25.9	26.5	27.0	27.6	28.2	28.8	29.4	32.5	32.8	33.1	33.5	33.8	34.1	34.4	34.8	35.1
92 to 94	25.4	26.0	26.6	27.2	27.8	28.4	29.0	29.6	30.2	33.3	33.6	33.9	34.3	34.6	34.9	35.3	35.6	35.9
95 to 97	26.1	26.7	27.3	27.9	28.5	29.1	29.7	30.3	30.9	34.1	34.4	34.7	35.1	35.4	35.7	36.1	36.4	36.7
98 to 100	26.8	27.4	28.0	28.6	29.2	29.8	30.4	31.0	31.6	34.8	35.2	35.5	35.8	36.2	36.5	36.8	37.2	37.5
101 to 103	27.5	28.1	28.7	29.3	29.9	30.5	31.1	31.7	32.3	35.6	65.9	36.3	36.6	36.9	37.3	37.6	37.9	38.3
104 to 106	28.2	28.8	29.4	30.0	30.6	31.2	31.8	32.4	33.0	36.3	36.7	37.0	37.3	37.7	38.0	38.3	38.7	39.0
107 to 109	28.9	29.5	30.1	30.7	31.3	31.9	32.5	33.1	33.7	37.1	37.4	37.7	38.1	38.4	38.7	39.1	39.4	39.7
110 to 112	29.6	30.2	30.8	31.4	32.0	32.6	33.2	33.8	34.4	37.8	38.1	38.4	38.8	39.1	39.4	39.8	40.1	40.5
113 to 115	30.2	30.8	31.4	32.0	32.6	33.2	33.8	34.5	35.1	38.5	38.8	39.1	39.5	39.8	40.1	40.5	40.8	41.1
116 to 118	30.9	31.5	32.1	32.7	33.3	33.9	34.5	35.1	35.7	39.1	39.5	39.8	40.1	40.5	40.8	41.1	41.5	41.8
119 to 121	31.5	32.1	32.7	33.3	33.9	34.5	35.1	35.7	36.4	39.8	40.1	40.4	40.8	41.1	41.5	41.8	42.1	42.5
122 to 124	32.1	32.7	33.3	33.9	34.5	35.1	35.8	36.4	37.0	40.4	40.7	41.1	41.4	41.8	42.1	42.4	42.8	43.1
125 to 127	32.7	33.3	33.9	34.5	35.1	35.8	36.4	37.0	37.6	41.0	41.4	41.7	42.0	42.4	42.7	43.1	43.4	43.7
128 to 130	33.3	33.9	34.5	35.1	35.7	36.4	37.0	37.6	38.2	41.6	41.9	42.3	42.6	43.0	43.3	43.7	44.0	44.3

B.M.I. Calculator

Height \ Weight	100	105	110	115	120	125	130	135	140	145	150	155	160	165	170	175	180	185	190	195	200	205	210	215	220	225	230	235	240	245	250
5'0"	20	21	21	22	23	24	25	26	27	28	29	30	31	32	33	34	35	36	37	38	39	40	41	42	43	44	45	46	47	48	49
5'1"	19	20	21	22	23	24	25	26	26	27	28	29	30	31	32	33	34	35	36	37	38	39	40	41	42	43	43	44	45	46	47
5'2"	18	19	20	21	22	23	24	25	26	27	27	28	29	30	31	32	33	34	35	36	37	37	38	39	40	41	42	43	44	45	46
5'3"	18	19	19	20	21	22	23	24	25	26	27	27	28	29	30	31	32	33	34	35	35	36	37	38	39	40	41	42	43	43	44
5'4"	17	18	19	20	21	21	22	23	24	25	26	27	27	28	29	30	31	32	33	33	34	35	36	37	38	39	39	40	41	42	43
5'5"	17	17	18	19	20	21	22	22	23	24	25	26	27	27	28	29	30	31	32	32	33	34	35	36	37	37	38	39	40	41	42
5'6"	16	17	18	19	19	20	21	22	23	23	24	25	26	27	27	28	29	30	31	31	32	33	34	35	36	36	37	38	39	40	40
5'7"	16	16	17	18	19	20	20	21	22	23	23	24	25	26	27	27	28	29	30	31	31	32	33	34	34	35	36	37	38	38	39
5'8"	15	16	17	17	18	19	20	21	21	22	23	24	24	25	26	27	27	28	29	30	30	31	32	33	33	34	35	36	36	37	38
5'9"	15	16	16	17	18	18	19	20	21	21	22	23	24	24	25	26	27	27	28	29	30	30	31	32	32	33	34	35	35	36	37
5'10"	14	15	16	17	17	18	19	19	20	21	22	22	23	24	24	25	26	27	27	28	29	29	30	31	32	32	33	34	34	35	36
5'11"	14	15	15	16	17	17	18	19	20	20	21	22	22	23	24	24	25	26	27	27	28	29	29	30	31	31	32	33	33	34	35
6'0"	14	14	15	16	16	17	18	18	19	20	20	21	22	22	23	24	24	25	26	26	27	28	28	29	30	31	31	32	33	33	34
6'1"	13	14	15	15	16	16	17	18	18	19	20	20	21	22	22	23	24	24	25	26	26	27	28	28	29	30	30	31	32	32	33
6'2"	13	13	14	15	15	16	17	17	18	19	19	20	21	21	22	22	23	24	24	25	26	26	27	28	28	29	30	30	31	31	32
6'3"	12	13	14	14	15	16	16	17	17	18	19	19	20	21	21	22	22	23	24	24	25	26	26	27	27	28	29	29	30	31	31
6'4"	12	13	13	14	15	15	16	16	17	18	18	19	19	20	21	21	22	23	23	24	24	25	26	26	27	27	28	29	29	30	30

BMI Category	< 18.5	18.5 - 24.9	25 - 29.9	30-34	35-39	40+
Health Risk Based Solely on BMI	Minimal	Low	Moderate	High	Very High	Extremely High
Risk Adjusted for the Presence of Comorbid Conditions and/or Risk Factors	Low	Moderate	High	Very High	Extremely High	Extremely High

© 2002 The Leanness Lifestyle by David Greenwalt • www.leannesslifestyle.com

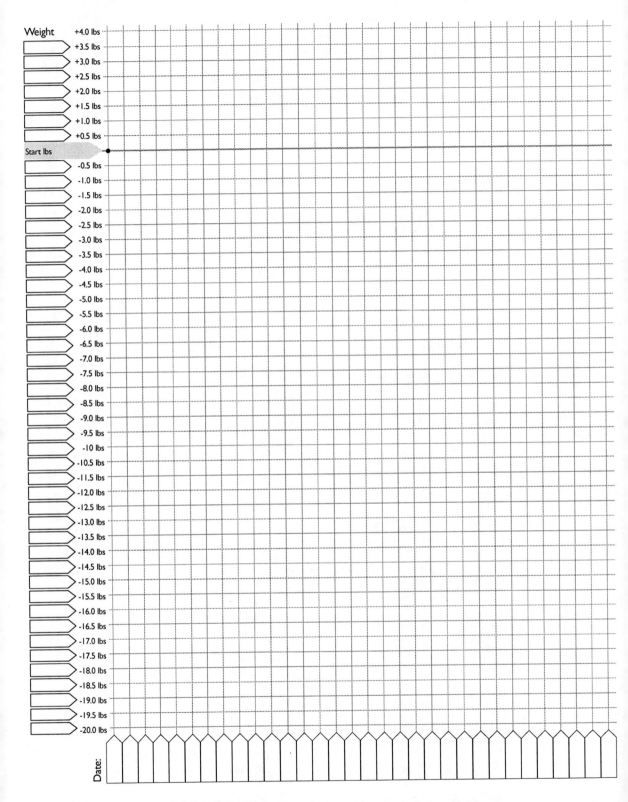

Basic Lifestyle Food Choices

• Fruits (Carbohydrates)

Apples, Apricots, Avocados, Bananas, Blackberries, Blueberries, Cherries, Citrus fruits, Cranberries, Grapes, Grapefruit, Grapefruit Jam or Jelly (all natural fruit like Polymers), Kiwi, Lemons, Mangos, Melons, Nectarines, Oranges, Orange juice (concentrate or with added Calcium), Papaya, Peaches, Pears, Peppers, Pineapple, Plums, Raisins, Raspberries, Strawberries, Tangerines, Tomatoes.

Remember this: Fresh is best, frozen next (any without extra added sugar) and canned is least (packed in water with no added sugar or syrups)

• Vegetables (Fibrous Carbohydrates)

Artichokes, Asparagus, Bok Choy, Broccoli, Broccoflower, Brussels Sprouts, Cabbage, Cauliflower, Celery, Carrots, Chili Peppers, Corn, Cucumber, Eggplant, Green Beans, Greens (turnip, mustard, collard), Kale, Lettuce (Butterhead, Romaine), Leeks, Mushrooms, Onions, Peas, Peppers, Popcorn (air popped without butter!), Potatoes, Pumpkin, Radishes, Spinach Leaf, Squash, Turnip Greens, V8 Juice (preferably low sodium), Yams, Zucchini

• Grains (Starchy Carbohydrates)

Barley, Bran muffin Bread (Whole Wheat are first two words on label), Cereal (whole-grain, 2 grams of fat or less per serving, 4-6 grams of sugar or less, no sulfured fruit or artificial color/flavor/sweetener, no coconut/palm oils), Crackers (whole-grain or mostly whole-grain; fat-free or low-fat), Cream of rice, Flour (whole-grain), High-protein pancake mix, Oats (slow-cooked), Okra, Pasta (low-fat and whole-grain), Pita, Pumpernickel bagel, Rice (all varieties), Soy milk, Tofu, Tortillas, Bulgur,

• Legumes (Starchy Carbohydrates and Some Protein)

Black Beans, Chick Peas, Kidney Beans, Navy Beans, Pinto Beans, Lentils, Peanuts, Peanut Butter

• Dairy (Protein primarily)

Cheese (Kraft makes great fat free slices and shredded cheddar), Cottage cheese (2%, 1% or fat-free), Cream Cheese (fat-free), Eggs, or egg white substitute, Powdered milk, Protein Powder, (nonfat) Skim milk, Sour Cream (fat-free), Spray butter (I Can't Believe It's Not Butter spray is great), Yogurt (low-fat)

Basic Lifestyle Food Choices

• Meats Including Beef (Protein), Fish (Protein & Essential Fats) and Fowl (Protein)

For beef look for U.S.D.A. "Select" (lowest fat) first, then "Choice" (next lowest fat) then "Prime" (highest fat). By trimming fat to less than 1/4 inch before cooking you can reduce fat by 20 percent! Do it! A study published in the June 1999 issue of the Archives of Internal Medicine provides further evidence you don't have to fear beef if you consume it in moderation. The conclusion of the 36 week study of 191 participants clearly indicated that "Lean red meat is just as good as lean white meat to curb bad cholesterol."

Center Loin (pork chops, pork roast), Chicken without skin, Clams, Cod, Crab, Emu, Eye of Round Steak, Flank, Flounder, Ground round, Ground sirloin, Haddock, Halibut, Lamb, Lobster, Mackerel, Monkfish, Mussels, New York Strip, Orange Roughy, Ostrich, Perch, Pike, Pollack, Red Snapper, Salmon (canned or fresh steak), Sardines, Scallops, Scrod, Sea Bass, Shrimp, Sirloin (tip, steak, or roast), Sole, Swordfish, Tenderloin (filet mignon, chateaubriand), Tenderloin (pork), Top Round Steak, Top Sirloin Steak, Trout, Tuna (Albacore packed in water or fresh steak), Turkey without skin, Yellowfin tuna

• Canned Goods (Carbohydrates primarily)

Apple Sauce (no sugar added), Chicken broth, Olives (go easy on these), Pickles (dill Kosher), Soups (low-fat, low-sodium), Spaghetti sauce (under 700 milligrams of sodium per serving, 30% or less of calories coming from fat), Tomato sauce, Whole tomatoes

• Beverages (Neutral or Carbohydrates)

Water, Coffee, Tea, Any artificially sweetened drink (no more than 12 ounces per day), Soda Non-Diet (no more than 12 ounces per day), Water (it needs repeating because it's the most important)

• Snacks (Carbohydrates)

Baked chips (3 g of fat or less per serving), Dry roasted nuts, Fig bars, Meal Replacement Shakes, Pretzels, Protein Bars, Protein Shakes, Rice Cakes, Sherbert, Sorbet/Fruit Ice, Yogurt (low-fat frozen)

Basic Lifestyle Food Choices

• Condiments (Neutral)

Almond extract, Barbecue sauce, Basil, Black pepper, Bouillon cubes, Cajun seasonings, Chicken broth, Chili powder, Cinnamon (ground), Clear broth, Coconut extract, Cocktail sauce, Cranberry sauce, Dill relish, Garlic salt, Garlic powder, Ginger (ground), Herbs (any), Honey, Horseradish, Iodized salt, Jams (natural all fruit), Ketchup, Lemon juice, Lime juice, Low-fat mayonnaise, Marinades (use sparingly), Marinara sauce, Mint sauce, Molly McButter, Mustards, Nutmeg, Onion (minced or bits), Oregano, Oyster sauce, Parsley, Parmesan cheese (fat-free), Pecante sauce, Pickles, Relishes, Salad Dressings (fat-free), Salsa, Soy sauce (low-sodium), Spices, Steak sauce, Sweet and sour sauces, Tabasco sauce, Teriyaki sauce (low-sodium), Thyme, Vanilla extract, Vinegars, Worcestershire sauce

• Cooking Sprays (Neutral)

Pam, Canola

• Nuts and seeds (Protein & Monounsaturated Fats)

Almonds, Almond butter, Cashews, Coconut, Macadamia, Pistachios, Sesame Seeds, Soybeans (Boiled), Tempeh, Tofu

giving it a shot, 188
glucagon, 176
gluconeogenesis, 176
glucose, 97, 110
glutamine, 422, 424
    anabolic or catabolic state, 422
    glycogen formation and, 422
    post-workout formula and, 422
    stress and, 422
glutathione, 129
glycemic index, 107, 108
glycogen, 91-92, 97, 106, 109, 173, 206, 362, 384
glycolytic, 361-363
goal achievers, 16
goals, 32-33, 60, 209-211, 214-224, 226, 228, 231, 268,
    293-294, 307, 433, 448
    barriers to setting, 224
    today, 218
    write them, 214
    write them, 215
gorging, 197, 203, 205, 217, 292, 319
grains, 98, 103, 115, 142
granola bar, 137
gratification, delaying, 278
gratitude, 269
grazer, 197, 198
ground beef, 123
guilt, 24
gyroscope, 436, 445

H

habits, routine, 31, 237, 436
HALT, 280
hamstring exercises, 393
headaches, 110, 113, 138, 140
healthy weight, 89, 162
healthy weight loss, 165, 167
heart attack, 63
heart disease, 98, 100, 103, 110, 120-121
heart rate monitor, 413
height, 211
height charts, 65
helping relationship, 45, 60-61, 320-321, 323
heredity, 433, 436
Hoarder, 267
holidays, 249, 251
honeymoon, 433, 437
hope, 22, 35
hoping, 33, 187-188, 195
hormones, 342
horrible, 58

hot flash, 33
hotel, 252, 255
housewives, 324
humiliation, 42-43
    public, 42, 43
hunger, 110-114, 117, 137-141, 251, 258-259, 280, 440-441
    emotional, 139, 140
    physiological, 139
    thirst, 139
hungry, 280
hunter-gatherer, 133, 142, 275
hydrodensitometry, 66, 184
hydrogenated fats, 124
hydrogenation, 119
hyperglycemia, 109
hyperplasia, 350
hypertension, 121
hypertrophy, 348-350, 355, 360-361, 372-373, 375
hypocaloric diet, 420
hypoglycemia, 110-111, 382
hypoglycemic, 382
hypothalamus, 434-435
hypothyroidism, 63

I

immovable date, 43-44
immune disorders, 120
immune system, 120, 422
immunoglobulins, 129
indifference, 293-294
inevitable crisis, 226, 329
influences, positive, 315, 438
insoluble fiber, 103
insulin, 97, 108-109, 114, 126, 197, 382
insulin management, 108
insulin resistance, 108
intensity, 358-359, 363
intentions, 32, 38, 215, 226, 285
interval solution, 409, 413
interval training, 408-409
    caloric expenditure, 408
    cortisol, 409
    EPOC, 408
    muscle fiber types, 409
    RMR, 408
intramuscular, 423
introspection, 439
inventory, personal, 210
irritability, 110, 113, 140
ischemia, 367
isometric, 359-360

P

pain, 39, 226, 264, 310
Paleolithic, 142
palpitations, 110
Pam, 429
pancreas, 108
paradigms, 226
parents, 312, 314, 329
parents, controlling, 332
parents, critical, 313-315
parents, negative, 312
parents, nurturing, 314-315
partners, 364
Pavlovian, 264, 307
pears, 212-213
peer pressure, 33
perceived exertion, 154-155
Percentage of Maximal Heart Rate, 404-405
perception, 20, 32, 72, 155-156, 258, 280, 287-288,
    290-291, 293
perfect practice, 15
perfection, 30
perfectionism, 308
performance goal, 210
performance goals test, 353, 371
performance measures, 65
periodization, 353-354, 356, 358, 367
periodization program, 395-397
    exercise number, 395
    intensity, 396
    load, 397
    macrocycle, 396
    mesocycle, 396
    momentary muscular failure, 396-397
    multi-joint exercises, 395
    repetitions, 396
    sets, 397
    single-joint exercises, 395
    tempo, 397
persistence, 225
personal record, 380
personal trainer, 46
phosphagen, 361-363
phosphatidyl serine, 421, 424
phosphorous, 132-133
photo album, 213
photographer, 52
photographers, professional, 418-419, 438
photos, 14, 36, 50-52
    After, 14
    Before, 52

photos, After, 416-417, 425-430, 433
    body fat and, 417
    depression and, 433
    subcutaneous water, 425
photos, Before and After, 417, 419
photos, progressive, 417-418
    body fat and, 418
    body weight change, 417
physical activity, 154, 340-341, 344
    arthritis and, 340
    benefits of, 340
    blood sugar and, 341
    cholesterol and, 340
    concentration and, 341
    coping and, 341
    endorphins, 341
    energy expenditure, 154
    fat burning and, 341
    heart disease and, 340
    immunity and, 340
    mood, 341
    muscle mass increases, 341
    osteoporosis, 340
    self-esteem and, 340
    sleep and, 340
    stress and, 341
physical exertion, 155
physique competition, 438
phytochemicals, 100-101
phytoestrogens, 431
Picker, 267
plan, 29, 31, 32, 209, 220, 224
planning, 28, 29, 206, 253
plateaus, 354, 356
Platemates, 379-380
PMS, 138, 335-337
polyunsaturated fatty acids, 116, 119-121
popcorn, 137
portions, 245
positive influences, 47
post-workout meal, 383-385
    carbohydrates and, 385
    glycogen synthesis and, 385
    insulin and, 385
    potassium and, 385
    protein and, 385
    remodeling muscle, 385
    sodium and, 385
potassium, 91, 384, 428
potassium, last day, 430
potassium, last week, 428-429

LaVergne, TN USA
30 May 2010
184318LV00004B/7/A